Strategic management essentials

1ST EDITION

Robert Grant

Peter A. Murray

Stuart Orr

Bella Butler

Pieter-Jan Bezemer

First edition published 2021 by
John Wiley & Sons Australia, Ltd
42 McDougall Street, Milton Qld 4064

Typeset in Times LT Std Roman 10/12 pt

Creators/contributors
Robert Grant (Author), Peter A. Murray (Author), Stuart Orr (Author), Bella Butler
(Author), Pieter-Jan Bezemer (Author), Bruce McKenzie (Case study author),
Janette Rowland (Case study author).

Wiley
Terry Burkitt (Director, Publishing and Course Development), Kylie Challenor (Senior
Manager, Education Content Management), Emily Brain (Production Editor), Tara Seeto
(Publishing Coordinator), Liam Gallagher (Production Assistant), Renee Byron
(Copyright & Image Research), Delia Sala (Cover Design)

Typeset in India by diacriTech

Printed in Singapore by
Markono Print Media Pte Ltd

10 9 8 7 6 5 4 3 2 1

BRIEF CONTENTS

CONTENTS

CHAPTER 6

Corporate-level strategy 127

CHAPTER 7

Cooperative strategies and alliances 160

Corporate governance and ethics   250

PREFACE

Strategic management in the 2020s

This resource combines the best of a research-based focus for applying theory to practice. Strategic management is evolving as rapidly as the world conditions that drive it. Global balances of power are shifting dramatically and technology routinely changes what was impossible yesterday into something that is commonplace today. These dynamic conditions make becoming skilled in strategic management more important than ever for business success. No matter how nimble the organisation, responding to the dynamic opportunities and changes in every market takes time and resources. Organisations that forecast these changes and prepare for them pre-emptively gain a first-mover advantage and stay ahead of the competition. Strategic management for the 2020s is based on a combination of proven concepts, such as maintaining adaptable resources that can respond to the market and technology changes and new concepts, such as short-term, high-level planning and developing global scale operations. Unlike the strategic management approaches of past decades, strategic management for the 2020s applies equally to all types of businesses — manufacturing, service, community, government and small business. Technology and global trends mean that the factors and approaches required for success now apply equally to all these different types of organisation.

This book has been developed with practice and application as a key feature. Each chapter includes a scene-setting case, with strategy capsules throughout that exemplify specific strategic management practices and act as a point of reference throughout the book. The chapters also contain a large variety of examples that strongly connect the concepts to practice. Discussion questions and exercise questions at the end of each chapter and learning objectives at the beginning of each chapter enable the reader to test their appreciation of all of the key concepts. The book is divided into four sections that represent the important stages on the path to a formidable strategy. Commencing with the key strategic concepts in part one, the book then introduces the tools of strategic analysis, which explain the internal and external environment of the organisation. Part three of the book describes the strategy formulation process and how competitive advantage is generated at the business and global levels. The final section of the book explains and demonstrates how strategy performance is assessed and how leadership and ethics can be used to drive performance and effective outcomes. Successful strategies for the 2020s require informed decision making and creative thought processes. This book is an invaluable companion for both and for your journey to success.

Unlike traditional textbooks, *Strategic Management Essentials* is an aggressively concise, high quality title that gives students the key content they need to succeed in their course. Content is designed around weekly retrieval practice, a pedagogical strategy that is proven to enhance and boost learning. Students are further supported with engaging questions and illustrative examples that provide focus and added clarity.

As an added benefit, this book concludes with a *Future Skills Guide*, which provides practical advice from experts across technology, wellbeing, social intelligence, ethics, skills and development, design thinking and the future of work. The Guide will help students build career-relevant skills and knowledge to complement their specialist knowledge in the field of strategy.

Stuart Orr
May 2020

ABOUT THE AUTHORS

Peter A. Murray

Peter A. Murray is a Professor of Management at the University of Southern Queensland. Peter specialises in applied research helping business leaders and firms to adapt, innovate and build social capital networks. Professor Murray has a background in change consultancies and strategic thinking to many of Australia's largest companies, including Hawker de Havilland, Energy Australia, Sunrice and Australian Nuclear Science Technology Organization, and across different sectors, such as local government, manufacturing and education, among others. A snapshot of his work appears in leading journals, including *Management Learning, Asia Pacific Journal of Management, Supply Chain Management* and *Government Information Quarterly*. Peter's research is located in the University of Southern Queensland's Institute of Resilient Regions. His most recent co-edited book is the *Palgrave Handbook of Knowledge Management*.

Stuart Orr

Stuart Orr is Professor of Strategic Management at Deakin University. He has worked in industry, consulting and academia, as well as having set up and operated two successful businesses. Stuart has been president of one of Australia's largest NGOs and a board member of several peak global academic associations, including the Decisions Sciences Institute. Stuart has published several articles, chapters and books on strategic management and international business. He is regularly interviewed on radio and television and in international magazines and media, such as Forbes and Bloomberg.

Bella Butler

Bella Butler an internationally recognised award-winning educator with over 30 years of experience in the tertiary sector. She is Senior Lecturer at School of Management, Curtin University, Australia. Bella has extensive experience teaching and coordinating a diverse teaching portfolio in Strategic Management, Corporate Strategy and Corporate Governance, and Organisational Change and Development. Bella teaches and coordinates these subjects at the main Curtin campus in Perth, Australia, as well as in Curtin transnational campuses in OAE (Dubai), Malaysia, Mauritius and Singapore. Bella's research and innovation in teaching resulted in the development and establishment of the Management HQ, a unique facility to the Australian Higher Education sector. The multipurpose facility, similar to corporate war rooms, is a simulation-powered boardroom with extensive opportunities for data accumulation, visualisation and transfer in teaching and research activities. Bella has published her research and presented her work in top international journals and conferences, including the annual conferences of the Academy of Management and Strategic Management Society.

Pieter-Jan Bezemer

Pieter-Jan Bezemer is a Senior Lecturer in Strategic Management at Edith Cowan University. Over the past 15 years he has taught strategy and corporate governance in Australia, Estonia, Italy, The Netherlands and New Zealand. Pieter-Jan's expertise centres around strategic decision making in the boardroom and the diffusion of contested management practices. His research has been published in leading journals, such as the *Academy of Management Journal, Corporate Governance: An International Review* and *British Journal of Management and Strategic Organization*. He is currently a member of the editorial review board at *Corporate Governance: An International Review* and the *International Journal of Business Ethics and Governance*. In Australia he has been involved in a series of formal boardroom evaluations, including financial institutions regulated by the Australian Prudential Regulation Authority.

UNDERSTANDING STRATEGY

CHAPTER 1

Strategic concepts and perspectives

LEARNING OBJECTIVES

After studying this chapter, you should be able to:

1.1 define what is meant by strategy and strategic management

1.2 explain the difference between emergent and intended strategy

1.3 define the four main types of strategy formulation process

1.4 understand how strategic management processes are used in practice in the digital age

1.5 explain how strategic thinking is used to achieve differentiation and create strategies that will lead to a sustainable competitive advantage

1.6 construct a statement of organisational purpose comprising the vision, values, ethics and stakeholder needs of an organisation

1.7 define the role of internal and external environmental analyses, strategic objectives and performance measures, including sustainability, in strategic management

1.8 distinguish between corporate, business- and functional-level strategies, comment on how strategy can be applied in the public sector, and explain the differences between offensive and defensive strategies.

The strategic problems behind Target Australia's poor performance

As Target Australia starts to shut down some of its retail activities, the consequences of the decline in sales over the last 10 years have become apparent.[1] Having been bought by the Coles supermarket chain, Target Australia (unrelated to Target US, having commenced operations in 1926 in Geelong, Victoria) was acquired along with the Coles supermarket chain by Wesfarmers (a major Australian holding company) in 2007. Target Australia is the largest retail chain in Australia with 289 stores.[2] Although highly successful due to extremely competitive pricing for most of its history, Target Australia has shown chequered performance since its acquisition by Wesfarmers.

Wesfarmers has been successful in the acquisition and subsequent process improvement of retail and primary industry businesses.[3] Wesfarmers enabled Target to grow significantly after its acquisition by merging it with a similar retail chain (Fossey's) and many new store openings. Wesfarmers also increased the focus of Target by shifting from competing through quite low prices to a more focused strategy of competing through value for money on higher quality products. Since 2000, international retail competition has increased customer quality expectations globally, making low-quality, low-cost products much less attractive.[4] Wesfarmers's repositioning of Target was a response to this change in the external environment.

This strategy made the process of running Target's inventory and supply chain much more challenging. In the past, Target had bought at the lowest prices and used the opportunities for low-cost supply as the basis of purchase and product decisions. The introduction of the quality standard meant that all merchandise that Target purchased needed to meet two criteria — quality and price — significantly reducing the supply opportunities available to Target.[5] Furthermore, this quality–cost balance on which Target was focusing was not static. Changes in economic conditions both in Australia and overseas resulted in large shifts in the quality and price that Target's customers were expecting.[6] By comparison, expectations of low-cost products and very high quality products are relatively static because the range of acceptable quality for low-cost products and the price for very high quality products is much larger than the accepted range for best-value products. This makes retail of best-value products a very dynamic process. The changes in economic conditions also introduced exchange rate fluctuations, which were now significant for Target, creating supply price variations for the quality range that Target was purchasing that were not always compatible with its best-value objective.

The result of this was that both inventory management and the supply chain became extremely difficult to manage. If stock was not sold quickly, shifts in customer preferences could mean that the price/quality ratio being offered was no longer attractive as customer quality expectations increased. Furthermore, Target could no longer rely on long-term supply relationships because its customer's expectations of both quality and price were constantly varying. Therefore, Target needed to constantly negotiate new supply contracts and supply chain structures in order to maintain an attractive quality/cost ratio.

The result has been that, while Target grew over the last 10 years and managed to produce an acceptable profit for a number of financial years, profitability was not strong when the quality/cost balance was difficult to sustain.[7] Wesfarmers's strategic approach to this issue has been to reduce costs by reducing the number of Target outlets. In addition, reducing sales volumes by reducing the number of outlets has made the supply chain smaller and easier to manage.

Introduction

The Target scene setter demonstrates the effect of strategic decisions on business performance and how strategy determines the direction of an organisation's development and its future. It is arguably the only business management activity that can make this claim. The trade war between the US and China has illustrated how economic conditions can quickly become difficult. Under conditions such as these, customers, suppliers and the government are unable to provide support and the only mechanism left to ensure the business's survival is its **strategic management**. Interestingly, the businesses that are able to survive a trade war will not only become more efficient and successful as a result of strategic improvements, they will also find that they have an increased market share, as a result of the closure of businesses unable to survive under those conditions.

Despite the clear benefits of strategic management, many organisations review their strategies thoroughly only during times of crisis, such as during a pandemic, or when a new chief executive officer (CEO) is employed.[8] One of the more popular topics in business-media interviews of incoming CEOs of large companies is how they will deal with the challenges of that company's performance. Incoming CEOs frequently find that the organisation's strategies are already out of date when they take up their new roles. Subsequently, one of the most common priorities of new CEOs is to introduce new strategies that are better matched to the organisation's current capabilities and external environment. The COVID-19 pandemic caused most organisations in Australia to review their strategies and many of them publicly described how they would remain (or become) effective during the crisis to assure customers.

Strategic management is an essential process, but it is not simple. Modern strategic management principles contain many concepts and each of these concepts contains a number of individual perspectives. This text will present the central themes of contemporary strategic management as a pattern of thought, creativity and planning. This chapter will provide an overview of strategic management in today's business environment, discuss its principal benefits and introduce some of the central themes upon which it is based. It is important to note that the principles presented in this chapter are equally applicable to commercial, non-government and not-for-profit organisations such as public-sector organisations and charities. Thus, wherever there is a reference to businesses and business-level strategy, the concepts will be equally applicable to multiple organisational contexts.

1.1 What is strategic management?

LEARNING OBJECTIVE 1.1 Define what is meant by strategy and strategic management.

Strategic management is the process of directing and strengthening the ability of an organisation to compete in its domain or industry. Strategic management theories explain why organisations succeed or fail.[9] Competitive actions have been shown to be more significant in determining an organisation's performance than the effect of its business environment. Strategies for these vary enormously between companies, even within a single industry. Within any industry there will be a broad range of organisations: small, large, public, private, manufacturing, service, domestic and global. These companies will experience a large variation in opportunities and will adopt different approaches to competing and different markets. Understanding these differences and how they impact on success is fundamental to the study of strategy.

Contemporary strategic management is based on the assumption that performance is first affected by the characteristics of the organisation and secondly by its environment. Strategic management is the process of matching the organisation's characteristics (e.g. strengths and weaknesses) to the external environment (which provides opportunities and threats).[10] This process of matching the organisation to its environment is a continuous process of analysis, synthesis, action-taking and evaluation as the environment is always changing.

An underlying assumption of strategic management is that those responsible for decision making can positively influence the success of their organisations through their decisions. Instead of simply responding to environmental factors, such as opportunities, senior decision makers make adjustments to direct the organisation along the path that they believe will lead to long-term success. Oster refers to this strategy planning and implementation as 'directed evolution'.[11] Mostly, these adjustments are relatively minor; however, they can sometimes be quite dramatic, such as a company's decision to exit a particular market where it is not successful.

Extensive surveys over the last decades have determined that strategy does indeed drive business success.[12] The relationship between strategy and success has been harder to demonstrate for public sector and small organisations because they frequently do not possess formalised and reportable strategies that can be measured, even if they are using strategy to create success. So, for these organisations, the jury is still out.

Strategy requires managers to make a continual stream of decisions to match their objectives, the external environment and the conditions within the organisation. This means that decision making is a fundamental component of strategy. Of course, not all organisational choices or decisions are 'strategic'.[13] Strategic decisions are focused on the long-term success of the organisation — short-term successes are more frequently the response of tactical and operational level decisions. However, sometimes these decisions can evolve into formal strategies, as we will discuss later on. In addition, strategies are almost exclusively aimed at achieving an advantage over competitors, no matter whether the objective is profitability, market share or funding. Finally, strategies determine the scope of the organisation's activities and the achievement of fit between the organisation and its environment.[14]

The commitment of key organisational resources is implicit in this view of strategic decisions. These resources will not be only financial; they will usually include key staff members, physical and information resources. The more irrevocable the commitment of these resources, the more 'strategic' becomes the decision to commit.[15] The military allegory of 'burning your bridges' demonstrates the importance of this commitment, as does the economics concept of 'sunk costs'. More recently, we have realised that changes to external conditions mean the value of specific resources also changes. This led to the concept of dynamic capabilities, which is the combination of resources and the competencies to be able to use them in order to adapt to changing external conditions. For example, if a professional organisation, such as a legal firm, had a dynamic capability in training that provided a competitive advantage, it would be able to adapt the type of training it offered as, for example, the opportunities for types of cases changed.

The pattern of decisions or actions taken by managers constitutes the organisation's strategy. Some strategy theorists believe that this pattern of decision making should be a rational and deliberate process of long-term planning. This is represented in Chandler's classic definition of strategy as 'the determination of the basic long-term goals and objectives of an enterprise and the adoption of courses of action and the allocation of resources necessary for carrying out these goals'.[16] Other strategists, such as Burgelman, suggest that 'strategy is a theory about the reasons for past and current success of the organisation'.[17] In other words, some strategies result from emergent, rather than planned, actions. Relying purely on planned strategy presumes that the organisation is totally in control of its destiny, which is rarely the case. This perspective on strategy will be discussed in more detail shortly.

Why does an organisation need strategy?

Apart from ensuring survival, a **strategy** acts as the key driver of how and where the organisation invests its resources. The strategy of an organisation will be evident in its pattern of resources. Strategies can also be responsible for ensuring that the organisation has sufficient flexibility to respond to environmental changes. This is a very important strategic outcome for many organisations. The complex global business environment is composed of constantly changing customer needs (for example, the needs of the Chinese middle-class, which is set to reach 750 million people by 2024, almost completely changes every six months).[18] In addition, the ability of competitors (local, regional, national and multinational) to take advantage of the weaknesses of other organisations is a major challenge. Strategy as the management of the interface between an organisation and its external environment must respond to these forces.

1.2 Strategic management approaches

LEARNING OBJECTIVE 1.2 Explain the difference between emergent and intended strategy.

The discipline of strategic management incorporates a range of different perspectives on the strategic management process. One of the most critical questions is 'how much can the strategy be planned and how much will emerge from day-to-day actions?' To help respond to this, Henry Mintzberg introduced the concept of the 'five Ps', shown in table 1.1.[19]

TABLE 1.1 Mintzberg's 'five Ps for strategy'

Strategy as *plan*	Consciously intended course of action
Strategy as *ploy*	Specific manoeuvre to outwit opponents
Strategy as *pattern*	Pattern in a stream of actions
Strategy as *position*	Position in relation to the organisation's environment
Strategy as *perspective*	The organisation's shared mindset

In most cases, strategy development constitutes a *plan*, a consciously intended course of action that is premeditated and deliberate with strategies realised as intended. Mintzberg's concept of strategy as *ploy* suggests engaging in specific tactics to outmanoeuvre or outsmart opponents. These two perspectives comprise the planned or *design* view of strategy.

Strategy can also be viewed as a *pattern* or 'stream of actions' resulting from day-to-day operational decisions. Strategy as a pattern suggests that strategy can also result from actions, rather than only as a plan.[20]

Mintzberg's concept of strategy as *position* concerns an organisation's strategic positioning in relation to its environment. By asking questions such as 'how is a market niche created?' or 'how can the organisation protect its position?', an organisation scans its external environment to identify trends that may affect the organisation and its environmental 'fit'. This suggests that strategy can be *opportunistic* and take advantage of changes in the environment, especially as the organisation develops or acquires new skills and competencies. Organisations that are skilled at anticipating or even precipitating environmental shifts and position themselves strategically to exploit these shifts ahead of competitors can draw on both *experience* and innovative *ideas*.

While strategy as position seeks to place the organisation in its external environment, the concept of strategy as *perspective* looks inside the 'mind' of the organisation and tries to understand its shared world view. Strategy as perspective 'is to the organisation what personality is to the individual'.[21] Perspective represents the shared values which frame the organisation's action and behaviour. Strategy as perspective has strong parallels with the concept of organisational culture.

Weick took the concept of strategy as *position* further and argued that there are a number of substitutes for strategic planning that can still result in successful organisational performance.[22] These include staff members' skills, the type of work that the organisation performs, the choice of the way operations are managed and the principal features of its environment — all of which force the organisation to take certain actions. Weick suggested that strategy can be represented by the day-to-day behaviours of staff, rather than the result of a formal process, directed by senior management. These behaviours, or tactics, are different to formal strategic management as they are responsive, rather than premeditated. Strategy capsule 1.1 explains how the Australian business Canva used a subscription service for its web-based publication design tools (a tactic, rather than a complete organisational strategy) to attract corporate customers.

Creating your own strategy canvas — Canva's success

Having commenced operations in 2012, Canva, a Sydney-based design and publishing web-based service, is now valued at over US$1 billion, has over 800 employees worldwide and posts an annual profit of over US$2 million per year.[23] The company's success has been due to its innovative and aggressive product development, which closely maps its target customers' needs.[24] Having initially created a subscription service for its web-based publication design tools, Canva was able to capture a significant corporate customer market.[25] It has subsequently moved on to acquire several smaller related publishing businesses to increase and broaden its product range to better service its target market.

As a creative organisation, staff are a key feature in Canva's ability to innovate.[26] The directors focus carefully on creating an attractive workplace and, in 2018, Canva was awarded the 'Best Place to Work' award for organisations with between 100 and 999 employees.[27] Canva's strategy reflects a strong resource-based view (attracting the best employees), a dynamic capabilities focus (using acquisitions to acquire new resources and capabilities in order to follow the market), innovation and entrepreneurialism (growing quickly when it can to achieve economies of scale and a large resource base).

As described in strategy capsule 1.1, Canva's tactic of using a web-based subscription service for the delivery of its publication design tools to make them attractive to corporate customers was very successful, enabling it to grow very rapidly. Whether this will continue to be sufficient to ensure its competitive position, however, is less clear and a more sophisticated strategy may be required. Inkpen and Choudhury support this view and argue that the absence of formal strategy can introduce a level of flexibility which is advantageous under some conditions.[28] This flexibility may be critical in organisations that are operating in turbulent environments when long-term planning is impossible and no organisation can make irrevocable commitments to a specific strategy. They point out that strategies 'may act like blinders and block out an organisation's peripheral vision'.[29]

The absence of formal strategy may foster flexibility and innovation in some cases, leading to successful new ideas and products. History is littered with examples of this, such as the development of the magnetic audio tape by BASF, a large German chemical manufacturer. One of its engineers developed a technique for incorporating iron oxide into a plastic strip and created the magnetic audio tape. BASF, however, had no intention of entering the audio recording equipment industry and instead licensed the technology to Sony.

Emergent strategy

Mintzberg's description of strategy as possessing an unplanned dimension introduces the idea of emergent strategy. **Emergent strategies** are unplanned strategies that result from decisions made by management at various levels in the organisation, which end up having a significant impact upon the performance of the organisation and, ultimately, become part of its strategy. Emergent strategy is reflected in the behaviours of companies such as BASF, discussed previously, and Microsoft Corporation. Emergent strategies also tend to evolve from the organisational flexibility that Inkpen and Choudhury identified as important for more turbulent business environments.

Emergent strategies will be considered in the section on strategy implementation at the end of this chapter. However, not only do they arise from decisions made that have a strategic impact upon the organisation, they can also result from environmental changes that force the organisation to react. For example, Woolworths, the leading supermarket chain in Australia, entered into a partnership with Caltex Australia to retail petrol. This partnership gave Woolworths access to the benefits of the petrol retail industry. This partnership created a major change to the environment of Woolworths' principal competitor, Coles. Coles was forced to diversify into the petrol retail industry as well.[30] Coles decided that acquisition of a petrol retail licence from Shell (a global petrochemical company) was the most appropriate approach to take and so an emergent strategy for Coles of developing a petrol retail division resulted.

Studies have shown that organisations do not usually adopt purely emergent or purely planned strategies, but normally end up with a combination of both. The more rapid the rate of change in the organisation's external environment, the more significant the emergent component of the strategy becomes.[31] Interestingly, there is no evidence for whether an emergent or a planned strategy will result in a greater level of performance. On the other hand, strategies that fit the external environment better have been shown to increase business performance.[32]

1.3 Applying strategy — the formulation process

LEARNING OBJECTIVE 1.3 Define the four main types of strategy formulation process.

Strategic management is influenced by diverse and often conflicting theories; so, how can it be applied in a manageable way? Whittington suggested strategy be viewed as comprising four overarching processes: classical, evolutionary, processual and systemic. These processes are measured using two dimensions:[33]

1. the extent to which the perspective assumes a single profit-maximising motive versus a broader (pluralist) one
2. the extent to which the theories assume that strategic management is a deliberate, rational planning process versus an emergent process.

These processes and their dimensions are illustrated in figure 1.1.[34]

Classical formulation adopts profit as the principal objective and pursues this in a rational and calculating manner. It has strong connections with both military history and classical economics theory where the strategy is driven by a single decision maker with a single objective. In military history, it is the general who dictates actions; in economics, the economist pursues clear, financial goals through rational and analytic means.[35]

Evolutionary formulation reflects the environment, more than internal planning, in the decisions. The environment is considered to be the key determinant of the success of organisations. This approach can provide a powerful 'reality check' for strategic decisions made using any formulation process.

Processual formulation reflects the realities of organisational life, which are influenced by politics, the divergent interests of multiple stakeholders and organisational culture. This formulation approach incrementally develops strategy and leads to a compromise between a planned strategy and a strategy that can be successfully implemented.

FIGURE 1.1   Generic perspectives on strategy

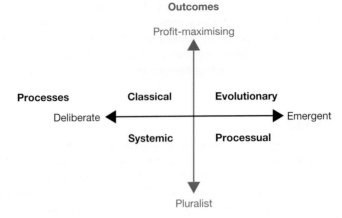

Source: Based on Whittington, p. 28, 1993.

Systemic formulation reflects the internal and external context in which strategy takes place. It allows for the behaviour of people, institutions and organisations, and is influenced by social and economic systems. It also introduces the limitations to strategies that these external systems create.

While all of these approaches will have something to offer any situation, it is not possible to specify a particular formulation process for a specific condition because the formulation of strategy is not a predictable process — it is creative. Strategy reflects how the stakeholders believe the organisation should develop and how they understand the environment. This makes the strategy formulation process complex. However, according to Lovallo and Sibony, the formulation process typically results in individual or sets of fundamental decisions that produce strategic outcomes, habitual 'strategic' decisions that do not actually produce strategic outcomes and incidental decisions that unexpectedly produce strategic outcomes.[36]

One problem that successful organisations experience is that past successes will tend to drive future strategic thinking. As a result, it often becomes extremely difficult to stop the longstanding routines and behaviours that were established to support past successes, but which may no longer be appropriate.[37] In their study of change at BHP, Lewis, Clark and Moss observed a rigid commitment to past approaches, even when confronted with their failure to produce results in the present.[38] They concluded that organisations 'become frozen by the emphatic success of the past'. Innovation can become stifled as managers become hesitant to take risks and performance suffers.

Adopting the correct strategy formulation process can help to avoid this trap by producing creative strategies. Another, more process-oriented, alternative to Whittington's categorical framework, which supports creative strategies, is composed of four approaches.

Sequential approach

The sequential or classic strategy formulation approach is often considered to be the 'standard' approach and is sometimes thought to be a strict sequence of steps. The sequential approach comprises:
- gathering information about your situation and the environment
- determining the directions to take, given the information available
- selecting a specific direction
- taking steps to implement your decision
- managing, monitoring and controlling your actions to achieve the desired outcome.

The sequential approach is a simple and frequently adopted model that incorporates an important dimension of creative strategy formulation — strategic thinking. The need for specific information at each stage means that this strategy formulation process cannot be a rigid sequence of steps. For example, the analysis required to help set the strategic direction will need to be finetuned as the appropriate direction becomes apparent and more information on specific direction is required. In addition, the implementation of the strategy may identify issues that require a modification of the selected direction and a possible demand for more analysis.

Incremental and interactive approach

The sequential view of strategy formulation above is heavily reliant on the availability of very specific information and the opportunity to make decisions after each step. It is an iterative process and so some strategic opportunities may no longer be available later in the process as a result of earlier decisions.

By comparison, the incremental approach will produce an evolutionary and gradual development of strategy, which is a significant contrast to the more dramatic changes often developed during intensive strategy workshops.[39] This logical incrementalism may result in a more 'ordered' evolution of strategy, but it will be inappropriate for any organisation with a rapidly changing environment.[40]

Hierarchical approach

A hierarchical approach to formulating strategy makes decisions based on information available at a specific level of the organisation. This leads to a stratified form of strategy and tends to produce strategic responses to strategy demands from the next highest level. It is more common in large, highly diversified organisations in which corporate strategy mainly focuses on identifying the industries and markets where the organisation should compete. The business level strategy then becomes a response from business unit managers to the corporate level decision about how to best compete in that particular environment. Divisional managers then make strategic decisions about how that approach to competition will be achieved in practice (e.g. marketing, purchasing and design decisions). The result of this approach is that the opportunities for introducing innovation at the lower levels are reduced.

Revolutionary approach

The revolutionary approach to formulating strategy, developed in the 1990s, is defined by Hamel and Markides[41] as being part planning and part trial and error until a successful approach is identified. Recently, the 'agile' approach (a process originally developed for producing innovative software) is being assessed as a more structured method for creating revolutionary strategy. This process involves:[42]

- identifying the objective of strategy development in the organisation
- development of different responses by teams
- strategy owner feedback regarding the responses to refine (discourse).

1.4 Strategic management in the digital age

LEARNING OBJECTIVE 1.4 Understand how strategic management processes are used in practice in the digital age.

The strategy formulation approaches that have been considered to this point create strategy deliberately either through evolution or by direct intent. However, is this how strategies are developed in practice? The growth and international success of many successful companies (e.g. Ebay, Tesla) are primarily due to the focus on providing a service or product that is valuable to the customer, in the best manner possible.

Henry Mintzberg has been a strong supporter of the importance of emergent strategies based on meeting needs and responding to opportunity since the 1980s.[43] Now the digital age provides information about opportunities and the ability to connect with customers at an unprecedented level. Companies are swamped with possibilities, but only have the capacity to invest in a small number of strategic level initiatives. Organisational resources simply don't allow for too much experimentation at the strategic level.

Furthermore, while the Internet of Things has increased access to information dramatically, the reliability and completeness of this information has not improved (or has even declined). Consequently, organisations must view the strategic opportunities that are available to them with discretion. This leads to a hybrid approach, combining traditional strategic planning, based on well understood information and emergent strategy resulting from responses to digital inputs and analytic systems such as AI.

It also brings about a greater diversity in decision making — traditional strategic planning occurring mainly at the board level and making significant demands on organisational resources, together with emergent strategy resulting from the decisions of managers embedded in various digital environments. The complex nature of digital information and analysis systems also means that knowledge specialists have an increasingly large influence on strategy.[44]

The optimal balance for these two dimensions of strategy depends on the stability of the external environment. For example, energy companies mostly experience stable environments, in which demand changes predictably and technology introduction is slow. Project planning in these companies allows for the long-term optimisation of high-value resources such as power lines and power stations and leaves little room for emergent strategy. Companies operating in the social media sector, however, must limit their strategic planning to a few strategic principles and guidelines; the rest of their strategies emerge in response to new developments. LinkedIn, for example, is driven by a clear statement of both mission and objectives, which is well understood throughout the organisation, combined with weekly meetings of all executives to draw ideas from all sections about how those goals can be achieved. CEO Jeff Weiner is prepared to make a major strategic decision at any time.[45]

Strategic intent

Strategic intent focuses on what the organisation will become in the future. Strategic intent is a set of aspirations intended to motivate and inspire the organisation. Hamel and Prahalad argue that:[46]

> strategic intent creates an extreme misfit between resources and ambitions. Top management then challenges the organisation to close the gap by building new competitive advantages.

Toyota and the Virgin Group have shown that a company can perform by developing a clear strategic intent and being innovative, in order to encourage staff to apply all resources to achieving the organisation's principal goals. The cost of resources encourages prioritisation and focus on strategies that lead to critical goals. It also creates a simple work environment which encourages innovations. The Walt Disney Company and 3M have utilised strategic intent to develop rapidly through high-level employee commitment and focus, and the ability to make innovative decisions.[47] Strategic intent is the reason that many successful organisations have inspirational vision and mission statements, such as the Australia Department of Health's 'Better health and wellbeing for all Australians, now and for future generations'.[48]

Strategic thinking

Strategic thinking extends the idea of strategic intent to cover the whole strategy formulation process and not just the broad thrust and objectives. Strategic planning assumes that the external environment is sufficiently static and predictable that carefully executed changes will still be relevant when they are implemented. As we have discussed, however, external events, such as the worldwide outbreak of COVID-19, mean that planning, and even digitally driven strategy, will not always provide the correct direction. Richard Branson's Virgin Group provides a good example of the art of **strategic thinking**. Strategic thinking is the process of achieving a balance between environmental conditions, the organisation's objectives and its resources. The appearance of big data has changed this process by introducing much more information about environmental conditions.[49] This has allowed organisations to respond more strongly to environmental conditions because they are more informed about those conditions. Richard Branson displays a strong capacity for strategic thinking, driving his Virgin Group to make quick decisions about new opportunities, using the decision-making heuristics resulting from the group's strategic thinking.[50]

Strategic thinking encourages the organisation to develop the responsiveness to unanticipated events. For example, if a business operates in a turbulent environment with a well-formulated strategy, strategic thinking will conclude that the strategy must embrace flexibility and responsiveness. As Michael Porter notes, strategy is not about doing things better — this is the concern of operational effectiveness — strategy is about making choices.[51]

1.5 Strategy and differentiation

LEARNING OBJECTIVE 1.5 Explain how strategic thinking is used to achieve differentiation and create strategies that will lead to a sustainable competitive advantage.

It will be apparent by now that a central objective of strategic management is to create **differentiation** between competing organisations (e.g. industry competitors or municipal bodies competing for funding and resources). As an objective, differentiation is the apparent difference between the services and product offerings of the organisation that leads **stakeholders** — particularly primary customers and other users — to prefer one organisation over another. Increasingly, intermediaries such as internet content aggregating services have reduced the opportunity to differentiate on the basis of support by eliminating the personal service element of the transaction.[52] This leaves only the product and service features as sources of differentiation, which can be difficult in many industries, such as commodity industries, where products and services are very standardised.

When making decisions about differentiation, the first question is 'how can a competitive advantage be achieved?' A **competitive advantage** is defined as any source of difference between one organisation and its competitors that will assist the organisation to achieve its objectives.

Essentially, there are two approaches to creating a competitive advantage. One approach is to set the price of the product or service lower than that of competitors. The alternative is to incorporate an 'added value' in the product or service that differentiates the product or service in the eye of the customer. This approach relies on the customer perceiving that the added feature is sufficiently attractive to influence their decisions. This can take the form of higher quality, extra features, compatibility or web-based support. Internet markets, such as eBay, have meant that other forms of service differentiation, such as speed of delivery, are not effective.

Core competencies

The development of internal processes and assets that create a competitive advantage will be the result of the organisation's **core competencies**.[53] When processes and core competencies are characterised by complexity, path dependency and casual ambiguity, they are difficult to imitate or transfer.[54] Possessing competitive advantages with these characteristics, however, is not an automatic guarantee of sustainable competitive advantage. Changes to the external environment can quickly destroy the basis of a competitive advantage and make the core competencies that created it redundant. For example, accounting software has made the competency of managing double-entry accounting records unnecessary. Core competencies and the organisational assets associated with them can even become a disadvantage if they interfere with the organisation's adaptation to new environmental conditions.

Strategic resources

The **resource-based view (RBV)** assumes that success is due to the **strategic resources** that are available for competition. This perspective is well supported by evidence. For example, a four-year longitudinal study of 2800 US businesses in the mid 1990s determined that, while industry conditions explained 4 per cent of profitability variation, individual company resources explained 44 per cent of profitability variation across the companies.[55] A more recent study in Spain, involving 1642 organisations, found that industry conditions explained 3 per cent and company resources explained 36 per cent of performance variation.[56] As a result, the RBV has remained one of the most popular contemporary strategy perspectives. As strategy capsule 1.3 demonstrates, Australia Post has focused on maximising its resource utilisation to increase its competitiveness in the global postal/logistics industry.

Dynamic capabilities

In addition to the concept of core competencies, the concept of dynamic capabilities was developed to reflect the ability of organisations to create capabilities that tracked and responded to changes in the external environment.[57] These capabilities enable the organisation to continue to hold a competitive advantage, even when what was required to achieve that had changed. For example, a traditional face-to-face medical service may move to a web-based consultation service due to customer demand or in response to a pandemic, if the medical staff are able to apply their skills in the online environment. The ability of the medical clinicians to apply their skills in either a face-to-face or online environment is an example of a dynamic capability.

Industry strategies

Achieving cost leadership or differentiation are not the only ways in which an organisation can compete. Contributing to the development of an industry strategy can increase the competitiveness of all the organisations in an industry, relative to other industries. These strategies are known as **industry strategies**.

The benefits of an industry strategy are particularly important for the public sector. Australian universities, for example, frequently adopt similar strategies, structures and course profiles when competing for status, research funding, new staff and students with the best credentials.[58] New universities will adopt these strategies because they are the fastest route to legitimacy within the higher education industry.[59] Adopting a standard approach demonstrates that the institution is dependable to students and deserving of support and resources to the governments that fund the universities. In industries where the institutional environment is strong, the legitimacy provided by industry strategies increases the entire industry's competitiveness.[60] For example, a recent study found that the New Zealand sheep farming industry would become much more competitive if the entire industry focused on customer responsiveness, innovation and sustainability. The study also found that if the entire industry displayed these characteristics, all New Zealand sheep products would be much more competitive in the global market and this would benefit all sheep farmers in New Zealand.[61]

1.6 Organisational purpose

LEARNING OBJECTIVE 1.6 Construct a statement of organisational purpose comprising the vision, values, ethics and stakeholder needs of an organisation.

Strategic thinking requires the answers to two critical questions.

1. Where should the organisation compete?
2. How should the organisation compete?

To be able to answer these questions, the organisation must first clearly identify its **organisational purpose**. Understanding the role of the organisation in its industry and society is fundamental to identifying long-term strategies and goals. This is no simple task, however, as it needs to represent the expectations of all stakeholders, both internal and external.

This understanding is particularly useful for complex and uncertain environments. It can provide direction when trends and preferences are not apparent. Consider, for example, the travel agency Flight Centre, which is listed on the Australian Securities Exchange (ASX). The purpose of this organisation is to provide travel-related services to clients. Competition with international flight agencies, crises such as the COVID-19 pandemic and plummeting demand make strategic decisions difficult in this industry. In this environment, an organisational purpose statement would help Flight Centre to decide whether it should compete as an agent which (a) provides advice and helps customers to plan dependable holidays, (b) books accommodation and tickets, or (c) helps customers if their travel plans go wrong. Focusing on all three of these areas would dilute Flight Centre's resources across too many activities. It is more likely to be successful if it excels in one area, rather than providing an average performance across the three. How can Flight Centre choose which approach is best in such an uncertain industry? Having a clear and up-to-date purpose would indicate which is the correct approach.

Organisational purpose is very important to strategy in the service industry. Through several corporate owners, the Australian travel guide company Lonely Planet has maintained a focus on accuracy and dependability of its travel reviews targeted to the economy-minded traveller. Despite the turbulence of the travel industry, this single-minded focus has kept the business successful for almost 50 years.[62]

When determining the organisation's purpose, five perspectives should be considered: (1) corporate governance, (2) stakeholder expectations, (3) mission, (4) values and ethical standards and (5) culture. The following questions should be asked.

- Who are the stakeholders?
- What are their interests?
- What influences their expectations?
- Should the organisation take their interests into account?
- Should the organisation serve wider societal interests?
- How are conflicting interests prioritised?
- How do national, industry and professional cultures impact on decisions?
- What is the ethical stance of stakeholders and the organisation?
- How does the organisational mission reflect all of these factors?

Organisational vision and mission

The mission and vision of the organisation are a good starting point for defining organisational purpose. They can be imaginative or pragmatic. The **vision** is a long-term view of where the organisation will be in the distant future, while the **mission** provides a contemporary statement of how the organisation competes in the current environment and who the target customers are. The mission should also describe the organisation's anticipated position within the industry, key values and ethical standards. For example, the vision of the Cancer Council (of Australia) is 'a cancer-free future' and the mission is to 'lead a cohesive approach to reduce the impact of cancer' by 'undertaking and funding cancer research, preventing and controlling cancer, and providing information and support for people affected by cancer'.[63]

Values

Organisations frequently include their corporate social responsibility (CSR) in their **value statements**. For example, BHP Billiton's CSR statement (called their Charter) states that it must involve stakeholders and create ethically acceptable operations. It also indicates that this should be a feature of the behaviours of its staff and culture. A large organisation such as BHP Billiton needs to take a broad approach to its value statements because of its diverse range of investors and stakeholders. Without incorporating all its stakeholders, investor confidence would be diminished and investment and share prices would be negatively affected.

Ethical position

When deciding upon the organisation's purpose, the **ethical position** of the organisation should be considered, along with its mission, vision and values. Important aspects of the organisation's ethical position include transparency to customers, attitudes towards human rights and the natural environment, and working conditions.

Unsurprisingly, aspects of the ethical position will overlap with the organisation's values. The principal difference, however, is that the values of an organisation can be quite individualised, while an ethical position will reflect the stakeholders' cultures and societies. In multinational organisations, reflecting stakeholders' cultures can make finding a broadly acceptable ethical position challenging if the different stakeholders' cultures have significantly different ethics expectations. For example, whaling is still considered to be an acceptable undertaking in some countries, but is unacceptable in other countries. If an organisation undertakes whaling or is associated with the whaling industry only within the boundaries of countries where it is considered ethical, it may consider itself to be behaving ethically. Customers from cultures which consider whaling to be inappropriate would view the organisation's ethical position regarding whaling as unethical. In the same way, employment of child labour by third-tier suppliers (e.g. organisations that supply other organisations which, in turn, supply other organisations that then supply manufacturers) has challenged large sports footwear manufacturers (e.g. Nike and Adidas) for many years. While many of their customers in developed countries view child labour as unethical, in some countries where the shoes are manufactured, child labour is considered to be acceptable as it provides essential financial support for poorer families. These challenges mean that an organisation's ethical position must be constantly reviewed to ensure that it continues to meet the expectations of its stakeholders, especially when the organisation introduces new stakeholders (e.g. introducing a new subsidiary, new suppliers or a new market). Ethics as part of organisational purpose will be considered in further detail in the chapter on corporate governance and ethics.

Key organisational stakeholders

The preceding discussion of the role of stakeholders in organisational purpose, value and ethical statements shows how important stakeholders are in providing direction to the organisation. As a result, selecting the correct stakeholders is also important. Robbins and Barnwell argue that stakeholders are agents that exert a large influence on the organisation.[64] Johnson et al. support this and state that stakeholders 'are those individuals or groups who depend on the organisation to fulfil their own goals and on whom, in turn, the organisation depends'.[65] However, De Wit and Meyer argue that this view is too narrow and that stakeholders should be divided into direct and indirect stakeholders.[66] Direct stakeholders are the 'direct participants in the economic value creation process' and indirect stakeholders are other 'parties affected by the organisation's activities'. Daft is more inclusive and suggests that stakeholders are 'any group within or outside an organisation that has a stake in the organisation's performance'.[67]

The key stakeholders to consider in relation to mission, vision, values and ethical position include:

- owners
- staff members
- staff members' representative groups (e.g. unions)
- customers
- regulatory authorities
- government
- communities in which the organisation operates
- sectors of society that benefit indirectly from the organisation's operations.

Determining each of these groups' views and expectations is not difficult; however, as discussed above the disparity between their views can make their integration into values, mission and ethical positions difficult. In situations where stakeholder views conflict, it is quite likely that a compromise will simply leave both parties dissatisfied. The conflict between unions and management when staff have been terminated due to the effect of the COVID-19 pandemic on sales is a good example. Managers are stakeholders who will view reducing staffing levels as the most appropriate way to reduce operating costs because the alternative of reducing infrastructure is slow and wasteful. The unions, who are also stakeholders, will have an opposing view because of the negative impact upon their members plus the subsequent loss of union membership resulting from lay-offs. It is unlikely that there is a compromise that will meet the needs of both parties in this case.

Changes to stakeholder groups (e.g. moving operations offshore) and the constant evolution in societal expectations can provide opportunities for resolving such conflicts. Therefore, awareness of the current state of stakeholder expectations is critical. Table 1.2[68] provides a list of common stakeholders and their typical expectations of an organisation.

TABLE 1.2	Typical expectations of key stakeholder groups
Stakeholder	**Typical expectations of organisations**
Owners	• return on investment • growth in earnings
Staff members	• pay • fringe benefits • satisfaction with working conditions
Customers	• satisfaction with price, quality and service
Suppliers	• satisfaction with payments • future sales potential
Creditors	• ability to pay debts
Unions	• competitive wages and benefits • satisfactory working conditions • willingness to bargain fairly
Local community officials	• involvement of organisation's members in local affairs • lack of damage to the community's environment
Government agencies	• compliance with laws • avoidance of penalties and reprimands

Source: Adapted from Robbins & Barnwell © 2006. Reprinted by permission of Pearson Education, Inc., Upper Saddle River, NJ.

The characteristics of some key stakeholders will now be considered.

Owners

Organisations can have a range of owners with very different expectations. Institutional investor owners will be seeking short-term investment returns (dividends, profits and share growth) and provide limited support for investments that result in a long-term benefit. Family owners, by comparison, will usually have a strong sentimental attachment to the organisation and its staff and be supportive of long-term investments. The Myer family in Australia, founders of a large and successful retail chain, demonstrated how strong the attachment of family owners can be for their businesses. Over its 110 years of operations, the family has retained a significant shareholding in the retail chain, through several ownership changes. Even though the share price has diminished dramatically over the last 20 years, the Myer family still remains loyal to both the organisation and its employees.

Staff members

Staff are very visible stakeholders and, in some regions (e.g. central Europe), different members of staff even participate in the strategic management process. Their needs are complex and varied and may be linked to other organisations, such as professional associations. The needs of these internal stakeholders, however, do not always reflect the external environment and may reflect a desire to maintain the status quo. This means that strategic decision processes which incorporate significant staff input are often slow to respond to environmental conditions.[69] It is not clear whether the loss of tactical responsiveness is compensated for by improved long-term planning; however, the involvement of staff with long-term experience in the industry is likely to improve the reliability of long-term strategies.

Local communities

The needs of local communities must also be considered when the organisation is a major employer or has a significant (e.g. economic) impact on a community. For example, Australia's only nuclear research facility (the Lucas Heights nuclear reactor) was established in 1958 in a non-residential area, about 30 kilometres south of Sydney.[70] Over time, residential properties were sold around the facility by local landowners. As a result, the research facility now has a new stakeholder group to consider — the local community — and they have very different views to the government, which owns the facility.[71] A similar scenario applies to airports which have expanded to accommodate increased air traffic. They will find that their community stakeholders change as they expand their boundaries and that the needs of the stakeholders change as the air traffic increases. Strategy capsule 1.2 demonstrates how a charitable organisation responds to changes in the needs of its community.

STRATEGY CAPSULE 1.2

Cancer Council Australia — integrating the Indigenous community

Cancer Council Australia commenced operations in 1961, as a federal body formed by the combination of six state-level cancer councils. This amalgamation significantly increased the complexity of the community needs which the Council was required to integrate into its organisational purpose. Due to environmental and lifestyle differences, cancer-related issues and research focus varied significantly across Australia. In 1997, due to increased demand from all its communities, the organisation also increased its political purpose: to help Australia establish appropriate policies and systems for dealing with cancer, including extending services into education.[72] One of the most important aspects of this extension was to increase the needs of the Indigenous community in its organisational purpose.

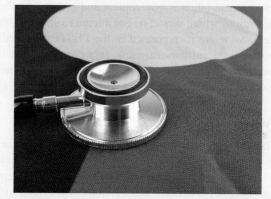

The Indigenous community in Australia has significantly different needs to the remainder of the Australian community. This community is experiencing increased rates of cancer and less effective diagnosis than the remainder of the Australian community.[73] Identifying how to engage with and incorporate the needs of this community was particularly challenging because of the lack of Indigenous staff within the Cancer Council. This made it particularly difficult to establish sustained relationships with Indigenous organisations, which was necessary for the Council to understand their needs. Internal education regarding this community's culture and values was the first step taken by the Council to increase the capacity to engage with this community. The Council adopted programs to increase Indigenous appointments, particularly in the volunteer area, however, this has not been extensively adopted across the organisation. Ongoing learning, however, appears to have improved the ability to understand and incorporate the needs of this community into the Cancer Council's goals and mission.[74]

1.7 A framework for strategic management

LEARNING OBJECTIVE 1.7 Define the role of internal and external environmental analyses, strategic objectives and performance measures, including sustainability, in strategic management.

Planning for strategic management requires considering seven key factors:
1. the external environment
2. the internal characteristics

3. the setting of objectives
4. the crafting of strategies
5. implementation of the necessary change
6. performance measurement
7. plan adjustment.

The following chapters in this book will consider each of these factors in detail. Each will now be briefly considered to provide a context for those chapters.

Analysis of the environment

Igor Ansoff's 1957 product–mission matrix suggested that different strategic approaches are required for different environmental conditions. This concept was the foundation for present-day strategic management environmental analysis approaches.[75] In contemporary strategic management, the external environment is considered to comprise of the macro environment (which can experience large-scale change due to global events such as the COVID-19 pandemic) and the industry environment (in which competitors, suppliers, customers and new market entrants create dynamic competition). The two dimensions of the external environment are analysed using the **PESTEL analysis** for the macro environment and the five forces analysis for the industry environment. An alternative approach involves the use of scenario planning, which was developed in the 1980s as a tool for identifying likely impact of future dramatic events on the organisation. This approach usually includes both macro and industry external environment conditions.

The institution-based view is another environmental analysis framework which is being used for external environmental analysis in strategic management. This view suggests that the institutions in the external environment (such as government and society) create expectations, accepted perspectives, and rules and regulations which should be considered in strategic management.[76] The major elements of the institution-based view are incorporated in the PESTEL analysis framework and it can be assumed to reasonably represent the institutional view. In a context where institutional forces are very strong, considering the institutional view directly may help to identify further external environmental forces which may be overlooked when conducting a more general PESTEL analysis.

Analysis of the organisation

The contribution of strategic management to the performance of the organisation will be largely determined by how well it matches the external and internal environment. The nature of the external environment is usually beyond the control of the organisation (except in the case of very large organisations) and so the matching of the external and internal environment will be achieved by adjusting the internal environment. This means making changes to skills, resources and processes to make the outputs of the organisation as attractive to the market as possible. To start this process, it is necessary to identify:

- the organisation's core competencies and the competencies it lacks, but are important in the current external environment
- the resources it has available for competition
- the suitability of the structure of the organisation for the selected approach to competing in its environment (e.g. a highly bureaucratic structure will make it difficult to compete in a rapidly changing external environment)
- the suitability of the organisational culture for the core competencies and external environment.

Although Mintzberg and the strategy theorists considered earlier in this chapter criticised an analytical-only approach to strategy formulation, a systematic internal analysis is vital for strategic management. Without a deep understanding of the external environment and the conditions in the organisation, strategic decisions are unlikely to increase competitiveness. Understanding the external environment, in particular, will provide a focus for strategic thinking, engaging with stakeholders and establishing sufficient communication and consensus for a successful strategy implementation. This process will be considered in more detail in the chapter on internal analysis of capabilities and core competencies. As strategy capsule 1.3 demonstrates, Australia Post has focused on understanding the global postal/logistics industry and maximising use of its resources to increase its competitiveness with international courier companies.

Australia Post — responding to the digital world

Australia Post is a fully government-owned organisation, which commenced operations in 1809 through its first post office located in George St, Sydney. The organisation was always future focused, taking responsibility for the national telephone services in 1902 and operating over 5000 post offices.[77] More recently, however, the organisation faced the twin threats of digital communication reducing the need for mail delivery and major international couriers replacing the need for a national parcel delivery service. In response, Australia Post underwent several strategic changes, drawing upon its core resources and developing new resources to remain competitive.

Despite the effect of the ongoing reduction in the demand for mail deliveries, Australia Post achieved a revenue of A$7 billion and a profit before tax of A$41 million in 2019.[78] How did this government organisation transform itself while making use of resources developed for a very traditional set of operations? Firstly, as a result of continuing to develop their technological resources to support traditional mail services, Australia Post developed a sophisticated parcel tracking system. In response to the threat of large international couriers, Australia Post struck a deal with the postal services of many countries including China Post and Japan Post to create an international courier service.[79] This service utilised the Australia Post parcel tracking system to enable customers to send parcels overseas using their local postal service, which worked in partnership with the national postal service in the destination country to provide a courier service. This service proved to be very successful because of the large economies of scale that each of the national postal services provided, resulting in a very efficient and competitive parcel delivery system.

Through further extensions of the capabilities of this tracking system, the new global postal service network was also able to make this courier service available as an integrated component of e-commerce systems. This meant that e-commerce platforms, such as eBay, were able to directly integrate the postal network's services with sales. The low cost of the postal service based parcel delivery has ensured that a large volume of global e-commerce sales now passes through this network. Using existing resources which were developed for its own national services, Australia Post was able to take significant advantage of the e-commerce sales occurring around the globe.

While all this was going on, Australia Post continued to adapt the retail sales side of its business. Australia Post had always viewed its postal outlets as a retail business as well as a service point. In addition to the banking and bill-paying services that Australia Post had been providing for some time, it began to increase retail product sales, such as computer peripherals and gifts. These activities now contribute 10 per cent to its total operating revenue[80] and have led to the opening of a large number of postal 'superstores'.[81] The organisation is even opening dedicated postal outlets for the growing number of Chinese expatriates selling prestige products from countries such as Australia to customers in China through social media.[82]

A knowledge-based view

The knowledge-based perspective is an alternative view to the resource-based view for analysing the internal operations of an organisation. It is based on the theory that it is faster and cheaper to transfer information within an organisation than to create it. It suggests that a competitive advantage should be achievable from the management of knowledge within the organisation. However, not all knowledge is strategic. The knowledge must possess an intrinsic value of its own. Also, the difficulties associated with the transfer of information (cost of governance) are dependent upon the backgrounds of the people holding and those receiving the knowledge.[83] For example, staff from the HR department may need more assistance when utilising knowledge generated by the research and development department, because they may use different 'language' and concepts. In this text, knowledge is treated as an organisational resource and incorporated in the resource-based view. This perspective is supported by much of the research that has been conducted on organisational resources in the last 60 years.[84]

Strategic objectives

Without appropriate objectives, an organisation lacks the concrete goals that can be utilised to justify the cost of appropriate strategies and to reject inappropriate strategies. These objectives must reflect the needs of the key stakeholders, the organisation's purpose, the industry conditions and the improvements that senior management wish to achieve. Several philosophies exist for the most important characteristics of **strategic objectives**; however, it is generally considered that strategic objectives should be singular, measurable (and therefore assessed by performance measurement) and represent a challenge (so as to focus activities in the organisation).[85]

Sustainability

Sustainability is a critical strategic objective for organisations in almost every industry, private and public, service and manufacturing. While environmental sustainability has been an objective for many organisations for some time, social and, more recently, economic, sustainability are becoming important strategic objectives as well. Social sustainability objectives are frequently linked with **corporate social responsibility (CSR)** outcomes. Corporate social responsibility includes the impact the organisation has on the community in which it operates[86] and the support it provides (for example, through benevolent activities). At this stage, economic sustainability objectives are limited to certain industries such as the banking and mining industries.[87]

Crafting of strategies

With a set of strategic objectives in place, organisations need to consider the interplay between the internal resources and the external conditions and develop approaches to meet the objectives under these and anticipated future conditions. This is referred to as crafting because of a number of factors. Firstly, uncertainty in the external environment and the plurality of most objectives means that the approach required will not be simple. Rather, a suite of actions will be required to jointly produce a suite of outcomes. These actions are likely to interact with each other as well as create the desired outcomes, which makes it difficult to predict which outcomes will result from specific activities. For example, a strategic objective of increasing customer satisfaction might result from a combination of related quality, training and operations improvement initiatives. It will be difficult, however, to determine which of these initiatives was the main cause of the improvement in customer satisfaction. This is further complicated by the fact that strategies are also applied in different ways at different hierarchical levels in the organisation. The strategies undertaken at each level will have a combined effect on specific strategic objectives, which will also be difficult to separate. As a result, strategy needs to be developed as a suite of interacting and complimentary actions designed to produce a suite of outcomes.

Implementation of the change

Strategic change tends to have a large impact. It also takes much longer than other forms of organisational change, such as promotion activities, training or schedule adjustments. Finally, it occurs much less frequently than changes to other areas of operations. As a result, resources need to be especially assembled for each strategic change, using approaches such as taskforces.

Performance measures

Strategic performance measures are principally used to assess organisational achievements relative to strategic objectives, or milestones on the way towards those objectives. Strategic performance measures are usually separate from operational performance, focusing on outcomes different to those which are used for operations management.[88] The most appropriate measures typically reflect strategy achievement and external perception.[89]

Plan adjustment

Emergent strategies mean that strategic plans are not always successfully implemented or that strategies end up being implemented together with unanticipated strategies. The result of this is that planned objectives may not be achieved as anticipated. A regular review of progress towards strategic objectives, along with strategic thinking can be used to determine what changes should be made to the planned strategies to improve performance in areas where the strategies are not working or whether the objectives need to be revised.

1.8 Types of strategies

LEARNING OBJECTIVE 1.8 Distinguish between corporate-, business- and functional-level strategies, comment on how strategy can be applied in the public sector, and explain the differences between offensive and defensive strategies.

Strategy for different levels of the organisation

Corporate- and business-level strategies were briefly considered in the earlier discussion of strategy formulation processes. The concepts of corporate-, business- and functional-level strategies provide a valuable perspective through which to view different aspects of an organisation's strategy. Separating the organisation's strategy into each of these three levels simplifies the strategy. This approach is very helpful for strategy setting in larger organisations, such as diversified businesses like Wesfarmers, a large, publicly listed Australian conglomerate.

Corporate-level strategy represents the broadest level of strategy. It includes the purpose of the organisation and the interests of its owners or major stakeholders. Corporate-level strategy defines the scope of the organisation's activities and the industries and countries in which it operates. Corporate-level strategy is particularly valuable to companies listed on stock exchanges which need to present cohesive and well-argued strategies to investors.

Business-level strategy, by comparison, refers to how an individual business unit will compete within a particular market. A diversified organisation will have multiple business-units and each will have an individual strategy to reflect the business conditions in its markets. For example, the electronics giant Siemens competes in computer hardware manufacturing, electricity, medical equipment, industrial automation, mobile phones and information services. It has a business-level strategy for each of its business units operating in each of these industries. In local government, the business-level strategy equates to how the organisation seeks to meet the needs of clients, through divisions such as libraries, construction and maintenance, recreation facilities and recycling or waste removal facilities.

Functional-level strategy is concerned with how the organisation supports its business-level strategies by allocating resources and organising operations to create competitive advantage.

Strategy in the public sector

The fundamental basis for strategic management in any type of organisation is the same, whether the organisation is not-for-profit, private or public sector. The external environment does account for some differences in the way in which strategic management is implemented in the public sector and is worthy of consideration.

Public sector organisations have traditionally only been responsible to their government, rather than the range of stakeholders to which most commercial organisations are responsible. In most countries, for example, the taxation office is an income-generating government department and does not provide a service to the businesses from which it collects taxes.

However, this situation is changing rapidly: public demand for increased transparency means that most public sector organisations are now focusing on value creation and external stakeholder needs. Some find themselves in direct competition with commercial organisations that provide the same service (e.g. public utilities, such as energy generators). Even the public sector organisations that enjoy a monopoly position (e.g. central banks) are still under close scrutiny. This is driving public sector organisations to invest more in formal strategic management and adopt strategies which are similar to those of the commercial sector.[90]

At the national level, two approaches to public sector strategy are beginning to emerge. In Australia, the dominant approach appears focused on improvement in management processes, especially governance and innovation. In the United States, the strategic planning process appears to be more revolutionary and is focused on reinventing the way in which these organisations function. In both these countries and in most developed countries, however, there is a strong overall trend towards a reduction in centralised control and an increased autonomy for public sector organisations.[91]

Strategic approaches developed for the commercial sector can be applied to the public sector. Both the realisation of planned strategy and the development of emergent strategy in the public sector are the same as for commercial organisations.[92] One of the most important recent developments in public sector strategy is the shift away from basing decisions on political expediency and internal issues towards creating an environment for performance improvement and organisational learning.[93] Public sector strategies had traditionally been risk adverse and, consequently, tended to ignore opportunities that have not been mandated or, at least, supported by the government sector. For example, further education has tended to be less common among managers in the public sector because it has been less important for promotion, while network connections are more important. One of the most important consequences of this network effect is that public sector strategy changes very slowly.[94]

Changing the industry structure has a unique effect in the public sector. If two commercial organisations operating in one market offer the same products or services, they will compete by increasing their efficiency or adding attractive features. When two public sector organisations service the same customers, they will not compete in the market. Instead they will compete internally to gain the most resources. Government allocations determine the share of the market that each organisation gets and the organisation with the greatest resources will be awarded the largest share of the market. This process does not create beneficial competition and leads to duplication of resources and inefficiency. Privatising public sector organisations has reduced this behaviour and driven them to differentiate in the market.

Modern public sector strategy approaches

Complexity theory can be used to examine strategies of public sector organisations. It suggests that informal decision-making processes and alternative processes exist in public sector organisations which create internal chaos — even while assisting the organisation to achieve its objectives. A combination of a complex and a structured approach to setting and implementing strategy can provide significant benefits. These benefits can be achieved by developing information collection processes for key areas of the organisation and utilising transition techniques to enable the organisation to keep the same objectives while alternating between informal and formal strategies.[95]

Performance measures are also important for public sector strategy and should be transparent to be most effective.[96] The performance of public sector organisations should be defined as the creation of public value, which would lead to public value being an objective for public sector strategies.[97]

From time to time, even public sector organisations will need to be rescued. This process is quite similar to the turnaround strategy adopted by commercial organisations.[98] It involves reducing costs through staff retrenchment, adjusting the structure to make it more efficient and removing unviable processes through outsourcing or closing down non-core business units and operations. It can be more difficult to implement in public sector organisations because union resistance in this sector makes retrenchment more difficult and legislation often interferes with restructuring and repositioning the objectives of the organisation.

Offensive and defensive strategies

Two of the most common categories of strategy are offensive and defensive strategies. These represent the two most general modes of competition. **Offensive strategies** are intended to enable the organisation to expand into new markets and with different products and services, while defensive strategies are intended to protect existing markets and strengthen the position within those. While most strategies have merit and clearly direct resources, offensive strategies have been found to result in longer-term survival. An offensive strategy forces competitors to adopt a defensive strategy and expend resources defending their position.

Defensive strategies generally leave the organisation with nowhere to retreat, and provide competitors with sufficient time to erode markets by developing superior competitive advantages (e.g. pricing, features or service). Improvements in the speed of transportation and information management have made it easy for organisations to compete in any other organisation's markets. No organisation can resist this level of competition in the long term.

Offensive strategies can introduce the organisation to new markets and opportunities. They are an important form of strategy which introduces new opportunities and methods for competing.[99] Any organisation can adopt offensive strategies — even public sector and charitable organisations. Competition for income and resources means that public sector and charitable organisations frequently need to adopt offensive strategies to enable them to meet their objectives. As illustrated in strategy capsule 1.4, World Vision is a good case in point. There were many barriers to World Vision's initiatives for combating COVID-19, internally and externally. Without a very strongly shared organisational purpose and mission, together with highly developed strategy implementation capabilities, this organisation would not have been able to respond so quickly and effectively to COVID-19. A defensive approach would not have allowed it to redirect its internal resources and use learning from prior experience to implement the strategy described in the capsule.

World Vision takes on COVID-19

World Vision Australia is Australia's largest non-government organisation. It is part of a Christian religious relief and development partnership comprising 18 national divisions, supporting operations in 90 countries and operating as a global federation. Its 2019 annual turnover was $500 million and it has 378 projects underway globally at present.[100] The global federation has core fundraising offices in the United States, Canada, Australia and New Zealand. In response to the COVID-19 pandemic, the first stage of World Vision Australia's strategy was to identify the communities at the greatest threat from the coronavirus.[101] This organisation is highly adept at deployment and redeployment of its key resources. In support of this strategy, World Vision Australia redirected their existing operations in these communities and transferred operations from other lower risk communities to provide self-help oriented education and protective equipment to the targeted communities. Prior experience with other crises informed them that this would be the most effective way of implementing their strategy. World Vision operatives in these communities also engaged strongly with 'faith leaders', training them to actively combat fear, stigma and misinformation, and to encourage important behaviours such as regular hand washing.[102] This increased the resources which they were able to apply to implementing this strategy. They engaged government health authorities to further extend the local resources supporting the strategy and provided psychosocial support to the communities to ensure that the actions of these teams were as effective as possible.[103]

Although this initiative was launched quickly and early in the spread of COVID-19, it came at a time when World Vision Australia was struggling with allegations of poor management practices and had just lost its CEO.[104] The crisis management capability of the organisation, however, was not affected by these internal problems and the implementation of this strategy was not delayed. The ability to direct key resources to this strategy without being disrupted by the internal conflict was directly due to the very clear mission of World Vision, which is 'to be a Christian organisation that engages people to eliminate poverty and its causes' and the organisational culture that it had developed over 60 years.[105] The values and organisational purpose of World Vision provided direction and guidance when management attention was lacking due to the internal conflict. Staff were also well trained in strategy execution and were able to adapt learnings from previous executions to the current environment, quickly correcting the misunderstandings of the target communities and assisting them to survive the pandemic.[106] These dynamic capabilities make World Vision Australia extremely effective at strategy implementation.

As a charitable organisation, World Vision has had to be both careful and innovative in its choice of partnerships. Charitable organisations are sometimes offered funding from successful commercial enterprises wishing to improve their social standing by aligning with charities. However, they are not always suitable partners. For example, the major national lottery company at the time, Tattersalls, offered a significant donation to World Vision for its Asian tsunami appeal, but was rejected because of World Vision's ethical position on gambling.

Strategy implementation

Implementation is a critical stage of strategic management. Until a strategy is implemented, it is only an idea. The process of strategy implementation is time consuming, costly and not always successful. As most strategies stretch the capacities of the organisation (see the earlier section, 'Strategic intent'), they are, by their very nature, a challenge to implement. Partially completed strategy implementations are often a source of emergent strategy outcomes.

Strategy implementation often takes years to complete. For example, the Coles supermarket chain's decision to enter the petrol retail market by purchasing 300 petrol stations took two years. In addition, it took several more years before this strategy produced the expected increase in customer loyalty.

five forces analysis (customers, suppliers, new market entrants, rivals and substitutes analysis) An evaluation framework that identifies the features of the industry environment that may affect the organisation.

functional-level strategy The development and coordination of resources through which business-level strategies can be executed effectively and efficiently.

industry strategies Collective approaches to competition adopted by whole industries.

mission A contemporary statement of the goals, values and focus of the organisation.

offensive strategy A strategy intended to increase the market share or leadership position of an organisation at the expense of competitors.

organisational purpose What that organisation is intended to do and for whom.

PESTEL analysis (political, economic, social, technological, environmental and legal analysis) An evaluation framework that helps to identify the features of the macro environment that may affect the organisation.

resource-based view (RBV) A strategic management perspective that connects building and maintaining critical strategic resources and organisational performance.

scenario planning An analysis of the likely impact of potential future external environmental events.

stakeholders Organisations and individuals to whom the organisation has a commitment and who have expectations of what the organisation does.

strategic intent The direction in which the organisation is heading, which strategy must support.

strategic management The process of thinking strategically; setting objectives for the organisation; planning and responding to unexpected events; implementing changes and measuring outcomes.

strategic objectives The measurable achievement expectations set for the organisation and its strategies.

strategic performance measures Measures of organisational achievement relative to strategic objectives and other strategy milestones.

strategic resources Special resources that are possessed by the organisation which increase competitiveness because they are valuable, rare, difficult to imitate and well organised within the business.

strategic thinking Understanding the environmental conditions, particularly those that are most critical to the organisation, and developing an organisation that will perform as strongly as possible in those conditions.

strategy The plans and actions a company adopts to achieve its strategic goals.

sustainability Minimising or even neutralising the impact of the organisation on its external environment.

tactics The actions an organisation takes in response to its environment, which are extensions of its normal day-to-day operations.

value statement A brief description of the stakeholders and behaviours the organisation considers most important.

vision The long-term future state of the organisation.

SELF-STUDY QUESTIONS

1 Can an organisation survive without strategy? Why?
2 What are the main characteristics of the four different types of strategy formulation process?
3 Why must managers consider the external environment when developing strategy? Why can't outcomes be driven from within?
4 What is strategic thinking?
5 What are the mechanisms by which sustainability can be incorporated into strategic management?
6 Define competitive advantage, dynamic capabilities and core competency.
7 How do strategic concepts apply to not-for-profit organisations and non-government organisations?
8 Identify the different levels at which strategy can be created in an organisation.

DISCUSSION QUESTIONS

1 Does an organisation always need a formally expressed strategy? Why?
2 How can different parts of the organisation be engaged in the strategy formulation process?

3 Which members of the external community would be interested in an organisation's strategies? Why?

4 Are various levels of strategy created separately or are they normally the result of an integrated process? Explain your reasoning.

5 Can an organisation be successful if it only focuses on responding to the external environment? Why?

EXERCISES

1 Identify the resources that give the company in this chapter's scene setter a competitive advantage.

2 Review the mission and values statements of the Body Shop (www.bodyshop.com/en-au). Identify what you think the needs of their key stakeholders would be. Explain whether the mission and values statements match the stakeholder needs you have identified.

3 Visit the Wesfarmers website (www.wesfarmers.com.au) and review the latest annual report. Identify what strategic actions Wesfarmers has taken in reaction to the coronavirus crisis and its ongoing effects.

4 Visit the BHP Billiton website (www.bhpbilliton.com) and view its sustainability report. Compare this with its strategic objectives outlined in its CSR statement. Determine whether environmental performance is slightly, strongly or fully represented in its core strategies.

FURTHER READING

Haans, RFJ 2018, 'What's the value of being different when everyone is? The effects of distinctiveness on performance in homogeneous versus heterogeneous categories', *Strategic Management Journal,* vol. 40, no. 1, 3–27.

Volberda, HW 2017, 'Comments on "Mastering strategic renewal: Mobilising renewal journeys in multi-unit firms"', *Long Range Planning,* vol. 50, no. 1, 44–47.

Rodrigues M & Franco, M 2019, 'The corporate sustainability strategy in organisations: a systematic review and future directions', *Sustainability,* vol. 11, no. 22, 6214.

Jacobides, MG 2010, 'Strategy tools for a shifting landscape', *Harvard Business Review*, vol. 88, no. 1, 76–84.

Hamel, G 2009, 'Moon shots for management', *Harvard Business Review*, vol. 87, no. 2, 91–98.

Porter, ME 2008, 'The five competitive forces that shape strategy', *Harvard Business Review*, vol. 86, no. 1, 78–93.

ENDNOTES

1. D Powell, '"It will be a smaller business": Target store closures flagged in tough environment,' *Sydney Morning* Herald, 27 August 2019, www.smh.com.au/business/companies/it-will-be-a-smaller-business-Target-stores-closures-flagged-in-tough-environment-20190827-p52l8m.html.

2. Target Australia, 'Our History', 2020, www.Target.com.au/company/about-us/our-history.

3. A Clark, 'The secret to Wesfarmers Ltd. financial success', *Fdfworld.com*, June 2014, www.fdfworld.com/retail/secret-wesfarmers-ltd-financial-success.

4. Salesforce.Com, 'What are customer expectations (and how have they changed)?', 2020, www.salesforce.com/research/customer-expectations.

5. N Cameron, 'CMO interview: turning around Target', *Cmo.com.au,* 2018, www.cmo.com.au/article/649285/cmo-interview-turning-around-Target.

6. R Mohammed, 'The good-better-best approach to pricing', *Harvard Business Review*, September 2018, https://hbr.org/2018/09/the-good-better-best-approach-to-pricing.

7. A Carey, 'Target in Australia: retailer's future in doubt', *News.com.au,* 6 February 2018, www.news.com.au/finance/business/retail/a-tale-of-two-retailers-Target-stores-could-be-converted-into-kmart-following-profit-crash/news-story/5192e281d208cc143e963dd1dc67c7b4.

8. M Birshan, T Meakin, A West, 'A deal-making strategy for new CEOs', *McKinsey Quarterly*, no. 2, 2017, 69–69.

9. ME Porter, *Competitive strategy*, New York: Free Press, 1980.

10. R Whittington, *What is strategy and does it matter?*, London: International Thomson Business Press, 1993.

11. S Oster, *Modern competitive analysis*, 2nd edn, New York: Oxford University Press, 1994.

12. MC Mankins and R Steele, 'Turning great strategy into great performance', *Harvard Business Review*, vol. 83, no. 7/8, 2005, 64–72; R Andrews, GA Boyne, J Law & RM Walker, 'Strategy formulation, strategy content and performance', *Public Management Review*, vol. 11, no. 1, 2009, 1–22; R Gulati, N Nohria & F Wohlgezogen, 'Roaring out of recession', *Harvard Business Review*, vol. 88, no. 3, 2010, 62–69.

13. S Oster, op. cit., p. 4; R Gulati, N Nohria and F Wohlgezogen., op. cit.

14. J Bundy, RM Vogel and MA Zachary, 'Organization-stakeholder fit: A dynamic theory of cooperation, compromise, and conflict between an organization and its stakeholders', *Strategic Management Journal*, vol. 39, no. 2, 2018, 476–501.

15. J Davis and T Devinney, *The essence of corporate strategy*, St Leonards: Allen & Unwin, 1997.

16. AD Chandler, *Strategy and structure*, Cambridge, MA: MIT Press, 1962.

17. RA Burgelman, 'A model of the interaction of strategic behaviour, corporate context, and the concept of strategy', *The Academy of Management Review*, vol. 8, no. 1, 1983, 61–70.

18. Sofya_Manager, 'The changing landscape of the Chinese middle class', *Daxueconsulting.com,* 26 August 2019, https://daxuec onsulting.com/the-chinese-middle-class.

19. H Mintzberg, 'The strategy concept 1: five Ps for strategy', *California Management Review*, Fall 1987, 11–17.

20. H Mintzberg and J Waters, 'Of strategies, deliberate and emergent', in *Strategy: process, content: an international perspective*, R de Wit and R Meyer (eds), St Paul, MN: West Publishing Company, 1994, pp. 12–21.

21. Mintzberg, 1987, op. cit.

22. KE Weick, 'Substitutes for strategy', in D Teece (ed.), *The competitive challenge: strategies for industrial innovation and renewal*, Business Strategies Series, Cambridge, MA: Ballinger Publishing, 1987.

23. M Bailey, '"Unicorn" Canva reports maiden profit in second half of 2017', *Australian Financial Review, Australian Financial Review*, 3 October 2018, www.afr.com/work-and-careers/careers/unicorn-canva-reports-maiden-profit-in-second-half-of-2017-20181003-h165qo.

24. 'Canva: Melanie Perkins', 2019, *NPR.org,* 28 January 2019, www.npr.org/2019/01/24/688299882/canva-melanie-perkins.

25. C Kruger, 'Rare billion-dollar beast: Aussie tech unicorn Canva makes a profit', *Sydney Morning Herald,* 14 September 2018, www.smh.com.au/business/companies/rare-billion-dollar-beast-aussie-tech-unicorn-canva-makes-a-profit-20180914 -p503s3.html.

26. S Nanclares, 'Just ask: four ways startups can create a culture of feedback just like Canva's', *SmartCompany*, 17 January 2019, www.smartcompany.com.au/startupsmart/advice/four-steps-feedback-culture-canva.

27. Kruger, op. cit., 2018

28. A Inkpen and N Choudhury, 'The seeking of strategy where it is not: towards a theory of strategy absence', *Strategic Management Journal*, vol. 16, 1995, 313–323.

29. ibid., p. 318.

30. A Ferguson, 'Coles close to Shell deal*', BRW*, vol. 25 no. 18, 2003, 29.

31. RJ Harrington, DJ Lemak, R Reed and KW Kendall 'A Question of fit: the links among environment, strategy formulation, and performance', *Journal of Business & Management*, vol. 10, no. 1, 2004, 15–38.

32. ibid.

33. Whittington, op. cit.

34. Whittington, op. cit., p. 28.

35. J Palmer and C Hardy, *Thinking about management: implications of organisational debates for practice*, London: Sage Publications, 2003, p. 140.

36. D Lovallo and O Sibony 2018, 'Broadening the frame: how behavioral strategy redefines strategic decisions', *Strategy Science*, vol. 3, no. 4, 658–667.

37. B Blumenthal and P Haspeslagh, 'Toward a definition of corporate transformation', *Sloan Management Review*, Spring 1994, 101–106.

38. G Lewis, J Clark and B Moss, BHP reorganises for global competition, in *Australian strategic management: concepts, context and cases*, G Lewis, A Morkel and G Hubbard (eds), Sydney: Prentice Hall, 1988.

39. A Khalifa, 'Strategy: restoring the lost meaning', *Journal of Strategy and Management*, vol. 13, no. 1, 2019, 128–143.

40. W Finnie, 'Leading the revolution: an interview with GaryHamel', *Strategy and Leadership*, vol. 29, no. 1, 2001, 4–10.

41. CC Markides, *All the right moves: a guide to creating breakthrough strategy*, Boston, MA: Harvard Business School Press, 2000.

42. K Pichel and A Mueller, 'Strategility: agility in strategic decisions', *International Journal of Strategic Management*, vol. 18, no. 1, 2018, 81–88.

43. H Mintzberg, 'The fall and rise of strategic planning', *Harvard Business Review*, January–February 1994, 107–114.

44. S Hossfeld, 'The advantage of digital decision making for strategic decisions: proofed by a supply chain Case', vol. 3, no. 5, 2017, 7–20.

45. First Round Review, 'The management framework that propelled LinkedIn to a $20 billion company', *First Round Review*, 2015, https://firstround.com/review/the-management-framework-that-propelled-LinkedIn-to-a-20-billion-company.

46. G Hamel and CK Prahalad, 'Strategic intent', *Harvard Business Review*, May–June 1989, 67.

47. JC Collins and JI Porras, *Built to last: successful habits of visionary companies*, New York: HarperCollins, 1995.

48. Australian Department of Health, www.health.gov.au.

49. J Mazzei M and D Noble, 'Big data and strategy: theoretical foundations and new opportunities' in *Strategy and behaviors in the digital economy*, 2020. doi:10.5772/intechopen.84819.

50. K Capell and W Zellner, 'Richard Branson's next big adventure', *Business Week*, 3873, 2004, 44.

51. M Porter, 'What is strategy?', *Harvard Business Review*, November–December 1996, 61–78.

52. T Kohlborn, A Korthaus, Axel, C Riedl and H Krcmar, 'Service aggregators in business networks', *Proceedings — IEEE International Enterprise Distributed Object Computing Workshop*, 2009, 195–202.

53. G Hamel and CK Prahalad, 'Strategy as stretch and leverage', *Harvard Business Review*, March–April, 1993, 75–84.

54. J Barney, 'The resource-based view of the firm: ten years after 1991', *Journal of Management*, vol, 27, no. 6, 2001, 625–641.

55. M Rumelt, 'How much does industry matter', *Strategic Management Journal*, vol. 12, 1991, 167–185.

56. VA Lopez, 'An overview review of the resource-based view of the firm, drawing on recent Spanish management research', *Irish Journal of Management*, vol. 22, no. 2, 2001, 105.

57. D Teece, G Pisano and A Shuen, 'Dynamic capabilities and strategic management', *Strategic Management Journal*, vol. 18, no. 7, 1997, 509–533.

58. See for example, S Marginson, 'Diversity and convergence in Australian higher education', *Australian Universities Review*, vol. 42, no. 1, 1999, 12–23.

59. ibid.

60. C Oliver, 'The influence of institutional and task environment relationships on organisational performance: the Canadian construction industry', *Journal of Management Studies*, vol. 34, no. 1, 1997, 99–124.

61. N Lees and I Lees, 'Competitive advantage through responsible innovation in the New Zealand sheep dairy industry', *International Food & Agribusiness Management Review* vol. 21, no. 4, 2018, 505–23.

62. T Wheeler, 'The long journey of Lonely Planet', *Financial Times*, 24 May 2018, www.ft.com/content/67706fe6-5da3-11e8-ad 91-e01af256df68.

63. Cancer Council, *About Us*, 2020, cancer.org.au, accessed 25 March 2020.

64. SP Robbins and N Barnwell, *Organisation theory: concepts and cases*, 5thd edn, New York: Pearson Australia, 2006.

65. G Johnson, R Whittington, K Scholes, A Angwin and P Regner, *Exploring strategy*, 11th edn, London: Pearson, 2017.

66. R De Wit and R Meyer, *Strategy: process, content and context*, 4th edn, Andover (UK): Cengage, 2010.

67. R Daft, *Organization theory and design*, 12th edn, Boston: Cengage, 2015.

68. Adapted from Robbins and Barnwell, op. cit.

69. P Rogers and Blenko, M. 'Who has the D?', *Harvard Business Review*, vol. 84, no. 1, 2006, 52–61.

70. BH O'Connor, AR Chivas, DW Mather, JDC Studdert and AE Binnie, AINSE: An institute for research and training excellence in nuclear science: the first 50 years: a history of the Australian Institute of Nuclear Science and Engineering, Menai NSW: AINSE, 2008.

71. New South Wales Government, Lucas Heights Nuclear Reactor Proposal, 2000, Parliament of New South Wales, www.parliam ent.nsw.gov.au.

72. Cancer Council Australia, *History*, September 6, 2019. Retrieved March 26, 2020, from Cancer.org.au website: www.cancer. org.au/about-us/history.html

73. J Brands, G Garvey, K Anderson, J Cunningham, J Chynoweth, I Wallington, B Morris, V Knott, S Webster, L Kinsella, J Condon, and H Zorbas, 'Development of a national Aboriginal and Torres Strait Islander cancer framework: a shared process to guide effective policy and practice', *International Journal Of Environmental Research And Public Health*, 2018, vol. 15, no. 5, 1–16.

74. S Shahid, K Beckmann and S Thompson, 'Supporting cancer control for Indigenous Australians: initiatives and challenges for cancer councils', *Australian Health Review*, vol. 32, no. 1, 2008, 56–63.

75. M Namaki, 'Does the thinking of yesterday's management gurus imperil today's companies?', *Ivey Business Journal*, vol. 76, no. 2, 2012, 10–13.

76. MW Peng, SL Sun, B Pinkham and C Hao, 'The institution-based view as a third leg for a strategy tripod', *Academy of Management Perspectives*, vol. 23, no. 3, 2009, 63–81.

77. Australia Post, 'Heritage Strategy', accessed 22 February 2020, https://auspost.com.au/content/dam/auspost_corp/media/docu ments/heritage-strategy.pdf.

78. Australia Post, 'Annual report', 2019, https://auspost.com.au/content/dam/auspost_corp/media/documents/publications/2019-a ustralia-post-annual-report.pdf.

79. Australia Post, 'Our customer network', 2016, https://auspost.com.au/annualreport2016/our-customer-network.html.

80. Australia Post, op cit., 2019.

81. Australia Post, op. cit., 2016.

82. TF Chan, 'Inside the Australia Post "concept store" that's stocked with baby formula and will only ship to China', *Business Insider Australia*, 24 May 2018, www.businessinsider.com.au/australia-post-store-for-daigou-who-ship-products-to-china-201 8-5?r=US&IR=T.

83. L Håkanson, 'The firm as an epistemic community: the knowledge-based view revisited', *Industrial & Corporate Change*, vol. 19, no. 6, 2010, 1801–1828.

84. F Acedo, C Barroso and J Galan, 'The resource-based theory: dissemination and main trends', *Strategic Management Journal*, vol. 27, no. 7, 2006, 621–636.

85. N Liviu, 'How to establish the objectives within a strategic system', *Annals of The University of Oradea, Economic Science Series*, vol. 17, no. 4, 2008, 442–446.

86. A Kleine and M von Hauff, 'Sustainability-driven implementation of corporate social responsibility: application of the integrative sustainability triangle', *Journal of Business Ethics*, vol. 85, 2009, 517–533.

87. D Baraldi, 'Banking on sustainability — what's next?', *World Economic Forum*, 21 September 2019, www.weforum.org/agend a/2019/09/how-banks-can-be-more-sustainable.

88. ML Frigo, 'Strategy-focused performance measures', *Strategic Finance*, vol. 84, no. 3, 2002, 10–15.

89. BS Chakravarthy, 'Measuring strategic performance', *Strategic Management Journal*, vol. 7, no. 5, 1986, 437–458.

90. B Caemmerer and M Banerjee, 'An exploration of assimilating service relation strategies in the private and the public sector', *Journal of Relationship Marketing*, vol. 8, no. 1, 2009, 68–79.

91. BG Peters, 'Debate: the two futures of public administration', *Public Money & Management*, 2008, 195–196.

92. Personnel Today 2008, 'Freedom to improve is key to public productivity,' *Personnel Today*, Reed Business Information Ltd.

93. N Ryan, T Williams, M Charles, and J Waterhouse, 'Top-down organizational change in an Australian Government agency', *International Journal of Public Sector Management*, vol. 21, no. 1, 2008, 26–44.

94. B Frew, 'Valuing heterarchy in the public sector,' *People & Strategy*, vol. 32, no. 1, 2009, 11–12.

95. E McMillan and Y Carlisle, 'Strategy as order emerging from chaos: a public sector experience', *Long Range Planning*, vol. 40, no. 6, 2007, 574–593.

96. B Behn, 'No perfect performance measure,' *PA Times*, vol. 32, no. 4, 2009, 7; E Tappin, 'Strategy in the public sector: management in the wilderness', *Journal of Management Studies*, vol. 40, no. 4, 2003, 955–982.

97. C Talbot, 'Public value: the next big thing in public management?', *International Journal of Public Administration*, vol. 32, no. 3/4, 2009, 167–170.

98. GA Boyne, 'Strategies for public service turnaround: lessons from the private sector?', *Administration & Society*, vol. 38, no. 3, 2006, 365–388.

99. Markides, op. cit., p. ix.

100. World Vision, *2019 annual review*, 2019.

101. World Vision, 'World Vision takes action in response to the coronavirus', retrieved 26 March 2020, www.worldvision.com.au.

102. S Omer, 'What is the coronavirus? Facts, symptoms, and how to help', *World Vision*, 25 March 2020, www.worldvision.org/ disaster-relief-news-stories/what-is-coronavirus-facts.

103. Anon, 'World Vision launches 17-country response as coronavirus "tsunami" set to devastate vulnerable', 19 March 2020, www.miragenews.com/world-vision-launches-17-country-response-as-coronavirus-tsunami-set-to-devastate-vulnerable.

104. N McKenzie and R Barker, 'Charity World Vision in allegations of corruption and nepotism", *Sydney Morning Herald*, 8 March 2020, www.smh.com.au/national/charity-world-vision-in-allegations-of-corruption-and-nepotism-20200306-p547ng.html.

105. World Vision, 'Our mission, motivation and values', *World Vision Australia*, 2015, www.worldvision.com.au/about-us/our-mission-motivation-and-values.

106. J Sandeman, 'As Covid-19 moves into Africa, they await a "tsunami"', *Eternity News*, 25 March 2020, www.eternitynews.com.au/world/as-covid-19-moves-into-africa-they-await-a-tsunami.

107. *MarketWatch*, 'Shell/Coles Myer: alliance may prompt fuel price war', *MarketWatch:* Food 2003; Ferguson 2003, op. cit.

ACKNOWLEDGEMENTS

Photo: © Nils Versemann / Shutterstock.com

Photo: © bangoland / Shutterstock.com

Photo: © simez78 / Shutterstock.com

Photo: © ArliftAtoz2205 / Shutterstock.com

Photo: © Casimiro / Alamy Stock Photo

Figure 1.1: © Based on R Whittington, *What is strategy and does it matter?*, p. 28, London: International Thomson Business Press, 1993.

Table 1.2: © Adapted from Table 3.3 Typical Organizational Effectiveness Criteria of Selected Strategic Constituencies from SP Robbins and N Barnwell, *Organisation theory: concepts and cases*, 5thd edn, New York: Pearson Australia, 2006.

THE TOOLS OF STRATEGIC ANALYSIS

CHAPTER 2

External and industry analysis

LEARNING OBJECTIVES

After studying this chapter, you should be able to:

2.1 explain why an understanding of the competitive environment is critical to strategic analysis

2.2 conduct a political, economic, social, technological, environmental and legal (PESTEL) analysis

2.3 explain the use of Porter's diamond for assessing determinants of national competitive advantage

2.4 conduct a five forces analysis

2.5 describe an industry's structure

2.6 conduct a network environment analysis

2.7 develop scenarios and explain their uses

2.8 identify key success factors and strategic groups.

China Inc — open for business

Why is everyone setting up business in China? Ten years ago, businesses set up operations in China to manufacture cheaply. Now, businesses set up in China to access the market.[1] But is that the only motivation? The business environment in China offers a number of different features which make it extremely attractive — particularly to manufacturers. While Chinese wage rates (particularly for skilled workers) have increased significantly over the last 10 years, the technological capacity of the country has also developed dramatically. This capacity has made the Chinese business environment attractive to a larger number of businesses.

For example, China recently developed the capability to refine a commonly occurring crystalline material which produces large quantities of methane and represents a viable and large-scale fossil fuel resource.[2] This development may significantly reduce the cost of energy in China.

China's business environment is in a state of rapid development. Ten years ago, disputes were still mainly settled through informal arbitration rather than through the court system; however, this is rapidly changing, providing western companies, used to dealing with business through contracts, with a much greater level of certainty. In addition, China has introduced 27 special economic zones (SEZs), which are responsible for 22 per cent of china's GDP, 45 per cent of foreign investment and 60 per cent of exports.[3] These SEZs provide low taxation, simplified regulations and well-developed infrastructure. Huge numbers of foreign companies invest there because they provide such an attractive commercial environment.

The Chinese SEZs have been in place since the 1980s, however, they were not as attractive to foreign direct investment as they are now. Their increased attractiveness results from China's large and rapidly growing middle class, increased technological capability, well-developed infrastructure (in the SEZs) and the establishment of foreign chambers of commerce (such as the Australian Chamber of Commerce) throughout the major cities.[4] This has made establishing operations in China much more attractive to foreign enterprises and has also attracted a very large number of small businesses to China. Australian small business are big investors in China, with 1300 small Australian businesses currently operating there.[5] e-commerce has also become a big phenomenon in China, operating at a much greater business transaction speed than in most western countries and creating very fast business exchanges. While attractive, this environment is very dynamic. It is not a good environment for cautious and slow-moving enterprises, however, those companies that are able to adapt to the rapidly changing business environment in China are rewarded with business opportunities that they would not experience at home.

Introduction

This chapter focuses on one of the most important strategic management activities: understanding the external environment. Understanding the external environment can be central to the survival of the organisation. Before critical decisions can be made that affect an organisation's purpose, values, resource deployment or products and services, the organisation's current and future circumstances must be understood. Strategic plans require the commitment of resources to a particular competitive approach and so reduce the availability of these resources for other strategic opportunities. Understanding the conditions in the external environment helps with decisions about which opportunities are the most attractive. In order to gain a thorough understanding of the key features of the external environment, strategic planners deploy a range of analytical tools and techniques. These tools are designed to focus attention on specific features of the external environment that are typically important for strategic decision making. This chapter will present a number of these tools and demonstrate their use. Each of these tools provides a filter through which one aspect of the environment can be examined in detail. Armed with an understanding of the key features of the environment, the likelihood of selecting and implementing a successful strategy is significantly increased.

2.1 Macro environmental influences

LEARNING OBJECTIVE 2.1 Explain why an understanding of the competitive environment is critical to strategic analysis.

The **macro environment** is the environment external to the organisation, its operations and its industry. Macro environmental factors strongly influence the medium-and long-term features of the strategy the organisation must adopt to compete successfully within its markets and remain viable. The main forces present in the macro environment are usually independent of the organisation and its activities; and so the organisation has little influence on them. For example, the financial success of a single organisation will have little effect on the economic conditions in the country in which it is located. Conversely, however, the country's economic conditions will have a significant effect on the sales and profitability of organisations operating there and even affect products and services that customers seek. Post COVID-19, the challenging economic conditions in many countries has meant that customers are more interested in lower cost products and services. Organisations must also adjust their strategies to changing external environmental conditions.

The trends that macro environment forces show is one of their most important characteristics. Individual forces in the macro environment will increase and decrease, creating cycles, and the organisation must follow these conditions in its strategic planning. China's increasing rate of technological development, for example, is making the force of technology a more important environmental factor in countries across the globe. Even charitable organisations need to adapt to changes in the macro environment; animal welfare charities, for example, took advantage of increased social concern for the plight of Australian native animals after 1 billion animals died in the 2019 bushfires.[6] One of the best tools for identifying trends in the macro environment is the PESTEL analysis, which will now be considered.

2.2 PESTEL analysis

LEARNING OBJECTIVE 2.2 Conduct a political, economic, social, technological, environmental and legal (PESTEL) analysis.

The most popular and useful tool (or perspective) for analysing the external macro environment is the political, economic, social, technological, environmental and legal framework, or **PESTEL analysis**. This analysis examines global scale environmental factors (such as economic cycles). Macro environment forces influence the nature of competition in every industry, as well as opportunities for organisational growth and profitability. COVID-19 demonstrated how quickly buoyant economic conditions can change to economic difficulty as the global shutdown ravaged all but a small number of (mainly medical and food) industries. Despite their significant effect, however, macro environmental forces are frequently overlooked in strategic thinking and planning.[7] If the organisation is performing well, strategic thinking will tend to focus on industry-level forces and internal operational issues. Successful organisations, in particular, tend to look for internal opportunities, such as increasing efficiency, and forget to keep an eye on the external macro environment. Figure 2.1 shows the elements of PESTEL analysis.

| **FIGURE 2.1** | Six elements of PESTEL analysis |

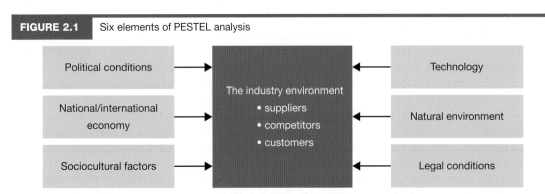

As figure 2.1 shows, the external macro environment comprises six dimensions. The *political* conditions in many countries remain static for long periods. Some variation can occur, improving conditions for some industries and making other industries less attractive during key events in the political cycle, such as the lead-up to elections when the parties in power introduce policies designed to improve their popularity. The current world political environment is a significant source of uncertainty for organisations in every country.

As the politically driven trade conflicts between China and the US continue, both countries' responses affect industries across the globe.

National and international *economic* conditions are rarely static and are characterised by trends known as economic cycles. Many countries around the world experienced a continual boom that ran from the end of the 2008 GFC right through to the COVID-19 pandemic, although the boom had started to taper off for some countries in the years preceding 2020. Understanding where the global economy is located in such cycles is vital information for strategic thinking. As this example shows, economic cycles can last more than ten years and so affect long-term strategic plans.

Sociocultural factors can have a significant impact on conditions in an industry. Significant sociocultural trends include the increasing concern about environmental, economic and social sustainability. Social concern for these factors will continue to increase for some time, especially so when economic conditions are positive, and companies will need to continue to improve their performance in this area in response to these sociocultural expectations.

Technology developments can have interesting consequences, particularly for commercial organisations. **Disruptive technology** significantly alters the nature of business and industries and shifts competitive advantage from one organisation to another. It can appear suddenly, without warning. It is usually independent of the industry as well and any organisation, large or small, can often adopt disruptive technology to gain an immediate competitive advantage. For example, the National Broadband Network in Australia disrupted competitiveness in the Australian telecommunications industry. It seriously challenged the competitive position of Telstra, the previously dominant provider. Telstra was forced to react by dividing its operations into two separate businesses in order to remain competitive.[8]

Many organisations choose to increase their competitiveness through acquired technology. The rapid rate of technology development globally means that a competitive advantage provided by new technology will be short lived. Once one organisation has demonstrated that a competitive advantage can be gained from a technology, competitors will quickly acquire the same or a comparable technology. For example, astronomical observatories usually compete for dominant capability and attract major world astronomical projects by acquiring the largest supercomputers available.[9] Typically, these computers provide a two-year advantage before another machine that can be up to 10 times faster becomes available.

Environmental sustainability is an important consideration for every type of organisation — government, not-for-profit, NGO, commercial, entertainment and agricultural companies must consider their sustainability as part of their strategic planning. While environmental sustainability has become a standard expectation of organisations, the expectations for social and economic sustainability (of communities) will continue to grow. These environmental expectations tend to divide organisations into two groups — those that comply with regulatory requirements and those that attempt to be sustainability leaders. Sustainability leaders take up the challenge to improve the natural environmental, social and economic conditions in the communities in which they operate.[10]

Legal conditions are frequently connected to political conditions. For example, the Australian government's decision to ratify the Kyoto protocol (a carbon emission reduction agreement) ultimately resulted in carbon credit and carbon tax schemes. Organisations that had started to work to reduce their carbon emissions were advantaged relative to those that had not identified this environmental factor and had not taken any action.

Applying the PESTEL analysis

Each of the six PESTEL elements should be examined as both a current force and a trend (i.e. the force increases or decreases in the future). The current strengths and trends of these forces can represent an opportunity or a threat (or possibly both). For example, a legal environmental force trend of increasingly tough corporate governance responsibility regulations may provide an opportunity for a business with a sophisticated corporate governance system when seeking capital for its future development. Under these conditions, lending organisations (or capital markets) may favour customers with strong corporate governance systems.

It is important to decide how far forward to project the analysis of the trends of factors in the macro environment. In industries where change is rapid, such as information technology industries, it may be practical to project only two years ahead. Rapid rates of change can lead to dramatic changes in industry structure. The resulting industry structural changes can have even more effect than the macro environmental changes that caused them. There are few industries where the macro environmental factors change slowly; however, in such environments, three- to five-year macro environmental forecasts may be sufficient for strategic thinking.

2.3 National competitive advantage

LEARNING OBJECTIVE 2.3 Explain the use of Porter's diamond for assessing determinants of national competitive advantage.

This section discusses Porter's view on **national competitive advantage**, also known as Porter's diamond.[11] The four national competitive conditions that this diamond draws attention to are factor conditions; demand conditions; related and supporting industries; and industry strategy, structure and rivalry. Each of these conditions reflects the home country government's support for local industry. Government industry support through policy is a macro environmental force. As figure 2.2 shows, this analysis approach breaks government support down into more detail and combines it with other local conditions to specify the competitive conditions at the national level for any given industry.

FIGURE 2.2 Porter's diamond of national competitive advantage

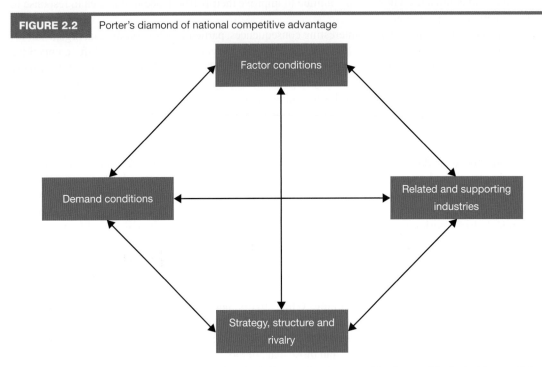

Multinational companies will seek national environments that provide them with desirable conditions, such as a supportive government policy or a highly-trained local workforce. This explains industry concentrations in the 27 special economic zones in China where taxes are low and government regulation is simplified (see the scene setter), as well as the technology precincts in Silicon Valley in the United States. The national competitive positions can have a significant effect on the success of an organisation. For example, the Australian wine industry has become the world's largest exporter of wine to China on the basis of the national competitive conditions of its pristine farming conditions and advanced winemaking technological skills.[12]

Factor conditions relate to business conditions (cost of capital, cost and skill of labour, and cost and availability of resources, including technology and information) and infrastructure. All of these factors may be influenced by government policy. *Demand conditions* refer to the market and customer expectations. Porter argued that the higher the demands placed on organisations by their customers, the more likely it is that organisations will develop a competitive strength. *Related and supporting industries* help the organisation with technological development and market information. *Industry strategy, structure and rivalry* is reflected in domestic rivalry, which may force industry members to become more competitive and industry strategies and structure will drive industry members to develop specific resources.

Porter's diamond is particularly valuable in informing government policy as governments can influence factor conditions, such as education levels, encourage the development of industries that support desirable industries (such as IT) and provide leadership in the development of specific industry strategies. Porter's diamond has become somewhat less relevant to today's globalised environment, however, as many of these conditions are accessed at the global, rather than the national, level. Trading blocks and geographical regions, however, can bear similar characteristics to national environments and so Porter's model is still useful for considering global development-based initiatives. For example, operating in the European market will expose a company to large customer demands with strong expectations in areas such as sustainability and technology. Operating in Asia will introduce the organisation to different related and supporting industries, as well as different industry strategies and structures. Both of these conditions will result in the development of new but different resources. Some global environments are very dynamic, however, and, as the China scene setter shows, an organisation has to be ready to adapt to changes in these conditions and take advantage of the new opportunities they present. Strategy capsule 2.1 shows how Seqirus's operations in multiple countries enables it to combine the national competitive conditions of each country to become the leading vaccination producer globally.

Seqirus Australia

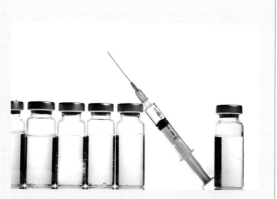

Seqirus is the world leader in vaccination development and manufacturing. Located in Australia with manufacturing in the US, UK and Europe, it is part of Commonwealth Serum Laboratories (CSL) in Australia. CSL was established in Melbourne in 1916, in response to the Spanish influenza pandemic ravaging the globe at that time.[13] In addition to providing a large portion of the flu vaccinations used globally every year, it has provided vaccinations for pandemics in different parts of the globe regularly since its inception. It currently has research, manufacturing and or subsidiaries in 20 countries.[14]

Seqirus has gained a substantial competitive advantage from operating production facilities in several countries by combining the national competitive advantage of each country into its global operations.[15] Operating production in these countries has meant that Seqirus has embedded itself in all the major global bioresearch locations. Access to research developments that occur in each of these countries, especially those that result from industry strategy and rivalry, provides it with alternative approaches to vaccination development and helps it maintain its level of innovation. Operating in a number of countries also means that it can trial and adopt technologies as they develop in each of the countries, rather than waiting for the technology to mature and become available globally. Its presence in different locations also enables it to take advantage of factor conditions and allocate its different production activities to the environments where the local factors (such as specialised staff availability) are most attractive. Finally, and most importantly, production in different locations enables it to respond more quickly to demand conditions. As influenza conditions develop in specific countries, for example, it can respond locally and therefore more quickly — providing a better service than would be available from imported vaccines.

2.4 Industry environment analysis

LEARNING OBJECTIVE 2.4 Conduct a five forces analysis.

In addition to the macro environment, organisations need to respond to the local environment within their industry. For most organisations, these are the most familiar and immediate environmental conditions.

Industry conditions are the result of the influence of substitute products or services and the behaviours of other competitors, industry suppliers, industry customers and organisations attempting to enter the industry. The most efficient way of assessing these is through Porter's five forces model.

Porter's five forces of competition framework

Porter's five forces model represents the significant components of an industry environment in an opposing (or balancing) framework, as shown in figure 2.3.[16] Porter suggested that it is not sufficient to just identify industry forces; an industry analysis must determine how they affect a particular organisation. While trends in industry environmental forces are significant considerations, the interactions between these forces are even more important. For example, an industry possessing both customers and suppliers imposing demands on the organisation creates a very challenging environment. If the organisation is not effective in negotiating with both suppliers and customers, it will find it difficult to maintain profitable operations. If only the suppliers were able to impose demands, however, the organisation could transfer some of the cost associated with meeting supplier demands to their customers. A similar transference option would be possible where customers were influential, but suppliers were not.

FIGURE 2.3   Porter's five forces of competition framework

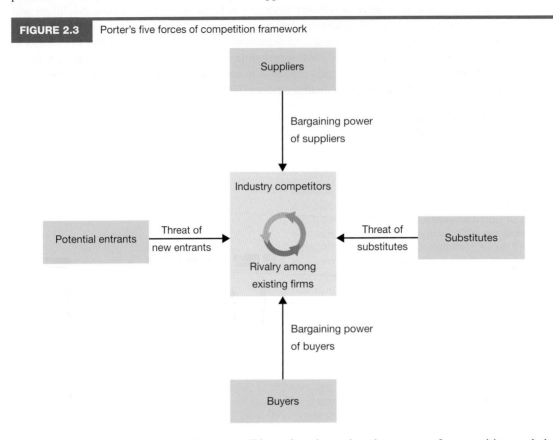

In practice, there are many industry conditions that determine the nature of competition and the attractiveness of an industry. Porter's five forces framework can be used to determine the attractiveness of an industry by considering the impact of the five sources of competitive pressure. These five forces of competition include three sources of 'horizontal' competition — competition from substitutes, competition from entrants and competition from established rivals — and two sources of 'vertical' competition — the power of suppliers and the power of customers.

Competition from substitutes

Substitute products normally come from a different market to the one that the industry serves. When there are few attractive substitutes for a product (e.g. housing is substituted by temporary accommodation and hotels) customers will be comparatively insensitive to price; that is, demand is inelastic with respect to price. For example, the high price of real estate in Australia reflects Australians' preference to live in specific locations and the absence of substitutes. When a close substitute exists, customers may switch easily in response to factors such as price. During the COVID-19 confinement period in many countries, online shopping became a very competitive alternative to traditional forms of shopping.

Substitutes can become attractive because of price or value, convenience and other differentiating factors such as quality or ethical expectations. For example, organic food is a substitute for food not certified as organic even though it is more expensive, because of its appeal to customer health and ethical motivations.

Threat of entry

New competitors are attracted by industry growth, profitability and low barriers to entry, such as low levels of competition or regulation. Attractive industries can become fragmented when large numbers of new companies enter the market. This can create uncertainty about industry standards and the viability of specific industry strategies, such as cost-based competition. This tends to lead to greater operating costs as organisations invest in advertising and product development in order to reduce uncertainty in the industry. During crises such as bushfires, for example, even charities engage in greater levels of advertising and more sophisticated appeals to customers in an attempt to bring certainty into their industry environment.

Research shows industries protected by high entry barriers tend to produce above-average rates of return.[17] The effectiveness of barriers to entry depends on the resources and capabilities that potential entrants possess. Barriers that are effective against 'start-up company' new entrants may be ineffective against established organisations and those diversifying from other industries.[18] Well-established companies will possess resources that allow them to overcome entry barriers and directly compete with market leaders. For example, the Mars Group used the strength of its confectionery manufacturing in Australia to enter the ice-cream market.

Creating barriers to entry

High levels of competition are a common barrier to industry entry. These higher levels of competition will be connected to individual organisational strategies, such as price or product/service based competition. The automotive manufacturer Lamborghini, for example, produces cars with high levels of quality and technology that create barriers to entry for other manufacturers attempting to enter its market niche. Tesla was able to successfully enter this market niche, but only by adopting an entirely different engine technology.

Economies of scale also provide an important mechanism for reducing operating costs and introducing operating efficiency-based barriers to entry. The mining giants BHP Billiton and Rio Tinto possess extraordinary economies of scale, which reduce their operating costs. The resultant industry pricing structure and capital investment required to achieve similar economies of scale make it extremely difficult for new mining companies to enter the industry. Sometimes new entrants can be successful, however, despite the existence of barriers to entry. For example, Budget Rent a Car challenged the international car rental organisations Hertz and Avis in the airport car rental industry. Budget Rent a Car entered the industry on a medium scale and, competing through price, eventually managed to gain a reasonable market share. In this industry, there were several keys to opening the barriers to entry, which Budget was able to utilise — including the ease with which customers could switch between rental car suppliers (switching costs) and the low levels of regulatory constraints in the industry.

As the above examples show, organisations need to meet certain criteria to become new market entrants. Some of these criteria will now be considered.

Capital requirements

The capital costs of setting up operations in an industry can represent a barrier to entry. For example, the manufacture of large passenger jets requires the establishment of advanced manufacturing facilities and advanced research and development facilities. Only companies with huge resources can set up operations that are competitive with Boeing and Airbus. Entrants to this industry, such as Canadian aircraft manufacturer Bombardier, stay in the smaller aircraft niche where the establishment costs are much less. By comparison, the new Chinese aircraft manufacturer Comac was established to compete directly with Airbus and Boeing and has used the financial support of the Chinese government to enable it to establish competitive operations.[19]

In other industries, entry costs vary as well. A juice bar food franchise in Australia can be purchased for A\$250 000[20], while a McDonald's franchise ranges between A\$600 000 and A\$1.8 million, depending on the location and size. Pop-up stores, on the other hand, require very little capital investment — just a short-term lease and stock that is to be sold. This means that the capital-based barriers to entry for this type of business are very low.[21] The ability to enter an industry does not ensure survival, of course, and competitive capabilities still need to be developed.

Economies of scale

Achieving efficiency in industries that are capital, research or advertising intensive requires large-scale operations. As a rule, the greater the volume of a business activity, the lower the set-up and operating costs per unit of that activity. This is due to the fixed and variable costs associated with introducing a product to a market. Some costs, such as facilities, systems and R&D are fixed, while other costs, such as staffing levels, are variable. The fixed costs are amortised over the total volume of activity, so as the level of activity increases, the individual fixed cost component per unit of activity decreases. In some industries, the fixed costs are quite large. The cost of developing and launching a new car model in Australia is typically A\$1.2 billion.[22] This has made it difficult for the Australian automotive industry to compete internationally as this fixed cost was amortised over a relatively small production volume, compared to the industry and other countries. The aircraft industry is even worse — the Airbus A380 cost A\$15 billion to develop, meaning that Airbus had to sell 300 planes just to break even, which they never managed![23]

New market entrants with smaller sales volumes in industries where competitors possess large economies of scale have an operating cost disadvantage. Cost-effective car manufacturing, for example, requires a scale of economy equivalent to the production of at least three million vehicles per year to become cost competitive. Subsequently, only government-supported companies such as Great Wall and Cherry in China and Tata Motors in India have achieved the economies of scale to enter the mainstream automotive industry in recent years. Companies like Tesla have remained in niches where economies of scale are relatively low for all competitors.

Absolute cost advantages

Businesses that have been in an industry for a while usually have an experience advantage over new entrants. This is due to *learning curve* effects in which time spent developing and producing a product or service develops the organisation's skills, network and knowledge. While these can translate to product and service features, they also tend to reduce operating costs by translating to improved efficiencies and better supplier agreements. They may also have territorial or proprietary rights which are difficult to imitate. For example, Saudi Arabia's largest petrochemical company, Saudi Aramco, has access to the world's largest and most accessible oil reserves, which means that its operating costs per barrel of oil are 30 per cent of those of Shell, Exxon Mobil and BP.[24]

Distribution network advantages

In countries such as Japan, the challenges of accessing distribution channels is a significant barrier to entry for foreign goods producers. In countries such as India, the limitations in the availability of refrigerated transport are a barrier to entry for foreign perishable goods.[25] Similarly, securing sufficient shelf-space in supermarkets is one of the biggest barriers to entry for the food retail industry in many countries. By comparison, however, e-commerce combined with courier delivery have reduced the barriers to entry in many industries.

Governmental and legal barriers

Government legislation creates many entry barriers at the industry and country level. The trade barriers of import tax and requirements such as mandated local content or ingredient quotas create entry barriers for foreign companies. Government regulations such as the requirement of licenses or certification create entry barriers for individual industries, especially when the availability of licenses is limited. For example, no new free-to-air television broadcasting licences were granted in Australia between 1970 and 2000,[26] creating a huge barrier to entry for the television industry. Patents, copyrights and other forms of intellectual property protection are also important barriers to entering knowledge-intensive industries. In developing economies, such as Indonesia, intellectual property rights protection is limited, however, eliminating this barrier to new market entrants.[27]

Rivalry between established competitors

Rivalry is a major contributor to competition in most industries. Rivalry can even drive organisations to compete so aggressively that their prices drop below their operating costs. For example, to compete with Boeing in the jumbo aircraft category, Airbus introduced the A380 and then frequently sold this product below cost in order to get it into the market. In the end, they had to retire the product without ever having made a profit from it.[28] Other industries exhibit *healthy competition* that motivates company capability and knowledge development, which ultimately circulates through the industry as employees change companies, but does not stifle profitability.

Concentration

Concentration is the number and size distribution of organisations competing in an industry. It is commonly measured using the **concentration ratio (CR)** — the combined share of the market held by the largest organisations. For example, the four-organisation concentration ratio (CR4) is the market share of the four largest producers. It represents the control of the key companies over the conditions in the market. In markets dominated by a single organisation, for example, such as Australia Post and the domestic mail market, the dominant organisation can exercise considerable discretion over prices. In highly concentrated markets, price-based competition is rare because the major competitors operating in the market will be reluctant to compete on the basis of price against other market dominators and will tolerate their current market share.[29] Competitors in markets dominated by two companies, such as Samsung and Apple or

Coca-Cola and Pepsi, tend to offer similar prices and compete on the basis of advertising, promotion and product development.

Diversity of competitors

In a highly dynamic industry, strategies and resources can vary considerably between competitors and so aggressive competition on price or service features can lead to a greater market share. Where there is limited diversity in competitors, however, such as in a mature and static market, the opportunities to offer significant differences to customers have all been explored and all competitors will have developed similar internal resources. For example, the Australian petrol retail industry is mature and there is very little diversity between the various retailers (such as Shell, BP Australia and Caltex Australia), resulting in limited competitive activity. When COVID-19 reduced transportation activity, each of these petrol retailers displayed exactly the same response in terms of reducing prices and consolidating services.[30]

Product differentiation

Organisations offering very similar products, such as USB drives, will often compete aggressively on price. In these situations, the product is a commodity and competition is mainly through price. Similarities between the products of competing organisations, however, should not be confused with a similarity in organisational resources or strategies. The ease with which customers can switch between commodity products can drive organisations to compete aggressively. This occurs in agriculture, where the opportunities for product differentiation are limited. The Dutch flower auctions demonstrate how dominant price-based competition can become if the industry conditions are suitable. These auctions are based in Amsterdam and sell 20 million cut flowers each day — purely on the basis of price (there is no inspection of quality).[31] Price-based competition is rare in industries where products are highly differentiated (such as perfumes, advanced pharmaceuticals, restaurants and management consulting services), even if there are many competitors.

Excess capacity and exit barriers

Why does industry profitability tend to fall drastically during crises? These events usually lead to a reduction in demand, resulting in unused capacity, which encourages organisations to cut prices in order to increase sales. Organisations require continuous cash flow to pay staff, operating costs and debts. A similar phenomenon occurs when an industry matures and demand growth slows, leading to an overshoot in the production capacity of the industry. Figure 2.4 shows how capacity can initially lag and then exceed demand. Unmet demand usually exists during the introduction of a new product or service and excess capacity exists once

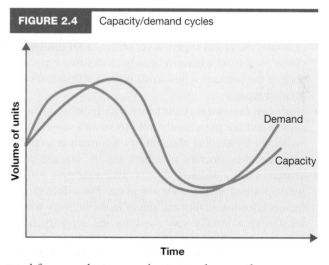

FIGURE 2.4 Capacity/demand cycles

demand plateaus and starts to decrease. Demand for a product or service may subsequently recover as a result of changes or innovations to the product or service. In this way, the cycle can repeat. The hotel industry is a good example of an industry that displays significant demand–capacity gaps.

Excessive industry capacity and the price-based competition it generates may encourage an organisation to leave the industry. This will cause it to encounter **barriers to exit**. Industry specific resources and industry skilled employees with job protection can make it difficult to exit industries.[32] In the Australian wool industry, for example, excess capacity together with high exit barriers devastated industry profitability. The impact of capacity–demand mismatch and exit barriers explains why companies in developing industries generally earn higher profits than companies in slow-growing or declining industries.

Bargaining power of customers

All organisations deal with two types of markets: markets for inputs and markets for outputs. Organisations purchase labour services, materials, components and finance from input markets. Organisations sell their goods and services to customers (who may be distributors, consumers or other manufacturers) in output markets. The customers' influence in output markets depends on the importance of the products to them and their bargaining power.

Importance of product to customers

The importance of the product or service to customers is affected by three factors.

1. *The cost of that product or service, relative to the customer's normal purchases.* For example, a customer spending $450 on shopping for a family will place a low level of importance on a box of matches that sells for 30 cents. Similarly, a jewellery retailer specialising in pearls which start at $1000 per string will place limited importance on packaging materials costs. Beverage manufacturers, by contrast, are highly sensitive to the cost of aluminium cans, which make up a significant component of the overall product cost. Conversely, most companies are not sensitive to the fees charged by their finance auditors, since auditing costs are small compared to overall company expenses. Most organisations will be more concerned about the credentials of the auditor than the fee since auditing is an important component of corporate governance.

2. *The amount of differentiation in the product or service.* The manufacturers of consumer products, such as light bulbs, are in a weak bargaining position with their direct customers, the supermarket chains, because of the supermarket chains' share of the light bulb retail market and their ability to purchase nationally. Supermarkets will switch suppliers in order to reduce the purchase price by 1 per cent.

3. *The importance of specific features of the product to the customer.* For example, the buying power of personal computer manufacturers over the microprocessor manufacturers (e.g. Intel and AMD) is limited because of the crucial importance of these components to the functionality of computers.

Relative bargaining power

The bargaining power of customers is based on their ability to switch suppliers. This results from the following.

- *Size and concentration of customers relative to suppliers.* The smaller the number of customers and the more they purchase, the greater their power. Excess capacity and unsold products resulting from losing a major customer can affect profitability or stop not-for-profit organisations from covering costs. For example, the global supermarket chain ALDI discussed in strategy capsule 2.3 has significant buying power in Australia because it only stocks two types of each product. This means that the volume of each of the products it purchases is greater than that of its competitors who stock a large range of each product type.

- *Customer knowledge.* Customers with industry knowledge are more aware of alternative sources of supply and are more easily able to switch suppliers. Some industries attempt to minimise supplier switching by keeping the industry information available to customers at a minimum. For example, market traders, doctors, plumbers, electricians and lawyers do not normally advertise the prices they charge. Their customers do not have extensive information about how they operate and are in a weak position to negotiate on price. For effective negotiation, customers need to understand the factors affecting quality and prices in the industry with which they are negotiating. Customer industry knowledge is usually very weak for the dentistry, hairdressing, interior design and financial advice industries, resulting in a reluctance to switch suppliers.

- *Ability to integrate vertically.* Another source of bargaining power is the ability of the customer to meet their own supply. For example, large food-processing companies (e.g. Heinz and Campbell Soup) produce their own metal cans to reduce their dependence on outside manufacturers. This is known as backward vertical integration. When there is a poor concentration of suppliers (leading to strong supply bargaining power) and the features and quality levels provided by the suppliers are not satisfactory, the motivation for backward vertical integration will be strong.

Bargaining power of suppliers

The power balance between an organisation and its suppliers is driven by the same type of factors that drive the balance of power between the organisation and its customers. The power of suppliers is determined by the importance of what they are supplying and the cost of switching suppliers.

Groups of small suppliers, such as dairy farmers, may form cartels or cooperatives (groups of producers trading and negotiating under a single name) to increase their bargaining power with suppliers. Global-scale cartels, such as the Organization of the Petroleum Exporting Countries (OPEC), the International

Coffee Organization and some labour unions have a strong influence on their suppliers and, in the case of OPEC, even on entire countries which supply them. Conversely, the suppliers of inputs to the organisation which are complex and technically sophisticated (such as design consultants) may be able to exert considerable bargaining power because their capabilities are rare. The reason for Google's constant product development is the desire to create new markets where there are few suppliers with Google's level of technical expertise and the power of suppliers is strong.

Identifying industry attractiveness

The above discussion shows that Porter's five forces model can be used as a framework for identifying the interactions between the major forces in the industry environment. These interactions can be used to identify (1) industry attractiveness and (2) the conditions on which the organisation's strategy should focus.

Industry attractiveness

While an industry that is composed only of high-level forces is likely to be unattractive, few industries comprising only low-level forces exist in practice. For example, low levels of rivalry, customer power and supplier power result in low barriers to entry and will lead to increased competition from new entrants. Most attractive industries will contain a balance of strong and weak forces. There are a large number of combinations of balancing forces that lead to industry attractiveness. For example, in an industry where customers had low power and suppliers had medium power, as long as the forces of rivalry and substitutes were not too high, barriers to new market entrants would be significant and the industry could be described as attractive. If the power of suppliers changed from medium to high, however, the competitors in the industry would be trapped between the power of its customers and its suppliers and would become unattractive.

Areas for focus

The balance of industry forces also indicates where the organisation's strategy should focus. Porter's model suggests that certain forces can combine to alter the balance of power in the organisation's environment. For example, in an industry where rivalry and the power of suppliers are high, an organisation's strategy should focus on identifying and reacting to events that could affect the relative power of rivals and suppliers, such as process innovations.

STRATEGY CAPSULE 2.2

Your overseas shopping agent — Chinese *daigou* in Australia shopping for friends and family at home

Daigou are Chinese living overseas who earn extra income by buying products in their country of residence and sending them back home to relatives and contacts in China that they have made through social media. The global *daigou* market is valued at about A$8 billion per year and approximately 150 000 of the world's *daigou* operate in Australia. While most operate as sole traders, some *daigou* have created businesses and generate hundreds of thousands of dollars per year in sales. Australia Post has even established a special post office for these entrepreneurs in Sydney which also sells the merchandise that they normally purchase to send to their customers in China. Typical products for *daigou* sales include vitamins, milk powder and health products.[33]

Daigou are great examples of entrepreneurs who manage their industry five forces very well. Firstly they exhibit a high degree of power over their suppliers because they purchase from intermediate suppliers such as chemist chains, supermarkets and even specialty *daigou* retail suppliers. For example, one of the staple *daigou* products is powdered baby milk formula. When the company Bellamy's decided to try to bypass the *daigou* supply chain and sell directly to China, the *daigou* community stopped promoting Bellamy's formula in China in favour of other brands and Bellamy's sales and share price plummeted. The *daigou* demand was so strong that Bellamy's was unable to supply both *daigou* and Bellamy's other customers — leading to shortages in regular supermarkets.[34] Although the *daigou's* reaction would have had some negative effect on *daigou* sales, their portfolio product range approach would have allowed them to switch focus to other more available products. Following this, when the Chinese government introduced trade barriers that made it less attractive to import vitamins and milk products, the *daigou* switched to trading in other products. The loss of sales had an immediate negative impact on the share price of the milk and vitamin product companies.[35]

Customers are a powerful force in the *daigou* industry, however, *daigou* operate businesses which are so flexible that they can accommodate a huge range of customer requirements. *Daigou* do not carry stock and purchase directly to order. This means that they can supply any product in any volume that their customers request and they can send the product straight to their homes as soon as it is acquired.[36]

Daigou do face some risk from new market entrants; however, as the Bellamy's example shows, only other *daigou* entering the market could be successful competitors. As each *daigou* services a community of relatives, friends and contacts, it is unlikely that a new market entrant will be able to capture their individual customers. Furthermore, as *daigou* do not compete on price, offering a trustworthy transaction instead, this makes it difficult for new market entrants to take their individual customers. Chinese are very particular about the trustworthiness of products such as health products and infant formula, which is why they seek a trustworthy supplier. Substitutes are a possible risk for the *daigou* but, again, their flexibility and contemporary demand focus means that they are aware of the potential for substitutes and can adapt.[37] For example, retail outlets that offer the same level of trustworthiness as the *daigou* may, in time, establish themselves in China. Treasury wines has done a good job of this, however, it took 20 years to achieve a sufficiently trustworthy status.[38] These substitutes enable the Chinese to purchase trustworthy products directly, so they do not need to purchase through the *daigou*. *Daigou*, however, are a delivery service and therefore they can simply move to the supply of other products which have not yet established themselves as trustworthy in the Chinese market. In addition, the extremely dynamic tastes of the rapidly growing Chinese middle-class (there are already over 500 million middle-class Chinese) mean that demand is constantly changing and the successful *daigou* substitute would need to be as flexible as the *daigou* themselves.

Complements — a missing force in Porter's model?

In later developments a new dimension — *complements* — was added to Porter's framework. The idea of complements originates in economic theory. While the presence of substitutes reduces the perceived value of a product, the presence of complements increases its value. For example, Microsoft realised that complimentary products would increase the value of its Windows operating system. Instead of protecting it from third-party software producers, Microsoft allowed any software writer to produce applications that worked with Windows. This resulted in more applications being developed for Windows than any other operating system.

Figure 2.5 shows how complements are added to Porter's five forces. The benefit that each of the producers of complements receives is determined by their relationship with the provider of the principal product or service. For example, Nintendo earned huge profits during the early 1990s through sales of video game consoles and the associated games software. Most of this revenue came from the games purchased by customers because Nintendo controlled the manufacture and distribution of the game cartridges and earned royalties from the game sales.[39] As this example shows, complimentary products are usually not valuable individually (e.g. a left shoe is not valuable without the right shoe).

2.5 Describing industry structure

LEARNING OBJECTIVE 2.5 Describe an industry's structure.

Porter's five forces framework provides a good basis for identifying the principal features of an industry's structure. An industry can be described through its competitors, customers, suppliers and producers of substitute goods. The key characteristics of each of these groups determine the overall level of competition in the industry.

The structure of manufacturing industries is usually easily identified. The structure of service industries, however, can be more complicated. For example, it is difficult to identify the customers and the suppliers in the pay TV program production industry, due to the complex interrelationship between finance, production facilities, marketing, licensors and streaming channels. With providers such as Netflix, high levels of vertical integration exist where production, control and financing all occur within a single organisation; with other streaming providers, third parties outside the organisation undertake all of these activities.

Industry structure can also be complex when some parts of a product or service are fully vertically integrated and other parts are supplied by multiple external suppliers. In the case of a television series, the basic filming work may occur in a vertically integrated manner in which the company is responsible for writing, scenery, filming and post-production. Special effects, however, may be constructed by external providers in several stages and then integrated into the finished product at the end.

| FIGURE 2.5 | Porter's five forces framework extended with complements |

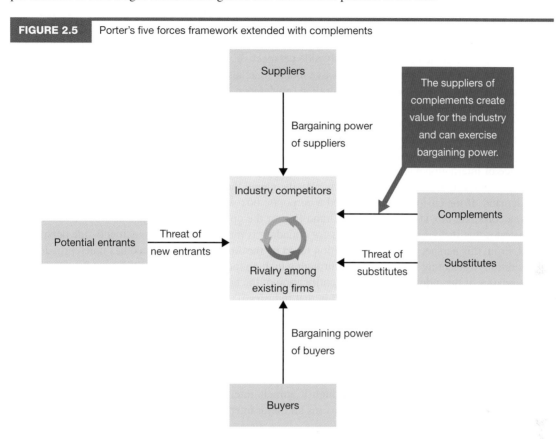

Structure can also vary across different segments of an industry. Pay TV on demand providers combine with free-to-air and free-to-air demand providers in the larger television program industry. Free-to-air service providers use a mix of internally and externally produced local and international programs, while pay TV providers such as Disney Plus use only internally generated programs produced by a suite of production companies that they have acquired.

Defining the boundaries of the industry

Identifying the boundaries of an industry can make analysis of its structure much simpler. The Australian and New Zealand Standard Industrial Classification (ANZSIC) offers a guide for the boundaries of most industries, however, this classification is only a starting point. Industry reports, such as those produced by Standard & Poor's, IBISWorld and Datamonitor, provide industry overviews that can help to further define the boundaries.

Once the boundaries of an industry have been identified, the segment of the industry most relevant to the organisation must be identified. For example, Seqirus's industry could be defined by a number of different boundaries (see strategy capsule 2.1). This medical product manufacturer could consider itself part of the Professional and Scientific Equipment Manufacturing (ANZSIC 241) industry, the Medical and Surgical Equipment Manufacturing (ANZSIC 2412) industry, or the Scientific Research Services (ANZSIC 6910) industry. In addition, it could view its industry as national (Australia), regional (Australia, New Zealand and South-East Asia), or global.

Industries and markets

When defining industries, it is important to clarify what is meant by the term 'industry'. Economists define an **industry** as a group of organisations that supplies a market. Hence, a close correspondence exists between markets and industries. The principal difference between analysing industry structure and analysing market structure is that industry analysis assesses industry attractiveness on the basis of competition between specific elements — such as suppliers, customers and substitutes — within the overall industry's market, while analysing market structure focuses predominantly on the customers alone.

It can be useful to consider the boundaries of an industry from the demand side. A **demand-side** definition of an industry regards the industry from the customer's viewpoint.

This is different from the market perspective or **supply-side** definition of an industry. For example, two very different definitions of the Australian Open — an international tennis competition — will result from defining it from the demand- or supply-side perspective. The supply-side definition would consider the Australian Open to be the spectacle of live tennis matches. The only competition would come from other similar spectacles — such as the Australian (golf) Open. Luckily these two opens occur at different times, however, other spectacles occurring at the same time, such as the Great Ocean Road Race (a bicycle race), do compete. The demand-side definition would consider the customer perspective — what customers expect to gain from attending or watching one of the spectacles. If it is an afternoon's entertainment, this need can also be met by meeting friends or going to the cinema. If the customer's expectation is first-hand experience of international sports stars in action, then any event with big 'stars' will fill their need. If the customer is interested in seeing how experts play the game, then tennis videos or lessons might meet the same demand. If the customer had reserved a corporate box with catering to entertain and impress their clients, a corporate box at the Formula 1 Grand Prix or the opera might work just as well. This example demonstrates that the definition of the industry boundary is much broader if the demand-side perspective is used. From this perspective, the competition faced by the Australian Open becomes much broader.

In addition to selecting the perspective through which an industry is viewed, it is important to identify the boundaries of the industry. Incorrect identification of the boundaries can lead to incorrect conclusions about the forces that would be experienced in that industry. Typically, an industry is identified as a fairly broad group of organisations that produce similar products or services (such as automotive manufacturers), while markets represent specific customer groups. As a result, markets are usually subsets of industries. For example, the packaging industry competes in many distinct markets, each containing different group customers — purchasers of glass containers, steel cans, aluminium cans, paper cartons and plastic containers.

Geography can sometimes assist in defining industries. For example, the Australian Open is an Australian tennis industry event (even though it attracts international visitors), which is sanctioned by the International Tennis Federation that governs all major international tennis events.

Competitor analysis

Determining the nature of competitors is an important and developing area of external environmental analysis. It is now the focus of a number of books,[40] a dedicated journal,[41] specialist consulting organisations and professional associations.[42] Most competitor analyses are based on information that is available in the public domain. In the United States, about 25 per cent of commercial enterprises have competitive intelligence units, however, competitive intelligence units are less common in Australia and most European countries.

The main purposes of a **competitor analysis** are to:
1. forecast competitors' future strategies and decisions
2. predict competitors' likely reactions to an organisation's strategic initiatives
3. determine how competitors' behaviour can be influenced to make it more favourable.

A framework for predicting competitor behaviour

The objective of this analysis is to be able to understand what drives competitors. A characteristic of great generals from history, from Hannibal to Patton, has been their ability to go beyond military intelligence and to 'get inside the heads' of their opposing commanders. The public domain is filled with information about competitors, but most of it will be too general or not relevant to a strategic competitor analysis. Porter proposes a four-part framework which can be used to sort this information and predict competitor behaviour, as shown in figure 2.6.

FIGURE 2.6 | Porter's framework for competitor analysis

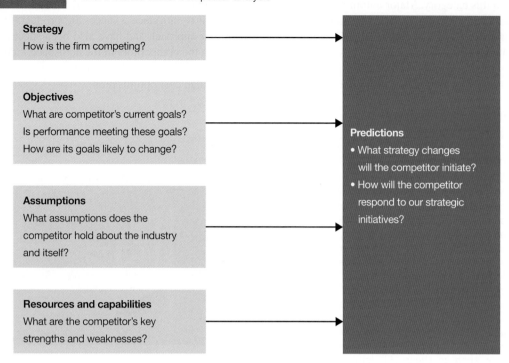

The four parts of the framework are as follows.

1. *Competitor's current strategy.* The company's website, annual reports and press releases will provide information on specific strategies that the organisation claims it is pursuing. As noted in the chapter on strategic concepts and perspectives, however, only some of these strategies will be realised in practice. The purpose of analysing the competitor's current strategy is to identify the strategies which have been implemented. The specific strategic actions the competitor will take (such as acquiring new businesses or restructuring) and the competitive advantages the organisation possesses are important features of an assessment of the competitor's current strategy.

2. *Competitor's objectives.* Most organisations will be driven by a combination of financial and non-financial goals, such as market share or performance targets. A company whose primary goal is attaining a specific market share is likely to be a much more aggressive competitor than one that is mainly interested in achieving profitability or maintaining quality standards (e.g. maintaining an ISO 9000 quality accreditation). For example, the Australian banking industry focused on maintaining profitability during the COVID-19 crisis and did not pursue many opportunities to acquire struggling competitors as they represented a profitability risk in the medium term.

3. *Competitor's assumptions about the industry.* A competitor's strategic behaviours are likely to reflect their interpretation of industry forces and key success factors. It is quite common for managers to become entrenched in their perception of the industry. It is also quite common for decision makers of the organisations in an industry to converge, over time, on the same shared views.[43] This is particularly true in traditional industries such as the wine industry. If these views are incorrect or outdated, they represent weakness in the strategies of competitors. The Australian wine industry, for example, converged on the belief that quality and consistency in winemaking resulted from technical excellence. This led wine producers to invest excessively in the pursuit of technical excellence and ignore the creativity and traditions associated with wine making. The excessive focus on technology negatively affected the perception of the Australian wine products in international markets – they were too consistent. Subsequently, the industry learnt to blend technology, creativity and tradition and has become very successful internationally.

4. *Competitor's resources and capabilities.* The strength of a competitor's resources and capabilities is an important indicator of their competitive ability. For example, if a small, independent petrol station attempts to attract more customers by dropping prices, other petrol stations will do the same and a price war will quickly develop. Local petrol stations owned by major international petroleum companies will be able to sustain the lower prices longer than independent associations, and the independent petrol station's strategy will be unsuccessful. Smaller competitors are much more successful when they use

their flexibility and focus on a competitor's major weakness. Elon Musk's group of businesses fits into this category. Major automotive producers are not skilled at producing high-performance electric vehicles, allowing Tesla to develop this capability and use it to introduce a successful product. Other companies, such as BYD (from China) have taken a similar approach and have also been successful. Musk's SpaceX company focuses on an area of weakness in the competitors in the aerospace industry — providing low-cost space transport services. SpaceX has been successful because aerospace industry competitors are focused on technology development rather than cost optimisation.

ALDI versus Woolworths and Coles in Australia

ALDI has been in operation in Australia since 2001, and now has 500 Australian stores.[44] ALDI has competed successfully with the large supermarket retailers Woolworths and Coles, holding 11 per cent of the Australian grocery market, compared to 28 per cent for Coles and 34 per cent for Woolworths.[45] ALDI competes on the basis of price, offering a much smaller product range (only 1700 products, compared with around 30 000 products for the major supermarket chains) which gives it economies of scale that enable it to undercut Coles and Woolworths on those products. ALDI also offers a range of weekly specials on a rotating  basis, such as cheap ski clothing, to make the shopping experience more interesting (and increase sales). Both price-based competition and special items are ALDI global strategy. ALDI Australia, however, extended the strategies by observing their key competitors' strategies and introducing a new feature which gave them a substantial edge.

ALDI saw that their competitors competed by carrying very large product ranges, operating very large numbers of stores (Woolworths has 3000 stores[46]) and forming partnerships (Woolworths partners with Caltex petrol stations as another outlet for their supermarket products). This made it difficult for both Woolworths and Coles to focus on individual products and so they predominantly sell brand-name products. ALDI focused on making their products different and special by negotiating individual contracts with suppliers and selling under their own brand. For example, when a study by the Australian Olives Association found that 85 per cent of extra virgin olive oil sold in Australian supermarkets did not meet extra virgin standards, ALDI introduced independent testing for their olive oils.[47] Having a small range of olive oil made this a viable activity for ALDI, however, the very large range of local and imported olive oils sold by Coles and Woolworths made this type of assurance impossible.

2.6 Network environment analysis

LEARNING OBJECTIVE 2.6 Conduct a network environment analysis.

Networks have become a very important feature of the competitive landscape. The chapter on co-operative strategies and alliances considers the impact of networks on competitive advantage in detail. Their role in the external environment will be considered in this section. An environmental analysis of networks identifies the characteristics and scope of the external networks (**network factors**) that support or interfere with an organisation's operations. Network factors are usually industry-specific, but may vary between the individual markets served by an industry.

The relationship between network factors is shown in figure 2.7. The nature of the *characteristic* and *scope factors* reflect the industry conditions. These factors and the conditions that create them are the result of interactions between different organisations in the industry and in supporting industries. In many instances, networks operate in the background and their influence on an industry is often overlooked. However, in some environments (especially political and highly competitive environments), the impact of networks should not be ignored. The conditions that create the networks are common to most industry contexts and include *trust levels, transparency, transferability* (of benefits), *network membership, ongoing membership requirements* and network member *attributes* (such as professional qualifications).[48] *Scope factors* include *geographical coverage*, the *size of the network* (numbers of members), *areas of the impact* (e.g. politics, capital market access and competition), *influence* of the network relative to other local institutions such as government and professional associations, and the *longevity* of the network.

Trust levels are particularly important characteristics of networks — the level of trust determines the *influence level* and *longevity* of the network. Trust results from the shared understandings, experiences and (industry) language of the network. Network *transparency* is measured relative to the *trust levels* and reflects the level of openness of purpose and procedure. The greater the levels of trust, the more important transparency becomes. *Transferability* occurs between individuals in networks and may be delayed until required. *Network membership* usually includes entry hurdles, such as experience, resources and knowledge, which are strongly related to *attributions*. *Attributions* are the qualifications (both professional and personal) required for *network membership*. Some networks may have low attribution requirements (e.g. industry experience), while professional networks require qualifications and other demonstrated achievements. *Ongoing requirements* are the contributions to the network necessary to retain *network membership* and *transferability* rights.

FIGURE 2.7 Hierarchy of network factors

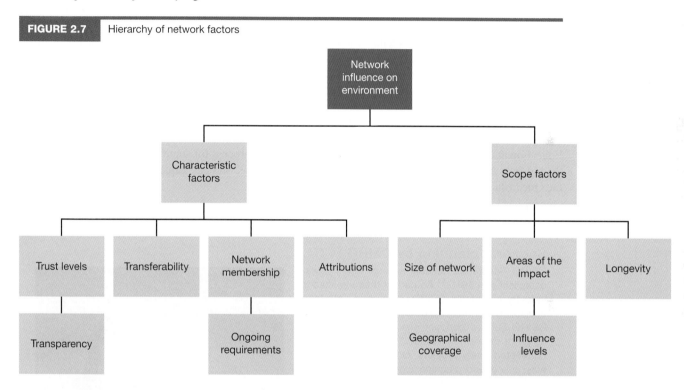

Not only does the *size of the network* determine the *level of influence* it exerts on an industry, it also determines the extent of the industry which is influenced (such as customers, rivals and suppliers). *Geographical coverage* is usually influenced by the *size of the network*. Larger networks will generally seek to increase *geographical coverage*. The *areas of impact* are industry features which are influenced by the network, such as new technology developments, regulation, industry peak bodies, suppliers and customers. The *influence levels* of these areas of impact are increased by the *size* or *geographical coverage* of the network. They are also increased by the *influence* of the individual network members. For example, network members who hold influential government positions can increase the network's effect on government regulations. *Longevity* is a separate network factor which reflects the time over which the network has an effect and, subsequently, the aggregated effect of the network on the industry.

2.7 Scenario planning

LEARNING OBJECTIVE 2.7 Develop scenarios and explain their uses.

Scenarios are stories or other evocative representations about what the future might look like. Schoemaker argues that scenarios:[49]

> highlight dynamic interactions (i.e. how we might get from here to there) . . . reflect a variety of viewpoints . . . [and] cover a broad range of possibilities. Scenarios are not . . . statistical predictions . . . but [aim to] bound and better understand future uncertainties.

Schoemaker was one of a group of strategic planners at Royal Dutch Shell who promoted the method and benefits of scenario planning in strategic management. **Scenario planning** is particularly useful for organisations that face significant environmental uncertainty and complexity. When an environmental analysis identifies the existence of a limited number of highly uncertain — but very important — environmental factors or trends, scenario planning can be used to identify how they might interact to affect the conditions and environment.

The process through which scenarios are generated is very structured. Good research, logical analysis and creativity are necessary to ensure that genuinely testing and diverse scenarios are identified. Scenarios are useful only insofar as they enable an understanding of possible future developments and the incorporation of appropriate actions into the organisation's strategy.[50] Relative to other forms of environment analysis, scenario planning can:

- generate more creative and plausible descriptions of complex external environments than extrapolating trends of past behaviours into the future
- assist with the exploration of ideas and build consensus around various possibilities, rather than focusing on only one future
- create evocative pictures of potential future events that are more easily understood by those not involved in the development of the external environmental analysis.

Effective scenario planning requires considerable organisational skills and very high levels of industry knowledge. In addition, it requires creative and comparative approaches that may not be consistent with an organisation's normal strategy formulation process. In Australia, scenario planning has been used more often in the public sector than the private sector, although this is changing. Organisations such as the Queensland Department of Natural Resources and Water, the Victorian Office of Training and Further Education and the Australian Taxation Office have used this process for some time. More recently, two of the big four Australian banks have begun using this technique. Strategy capsule 2.4 briefly outlines how the Queensland transport authority utilised scenario planning.

Scenario planning by CSIRO

CSIRO, Australia's national science agency, was established in 1916.[51] As part of their services to industry in Australia, CSIRO established a strategic advisory department called CSIRO Futures in 2014. CSIRO Futures conduct scenario planning for a range of different industries.[52] To date, they have completed many projects. One of these projects was a scenario planning exercise conducted in 2018 for the Queensland transport authority — considering potential transport developments until 2048. This study identified emerging social and business trends that affected transport in the region, the uncertainties in these trends and the

effect on the communities that the transport authority serviced.[53] This report divided scenarios into geopolitical events, cultural shifts, population growth and dispersion, technology effects and slower than expected introductions of factors such as autonomous vehicles.

The study resulted in a range of recommended policy considerations for the transport authority, including the adoption of a road fee to replace vehicle registration (reflecting the possibility of reduced vehicle ownership in the future), the development of rideshare applications integrated with mass transport to reduce congestion resulting from uncontrolled ridesharing, and a shift in focus for the authority from being a service provider to being a service broker. This would mean changing from a focus on routine transactions such as vehicle registration to brokering collaboration with commercial enterprises for Queensland transportation users, such as negotiating car insurance deals.[54]

2.8 Identifying key success factors

LEARNING OBJECTIVE 2.8 Identify key success factors and strategic groups.

In addition to understanding the nature of competition and attractiveness of an industry, an external environmental analysis such as a PESTEL or five forces analysis can identify the factors that enable an organisation to be competitive in that industry. These are known as the industry **key success factors** (KSFs). These industry KSFs represent behaviours that may result in a competitive advantage, however, they only represent what is already successful in the industry. Internal resources can lead to alternative ways to compete in an industry, such as a novel supply chain management approach, which have not been previously considered or tested.

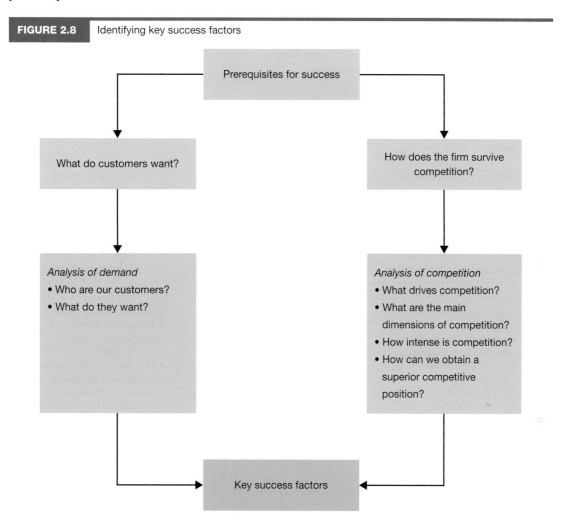

FIGURE 2.8 Identifying key success factors

KSFs can be identified using the process shown in figure 2.8. The figure shows that customers are an important factor in the identification of KSFs. In this analysis, it is important to take a stakeholder perspective and view customers as key stakeholders and even as the fundamental reason for the existence of the industry. For example, customers' choice of supermarket may be based primarily on accessing the lowest prices. A supermarket's ability to charge low prices depends on maintaining low costs. Therefore, a supermarket industry KSF would be to achieve low operational costs. Low operational costs could be achieved by purchasing goods from wholesalers at competitive prices and would enable goods to be resold at low prices to customers. Successful supermarket chains such as ALDI and Costco use this principle.

In highly competitive industries, knowing the KSFs may not be sufficient to make the organisation competitive. For example, in the mobile phone market, introducing a feature that customers did not know they wanted, developing superior financial management capabilities (mobile phone development is very expensive) or having the capability to negotiate special deals with governments that support establishing manufacturing in new countries can also increase competitiveness, but would not be identified as KSFs for this industry. As a result, KSFs alone are not a sufficient basis for strategic thinking.[55] KSFs should, instead, be used in strategic thinking to ensure that external environmental conditions are adequately represented in relation to competitive advantage. Each industry is different in terms of what motivates customers and how competition works. Developing a unique set of resources and capabilities that respond to the environment is the best basis for establishing competitive advantage. Table 2.1 provides some examples of the industry KSFs for three different industries in 2020.

TABLE 2.1   Key success factors for Australian steel, clothing and tourism industries

	External forces/Needs	Industry responses	Key success factors
Iron and steel manufacture[56]	• Overseas competitors will expand, reducing domestic markets, while international markets are uncertain • Challenging conditions will reduce the number of producers operating in Australia • Increased automation will be needed to reduce costs • Steel production in India and China will increase • Technology change is occurring at a medium pace	• The industry is patenting new technologies at a high rate, indicating innovation • Increased costs have driven producers to increase efficiencies • Automation levels continue to increase • Low performing producers are exiting the industry	• Ability to reduce costs • Innovative introduction of technology • Vertical integration into downstream industries to bypass cheap imported steel • Operation in low-labour cost countries
Clothing retailing[57]	• Demand likely to increase at 2 per cent per year • Strong competition with retail outlets who offer lower prices • International retailers with bigger supply chains expand local presence • Online shopping demand increasing • Narrower demand requirements due to segmented shopping practices	• Compete on the basis of price, quality, brand, marketing, customer service and location • Increasing frequency of virtual stores and adaptive storefronts • Struggling to keep up with changing customer preferences • Constant mergers and acquisitions to increase economies of scale	• Ability to control stock • Cash flow management • Clear and consistent industry position • Customer demand understanding • Proximity to key markets • e-commerce capability
Tourism[58]	• Increasing demand driven by low Australian dollar • Largest spend from Chinese tourists • Growing attention from Indian tourists • East Coast most popular with domestic tourists • Increasing digital activity • Infrastructure development inadequate • Growing competition with international tourism for domestic market	• Australian government to introduce new tourism campaign • Increase in capacity in response to increased demand • Stimulation of word-of-mouth recommendations • increased capacity to adapt to new technologies • Use of casual workers to adjust capacity to meet demand • Increased quality of inputs (e.g. food)	• Online booking capability • Integration with online platforms such as social media • Proximity to key markets • Multiskilled workforce • Capacity utilisation optimisation • Marketing capabilities

Strategic groups

A **strategic group analysis** identifies clusters of organisations in the industry which compete using the same strategies. A **strategic group** is a single 'group of organisations following the same or a similar strategy in an industry'.[59] The strategies are usually represented on the basis of two dimensions drawn from strategy features such as product range, geographical breadth, choice of distribution channels, level of product quality, degree of vertical integration and choice of technology. Figure 2.9 shows the strategic groups making up the global automobile industry. The groups of companies that have adopted similar strategies are represented as strategic groups by selecting the appropriate dimensions (geographical coverage and product range) to represent their strategies.

The strategic group analysis technique presumes that mobility barriers stop organisations moving between strategic groups, which is why different strategic groups are consistently more successful than other strategic groups.[60] Strategic group analyses are useful for identifying strategic niches within an industry and selecting the most attractive strategies for that niche. They are less useful for analysing differences in business performance as the companies in the strategic group may experience different local environments, especially if the industry is international.[61]

The SWOT analysis

The SWOT (strengths, weaknesses, opportunities, threats) analysis is probably the most familiar and simple strategic analysis tool. The opportunities and threats components of this analysis tool provide a simple external environmental analysis. The strengths and weaknesses components provide a simple assessment of the internal resource conditions in the organisation. The greatest drawback of this simple analysis technique is that it usually identifies too large a range of factors to inform strategic thinking and does not incorporate a framework for prioritising the factors that it identifies. Another concern is that it also takes a static view of the internal and external environment and does not adequately represent trends in key conditions.

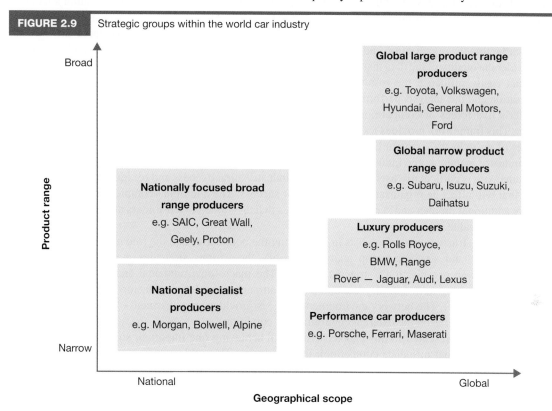

FIGURE 2.9 Strategic groups within the world car industry

Some authors recommend reversing the acronym and conducting this analysis as TOWS. This approach brings the external environmental components of threats and opportunities to the opening of the analysis and provides an environmental context for assessing the weaknesses and strengths. This is a useful perspective, as an environmental condition that represents a threat for one organisation could represent an opportunity for another.

The most effective approach for conducting a SWOT (or TOWS) analysis is as a basis for generating discussion about internal and external conditions and as a warm-up for a strategic thinking exercise. As long as a more thorough and framework-based analysis is conducted, a SWOT analysis can be used to quickly draw issues of concern to decision makers' attention.

Relationship of environmental analysis to strategic plans

As Porter noted, an awareness of the external environment enables the organisation to focus its strategies on the particular segment of the environment which offers the greatest opportunity for success.[62] While an environmental analysis may reduce uncertainty about the future, it is important to remember that business success is not entirely depended on understanding the external environmental. Internal strengths and resources have a significant impact upon organisational success as well. Environmental analysis can form a valuable foundation for strategic thinking about the effect of the external environment and it can also provide a basis for evaluating the value of internal capabilities. De Wit and Meyer refer to these two approaches as the paradox of markets and resources.[63] Organisations that adopt a demand perspective commence strategic thinking with the needs of the market and the customers. This is also called the positioning approach because organisations take up a particular position in the market relative to customer needs. For example, ALDI has positioned itself as a low-cost supermarket in response to perceived customer needs.

Organisations that commence strategic thinking by considering the value of internal capabilities will adopt a supply perspective and seek opportunities to generate an advantage in the external environment from the organisation's resources. For example, Seqirus (see strategy capsule 2.1) focuses on developing vaccinations that have the greatest benefit to the community on an annual basis — forecasting the type of vaccines required each year and developing them accordingly. It attempts to compete by producing the most attractive general influenza vaccines available on the market.

SUMMARY

The tools discussed in this chapter provide a systematic approach to analysing an organisation's industry environment in order to evaluate the industry's attractiveness and the sources of competitive advantage. They can improve decision making by providing insights and reducing uncertainty about the external factors affecting the organisation and industry. When conducting analysis using these tools, it is important to consider the quality of the data that is being utilised and factors such as the time period being considered. Bias can easily influence the results of such analyses, especially if all the data is collected by the organisation and the analysis performed only by internal staff, or staff in a single department.

Porter's five forces of competition framework is one of the most important tools considered in this chapter. This framework provides a simple yet powerful organising framework for classifying the relevant features of an industry's structure and predicting the implications for competitive behaviour. Although every industry is unique, the industry structure will influence competition and opportunities for success. The framework is particularly useful for predicting industry attractiveness and for identifying the industry forces that will affect an organisation's potential for success. The additional complements force helps to identify additional product and service characteristics that are valued by customers and how to exploit the sources of this value.

The industry structure analysis assists in identifying the boundaries and the true nature of the industry. The competitor and strategic group analyses identify the various strategies at play in an industry and can inform an organisation's strategic choices. The macro environmental analysis focuses on the most significant long-term industry conditions and attractiveness-defining factors (e.g. economic and technological trends). The network environment analysis provides an assessment of the likely impact of the industry's networks on the external environmental conditions.

All of the tools presented in this chapter assist with achieving one important strategic understanding — the key factors that influence competition in an industry. This understanding is critical for effective strategic thinking.

KEY TERMS

barriers to exit The costs of or impediments to exiting the industry.

competitor analysis An analysis of the strategies through which competitors create a competitive advantage.

concentration ratio (CR) The percentage of the market that is held by a set number of the largest organisations.

demand-side Pertaining to the perspective of customers.

disruptive technology A technology that appears with little warning and has a significant impact on how business is conducted in an industry.

industry A group of organisations that supplies a particular market.

industry environment The conditions in the organisation's industry (i.e. in the environment immediately surrounding the organisation).

key success factors (KSFs) The characteristics defined by industry conditions that are important for the success of an organisation.

macro environment The environment external to the organisation, its operations and its industry.

national competitive advantage The features of the local environment that provide a competitive advantage.

network factors The nature and scope of networks that affect the conditions in the external environment.

PESTEL analysis (political, economic, social, technological, environmental and legal analysis) A framework for identifying features of the macro environment that may affect the organisation.

scenario planning An analysis of the likely impact on the organisation of potential future external environmental events.

strategic group A group of organisations in an industry with similar strategies.

strategic group analysis An analysis of the different strategy groupings present in industry, represented on two common strategic dimensions.

supply-side Pertaining to the perspective of suppliers.

SELF-STUDY QUESTIONS

1 Identify the characteristics and principal elements of a PESTEL analysis.

2 Describe the purpose and basic method of scenario planning.

3 Describe the major elements of a five forces analysis.

4 Explain the difference between complements and the five principal forces in a five forces analysis.

5 Describe the four components of Porter's framework for competitor analysis.

6 List and describe the major components of the characteristic and scope factors of a network environment.

7 Describe why a strategic group analysis is conducted.

8 Describe the framework for competitor analysis.

DISCUSSION QUESTIONS

1 The NBN telecommunications network in Australia has had a major levelling effect on the telecommunications industry. Using the five forces of competition framework, explain how competition may have changed between the telecommunications providers, now that they all have equal access to the national network.

2 Manufacturers of inkjet printers (e.g. HP, Canon, and Lexmark) make most of their profits on the sales of ink cartridges. Why are cartridges more profitable than printers? If cartridges were manufactured by different organisations to those that make the printers, would the situation be different? Explain.

3 COVID-19 has had a significant impact on many industries, especially the transportation energy industry. Considering the changes to transportation, especially private transportation, describe two potential scenarios that might inform strategic decision making in the petrochemical industry.

4 Why is rivalry not a major competitive force in the generic pharmaceuticals industry?

5 The ALDI supermarket chain competes on the basis of price. Identify the relative strengths of the five forces to which ALDI is responding and identify any complements that ALDI has utilised to help it compete. Explain why these complements are effective in increasing ALDI's competitiveness.

6 China has made great progress in improving the environmental sustainability of its manufacturing industries and has made some progress in terms of social sustainability as well. Read about some of these initiatives in the media and identify three reasons why China has decided to take a leadership role in this area.

7 List the key success factors for:

    (a) the rideshare industry (e.g. Uber)

    (b) the airline industry.

EXERCISES

1 Audit an 'industry' environment of your choice. Which of the influences you identified in the audit are likely to be the main 'drivers for change' in the future? Why?

2 Assume you have just become executive assistant to the CEO of a major bank, either in Australia or in another country with which you are familiar. The CEO knows you are currently completing a degree in business and asks you to prepare a report summarising if and how scenario planning may be useful to help in the bank's strategic planning process. What would you write?

3 Apply Porter's five forces framework to the competitive environment of the Australian domestic airline industry. Since Virgin Blue entered the Australian market in 2000, this industry has radically altered. Qantas and Virgin Blue are now the only key players left.

    a. Can you identify how some of the five forces have changed in the past five years?

    b. Can you foresee how some of the forces might change again in the next five years?

4 Conduct a scenario planning exercise for the resources industry in Western Australia, with particular attention to the Chinese market.

5 What are some of the ways that you have observed managers and/or strategic analysts conducting imperfect analysis, or reaching imperfect conclusions? If you do not have your own experience of this, provide examples of organisational or strategic failure you have seen in the business media.

6 Access Telstra's current annual report from the company's website (www.telstra.com.au). Review the description of the industry conditions in the report. How do these conditions compare with the statement that 'Telstra is one of the most attractive Australian shares'? Explain.

7 Review the assessment of the external environment provided by the Myer retail chain (http://investor.m yer.com.au) in its financial statements. Compare these financial statement results with the Myer share results on the Australian Securities Exchange. What are your conclusions?

FURTHER READING

Cornelius, P, Van de Putte, A & Romani, M 2005, 'Three decades of scenario planning in Shell', *California Management Review*, vol. 48, no. 1, 92–111.

Hamel, G 2000, *Leading the revolution*, Boston MA: Harvard Business School Press.

Humphreys, J 2004, 'The vision thing', *MIT Sloan Management Review*, vol. 45, iss. 4, 6.

Jacobides, MG 2010, 'Strategy tools for a shifting landscape', *Harvard Business Review*, vol. 88, no. 1, 76–84.

Panagiotou G 2003, 'Bringing SWOT into focus', *Business Strategy Review*, vol. 14, no. 2, 8–10.

Porter, ME 1980, *Competitive strategy: techniques for analyzing industries and competitors*, New York: Free Press.

Porter, ME 2008, 'The five competitive forces that shape strategy', *Harvard Business Review*, vol. 86, no. 1, 78–93.

Yunggar, M 2005, 'Environment scanning for strategic information: content analysis from Malaysia', *Journal of American Academy of Business*, vol. 6, no 2, 324–331.

ENDNOTES

1. S Orr, J Menzies, C Zheng and S Maddumage, *Innovation and internationalisation: successful SMEs' ventures into China*, Abington: Routledge, 2017.
2. R Jennings, 'Discovery of unusual natural gas sharpens China's maritime sovereignty claims', *Voice of America*, 30 March 2020, www.voanews.com/east-asia-pacific/discovery-unusual-natural-gas-sharpens-chinas-maritime-sovereignty-claims.
3. 'China's special economic zones experience gained', World Bank, 2015, www.worldbank.org/content/dam/Worldbank/Event/Africa/Investing%20in%20Africa%20Forum/2015/investing-in-africa-forum-chinas-special-economic-zone.pdf.
4. Orr et al., op cit.
5. S Orr, J Menzies and M Donnelly, 'Born in China: a new type of Australian business,' *The Conversation*, 28 June 2017, https://theconversation.com/born-in-china-a-new-type-of-australian-business-79037.
6. '1 billion animals killed in Australian bushfires', The Wildlife Society, 2020, https://wildlife.org/1-billion-animals-killed-in-australian-bushfires.
7. J Bigley, 'Assembling frameworks for strategic innovation enactment: enhancing transformational agility through situational scanning', *Administrative Sciences*, vol. 8, no. 3, 2018.
8. Department of Infrastructure, Transport, Regional Development and Communications, 'Telstra's separation framework', 30 April 2015, www.communications.gov.au/what-we-do/internet/competition-broadband/telstras-separation-framework.
9. 'World's fastest supercomputer processes huge data rates in preparation for mega-telescope project — ICRAR', *ICRAR*, 22 October 2019, https://www.icrar.org/summit.
10. M Malik, S Abdalla, S Orr and U Chaudhary, 'The differences in agent effects on sustainable supply chain management: an activity theory construction', *Supply Chain Management*, vol. 24, no. 5, 2019, 637–65.
11. For a review of the Porter analysis, see RM Grant, 'Porter's competitive advantage of nations: an assessment', *Strategic Management Journal*, vol. 12, 1991, 535–548.
12. Wine Australia, 'Australian wine exports to China reach new record', 2019, www.wineaustralia.com/news/media-releases/australian-wine-exports-to-china-reach-new-record.
13. Seqirus, 'Our company, 2015, www.seqirus.com/our-company.
14. ibid.
15. Seqirus, 'Gordon Naylor President Presentation', Macquarie Australia Conference, May 2017, www.csl.com/-/media/csl/documents/seqirus-president-presentation-to-the-macquarie-australia-conference-sydney.pdf?la=fr-fr&hash=20CE1CBD225391E62A58B62F55E876C149EB9C8E.
16. ME Porter, *Competitive strategy: techniques for analyzing industries and competitors*, New York: Free Press, 1980, chapter 1. For a summary, see article, 'How competitive forces shape strategy', *Harvard Business Review*, vol. 57, March/April 1979, 86–93.
17. B Maury, 'Sustainable competitive advantage and profitability persistence: sources versus outcomes for assessing advantage', *Journal of Business Research*, 84, 2018, 100–113.
18. GS Yip, 'Gateways to entry', *Harvard Business Review*, vol. 60, September–October 1982, 85–93.
19. Comac, 'About us', 2020, http://english.comac.cc/introduction.
20. Boost Juice, 'Franchising', www.boostjuice.com.au.

21. Australian Franchises, 'Fast food franchise opportunities', 2020, www.australianfranchises.com.au; WSI, 'McDonalds franchise for sale Australia', 2020, www.wsicorporate.com.

22. R Blackburn, 'Holden confirms it will design and engineer a new hatch', 3 June 2009, *Drive*, www.drive.com.au.

23. D Reed, 'The plane that never should have been built: the A380 was designed for failure', *Forbes*, 15 February 2019, www.forbes.com/sites/danielreed/2019/02/15/the-plane-that-never-should-have-been-built-the-a380-was-designed-for-marketplace-failure/#15f783ec3c59.

24. Saudi Aramco, 2020, www.saudiaramco.com.

25. M Balaji and K Arshinder, 'Modeling the causes of food wastage in Indian perishable food supply chain', *Resources, Conservation and Recycling*, vol. 114, 2016, 153–67.

26. Australian Bureau of Statistics, *Radio and Television Services*, 2020, www.abs.gov.au.

27. K Paulson, 'Intellectual property protection: key to accelerating Indonesia's economic growth', *Defence Technical Information*, 2018, https://apps.dtic.mil/docs/citations/AD1077879.

28. Reed, op. cit.

29. H Beladi, S Marjit and R Oladi, 'Inflating profits and industry competitiveness', *International Journal of Economic Theory*, vol. 15, no. 3, 2018, 281–87.

30. IBISWorld, 'Fuel retailing in Australia — Market research report', *IBISWorld*, 2020.

31. FloraHolland, 'Auctioning', www.flora.nl.

32. The problems caused by excess capacity and exit barriers are discussed in C. Baden–Fuller (ed.), *Strategic Management of Excess Capacity*, Oxford: Basil Blackwell, 1990.

33. J Hollingsworth, 'Daigou down under: the Chinese shopping trend taking Australia by storm (and a public listing to boot)', *South China Morning Post*, 3 September 2017, www.scmp.com/week-asia/business/article/2109396/daigou-down-under-chinese-shopping-trend-taking-australia-storm.

34. T Flanagan, 'The Australian baby formula frenzy: is China really bleeding the nation dry?', *Yahoo News*, 10 August 2019, https://au.news.yahoo.com/baby-formula-australia-china-daigou-032543894.html.

35. 'Bellamy's jumps after getting nod from China', *Sydney Morning Herald*, 24 April 2019, www.smh.com.au/business/companies/bellamy-s-jumps-after-getting-nod-from-china-20190424-p51gxq.html.

36. B Xiao, '"You must embrace them": Inside the world of the Chinese shoppers that have unnerved Australians", *ABC News*, 30 July 2019, www.abc.net.au/news/2019-07-31/chinese-daigou-changing-influencing-australian-business/11221498.

37. T Flanagan, 2019.

38. S Evans, 'Treasury wines says China business is strong', *Australian Financial Review*, 30 April 2019, www.afr.com/companies/agriculture/treasury-wines-says-china-business-is-strong-20190501-p51iux.

39. See A Brandenburger and B Nalebuff, 'The right game: use game theory to shape strategy', *Harvard Business Review*, July/August 1995, 63–64; and A Brandenburger, J Kou and M Burnett, *Power play (A): Nintendo in 8-bit video games*, Harvard Business School Case No. 9-795-103, 1995.

40. L Field, *The secret language of competitive intelligence*, New York: Random House, 2006; JE Prescott and SH Miller, *Proven strategies in competitive intelligence: lessons from the trenches*, New York: John Wiley & Sons, 2001.

41. *Competitive Intelligence Review*, New York: John Wiley & Sons.

42. The Society of Competitive Intelligence Professionals, www.scip.org.

43. J-C Spender, *Industry recipes: the nature and sources of managerial judgement*, Oxford: Basil Blackwell, 1989; A Huff, 'How social interaction promotes convergence of perceptions and beliefs is discussed in 'Industry influences on strategy reformulation', *Strategic Management Journal*, no. 3, 1982, 119–131.

44. ALDI, 'About ALDI — ALDI Australia', 2020, https://corporate.aldi.com.au/en/about-aldi.

45. ABC, 'Supermarket market share', 3 May 2019, www.abc.net.au/news/2019-05-03/supermarket-market-share-roy-morgan-single-source/11073926.

46. Woolworths group, 'About us', 2019, www.woolworthsgroup.com.au/page/about-us.

47. E Han, 'Imported "extra virgin" olive oil increasingly failing quality tests', *The Sydney Morning Herald*, 5 May 2016, www.smh.com.au/business/consumer-affairs/imported-extra-virgin-olive-oil-increasingly-failing-quality-tests-20160504-golr7y.html; ALDI, 'Olive oil', 2020, www.aldi.com.au/en/groceries/pantry/olive-oil.

48. S Orr and JL Menzies, 'Using social networks and the Guanxi in case study research on Australian firms doing business in China', *Australasian Journal of Market & Social Research*, vol. 20, no. 1, 2012, pp. 22–33, Australian Market & Social Research Society, Glebe, NSW; JL Menzies and S Orr, 'The impact of political behaviours on internationalisation: the case of Australian companies internationalising to China', *Journal of Chinese Economic and Foreign Trade Studies*, vol. 3, no. 1, pp. 24–42, Emerald Group Publishing Ltd, United Kingdom.

49. P Schoemaker, 'Multiple scenario development: its conceptual and behavioural foundation', *Strategic Management Journal*, vol. 14, 1993, 196.

50. ibid.

51. CSIRO, 'Our history', 2020, www.csiro.au/en/About/History-achievements/Our-history.

52. CSIRO, 'CSIRO futures', 2020, www.csiro.au/en/Showcase/CSIRO-Futures.

53. C Naughtin, J Horton, O Marinoni, M Mailloux, A Bratanova and K Trinh, 'Time travel: Megatrends and scenarios for Queensland transport out to 2048', 2018, Brisbane: CSIRO Data61.

54. ibid.

55. P Ghemawat, *Commitment: the dynamic of strategy*, New York: Free Press, 1991, p. 11.

56. 'Iron smelting and steel manufacturing in Australia', *IBISWorld*, October 2019.

57. T Miller, 'Clothing retailing in Australia', *IBISWorld*, August 2019.

58. N Cloutman, 'Tourism in Australia', *IBISWorld*, March 2020.

59. ME Porter, *Competitive strategy*, New York: Free Press, 1980, p. 129; M Porter, 'The structure within industries and companies' performance', *Review of Economics & Statistics*, vol. 61, no. 2, 1979, 214.

60. Ibid.

61. K Smith, C Grimm and S Wally, 'Strategic groups and rivalrous organisation behaviour: toward a reconciliation', *Strategic Management Journal*, vol. 18, 1997, 149–157.

62. M Porter, 'What is strategy?', *Harvard Business Review*, 1996, vol. 74, no. 6, 61–78.

63. B De Wit and R Meyer, *Strategy: process, content and context*, 3rd edn, London: Thomson Learning, 2004.

ACKNOWLEDGEMENTS

Photo: © Getty Images

Photo: © Nikolay Litov / Shutterstock.com

Photo: © Tirachard Kumtanom / Shutterstock.com

Photo: © TK Kurikawa / Shutterstock.com

CHAPTER 3

Internal analysis of capabilities and core competencies

LEARNING OBJECTIVES

After studying this chapter, you should be able to:

3.1 explain the nature of 'competitive advantage'

3.2 discuss the concept of the value chain and its links to competitive advantage

3.3 describe the role of an organisation's resources and capabilities as a basis of competitive advantage

3.4 identify the resources and capabilities of an organisation.

Bunnings — continuous development of a successful formula

Why do some companies perform better than their rivals? And why are some competitors successful in challenging and fast-changing industries while many others are not? An explanation may be found in the ability of successful companies to continuously reassess their business models and challenge existing assumptions. This is illustrated by the retailer Bunnings, a business owned by ASX-listed entity Wesfarmers Limited. Over the years the company has been able to develop and refine its business model and its financial performance has been contributing significantly to the success of Wesfarmers.

The origins of Bunnings go back to 1886 when the two founders of the company arrived in Western Australia and started operating a sawmill. In the decades thereafter the company grew and during the 1950s the company went public and moved into the building supply industry. It took the company until around the 1990s to start acquiring other Do It Yourself businesses, also in other parts of Australia. In 1994 the business opened its first Bunnings Warehouse in Victoria, the large-scale home improvement and outdoor living stores for which the company is now best known. In 2001 the company ventured into the New Zealand market, in which they currently are the market leader as well. During the 2019 financial year the company had a total revenue of A\$13.1 billion and employed over 44 000 people.[1]

The specific drivers of the continuing success of Bunnings are hard to pinpoint, as a combination of factors have contributed.[2] The company has long been known for its role in Australian communities (via such activities as its famous sausage sizzles), smart marketing and a wide range of products, services and solutions offered under one big roof. Bunnings also trains its employees to be experts in specific areas, thus enabling them to provide customised advice to customers. For a long time the company's slogan was 'lowest prices are just the beginning', promising to undercut the price if the same product is sold at a lower price by competitors.[3] As such, the business has positioned itself around having low prices, stocking the widest range of products and offering the best service in this industry. And so far, competitors have been struggling to challenge Bunnings, which was clearly visible in the failed efforts of Woolworths to set up a Masters Home Improvement chain in Australia.

While being the market leader, the company has been busy further strengthening its position. During 2019 Bunnings went digital by establishing an online selling platform and investing in a data centre in Bangalore, India.[4] Bunnings' online strategy appears to be working, with the company moving into the top four of the recent Power Retail ranking of online retailers in Australia.[5] The digital strategy allows Bunnings to sell products and services beyond those offered in stores, thereby targeting a broader part of the market. At the same it provides existing customers more flexibility around how and when they can buy products and services from Bunnings. Whereas the jury is still out as to whether the new digital strategy is going to work, it at least appears to be an interesting strategic response to the quickly changing and increasingly competitive retail sector in Australia.[6]

A note of caution when driving strategy from a business's resources and capabilities is that different or new competitive conditions can undermine the advantage. In 2016 Bunnings pursued international growth by acquiring Homebase in the United Kingdom for A\$1.7 billion. The idea was to leave the Homebase stores intact and start trialling with new Bunnings stores in that market.[7] After two years of disappointing revenues and losses, however, Bunnings decided to sell the company to Hilco for the symbolic sum of one British pound. The Bunnings formula clearly did not work in a context with other similar competitors and different customer preferences.[8]

Introduction

In the chapter on strategic concepts and perspectives, the shift in strategic thinking from the external to internal environment was discussed. Indeed, this transition leads to the question of why, in the same industries, some companies outperform competitors. As Rumelt, a professor of strategy, noted 'being in the right industry does matter, but being good at what you do matters a lot more'.[9]

This chapter will focus on the organisation's performance: what does the organisation do better than its rivals that is valuable to its customers and difficult for competitors to imitate? As the scene setter shows, successful companies do not rely on their current resource base; rather, they continuously re-invent their resources and develop new capabilities. Bunnings has built their core competence in consistently delivering a wide range of home improvement products for a quality–price combination that is not yet matched by competitors. The company is currently developing an online presence which will enable them to remain competitive in an increasingly challenging retail context. This chapter will discuss the role of organisational capabilities, including dynamic capabilities, in a company's ability to build and sustain its competitive advantage.

3.1 The nature of competitive advantage

LEARNING OBJECTIVE 3.1 Explain the nature of 'competitive advantage'.

Ongoing innovation is a source of superior performance in business. For any company, the creation and sustainability of **competitive advantage** is a main consideration when it formulates its strategy. Competitive advantage is displayed by superior performance and **value** created for the organisation's customers.

Value creation can be defined in many ways; for example, the ability to increase shareholders' wealth by charging higher prices and achieving higher profits, the ability to achieve greater customer satisfaction via improved product attributes, or the ability to increase a company's profit by reducing manufacturing costs. Although a competitive advantage of the organisation is manifested in superior customer satisfaction and higher profit, in some cases an increased profit may be a result of reduced expenses on research and development (R&D), which in the long term will lead to lost competitive advantage and reduced profit. The focus of this chapter is on the analysis of how the various resources, activities and product offerings are employed by organisations to create a competitive advantage.

The ability of organisations to develop a competitive advantage depends on their ability to position their business system in the business environment. A **business system** comprises resources (inputs), activities (throughputs) and product/service offerings (outputs) intended to create value for customers — this is how the company conducts its business. All three elements of the business system must be aligned to create a competitive advantage. First, competitive advantage can be created only if a business system creates superior value for customers. This means that the organisation's products or services are a better fit with the needs of buyers than are the offerings of competitors. Such a better fit can be achieved if every element of an organisation's product/service offerings (e.g. availability, features, reliability, colour, taste, image, reputation, price) satisfies the demands of a particular segment of the market. Next, a competitive organisation should be efficient and effective in performing the required value-creating activities such as logistics, production, R&D, marketing and sales, which are jointly referred to as the value chain. Last, a competitive advantage can be created only if an organisation has the resource base necessary for performing the value-adding activities. Distinctive resources and capabilities of an organisation can build the basis of a superior value proposition. This chapter will explain how each element of an organisation's business system contributes to its ability to create and sustain a competitive advantage. Strategy capsule 3.1 describes how New Zealand's Rocket Lab is positioning its business system to build and sustain a competitive advantage in the global space industry.

Rocket Lab — making New Zealand a player in the space industry

On 11 November 2018 Rocket Lab successfully launched its first commercial rocket from its launch site in Mahia, New Zealand. With this launch 12 years of rocket pioneering by Rocket Lab came to fruition as New Zealand officially joined the international space industry. Morgan Stanley since then has labelled the company 'a disruptive front runner among 117 possible competitors' and 'best positioned to take advantage of the smaller private satellite launch market'.[10] The company in the meantime has already reached unicorn status with an estimated value of more than $1 billion and its

investors include organisations such as Lockheed Martin, Bessemer Venture Partners and Future Fund.[11] The firm has grown rapidly and nowadays employs about 500 staff members.[12] With its business rapidly expanding, particularly in the United States, the business has changed its incorporation to Delaware and its headquarters is currently located in California.

Rocket Lab was founded by Peter Beck in 2006 in New Zealand. In 2009 the company managed to reach space for the first time and since then has developed its Electron rocket, the vehicle it is currently using to launch satellites into space. While the Electron is smaller than many of its direct competitors, Rocket Lab realised early on that a smaller rocket would give them an advantage in the industry, both in terms of lowering the costs of manufacturing and launching rockets, but also in making it easier to embed cutting-edge technology in the design. In particular, 3D printing technology played an important role, as it allowed for a structure that otherwise would not have been possible.[13] Interestingly, being able to secure access to funding turned out to be equally important. In 2019 the CEO remarked that 'we learnt that it took the same amount of capital to go from "zero" to first flight as it did to go from first flight to where we are now. The barriers to entry in this market are just extreme'.[14] As such, making the Electron rocket, which already has a backlog of orders, a sustainable commercial success is not an easy feat.

One of the things working for the company is its launch location in New Zealand. With less air traffic to worry about and government approval to launch 120 rockets a year, the company can provide its customers with a lot of options to launch their satellites. The New Zealand government's Provincial Growth Fund has also announced an upgrade of the road infrastructure surrounding the launch platform to enhance local economic activity.[15] Rocket Lab's CEO recently highlighted that 'any other site is sub-optimal',[16] meaning Rocket Lab's site gives it a clear first-mover, locational advantage. Currently work is under way to increase the capacity of the Mahia site, with another launch location being added in the United States as well.

The company does not stop there. In 2020 Rocket Lab announced it would be moving into the satellite business to become a more all-round space company. Based on its learning over the past decade, the company sees an opportunity to develop its own satellite platform, called Photon, which would reduce the lead time for potential customers. Moreover, the company is investigating the possible reuse of parts of launched rockets so as to further enhance the sustainability of the business.[17]

Product/service offerings

To achieve an attractive fit with customers' needs an organisation must know its target segment of the market. The decision regarding the target customer is an important one.[18] Organisations divide customers into groups according to the differences in customers' needs. This is referred to as **market segmentation**. In soft drink manufacturing, for example, the needs for beverages differ among people depending on their tastes, habits and health concerns. Gatorade offers a range of drinks for active people who train intensively and need to regain energy when they are training. The most common characteristics on which customers' needs vary include demographic factors (e.g. age and income), socioeconomic factors (e.g. stage in the family life cycle and social class), geographic factors (e.g. national and regional differences), psychological factors (e.g. lifestyle and personality), consumption patterns (e.g. regular, moderate and occasional users), and perceptual factors (perceived benefits).[19] Needs of industrial customers differ based on product factors (e.g. technological differences), geographic factors, common buying factor segments and customer size.[20] **Market segments** can be defined on the basis of buying criteria employed and/or buyer behaviour exhibited. Market segmentation should allow an organisation's strategists to gather a better insight into customers and lead to new opportunities for developing product/service offerings that are tailored to the needs of target customers.[21] Competitive advantage can be achieved only if a company is able to satisfy its chosen market segment. In other words, 'without customers, you do not have a business'.[22]

The process of focusing an organisation's business system to satisfy certain needs of a targeted market segment of customers that distinguishes the company among its competitors is called **positioning**. Positioning is achieved by alignment of the three elements of the business system: product/service offering, value chain and the resources base. Positioning is concerned with the decisions 'where to compete' and 'how to compete'.[23] The choice of certain product/market combinations in which a company wants to participate is referred to as the choice of competitive scope. The choice of how to outperform competitors for a product/service offering is the matter of competitive advantage. These two issues are interrelated because organisations have to create a competitive advantage within a chosen competitive scope. Organisations can outperform competitors and create competitive advantage in a chosen product/market using many dimensions along which performance can be compared. Some of the most important bases of competitive advantage are as follows.

- *Price*. The ability to charge a lower price than competitors charge for a comparable quality.
- *Product features*. The different functional characteristics that are provided.

- *Quality*. The product and its features do not have to be fundamentally different from competitors' products, particularly, in the commodity markets; the products just have to be better.
- *Availability*. The way the product is distributed to reach its customers can also be the main competitive advantage for an organisation's positioning. Providing customers with the right product in the right way at the right place can be more appreciated by customers than the product features and quality.
- *Image*. An advantage can be created by having a more appealing image than competitors. Customers often remain loyal to their favourite brands; brands can improve customers' perception of products as more reliable and having a higher quality.
- *Bundling*. Selling a package of products and/or services 'wrapped together' (e.g. renovation services, including interior design and outdoor landscaping features) offers customers the convenience of 'one stop shopping' and promotes products and services that fit together.

According to Porter,[24] all the specific forms of competitive advantage listed above can be presented as two main categories: cost leadership and differentiation. These two forms of competitive advantage will be discussed in detail in the chapter on business-level strategy and competitive advantage. This chapter will now discuss how a company's activities (throughputs) contribute to competitive advantage.

3.2 Value chain analysis

LEARNING OBJECTIVE 3.2 Discuss the concept of the value chain and its links to competitive advantage.

There are many activities and functions of the organisation (e.g. R&D, logistics, production, marketing and sales) that enable it to create value for customers. Value chain analysis enables organisations to understand which activities create value and which do not. The **value chain** is a template used by an organisation to identify its cost position, and the means that might be used to facilitate implementation of a chosen business-level strategy. The value chain shows how a product moves from the raw materials stage to the end customer. A competitive advantage can be created if the company's value chain creates additional value without incurring significant extra costs. As shown in figure 3.1, an organisation's value chain is divided into primary and support activities.

| **FIGURE 3.1** | Porter's value chain |

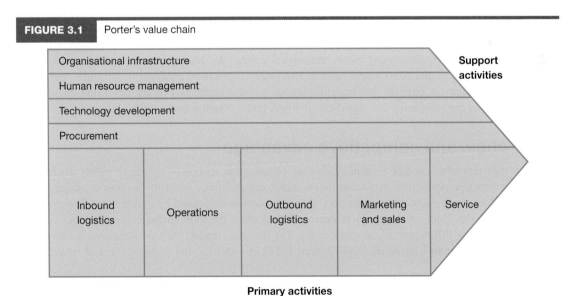

Primary activities

Primary activities

Primary activities are directly associated with production, delivery, sales and services. The primary activities are: inbound logistics, operations, outbound logistics, marketing and sales, and service.

Inbound logistics involves activities such as materials handling, warehousing and inventory control, which are used to receive, store and disseminate inputs to a product.

Operations includes machining, packaging, assembly and equipment maintenance. These activities transform the inputs provided by inbound logistics into the final product, and create value by performing activities efficiently, which leads to lower costs. Operations can increase the quality of products, leading to differentiation and lower costs.

Outbound logistics includes finished goods warehousing, materials handling and order processing. These activities collect, store and physically distribute the final product to customers.

Marketing and sales involve advertising and promotional campaigns, and the choice and development of distribution channels and sales forces. These activities provide the means through which products and services can reach the customer. Marketing can improve the customers' perception of a brand and product, which also increases customer value. In addition, marketing can identify customers' unsatisfied needs and communicate these needs to the production function of the company. This information can help develop products that then better satisfy customers' needs.

Service is concerned with installation, adjustment, repair, after-sales support and training. These activities enhance and maintain a product's value. Service can also improve customers' perception of the organisation and its products by supporting customers' use of the product. For example, Toll Holdings, an Australian-based subsidiary of Japan Post, does not only provide international delivery services, but also manages the entire supply chain of its customers.

Support activities

Support activities are concerned with the assistance necessary for the primary activities to take place. They include human resource management, procurement, technology development and support of infrastructure.

Organisational infrastructure includes activities such as planning, finance, accounting, legal support, general management and governmental relations, which are necessary to support the functioning of the entire value chain. The administrative infrastructure enables managers to identify external opportunities and threats as well as internal resources and capabilities to implement chosen strategies.

Human resource management includes activities such as recruiting, hiring, training, developing and rewarding the company's staff. This activity is very powerful in value creation because it is responsible for the right mix of skilled staff to perform value chain activities effectively. It also ensures personnel are appropriately trained, motivated and rewarded to perform value creation activities.

Technology development includes process equipment, research and product design and development, and servicing procedures which underpin the company's products and the processes used to manufacture them. Technology development can enable the company to produce its products more efficiently and effectively, leading to lower production costs. It also can assist the company to differentiate its products and increase value via improvement of product attributes.

Procurement involves purchasing items consumed during the manufacture of products (e.g. raw materials and supplies) and fixed assets such as machinery, laboratory equipment, buildings and office equipment. Procurement controls the transmission of physical materials along the value chain. This activity, if carried out efficiently, can significantly lower costs, creating more value.

Value chain and competitive advantage

The activities described in this section enable an organisation to create customer value. To be able to create a superior perception in a customer's mind, organisations need to develop a unique set of activities that reinforce each other in use and, therefore, cannot be copied by competitors. For example, the Commonwealth Bank of Australia is determined to offer the best customer service, and is committed to making a difference in the community. On the other hand, DuPont Australia, a diversified chemical company, builds its value chain around R&D in order to stay competitive and maintain its superior performance.

The importance of the value chain is found in its ability to assist managers to identify value-creating activities, both current and future. By understanding where the company creates its value at each element of the value chain, it can link value-creating activities to strategies and customers' needs. Having a unique set of value chain activities and ways they are integrated makes it difficult for competitors to copy the value chain of an organisation, thereby establishing a longer lasting competitive advantage for the organisation.

Core competencies, distinctive competencies and competitive capabilities

As discussed earlier, the value chain analysis assists organisations to identify value-creating activities. However, in order to build competitive advantage, organisations should also understand what they are good at, and what capabilities they possess for competing against their rivals. An organisation's

competence is the product of learning and experience and represents real proficiency in performing an internal activity. Organisations deliberately develop their competencies over time by making efforts to do something — however imperfectly or inefficiently at first. These efforts include selecting people with the required knowledge and skills, upgrading or expanding individual abilities as needed, and combining individual efforts into a cooperative group effort to create organisational capability. As experience is being accumulated, the organisation reaches a level of ability to perform the chosen activity consistently well and at an acceptable cost. This ability has then evolved into a true competence. Examples of competencies include the ability to build working relationships with customers and suppliers, just-in-time delivery, expertise in a specific technology and effective managerial practices. Competencies represent the combination of skills, resources and technologies, as opposed to a single specific skill or resource.

An organisation's competence serves as a **competitive capability** if it is appreciated by customers and helps to distinguish a company from its rivals. In general, every organisation has a collection of capabilities, some of them stronger and more competitive than the others.

Core competencies are activities that a company performs better than its other internal activities and that are the most important for the organisation's competitiveness and profitability. Core competencies may reside, for example, in the company's people, technology, ability to build networks and systems which enable electronic commerce, or skills in manufacturing innovative products.

The concept of distinctive competencies is related to the concept of core competencies: a core competence is something that a company does well relative to other internal activities; a **distinctive competence** is something a company does well relative to its rivals. Most organisations perform some important activities better than others. These activities are core competencies. However, what the organisation does best internally only translates into a distinctive competence if the company performs these activities better than its competitors. For instance, many tea shops have their own special recipes for this popular beverage. An Australian organisation that in 2013 became a subsidiary of Unilever, T2 is enjoying superior customer perception and popularity in this sector.[25] This popularity is evident by the number of customers waiting to purchase tea products at their outlets in relation to their competitors. A core competence of T2 is the ability to create a multi-sensory purchase experience (with the aid of tasting stations and atmospheric visual merchandising), whereby the 'ceremony' of tea making is emphasised rather than treating the product as a commodity.[26] This is recognised by its customers in greater sales; thus, a core competence has become a distinctive competence and serves the company as a basis for competitive advantage. *Generally, a core competence becomes a basis for competitive advantage only when it is a distinctive competence.*[27]

The following section will discuss the role of resources and capabilities in crafting competitive advantage.

3.3 The role of resources and capabilities for creating competitive advantage

LEARNING OBJECTIVE 3.3 Describe the role of an organisation's resources and capabilities as a basis of competitive advantage.

As discussed in the scene setter, the rapidly changing external environment poses a challenge for organisations to sustain their competitive advantage. Unless organisations continuously produce innovative products or re-invent their way of doing business, they are unlikely to sustain their advantage. So far, the emphasis of this text has been on identifying profit opportunities in the market and industry environment. Now this emphasis shifts from the interface between strategy and the external environment towards the interface between strategy and the internal environment of the organisation; specifically, the resources and capabilities of the organisation (see figure 3.2).

The dominant strategic thinking in the 1970s and 1980s advocated the role of the industry in company performance; for example, the work of Porter[28] and others as outlined in the chapters on strategic concepts and perspectives, and external and industry analysis. This emphasis on industry analysis represented a shift from the 1950s and 1960s, which explored the role of the internal resources of organisations; for example, the work of Penrose.[29] However, in the 1980s and 1990s other scholars observed differences in profitability and other performance indicators among organisations operating in the same industries and shifted the emphasis towards the resources and capabilities of companies.[30]

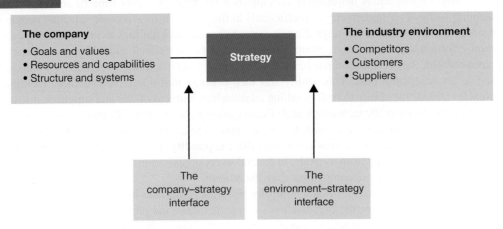

FIGURE 3.2 Analysing resources and capabilities: the interface between strategy and the company

The resource analysis and competitive advantage: the resource-based view

During the past 30 years, ideas concerning the role of resources and capabilities as the principal basis for company strategy and the primary source of profitability coalesced into what has become known as the **resource-based view (RBV)** of the company, one of the standard theories in the field of strategy.[31] This theory has evolved over the years as a result of the contributions of many scholars.

The central question of the RBV is 'Why do some companies in the same industry outperform others?' When Rumelt explored the sources of profits in major US corporations in the 1970s, he concluded that the greatest contributor to overall company profitability was at the individual company level rather than at the corporate or industry level.[32] There are other examples that show the differences in performance of companies in the same industries. For example, Toyota and Honda (which both originated in Japan) achieved success worldwide in the car manufacturing industry. In the United States, however, General Motors and Ford experienced losses even in their home markets at different times throughout the 1990s and the first decades of the 2000s. Similarly, in the personal computer industry, by the end of the 1990s, Acer (Taiwan) and Dell (United States) demonstrated growth, while previous industry leader IBM (a US company) was losing market share. The RBV emphasises the role of the individual resources of companies in their ability to create and sustain competitive advantage.

Prahalad and Hamel pointed to the potential for capabilities to be the 'roots of competitiveness', the source of new products and the foundation for strategy.[33] Examples are as follows.

- Honda Motor Company is the world's biggest motorcycle producer and a lead supplier of vehicles. However, it has never defined itself either as a motorcycle company or a motor vehicle company. Since its founding in 1948, its strategy has been built around its expertise in the development and manufacture of engines; this capability has successfully carried it from motorcycles to a wide range of petrol-engined products (see figure 3.3).
- Canon Inc. had its first success producing 35 mm cameras. Since then it has gone on to develop fax machines, calculators, copy machines, printers, video cameras, camcorders, semiconductor manufacturing equipment and many other products. Almost all Canon products involve the application of three areas of technological capability: precision mechanics, microelectronics and fine optics.
- 3M Corporation expanded from sandpaper into adhesive tapes, road signs, medical products, and storage media. Its product list comprises more than 30 000 separate products. Is it a conglomerate? Certainly not, claims 3M. Its vast product range rests on a foundation of key technologies relating to adhesives and thin-film coatings, and its remarkable ability to manage the development and marketing of new products (see figure 3.4).

In general, the greater the rate of change in a company's external environment, the more likely it is that internal resources and capabilities will provide a secure foundation for long-term strategy. In fast-moving, technology-based industries, new companies are built around specific technological capabilities. The markets where these capabilities are applied are a secondary consideration. Motorola, the Texas-based supplier of wireless telecommunications equipment, semiconductors and direct satellite communications, has undergone many transformations, from being a leading provider of TVs and car radios to its current focus on telecommunications equipment. Yet, underlying these transformations has been a consistent focus on wireless electronics.

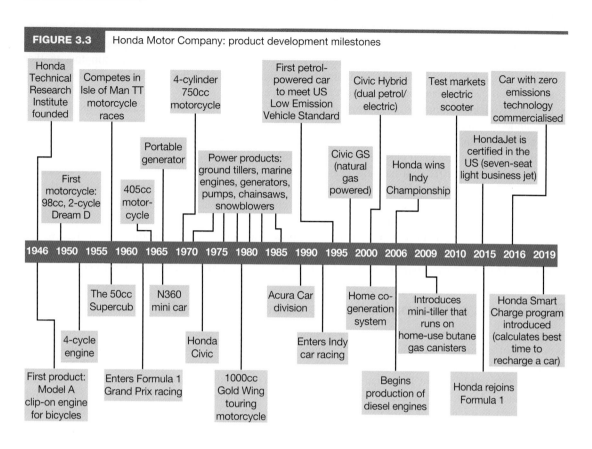

FIGURE 3.3 Honda Motor Company: product development milestones

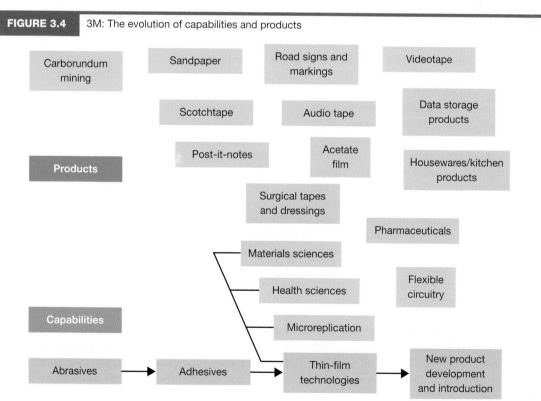

FIGURE 3.4 3M: The evolution of capabilities and products

When a company faces the imminent obsolescence of its core product, should its strategy focus on continuing to serve fundamental customer needs or on deploying its resources and capabilities in other markets?

- When Olivetti, the Italian typewriter manufacturer, faced the displacement of typewriters by micro-computers during the 1980s, it sought to maintain its focus on serving the word processing needs of businesses by expanding into PCs. The venture was a costly failure.[34] By contrast, Remington, another leading typewriter manufacturer, moved into products that required similar technical and manufacturing skills: electric shavers and other personal care appliances.[35]
- Eastman Kodak's dominance of the world market for photographic products based on chemical imaging was undermined by the advent of digital imaging. Over the years, Kodak invested billions of dollars developing digital technologies and digital imaging products. However, profits and market leadership in digital imaging remained elusive for Kodak, to the point where it was forced to file for bankruptcy protection in early 2012.[36] It has now ceased producing digital cameras, choosing instead to license its brand out to other manufacturers, in order to focus on photo printing and desktop inkjet services.[37] Might Kodak have been better off sticking with its chemical know-how and developing its interests in specialty chemicals, pharmaceuticals and healthcare?

The difficulties experienced by established companies in adjusting to technological change within their own markets are well documented — in typesetting and in disk-drive manufacturing, successive technological waves have caused market leaders to falter and allowed new entrants to prosper.[38]

Resources and capabilities as sources of profit

The distinction between industry attractiveness and competitive advantage (based on superior resources) as sources of a company's profitability corresponds to economists' distinction between different types of profit (or rent). The profits arising from market power are referred to as monopoly rents; those arising from superior resources are Ricardian rents, named after the 19th-century British economist Ricardo. Ricardo showed that, even when the market for wheat was competitive, fertile land would yield high returns. Ricardian rent is the return earned by a scarce resource over and above the cost of bringing it into production.[39]

Distinguishing between profit arising from market power and profit arising from resource superiority is less clear in practice than in principle. A closer look at Porter's five forces framework suggests that industry attractiveness derives ultimately from the ownership of resources. Barriers to entry, for example, are the result of patents, brands, distribution channels, learning or some other resource possessed by incumbent companies. Similarly, the lack of rivalry resulting from the dominance of a single company (monopoly) or a few companies (oligopoly) is usually based on the concentrated ownership of key resources such as technology, manufacturing facilities or distribution facilities.

The resource-based approach has profound implications for organisations' strategy formulation. When the primary concern of strategy was industry selection and positioning, organisations tended to adopt similar strategies. The resource-based view, by contrast, emphasises the uniqueness of each company and suggests that the key to profitability is not through doing the same as other companies, but rather through exploiting differences. Establishing competitive advantage involves formulating and implementing a strategy that exploits the uniqueness of a company's portfolio of resources and capabilities.

The remainder of this chapter outlines a resource-based approach to strategy formulation. Fundamental to this approach is recognising that a company must seek a thorough and profound understanding of its resources and capabilities. Such understanding provides a basis for:

1. selecting a strategy that exploits the company's key strengths. Air New Zealand's strategy to continuously develop and improve its operations (see strategy capsule 3.2) is an example of ongoing efforts to exploit a company's underlying resources more effectively
2. developing the company's resources and capabilities. Resource analysis is not just about deploying existing resources; it is also concerned with filling resource gaps and building capability for the future. Apple, Microsoft, and Asia–Pacific companies such as retailer Bunnings (see this chapter's scene setter), airline Air New Zealand (see strategy capsule 3.2) and hearing implant producer Cochlear (see strategy capsule 3.3) are all companies whose long-term success owes much to their commitment to nurturing talent, developing technologies, and building capabilities that allow adaptability to their changing business environments.

Developing core resources and capabilities at Air New Zealand

Established in 1940, Air New Zealand is one of the key airlines in the Pacific Rim, serving around 17 million passengers a year. The airline has a fleet of 114 aircraft and its planes on average leave the tarmac 3400 times a week. Over 12 500 employees work for the company and in 2018 its revenues were around the NZ$45.5 billion.[40] At the end of 2019, Air New Zealand was announced the world's number one airline for 2020 by airlinerating.com,[41] clearly illustrating what this relatively small airline, operating in a corner of the world, is all about.

The company's good reputation is built on a strong desire to continuously develop its resources and capabilities, with technological innovation being central. Already in 1950, the airline was the first one to be able to boil water in-flight and since then Air New Zealand has been innovating. More recently, its Skycouch has attracted attention, giving economy class passengers the possibility to convert their row of seats into a bed. The airline is also experimenting with virtual reality to enhance passengers' experiences, and uses 3D printing to improve the layout of aircraft cabins.[42] All these technological advancements are supported by marketing efforts that try to differentiate the airline from its main competitors. For instance, Air New Zealand's creative safety movies are renowned for their ability to tap into contemporary themes, such as the Hobbit movies and the All Blacks' success.[43]

Interestingly, the company appears to realise it cannot do all of this without its key stakeholders. In February 2020 the new chief executive officer, Greg Foran, commented that 'as I travel around the various parts of the business, it is clear that what makes Air New Zealand stand out from its global competitors is the enthusiasm and dedication of our people. Their focus on providing our customers with the best service will continue to be a key differentiator as we look to set the airline up for future success'.[44] In 2019 the company also organised a supplier awards night, recognising the important role suppliers play in the continued success of Air New Zealand. The then chief executive officer, Christopher Lyon, highlighted that 'Air New Zealand has more than 4000 suppliers who are each a vital part of our extended enterprise. We've been on a journey with them over the past couple of years, looking at ways we can work better together and grow our partnerships'.[45] Central to these partnerships has been a commitment to making the procurement more sustainable.

With the industry hitting turbulence due to increased competition across the Tasman and slowing demand as a result of the coronavirus pandemic that started in 2019, the company appears to be in a good position to face these challenges. The various parts of Air New Zealand's value chain appear to be well-aligned and are based on the principles that have been core to this company for some time.

Global leadership via ongoing innovation at Cochlear

Australian company Cochlear is a classic example of global competitiveness based on internal growth, despite the economic cycle. Cochlear today is the global leader in medical hearing devices, holding a 67 per cent market share. The company is based in Sydney and sells its products in more than 100 countries. It employs over 4000 employees around the world. The long-term vision of the company is to help the hearing impaired. How did Cochlear's unique technology originally evolve?

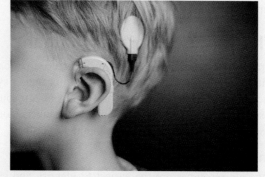

In the 1960s, the company's founder Graeme Clark (an ear, nose and throat doctor) began research into the possibility of an electronic, implantable hearing device. He persevered despite the resistance of his colleagues.

The idea of a bionic ear evolved gradually through the integration of research from numerous disciplines. Apart from audiology and surgery, these included biology, psychophysics, speech science and electrochemistry. Clark strengthened his research after being appointed professor and chairman of the Department of Otolaryngology at the University of Melbourne. He established partnerships with a leading expert in sound quality and a small local company conducting pioneering research on heart pacemakers.

The critical contribution to the progress was made by engineers Jim Patrick and Ian Foster who designed the circuit diagram for the Mastermos silicon chip to provide circuitry for one of the ten stimulus channels of the first bionic ear. The first Cochlear implant from multichannel research was developed in 1978. The lengthy delay was due largely to the indifference of the medical community and the lack of financial support. Fundraising continued to be a major obstacle and the leading Australian research institutions repeatedly rejected Clark's applications for research grants.[46]

The first major breakthrough came in 1974 when Clark persuaded the proprietor of a new television channel to conduct a fundraising 'Telethon', which provided the finance to produce a prototype. A year later, Clark began partnering with a group of medical equipment manufacturers who had offered to commercially develop the bionic ear. In 1982 Cochlear was listed on the stock exchange and became a public company. This was the turning point for Cochlear and the company became engaged in a significant development process. At that stage, obtaining the support of surgeons and hearing aid professionals around the world was a formidable challenge. 'Because of the unique controls and sensitivities associated with medical technology, and despite the enormous credibility Cochlear has earned, there will be no respite for top management. They will always be evangelists and increasingly educators.'[47]

Cochlear was twice named the most innovative company in Australia[48] and in 2011 featured as number 30 in Forbes' most innovative growth companies list.[49] The company today has provided more than 550 000 devices to people worldwide, with its main product — Nucleus — in particular being well renowned. As part of its services, it provides support for both medical professionals and implant recipients.

The company invests a significant portion of its revenue (around 12 per cent of sales revenue) into research and development. Cochlear is involved with over 100 collaborative research programs focused on implantable hearing solutions and part of its research investment is geared towards redesigning its products so that they can be scaled up to mass production.[50] As Clark stated, 'Good science is absolutely essential to making progress. Cochlear strives to not only develop a product but to underpin it with a good science'.[51]

What can be learned from Cochlear is that a relatively small company managed to achieve global leadership through organic growth and innovation. The company's growth was driven by its internal desire to create value for customers and the strong vision of Clark.

3.4 Organisational resources and capabilities

LEARNING OBJECTIVE 3.4 Identify the resources and capabilities of an organisation.

The starting point to better understand how resources and capabilities of a company add strategic value is to identify and assess the resources and capabilities currently available to the company. It is important to distinguish between the resources and the capabilities of the company — resources are the productive assets owned by the company; capabilities are what the company can do. Individual resources do not confer competitive advantage; they must work together to create organisational capability. Organisational capability is the essence of superior performance. Figure 3.5 shows the relationships among resources, capabilities and competitive advantage.

The resources of the company

Drawing up an inventory of a company's resources can be surprisingly difficult. No such document exists within the accounting or management information systems of most corporations. The corporate balance sheet provides a limited view of a company's resources — it comprises mainly financial and physical resources. To take a wider view of a company's resources it is helpful to identify three principal types of resource: tangible, intangible and human resources.

Tangible resources

Tangible resources are the easiest to identify and evaluate: financial resources and physical assets are identified and valued in the company's financial statements. Yet, balance sheets are renowned for their propensity to obscure strategically relevant information, and to under-or overvalue assets. However, the primary goal of resource analysis is not to value a company's assets, but to understand their potential for creating competitive advantage. For example, knowing that in June 2019 airline Air New Zealand possessed tangible assets with a book value of NZ$7.570 billion is of little use in assessing their strategic value.[52] To assess Air New Zealand's ability to compete effectively in the airline industry, information is needed about the composition of the fleet, location of facilities, the types of equipment and their age, and so on.

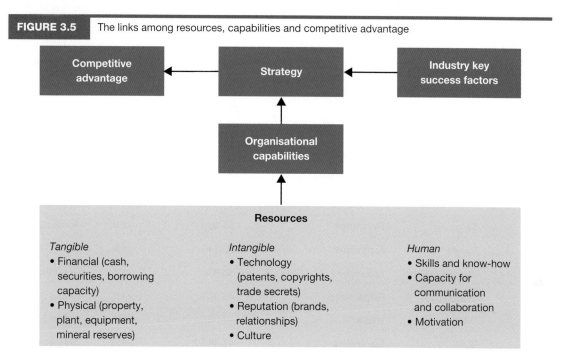

FIGURE 3.5 The links among resources, capabilities and competitive advantage

Once more information is known about a company's tangible resources, it can then be explored how additional value can be created from them. This requires two key questions to be addressed.

1. *What opportunities exist for economising on their use?* It may be possible to use fewer resources to support the same level of business, or to use the existing resources to support a larger volume of business. In the case of Air New Zealand, there may be opportunities for further development of partnerships with other airlines to increase the number of overseas destinations served or reduce overcapacity on certain routes that are not profitable enough.

2. *What are the possibilities for employing existing assets more profitably?* Could Air New Zealand generate better returns on some of its assets by redeploying them to serve new customers on different routes? How would an economic downturn or pandemic affect the company's expansion and the ability to employ its resources?

Intangible resources

For most companies, intangible resources are more valuable than tangible resources. Yet, in company financial statements, intangible resources remain largely invisible — particularly in the United States where R&D is expensive. Among the most important of these undervalued or unvalued intangible resources are brand names. Table 3.1 shows companies owning brands valued at US$25 billion or more.[53]

Brand names and other trademarks are a form of *reputational asset*: their value is in the confidence they instil in customers. This value is reflected in the price premium that customers are willing to pay for the branded product over that for an unbranded or unknown brand. Brand value (or 'brand equity') can be estimated by taking the price premium attributable to a brand, multiplying it by the brand's annual sales volume, then calculating the present value of this revenue stream. The brand valuations in table 3.1 involve estimating the operating profits for each brand (after taxation and a capital charge), estimating the proportion of net operating income attributable to the brand, and then capitalising these returns. The value of a company's brands can be increased by extending the product/market scope over which the company markets those brands. In recent years particularly the companies operating in information technology have been successful in improving the value of their brand in such a way.

Reputation may be attached to a company as well as to its brands. Companies depend on support from employees, customers, investors and governments.[54] In Australia, Air New Zealand scored the best in the 'annual corporate reputation index', followed by Qantas, JB Hi-Fi, Toyota, Mazda and Aldi.[55] Interestingly, whereas retailers such as Woolworths, Myer, Coca-Cola, Coles and 7-Eleven reported huge improvements from 2018 to 2019, the opposite was the case for Australia's financial institutions. The findings of the Banking Royal Commission (see the chapter on corporate governance and ethics) had a huge negative impact on the reputation ratings of the likes of AMP, NAB, Westpac and ANZ, with all losing more than nine positions from 2018 to 2019.

TABLE 3.1	The world's most valuable brands				
Rank 2019	Brand	Sector	Brand value in 2012, $ billion	Change from 2018	Country of origin
1	Apple	Electronics	234.241	+9%	United States
2	Google	Internet services	167.713	+8%	United States
3	Amazon	Online retail	125.263	+24%	United States
4	Microsoft	Computer software	108.847	+17%	United States
5	Coca-Cola	Beverages	63.365	−4%	United States
6	Samsung	Electronics	61.098	+2%	South Korea
7	Toyota	Automotive	56.246	+5%	Japan
8	Mercedes Benz	Automotive	50.832	+5%	Germany
9	McDonalds	Restaurants	45.362	+4%	United States
10	Disney	Media	44.352	+11%	United States
11	BMW	Automotive	41.440	+1%	Germany
12	IBM	Computer services	40.381	−6%	United States
13	Intel	Electronics	40.197	−7%	United States
14	Facebook	Social media	39.857	−12%	United States
15	Cisco	Business services	35.559	+3%	United States
16	Nike	Sportswear	32.376	+7%	United States
17	Louis Vuitton	Luxury	32.223	+14%	France
18	Oracle	Business services	26.288	+1%	United States
19	General Electric	Diversified	25.566	−22%	United States
20	SAP	Computer software	25.092	+10%	Germany

Note: Brand values are calculated as the net present value of future earnings generated by the brand. The Interbrand Best Global Brands is provided by Interbrand for informational purposes only, and is based on methodology that includes subjective components. It should not be construed as a recommendation or advice. You can view the full Terms and Conditions of accessing the Interbrand Best Global Brands rankings at www.interbrand.com/best-global-brands-terms-and-conditions.
Source: Interbrand, 2019.

Like reputation, technology is an intangible asset whose value is not evident from most companies' balance sheets. Intellectual property — patents, copyrights, trade secrets and trademarks — comprise technological and artistic resources where ownership is defined in law. Over the past 20 years, companies have become more attentive to the value of their intellectual property. Texas Instruments was one of the first companies to begin managing its patent portfolio in order to maximise its licensing revenues. For some companies, ownership of intellectual property is a key source of market value. For example, Qualcomm's patents relating to CDMA digital wireless telephony make it one of the most valuable companies in the telecommunications sector, while IBM's position as the world's biggest patent holder results in a royalty stream of over US$1.2 billion a year.

Human resources

The human resources of the company are the expertise and effort offered by its employees. Human resources do not appear on corporate balance sheets for the simple reason that people are not owned: they offer their services under employment contracts. Identifying and appraising the stock of human resources within a company is complex and difficult. Human resources are appraised at the time of recruitment and throughout the period of employment, for example, through annual performance reviews.

Companies are continually seeking more effective methods to assess the performance and potential of their employees. Over the past decade, human resource appraisal has become far more systematic and sophisticated. Organisations are relying less on formal qualifications and years of experience and more on attitude, motivation, learning capacity and potential for collaboration. Competency modelling involves identifying the set of skills, content knowledge, attitudes, and values associated with superior performers within a particular job category, then assessing each employee against that profile.[56] The results of such competency assessments can then be used to identify training needs, make selections for hiring or promotion and determine compensation. A key outcome of systematic assessment has been recognition of the importance of psychological and social aptitudes in linking technical and professional abilities to overall job performance. Recent interest in emotional intelligence reflects growing recognition of the importance of social and emotional skills and values.[57]

The ability of employees to harmonise their efforts and integrate their separate skills depends not only on their interpersonal skills but also the organisational context. This organisational context as it affects internal collaboration is determined by a key intangible resource: the culture of the organisation. The term *organisational culture* is notoriously ill defined. It relates to an organisation's values, traditions and social norms. Building on the observations of Peters and Waterman[58] that 'firms with sustained superior financial performance typically are characterised by a strong set of core managerial values that define the ways they conduct business,' Barney identifies organisational culture as a company resource of great strategic importance that is potentially very valuable.[59]

Organisational capabilities

Resources are not productive on their own. A brain surgeon is close to useless without a radiologist, anaesthetist, nurses, surgical instruments, imaging equipment and a host of other resources. To perform a task, a team of resources must work together. Moreover, only some resources are inputs to a productive process. In fact, resources have to be coordinated in order to be effectively productive. An **organisational capability** is a company's capacity to deploy resources for a desired result.[60] Just as an individual may be capable of playing the violin, ice skating and speaking Mandarin; so too can an organisation possess the capabilities needed to manufacture widgets, distribute them throughout South-East Asia and hedge the resulting foreign exchange exposure. The terms *capability* and *competence* are used interchangeably.[61]

Of primary interest are those capabilities that can provide a basis for competitive advantage. Selznick used the term *distinctive competence* to describe those things that an organisation does particularly well relative to its competitors.[62] Prahalad and Hamel coined the term *core competencies* to distinguish those capabilities fundamental to a company's strategy and performance.[63] Core competencies, according to Hamel and Prahalad,[64] are those that:

- make a disproportionate contribution to ultimate customer value, or to the efficiency with which that value is delivered
- provide a basis for entering new markets.

Prahalad and Hamel criticise US companies for emphasising product management over competence management. They compare the strategic development of Sony and RCA in consumer electronics. Both companies were failures in the home video market. RCA introduced its videodisc system; Sony, its Betamax videotape system. For RCA, the failure of its first product marked the end of its venture into home video systems and heralded a progressive retreat from the consumer electronics industry. RCA was acquired by GE, which then sold off the combined consumer electronics division to Thomson of France. Sony, on the other hand, acknowledged the failure of Betamax, but continued to develop its capabilities in video technology. This continuous development and upgrading of its video capabilities resulted in a string of successful video products from camcorders and digital cameras to the PlayStation game console.

Classifying capabilities

To identify a company's capabilities, there needs to be some basis for classifying and disaggregating its activities. Two commonly used approaches are as follows.

1. A *functional analysis* identifies organisational capabilities in relation to each of the principal functional areas of the company. Table 3.2 classifies the principal functions of the company and identifies organisational capabilities pertaining to each function.
2. A *value chain analysis* discussed earlier in this chapter (see figure 3.1) separates the activities of the company into a sequential chain. Porter's representation of the value chain distinguishes between primary activities (those involved with the transformation of inputs and interface with the customer) and support activities. Porter's generic value chain identifies a few broadly defined activities that can be disaggregated to provide a more detailed identification of the company's activities (and the capabilities that correspond to each activity). Thus, marketing might include market research, test marketing, advertising, promotion, pricing and dealer relations.[65]

TABLE 3.2 **A functional classification of organisational capabilities**

Functional area	Capability	Exemplars
Corporate functions	Financial control	Exxon Mobil, Wesfarmers
	Strategic management of multiple businesses	General Electric, Virgin
	Strategic innovation	Google, Cochlear
	Multidivisional coordination	BHP Billiton, Time Warner
	Acquisition management	Disney
	International management	AirBnB, McDonalds
Management information	Comprehensive, integrated MIS network linked to managerial decision making	Facebook, McDonalds
Research and development	Research	Johnson & Johnson, Samsung
	Innovative new product development	Tesla, Square
	Fast-cycle new product development	3M, Inditex (Zara)
Operations	Efficiency in volume manufacturing	Caltex, Visy
	Continuous improvements in operations	Toyota, Qantas
	Flexibility and speed of response	Cisco, Google
Product design	Design capability	Apple, Ferrari
Marketing	Brand management	Coca Cola, Mercedes Benz
	Promoting reputation for quality	Toyota, RM Williams
	Responsiveness to market trends	Facebook, Netflix
Sales and distribution	Effective sales promotion and execution	Redbull, Nike
	Efficiency and speed of order processing	L. L. Bean, Dell Computers, Ebay
	Speed of distribution	Amazon, Alibaba
	Quality and effectiveness of customer service	Singapore Airlines, Disney

The dynamic capabilities view

The previous sections discussed the role of resources and capabilities of companies in creating value and competitive advantage from the position of the resource-based view of strategy. Although this theory has been extensively developed over the past 30 years by many empirical studies, some scholars note the shortcomings of this theory. For example, some scholars argue that the theory is essentially a tautology.[66] Others argue that while heterogeneity of capabilities and resources of companies is one of the main postulates of the RBV theory, this theory does not explain how this heterogeneity arises. 'Absent an understanding of where heterogeneity in resources and capabilities comes from, it is difficult . . . to fully explain how firms use resources and capabilities to create competitive advantage'.[67] Another limitation to RBV is that it does not set out to address how and why certain companies exhibit timely responsiveness in unpredictable situations.[68]

The RBV of a competitive advantage emphasises the deployment and protection of unique resources rather than the need for resources and competencies to develop over time. Rapid and unpredictable environmental changes and market complexity require companies to accumulate competitive advantage through learning and knowledge creation processes in order to respond to such dynamics. Considerations such as how resources are developed, how they are integrated within the company and how they are released have been addressed by the knowledge-based view of strategy. Dynamic capabilities are attempting to act as:

> a buffer between firm resources and the fast-changing business environment. Dynamic resources help an organisation to adjust its resource-mix. The RBV emphasises on resource choice. In contrast, dynamic capabilities emphasise resource development and renewal, and sustain a firm's competitive advantage.

The concept of dynamic capabilities is relatively new and still evolving.[69]

Although the dynamic capabilities view is a relatively recent stream in the strategic management literature, it has attracted increasing attention from researchers and practitioners who explore the role of dynamic capabilities in obtaining competitive advantage. Teece et al. defined dynamic capabilities as 'the firm's ability to integrate, build, and reconfigure internal and external competencies to address rapidly changing environments'.[70] This definition opened the opportunity to incorporate managerial action into discussions of the sources of competitive advantage. This definition and its attention to managerial action was further emphasised by Eisenhardt and Martin,[71] who defined dynamic capabilities in terms of process. Other scholars also believe that a process view of dynamic capabilities has some benefits.[72] Ongoing collaboration with customers allows companies to reconfigure existing resources and thus develop dynamic capabilities in response to customer needs and suggestions.

The VRIO framework — evaluating competitive resources and capabilities

As discussed earlier in this chapter, some of a company's heterogeneous resources and capabilities hold the potential for sustained competitive advantages. As Barney[73] suggests, to have this potential:

> a firm resource must have four attributes: a) it must be valuable, in the sense that it exploits opportunities and/or neutralises threats in a firm's environment, b) it must be rare among a firm's current and potential competition, c) it must be imperfectly imitable, and d) it must be able to be exploited by a firm's organisational processes. These attributes of company resources can be thought of as indicators of how heterogeneous and immobile a firm's resources are, and thus how useful these resources are for generating sustained competitive advantages.

These attributes have been further developed into a framework — the value, rarity, imitability and organisation (VRIO) framework — that can be applied in assessing the potential of a broad range of company resources to be sources of sustained competitive advantage. These analyses not only specify the theoretical conditions under which sustained competitive advantage might exist, they also suggest specific empirical questions that need to be addressed before the relationships between a particular company resource and sustained competitive advantage can be understood. A description of the four components of the VRIO framework follows.

1. The question of *value*: Do a firm's resources and capabilities enable the company to respond to environmental threats or opportunities? The traditional strengths, weaknesses, opportunities and threats (SWOT) model suggests that companies can improve their performance only if their strategies exploit opportunities or neutralise threats. Companies might have other characteristics that can serve as sources of competitive advantage (e.g. rarity, inimitability and organisational abilities/processes) but these characteristics become valuable resources only when they exploit opportunities or neutralise threats

in the company environment.[74] A company must have valuable resources in order to create economic value and increase the willingness of customers to pay, decrease its costs, or both.

2. The question of *rarity*: Is a resource currently controlled by only a small number of competing companies? Valuable resources of a company that are also possessed by large number of competitors cannot serve as a source of competitive advantage. Each of these companies has the capability of exploiting that resource in the same way and implementing a common strategy which would not allow one company to create a competitive advantage.[75] In order to implement some strategies, companies need to form bundles of resources and these bundles have to be valuable to enable companies to create a competitive advantage. Companies must still maintain valuable but common resources. These help companies to survive when they are exploited to create competitive parity, a condition under which no one company is able to create a competitive advantage. According to Porter,[76] companies increase their probability of economic survival under conditions of competitive parity. The question of how rare a valuable company resource should be in order to serve as a source of a competitive advantage does not have a common answer. Barney and Clark[77] assert that:

> as the number of firms that possess a particular valuable resource (or a bundle of valuable resources) is less than the number of firms needed to generate perfect competition dynamics in an industry, that resource has the potential of generating a competitive advantage.

3. The question of *imitability*: Do companies without a resource face a cost disadvantage in obtaining or developing it? Companies with valuable and rare resources can enjoy a first mover advantage, acting as innovators because their resources allow them to conceive and engage in strategies that other companies could not conceive nor implement due to the lack of relevant resources. On the other hand, valuable and rare resources help companies to sustain their competitive advantage only if competitors cannot obtain these resources by direct duplication or substitution.[78] It depends on how difficult or costly it is to imitate the company's resources, which can be attributed to the following three main reasons.

   (a) **Unique historical conditions** determined the path a company followed to arrive at its current situation, and the company's long-term performance. Barney and Clark suggest that unique historical conditions can lead to a sustained competitive advantage in at least the following two ways.[79]

   > First, it may be that a particular firm is the first in an industry to recognize and exploit an opportunity, and being first gives the firm a first-mover advantage. Second, when events early in the evolution of a process have significant effects on subsequent events, path dependence allows a firm to gain a competitive advantage in the current period based on the acquisition and development of resources in earlier periods.

   (b) There is **causal ambiguity** in the link between the resources controlled by the company and its competitive advantage. This link is either not understood or not understood clearly. The main situations in which managers may not fully understand their sources of competitive advantage include: when the resources and capabilities are invisible (e.g. relationships with customers and/or suppliers, and organisational culture); when managers are unable to evaluate which resources and capabilities or their combinations create a competitive advantage; and when the resources and capabilities are complex networks of relationships between individuals, groups and technology. This last source of competitive advantage is referred to as interconnectedness of asset stocks and asset mass efficiencies.[80] In general, when sources of competitive advantage are widely spread across processes of the company, locations and people, these sources are difficult to understand and costly to imitate.

   (c) **Social complexity** of a company's resources means that it is beyond the company's ability to systematically manage and influence these resources. A wide variety of resources may be socially complex, for example, the interpersonal relationships among managers in a company,[81] a company's culture,[82] and its reputation among customers and suppliers. Often it is clear how these socially complex relations add value to the company and thereis little or no causal ambiguity about the link between these resources and competitive advantage. At the same time, such understanding does not necessarily lead companies without these socially complex resources to the process of their creation.

4. The question of *organisation*: Are a firm's other policies and procedures organised to support the exploitation of its valuable, rare and costly-to-imitate resources? Valuable, rare and inimitable resources can serve as a source of competitive advantage if the company is organised to exploit the potential

offered by these resources. Organisational processes assist companies in building and sustaining competitive advantage. The following components allow companies to exploit the full competitive potential of their resources and capabilities: their formal reporting structure, explicit management control systems and reward policies. These components are often referred to as complementary resources and capabilities as they have limited ability to generate competitive advantage in isolation. It is in combination with other resources and capabilities they can enable a firm to realise its full potential for competitive advantage.[83]

Bringing these questions of value, rarity, imitability and organisation together provides a single framework to understand the return potential associated with exploiting any of a company's resources and capabilities. This framework is summarised in table 3.3.[84]

TABLE 3.3 **The VRIO framework**

Is a resource or capability . . .					
Valuable?	Rare?	Costly to imitate?	Exploited by organisation?	Competitive implications	Economic performance
No	—	—	No	Competitive disadvantage	Below normal
Yes	No	—	—	Competitive parity	Normal
Yes	Yes	No	—	Temporary competitive advantage	Above normal
Yes	Yes	Yes	Yes	Sustained competitive advantage	Above normal

The RBV asserts that the individual resources capabilities of companies provide a stronger basis for strategy development than industry analysis. The main argument for this view is that it will identify those resources and capabilities that are outstanding and thus have the potential for sustainable competitive advantage.

SUMMARY

The creation and sustainability of competitive advantage is a main consideration of managers of any company when they formulate the company strategy. Competitive advantage is displayed by superior performance and value created for the company's customers. Value is measured by a product's performance characteristics and by its attributes for which customers are willing to pay. The ability of a company to develop a competitive advantage depends on its ability to position its business system in the business environment. A business system comprises resources (inputs), activities (throughputs) and product/service offerings (outputs) intended to create value for customers — this is how the company conducts its business.

There are many activities and functions of the company (e.g. research and development (R&D), logistics, production, marketing and sales) that enable it to create value for customers. Value chain analysis enable companies to understand which activities create value and which do not. The value chain is a template used by a company to identify its cost position and the means that might be used to facilitate implementation of a chosen business-level strategy. The value chain shows how a product moves from the raw-material stage to the end customer. A competitive advantage can be created if the company's value chain creates additional value without incurring significant extra costs. A company's value chain is divided into primary and support activities. To be able to create a superior perception in the customer's mind, companies need to develop unique set of activities which reinforce each other in use and therefore cannot be copied by competitors. A company competence is the product of learning and experience and represents real proficiency in performing an internal activity. A company core competence is something which a company does well relative other internal activities, whereas a distinctive competence is something a company does well relative to its rivals. A core competence becomes a basis for competitive advantage only when it is a distinctive competence.

The external and industry analyses give a company the information to make decisions on what it *can* do. For strategy analysis, the key issue is what the company *should* do. This requires looking at the resources of the company and the way resources combine to create organisational capabilities. Of interest is the potential for resources and capabilities to establish a sustainable competitive advantage. Systematic evaluation of a company's resources and capabilities provides the basis for formulating (or reformulating) strategy. How can the company deploy its strengths to maximum advantage? How can it minimise its vulnerability to its weaknesses? How can it develop and extend its capabilities to meet the challenges of the future?

Despite the progress that has been made in the past decades in understanding resources and capabilities, there is much that remains unresolved. Little is known about the microstructures of organisational capabilities and how they are established and developed. Can companies develop entirely new capabilities, or must top management accept that distinctive capabilities are the result of experience-based learning over long periods of time through processes that are poorly understood? If that is the case, strategy must be concerned with exploiting, preserving and developing the firm's existing pool of resources and capabilities, rather than trying to change them. There is much to learn in this area.

Although much of the discussion has been heavy on concepts and theory, the issues are practical. The management systems of most companies devote meticulous attention to the physical and financial assets that are valued on their balance sheets; much less attention has been paid to the critical intangible and human resources of the company, and even less to the identification and evaluation of organisational capability. Most senior managers are now aware of the importance of their resources and capabilities, but the techniques of identifying, assessing and developing them are woefully underdeveloped. Because the resources and capabilities of the company form the foundation for building competitive advantage, the concepts of this chapter will be returned to again and again.

KEY TERMS

business system The resources (inputs), activities (throughputs) and product/service offerings (outputs) intended to create value for customers.

causal ambiguity The situation in which the link between the resources controlled by the company and its competitive advantage is unclear or not understood.

competence The product of learning and experience that represents real proficiency in performing an internal activity.

competitive advantage A characteristic, feature or opportunity that an organisation possesses that will make it more attractive than its competitors.

competitive capability A competence that is appreciated by customers and distinguishes the organisation from its rivals.

core competencies Activities that an organisation performs better than its other internal activities and that are the most critical to competitiveness and profitability.

distinctive competence An activity an organisation does well relative to its rivals.

market segmentation The process that clusters people with similar needs into identifiable groups.

market segments Groups of customers with similar criteria for buying decisions and/or similar buying behaviours.

organisational capability An organisation's capacity to deploy resources for a desired result.

positioning The process of focusing an organisation's business system to satisfy certain needs of a targeted market segment of customers to distinguish the organisation from competitors.

primary activities Actions directly associated with production, delivery, sales and service: inbound logistics, operations, outbound logistics, marketing and sales, and service.

resource-based view (RBV) Research into the role of a company's resources and competitive capabilities in crafting strategy and in determining company profitability.

social complexity The degree to which sociocultural forces are organised.

support activities Actions that enable primary activities to take place, including human resource management, procurement, technology development and support of infrastructure.

unique historical conditions Circumstances that determined the path a company followed to arrive at its current situation and the company's long-term performance.

value A product's performance characteristics and attributes for which customers are willing to pay.

value chain A template that identifies the activities of a company from raw materials to customer, the value added by each activity and the cost of each activity, and that facilitates implementation of business-level strategy.

SELF-STUDY QUESTIONS

1 Define competitive advantage.

2 Why do companies use the value chain analysis?

3 How does the resource-based view (RBV) explain the role of resources and capabilities in the ability of companies to create competitive advantage?

4 What are core competencies of companies?

5 What role do dynamic capabilities play in the ability of companies to create competitive advantage in rapidly changing environments?

DISCUSSION QUESTIONS

1 Discuss the difference between resources and capabilities, and what it means for the ease with which competitors will be able to copy specific resources and capabilities.

2 Bunnings is currently expanding into online retailing to further develop its resources and capabilities (see the scene setter). Do you think it was wise for the organisation to wait relatively long before pursuing this avenue? And what could be potential dangers related to this strategic move?

3 Rocket Lab is quickly adapting itself to the demands of the global space industry (see strategy capsule 3.1). What are the dynamic capabilities this company will need to be able to survive and thrive over the years to come? Can competitors imitate those dynamic capabilities easily? Explain why.

4 Does every company have a core competence? If not, what are the strategic implications if a company would not have a distinctive core competence?

5 Which is more important in explaining the success and failure of companies in the rapidly changing environment: the ability to improvise or strategise? Why?

EXERCISES

1 Consider a company you know well or have researched. What do you think are the strategic capabilities of this company? Use the functional classification of organisational capabilities presented in table 3.2 for your analysis.

2 Draw a value chain for a company you know well or have researched (e.g. choose your university, local recreation centre or travel agency). Explain the implication of your study for competitive advantage.

3 Using the evidence from strategy capsule 3.3 (Cochlear), identify the main elements of Cochlear's competitive advantage.

4 Visit the Singapore Airlines website, www.singaporeair.com, and explain what resources and capabilities the company uses as a base of its competitive advantage.

5 Select two sports teams that participate in the same competition but vary in their long-term performance. Use the VRIO model to identify the resources and capabilities that could explain why one of the teams has outperformed the other for so long.

FURTHER READING

Teece, DJ 2020, 'Fundamental issues in strategy: Time to reassess?', *Strategic Management Review,* vol. 1, 103–144.

Helfat, CE & Winter, SG 2011, 'Untangling dynamic and operational capabilities: strategy for the n(ever)-changing world', *Strategic Management Journal,* vol. 32, 1243–1250.

Hamel, G & Prahalad, CK 1989, 'Strategic intent', *Harvard Business Review*, May–June, in H Mintzberg, J Lampel, JB Quinn & S Goshal 2003, *The strategy process,* Harlow: Pearson Education.

Schoenmaker, PJH, Heaton S & Teece DJ, 2018, 'Innovation, dynamic capabilities, and leadership', *California Management Review,* vol. 61, 15–42.

ENDNOTES

1. See more about the company's history and origins on their website www.bunnings.com.au/about-us; website visited on 13 March 2020.
2. D Killalea, 'Bunnings ditches iconic advertising slogan', *News Corp Australia*, 15 September 2016, www.new.com.au.
3. B Brook, 'The Bunnings effect: Secrets behind its success', *News Corp Australia*, 14 February 2020, www.new.com.au.
4. J Bajkowski, 'Bunnings goes to Bangalore for new dev centre', *IT News*, 19 February 2020, www.itnews.com.au.
5. A Santoreneos, 'Woolworths delivers huge blow to Coles', *Yahoo Finance*, 21 February 2020, au.finance.yahoo.com.
6. S Mitchell, 'Bunnings to sell 60,000 products online', *Financial Review*, 21 March 2019, www.afr.com.
7. S Bartholomeusz, 'Going off script: how the $1.7b Bunnings UK disaster unfolded', *The Sydney Morning Herald,* 28 May 2018, www.smh.com.au.
8. A Robertson, 'Bunnings fails to learn from Masters mistakes in UK hardware push', *ABC News*, 28 February 2018, www.abc.net.au.
9. DP Lovallo and LT Mendonca, 'Strategy's strategist: an interview with Richard Rumelt', *McKinsey Quarterly*, November 2007, www.mckinseyquarterly.com.
10. M Sheetz, 'Morgan Stanley says Rocket Lab is the up-and-coming space company to watch', *CNBC*, 2 April 2019, www.cnbc.com.
11. R Stock, 'Government's $300m venture capital fund seeks 'unicorn' technology companies', *Stuff Limited*, 4 March 2020, www.stuff.co.nz.
12. J Foust, 'Rocket Lab turns attention to satellite efforts', *Space News,* 6 February 2020, www.spacenews.com.
13. Sheetz, op. cit.; G Autry, 'Is space launch overheating? I ask five rocket startups', *Forbes*, 21 May 2019, www.forbes.com; M Joass, 'Rocket Lab: The Kiwis winning the new Space Race', *Matt Joass Blog*, 71 December 2018, mattjoass.com.
14. T Pullar-Strecker, 'Rocket Lab keeps tabs on 117 rivals, but that's not what's keeping it busy', *Stuff Limited*, 9 June 2019, www.stuff.co.nz.
15. A van Delden, 'PGF funding to help Rocket Lab up the ante on launches', *Radio New Zealand*, 26 February 2020, www.rnz.co.nz.
16. Pullar-Strecker op. cit.
17. Foust, op. cit.
18. A Reed and LE Bolton, 'The complexity of identity', *MIT Sloan Management Review*, vol. 46, no. 3, 2005, 11–22.
19. SC Jain, *Marketing planning and strategy*, Cincinnati: South-Western College Publishing, 2004.
20. ibid.
21. B De Wit and R Meyer, *Strategy synthesis*, London: South-Western Cengage Learning, 2005.
22. D Peppers and M Rogers, 'Customers don't grow on trees', *Fast company*, iss. 96, 1 July 2005, 25–26.
23. ME Porter, *Competitive strategy: techniques for analysing industries and competitors*, New York: The Free Press, 1980.
24. ibid.
25. Boost juice bars, www.boostjuicebars.com.

26. M Steffens, 'T2's touch of ceremony proves recipe for success', *Sydney Morning Herald*, 20 February 2012.

27. AA Thompson Jr and A Strickland, *Strategic management: Concepts and cases*, McGraw-Hill Irwin.

28. Porter, op. cit.

29. E Penrose, *The theory of the growth of the firm*, Oxford: Basil Blackwell; I Ansoff, *Corporate strategy*, New York: McGraw-Hill, 1965.

30. For example, JB Barney, 'Strategic factor markets: expectations, luck, and business strategy', *Management Science*, vol. 32, no. 10, 1986a, 1231–1241; JB Barney, 'Firm resources and sustained competitive advantage,' *Journal of Management*, vol. 17, 1991, 99–120; MA Peterlaf, 'The cornerstones of competitive advantage: a resource-based view', *Strategic Management Journal*, vol. 14, 1993, 179–192; RP Rumelt, 'Towards a strategic theory of the firm', *Competitive Strategic Management*, RB Lamb (ed.), Englewood Cliffs, NJ: Prentice-Hall, pp. 566–570; B Wernerfelt, 'A resource based view of the firm', *Strategic Management Journal*, vol. 5, 171–180, 1984.

31. Wernerfelt, op. cit.; Barney 1991, op. cit.

32. R Rumelt, 'How much does strategy matter?', *Strategic Management Journal*, March 1991, 64–75.

33. CK Prahalad and G Hamel, 'The core competence of the corporation', *Harvard Business Review*, May–June 1990, 79–91.

34. 'Olivetti: on the ropes', *Economist*, May 20, 1995, 60–61; 'Olivetti Reinvents itself once more,' *Wall Street Journal*, 22 February 1999, A.1.

35. Remington, www.remington-products.com.

36. 'Eastman Kodak: 'Meeting the digital challenge', in RM Grant, *Cases to accompany contemporary strategy analysis*, 6th edn, Oxford, Blackwell, 2008.

37. 'Kodak ditches digital camera business', *CNN*, 9 February 2012. http://money.cnn.com/2012/02/09/technology/kodak_digital_cameras.

38. M Tripsas, 'Unraveling the process of creative destruction: complementary assets and incumbent survival in the typesetter industry', *Strategic Management Journal*, vol. 18, Summer Special Issue, 1997, 119–42; J Bower and CM Christensen, 'Disruptive technologies: catching the wave', *Harvard Business Review*, January–February 1995, 43–53.

39. JW Trailer, 'On the theory of rent and the mechanics of profitability', CSU Chico, 2002, www.csuchico.edu.

40. See more about the company's history and origins on their website www.airnewzealand.com.au/corporate-profile; website visited on 13 March 2020.

41. C Kelly, 'This is the world's 'most excellent' airline for 2020', *The New Daily*, 2 December 2019, www.thenewdailly.com.au.

42. L Parker, 'Is Air New Zealand the most tech-savvy airline in the world?', *Forbes*, 20 July 2019, www.forbes.com.

43. L Bennett, 'Air New Zealand: Standing out on the world's tarmac', *AD News*, 16 October 2018, www.adnews.com.au.

44. S Edmunds, 'Air New Zealand blames slower demand for drop in profits', *Stuff Limited,* 27 February 2020, www.stuff.co.nz.

45. 'Air New Zealand celebrates its suppliers', *Scoop*, 7 August 2019, www.scoop.co.nz.

46. Cochlear, www.cochlear.com.au.

47. J Milton-Smith, 'Framework facilitates innovation growth', *Western Australian Business News*, 11 March 2009, 38.

48. 'Cochlear named most innovative company', *Sydney Morning Herald*, 17 November 2003, www.smh.com.au.

49. 'Most innovative growth companies', Forbes, www.forbes.com, website visited on 16 March 2020.

50. InvestSMART, 'Cochlear Limited (COH)', www.investsmart.com.au.

51. J Milton-Smith, 'Framework facilitates innovation growth', *Western Australian Business News*, 11 March 2009, 38; Cochlear, www.cochlear.com.au.

52. Air New Zealand, *Annual Shareholder Review 2019*, 22 August 2019, www.airnewzealand.com.au.

53. Interbrand, www.interbrand.com.

54. C Fombrun, 'The value to be found in corporate reputation,' *Financial Times Mastering Management Series*, 4 December 2000, 8–10.

55. D Rose, 'Australia's most-trusted brand isn't Australian', *Financial Review*, 17 April 2019, www.afr.com.

56. E Lawler, 'From job-based to competency-based organizations,' *Journal of Organizational Behavior*, vol. 15, 1994, 3–15; L Spencer, D McClelland, and S Spencer, *Competency assessment methods: history and state of the art*, Hay/McBer Research Group, 1994; L Spencer and S Spencer, *Competence at work: models for superior performance*, New York: John Wiley & Sons, Inc., 1993.

57. D Goleman, *Emotional intelligence*, New York: Bantam, 1995.

58. TJ Peters and RH Waterman, *In search of excellence: lessons from America's best run corporations*, New York: Harper and Row, 1982, p. 47.

59. JB Barney, 'Organizational culture: can it be a source of sustained competitive advantage?', *Academy of Management Review*, vol. 11, 1986b, 656–665.

60. CE Helfat and M Lieberman, 'The birth of capabilities: market entry and the importance of prehistory', *Industrial and Corporate Change*, vol. 12, 2002, 725–760.

61. G Hamel and CK Prahalad argue that 'the distinction between competencies and capabilities is purely semantic', in *Harvard Business Review*, May–June 1992, 164–165.

62. P Selznick, *Leadership in administration: a sociological interpretation*, New York: Harper & Row, 1957.

63. CK Prahalad and G Hamel 1990, op. cit.

64. G Hamel and CK Prahalad 1992, op. cit., 164–165.

65. Porter's value chain is the main framework of his competitive advantage, Porter, op. cit.; McKinsey & Company refers to the firm's value chain as its 'business system', see: CF Bates, P Chatterjee, FW Gluck, D Gogel, and A Puri, 'The business system: a new tool for strategy formulation and cost analysis', in *McKinsey on Strategy*, Boston: McKinsey & Company, 2000.

66. For example, see P Bromiley and L Fleming, 'The resource based view of strategy: an evolutionist's critique', *The economics of choice, change, and organisations: essays in memory of Richard M. Cyert*, M Auger JG March (eds), Cheltenham: Edward Elgar, pp. 319–336, 2002; RL Priem and JE Butler, 'Is the resource-based 'view' a useful perspective for strategic management research?', *Academy of Management Review*, vol. 26, no. 1, 2001, 22–40.

67. See CE Helfat and MA Peteraf, 'The dynamic resource-based view: capability lifecycles', *Strategic Management Journal*, vol. 24 (special issue), 2003, 997–1010.

68. K Eisenhardt and M Martin, 'Dynamic capabilities: What are they?', *Strategic Management Journal*, October–November Special Issue 21, 2000: 1105–1121; E Døving and PN Gooderham, 'Dynamic Capabilities as antecedents of the scope of related diversification: the case of small firm accountancy practices', *Strategic Management Journal*, vol. 29, 2008, 841–857.

69. M Holzweber, J Mattsson, D Chadee and R Raman, 'How dynamic capabilities drive performance in the Indian IT industry: the role of information and co-ordination', *The Service Industries Journal*, vol. 32, no. 4, 2012, 533.

70. DJ Teece, G Pisano, and A Shuen, 'Dynamic capabilities and strategic management', *Strategic Management Journal*, vol. 18, no. 7, 1997, 509–553.

71. Eisenhardt and Martin, op. cit.

72. See C Helfat, S Finkelstein, W Mitchel, MA Peteraf, H Singh, D Teece, and S Winter, *Dynamic capabilities: understanding strategic change in organisation*, Malden, MA: Blackwell, 2007; M Easterby-Smith, MA Lyles, AA and Peteraf, 'Dynamic capabilities: current debates and future directions', *British Journal of Management*, vol. 20, 2009, S1–S8.

73. JB Barney and DN Clark, *Resource-based theory. Creating and sustaining competitive advantage*, Oxford University Press, 2007, pp. 57, 69–70.

74. ibid., p. 57.

75. ibid., p. 58.

76. Porter, op. cit.

77. Barney and Clark, op. cit., p. 59.

78. ibid.

79. ibid., p. 61.

80. I Dierickx and K Cool, 'Asset stock accumulation and sustainability of competitive advantage', *Management Science*, vol. 35, 1989, 1504–1511.

81. D Hambrick, 'Top management teams: key to strategic success', *California Management Review*, vol. 30, 1987, 88–108.

82. Barney 1986b, op. cit.

83. Barney and Clark 2007, op. cit., p. 67.

84. ibid., p. 70.

ACKNOWLEDGEMENTS

Photo: © Scott Kenneth Brodie / Shutterstock.com

Photo: © Rocket Lab / Alamy Stock Photo

Photo: © ChameleonsEye / Shutterstock.com

Photo: © Ivan_Shenets / Shutterstock.com

Extract: © Air New Zealand 2020, 'Air New Zealand reports interim profit of $198 million and maintains interim dividend', media release, 27 February.

Table 3.1: © Interbrand 2019, 'Best Global Brands 2019 Rankings', www.interbrand.com/best-brands/best-global-brands/2019/ranking.

PART III

STRATEGIC FORMULATION AND COMPETITIVE ADVANTAGE

The nature and sources of competitive advantage

LEARNING OBJECTIVES

After studying this chapter, you should be able to:

4.1 identify the circumstances in which a company can create a competitive advantage and understand the contribution of responsiveness and innovation

4.2 describe the variation of competitive advantage in different market settings

4.3 recognise the different stages of industry development and understand the factors that drive the process of industry evolution

4.4 distinguish between slow-, standard- and fast-cycle market characteristics

4.5 analyse various levels of strategy, describe how strategic advantage can be sustained at each level and explain how different kinds of strategies create competitive advantage.

Singapore Airlines (SIA)

Over the past four decades, Singapore Airlines (SIA) has developed an enviable reputation for providing its passengers with a high-quality air travel experience. The company prides itself on being the 'most awarded airline', a title it has gained through winning many prizes for its customer service standards. It was also ranked 18th in *Fortune* magazine's 'World's Most Admired Companies' in 2019.[1]

A brief history of SIA

The company can trace its roots back to 1947 but really took off as an independent entity in the early 1970s when it severed its ties with what would eventually become Malaysia Airlines. During the 1970s, the company grew rapidly, extending its scheduled routes from its Singapore hub to many destinations in India and Asia. In the 1980s, it added routes to the US, Canada and Europe, and has continued to expand its network over time. Since its incorporation in 1972, SIA has been partly owned by the Singapore government, which has a 'golden share', but operationally it is free from government intervention.

SIA's strategy

SIA has based its strategy on two main pillars: its planes and its people. In terms of its aircraft, the company tries to keep its fleet 'young'. In April 2014, it was estimated that the average age of the SIA fleet was 81 months as opposed to the industry average of around 128 months.[2] SIA was the first airline to launch the Airbus A380 high-capacity jet and has continued to invest significant sums both in new aircraft and in new cabin products such as in-flight entertainment systems and economically designed seats. The policy of operating a young fleet also means that SIA's aircraft are more fuel efficient and require less repair and maintenance than those of its rivals. Heracleous and Wirtz report that 'in 2008 repairs accounted for 4% of SIA's total costs compared with 5.9% for United Airlines and 4.8% for American Airlines'.[3] SIA's aircraft also spend less time in hangars and more time in the air — 13 hours on average per day versus the industry average of 11.3 hours.

In terms of its people, the Singapore International Airlines group as a whole (including cargo, repair and maintenance service etc.) employed just under 23 000 people in 2013, of which 14 000 were employed by the airline business. While the company pays only average Singapore wages, it manages to attract first-class university graduates because it has a reputation for offering excellent training and experience. The company spends around $70 million a year putting each of its employees through 110 hours of retraining annually. Much of this training is focused on embedding the culture of customer service into everything employees do. Staff are, for example, trained to appreciate subtle cultural differences and to look for clever ways of personalising passengers' flying experience — for example, noticing that a laptop is out of power or a mother needs assistance with her child. As a consequence, crew members who leave the company usually find it easy to find employment with other operators.

While emphasis is given to customer service, any opportunity to cut costs, however small, is taken. The headquarters of the airline is housed in modest premises near Changi airport in Singapore and the central head count is kept to a minimum. Training takes place within the airline's offices and is delivered by senior members of the airline's own crew rather than by outside trainers. Staff are encouraged to find ways of reducing waste and bonus schemes are in place that incentivise cost-cutting behaviour. For example, even though two brands of high-quality champagne are available to business class travellers, cabin crew are encouraged to pour drinks from whichever bottle is open unless the passenger requests a specific brand. Similarly, pots of jam, which cabin crew noticed were frequently wasted, are now provided only on request. To make sure that cabin crew can give passengers personal attention SIA flights usually carry more flight attendants than other airlines, but this is reported to add only about 5 per cent to labour costs and, as an expense that contributes strongly to the airline's reputation for excellent customer service, allows SIA to compete on factors other than price.

SIA tries to achieve both differentiation and cost saving through its approach to innovation. The company is willing to experiment and is fast to adopt any incremental innovations that improve customer service. It was one of the first airlines to introduce fully reclining seats (slumberettes), in-flight mobile telephones, fax services and biometric technology to simplify and speed up check-in times following global health scares. However, unlike some of its rivals, it has not developed highly customised and sophisticated yield management and other back-office software, preferring instead to buy tried-and-tested applications. It has also outsourced responsibility for maintaining non-strategic hardware and software to low-cost service providers in India.

Recent challenges

While the company seems to have very successfully reconciled the apparently contradictory strategies of cost minimisation and differentiation, it does face problems. The company dominates the business class market segment on many of its routes and it is this segment that is particularly sensitive to the level of economic activity. The company was badly hit by the 2008 financial crisis and in 2009 posted its first full-year loss.[4] The company responded by cutting staff, reducing working hours and reviewing its routes and schedules. By 2013, it had returned to profit and continued to exceed industry average performance.

Competition, however, remains intense, particularly in the premium air travel segment, which has been aggressively targeted by Middle Eastern airlines such as Emirates, Etihad Airways and Qatar Airways.

To avoid excessive dependence on mature markets, SIA has also entered the low-cost segment of the airline business, first by acquiring shares in Tigerair (a budget carrier serving the Asia–Pacific region) and then by launching its own budget airline, Scoot, in 2012. Scoot operates medium- and long-haul flights from Singapore to Australia and China. At present, little is known about Scoot's performance but there is a danger that this low-cost subsidiary could cannibalise its parent's traditional market and dilute its yield. It remains to be seen whether the distinctive culture of the company can remain intact as SIA seeks to simultaneously operate a budget and full-service airline.

The impact of the global pandemic

In 2020, the airline industry experienced major destruction as a result of the global spread of COVID-19, an infectious disease caused by a new virus. Demand on airline transportation has drastically reduced because of the pandemic. As a result, international airline companies grounded most of their planes, transferred staff on leave and tried to raise more cash to avoid financial collapse.

Singapore Airlines managed to raise to S$19 billion ($13 billion) of cash to help see it through the coronavirus crisis and recover afterward, when demand on airline transportation will eventually return.[5]

Singapore Airlines will receive a loan of $4 billion from the biggest bank of Singapore, DBS Group. 'This transaction will not only tide SIA (Singapore Airlines) over a short term financial liquidity challenge, but will position it for growth beyond the pandemic,' clarified Dilhan Pillay Sandrasegara, Temasek International Chief Executive. In response to the situation, Singapore Airlines will put on hold for the next few years the order of a new-generation aircraft, which will provide improved fuel efficiency across the fleet once SIA is in a position to expand their capacity.[6]

Introduction

A company can achieve superior profitability either by locating in an attractive industry or by establishing a competitive advantage over its rivals. Of these two options, competitive advantage offers the more important competitive edge because an attractive industry will likely draw more competitors and the advantage will very soon vanish. As competition has intensified across almost all industries, very few industry environments can guarantee stable returns; hence, the primary goal of a corporate-level strategy is to establish a position of sustainable competitive advantage for the company. The scene setter illustrates the point about sustainable advantage in both cost advantage and differentiation through continuous approach to innovation. It also provokes other questions about how large companies in highly competitive markets (e.g. international airlines) actually create competitive advantage when costs are high and demand is variable. Further examining SIA's competitive advantage, we can observe how the company extends its operations into new segments to avoid its dependence on the highly competitive premium air travel segment, especially in mature markets. As we shall see in this chapter, companies, in particular large ones with higher bargaining power, create competitive advantage through entering into new niches and segments through low-cost differentiation, which allows these companies to expand not only through exports but through supplier relationships in emerging countries.

There are three big questions that concern competitive advantage.[7]

1. Where do competitive advantages come from, and how are they sustained?
2. Why do some companies consistently outperform their competitors?
3. Why do some companies succeed in the same industry environments where others fail?

Competitive advantage can be approached from two perspectives. From a *longitudinal* perspective, strategy formulation and implementation can be analysed in relation to competitive advantages at various stages of the industry life cycle (which includes introduction, growth, mature and declining stages). From a *hierarchical* perspective, three basic levels of strategies within an organisation (namely corporate, business and functional levels) can be examined. In addition, how a company can obtain competitive advantage at the network and global levels will be addressed, as these are both very important factors for the consideration of market competition in this modern, boundaryless world.

4.1 The emergence of competitive advantage

LEARNING OBJECTIVE 4.1 Identify the circumstances in which a company can create a competitive advantage and understand the contribution of responsiveness and innovation.

What is the meaning of competitive advantage? Why is it important? How does competitive advantage emerge? To understand how competitive advantage emerges, it is first necessary to understand what competitive advantage is. Competitive advantage is often easily recognised: Microsoft has a competitive advantage in the supply of computer operating software, Toyota has a competitive advantage in making cars, Apple has a competitive advantage in innovation in a large range of electronic products. Defining **competitive advantage** precisely is not easy. However, at a basic level it can be defined as follows: when two or more companies compete within the same market, competitive advantage is a condition that enables a company to operate in a more efficient or responsive manner than its competitors, and which results in higher potential to earn a persistently higher rate of profit.

It should be noted that competitive advantage may not be necessarily revealed immediately in higher profitability — a company may forgo current profit in favour of investment in market share, technology, customer loyalty or executive perks.[8] It is, therefore, important to have a long perspective on strategy formulation and implementation.

How competitive advantage emerges from external sources of change

Companies that do not compete effectively will be eliminated from the market eventually. Competitive advantage is the key success factor of a company's survival. However, the competitive advantage of a company cannot last forever. When the market changes, the competitive advantage possessed by companies may also change. For example, the introduction of digital camera technology has caused significant damage to the traditional film camera market. No matter how effective or efficient a film camera producer is, most consumers are no longer interested in its products.

Various types of competitive advantages emerge when change occurs. The source of the change may be external or internal to the industry (see figure 4.1). For an external change to create competitive advantage, the change must have differential effects on companies because of their different resources and capabilities or strategic positioning. When will external change create competitive advantage and disadvantage? It depends on the magnitude of the change and the extent of companies' strategic differences. The more turbulent an industry's environment, the greater the number of sources of change. The greater the differences in companies' resources and capabilities, the greater the dispersion of profitability within the industry.

In the world tobacco industry, the external environment is comparatively stable and the leading companies pursue similar strategies with similar resources and capabilities. The result is that competitive advantages, as reflected in inter-company profit differentials, tend to be small. The toy industry, on the other hand, experiences rapid and unpredictable changes in demand, technology and fashion. The leading companies pursue different strategies and have different resources and capabilities. As a result, profitability differences are wide and variable over time.

Competitive advantage from responsiveness to change

The impact of external change on competitive advantage depends on a company's ability to respond to change. Any external change creates opportunities for the organisation. The ability to identify and respond to opportunity lies in the core management capability of entrepreneurship.[9] To the extent that external opportunities are fleeting or subject to first-mover advantage, speed of response is critical to exploiting business opportunity. An unexpected rain shower creates an upsurge in the demand for umbrellas. Those street vendors who are quickest to position themselves outside a busy railway station will benefit most.

As markets become increasingly turbulent, so responsiveness to external change has become increasingly important as a source of competitive advantage. The competitive landscape is rapidly changing and competitive advantage is increasingly based on the business connectivity, interdependence and co-evolution of companies, technologies and institutions. More and more companies develop their competitive advantage through innovation in ecosystems. For example, Amazon continually enters new market segments and niches and its ecosystem consists of various content creators, product and service providers, influencers and app developers who all utilise market opportunity on the Amazon platform.[10]

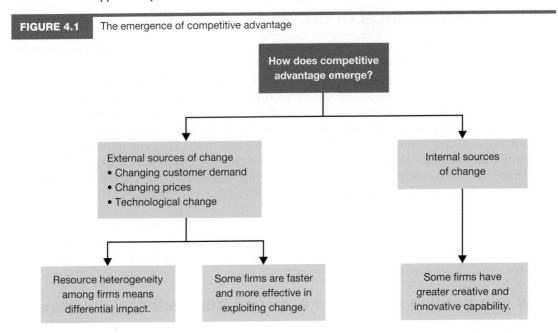

FIGURE 4.1 The emergence of competitive advantage

Responsiveness to the opportunities provided by external change requires one key resource (information) and one key capability (flexibility). Information is necessary to identify and anticipate external changes. This requires environmental scanning.

As the pace of change has accelerated, companies are less dependent on conventional analysis of economic and market research data and more dependent on 'early warning systems' through direct relationships with customers, suppliers and competitors. The faster a company can respond in real time to changing market circumstances, the less it needs to forecast the future. Short cycle times have become a key requirement for fast response capability.

Fast market changes and dynamic environments challenge companies to develop an **entrepreneurial orientation (EO)**, the strategic process by which organisations identify new opportunities and implement entrepreneurial actions.[11] Entrepreneurial orientation involves a continuous behaviour of an entrepreneurial organisation for the purpose of the identification and generation of new business, which will create and sustain a competitive advantage.[12] Artificial Intelligence (AI) allows organisations to develop competitive advantage through timely and accurate response to environmental changes, for example, AI enables companies to scale and utilise unlimited opportunities of digital marketing.

Competitive advantage from innovation: 'new game' strategies

The changes that create competitive advantage may be internal as well as external. Internal change is generated through innovation. Innovation not only is a source of competitive advantage, it provides a basis for overturning the competitive advantage of other companies. Innovation is typically thought of in its technical sense: the new products or processes that embody new ideas and new knowledge. In a business, however, innovation includes new approaches to doing business.

What does 'strategic innovation' involve? Most commonly it involves creating value for customers from novel experiences, products, product delivery or bundling. For example, competition in the retail sector is driven by a constant quest for new retail concepts and formats. This may take the form of bigger stores with greater variety (Woolworths and Metcash) or novel approaches to display and store layout (Coles).

Strategic innovation may also be based on redesigned processes and novel organisational designs, as in the following examples.

- Costco operates an international chain of membership warehouses, under the 'Costco Wholesale' name, that carry quality, brand-name merchandise at substantially lower prices than are typically found at conventional wholesale or retail sources. The company uses an intensive distribution strategy of its highly successful brand name into different regional areas to promote its unique form of competitive advantage.

- Nike built its large and successful businesses on a business system that totally reconfigured the traditional shoe-manufacturing value chain. To begin with, Nike does not manufacture shoes — indeed, it manufactures little of anything. It designs, markets and distributes shoes, but its primary activity is the coordination of a vast and complex global network involving design and market research (primarily in the United States), the production (under contract) of components (primarily in Korea and Taiwan), and the contract assembly of shoes (in China, the Philippines, India, Thailand and other low-wage countries).
- Apple's resurgence between 2003 and 2006 is the result of its reinvention of the recorded music business by combining an iconic MP3 player, the iPod, with its iTunes music download service. In 2007, Apple Computer Inc. changed its name to Apple Inc. to reflect that it no longer considers itself strictly a computer manufacturer. This shift was evidenced by the development of the highly innovative, multifunctional iPad, which, in 2013, continued to dominate the global tablet market.

Formulating innovative strategies

How do organisations go about formulating innovative strategies? Are new approaches to competing and delivering superior value the result of pure creativity, or are there analyses and ways of thinking that can lead an organisation in the right direction? The management literature suggests several approaches.

- Chesbrough and Bogers view open innovation based on inter-organisational alliances as an alternative to a vertically integrated, closed innovation model in which all innovation activities are internal to organisations. They define open innovation as 'a distributed innovation process based on purposively managed knowledge flows across organisational boundaries, using pecuniary and non-pecuniary mechanisms in line with the organisation's business model' and suggest it is a means by which organisations can share risk.[13]
- Hamel argues that strategic innovation extends beyond new products, new markets and new technologies. Innovations in management — Procter & Gamble's invention of brand management, General Electric's unique approach to management development, Toyota's lean production system — are the strongest foundation for competitive advantage.[14]
- Kim and Mauborgne's blue ocean strategy emphasises the attractions of creating new markets. Blue oceans may comprise entirely new industries (e.g. Apple's pioneering of the personal computer industry) or the re-creation of existing industries (e.g. Cirque du Soleil in the circus business).[15]
- McKinsey & Company's concept of new game strategy involves reconfiguring the industry value chain in order to change the 'rules of the game'.[16]

Sustaining competitive advantage

A company cannot live on its current competitive advantage forever. Once established, competitive advantage is subject to erosion by competition. The speed with which competitive advantage is undermined depends on the ability of competitors to challenge by imitation or innovation. Imitation is the most direct form of competition; thus, for competitive advantage to be sustained over time, barriers to imitation must exist. In most industries the erosion of the competitive advantage of industry leaders is a slow process.

To identify the sources of isolating mechanisms, the process of competitive imitation needs to be examined. For one company to imitate the strategy of another, it must meet four conditions.

1. *Identification.* The company must be able to identify that a rival possesses a competitive advantage.
2. *Incentive for imitation.* There must be a profit incentive. If a company can persuade rivals that imitation will be unprofitable, it may be able to avoid competitive challenges. A company can also deter imitation by pre-emption — occupying existing and potential strategic niches to reduce the range of investment opportunities open to the challenger.
3. *Diagnosis.* If a company is to imitate the competitive advantage of another, it must understand the basis of its rival's success. In most industries, there is a serious identification problem in linking superior performance to the resources and capabilities that generate that performance.
4. *Resource acquisition.* A company can acquire resources and capabilities in two ways: it can buy them or it can build them. The period over which a competitive advantage can be sustained depends critically on the time it takes to acquire and mobilise the resources and capabilities needed to mount a competitive challenge.

Figure 4.2 illustrates these stages and the types of isolating mechanism that exist at each stage. In addition, a company can develop inimitable competitive advantage through continuous innovation. For instance, Apple Inc., the American company that produces iMac, iPod, iPhone and iPad, adopts a strategy of continuous innovation to build up its competitive advantage in the market.

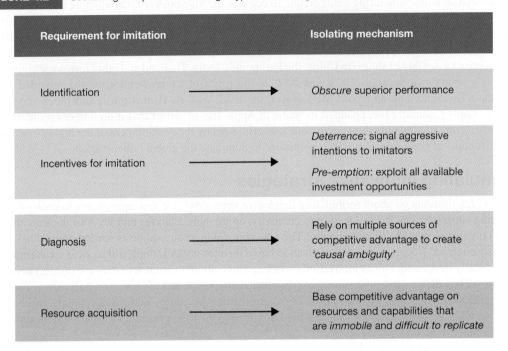

Requirement for imitation	Isolating mechanism
Identification	*Obscure* superior performance
Incentives for imitation	*Deterrence*: signal aggressive intentions to imitators *Pre-emption*: exploit all available investment opportunities
Diagnosis	Rely on multiple sources of competitive advantage to create *'causal ambiguity'*
Resource acquisition	Base competitive advantage on resources and capabilities that are *immobile* and *difficult to replicate*

First-mover advantage

A company's ability to challenge an incumbent depends on the extent and the sources of **first-mover** advantage in the market. The idea of first-mover advantage is that the initial occupant of a strategic position or niche gains access to resources and capabilities that a follower cannot match. The simplest form of first-mover advantage is a patent or copyright.

First movers can also gain preferential access to scarce resources, such as a prime retail location. First movers may also be able to use the profit streams from their early entry to build resources and capabilities more rapidly than latecomers.[17] While figure 4.2 illustrates ways to maintain first-mover advantage and thus sustained performance over time, there are many examples where innovators have more recently benefited by greater knowledge spillovers. For example, when Intel established superior advantage by developing sophisticated microprocessor capabilities, companies such as AMD benefited from this knowledge as it became available. The natural tendency for companies is to prevent spillovers and to protect proprietary assets such as investment-rich resources in technologies and capital investments. This belief is based on a classical view that knowledge spillovers (e.g. detailed technical specifications, process techniques) commonly shared over time with competitors are highly beneficial to imitators but detrimental to innovators.[18] More recent research suggests that deliberately withholding knowledge may force imitators to speed up innovative attempts to replicate the innovator's first-mover advantage.[19] However, rather than maintaining isolating mechanisms (outlined in figure 4.2), the practice of 'free revealing' — that is, the provision of a minimal level of spillover knowledge to rivals — may prove more beneficial for the innovator, in that it encourages followers to adopt an imitative development strategy rather than a concurrent one. This means that innovators or leaders with first-mover advantage can slow down their own development activities and reduce development costs.

4.2 Competitive advantage in different market settings

LEARNING OBJECTIVE 4.2 Describe the variation of competitive advantage in different market settings.

Profiting from competitive advantage requires that the company first establishes a competitive advantage, and then sustains its advantage for long enough to reap the rewards. To identify opportunities for establishing and sustaining competitive advantage requires an understanding of the competitive process in the specific market. For competitive advantage to exist, there must be some imperfection of competition. To understand these imperfections in the competitive process, it is necessary to identify the types of resources and capabilities necessary to compete and the circumstances of their availability.

There are two types of value-creating activity: trading and production. Trading involves arbitrage across space (trade) and time (speculation). Production involves the physical transformation of inputs into outputs. These different types of business activity correspond to different market types: trading markets and production markets (see figure 4.3). But first, a special type of trading market — an efficient market — is discussed.

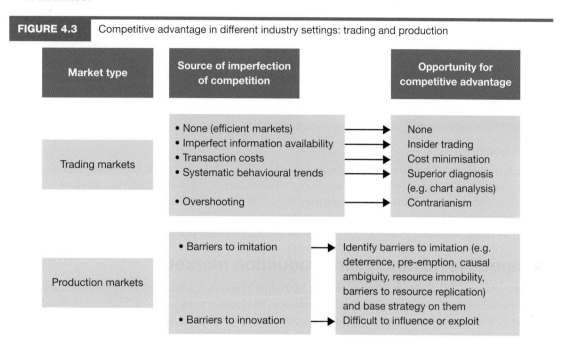

FIGURE 4.3 Competitive advantage in different industry settings: trading and production

Efficient markets: the absence of competitive advantage

Economic theories state that perfect competition exists where there are many buyers and sellers, no product differentiation, no barriers to entry or exit, and free flow of information. The closest real-world examples of perfect competition are financial and commodity markets (e.g. the markets for securities, foreign exchange, and grain futures). These markets are sometimes described as efficient. An efficient market is one in which prices reflect all available information. Because prices adjust instantaneously to newly available information, no market trader can expect to earn more than any other. Any differences in profit reflect either different levels of risk selected by different traders or just pure luck. Because all available information is reflected in current prices, no trading rules based on historical price data or any other available information can offer excess return. In other words, competitive advantage is absent.

The absence of competitive advantage in efficient markets can be linked to resource availability. If financial markets are efficient, it is because only two types of resource are required to participate — finance and information. If both are equally available to all traders, there is no basis for one to gain competitive advantage over another.

Competitive advantage in trading markets

For competitive advantage to emerge, there must be some imperfections that exist in the competitive process. Using trading markets as an example, the following introduces different sources of imperfection to the competitive process, showing how these imperfections create opportunities for competitive advantage.

Superior access to information

In financial markets (and most other trading markets), competitive advantage depends on superior access to information. The most likely source of superior information is privileged access to private information. Trading on the basis of such information normally falls within the restrictions on 'insider trading'. Though insider information creates advantage, such competitive advantage tends to be of short duration. Once a market participant begins acting on the basis of insider information, other operators are alerted to the existence of the information. Even though they may not know its content, they are able to imitate the behaviour of the market leader.

Transaction costs

In stock markets, low transaction costs are attained by traders who economise on research and market analysis and achieve efficient portfolio diversification. Studies of mutual fund performance show that, on average, managed funds underperform index funds and the amount of that underperformance is roughly equal to the additional expenses incurred by the managed funds.[20]

Systematic behavioural trends

In general, there is evidence that prices in financial markets follow systematic patterns that are the result of 'market psychology', which is reflected in the trends, the turning points of which can be established from past data. Chart analysis uses hypotheses concerning the relationship between past and future price movements for forecasting. Despite mixed evidence on the success of chart analysis in financial markets,[21] systematic behavioural trends do occur in most markets, which implies that competitive advantage is gained by traders with superior skill in diagnosing such behaviour.

Overshooting

One well-documented behavioural aberration is the propensity of market participants to overreact to new information, with the result that prices overshoot.[22] Such overreaction is typically the result of imitative behaviour resulting in the creation of bandwagon effects. On the assumption that overshooting is temporary and is eventually offset by an opposite movement back to equilibrium, then advantage can be gained through a contrarian strategy: doing the opposite of the mass-market participants.

Competitive advantage in production markets

The transitory nature of competitive advantage in trading markets is a result of the characteristics of the resources required to compete: finance and information. Production markets are quite different. Production activities require complex combinations of resources and capabilities, and these resources and capabilities are highly differentiated. The result is that each producer possesses a unique combination of resources and capabilities.

In the airline industry, the growing diversity of companies has expanded opportunities for competitive advantage and widened the profit differentials between them. For instance, Qantas (Australia's leading airline) operates a fleet of over 200 aircraft and, at the same time, has diversified its airline operations to include regional carrier QantasLink, as well as a low-fare carrier, Jetstar Airways, both of which operate in Australia and elsewhere in the Asia–Pacific region. The nature of competition in the airline industry is significantly impacted by the global COVID-19 pandemic. In 2020, demand on airline transportation plunged and most of the global airline companies grounded their fleet. When demand is likely to recover after the crisis, recovery capabilities will be crucial for airlines' ability to compete.

Differences in resources of companies have an important impact on the process by which competitive advantage is eroded. Where companies possess very similar bundles of resources and capabilities, imitation of the competitive advantage of the incumbent company is most likely. Where resource bundles are highly differentiated, competition is likely to be less direct. Using different resources and capabilities, a company may substitute a rival's competitive advantage.[23] It is misleading, however, to suggest that resources and capabilities are the main source of competitive advantage — the integrative effects of strength and weakness sets on relative performance also need to be considered. That is, if resources are influenced by both strengths and weaknesses of a given organisation, then we need to think about the combined effect of capabilities/weaknesses on competitive advantage. Research[24] indicates that it is not just resources that lead to sustained competitive advantage because this misrepresents the power of strategic liabilities. While resource-based theory (RBV) suggests that valuable and rare resources create a competitive advantage, this is relative to competitors — meaning that organisations cannot rely on the absolute quality of capabilities. Consequently, strengths and weaknesses create a dynamic interdependence between multiple rivals competing in the same marketplace.[25]

Hence, the durability of competitive advantage over time depends on the environment and organisation-specific factors, and this is limited because strengths and weakness sets change significantly. Research confirms that there is a negative outcome on relative organisation performance from weakness sets,[26] which probably accounts for temporary advantage rather than sustained competitive advantage. Many factors lead to attacks on an organisation's competitive advantage including, but not limited to, organisational inefficiencies (what Dorothy Leonard-Barton calls rigidities[27]) and inability to exploit opportunities. When an organisation has many weaknesses, the number and intensity of attacks upon it are likely to be higher and stronger. Figure 4.4[28] illustrates that relative high or low weaknesses need to be offset with high or low strengths.

FIGURE 4.4	Performance effects of relative strengths and weaknesses

		Relative strength set	
		Low	**High**
Relative weakness set	**Low**	I Offsetting — undifferentiated Neutral performance effect	II Robust advantage Positive performance effect
	High	III Undermining Negative performance effect	IV Precarious advantage Positive performance effect

Quadrant II in figure 4.4 indicates that a set of strengths will overwhelm a set of weaknesses, leading to a robust advantage. This fits RBV logic that more capabilities from resources than weaknesses create competitive advantage. Quadrant III, however, indicates that a low strength set coupled with a high weakness set will have a negative effect on relative performance because the weaknesses undermine the strengths set's positive contribution. In quadrant I, there is little to differentiate between competitors since strengths and weaknesses offset each other. Lastly, in quadrant IV, the strength and weakness sets neutralise each other. Precarious advantage in quadrant IV is less durable because a high level of weaknesses makes an organisation more vulnerable to rivals' attacks and there is greater performance variation than with robust advantage (quadrant II). Notice that in quadrant III, organisations possess an overall competitive disadvantage while in quadrant I, at best, competitors achieve parity but the absence of any real capabilities does not create competitive advantage in production markets. The overall logic of figure 4.4 is that organisations are more likely to achieve temporary advantage because of constant changes to organisation-specific resources and shifting environments. In such circumstances, organisations need to develop a differentiated stock of capabilities in dynamic markets that are constantly shifting. To achieve sustained competitive advantage, organisations will need to constantly develop their capabilities and not stay static after recent successes.

Note the following examples of two organisations' constantly developing capabilities.

- Canon, a Japanese company, substituted for Xerox's technical service capability in copiers by developing high reliability copiers that needed little service.
- Lenovo, the Chinese company that purchased IBM's PC business, is now moving the focus back to the Chinese PC market which provides a sustainable home-based competitive advantage.

Since substitute competition can come from many directions — alternative resources, technological innovations or new business models — it is difficult to counter. The key is to persuade potential competitors that substitution is unlikely to be profitable. This can be achieved through committing the company to continuous improvement, locking in customers and suppliers, and market deterrence.[29]

Industry conditions conducive to the emergence of sustained competitive advantage

The opportunities for establishing competitive advantage in production markets depend on the number and diversity of the sources of change in the business environment. Consider the wireless telecommunication services industry. The industry is subject to a vast array of dynamic forces — regulatory change, technological change, changing customer preferences, to mention but a few. All of these forces offer opportunities for competitive advantage. The complexity of the industry also determines the variety of opportunities for competitive advantage.

The extent to which competitive advantage is eroded through imitation will also depend on the characteristics of the industry. Examples include the following.

- *Information complexity.* Industries where competitive advantage is based on complex, multilayered capabilities tend to have more sustainable competitive advantages. In movie production, the long-established leadership of studios such as Paramount, Columbia (Sony), Universal, Fox and Disney reflects the difficult-to-diagnose secrets of producing 'blockbuster' movies, even though the individual resources (scripts, actors, technicians and directors) can be hired from the market.
- *Opportunities for deterrence and pre-emption.* Industries in which the market is small (relative to the minimum efficient scale of production), essential resources are scarce or tightly held, or economies of learning are important, allow first movers to establish and sustain competitive advantage by

pre-emption and deterrence. The local market dominance of Australian banks such as the Commonwealth Bank and National Australia Bank (NAB) ensure that foreign banks are relatively uncompetitive in their development of effective local business networks and efficient customer services.

- *Difficulties of resource acquisition.* Industries differ according to the availability of strategically important resources. The securities underwriting business (whether for initial public offerings or corporate bond issues) offers more sustainable advantages because the key resources and capabilities (market expertise, reputation, relationships, retail distribution links and massive financial reserves) are difficult to assemble.

4.3 Industry evolution and strategic advantage

LEARNING OBJECTIVE 4.3 Recognise the different stages of industry development and understand the factors that drive the process of industry evolution.

Everything is in a state of constant change — the business environment especially. The greatest challenge of management is to ensure that adaptation of the enterprise matches the changes occurring within the business environment, while upholding the company's strategic advantage.

Change in the industry environment is driven by a number of forces — technology, consumer preferences, economic growth and a host of other influences. In some cases, these forces for change may combine to create massive, unpredictable changes. For example, in telecommunications, new digital and wireless technologies combined with regulatory changes have resulted in the telecommunications industry in the twenty-first century being almost unrecognisable from that which existed 20 years previously. In other industries — food processing, car production and wedding services — change is more gradual and more predictable. Change is the result both of external forces and the competitive strategies of the companies within the industry.

Industry life cycle

One of the best-known and most enduring marketing concepts is the product life cycle.[30] Products are born, their sales grow, they reach maturity, they go into decline, and they ultimately die. If products have life cycles, so too do the industries that produce them.

The **industry life cycle** is the supply-side equivalent of the product life cycle and is likely to be of longer duration than that of a single product. The life cycle comprises four phases: introduction (or emergence), growth, maturity, and decline (see figure 4.5). The characteristic profile of such a life cycle is an S-shaped growth curve.

- In the *introduction* stage, sales are small and the rate of market penetration is low because the industry's products are little known and customers are few. Customers for new products tend to be affluent, innovation-oriented and risk-tolerant.
- The *growth* stage is characterised by accelerating market penetration as product technology becomes more standardised and prices fall. Ownership spreads from higher income customers to the mass market.
- Increasing market saturation causes the onset of the *maturity* stage and slowing growth as new demand gives way to replacement demand. Once saturation is reached, demand is wholly for replacement, either by customers replacing old products with new products or by new customers replacing old customers.
- Lastly, as the industry becomes challenged by new industries that produce technologically superior substitute products, the industry enters its *decline* stage.

Driving forces of an industry life cycle

The industry life cycle is driven by two forces.
1. The life cycle and the stages within it are defined primarily by changes in an industry's growth rate over time.
2. The second driving force of the industry life cycle is knowledge. New knowledge in the form of product innovation is responsible for an industry's birth, and the dual processes of knowledge creation and knowledge diffusion exert a major influence on industry evolution.

The life cycle model is a useful approach to exploring the impact of temporal processes of market saturation and technology development and dissemination and their impact on industry structure and the basis of competitive advantage. Classifying industries according to their stage of development can in itself be an insightful exercise, for the following reasons.

- It acts as a shortcut in strategy analysis. Categorising an industry according to its stage of development can suggest the type of competition likely to emerge and the kinds of strategy likely to be effective.
- Classifying an industry encourages comparison with other industries. By highlighting similarities and differences with other industries, such comparisons can provide a deeper understanding of the strategic characteristics of an industry.
- It directs attention to the forces of change and direction of industry evolution, thereby helping anticipate and manage change.

FIGURE 4.5 The industry life cycle

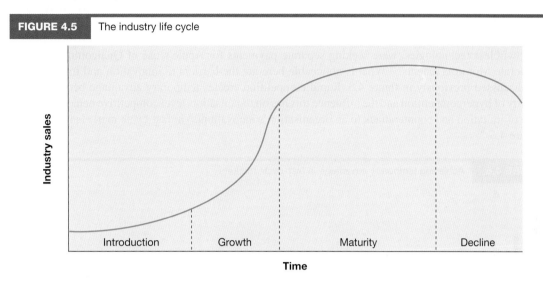

Industry life cycle can also explain how international migration of production started to prevail in the 1980s.

While various management consultants and commentators advocate radical and continuous change among established companies, there is little evidence that most companies have the capacity to manage such change. Certain tools and techniques — scenario analysis, in particular — may help managers understand and cope with change in the external environment. Nevertheless, the fundamental truth is that, so long as developing new capabilities is slow and risky, a company's capacity to successfully undergo radical change is inherently uncertain.

4.4 Industry life cycle and cycle markets

LEARNING OBJECTIVE 4.4 Distinguish between slow-, standard- and fast-cycle market characteristics.

As we discussed earlier, market growth-to-saturation and technology development and dissemination have a significant impact on industry structure and the basis of competitive advantage. However, industry life cycle cannot be defined or highlighted in such discrete terms. This is because the pace of change or the competitive dynamics within a particular industry and market dictate the life of products and innovations at each stage of the life cycle. So, it is often useful to think of industry life cycles in terms of cycle markets: slow, fast and standard. **Slow-cycle markets** are defined here as products and innovations that have *high* barriers to competitive imitation protecting an organisation's strategic advantage over time. An example is B. Braun in Malaysia, which manufactures high precision surgical equipment where each product is patented and protected. While companies may imitate over time, the capability and production related to 'high precision' are more difficult to copy. For instance, B. Braun has a unique set of competencies and capabilities that are hard to replicate, and the company possesses many unique in-house innovations.

Standard-cycle markets by comparison are defined as products and innovations that have *measured* barriers to competitive imitation protecting a company's strategic advantage over time. Here, companies compete in high-volume markets that experience severe competition. However, as outlined in figure 4.4 earlier, continuing investments in resources and capability strengths create robust advantage over time, allowing companies to stay ahead of their competitors. Continuous investments in people through skill equipping, process technology investments, and general organisational know-how assist these companies to sustain their advantage over time. Rather than seeking to understand product and industry life cycles with discrete starts and ends, viewing markets as a compilation of capabilities that are earnestly defended makes equal sense. In many ways, precarious advantage (see figure 4.4) aptly fits standard-cycle organisations when imitators achieve parity in design and innovation. Here, precarious advantage suggests an equal number of strengths and weaknesses for a time when competitors have roughly the same quality of resources. However, standard-cycle organisations make strategic investments in new and related products and processes, enabling them to maintain advantages longer and thus make performance gains relative to competitors.[31]

Fast-cycle markets are different because of the pace of disruption. **Fast-cycle markets** are defined as products and innovations that cannot be protected because of intense and rapid competitive moves that *erode* and *destroy* competitive advantage.[32] An example here was the fast imitation by Samsung of Apple iPhone patents and designs in their Android 4.0 platform.[33] At the same time, Motorola, who owns patents to key wireless technologies, were seeking separate payments for Apple's use of Qualcomm chips that incorporate Motorola patents.[34] What is noticeable here are the barriers to innovation and imitation that were discussed previously in figure 4.3. Rapid competition creates temporary advantage because of the volatility of hypercompetition and the influence this has on organisation-level competitive behaviour.[35] The nature of imitation and counterattack to an organisation's innovation(s) in fast-cycle markets is illustrated in figure 4.6.[36]

| **FIGURE 4.6** | Achieving temporary advantage in fast-cycle markets |

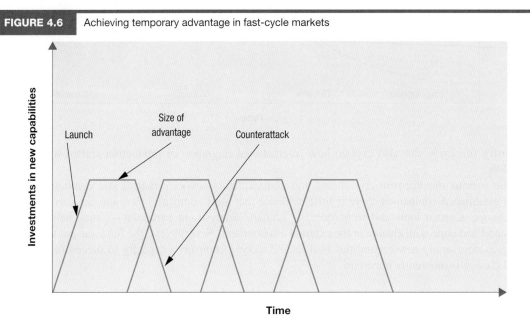

Competitive advantage at the introduction and growth stages

In emerging industries at the introduction and growth stages, nurturing and exploiting innovation is the fundamental source of competitive advantage. This means that the practices of effective strategic management are fundamentally different in emerging industries from other types of business environments.

A common problem in emerging industries is the speed of change and the difficulty of forecasting change. It means that traditional approaches to strategy formulation based on forecasting must be abandoned in favour of strategic management approaches that combine a clear sense of direction based on vision and mission, with the flexibility to respond to and take advantage of the unexpected.

Despite this turbulence and uncertainty, the principles of strategic analysis are critical in guiding the quest for competitive advantage in emerging industries. Key issues include:

- whether an innovation has the potential to confer sustainable competitive advantage
- the relative merits of alternative strategies for exploiting an innovation
- the factors that determine the comparative advantages of being a leader or a follower in innovation.

The key to successful innovation is not resource allocation decisions, but creating the structure, integration mechanisms and organisational climate conducive to innovation. Strategies aimed at the exploitation of innovation, choices of whether to be a leader or a follower and the management of risk must take careful account of organisational characteristics.

Emerging industries also reveal some of the dilemmas that are a critical feature of strategic management in complex organisations and complex business environments. For example, emerging industries are difficult to predict, yet some investments in technology have time horizons of a decade or more, for example, LCD televisions. Successful strategies must be responsive to changing market conditions, but successful strategies also require long-term commitment. The fundamental dilemma is that innovation is an unpredictable process that requires creating a nurturing organisational context, whereas strategy is about resource-allocation decisions.

The increasing pace of technological change and intensifying international competition suggest that the advanced, industrialised countries will be forced to rely increasingly on their technological capabilities as the basis for international competitiveness. Strategies for promoting innovation and managing technology will become more important in the future.

Strategic innovation at the growth stage

Innovation is not easy, and it is often expensive. Although in some heavy industries — steel, textiles, food processing, insurance and hotels — research and development (R&D) expenditure is below 1 per cent of sales revenue, in manufacturing as a whole just three sectors — computers and electronics, pharmaceuticals, and aerospace — account for more than half of research and development spending.[37]

At the early growth stage of a company, the pressure of competition and the opportunities for technology-based advantage create impetus for innovation in competitive strategy. While product and process innovation is definitely important, it is possible that there is another phase of innovation — **strategic innovation** — which becomes most prominent once product and process innovation have begun to develop.

Imagine what will happen when most competitors have started to explore similar technologies — the initial competitive advantage enjoyed by a company at the introduction stage will be eroded later when it intends to grow further. Strategic innovation will then become important for competition.

Strategic innovation may also result from redefining markets and market segments.[38] This may involve the following.

- *Embracing new customer groups.* The ability to break away from conventional wisdom and establish a unique positioning or novel form of differentiation may be critical in mature industries. This is particularly important in finding new customers. For example, Sony, through its product, the PlayStation 4 console, has extended video gaming from teenage boys to girls, adults and retirees.
- *Adding products and services that perform new but related functions.* Many of the innovative forms of differentiation involve the creation of entirely new customer experiences. Some companies go beyond providing a product or service that meets a clearly defined customer need and involve their customers in a process that engages them at the emotional, intellectual, or even spiritual, level.[39]

Embracing new customer groups and adding new products and services can be done by adopting a blue ocean strategy.[40]

Dynamic contexts encourage organisations to seize opportunities that arise with changes in technology and demand through **entrepreneurial orientation**, the strategic process by which organisations identify new opportunities and implement entrepreneurial actions.[41]

Following an entrepreneurial orientation approach, Chinese manufacturers have adapted the tightly integrated product architecture of Japanese motorcycle manufacturers by outsourcing to local suppliers and taking a more flexible and modular approach. In prescribing to suppliers only the design blueprints and specifying broad parameters, this left local innovators and manufacturers to design their own components and subsystems. Through improvisation, local manufacturers then used 'process networks' to mobilise dozens of specialised companies to modularise production in parallel. As such, detailed design drawings of components and subsystems are therefore irrelevant. Rather, suppliers improvise within broad constraints, take collective responsibility for the detailed design of components and subsystems and rapidly cut costs and improve quality.

This has enabled China to make rapid gains in export markets, where they now account for half of global motorcycle production. The 'blowback' for Japanese manufacturers has been immense — for example, in Vietnam, Honda's share of exports fell from 90 per cent to 30 per cent against the popularity of Chinese motorcycle products. What Chinese manufacturers have done through production modularity is change the rules of the game as Gary Hamel and CK Prahalad talked about in their article 'Strategic Intent' HBR (1989).[42] While an advanced country such as Japan might complain about Chinese manufacturers copying their designs, this approach to strategic innovation is about encouraging local innovation at the component and subsystem level at a fraction of the cost of the resource allocations used in traditional designs. Similarly, in the apparel industry in Hong Kong, the experiences of Li & Fung testify to the importance of the second aspect of strategic innovation: process networks. Li & Fung have developed a network of 7500 specialised businesses as partners who create customised supply for each new apparel line. These 'process orchestrators' decide which companies will participate in the network, what the party's role will be, and guarantee performance for a fair price.[43] From a strategic innovation perspective, mobilised process networks require unique performance parameters, access to reliable suppliers, and ways to reduce the cost of interaction among network participants. So, why are production-driven modularity and process-driven networks important? The answer is because they potentially disintegrate vertically by outsourcing the innovation entirely, effectively turning traditionally-designed resource components on their head. In turn, emerging economies can take advantage of these dispersed aspects of production and networks by developing their own products and exporting them to developed countries (the blowback effect).

Competitive advantage in mature industries

An analysis of the industry life cycle suggests that maturity has two principal implications for competitive advantage: first, it tends to reduce the number of opportunities for establishing competitive advantage; second, it shifts these opportunities from differentiation-based factors to cost-based factors.

Diminishing opportunities for sustainable competitive advantage in mature industries stem from:

- less scope for differentiation advantage resulting from increased buyer knowledge, product standardisation and less product innovation
- diffusion of process technology, which means that cost advantages based on superior processes or more advanced capital equipment methods are difficult to obtain and sustain; once a cost advantage is established, it is vulnerable to exchange rate movements and the emergence of low-cost overseas competitors
- a highly developed industry infrastructure together with the presence of powerful distributors, which makes it easier to attack established companies that occupy particular strategic niches.

This trend towards deteriorating industry profitability is a constant threat in mature industries. As rivalry encourages overinvestment in capacity, international competition increases and differentiation is undermined by commoditisation, attaining a competitive advantage becomes essential to achieving positive economic profits.

Cost advantage

Cost is the overwhelmingly important key success factor in most mature industries. What are the primary sources of low cost? Three cost factors tend to be especially important.

1. *Economies of scale.* In capital-intensive industries, or where advertising, distribution or new product development is an important element of total cost, economies of scale are important sources of intercompany cost differences. The significance of scale economies in mature industries is indicated by the fact that the association between profitability and market share is stronger in mature industries than in emerging industries.[44]
2. *Low-cost inputs.* Where small competitors are successful in undercutting the prices of market leaders in mature industries, it is frequently through their access to low-cost inputs. Established companies can become locked into high salaries and benefits, inefficient working practices, and bloated overheads inherited from more prosperous times. New entrants into mature industries may gain cost advantages by acquiring plant and equipment at bargain-basement levels and by cutting labour costs. The acquisition of retailers, hotels, hospital groups and chemical companies by private equity funds has been motivated in part by the attractions of substituting low-cost debt for high-cost equity.[45]
3. *Low overheads.* Some of the most profitable companies in mature industries tend to be those that have achieved the most substantial reductions in overhead costs. In retailing, the Coles Group in Australia is persistent in its parsimonious approach to lowering overhead costs.

Segment and customer selection

Sluggish demand growth, lack of product differentiation, and international competition tend to depress the profitability of mature industries. Yet, even unattractive industries may offer attractive niche markets with strong growth of demand, few competitors, and abundant potential for differentiation. As a result, segment selection can be a key determinant of differences in the performance of companies within the same industry.

In the car industry, there is a constant quest to escape competition by creating new market segments with 'crossover' vehicles that span existing segments. Opportunities for establishing new segments can arise from the strategies of market leaders. The more that incumbents focus on the mass market, the more likely it is that new entrants can carve out new market niches by supplying under-served customer needs.[46]

The logic of segment focus implies further disaggregation of markets — down to the level of the individual customer. Information technology permits new approaches to customer relationship management (CRM), making it possible to analyse individual characteristics and preferences, identify individual customers' profit contribution to the company, and organise marketing around individualised, integrated approaches to customers. Banks, supermarkets, credit card companies and hotels increasingly use transaction data to identify their most attractive customers and those that are a drag on profitability. The next possible step in this process is to go beyond customer selection to actively target more attractive customers and transform less valuable customers into more valuable customers.

The quest for differentiation

Cost leadership is difficult to sustain, particularly in the face of international competition. Hence, differentiating to attain some insulation from the rigours of price competition is particularly attractive in mature industries. The problem is that the trend toward commoditisation narrows the scope for differentiation and reduces customer willingness to pay a premium for differentiation. Two examples are listed here.

1. In the domestic appliances industry, companies' investments in differentiation through product innovation, quality and brand reputation have generated disappointing returns. Vigorous competition, price-sensitive customers and strong, aggressive retailers have limited the price premium that differentiation will support.
2. Attempts by airlines to gain competitive advantage through offering more legroom, providing superior in-flight entertainment and achieving superior punctuality have met little market response from consumers. The only effective differentiators appear to be frequent flyer programs and services offered to first- and business-class travellers.

Standardisation of the physical attributes of a product and convergence of consumer preferences constrain, but do not eliminate, opportunities for meaningful and profitable differentiation. In consumer goods, maturity often means a shift from physical differentiation to image differentiation. Entrenched consumer loyalties to specific brands of cola or cigarettes are a tribute to the capacity of brand promotion over long periods of time to create distinct images among near-identical products.

Rejuvenation represents a formidable challenge to a mature enterprise. Resistance to innovation and renewal arises not just from entrenched structures and systems but also from the propensity for managers to be trapped within their industry's conventional thinking about key success factors and business practices. Some companies are able to adapt better than others.

Strategy implementation in mature industries: structure, systems and style

If the key to success in mature industries is achieving operational efficiency and reconciling this with innovation and customer responsiveness, achieving competitive advantage in mature businesses requires implementing structures, systems and management styles that can mesh these multiple performance goals.

If maturity implies greater environmental stability, slower technological change and an emphasis on cost efficiency, what types of organisation and management approaches are called for? The conventional prescription for stable environments was 'mechanistic' organisations characterised by centralisation, well-defined roles and predominantly vertical communication.[47]

Efficiency of a mature company can be achieved through standardised routines, division of labour and close management control based on bureaucratic principles. Division of labour extends to management as well as operatives — high levels of vertical and horizontal specialisation are typical among managers. Vertical specialisation is evident in the concentration of strategy formulation at the apex of the hierarchy, while middle and junior management supervise and administer through the application of standardised rules and procedures. Horizontal specialisation takes the form of functional structures.

Strategies for declining industries

The transition from maturity to decline can be a result of technological substitution (e.g. typewriters and railways), changes in consumer preferences (men's suits), demographic shifts (baby products in Australia where the birth rate is declining) or foreign competition (computers from Japan and the United States). Shrinking market demand gives rise to acute strategic issues. Among the key features of declining industries are:
• excess capacity

- lack of technical change (reflected in a lack of new product introduction and stability of process technology)
- a declining number of competitors, but some entry as new companies acquire the assets of exiting companies cheaply
- high average age of both physical and human resources
- aggressive price competition.

Some declining industries can still earn surprisingly high profits. These include electronic vacuum tubes, cigars and leather tanning. However, elsewhere — notably in prepared baby foods, rayon and meat processing — decline has been accompanied by aggressive price competition, company failures and instability.[48]

What determines whether or not a declining industry becomes a competitive blood-bath? Two factors are critical: the balance between capacity and output; and the nature of the demand for the product.

Adjusting capacity to declining demand

The smooth adjustment of industry capacity to declining demand is the key to stability and profitability during the decline phase. In industries where capacity exits from the industry in an orderly fashion, decline can occur without trauma. Where substantial excess capacity persists, as has already occurred in some industries in Asia–Pacific economies, such as shipbuilding in Japan and Korea, and the clothing and footwear industry in Australia, the potential exists for destructive competition. The ease with which capacity adjusts to declining demand depends on the following factors.

- *The predictability of decline.* If decline can be forecast, it is more likely that companies can plan for it. The decline of traditional photography with the advent of digital imaging was anticipated and planned for by most companies. The more cyclical and volatile the demand, the more difficult it is for companies to perceive the trend of demand even after the onset of decline.
- *Barriers to exit.* Barriers to exit impede the exit of capacity from an industry. The major barriers are as follows.
  - *Durable and specialised assets.* Just as capital requirements impose a barrier to entry into an industry, those same investments also discourage exit. The longer they last and the fewer the opportunities for using those assets in another industry, the more companies are tied to that particular industry.
  - *Costs incurred in plant closure.* Apart from the accounting costs of writing off assets, substantial cash costs may be incurred in redundancy payments to employees, compensation for broken contacts with customers and suppliers, dismantling the plant, and environmental clean-up.
  - *Managerial commitment.* In addition to financial considerations, companies may be reluctant to close plants for a variety of emotional and moral reasons. Resistance to plant closure and divestment arises from pride in company traditions and reputation, managers' unwillingness to accept failure, and loyalties to employees and the local community.
- *The strategies of the surviving companies.* The sooner companies recognise and address the problem of the decline, the more likely it is that independent and collective action can achieve capacity reduction. Stronger companies in the industry can facilitate the exit of weaker companies by offering to acquire their plants and take over their after-sales service commitments.

The nature of declining demand

Where a market is segmented, the general pattern of decline can obscure the existence of pockets of demand that are not only comparatively resilient, but also price inelastic. For example, despite the obsolescence of vacuum tubes after the adoption of transistors, GTE Sylvania and General Electric earned excellent profits supplying vacuum tubes to the replacement and military markets.[49] In fountain pens, survivors in the quality pen segment such as Cross and Mont Blanc have achieved steady sales and high margins through appealing to high-income professionals and executives. Despite overall decline of the cigar market, quality cigars have benefited from strong demand and attractive margins.

Choosing the most appropriate strategy requires a careful assessment of the profit potential of the industry and the competitive position of the company. Harrigan and Porter[50] pose four key questions.

1. Can the structure of the industry support a hospitable, potentially profitable decline phase?
2. What are the exit barriers that each significant competitor faces?
3. Do your company strengths fit the remaining pockets of demand?
4. What are your competitors' strengths in these pockets? How can their exit barriers be overcome?

Selecting an appropriate strategy requires matching the opportunities remaining in the industry to the company's competitive position.

Beyond bureaucracy in mature and declining industries

The past two decades have seen growing unpopularity of bureaucratic approaches to management, especially in mature and declining industries. Factors contributing to this trend include the following.

- *Increased environmental turbulence.* Bureaucracy is conducive to efficiency in stable environments. However, the centralised, structured organisation cannot readily adapt to change. Achieving flexibility to respond to external change requires greater decentralisation, less specialisation and looser controls.
- *Increased emphasis on innovation.* The organisational structure, control systems, management style and interpersonal relationships conducive to efficiency are likely to hinder innovation. As mature enterprises sought new opportunities for competitive advantage, so the disadvantages of formalised, efficiency-oriented organisations became increasingly apparent.
- *New process technology.* The efficiency advantages of bureaucratised organisations arise from the technical virtues of highly specialised, systematised production methods. As automation displaces labour-intensive, assembly-line manufacturing techniques, there is less need for an elaborate division of labour and greater need for job flexibility. At the same time, the electronic revolution in the office is displacing the administrative bureaucracy that control and information systems once required.

Companies in mature industries have undergone substantial adjustment over the past decade. Among large, long-established corporations management hierarchies have been pruned, decision making decentralised and accelerated, and more open communication and flexible collaboration fostered. The trend began in North America, spread to continental Europe, and is now evident in Australia, Japan and Korea. The changes are apparent in:

- strategic decision processes that increase the role of business-level managers and reduce the role of corporate management; an emphasis on the strategy formulation process as more important than strategic plans per se
- a shifting of decision-making power to the business level accompanied by shrinking corporate staffs
- less emphasis on economies of large-scale production and increased responsiveness to customer requirements together with greater flexibility in responding to changes in the marketplace
- increased emphasis on teamwork as a basis for organising separate activities to improve interfunctional cooperation and responsiveness to external requirements
- wider use of profit incentives to motivate employees and less emphasis on controls and supervision.

Despite the changes, the primary emphasis on cost efficiency remains. However, the conditions for cost efficiency have changed. The most powerful force for organisational change in mature industries has been the inability of highly structured, centralised organisations to maintain their cost efficiency in an increasingly turbulent business environment. By relying more on performance targets and less on approvals and committees, the old corporate empires need to become more flexible and responsive while maintaining a strong focus on efficiency.

4.5 Competitive advantage at various levels of a company

LEARNING OBJECTIVE 4.5 Analyse various levels of strategy, describe how strategic advantage can be sustained at each level and explain how different kinds of strategies create competitive advantage.

Competitive advantage is considered the basis for superior company performance. A company has to nurture an evolving system of competitive advantages to carry it through competition and over time. What are the various possible types of such advantages at various levels of strategy? How can a company systematically analyse the multiple advantages it could possess and use them to achieve and maintain superior performance?

Answers to these questions can contribute to managers' knowledge about the nature and content of competitive advantage at different levels of organisations. Such knowledge can help managers nurture, sustain and renew their company's advantages more effectively through time.

In general, there are several levels of strategy associated with the strategic advantage of business organisations (as shown in figure 4.7).

- A *corporate-level strategy* defines the organisation's purpose and the type of businesses in which it plans to operate, providing the overarching direction for the organisation. It also considers the structure of the organisation.
- A *business-level strategy* is the blueprint that should enable an organisation to leverage its resources in order to differentiate itself from the competition within a particular line of business. If an organisation

only operates in one line of business, its corporate-level strategy and business-level strategy are effectively one and the same.

- A *functional-level strategy* serves to support the organisation's business-level strategy by providing direction for the appropriate short-term activities required by each functional area to meet the goals established in the business-level strategy.
- A *network-level strategy* helps the organisation to form alliances with other companies for seeking valuable resources and information.
- A *global-level strategy* provides an opportunity for the company to develop overseas markets, especially when local markets have matured.

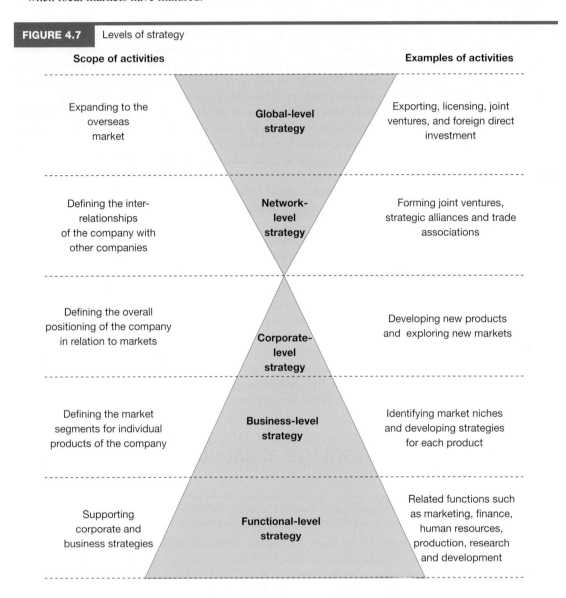

FIGURE 4.7 Levels of strategy

Scope of activities		Examples of activities
Expanding to the overseas market	**Global-level strategy**	Exporting, licensing, joint ventures, and foreign direct investment
Defining the inter-relationships of the company with other companies	**Network-level strategy**	Forming joint ventures, strategic alliances and trade associations
Defining the overall positioning of the company in relation to markets	**Corporate-level strategy**	Developing new products and exploring new markets
Defining the market segments for individual products of the company	**Business-level strategy**	Identifying market niches and developing strategies for each product
Supporting corporate and business strategies	**Functional-level strategy**	Related functions such as marketing, finance, human resources, production, research and development

Consequently, having properly aligned strategies at corporate, business, functional, network and global levels aids an organisation in its efforts to accomplish its goals, thereby strategically positioning itself to successfully compete within the marketplace. An organisation must view strategies for developing and managing its employees as a part of its overarching corporate-level strategy if it desires to have highly differentiated and efficient human capital in today's competitive, global environment.

Competitive advantage will always be established through one or more business-level strategies as well. Here, business-level strategies such as low cost or low-cost differentiation are required because, as discussed earlier, companies produce capabilities that attack cherished company positions. Other companies will always want to take market share away from those who possess it. They do this through different combinations of business-level strategy inputs such as low cost/high quality or more product differentiation by including and designing more features. As much as companies build in competitive advantage, this is frequently counter-attacked (as shown in figure 4.6). For example, the innovator might respond with another dose of business-level strategy by either adjusting prices, adding new features, lowering costs in production cycles and, if the innovator is a smaller business, perhaps focusing on a niche market to capture new business. In the chapter on business-level strategy and competitive positioning, we describe how these strategies unfold in different ways and how the value chain is one way of developing various responses to competitive attacks to existing products and services.

Competitive advantage at the network level

Companies cannot survive by themselves. They need at least suppliers and customers. Sometimes companies work together with other organisations to develop and enhance their competitive advantage. This type of inter-organisational cooperation is often done in the form of inter-organisational networks, which are informal collaborations that provide resource exchanges among these organisations to economise on production and information costs while maintaining flexibility.[51]

A **network strategy** is a cooperative strategy used by several companies to form multiple partnerships based on shared objectives. A network strategy can provide access to greater resources than the member organisations could access on their own. Network strategies are an alternative to vertical integration and diversification, and have become central to competitive success in fast-changing global markets.[52]

Resource exchange relationships are regarded as critical requirements of business organisations. The control and distribution of valuable resources is a major role played by inter-organisational networks, which facilitate the provision of valuable resources for the embryonic development of the new organisation up to its maturity. These networks can act as a resource to facilitate organisational development. It is viewed as a strategic mechanism to improve a company's competitive advantage through cost minimisation while maintaining flexibility, thus allowing companies to economise on information costs and accelerate technological innovation.

Types of network relationships

The relationships within a business network can be very complex and multilayered. In general, there are four basic types of network relationship.[53]
1. *Upstream vertical (supplier) relationships.* These are the relationships of a company with its suppliers that provide raw materials, parts, machinery and services to the company.
2. *Downstream vertical (buyer) relationships.* These are the relationships of a company with its buyers that purchase its products and services.
3. *Direct horizontal (industry insider) relationships.* These represent the relationships of a company with its competitors in the same industry.
4. *Indirect horizontal (industry outsider) relationships.* These are the company's relationships with companies outside its industry.

Leadership strategy in networks

A typical business network comprises one or a few leading participants, with most of the rest being smaller companies. There are two leadership strategies in networks.[54]
1. *Keystone strategy.* Keystone leaders typically exercise a system-wide role in the networks by setting the rules and standards of the business operations. However, a keystone leader tends not to become overly dominant and leaves room for other network participants to operate their businesses. Microsoft is a good example of the keystone profile. While it remains the most influential player in software provision, its market capitalisation as a percentage of this domain has never gone above 40 per cent of the whole industry.
2. *Dominator strategy.* A dominator is a leading company in a network, which tends to use its powerful position to extract as much value as possible from the network. Other smaller participants will eventually find the network unattractive. As a result of such domination, it will very likely diminish the attractiveness of the network to new entrants. Examples can be found in the microprocessor (Intel) and operating system (Microsoft) markets.

Companies that are not the leaders in their inter-organisational networks usually play the role of followers by participating in the majority of the network's activities in terms of the provision of differentiated products and services. However, they must be careful not to become too tightly linked to the network and limit their opportunities of further development in other business networks.

Success at the network level

Ever-increasing connectivity, interdependence of diverse organisations, technologies and institutions challenge managers to understand and apply new business models. The idea of understanding 'markets as networks'[55] was introduced to view the changes of companies' customer and supplier relationships within the broader context of deeper supplier networks, cooperative arrangements and competitive coalitions. According to Möller and Halinen, 'the competitive environment of firms is undergoing a fundamental change. Traditional markets are being rapidly replaced by networks'.[56] The biggest challenge of a successful network-level strategy is the combination of the internal and external competencies of the company in order to maximise the value gained from the business network. Participating companies will need to carefully consider the effective design and management of complex marketplaces in these networks.

From networks to business ecosystem

Many companies develop and expand their operations and distribution through building up their own business networks. A business ecosystem is a well-developed network of suppliers and support organisations operating within a particular business environment, which collaborate in an economic web of relationships with a powerful company as the centre of the network.[57] Such a system is very effective because it can attract a diverse set of specialised participants with a wide range of capabilities willing to make their own specific investments in the business network to further enhance its value.

When there is a well-established business ecosystem in an industry, new competitors will find difficulties in entering the market. A company's choice of ecosystem strategy is governed primarily by the nature of its business as well as the business environment in which it operates (the general level of turbulence and the complexity of its relationships with others in the ecosystem).

The ecosystem approach to business development is illustrated by the leading Chinese e-commerce company, Alibaba Group.[58] Alibaba has cultivated a successful business ecosystem through its website design and innovative collaboration with partners, creating new potential profit streams for itself and its partners.[59] Alibaba's ecosystem approach to business development will be discussed in more detail in the chapter on cooperative strategies and alliances.

Discrete and embedded organisations

While business networks obviously can help a company build up their competitive advantage, not every company chooses to be part of extended networks. There are organisational leaders who believe that companies should be primarily competitive in their relationships to all outside forces and they should remain independent and interact with other companies under market conditions. This view is described as the discrete organisation perspective.

Other organisational leaders believe that companies should build up more cooperative relationships with key organisations in their environment. They argue that companies can reap significant benefits by surrendering a part of their independence and developing close collaborative arrangements with a group of other organisations. This view is referred to as the embedded organisation perspective.

Remember that these two views are only extreme cases and most business organisations are between these two extremes. Sometimes businesses like to work with other companies in the form of networks, for instance, supplier cooperatives; at other times, they prefer to work alone. Therefore, the choice of perspective is a matter of strategic decision. Network strategies are further considered in the chapter on cooperative strategies and alliances.

Competitive advantage from a global perspective

During the second half of the twentieth century, most barriers to international trade were removed and many companies began pursuing global-level strategies to gain a competitive advantage. However, some industries benefit more from globalisation than do others, and some nations have some comparative advantages over other nations in certain industries. To create a successful global-level strategy, managers first must understand the nature of global industries and the dynamics of global competition.

Sources of competitive advantage from a global-level strategy

A well-designed global-level strategy can help a company to gain a competitive advantage. This advantage is based on the following objectives of a global-level strategy.

- *Extended customer base.* A company's customer base is limited by the population and production capacity of industries in its home country. By exploring the global market, a company can significantly extend its customer base.
- *Innovation and learning.* A company can enhance first-mover advantage and become the only provider of a new product to a foreign market. It can also broaden learning opportunities due to the diversity of operating environments in other countries.
- *Efficiency in operations.* A global strategy can be built on the economies of scale from access to more customers and markets. A company can take advantage of another country's resources, including labour, raw materials and expertise.
- *Flexibility.* A company can enhance its operational flexibility by shifting production or markets to another country. It can also extend the product life cycle so that older products can be sold in less-developed countries.

In order to achieve these objectives, a company pursuing an international strategy can build on the following sources of competitive advantage.[60]

- *National differences.* Expanding into overseas markets can allow a company to exploit factor cost differences between countries. There are also learning and development opportunities arising from differences in management and organisation in different countries.
- *Scale economies.* The expansion into overseas markets provides an opportunity to achieve a more efficient production scale. Cost reduction is thus possible and the company can become even more competitive in offering cheaper products with equivalent quality in the home market.
- *Scope economies.* A company can enhance product diversification in the global market and, therefore, can share investment and costs among its overseas operations and develop shared learning across different activities.

Types of global-level strategies

In this era of globalisation, all companies have to be aware of global competition, even if they are not planning to expand their operation outside their home market. Even a local company has to understand global-level strategies used by multinational corporations whose penetration of a local market will change the competitive dynamics and capture a market share from local companies.

Nippon Express is an example of a global company that adapts its procurement and logistics strategies to each market. Nippon Express is a Japanese logistics company that operates a global network covering the key regions of Japan, the Americas and Europe, East Asia and South Asia/Oceania, with further potential for growth.[61] This highly diversified global company includes rail, truck, marine, warehousing, air, heavy haulage and construction and incidental operations. Nippon Express divides its market into various emerging, growth and mature markets in order to obtain competitive advantage within an industry with highly competitive product life cycles and establish a competitive advantage in each market with unique characteristics. For example, in Japan where it is headquartered, the company is more likely to focus on business solutions offering quality and cost competitiveness since other companies are equally sophisticated in their ability to match resource inputs. Nippon creates capabilities that enable competitive advantage in target markets with unique product/service and cost offerings and this will vary according to Nippon's size, breadth of geographic coverage, and actual capability-enhancing advantage. These unique business-level strategies and their impact on competitive advantage are discussed in the chapter on business-level strategy and competitive positioning, and in the chapter on global strategies and multinational corporation we expand upon specific global strategies and how different company structures are often necessary for their implementation. So, a standardisation strategy of taking a homegrown product(s) in design, engineering and manufacturing to mass markets (e.g. Honda cars) is different from a global adaptation strategy of adapting products to suit the particular characteristics of different markets. For this chapter, our key focus has been on how competitive advantage is achieved in different markets. Another point is that global standardisation may require a global matrix structure and global adaptation of a multinational networked structure (see also the chapter on strategic evaluation, implementation, structure and control for an explanation).

Creating competitive advantage in global markets is most likely related more to corporate strategy initially, until a company is established. Nippon Express manages its businesses as related strategic business units (see the chapter on corporate-level strategy) but this would not be so if they start acquiring or setting up new unrelated businesses. For Nippon Express, strategies used in market development are related since they are not moving away from their core businesses of distribution and procurement. However, unrelated corporate strategies include expansion into new unrelated markets, away from the company's existing business. Figure 4.8 illustrates some key strategies to create competitive advantage in unrelated industries. For instance, temporary (in some cases, permanent) advantage is gained by transferring existing capabilities to new markets. Organisations can exploit the new market when they are more efficient than those that currently exist in that market. That is, they use their capabilities to exploit the market opportunities. Similarly, they can use a range of product and service capabilities across their product portfolios of existing businesses to fend off rival counterattacks. Most assuredly, when new companies seek to enter a new market, they will receive a counterattack from existing ones since the latter do not want to lose established market share positions.

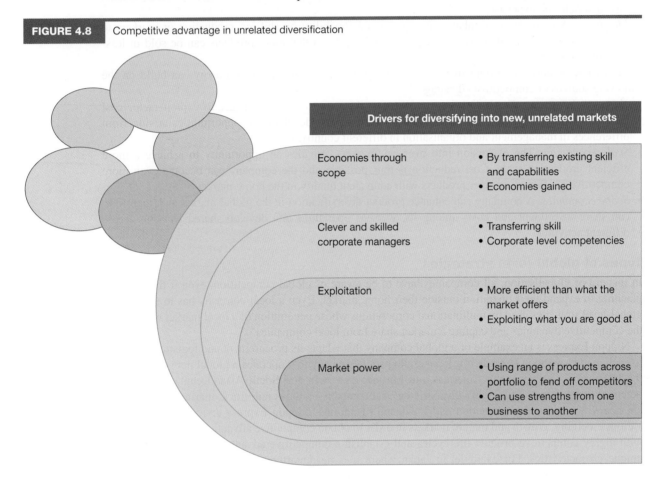

FIGURE 4.8 Competitive advantage in unrelated diversification

Developing global market entry methods

An important part of a global-level strategy is the method that the company will use to enter the foreign markets. There are four possible methods of global market entry.

1. *Exporting.* There are two ways to export: selling products or services directly to an international company or customer, or indirectly by using export agents or intermediaries that include commissioned agents, distributors and export or trading companies.
2. *Licensing (includes franchising).* Licensing is a contractual arrangement that gives rights to operate under another's trade mark name and using their business processes. In return, the trade mark owner receives marketing benefits and earns royalties on the sale of that product or service.
3. *Joint venture.* A joint venture with an already established overseas business may be the most effective way to gain entry into a foreign market. These are local businesses that know the market and have a distribution framework in place, meaning less capital is required.
4. *Foreign direct investment.* Foreign direct investment requires establishing a company's own facility under its direct supervision. The cost is high and the company has to bear all the risks of the operations in the overseas subsidiaries.

SUMMARY

Making money in business requires establishing and sustaining competitive advantage, which depends critically on the presence of some imperfection in the competitive process. Under perfect competition, profits are transitory. The relationship between strategies and competitive advantage needs to be considered at different levels, such as corporate, business and functional, as well as network and global levels. Competitive advantage can also be considered further in terms of industry life cycle and levels of strategies. Various stages in the industry life cycle — the introduction, growth, mature and declining stages — present challenging environments for the formulation and implementation of business strategies.

To compete in different markets and to pursue different levels of strategies, important and valuable resources and capabilities are required. There is a clear need for accessing resources and information, reducing production and transaction costs, and adopting appropriate strategies. Competitive advantage is the base on which companies can compete in the market.

KEY TERMS

competitive advantage A characteristic, feature or opportunity that an organisation possesses that will make it more attractive than its competitors.

entrepreneurial orientation The strategic process by which organisations identify new opportunities and implement entrepreneurial actions.

fast-cycle markets Products and innovations that cannot be protected because of intense and rapid competitive moves that erode and destroy competitive advantage.

first-mover The initial occupant of a strategic position or niche gains access to resources and capabilities that a follower cannot match.

industry life cycle The passage of an industry through the stages of introduction, growth, maturity and decline.

network strategy A cooperative strategy used by several companies to form multiple partnerships based on shared objectives.

slow-cycle markets Products and innovations that have high barriers to competitive imitation protecting an organisation's strategic advantage over time.

standard-cycle markets Products and innovations that have measured barriers to competitive imitation protecting an organisation's strategic advantage over time.

strategic innovation The development of new strategies of offering new products or services that will generate significant new value for customers and have the potential to change market demand.

SELF-STUDY QUESTIONS

1 What is competitive advantage? How can a company build its competitive advantage?
2 Describe the different stages of industry development.
3 How can competitive advantage be developed through strategic innovation?
4 Explain the concept of business ecosystems.

DISCUSSION QUESTIONS

1 Figure 4.1 implies that stable industries in which companies have similar resources and capabilities offer less opportunity for competitive advantage than industries where change is rapid and companies are heterogeneous. Select examples of these two types of industry, and look for any evidence that intercompany profit differences are wider in dynamic, heterogeneous industries than in stable, homogeneous industries.
2 Businesses in fast-cycle markets will have different differentiation features and influences than those in standard-cycle markets. List some of the features in each and discuss the differences.
3 Bunnings, the leading retailer of home improvement and outdoor living products in Australia and New Zealand and a major supplier to project builders, commercial tradespeople and the housing industry, offers a wide variety of products at the lowest price. While Bunnings has been successful

in Australia and New Zealand, its attempt to compete in Britain's home improvement sector was costly and disastrous. Bunnings's entry to the UK was implemented through the acquisition of Homebase, an established business in Britain's home improvement sector, to lower the risk. What are the principal challenges of a low-cost strategy in the home improvement sector? Design a low-cost strategy for a company operating in this sector entering another market, for example, China, India, Germany.

4 Ever since the Swiss company Nestlé created a new market segment by developing an innovative system for premium portioned coffee under the Nespresso brand, it has seen a remarkable growth in the global coffee market. How would you describe the stage of the premium coffee industry and what recommendations would you give to Nespresso to sustain their competitive advantage?

5 Consider the changes that have occurred in a comparatively new industry (e.g. wireless communications, video game consoles, medical diagnostic imaging, PDAs, online auctions, bottled water, courier delivery services). To what extent has the evolution of the industry followed the pattern predicted by the industry life cycle model? At what stage of development is the industry today? How is the industry likely to evolve in the future?

6 Department stores (e.g. Myer stores in Australia capital cities, Robinsons in Malaysia and Singapore, Takashimaya in Singapore) are facing increasing competition from specialised chain retailers (e.g. British India in Malaysia and Singapore) and discount stores (e.g. Tesco in Australia). What innovative strategies might department stores adopt to revitalise their competitiveness?

EXERCISES

1 Identify at least five products that you purchased in the past week. Are the companies that produce these products market leaders or followers? At which stages of industry life cycle are these five products? Identify at least two competitors of each of these five products and try to explain how they compete with each other.

2 Imagine that you are the CEO of a commercial bank. Your bank has recently considered expanding its business both locally and internationally. You are required to organise a consultative meeting with the functional managers of various departments such as the loans, marketing and accounting departments. Prepare a short speech with a view to convincing these functional managers to work more efficiently and effectively with you.

3 Form a small group with two or three peers. Select a newspaper or academic article that discusses how a certain company responded to drastic changes in the market. Why and how did this company manage to change its strategies? Identify some of the possible competitive advantages that this company tries to explore or maintain.

4 Perform an online search of some major competitors in a specific industry (e.g. garments, toys or banking). How do these companies compete in the selected industry? What are the possible competitive advantages each player has?

5 Visit Alibaba Group's website (www.alibaba.com) and examine the company's global-level strategies. List as many competitive advantages as you can see related to business-level strategy (such as differentiation and low cost) versus corporate-level strategy (such as new products into new markets). What kind of resource inputs exist in the group? How does the company leverage its capabilities to create new competitive advantage? Draw up a table with two columns — one with existing capabilities, the other with new capabilities — and compare the two. What has this told you about competitive advantage?

6 Explore the website of the National Australia Bank (NAB), www.nab.com.au. What does this website tell about the bank's business and strategy, especially its personal and business banking operations? Now, compare this site with that of the Commonwealth Bank of Australia, www.commbank.com.au. How do these two banks differ and in what ways are they similar?

7 Go to the website of the World Economic Forum, www.weforum.org, and look for its Global Competitiveness Report. Identify two countries (e.g. Australia and Japan) and compare them based on the 12 pillars of competitiveness as proposed in the report. Based on these 12 pillars, how should each of the countries you've selected improve their competitiveness?

FURTHER READING

Barney, J 2007, *Gaining and sustaining competitive advantage,* 3rd edn, Prentice-Hall.

Barney, JB 2012, 'Purchasing, supply chain management and sustained competitive advantage: the relevance of resource-based theory', *Journal of Supply Chain Management,* vol. 48, no. 2, 3–6.

Chen, MJ, Lin, HC & Michel, JG 2010, 'Navigating in a hypercompetitive environment: the roles of action aggressiveness and TMT integration', *Strategic Management Journal,* vol. 31, no. 13, 1410–1430.

Chesbrough, H, Lettl, C & Ritter, T 2018, 'Value creation and value capture in open innovation', Journal of Product innovation Management, vol. 35, no. 6, 930–938.

Di Pietro, L, Edvardsson, B, Reynoso, J, Renzi, MF, Toni, M & Mugion, RG 2018, 'A scaling up framework for innovative service ecosystems: lessons from Eataly and KidZania', Journal of Service Management, vol. 29, no. 1, 146-175.

Kim, W Chan & Mauborgne, R 2005, *Blue ocean strategy: how to create uncontested market space and make competition irrelevant,* Harvard Business Press.

Oh, D-S, Phillios, F, Park, S & Lee, E 2016, 'Innovation ecosystems: a critical examination', *Technovation,* vol. 54 (C), 1–6.

Sirmon, DG, Hitt, MA & Arregle, JL 2010, 'The dynamic interplay of capability strengths and weaknesses: investigating the bases of temporary competitive advantage', *Strategic Management Journal,* vol. 31, no. 13, 1386–1409.

ENDNOTES

1. www.skyscanner.com.au.
2. SIA Annual Report 2012/13.
3. L Heracleous and J Wirtz, 'Singapore Airlines' balancing act', *Harvard Business Review*, July–August 2010, 145–9.
4. J Burton, 'Singapore Airlines sees first full-year loss', *Financial Times*, 30 July 2009.
5. A Daga and J Freed, 'Singapore Airlines latest to get massive rescue amid coronavirus crisis', *yahoo!finance,* 26 March 2020, https://au.finance.yahoo.com/news/singapore-airlines-secures-13-billion-234530177.html.
6. 'Singapore Airlines Latest to Get Massive Rescue Amid . . .', NYTimes, 27 March 2020, www.nytimes.com/reuters/2020/03/27/business/27reuters-health-coronavirus-airlines.html
7. Theme of the Atlanta Competitive Advantage Conference 2009 Abstracting e-Journal, conference papers available at www.ssrn.com.
8. Richard Rumelt argues that competitive advantage lacks a clear and consistent definition, 'What in the world is competitive advantage', Policy Working Paper 2003–105, Anderson School, UCLA, August 2003.
9. According to Edith Penrose, 'Entrepreneurial activity involves identifying opportunities within the economic system', *Theory of the growth of the firm*, Oxford: Blackwell, 1959.
10. H Shaughnessy, 'Why Amazon succeeds', *Forbes,* 2012, www.forbes.com/sites/haydnshaughnessy/2012/04/29/why-amazon-succeeds/#79a89a00385a.
11. GG Dess and GT Lumkin, 'The role of entrepreneurial orientation in stimulating effective corporate entrepreneurship', *Academy of Management Perspectives*, vol. 19, no. 1, 2005, 147–156.
12. J Wiklund and D Shepherd, 'Knowledge-based resources, entrepreneurial orientation, and the performance of small and medium-sized businesses', *Strategic Management Journal*, vol. 24, no. 3, 2003, 1307–1314.
13. H Chesbrough and M Bogers, 'Clarifying an emerging paradigm for understanding innovation', in H Chesbrough, W Vanhaverbeke and J West, *New frontiers in open innovation*, Oxford: Oxford University Press, 2014, 3–28.
14. G Hamel, 'The why, what, and how of management innovation', *Harvard Business Review*, February 2006, 72–84.
15. W Chan Kim and R Mauborgne, 'Blue ocean strategy', *Harvard Business Review*, October 2004.
16. McKinsey & Company, www.mckinsey.com.
17. For an analysis of first-mover advantage, see M Lieberman and D Montgomery, 'First-mover advantages', *Strategic Management Journal*, vol. 9, 1988, 41–58; and M Lieberman and D Montgomery, 'First-mover (dis)advantages: retrospective and link with the resource-based view', *Strategic Management Journal*, vol. 19, 1998, 1111–1125.
18. D Harhoff and J von Heppel, 'Profiting from voluntary information spillovers: how users benefit by freely revealing their innovations', *Research Policy*, vol. 32, 2003, 1753–1769.
19. GP De-Almeida and PB Zemsky, 'Some like it free: innovators' strategic use of disclosure to slow down competition', *Strategic Management Journal*, vol. 33, no. 7, 2012, 773–793.
20. Australian Independent Financial Advisers 2006, The common sense truth about managed funds, www.travismorien.com.
21. SN Neftci, 'Naive trading rules in financial markets and Wilner-Kolmogorov prediction theory: a study of technical analysis', *Journal of Business*, vol. 64, 1991, 549–571.
22. W De Bondt and R Thaler, 'Does the stock market overreact?', *Journal of Finance*, vol. 42, 1985, 793–805.
23. JB Barney, 'Firm resources and sustained competitive advantage', *Journal of Management*, vol. 17, 1991, 99–120.
24. DG Sirmon, MA Hitt, JL Arregle and J Tochman Campbell, 'The dynamic interplay of capability strengths and weaknesses: investigating the bases of temporary competitive advantage', *Strategic Management Journal*, vol. 31, no. 13, 2010, 1386–1409.
25. ibid.
26. ibid., p. 1402.
27. D Leonard-Barton, 'Core capabilities and core rigidities: a paradox in managing new product development', *Strategic Management Journal*, vol. 13, 1992, 111–125.

28. Adapted from DG Sirmon, MA Hitt and JL Arregle, 'The dynamic interplay of capability strengths and weaknesses: investigating the bases of temporary competitive advantage', *Strategic Management Journal*, vol. 31, 2010, 1386–1409.

29. SK McEvily, S Das and K McCabe, 'Avoiding competence substitution through knowledge sharing', *Academy of Management Review*, vol. 25, 2000, 294–311.

30. For early work on the product life cycle, see EM Rogers, *The diffusion of innovations*, New York: Free Press, 1962; T Levitt, 'Exploit the product life cycle',*Harvard Business Review*, November–December 1965, 81–94; G Day, 'The product life cycle: analysis and applications', *Journal of Marketing*, vol. 45, Autumn 1981, 60–67.

31. op. cit., note 20.

32. RD Aveni, *Hypercompetition: managing the dynamics of strategic maneuvering*, New York: Free Press, 1994.

33. 'When Apple's Lawsuits get more coverage than Apple's Products', Technighttowl.com, 14 February 2012.

34. ibid.

35. MJ Chen, HC Lin and JG Michel, 'Navigating in a hypercompetitive environment: the roles of action aggressiveness and TMT integration', *Strategic Management Journal*, vol. 31, 2010, 1410–1430.

36. Adapted from LC Macmillan, 'Controlling competitive dynamics by taking strategic initiative', *Academy of Management Executive*, vol. 2, 1988, 111–118.

37. National Science Foundation, Research and development in industry: 2002, www.nsf.gov.

38. D Abell, *Managing with dual strategies*, New York: Free Press, 1993, 75–78.

39. BJ Pine and J Gilmore, 'Welcome to the Experience Economy', *Harvard Business Review*, July–August 1998, 97–105.

40. W Chan Kim and R Mauborgne, *Blue ocean strategy: how to create uncontested market space and make competition irrelevant*, Harvard Business Press, 2005.

41. Dess and Lumkin, op. cit.

42. See CK Prahalad and G Hamel, *Strategic Intent*. The authors in this article talk about how some companies do not play by the existing rules of the industry. In this case, Chinese motorcycle manufacturers have invented their own system of production which is different to the one imposed on them initially by Japanese producers.

43. ibid, note 26.

44. RD Buzzell and BT Gale, *The PIMS Principles*, New York: Free Press, 1987, p. 279.

45. 'European leveraged buy-outs', *The Economist*, 10 August 2006.

46. GR Carroll and A Swaminathan, 'Why the microbrewery movement? Organizational dynamics of resource partitioning in the American brewing industry', *American Journal of Sociology*, vol. 106, 2000, 715–762; C Boone, GR Carroll, and A van Witteloostuijn, 'Resource distributions and market partitioning: Dutch Daily Newspapers 1964–94', *American Sociological Review*, vol. 67, 2002, 408–431.

47. T Burns and GM Stalker, *The management of innovation*, London: Tavistock Institute, 1961.

48. KR Harrigan, *Strategies for declining businesses*, Lexington, MA: DC Heath, 1980.

49. KR Harrigan, 'Strategic planning for endgame', *Long Range Planning*, vol. 15, 1982, 45–48.

50. KR Harrigan and ME Porter, 'End-game strategies for declining industries', *Harvard Business Review*, July–August 1983, 111–120.

51. H Hung, 'Formation and survival of new ventures: A path from interpersonal to inter-organisational networks', *International Small Business Journal*, vol. 24, 2006, 359–378.

52. R Gulati, N Norhia and A Zaheer, 'Strategic networks', *Strategic Management Journal*, vol. 21, no. 3, 2000, 203–215.

53. B De Wit and R Meyer, *Strategy: process, content, context*, 3rd edn, Thomson, 2004.

54. M Iansiti and R Levien, *The keystone advantage*, Harvard Business School Press, 2004.

55. L-G Mattsson, '"Relationship marketing" and the "markets-as-networks approach" — A comparative analysis of two evolving streams of research', Journal of Marketing Management, vol. 13, no. 5, 1997, 447–461.

56. K Möller and A Halinen, 'Business relationships and networks: managerial challenges of a network era', *Industrial Marketing Management*, vol. 28, no. 5, 1999, p. 413.

57. M Iansiti and R Levien, 'Strategy as ecology', *Harvard Business Review*, vol. 82, no. 3, March 2004, 68–78.

58. Interview of Kishore Biyani with IndiaKnowledge @Wharton. 'Retailer Kishore Biyani: "We Believe in Destroying What We Have Created"'. Retrieved from knowledge.wharton.upenn.edu, November 1, 2007.

59. P Williamson and MW Jingji, 'Alibaba Group's Taobao: from intermediary to ecosystem enabler'. In B De Wit, *Strategy: an international perspective*, 6th Edition, Cengage Learning, 2017.

60. CA Bartlett and G Sumantra, *Managing across borders: the transnational solution*, Harvard Business Press, 2002.

61. *Global Logistics Solutions*, Nippon Express, Corporate Brochure, 2011, www.nipponexpress.com.

ACKNOWLEDGEMENTS

Photo: © Fedor Selivanov / Shutterstock.com

CHAPTER 5

Business-level strategy and competitive positioning

LEARNING OBJECTIVES

After studying this chapter, you should be able to:

5.1 describe how cost advantage and differentiation are fundamentally different approaches to achieving a competitive advantage through business-level strategy

5.2 identify the basic sources of cost advantage in an industry and appreciate its potential for creating competitive advantage

5.3 explain how value chain analysis is used to understand cost advantage

5.4 identify the basic sources of differentiation, recognise its different forms and appreciate its potential for creating competitive advantage

5.5 explain how value chain analysis is used to understand differentiation advantage

5.6 understand a focus strategy and appreciate its potential for creating competitive advantage

5.7 understand how competitive advantage can be created by an integration of cost advantage and differentiation.

CSL Limited — cost advantage and differentiation via innovation

CSL Limited, one of the larger listed companies on the Australian Stock Exchange, is a global biotechnology firm involved in the discovery, development and commercialisation of medical products aimed at the treatment and prevention of serious diseases. Over time CSL has developed and marketed a wide range of products, including antivenoms against snake poison and vaccines for diseases such as influenza, polio and tetanus. The company was founded in 1916 in Victoria and its headquarters is still based in Melbourne. Since 1916 the firm has steadily grown, with the company truly becoming a global player after the acquisitions of

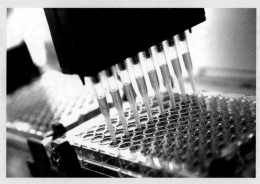

Aventis Behring, Nabi, Calimmune and parts of Novartis. To date, CSL still adheres to its original vision to 'save lives and protect the health of people who were stricken with a range of serious and chronic medical conditions'.[1] Not surprisingly, the company announced in February 2020 that they would join the fight against COVID-19, despite this type of virus not being within their typical range of expertise.[2]

Whereas innovation is naturally embedded in the DNA of most biotechnology companies, CSL aims to go beyond merely innovating their biotechnology products. One of the firm's most recent innovative initiatives is to incorporate artificial intelligence in its operations. The idea behind this move is that machine learning has the potential to allow CSL to more easily detect inefficiencies in its operations, leading to cost savings on both the research side and the manufacturing side of the business.[3] This potentially not only benefits CSL, but also doctors and patients, as earlier and more tailored medical interventions might be possible in the near future. In its 2018–19 annual report, the company confirmed its commitment by stating that artificial intelligence and data science are 'essential to CSL's future success'.[4]

CSL's innovation activities do not stop at developing and implementing artificial intelligence. The company is also busy experimenting with virtual reality in order to make its production processes more precise, quicker and more efficient. A practical example is that CSL has trialled employees wearing mixed reality glasses that map critical information on factory equipment, saving them time on the manufacturing floor. CSL is also critically reflecting on its impact on the natural environment by using innovation to reduce its ecological footprint. In Switzerland, for instance, one of the firm's plants has reengineered its operations so that its significant amount of wastewater is now used to generate about 20 per cent of the gas the plant needs.[5] As these examples show, the company appears to be using technological innovation to enhance its medical products, manufacturing processes and firm reputation, while also lowering the costs of its operations.

Introduction

As the scene setter illustrates, CSL's source of competitive advantage is based on its ability to innovate and develop medical products that are cutting-edge and reliable. For some industries, however, cost advantage is the predominant basis for competitive advantage — in commodities there is limited opportunity for competing on anything else. But even where competition focuses on product differentiation, intensifying competition has resulted in cost efficiency becoming a prerequisite for profitability. Some of the most dramatic examples of companies and industries being transformed through the pursuit of cost efficiency are in sectors where competition has increased sharply due to deregulation, such as airlines, telecommunications, banking and electrical power generation.

The CSL example also shows that the company is motivated to reduce its ecological footprint and enhance healthcare through the application of emerging technologies. At the same time, the new technology will enable the company to run their operations more cost effectively by optimising manufacturing processes and obtaining quicker approval for the commercial release of medical products. CSL's competitive advantage is therefore based both on the company's differentiation and cost advantage.

Every company has opportunities for differentiating its offering to customers, although the range of differentiation opportunities depends on the characteristics of the product. A vehicle or a restaurant offers greater potential for differentiation than cement, wheat or memory chips. These latter products are called 'commodities' precisely because they lack significant physical differentiation. Yet, even commodity products can be differentiated in ways that create customer value: 'Anything can be turned into a value-added product or service for a well-defined or newly created market,' claims Tom Peters.[6]

Companies can pursue both of these strategies — cost advantage and differentiation — on different, specific segments of the market by focusing on one or more specific customer groups via a focus strategy or a niche-oriented strategy. Earlier chapters explained how competitive advantage can be achieved via the external and internal characteristics of the company. This chapter will first discuss the primary business-level strategies that a company can use to exploit its competitive advantage and compete effectively in an industry.

5.1 Business-level strategies to achieve competitive advantage

LEARNING OBJECTIVE 5.1 Describe how cost advantage and differentiation are fundamentally different approaches to achieving a competitive advantage through business-level strategy.

As described in the chapter on the nature and sources of competitive advantage, a company can achieve a competitive advantage over rivals through either:

- *cost advantage:* supplying an equivalent product or service at a lower cost, or
- *differentiation:* differentiating its product or service in such a way that customers are willing to pay a price premium that exceeds the cost of creating the differentiation.

Each represents a fundamentally different approach to business-level strategy. Porter initially viewed cost leadership and differentiation as mutually exclusive strategies, suggesting that trying to combine elements of each almost guarantees poor profitability.[7] In practice, however, the market leader in most industries tends to be a business that has successfully reconciled effective differentiation with low cost.

Some scholars view the simultaneous pursuit of differentiation and low cost as a key element in the creation of 'blue ocean' opportunities. Common to the success of Japanese companies in consumer goods industries such as cars, motorcycles, consumer electronics and musical instruments has been the ability to reconcile low costs with high quality and technological progressiveness. New management techniques have helped. Total quality management has exploded the myth that there is a trade-off between high quality and low cost. Innovations in manufacturing technology and manufacturing management have produced simultaneous increases in productivity and quality.[8] Peters observes an interesting asymmetry.[9]

> Cost reduction campaigns do not often lead to improved quality; and, except for those that involve large reductions in personnel, they don't usually result in long-term lower costs either. On the other hand, effective quality programs yield not only improved quality but lasting cost reductions as well.

Having conquered the cost/quality trade-off, companies such as Honda, Toyota, Sony and Canon have gone on to reconcile world-beating manufacturing efficiency and outstanding quality with flexibility, fast-paced innovation, and effective marketing.

5.2 The sources of cost advantage

LEARNING OBJECTIVE 5.2 Identify the basic sources of cost advantage in an industry and appreciate its potential for creating competitive advantage.

The key to cost analysis is to go beyond mechanistic approaches such as the experience curve and probe the factors that determine a company's cost position. There are major determinants of a company's unit costs (cost per unit of output) relative to its competitors; these are called *cost drivers* (see table 5.1).

TABLE 5.1   The major drivers of cost advantage and their definitions

Cost drivers	Definition
Economies of scale	Cost savings attributed to decreased fixed costs per unit when the volume of production and sales increases
Economies of learning	Cost savings attributed to cost reductions as a result of fewer mistakes and improvement in problem solving by repetition of operations
Process technology and process design	Cost savings attributed to improved efficiency via innovation of the production process

The relative importance of these different cost drivers varies across industries, across companies within an industry, and across the different activities within a company. By examining each of these different cost drivers in relation to a particular company it is possible to:

- analyse a company's cost position relative to its competitors and diagnose the sources of inefficiency
- make recommendations as to how a company can improve its cost efficiency.

The nature and the role of each of these major cost drivers will now be examined.

Economies of scale

The predominance of large corporations in most manufacturing and service industries is a consequence of economies of scale. **Economies of scale** exist wherever proportionate increases in the amounts of inputs employed in a production process result in lower unit costs. Economies of scale have been conventionally associated with manufacturing. Figure 5.1 shows a typical relationship between unit cost and plant capacity. The point at which most scale economies are exploited is the minimum efficient plant size (MEPS). Scale economies are also important in nonmanufacturing operations such as purchasing, research and development (R&D), distribution and advertising.

| **FIGURE 5.1** | The long-run average cost curve for a plant |

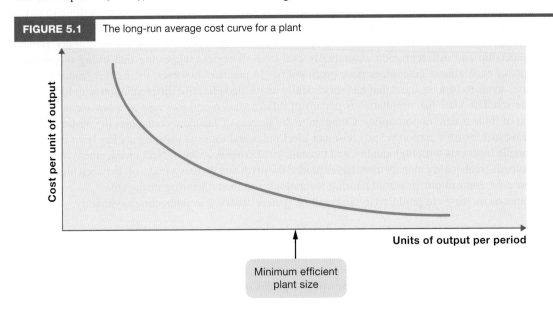

Scale economies arise from three principal sources.

1. *Technical input–output relationships.* In many activities, increases in output do not require proportionate increases in input. A 10 000-barrel oil storage tank does not cost five times as much as a 2000-barrel tank. Similar volume-related economies exist in ships, trucks, and steel and petrochemical plants.

2. *Indivisibilities.* Many resources and activities are 'lumpy' — they are unavailable in small sizes. Hence, they offer economies of scale, as larger companies are able to spread the costs of these items over larger volumes of output. An exploration project for discovery of new gas resources will cost much the same whether it is being undertaken by a multinational corporation or a small mining start-up. However, the costs as a percentage of sales will be much lower for the multinational because it has enormous sales volumes.

3. *Specialisation.* Increased scale permits greater task specialisation that manifests in greater division of labour. Mass production involves breaking down the production process into separate tasks performed by specialised workers using specialised equipment. Specialisation promotes learning, avoids time loss from switching activities, and assists in mechanisation and automation. Similar economies are important in knowledge-intensive industries such as investment banking, management consulting and design engineering, where large companies are able to offer specialised expertise across a broad range of know-how.

Limits to scale economies

Despite the prevalence of scale economies, small and medium-sized companies continue to survive and prosper in competition with much bigger rivals. For example, in countries such as the United States, New Zealand and Australia, microbreweries have been making inroads into the national beer markets while competing with the large, traditional breweries. In those cases, the efficiency advantages of scale are offset by three factors: first, the ability of smaller companies to differentiate their offerings more effectively; second, the greater flexibility of smaller companies; and third, the greater difficulty of achieving motivation and coordination in large units.[10]

Economies of learning

The experience curve is based primarily on learning-by-doing on the part of individuals and organisations. **Economies of learning** are the cost savings attributed to cost reductions as a result of fewer mistakes and improvement in problem solving by repetition of operations. Repetition develops both individual skills and organisational routines. In 1943, it took 40 000 labour hours to build a Convair B-24 bomber. By 1945, it took only 8000 hours.[11] The more complex a process or product is, the greater the potential for learning. Learning curves are exceptionally steep in semiconductor fabrication. When IBM introduced 0.18 micron copper-interconnector chips, yields increased from zero to over 50 per cent within the first two months. LCD flat screens are notoriously difficult to manufacture — a single defective chip may render an entire screen useless. The dominant position of LG and Samsung in flat screens is primarily a result of volume-based learning resulting in exceptionally high yields.[12] Learning occurs both at the individual level through improvements in dexterity and problem solving, and at the group level through the development and refinement of organisational routines.[13]

Process technology and process design

For most goods and services, alternative process technologies exist. **Process technology and process design** are cost savings attributed to improved efficiency via innovation of the production process. A process is technically superior to another when, for each unit of output, it uses less of one input without using more of any other input. Where a production method uses more of some inputs but less of others then cost efficiency depends on the relative prices of the inputs. For example, the budget airlines such as AirAsia implemented a different process using different inputs in comparison with traditional airlines. Their cost advantage was created by: choosing an alternative, less expensive airport (e.g. in Paris, Orly instead of Charles de Gaulle); using one type of aircraft (modern, with low maintenance costs); flying simple routes; and using online booking to minimise the fees to agencies.

As noted in the chapter on internal analysis of capabilities and core competencies, competitive advantage is created by organisational learning and the development of organisational capabilities. New technology and process design create conditions for learning new capabilities and routines which build cost advantages in various activities. Every business may be viewed as a collection of interrelated and interdependent value-creating activities. Strategy capsule 5.1 shows how a New Zealand supermarket chain has been continuously developing its interrelated value-creating activities in order to create cost advantage.

STRATEGY CAPSULE 5.1

The business model of PAK'nSAVE

PAK'nSAVE is one of the three largest supermarket chains in Aotearoa (New Zealand). The business opened its first store in 1985 and its network has since then grown to over 55 stores. The overarching mission of the business is 'to deliver New Zealand's lowest food prices and [help] New Zealanders live better for less' by 'being cheap as, fresh as, and sweet as, so customers can get everything they need at PAK'nSAVE'.[14]

The business aims to deliver on this promise by trying to realise cost advantages throughout its value chain. The lay-out of stores gives shoppers a 'warehouse feel'; the concrete floors and long aisles with bulk quantities of groceries and other household items, displayed without polish, make it a different experience than shopping at the Countdown or New World, the main two other players in the New Zealand market. Moreover, customers are expected to pack their own bags, with special packing areas provided after one leaves the checkout counter. The shops themselves are often located in

non-premium shopping areas, requiring customers to travel to the shops, yet saving the company location costs. The business is also known for its cost-effective marketing, with its simple 'Stickman-ads' contributing to a Kiwi brand with a high reputation in New Zealand.[15]

PAK'nSAVE does not stop there but is continuously trying to improve its successful business model. In 2019 the business went online by providing customers with the opportunity to 'click and collect' their groceries in 38 of their shops. The company has also been busy implementing software products from market leader SAP in order to make better, and where possible automated, decisions. Through an improved use of information analytics, the business expects to save further costs on staffing and logistics.[16] In 2019, one of the top executives of the company highlighted that customers are the main priority behind these initiatives: 'they have been asking us to help them save more money, they want to help us save time'.[17] The future will tell which other cost-saving initiatives PAK'nSAVE will be able to implement to further strengthen its cost leadership position in the New Zealand market.

5.3 Using the value chain to analyse costs

LEARNING OBJECTIVE 5.3 Explain how value chain analysis is used to understand cost advantage.

To analyse costs and make recommendations for building cost advantage, each activity has a distinct cost structure determined by different cost drivers. Analysing costs requires disaggregating the company's value chain to identify:

- the relative importance of each activity with respect to total cost
- the cost drivers for each activity and the comparative efficiency with which the company performs each activity
- how costs in one activity influence costs in another
- which activities should be undertaken within the company and which activities should be outsourced.

The principal stages of value chain analysis

A value chain analysis of a company's cost position comprises the following stages.
1. *Disaggregate the company into separate activities.* Determining the appropriate value chain activities is a matter of judgement. It requires understanding the chain of processes involved in the transformation of inputs into output and its delivery to the customer. Very often, the company's own divisional and departmental structure is a useful guide. Key considerations are:
   - the separateness of one activity from another
   - the importance of an activity
   - the dissimilarity of activities in terms of cost drivers
   - the extent to which there are differences in the way competitors perform the particular activity.
2. *Establish the relative importance of different activities in the total cost of the product.* The analysis needs to focus on the activities that are the major sources of cost. In disaggregating costs, Michael Porter suggests the detailed assignment of operating costs and assets to each value activity. Though the adoption of activity-based costing has made such cost data more available, detailed cost allocation can be a major exercise.[18] Even without such detailed cost data, it is usually possible to identify the critical activities, establish which activities are performed relatively efficiently or inefficiently, identify cost drivers, and offer recommendations.
3. *Compare costs by activity.* To establish which activities the company performs relatively efficiently and which it does not, unit costs for each activity are benchmarked against those of competitors.
4. *Identify cost drivers.* For each activity, what factors determine the level of cost relative to other companies? For some activities, cost drivers are evident simply from the nature of the activity and the composition of costs. For capital-intensive activities such as the operation of a body press in an automotive plant, the principal factors are likely to be capital equipment costs, weekly production volume, and downtime between changes of dies. For labour-intensive assembly activities, critical issues are wage rates, speed of work and defect rates.
5. *Identify linkages.* The costs of one activity may be determined, in part, by the way in which other activities are performed. AirAsia realises that operational costs can be reduced by using single-route flights and modern aircraft.

6. *Identify opportunities for reducing costs.* By identifying areas of comparative inefficiency and the cost drivers for each, opportunities for cost reduction become evident. Examples include the following.
   – If scale economies are a key cost driver, can volume be increased? One feature of Caterpillar's cost-reduction strategy was to broaden its model range and begin selling diesel engines to other vehicle manufacturers in order to expand its sales base.
   – Where wage costs are an issue, can wages be reduced either directly or by relocating production?
   – If a certain activity cannot be performed efficiently within the company, can it be outsourced?

   Figure 5.2 shows how the application of the value chain to vehicle manufacturing can yield suggestions for possible cost reductions.

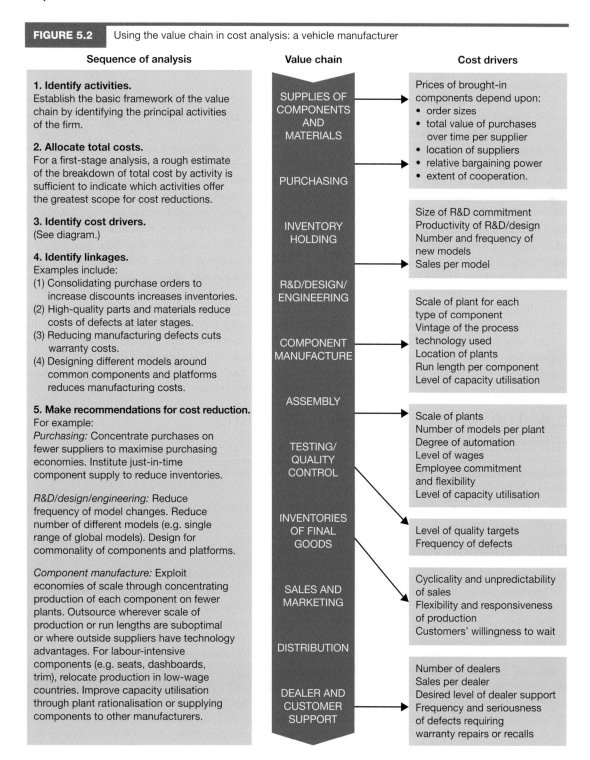

FIGURE 5.2   Using the value chain in cost analysis: a vehicle manufacturer

Risks of cost advantage

Although strategy analysis has traditionally emphasised cost advantage as the primary basis for competitive advantage, the cost leadership strategy offers a less secure basis for competitive advantage than does differentiation. The growth of international competition and online selling has revealed the fragility of seemingly well-established positions of domestic cost leadership. Australian retailers such as Kmart and Target have been increasingly struggling with online competition from businesses such as eBay Australia, Amazon and Kogan. Interestingly, the competition between these online players appears to be heating up as well, raising the question as to who will emerge as the true cost leader.

Cost advantage is also vulnerable to new technology and strategic innovation. US integrated iron and steel producers have lost ground to mini-mill producers — Nucor, Chaparral Steel and Steel Dynamics. Discount brokers such as Quick and Reilly, Brown & Company, Olde and Seibert have been undercut by online brokers such as Ameritrade and E-Trade. Internet telephony (VoIP) offered by Skype, Vonage and other start-ups has potentially devastating implications for the fixed-line businesses of established telecommunication providers such as Telstra.

In addition, cost advantage is highly vulnerable to unpredictable external forces. The slow fall of the Australian dollar against the US dollar since 2013 has seriously affected the cost competitiveness of many Australian companies reliant on imported materials and parts.

Hence, sustained high profitability is associated more with differentiation than cost leadership. Computer technology company Dell created its competitive advantage by using lean manufacturing and a direct sales model, but Dell's model also allowed it to differentiate its PCs by permitting customers to design their own computer system and offering complementary services such as online customer support, a three-year on-site warranty, web hosting and configuration of customer hardware and software. Similarly, AirAsia initially created its cost advantage by simple point-to-point routes, but it maintains the competitive advantage by providing high-quality service to its customers. Large companies that consistently earn a high return on equity — such as Colgate-Palmolive, Microsoft, Anheuser-Busch, Yum Brands, Kellogg's, Procter & Gamble, 3M and Wyeth — tend to be those that have pursued differentiation through quality, branding and innovation.

Analysing differentiation requires looking at both the company (the supply side) and its customers (the demand side). While supply-side analysis identifies the company's potential to create uniqueness, the critical issue is whether such differentiation creates value for customers, and whether the value created exceeds the cost of the differentiation. Hence, the next section will be concerned especially with the demand side of the market. By understanding what customers want, how they choose, and what motivates them, it is possible to identify opportunities for profitable differentiation.

5.4 The nature of differentiation and differentiation advantage

LEARNING OBJECTIVE 5.4 Identify the basic sources of differentiation, recognise its different forms and appreciate its potential for creating competitive advantage.

The following section explores what differentiation is and why it is such an important basis for competitive advantage.

Differentiation variables

The potential for differentiating a product or service is partly determined by its physical characteristics. For products that are technically simple (e.g. a pair of socks or a brick), that satisfy uncomplicated needs (e.g. a corkscrew or a nail), or must meet rigorous technical standards (e.g. a spark plug or a thermometer), differentiation opportunities are constrained by technical and market factors. Products that are technically complex (e.g. an aircraft), that satisfy complex needs (e.g. a vehicle or a holiday), or that do not need to conform to particular technical standards (e.g. wine or toys) offer much greater scope for differentiation.

Beyond these constraints, the potential in any product or service for differentiation is limited only by the boundaries of the human imagination. For seemingly simple products such as shampoo, toilet paper and bottled water, the proliferation of brands on any supermarket's shelves is testimony both to the ingenuity of companies and the complexity of customer preferences. Differentiation extends beyond the physical characteristics of the product or service to encompass everything about the product or service that influences the value customers derive from it. This means that differentiation includes every aspect of the way in which a company relates to its customers. Friends Restaurant, one of the top restaurants in

Perth, Western Australia, charges up to $45 for a main course and up to $25 for an entree. This ability rests not just on the quality of the dishes but also on the overall 'Friends Experience', which encompasses frequent live entertainment, a special atmosphere, the value the owners place on high standards of customer service and attention to detail. Differentiation is not an activity specific to particular functions such as design and marketing; it infuses all activities within the organisation and is built into the identity and culture of a company.

In analysing differentiation opportunities, tangible and intangible dimensions of differentiation can be distinguished. Tangible differentiation is concerned with the observable characteristics of a product or service that are relevant to customers' preferences and choice processes. These include size, shape, colour, weight, design, material and technology. Tangible differentiation also includes the performance of the product or service in terms of reliability, consistency, taste, speed, durability and safety.

Tangible differentiation extends to products and services that complement the product in question. There is little that is distinctive about the coffee offered at one of the most popular chains of Australian coffee shops, Dôme. The differentiation lies in the ability to create a relaxed café environment, speed of customer service, the combination of traditional flavours and introduction of the flavour or special dish of the season, the availability of popular newspapers and magazines, and convenient shopping centre locations.

Opportunities for intangible differentiation arise because the value that customers perceive in a product or service does not depend exclusively on the tangible aspects of the offering. There are few products where customer choice is determined solely by observable product features or objective performance criteria. Social, emotional, psychological and aesthetic considerations are present in choices over all products and services. The desires for status, exclusivity, individuality and security are powerful motivational forces in choices relating to most consumer goods. Where a product or service is meeting complex customer needs, differentiation choices involve the overall image of the company's offering. Image differentiation is especially important for those products and services whose qualities and performance are difficult to ascertain at the time of purchase ('experience goods'). These include cosmetics, medical services and education.

Successful differentiation involves matching customers' demand for differentiation with the company's capacity to supply differentiation.

Analysing differentiation: the demand side

Analysing customer demand enables an organisation to determine which product characteristics have the potential to create value for customers, customers' willingness to pay for differentiation, and a company's optimal competitive positioning in terms of differentiation variables.

Analysing demand begins with understanding why customers buy a product or service. What are the needs and requirements of a person who is purchasing a personal computer? What is motivating a company when it hires management consultants? Market research systematically explores customer preferences and customer perceptions of existing products. However, the key to successful differentiation is to understand customers. In gaining insight into customer requirements and preferences, simple, direct questions about the purpose of a product and its performance attributes can often be far more illuminating than objective market research data obtained from large samples of actual and potential customers.

The role of social and psychological factors

The problem with analysing product differentiation in terms of measurable performance attributes is that it does not delve very far into customers' underlying motivations. Very few goods or services are acquired to satisfy basic needs for survival; most buying reflects social goals and values in terms of the desire to find community with others, to establish one's own identity, and to make sense of what is happening in the world. Psychologist Abraham Maslow proposed a hierarchy of human needs. Once basic needs for survival are established, there is a progression from security needs, to belonging needs, to esteem needs, to self-actualisation needs.[19] Most suppliers of branded goods recognise that their brand equities have much more to do with status and conformity than to survival or security. What is so different about Louis Vuitton's popular, much-copied brown and black tote? What is so different in the commonly recognised designs of Gucci handbags? These customers are willing to pay a premium price for these branded products, not just for the physical features of these products, but also for intangible differentiation of self-identity and social affiliation. Indeed, the value conferred by leading consumer brands such as Louis Vuitton, Gucci, Coca-Cola, Harley-Davidson and Mercedes-Benz is less a warranty of the reliability and more an embodiment of identity and lifestyle. For these brands, advertising and promotion have long been the primary means of influencing and reinforcing customer perceptions.

Increasingly, consumer goods companies are seeking new approaches to brand development that focus less on product characteristics and more on 'brand experience', 'shared values' and 'emotional dialogue'.

Many Australian companies take serious consideration of social and psychological factors when positioning themselves in the market. For example, the Peters Ice Cream brand, despite a change of ownership, is perceived as an Australian national company that does not exploit low-cost labour and other resources in emergent economies. Australia's leading grocery retailer Woolworths positions itself as the 'Fresh Food People'.

If the key customer needs that a product satisfies are self-identity and social affiliation, the implications for differentiation are far reaching. In particular, to understand customer demand and identify profitable differentiation opportunities requires not only an analysis of the product and its characteristics, but also of customers, their lifestyles and aspirations, and the relationship of the product to these lifestyles and aspirations. Market research that looks behind the product and explores the demographic (e.g. age, sex, race, location), socio-economic (e.g. income, education), and psychographic (e.g. lifestyle, personality type) characteristics of potential customers may be of some value. However, effective differentiation is likely to depend on an understanding of what customers want and how they behave rather than the results of statistical market research. While the phenomenon is complex, the answer, according to Peters, is simple: business people need to 'get out from behind their desks to where the customers are [and] construct settings so as to maximise 'naive' listening.'[20]

In practice, understanding customer needs and preferences is likely to require more than listening. Typically, consumers cannot clearly articulate the motives that drive them and the emotions that different products trigger. Companies must observe their customers to understand their lives and their use of the product. The implication is that, for companies to understand their customers, they need to become involved with them. Going beyond functionality to explore the emotional and aesthetic aspects of consumers' relationships with products is central to Japanese companies' approaches to marketing.[21]

Analysing differentiation: the supply side

Demand analysis identifies customers' demands for differentiation and their willingness to pay for it, but creating differentiation advantage also depends on a company's ability to offer differentiation. To identify the company's potential to supply differentiation, it is necessary to examine the activities the company performs and the resources it commands.

The drivers of uniqueness

Differentiation is concerned with the provision of uniqueness. A company's opportunities for creating uniqueness in its offerings to customers are not located within a particular function or activity, but can arise in virtually everything that it does. Porter identifies a number of drivers of uniqueness that are decision variables for the company:

- product features and product performance
- complementary services (e.g. credit, delivery and repair)
- intensity of marketing activities (e.g. rate of spending on advertising)
- technology embodied in design and manufacture
- the quality of purchased inputs
- procedures influencing the conduct of each of the activities (e.g. rigour of quality control, service procedures and frequency of sales visits to a customer)
- the skill and experience of employees
- location (e.g. with retail stores)
- the degree of vertical integration (which influences a company's ability to control inputs and intermediate processes).[22]

5.5 Using the value chain to analyse differentiation

LEARNING OBJECTIVE 5.5 Explain how value chain analysis is used to understand differentiation advantage.

There is little point in identifying the product attributes that customers value most if the company is incapable of supplying those attributes. Similarly, there is little purpose in identifying a company's ability to supply certain elements of uniqueness if these are not valued by customers. The key to successful differentiation is matching the company's capacity for creating differentiation to the attributes that customers value most. For this purpose, the value chain provides a particularly useful framework.

Value chain analysis of producer goods

Using the value chain to identify opportunities for differentiation advantage involves four principal stages.

1. *Construct a value chain for the company and the customer.* It may be useful to consider not just the immediate customer, but also companies further downstream in the value chain. If the company supplies different types of customers (e.g. a steel company may supply steel strip to vehicle manufacturers and white goods producers), draw separate value chains for each of the main categories of customer.

2. *Identify the drivers of uniqueness in each activity.* Assess the company's potential for differentiating its product by examining each activity in the company's value chain and identifying the variables and actions through which the company can achieve uniqueness in relation to competitors' offerings. Figure 5.3 identifies sources of differentiation within Porter's generic value chain.

3. *Select the most promising differentiation variables for the company.* Among the numerous drivers of uniqueness that can be identified within the company, which one should be selected as the primary basis for the company's differentiation strategy?

4. *Locate linkages between the value chain of the company and that of the buyer.* The objective of differentiation is to yield a price premium for the company. This requires that the company's differentiation creates value for the customer. Creating value for customers requires either that the company lowers customers' costs or that customers' own product differentiation is facilitated. Thus, by implementing information technology support for customers of its logistics services, Toll Holdings managed to radically reduce distribution time and increase delivery reliability. This permits its customers to reduce transportation costs while simultaneously increasing reliability and the manageability of locations of specific projects (Toll Holdings' customers include international mining giants such as BHP Billiton and Rio Tinto, which are dependent on logistics services to ensure that projects are implemented on time).[23] To identify the means by which a company can create value for its customers it must locate the linkages between differentiation of its own activities and cost reduction and differentiation within the customer's activities. Analysis of these linkages can also evaluate the potential profitability of differentiation. The value differentiation created for the customer represents the maximum price premium the customer will pay. If the provision of just-in-time (JIT) delivery by a component supplier costs an additional $1000 a month but saves a vehicle company $6000 a month in reduced inventory, warehousing and handling costs, then it should be possible for the component manufacturer to obtain a price premium that easily exceeds the cost of the differentiation.

FIGURE 5.3 Using the value chain to identify differentiation potential on the supply side

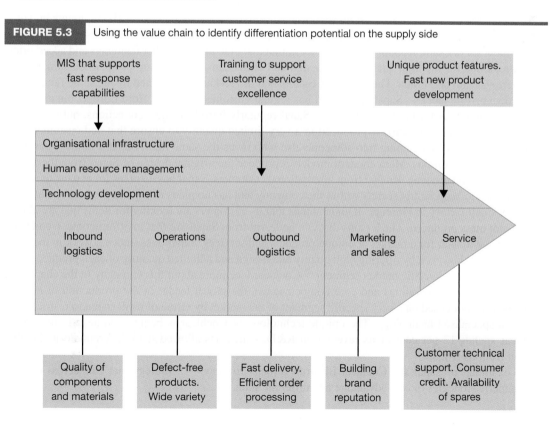

Value chain analysis of consumer goods

Value chain analysis of differentiation opportunities can also be applied to consumer goods. Few consumer goods are consumed directly; in most cases, consumers are involved in a chain of activities involving the acquisition and purchase of the product. Hence, even when the customer is a consumer, it is still feasible to draw a value chain showing the activities that the consumer engages in when purchasing and consuming a product.

In the case of consumer durables, customers are involved in a long chain of activities from search, purchase, financing, accessory acquirement, operation, service and repair, to eventual disposal. Complex consumer value chains offer many potential linkages with the manufacturer's value chain, with considerable opportunity for innovative differentiation. Japanese producers of vehicles, consumer electronics and domestic appliances have a long tradition of observing their customers' behaviour in selecting and utilising products, then using the information of customer usage and selection processes in planning product design and marketing.

Differentiation and segmentation

Differentiation is different from segmentation. Differentiation is concerned with how a company competes — the ways in which it can offer uniqueness to customers. Such uniqueness might relate to consistency (McDonald's), reliability (Australia Post), status (American Express), quality (BMW) and innovation (Apple). Segmentation is concerned with where a company competes in terms of customer groups, localities and product types.

Whereas segmentation is a feature of market structure, differentiation is a strategic choice by a company. A segmented market is one that can be partitioned according to the characteristics of customers and their demand. Differentiation is concerned with a company's positioning within a market (or market segment) in relation to the product, service and image characteristics that influence customer choice.[24] By locating within a segment, a company does not necessarily differentiate itself from its competitors within the same segment. Selling personal computers, Dell and HP are offering mini-laptop computers and are focused on this specific segment of computer manufacturing, yet their mini-laptops are not significantly differentiated from one another. Conversely, Toyota, McDonald's, Gloria Jeans and Dôme pursue differentiation, but position themselves within the mass market and span multiple segments.

Nevertheless, differentiation decisions tend to be closely linked to choices over the segments in which a company competes. By offering uniqueness in its offerings, a company may inevitably target certain market niches. For example, Sapaf, an upmarket Italian manufacturer of leather handbags and accessories, is well regarded for the high quality of its design and craftsmanship by its top business customers such as Roberto Cavalli and Prada. The company, established in 1954 and still owned by the same family, also has its own private label — Sapaf. This label has regular customers not only from Europe, but also from Japan, the United Arab Emirates and Russia. Sapaf regularly introduces new collections, but every item (e.g. a handbag, wallet or scarf) is produced in a very limited quantity to ensure that end customers will not be embarrassed by bumping into someone else who owns the same item. Sapaf's modern design is rooted in family traditions. Many modern models reproduce the original design of Sapaf from the 1950s. Despite strong and growing demand from international customers, Sapaf has no plans for expansion. Sapaf is determined to keep family secrets within the company and has no plans to expand production outside a relatively small factory in Florence. It understands that its customers are looking for items that are almost unique, not mass produced. The lessons that can be learnt from Sapaf are that to differentiate, a company does not have to look for a market of unique products and services. Sapaf does, indeed, work in the mass product market; however, by offering high quality and design and a limited quantity of each product, Sapaf is focused on a very specific market segment.[25] Cochlear (see more about this company in the chapter on internal analysis of capabilities and core competencies), the global leader in the production of hearing implants, is also focused on a very specific segment of the market by virtue of its decision to restrict itself to such a specialised technology. The unique technology of Cochlear is being continuously innovated. Cochlear spends 12 per cent of its revenue on R&D, which has allowed it to differentiate its hearing implant from its rivals.

The examples of Sapaf and Cochlear illustrate a *focus strategy* — a strategy that cuts across the two basic generic strategies of cost advantage and differentiation.

5.6 Focus strategy

LEARNING OBJECTIVE 5.6 Understand a focus strategy and appreciate its potential for creating competitive advantage.

A focus strategy allows companies to concentrate their resources on the chosen target market and advantage is achieved by a better understanding of the customers' needs and the ability to satisfy them. Strategy capsule 5.2 illustrates competitive advantage created by several social businesses using a focus strategy in the Asia–Pacific region.

STRATEGY CAPSULE 5.2

Targeting customers interested in sustainability

With increasing global concerns about climate change, the current use of scarce resources, pollution and the quality of life for future generations, a growing number of businesses is developing and implementing business models that explicitly incorporate sustainability considerations. Most of these initiatives specifically focus on those customers who feel strongly about making a difference by changing their shopping habits and can afford to do so. Many businesses operating in this space have seen tremendous growth over the past years. Some good examples from the Asia–Pacific region include the following businesses.

The Source Bulk Foods was founded in 2012 and since then has become the largest specialised bulk foods chain in Australia. The company describes its mission as follows: 'Bulk food is as much about providing nutritious products as it is about embracing a zero-waste goal. We nourish families, foster a healthy community, and in doing so, take a hands-on approach to nurturing our planet'.[26] Customers are encouraged to bring their own jars and containers to fill them up with often locally sourced bulk foods, thereby reducing the use of plastics. The business itself estimates that around 300 000 kilograms of waste and 50 000 000 plastic bags have already been saved through their efforts. The business model appears to work well, with The Source already opening more than 50 stores across Australia and venturing into the United Kingdom and Singapore.[27]

Another example is the Australian toilet paper seller Who Gives A Crap. In 2012 the three founding entrepreneurs used crowdfunding to set up their new business, whose aim is to produce toilet paper that is 'good for your bum and great for the world'.[28] Who Gives A Crap claims to produce all its toilet paper from recyclable materials and donates 50 per cent of its profits to help build toilets around the world. To date, the company claims to 'have donated over $2.6 million dollars to charity and saved a lot of trees, water and energy.'[29] Part of their success is that they have cut out all middlemen and directly sell to the customer.

A final example is provided by the Kiwi business Icebreaker. This high-end merino wool outdoor clothing company defines its purpose as follows: 'driven by the belief that nature has the solutions, we provide natural alternatives to synthetic based apparel to create a healthier more sustainable future for our species and the planet.'[30] Consequently, the business has incorporated sustainable practices in each part of its value chain, which is most clearly visible in the treatment of merino sheep. Farmers are being paid above average prices to take better care of their sheep and not engage in contested animal welfare practices.[31] In 2008 the company made headlines with the introduction of a 'Baacode', a barcode that makes it visible to customers from which sheep station the wool in their product was sourced. These days Icebreaker products can be found in many countries around the globe and in 2017 the company was sold to listed US-business VF Corporation for $288 million.[32]

5.7 Integrated approach of cost advantage and differentiation

LEARNING OBJECTIVE 5.7 Understand how competitive advantage can be created by an integration of cost advantage and differentiation.

When in 1980 Porter first introduced the three generic strategies — cost advantage, differentiation and focus[33] — many academics and practitioners questioned whether it was possible to use both cost advantage and differentiation successfully. Initially, Porter's response was negative. He argued that an attempt to create advantage via low costs and differentiation would lead companies to the position of 'stuck in the middle' where companies achieve neither cost leadership nor differentiation. Indeed, differentiation adds to cost. The direct costs of differentiation include higher-quality inputs, better-trained employees, more advertising, and better after-sales service. The indirect costs of differentiation arise through the interaction of differentiation variables with cost variables. If differentiation narrows a company's segment scope, it also limits the potential for exploiting scale economies, thus limiting the opportunities for cost advantage. If differentiation requires continual product redesign, it hampers the exploitation of learning economies and does not allow companies to achieve cost leadership. Strategy capsule 5.3 illustrates how an iconic Australian car brand indeed ran into trouble by getting 'stuck in the middle' with its strategy.

STRATEGY CAPSULE 5.3

Holden — the demise of a once very successful car brand

In February 2020, General Motors announced that it would discontinue its well-known Australian car brand Holden sometime in 2021. The announcement came after years of disappointing sales, the 2017 closure of Holden's manufacturing operations in Australia, and the axing of the brand's most successful model, the Holden Commodore, at the end of 2019. Australian Prime Minister Scott Morrison at the time responded by stating: 'I am disappointed but not surprised. But I am angry, like I think many Australians would be. (...) Australian taxpayers put millions into this multinational company. [General Motors] let the brand just wither away on their watch. Now they are leaving it behind'.[34]

It is a sad end to a brand that has been connected to Australia for a long time. Holden was founded as a saddle maker in South Australia in 1856, before the company moved into the automotive industry in the twentieth century. Over the decades Holden introduced a variety of new models and tried to stay at the cutting edge of technology through innovation. With the slogan 'Made in Australia, for Australia' the brand also strongly positioned itself as local, although the brand has been owned by US company General Motors since 1931.[35] Over the years, the Holden Commodore in particular turned out to be a massive success, with the model being Australia's bestselling car between 1996 and 2010.[36]

Dark clouds already started to gather on the horizon as early as the eighties. During those years Australia's car manufacturing industry started to struggle with relatively high labour costs, the emergence of more cost-efficient international competitors and the relatively small size of the local markets in Australia and New Zealand. When the global financial crisis hit and the Australian government cut its support for the sector, the industry really got into trouble.[37] At the time Holden was in a difficult strategic position, as the brand was increasingly facing competitors that offered better value for money, both in terms of differentiation and cost levels. Whereas the company tried to restructure and cut costs, for example, by no longer manufacturing the cars in Australia, this effort came too late to rescue the brand. In 2020 General Motors decided to pull the plug, as the company was facing a losing battle with not enough financial returns.

In 1985, however, Porter recognised the possibility of an integrated approach of cost advantage and differentiation.[38] One way of reconciling differentiation with cost efficiency is to postpone differentiation to later stages of the company's value chain. Economies of scale and the cost advantages of standardisation are frequently greatest in the manufacturing of basic components. Modular design with common components permits scale economies while maintaining considerable product variety. All the major car makers have reduced the number of platforms and engine types and increased the commonality of components across their model ranges, while offering customers a greater variety of colour, trim and accessory options.

New manufacturing technologies and the internet have redefined traditional trade-offs between efficiency and variety. Flexible manufacturing systems and JIT scheduling have increased the versatility of many plants, made model changeovers less costly, and made the goal of an 'economic order quantity of one' increasingly realistic. Increasingly, vehicle, motorcycle and domestic appliance plants are producing multiple models on a single assembly line.[39] Internet communication allows consumers to design their own products and quickly communicate their requirements to manufacturers. As already discussed, Dell created a cost advantage via lean manufacturing and direct sales, and the opportunity of customers to choose their own model differentiates Dell from its rivals. Similarly, IKEA enjoys its advantage from its ability to offer furniture at affordable prices. IKEA's business model is based on a showroom that displays the assembled furniture and other accessories. However, customers purchase flat-packs of unassembled furniture and have to assemble their purchased items at home. In the Australian fashion industry, the fashion chain Witchery also created advantage based on affordable prices and the frequent change of collections. The company's ability to offer fashionable clothing is similar to upmarket designers. Witchery is positioned much higher in the market compared to other mass-market designers. Its focus on trendiness and speedy updates maintains customer excitement and boosts their willingness to pay. What the customer is willing to pay is higher than the company's production costs. An interesting approach to broaden the customer base and reduce operating costs is currently being implemented at Telstra — an Australian telecommunications company. This approach is illustrated in strategy capsule 5.4.

STRATEGY CAPSULE 5.4

Telstra — simultaneously pursuing differentiation and cost savings

The telecommunications industry is generally considered to be a challenging context for the companies operating within it. Rapid technological developments, fierce competition, the presence of powerful suppliers, the required investments in network infrastructure and stringent government regulation all help to create a context in which it is not easy to develop and maintain a sustainable competitive advantage. This is also the case for the Australian telecommunications market leader, Telstra. The company in recent years has seen declining profits and therefore announced a new strategy labelled Telstra2022 (T22). The foundations of T22 are to reduce the number of products, simplify the organisational structure, reduce costs where possible and set up a special infrastructure business unit.[40] In essence, this major restructuring of the business is planned to enhance the experiences of the customer through the smarter use of technology, while simultaneously reducing the cost structure of the business, for instance, through the cutting of around 8000 jobs.

Telstra expects that this combination will deliver more value to existing customers, while also making its products and services more attractive to potential new customers.[41]

The verdict is still out on whether the integrated approach of differentiation and cost advantage is going to work for Telstra, with the company announcing a profit drop as a result of problems with the rollout of the national broadband network and the Australian bushfire crisis in the summer of 2019–20. The company, though, believes it is moving in the right direction with its CEO stating that 'we are starting to build positive underlying financial momentum'.[42] The changes might have come just in time for Telstra, as they will be facing another potentially strong rival after the merger between Vodafone and TPG was approved by the Federal Court on 13 February 2020.[43]

SUMMARY

The choice of business-level strategy is important because it is linked to profitability in today's hypercompetitive markets. In almost all industries it is a prerequisite for success. In industries where competition has always been primarily price-based — steel, textiles and mortgage loans — increased intensity of competition requires relentless cost-reduction efforts. In industries where price competition was once muted — airlines, banking and electrical power — companies have been forced to reconcile the pursuit of innovation, differentiation and service quality with vigorous cost reduction.

The foundation for a cost-reduction strategy must be an understanding of the determinants of a company's costs. The principal message of this chapter is the need to look behind cost accounting data and beyond simplistic approaches to the determinants of cost efficiency, and to analyse the factors that drive relative unit costs in each of the company's activities in a systematic and comprehensive manner.

Increasingly, competitive advantage is created via the ability of a company to differentiate its products and/or itself via differentiation. The attraction of differentiation over low cost as a basis for competitive advantage is its potential for sustainability. It is less vulnerable to being overturned by changes in the external environment and it is more difficult to replicate.

The potential for differentiation in any business is vast — it may involve physical differentiation of the product, it may be through complementary services, it may be intangible. Differentiation extends beyond technology, design and marketing to include all aspects of a company's interactions with its customers.

The essence of differentiation advantage is to increase the perceived value of the offering to the customer either more effectively or at lower cost than competitors. This requires that the company match the requirements and preferences of customers with its own capacity for creating uniqueness.

The value chain provides a useful framework for analysing both cost advantage and differentiation. By analysing how costs are decreased and how value is created for customers and by systematically appraising the scope of each of the company's activities for achieving differentiation, the value chain permits matching demand-side and supply-side sources of differentiation. Business-level strategies evolve with the company: at certain stages of a company's evolution, it uses different business-level strategies.

KEY TERMS

economies of learning Cost savings attributed to cost reductions as a result of fewer mistakes and improvement in problem solving by repetition of operations.

economies of scale Cost savings attributed to decreased fixed costs per unit when the volume of production and sales increases.

process technology and process design Cost savings attributed to improved efficiency via innovation of the production process.

SELF-STUDY QUESTIONS

1 What are the main cost drivers and how do they create cost advantage?
2 What is the relationship between economies of scale and the minimum efficient plant size?
3 How do companies achieve economies of learning?
4 Why is it important to analyse differentiation from both perspectives — the demand and supply sides?
5 What does the expression 'stuck in the middle' mean? Why is it perceived to be a negative position?
6 Why is a better understanding of the customers' needs important for successful implementation of the focus strategy?
7 How do companies achieve successful integration of cost advantage and differentiation?

DISCUSSION QUESTIONS

1 What advice would you offer Countdown, one of the leading supermarkets in New Zealand and a subsidiary of Australia's Woolworths, regarding how they should maintain (or possibly adjust) their differentiation advantage in conditions of growing competition from budget supermarkets such as PAK'nSAVE (see strategy capsule 5.1)?

2 What are the possible strategic moves social businesses could make to protect and further extend the success of their adopted focus strategies (see strategy capsule 5.2)?

3 How would centralisation or decentralisation of decision making within a company impact upon the achievement of cost leadership? (*Hint:* centralisation might lead to streaming of operations and, thus, to cost reduction; on the other hand, decentralisation allows more employees to exercise more initiative, which might also lead to costs savings.) Under which circumstances/industry conditions would centralisation be the preferred option?

4 What could the executives of Holden have done differently to not have ended up being 'stuck in the middle' (see strategy capsule 5.3)?

5 Discuss how understanding of consumer behaviour could be used to increase sales in the fast food sector of the hospitality industry.

EXERCISES

1 Imagine that you belong to a group of entrepreneurs contemplating opening a new video game store in your city. You are trying to decide what business-level strategy would lead this investment to the best competitive position. Identify which video game stores are the most profitable and why. On the basis of this analysis, decide what kind of video game store you want to open and explain why.

2 Identify a company that is 'stuck in the middle' and prepare a plan that may allow it to escape from this situation.

3 Choose an emerging social business in your country and explain which business-level strategy it is using to realise a sustainable competitive advantage.

4 Review the business-level strategies of online retailers such as Amazon, eBay and Kogan in the Australian context. Discuss which online retailer is most likely to emerge as the winner (if any). Explain your answer while using concepts from this chapter.

5 Search online for sites that sell running shoes in your country. What business-level strategies do the companies associated with these websites implement?

FURTHER READING

Bonn, I & Fisher, J 2011, 'Sustainability: the missing ingredient in strategy', *Journal of Business Strategy*, vol. 32, 5–14.

Drnevich, PL & Croson, DC 2013, 'Information technology and business-level strategy: toward an integrated theoretical perspective', *Mis Quarterly,* vol. 37, 483–509.

Ellram, LM, Tate, WL & Petersen, KJ 2013, 'Offshoring and reshoring: an update on the manufacturing location decision', *Journal of Supply Chain Management,* vol. 49, 14–22.

Nandakumar, MK, Ghobadian, A & O'Regan, N 2010, 'Business-level strategy and performance', *Management Decision,* vol. 48, 907–939.

Rachinger, M, Rauter, R, Müller, C, Vorraber, W & Schirgi, E 2019, 'Digitalization and its influence on business model innovation', *Journal of Manufacturing Technology Management,* vol. 30, 1143–1160.

ENDNOTES

1. See more about the company's history and origins on its website www.csl.com/our-company; website visited on 26 February 2020.
2. E Knight, 'Biotech giant CSL looks to join the defence against coronavirus', *Sydney Morning Herald*, 4 February 2020, www.smh.com.au.
3. N Khadem, 'CSL to draw blood donors' data with help of artificial intelligence', *Sydney Morning Herald*, 16 August 2018, www.smh.com.au.
4. CSL, *CSL Limited Annual Report 2018/19*, 2019, www.csl.com.
5. ibid.
6. T Peters, *Thriving on chaos*, New York: Knopf, 1987, p. 56.
7. ME Porter, *Competitive strategy*, New York: Free Press, 1980, p. 42.
8. See, for example, JR Meredith, 'Strategic advantages of the factory of the future', *California Management Review*, Winter 1989, 129–145.
9. Peters, op. cit., p. 80.
10. D Schwartzman, 'Uncertainty and the size of the firm', *Economica*, August 1963.
11. L Rapping, 'Learning and World War II production functions', *Review of Economics and Statistics*, February 1965, 81–86. See also KB Clark and RH Hayes, 'Recapturing America's manufacturing heritage', *California Management Review*, Summer 1988, 25.

12. 'Exploiting the flat screen frenzy', Forbes.com, 12 December 2003, www.forbes.com; 'Japan watches display market go flat', RedHerring.com, 10 January 2001.
13. L Argote, SL Beckman and D Epple, 'The persistence and transfer of learning in industrial settings', *Management Science*, vol. 36, 1990, 140–154; M Zollo and SG Winter, 'Deliberate learning and the evolution of dynamic capabilities', *Organization Science*, vol. 13, 2002, 339–351.
14. Foodstuffs, *Annual Report for Foodstuff's North Island Limited*, 2019, www.foodstuffs.co.nz.
15. C Smith, 'Air New Zealand named Kiwis' most respected brand', *New Zealand Herald*, 12 April 2019, www.nzherald.co.nz.
16. Foodstuffs, op. cit.
17. M Bain, 'Online shopping comes to Pak'n Save', *Stuff Limited*, 15 January 2019, www.stuff.co.nz.
18. On activity-based costing, see RS Kaplan and SR Anderson, 'Time-driven activity-based costing', *Harvard Business Review*, November 2004, 131–138; J Billington, 'The ABCs of ABC: activity-based costing and management', *Harvard Management Update*, May 1999.
19. A Maslow, 'A theory of human motivation', *Psychological Review*, vol. 50, 1943, 370–396.
20. Peters, op. cit., p. 149.
21. JK Johansson and I Nonaka, *Relentless: the Japanese way of marketing*, New York: HarperBusiness, 1996.
22. Porter 1985, op. cit., pp. 124–125.
23. See more about developments of special programs at Toll Holdings to improve customer satisfaction on the company website www.toll.com.au.
24. These distinctions are developed in more detail by PR Dickson and JL Ginter, 'Market Segmentation, Product Differentiation and Marketing Strategy', *Journal of Marketing*, vol. 51, April 1987, 1–10.
25. See more on Sapaf business model and philosophy on the company's website www.sapaf.it.
26. See more about the company's history and origins on their website www.thesourcebulkfoods.com.au; website visited on 3 March 2020.
27. ibid.
28. See more about the company's history and origins on their website au.whogivesacrap.org; website visited on 3 March 2020.
29. ibid.
30. See more about the company's history and origins on their website www.icebreaker.com; website visited on 3 March 2020.
31. Icebreaker, *Transparency Report 2018*, 2018, www.icebreaker.com.
32. A Shaw, 'Icebreaker sold to VF Corporation, owner of Vans and The North Face, for $288m', *New Zealand Herald*, 9 April 2018, www.nzherald.co.nz.
33. ME Porter, 'What is strategy?' in *Competitive strategy: techniques for analyzing industries and competitors*, New York: Free Press, 1980, chapters 2–4.
34. 'GM scraps historic Holden car brand in Australia', *BBC*, 17 February 2020, www.bbc.com.
35. 'A history of Holden in Australia – timeline', *The Guardian*, 19 February 2020, www.theguardian.com.
36. 'Holden axes Commodore range to focus on SUVs and utes as sedan sales dwindle', *ABC*, 10 December 2019, www.abc.net.au.
37. op. cit. 30.
38. ME Porter, *Competitive advantage: creating and sustaining superior performance*, New York: Free Press, 1985.
39. RJ Schonberger, World class manufacturing casebook: implementing JIT and TQC, New York: Free Press, 1987, pp. 120–123; J Pine, B Victor, A Boynton, 'Making mass-customization work', *Harvard Business Review*, September–October 1993, 108–116.
40. A Penn, 'T22 – our plan to lead', 28 February 2020, www.exchange.telstra.com.au.
41. ibid.
42. A Druce, 'Telstra first-half profit drops 7.6% after NBN rollout', *News Corp Australia*, 13 February 2020, www.new.com.au.
43. J Fernyhough, 'New telco giant takes aim at Telstra, Optus', *Financial Review*, 13 February 2020, www.afr.com.

ACKNOWLEDGEMENTS

Photo: © DavidBGray / Getty Images
Photo: © 1000 Words / Shutterstock.com
Photo: © Romolo Tavani / Shutterstock.com
Photo: © TK Kurikawa / Shutterstock.com
Photo: © TK Kurikawa / Shutterstock.com

CHAPTER 6

Corporate-level strategy

LEARNING OBJECTIVES

After studying this chapter, you should be able to:

6.1 understand the nature of corporate-level strategy and be able to identify and explain various types of corporate strategies

6.2 identify the conditions under which diversification creates value for shareholders

6.3 recognise the organisational and managerial issues arising from diversification and why diversification so often fails to realise its anticipated benefits

6.4 distinguish between mergers and acquisitions and determine their relative merits in exploiting the linkages between different businesses

6.5 assess the relative advantages of vertical and horizontal integration in organising related activities, understand the circumstances that influence these relative advantages, and advise a company whether a particular activity should be undertaken internally or outsourced

6.6 understand the purpose of turnaround and retrenchment strategies

6.7 critically evaluate corporate parenting and synergy connection in diversified portfolios

6.8 demonstrate applied knowledge of portfolio strategy by performing high-level analysis of diversified businesses at various growth phases.

Diversification at Disney

In his 2019 address at the annual meeting of share-holders, Robert Iger, chairman and chief executive officer of the Walt Disney Company, took pleasure in announcing that the company had released some of the most successful movies of the year, generating more than US$7 billion in total global box office, for the second year running, the only studio ever to do so.[1] In recent years, the company has had a stream of hit movies including *Frozen, The Avengers* and *Black Panther,* and its acquisition of Lucasfilm in 2012 added further creative momentum with the release of new *Star Wars* movies. Success in the movie business has had positive spin-off effects for

Disney consumer products and theme parks as well as its TV channel, Disney Junior, and games platform, Disney Infinity. As a result, total revenue was up 8 per cent and earnings per share were at an all-time high of US$8.36 billion.[2] This was quite an achievement for the leader of such a large and complex organisation, particularly given that Disney had been a troubled company when Iger took over from his predecessor, Michael Eisner, in 2006.

The background to the Walt Disney Company

The Walt Disney Company, founded by Walt and Roy Disney, started life as The Disney Brothers Cartoon Studio producing the cartoons that brought the world such memorable characters as Mickey Mouse and Donald Duck. Having achieved success with short films, the Disney Studio quickly moved into the production of feature-length animated films, including *Snow White and the Seven Dwarves, Pinocchio* and *Fantasia.* The brothers were introduced early in the company's existence to opportunities for diversification when a businessman, who wanted to use the image of Mickey Mouse to promote sales of a drawing tablet for children, approached them. The establishment of the Mickey Mouse Club for fans soon after this encounter suggests that the Disney brothers recognised immediately the potential for selling toys, books and other products linked to their animated characters. Over time, Disney added more and more businesses to its portfolio, transforming itself into the multinational media and entertainment company that we see today.

The scope of the company's business activities in 2019

The Walt Disney Company grouped its activities into five main areas: media networks, parks and resorts, studio entertainment, consumer products and interactive media, but beneath these five titles lay a multiplicity of different business activities.

The total revenue of these business groups in 2018–19 was US$59 434, with 41 per cent of that total generated by media networks (US$24 500), 34 per cent by parks and resorts (US$20 296), 17 per cent by studio entertainment (US$9 987), and 8 per cent by consumer products and interactive media (US$4 650).[3]

- *Media networks.* Disney's media network segment comprised the US television and radio networks and stations, international cable and broadcast networks, television production and distribution operations through which it distributed its media content to households. Having access to distribution channels was (and remains) a key success factor in the media industry because the high fixed costs of making films and television programs mean that profitability depends on gaining as broad an audience as possible. If a company controls both content and distribution, it can promote its own content and shape how and when its content is broadcast. As the media industry became more concentrated with large conglomerates like Time Warner and Bertelsmann dominating scheduling, the position of independent content providers became more precarious. In 1995, Disney acquired the TV and radio broadcasting company Capital Cities/ABC for the sum of US$19 billion. Disney paid a lot to acquire the company but the deal was of particular strategic importance because it secured Disney's access to media channels for its creative content. As the demand for cable services began to decline, growing their direct-to-consumer service offering became a top priority for Disney, leading to the 2019 introduction of Disney+ to their media network. This service offered Disney, Pixar, Marvel and Lucasfilm movies, exclusive original series and movies, and other titles from their film and television libraries.

- *Parks and resorts.* Among the first areas of business developed by Disney outside its animation and merchandising base were theme parks. The company opened Disneyland in California in 1955 and went on to establish the Walt Disney World Resort in Orlando, Florida in 1971. Disneyland resorts were subsequently developed in Tokyo (1983), Paris (1993), Hong Kong (2005) and Shanghai (2016). The theme parks were a natural extension of Disney's core business because the themes and characters that appeared in its films provided the basis for the rides and fantasy settings. A virtuous circle was created whereby the films promoted the parks and the parks promoted the films. As Disney acquired more movie disruption rights, the growth possibilities for the theme parks also increased with the introduction of related 'lands' such as *Toy Story* and *Star Wars: Galaxy's Edge*. Over time, the development of the theme parks took Disney into a new area. Visitors to the theme parks needed accommodation so Disney built and ran hotels; Disney became skilful in managing travel arrangements and the tourist experience and subsequently founded the Disney Vacation Club, the Disney Cruise Line and Adventures by Disney. Disney also planned and built retail, entertainment and dining complexes, which led to the establishment of the Disney Development Company.

- *Studio entertainment.* At the heart of Disney's operation lies its creative content. The early success of the company was based on its animated cartoons and the characters who populated them, but as audiences' tastes changed, Disney needed to move with the times by acquiring new content and embracing new animation technologies. To that end, in 2006, it acquired Pixar, a computer animation studio best known for films such as *Toy Story* and *Finding Nemo*. It purchased Marvel Entertainment, the owner of comic book characters such as Spider Man and the Hulk, in 2009, and, in 2012, bought Lucasfilm, the production company behind the *Star Wars* movies. In 2019 Disney acquired a number of Twenty-First Century Fox businesses, including their film and television studies, certain cable networks and their 30 per cent interest in Hulu (a streaming service). In addition, Disney acquired the rights to a number of other film, direct-to-video, musical and theatrical content.
- *Consumer products.* The consumer products division was the vehicle that Disney used to exploit its intellectual property by awarding licences to third parties to produce and sell merchandise based on its characters; publishing children's book, magazines and learning devices; and operating both physical and online Disney Stores. Its stores were generally located in shopping malls or retail complexes. By 2018, Disney owned and operated 214 stores in the US, 87 in Europe, 53 in Japan and 2 in China.
- *Interactive media.* This division focused on developing console, mobile, social and virtual world games that were marketed on a worldwide basis. While most of the game development activity took place in-house, Disney also licensed some third-party developers to develop games based on Disney material. From small beginnings the division grew relatively rapidly.

What drives success?

Unlike many other large conglomerates, Disney has been able to maintain momentum and improve its performance in all its major segments, raising the question of what drives success. Iger has suggested that there are three main elements underlying Disney's performance. First, he argues that, under his leadership, the company has made the production of high-quality, family-orientated content its priority with the ongoing development of creative content driving all parts of the business. Much of the creative impetus has come from acquiring companies but, once acquired, Disney has allowed these businesses to operate quasi-autonomously and has encouraged innovation. Second, he suggests that Disney is future-orientated and has succeeded by making its content more accessible and engaging through the use of digital technology. The company has been willing to learn from its mistakes, for example restructuring its interactive division and moving away from console games when this segment failed to make money. Finally, he places emphasis on building a portfolio of brands.

Disney's continuing success depends on its ability to consistently create and distribute films, broadcast and cable programs, online material, electronic games, theme park attractions, hotel and other resort facilities, travel experiences and consumer products that meet the changing preferences of a wide range of consumers, a growing number of whom are located outside the US. The linkages between businesses mean that success or failure in one part of the business can affect other parts. For example, if entertainment offerings like *Who Wants to be a Millionaire* or *High School Musical* cease to be popular with audiences then revenue from advertising, which is based in part on program ratings, falls and so does revenue from merchandising. In the worst-case scenario, if the company experiences successive content failures then viewers might cancel their subscriptions to cable channels or reduce their visits to entertainment parks where the themed rides are seen as passé. Disney has had its fair share of flops as well as hits, for example *The Lone Ranger, John Carter, A Wrinkle in Time* and even *Solo: A Star Wars Story* failed to make it at the box office. At the same time, changes in technology and different delivery formats such as television, DVDs, computer and web-based formats are affecting not only the demand for the company's entertainment products but also the cost of producing and distributing them.

Disney faces a fundamental tension, namely in expanding to exploit the benefits of scale and scope present in its business activities, the size and complexity of its organisation increases and makes it more difficult for the company to be agile and innovative. The challenge for Iger remains that of maintaining creative impetus while putting in place the structures and systems necessary to manage such a large and complex organisation.

Introduction

Unlike business-level strategy, which is primarily concerned with how business units of a company compete within specific markets, corporate-level strategy is about how and where a company grows and competes. We see this with Disney in this chapter's scene setter. While business-level or competitive strategy examines how a company succeeds in each business, corporate-level strategy answers the question about which businesses the company should select or occupy. Mostly, corporate-level strategy focuses on three things: (1) corporate parenting, (2) business portfolios (i.e. the range of strategic business units) and (3) portfolio matrices. First, since very large companies consist of multibusinesses, a corporate hierarchy exists as a corporate parent responsible for making corporate-level strategy decisions. Second, the parent decides which new businesses (business portfolio/ strategic business units) to support, what acquisitions to make, and whether to form joint ventures or alliances.[4] For Disney, they chose to expand their distribution network by developing their own direct-to-consumer streaming network, Disney+, as well as acquiring Twenty-First Century Fox businesses. Third, corporate managers need to analyse strategic decisions by using a range of portfolio matrices. Typically, the basis of corporate strategy is to develop strategies by which the corporate parent can create more value than rival parents in its portfolio compositions. Accordingly, the emphasis in this chapter is on corporate-level strategy that defines the scope of the company through product scope (diversification), vertical scope (vertical integration) and geographical scope (multinationality). The scope of corporate strategy can be broken into the following three areas.

- *Product scope.* How specialised should the company be in terms of the range of products it supplies? Coca-Cola (soft drinks), National Australia Bank (banking service), Gap (fashion retailing), and Insurance Australia Group (insurance) are specialised companies: they are engaged in a single industry sector. General Electric, Samsung and Wesfarmers are diversified companies: each spans a number of different industries.
- *Vertical scope.* What range of vertically linked activities should the company encompass? Walt Disney Company is a vertically integrated company: it produces its own movies, distributes them itself to cinemas and through its own TV networks (ABC and Disney Channel), and uses the movies' characters in its retail stores and theme parks. Nike is much more vertically specialised: it engages in design and marketing but outsources most activities in its value chain, including manufacturing, distribution and retailing.
- *Geographical scope.* What is the optimal geographical spread of activities for the company? In the restaurant business, Hungry Jack's has over 300 locations across Australia, Lotteria operates throughout the Asia–Pacific region, and McDonald's operates in 121 different countries.

Collectively, the corporate strategy framework is illustrated in figure 6.1.

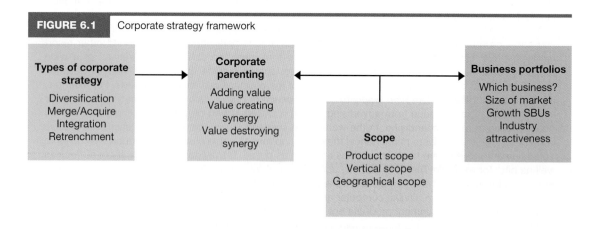

| FIGURE 6.1 | Corporate strategy framework |

Types of corporate strategy

Diversification
Merge/Acquire
Integration
Retrenchment

Corporate parenting

Adding value
Value creating synergy
Value destroying synergy

Scope

Product scope
Vertical scope
Geographical scope

Business portfolios

Which business?
Size of market
Growth SBUs
Industry attractiveness

6.1 Corporate-level strategy

LEARNING OBJECTIVE 6.1 Understand the nature of corporate-level strategy and be able to identify and explain various types of corporate strategies.

A useful way to think about corporate-level strategy to is focus on growth. The corporate parent needs to grow the company by adding and creating value to each of its individual businesses. If an organisation has been successful as a single-unit business and wants to grow by reinvesting its profits into new business areas, it will need to determine the scope of its growth. It will also need to establish new businesses by creating them and/or acquiring other related businesses or — in the case of conglomerate growth — unrelated businesses. To grow in strategic terms means to diversify the scope of a company's competitive strategy. If a company is standing still or not progressing competitively, it is regressing and going backwards. This is because the world moves against companies consistently. Prices increase; products become discontinuous because of fast-cycle markets; the cost of labour increases along with other variable costs; and competitors increasingly outflank other companies through better business strategies, by being better corporate parents, and by creating superior value in their business units faster than other parents. So, companies diversify for a number of reasons — namely, when:

- current objectives can no longer be met
- retained cash (often called cash reserves in general funds) exceeds the total expansion needs of the present portfolio
- diversification opportunities promise greater profitability than expansion opportunities that involve simply expanding into existing markets.[5]

Typical symptoms are important such as a drop in the rate of return, too many products in slow cycle markets due to market saturation and falling market share. Shareholders do not take kindly to CEOs of corporate parents, for instance, who hold large cash reserves but fail to reinvest this in growth. Shareholders expect more than average returns.

Setting direction

Corporate strategy is about generating the most profits from current businesses as well as diversifying by developing new business. Parents accordingly look for synergies in business units by matching these to growth opportunities. Synergy relates to a desired fit between a company and its new product–market entries.[6] Synergy suggests that a company seeks a product–market posture with a combined performance that is greater than the sum of its parts.[7] This is often described as the '2 + 2 = 5' effect, where synergies can be found in sales (where products might use common distribution channels or common sales administration). Similarly, synergies can be found in operations (higher utilisation of facilities), investments (joint use of plant and common raw materials inventories) and in management synergies (experience gained in previous business encounters results in stronger performance). Synergy will be discussed in more detail later in the chapter.

One way to think about diversification and seeking synergy in a company's current and new businesses is through the growth vector, which is often called the product–market matrix.[8] As figure 6.2 illustrates, the product–market matrix concerns the direction the company wants to consider for each of its portfolios of existing businesses or portfolio of new businesses.

In figure 6.2, quadrant 1 indicates that a company wants to create more value by taking present products into existing markets. Here, opportunities are not exhausted in existing markets that the company currently serves. Take, for example, a company in Malaysia that provides educational services but currently offers these only in Kuala Lumpur. More opportunities exist in Kuala Lumpur to grow existing products by providing more classes or a variety of course structures and delivery methods. New opportunities to provide educational services might also exist in Penang and Kuching, which present opportunities to create new customers. Put simply, the company's competitive posture in traditional markets may raise its future performance prospects to a level which will satisfy its objectives.[9] Similarly, quadrant 2 concerns taking existing products into new markets. Here, the company notes that existing synergies can be usefully matched to new markets. So, our educational company in Malaysia decides to grow into Singapore by opening up its education services and setting up an office in that location. There is a good reason for starting competitive analysis in existing markets. While discontinuities exist in nearly every competitive environment, they are familiar discontinuities to the extent that the educational company knows its market very well and has learned from past experience.

FIGURE 6.2   Product–market matrix

Products or service

	Existing	New
Existing	Market penetration 1	Product development 4
New	Market development 2	Diversification 3

(Markets — vertical axis label)

Source: Adapted from Ansoff, 1965.

Now we need to examine quadrant 3. Here, the company is interested in taking new products or services into new markets. This relates to corporate diversification (see the following discussion on diversification strategy for different forms of diversification and different kinds of corporate strategies). If, for instance, the research and development arm of the company has started to develop and identify new products/services, they may find these unsuitable for the existing market. Instead, the company will look for growth in new markets with new products. This can clearly be seen in Disney's strategies. Originally a cartoon studio, they soon diversified into consumer products linked to their characters. Their next step was into theme parks — with their movies and characters providing the inspiration for 'lands', rides and experiences. The success of these parks worldwide led to further diversification into accommodation, travel planning and retail development. They have also vertically integrated their original studio business by developing and acquiring distribution networks giving them control of both content and distribution.

By contrast, quadrant 4 (in figure 6.2) refers to the development of new products and services for existing markets. To use the education company example, new educational degrees might be developed for the existing market, representing another growth vector for the company.

Types of corporate-level strategy

This chapter examines different types of corporate strategy, beginning with diversification (see figure 6.3). Since diversification is one of the main reasons for corporate strategy development, much of the discussion and analysis relates to this area. Mergers and acquisitions, and integration and retrenchment will then be explored. An examination of the different ways to analyse corporate parenting (which encapsulates market growth in strategic business units) and various ways to perform portfolio analysis will follow.

6.2 Diversification strategy

LEARNING OBJECTIVE 6.2 Identify the conditions under which diversification creates value for shareholders.

A **diversification strategy** is a company's decision to expand its operations by adding new products and services, markets or stages of production to the existing business. The purpose of diversification is to allow the company to enter lines of business that are different from current operations.

There are two types of diversification. The first type, *related diversification* (or concentric diversification), is about the expansion of the business based on the common core of a company's existing resources and capabilities. With related diversification, synergy increases because the related activity can increase value and the economies of scale can save money. *Unrelated diversification* (or conglomerate diversification) is used to improve the profitability and lower the overall business risk of a company.

It occurs when there is no common thread of strategic fit or relationship between the new and old lines of business; the new and old businesses are unrelated. Essentially, it is like holding a portfolio.

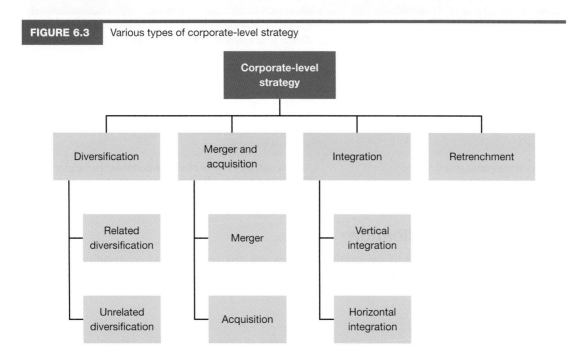

FIGURE 6.3   Various types of corporate-level strategy

Related and unrelated diversification

Given the importance of economies of scope in shared resources and capabilities, it seems likely that diversification into related industries should be more profitable than diversification into unrelated industries. Empirical research initially supported this prediction. Rumelt discovered that companies that diversified into businesses closely related to their core activities were significantly more profitable than those that pursued unrelated diversification.[10]

The lack of clear performance differences between related and unrelated diversification is troubling. Three factors may help explain the confused picture. First, related diversification may offer greater potential benefits, but may also pose more difficult management problems for companies such that the potential benefits are not realised. Second, the tendency for related diversification to outperform unrelated diversification might be the result of poorly performing companies rushing into unrelated diversification.[11] Third, the distinction between 'related' and 'unrelated' diversification is not always clear. Relatedness refers to common resources and capabilities, not similarities of products and technologies. Thus, champagne and luggage are not obviously related products; however, LVMH applies similar brand management capabilities to them.

If relatedness refers to the potential for sharing and transferring resources and capabilities between businesses, there are no unambiguous criteria to determine whether two industries are related — it all depends on the company undertaking the diversification. Empirical studies have defined relatedness in terms of similarities between industries in technologies and markets. These similarities emphasise relatedness at the operational level — in manufacturing, marketing and distribution — typically activities where economies from resource sharing are small and achieving them is costly in management terms. Conversely, some of the most important sources of value creation within the diversified company are the ability to apply common general management capabilities, strategic management systems and resource allocation processes to different businesses. Such economies depend on the existence of strategic rather than operational commonalities among the different businesses within the diversified corporation.[12]

The essence of such strategic-level linkages is the ability to apply similar strategies, resource allocation procedures and control systems across the different businesses within the corporate portfolio.[13] Table 6.1[14] lists some of the strategic factors that determine similarities and synergies among businesses in relation to corporate management activities. Unlike operational relatedness, where the benefits of exploiting economies of scope in joint inputs are comparatively easy to forecast, and even to quantify, relatedness at the strategic level may be much more difficult to appraise.

TABLE 6.1 The determinants of strategic relatedness between businesses

Corporate management tasks	Determinants of strategic similarity
Resource allocation	Similar sizes of capital investment projects Similar time spans of investment projects Similar sources of risk Similar general management skills required for business unit managers
Strategy formulation	Similar key success factors Similar stages of the industry life cycle Similar competitive positions occupied by each business within its industry
Performance management and control	Targets defined in terms of similar performance variables Similar time horizons for performance targets

Drivers for diversification

Diversification has been driven by three major goals: growth, risk reduction and profitability. As will be seen, although growth and risk reduction have been prominent motives for diversification, they tend to be inconsistent with the creation of shareholder value.

Growth

In the absence of diversification, companies are prisoners of their industry. For companies in stagnant or declining industries this is a daunting prospect — especially if the industry faces ultimate demise. However, the critical issue for top management is whether the pursuit of growth is consistent with the quest for profitability. In principle, widening the company's range of potential investment to include opportunities outside its existing industry should be entirely compatible with increasing profitability. Indeed, for companies such as Canon, deploying their capabilities in new product markets such as printers and business systems is a key source of value creation. However, the overall evidence is to the contrary. During the 1980s, Philip Morris diversified into soft drinks (7-Up), beer (Miller) and food (Kraft, General Foods), while Exxon diversified into copper and coal mining, electric motors, and computers and office equipment. In Australia, conglomerates such as Wesfarmers diversified into hardware retailing and forest products. It is notable that when underperforming public companies are threatened by investor discontent or a corporate raider, they frequently resort to selling off diversified businesses.[15]

Risk reduction

A second motive for diversification is the desire to spread risks. To isolate the effects of diversification on risk, consider the case of 'pure' or 'conglomerate' diversification, where separate businesses are brought under common ownership but the individual cash flows of the businesses remain unchanged. So long as the cash flows of the different businesses are imperfectly correlated, then the variance of the cash flow of the combined businesses is less than the average of that of the separate businesses. Hence, diversification reduces risk.

But does this risk reduction create value for shareholders? It is important to take account of the fact that investors hold diversified portfolios. If investors can hold diversified portfolios, what advantage can there be in companies diversifying for them? The only possible advantage could be if companies can diversify at lower cost than individual investors. In fact the reverse is true: the transaction costs to shareholders of diversifying their portfolios are far less than the transaction costs to companies diversifying through acquisition. Not only do acquiring companies incur the heavy costs of using investment banks and legal advisers, they must also pay an acquisition premium to gain control of an independent company.

Risk spreading through diversification may benefit other stakeholders. If cyclicality in the company's profits is accompanied by cyclicality in employment, then so long as employees are transferable between the separate businesses of the company, there may be benefits to employees from diversification's ability to smooth output fluctuations. Special issues arise when considering the risk of bankruptcy. For a marginally profitable company, diversification can help avoid cyclical fluctuations of profits that can push it into insolvency.

If there are economies to the company from financing investments internally rather than resorting to external capital markets, the stability in the company's cash flow that results from diversification may reinforce independence from external capital markets. For Exxon Mobil, BP and the other major oil companies one of the benefits of extending across upstream (exploration and production), downstream (refining and marketing), and chemicals is that the negative correlation of the returns from these businesses increases the overall stability of their cash flows. This in turn increases their capacity to undertake huge, risky investments in offshore oil production, transcontinental pipelines and natural gas liquefaction. These benefits also explain why companies pursue hedging activities that only reduce unsystematic risk.[16]

Profitability

If corporate-level strategy should be directed towards the interests of shareholders, what are the implications for diversification strategy? For companies contemplating diversification, Porter proposes three 'essential tests' to be applied in deciding whether diversification will truly create shareholder value.

- *The attractiveness test.* The industries chosen for diversification must be structurally attractive or capable of being made attractive. A critical realisation in Porter's 'essential tests' is that industry attractiveness is insufficient on its own. Although diversification is a means by which the company can access more attractive investment opportunities than are available in its own industry, it faces the problem of entering the new industry.
- *The cost-of-entry test.* The cost of entry must not capitalise all the future profits. This test recognises that the attractiveness of an industry to a company already established in an industry may be different from its attractiveness to a company seeking to enter the industry. Pharmaceuticals, management consulting and investment banking offer above-average profitability precisely because they are protected by barriers to entry. Companies seeking to enter these industries have a choice. They may enter by acquiring an established player, in which case not only does the market price of the target company reflect the superior profit prospects of the industry, but the diversifying company must also offer an acquisition premium of around 25 to 50 per cent over the market price to gain control.[17] Alternatively, entry may occur through establishing a new corporate venture. In this case, the diversifying company must directly confront the barriers to entry protecting that industry, which usually means low returns over a long period.[18]
- *The better-off test.* Either the new unit must gain competitive advantage from its link with the corporation, or vice versa.[19] This test addresses the basic issue of competitive advantage: if two businesses producing different products are brought together under the ownership and control of a single enterprise, is there any reason why they should become any more profitable? Combining different, but related, businesses can enhance the competitive advantages of the original business, the new business, or both.

Although the potential for value creation from exploiting linkages between the different businesses may be considerable, the practical difficulties of exploiting such opportunities are often complex and challenging. The chapter will now examine the issues systematically.

6.3 Competitive advantage from diversification

LEARNING OBJECTIVE 6.3 Recognise the organisational and managerial issues arising from diversification and why diversification so often fails to realise its anticipated benefits.

If the primary source of value creation from diversification is exploiting linkages between different businesses, what are the linkages and how are they exploited? The primary means by which diversification creates competitive advantage is through the sharing of resources and capabilities across different businesses. There is also the potential for diversification to enhance or exploit a company's market power.

Economies of scope

The most general argument concerning the benefits of diversification focuses on the presence of economies of scope in common resources. Economies of scope exist whenever there are cost savings from using a resource in multiple activities carried out in combination rather than carrying out those activities independently.[20] Economies of scope exist for similar reasons as economies of scale. The key difference is that the economies of scale relate to cost economies from increasing output for a single product; economies of scope are cost economies from increasing output across multiple products.[21] The nature of economies of scope varies between different types of resources and capabilities.

Tangible resources

Tangible resources (e.g. distribution networks, information technology systems, sales forces and research laboratories) can offer economies of scope by eliminating duplication between businesses through creating a single shared facility. The greater the fixed costs of these items, the greater the associated economies of scope are likely to be. Entry by cable TV companies into telephone services, and telephone companies into cable TV, are motivated by the desire to spread the costs of networks and billing systems over as great a volume of business as possible. Economies of scope also arise from the centralised provision of administrative and support services by the corporate centre to the different businesses of the corporation. Among diversified companies, accounting, legal services, government relations and information technology tend to be centralised — often through shared service organisations that supply common administrative and technical services to the operating businesses. Similar economies arise from centralising research activities in a corporate R&D laboratory. In aerospace, the ability of US companies such as Boeing and United Technologies to spread research expenditures over both military and civilian products has given these companies an advantage over overseas competitors with more limited access to large defence contracts.[22]

Intangible resources

Intangible resources such as brands, corporate reputation and technology offer economies of scope from the ability to extend them to additional businesses at low marginal cost.[23] Exploiting a strong brand across additional products is called brand extension. In Australia, Jacob's Creek (through Pernod Ricard) also managed to increase its sales after extending its wine range to new varietals such as pinot grigio, sauvignon blanc and pinot noir. Globally, Starbucks has extended its brand to ice cream, bottled drinks, home espresso machines and books.

Organisational capabilities

Organisational capabilities can also be transferred within the diversified company. For example, LVMH is the world's biggest and most diversified supplier of branded luxury goods. Its distinctive capability is the management of luxury brands. This capability comprises market analysis, advertising, promotion, retail management and quality assurance. These capabilities are deployed across Louis Vuitton (accessories and leather goods); Hennessey (cognac); Moët et Chandon, Dom Pérignon, Veuve Clicquot and Krug (champagne); Celine, Givenchy, Kenzo, Dior, Guerlain and Donna Karan (fashion clothing and perfumes); TAG Heuer and Chaumet (watches); Sephora and La Samaritaine (retailing); and some 25 other branded businesses. Another example is Sharp Corporation — a Japanese company originally established to manufacture metal products and the Ever Sharp Pencil — which developed capabilities in the miniaturisation of electronic products that it has deployed to develop and introduce a stream of innovative products, beginning with the world's first transistor calculator (1964), the first LCD pocket calculator (1973), LCD colour TVs, PDAs, webcams, ultraportable notebook computers, and 5G mobile telephones.

General management capabilities

Some of the most important capabilities in influencing the performance of diversified corporations are general management capabilities. General Electric possesses strong technological and operational capabilities at business level and it is good at sharing these capabilities between businesses (e.g. turbine know-how between jet engines and electrical generating equipment). However, its core capabilities are in general management and these reside primarily at the corporate level. These include its ability to motivate and develop its managers, its outstanding strategic and financial management that reconciles decentralised decision making with strong centralised control, and its international management capability. Similar observations could be made about Disney. While Disney's capabilities in technical know-how, new product development and international marketing reside within the individual businesses, it is the corporate management capabilities and the systems through which they are exercised that maintain, nourish, coordinate and upgrade these competitive advantages.[24]

Economies from internalising transactions

Although economies of scope provide cost savings from sharing and transferring resources and capabilities, does a company have to diversify across these different businesses to exploit those economies? The answer is no. Economies of scope in resources and capabilities can be exploited simply by selling or licensing the use of the resource or capability to another company. Walt Disney Company exploits the enormous value of its trademarks, copyrights and characters partly through diversification into theme parks, live theatre, cruise ships and hotels; and partly through licensing the use of these assets to producers of clothing, toys, music, comics, food and drinks, as well as to the franchisees of Disney's retail stores.

What determines whether economies of scope are better exploited internally within the company through diversification, or externally through market contracts with independent companies? The key issue is relative efficiency: what are the transaction costs of market contracts, as compared with the administrative costs of a diversified enterprise? Transaction costs include the costs involved in drafting, negotiating, monitoring and enforcing a contract. The costs of internalisation consist of the management costs of establishing and coordinating the diversified business.[25]

Though the returns to patents and brand names, such as those of Disney, can often be appropriated efficiently through licensing, complex general management capabilities may be near impossible to exploit through market contracts. For example, the only way for Apple Inc. to exploit its capabilities in innovation and user-friendly design outside its core computer business was for it to diversify into other areas of entertainment and consumer electronics.

The more deeply embedded a company's capabilities within the management systems and the culture of the organisation, the greater the likelihood that these capabilities can only be deployed internally within the company. In principle, Virgin could license its brand to other companies. In practice, the value of the Virgin brand depends critically on the dynamism of Virgin companies, the irreverence of the Virgin culture, and the personality of Richard Branson. The drivers for diversification coupled with the competitive advantage that accrues to the diversified company is illustrated in figure 6.4.

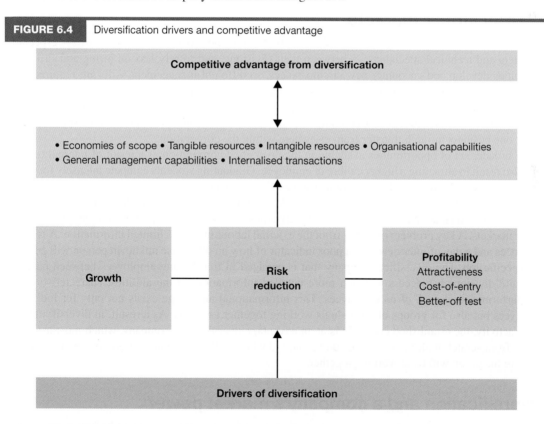

FIGURE 6.4 Diversification drivers and competitive advantage

The diversified company as an internal market

Economies of scope on their own do not provide an adequate rationale for diversification — they must be supported by the presence of transaction costs. However, the presence of transaction costs in any non-specialised resource can offer efficiency gains from diversification, even where no economies of scope are present.

Internal capital markets

Consider the case of financial capital. The diversified company represents an internal capital market: the corporate allocating capital between the different businesses through the capital expenditure budget.

Which is more efficient, the internal capital markets of diversified companies or the external capital market? Diversified companies have two key advantages.

- By maintaining a balanced portfolio of cash-generating and cash-using businesses, diversified companies can avoid the costs of using the external capital market, including the margin between borrowing and lending rates and the heavy costs of issuing new debt and equity.
- Diversified companies have better access to information on the financial prospects of their different businesses than that typically available to external financiers.[26]

Against these advantages is the critical disadvantage that investment funds within the diversified company are not allocated solely on the basis of potential returns. Corporate management is likely to be subject to goals other than shareholder value maximisation and capital allocation tends to be a politicised process. How do these conflicting factors balance out? Despite inconsistent findings, the balance of the evidence is that diversified companies exhibit key weaknesses in their internal capital markets, including a tendency to cross-subsidise their poorly performing divisions, to waste resources in internal political competition for funding, and reluctance to transfer divisional cash flows to the divisions with the best prospects.[27] However, overall averages obscure sharp differences in the efficiency of capital allocation between different diversified companies. Illustrative examples can be found in cases such as Wesfarmers of Australia, Hutchison Whampoa of Hong Kong, Bouygues and Lagardere of France, ITC of India, and Carso of Mexico. The common characteristics of these companies were: 'strict *financial* discipline, rigorous analysis and valuation, a refusal to overpay for acquisitions, and a willingness to close or sell existing businesses'.[28]

Internal labour markets

Efficiencies also arise from the ability of diversified companies to transfer employees — especially managers and technical specialists — between their divisions, and to rely less on hiring and firing. As companies develop and encounter new circumstances, so different management skills are required. The costs associated with hiring include advertising, the time spent in interviewing and selection, and the costs of 'head-hunting' agencies. The costs of dismissing employees can be very high where severance payments must be offered. A diversified corporation has a pool of employees and can respond to the specific needs of any one business through transfer from elsewhere within the corporation.

The broader set of opportunities available in the diversified corporation as a result of internal transfer may also result in attracting a higher calibre of employee. Graduating students compete intensely for entry-level positions with diversified corporations such as Canon, General Electric, Unilever and Nestlé in the belief that these companies can offer richer career development than more specialised companies.

The informational advantages of diversified companies are especially important in relation to internal labour markets. A key problem of hiring from the external labour market is limited information. A résumé, references and a day of interviews are a poor indicator of how an otherwise unknown person will perform in a specific job. The diversified company that is engaged in transferring employees between business units and divisions has access to much more detailed information on the abilities, characteristics and past performance of each of its employees. This informational advantage exists not only for individual employees but also for groups of individuals working together as teams. As a result, in diversifying into a new activity, the established company is at an advantage over the new company, which must assemble a team from scratch with poor information on individual capabilities and almost no information on how effective the group will be at working together.

Diversification and a company's market power

The potential for diversification to enhance profitability by increasing a company's market power and suppressing competition is of interest for large companies all over the world. Diversification can affect a company's market power through the following four mechanisms.

- *Predatory pricing.* Global corporations can derive strength from their ability to finance competitive battles in individual markets through cross-subsidisation. They can also use their size and diversity to discipline or even drive out specialised competitors in particular product markets through predatory pricing — cutting prices to below the level of rivals' costs.
- *Bundling.* A diversified company can extend its monopoly in one market into a related market by bundling the two products together. The US Justice Department claimed Microsoft abused its monopoly power in PC operating systems by bundling its Explorer web browser with Windows, thereby squeezing

Netscape from the browser market. The European Union made a similar case against Microsoft regarding its bundling of its media player with Windows.[29]

- *Reciprocal dealing.* A diversified company can leverage its market share across its businesses by reciprocal buying arrangements. One case involved Intel, which refused to supply microprocessors to Intergraph Corporation unless Intergraph licensed certain technology to Intel free of charge.[30] The potential for reciprocal dealing is greatest in those emerging market economies where a few large companies span many sectors.

- *Mutual forbearance.* It is argued that when one large conglomerate enterprise competes with another, the two are likely to encounter each other in a considerable number of markets. The multiplicity of their contacts may blunt the edge of their competition. Each conglomerate may adopt a mutual forbearance policy designed to stabilise the whole structure of the competitive relationship.[31] Empirical evidence suggests this is most likely among companies that meet in multiple geographical markets for the same product or service — the airline industry, for example.[32] Such tendencies may also exist where diversified companies meet in multiple product markets.[33] When working together, the four instruments effectively influence market power (see figure 6.5).

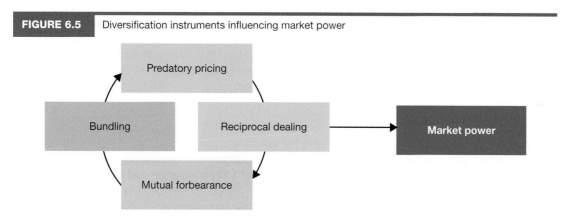

FIGURE 6.5   Diversification instruments influencing market power

Diversification and performance

Diversification has the potential to create value for shareholders where it exploits economies of scope and where transaction costs in the markets for resources make it inefficient to exploit these economies of scope through market contracts. How do these predictions work in practice?

The performance of diversified and specialised companies

Despite a large number of empirical studies over four decades, no consistent, systematic relationships have emerged between performance and the degree of diversification. However, there is some evidence that, beyond a certain point, high levels of diversification are associated with deteriorating profitability — possibly because of the problems of complexity that diversification creates. Among British companies, diversification was associated with increased profitability up to a point, after which further diversification was associated with declining profitability.[34] Other studies have also detected a curvilinear relationship between diversification and profitability.[35] Research by McKinsey & Company offers further evidence of the benefits of moderate diversification — 'a strategic sweet spot between focus and broader diversification'. Timing is the key, they note. Diversification makes sense when a company has exhausted growth opportunities in its existing markets and can match its existing capabilities to emerging external opportunities.[36] As with most studies seeking to link strategy to performance, a key problem is distinguishing *association* from *causation*. If diversified companies are generally more profitable than specialised companies, is it because diversification increases profitability or because profitable companies channel their cash flows into diversifying investments?

It is also likely that the performance effects of diversification depend on the mode of diversification. There is a mass of evidence pointing to the poor performance of mergers and acquisitions in general — for acquiring companies, the stock market returns to acquisition are unequivocally negative.[37] Among these, mergers and acquisitions involving companies in different industries appear to perform especially poorly.[38]

Some of the most powerful evidence concerning the relationship between diversification and performance relates to the refocusing initiatives by a large number of North American, European and Australian companies. The evidence, ranging from conglomerates such as General Electric in technology, media and financial services, UXC in IT and business solutions, and Rio Tinto in mineral resources, is that narrowing business scope leads to increased profitability and higher stock market valuation. Markides provides systematic evidence of the performance gains to diversified companies from divesting noncore activities.[39] This may reflect a changing relationship between diversification and profitability over time: the growing turbulence of the business environment may have increased the costs of managing complex, diversified corporations. The stock market's verdict on diversification has certainly shifted over time, with highly diversified companies having their earnings valued at a discount rather than a premium to the overall market, and takeover announcements being greeted by share price reductions for bidding companies.[40] As a result, diversified companies have fallen prey to leveraged buyout specialists seeking to add value through dismembering these companies.

6.4 Mergers and acquisitions

LEARNING OBJECTIVE 6.4 Distinguish between mergers and acquisitions and determine their relative merits in exploiting the linkages between different businesses.

This section builds on diversification since acquisitions are concerned with either diversifying existing businesses and/or buying new strategic business units (SBUs). This usually occurs through outright acquisitions, merging with other companies to share resources and/or joint ventures. Accordingly, mergers and acquisitions refer to the aspects of corporate-level strategy that deal with the buying, selling and combining of different companies that can help a company in a given industry grow rapidly without having to create another business entity. They are closely related to an integration strategy.

Acquisition

An **acquisition**, also known as a takeover or a buyout, is the purchase of one company by another. It usually refers to a purchase of a smaller company by a larger one. Sometimes, however, a reverse takeover exists when a smaller company obtains the control of a larger company and keeps its name for the combined entity.

An acquisition may be friendly or hostile. In the former case, the companies cooperate in negotiations. In the latter case, the takeover target is unwilling to be bought or the target's board has no prior knowledge of the offer. The acquisition process is very complex, with many dimensions influencing its outcome.

Types of acquisition

There are two types of acquisition.
- *Share acquisition.* The buyer acquires a controlling number of shares, and thereby takes control of the target company. Ownership control of the company in turn conveys effective control over the assets of the company. This form of transaction usually carries with it all of the liabilities accrued by that business over its past and all of the risks that company faces in its commercial environment.
- *Asset acquisition.* The buyer purchases the assets of the target company. The cash the target receives from the sell-off is paid back to its shareholders by dividend or through liquidation. This type of transaction leaves the target company as an empty shell, if the acquirer buys out the entire assets. This can be particularly important where foreseeable liabilities may include future, unquantified damage awards such as those that could arise from litigation.

Merger

A **merger** is a combination of two companies into a bigger company. Both companies' stocks are surrendered and new company stock is issued in its place.

Classifications of mergers

Mergers can be classified in various ways, as follows.
- *Horizontal merger.* The merger of two companies that are in direct competition in the same industry and that have similar product lines and markets.
- *Vertical merger.* The merger of a customer and company or a supplier and company.
- *Conglomerate merger.* A merger between two companies that have no common business areas.
- *Concentric merger.* A merger in which the two companies are in the same general industry, but have no mutual buyer/customer or supplier relationship, such as a merger between a bank and a leasing company. For example, Prudential's acquisition of Bache & Company.

Distinction between mergers and acquisitions

A merger is a transaction in which the assets of at least two companies are transferred to a new company so that only one separate legal entity remains. Acquisition is a transaction in which both companies in the transaction can survive but the acquirer increases its percentage ownership in the target.

From a legal point of view, the purchase of a company is called an acquisition when the target company ceases to exist, the new buyer takes in the business and the buyer's stock continues to be traded. However, a merger is when two companies agree to go forward as a single new company rather than remain separately owned and operated.

Financing mergers and acquisitions

Various methods of financing merger and acquisition deals exist, as follows.
- *Cash transaction.* Cash transactions refer to situations when shareholders of target companies are given cash for giving up their shares. A major issue in using cash for mergers and acquisitions is that it places a burden on the cash flow of the companies.
- *Share financing.* The acquirer's stock may be offered as consideration for the purchase of shares from shareholders of the target company.
- *Debt financing.* Financing capital may come from bank loans or the issue of corporate bonds. Acquisitions financed through debt are known as leveraged buyouts.

Reasons for mergers and acquisitions

Many companies actively engage in merger and acquisition activities to seek better financial performance. The following reasons are the most common.
- *Economies of scale.* Some costs, especially fixed costs, can be reduced by removing overlapping operations after a merger or acquisition.
- *Economies of scope.* Mergers and acquisitions often can extend the market and product portfolio of the companies when they are combined into one.
- *Tax benefits.* A profitable company can enjoy tax benefits by acquiring a money-losing business by incorporating the losses into their consolidated profits accounts.
- *Higher return on investment.* A company can increase its return on investment (ROI) by acquiring another company with a higher ROI.

Concerns about mergers and acquisitions

Despite the goal of performance improvement, results from mergers and acquisitions are often disappointing. Numerous empirical studies show high failure rates of mergers and acquisition deals.[41] Mergers and acquisitions very often cause social concern. For example, the ACCC showed concern when the Commonwealth Bank of Australia acquired Bankwest. The concern was primarily related to the fear of reducing competition in the banking business in Australia.

6.5 Integration strategy

LEARNING OBJECTIVE 6.5 Assess the relative advantages of vertical and horizontal integration in organising related activities, understand the circumstances that influence these relative advantages, and advise a company whether a particular activity should be undertaken internally or outsourced.

The purpose of an integration strategy is to develop a coherent and consistent approach that will guide implementation decisions and reduce costs on important projects. An effective integration strategy will generate a higher profit and decrease the total cost of operations over time.

A company seeking integration strategies faces a subset of choices: horizontal and vertical integration.
- *Vertical integration.* Vertical integration is integration up or down a supply chain through which a company will control the production and distribution of products. For example, if a retailer starts manufacturing the products it sells, it is increasing its level of vertical integration.
- *Horizontal integration.* The expansion or addition of business activities at the same level of the value chain is referred to as horizontal integration. By adopting a horizontal integration strategy, a company may decide to pursue new customers, new products and new geographic locations.

Vertical integration

Vertical integration refers to a company's ownership of vertically related activities. The greater the company's ownership and control over successive stages of the value chain for its product, the greater its degree of vertical integration. The extent of vertical integration is indicated by the ratio of a company's value added to its sales revenue. Highly integrated companies — such as the major oil companies that own and control their value chain from exploring for oil down to the retailing of petrol — tend to have low expenditures on bought-in goods and services relative to their sales.

Vertical integration can be either *backward*, where the company takes over ownership and control of producing its own components or other inputs, or *forward*, where the company takes over ownership and control of activities previously undertaken by its customers.

Vertical integration may also be full or partial.

- *Full integration* exists between two stages of production when all of the first stage's production is transferred to the second stage with no sales or purchases from third parties.
- *Partial integration* exists when stages of production are not internally self-sufficient. Among the oil and gas majors, 'crude-rich' companies (such as Statoil) produce more oil than they refine and are net sellers of crude; 'crude-poor' companies (such as Exxon Mobil) have to supplement their own production with purchases of crude to keep their refineries supplied.

Technical economies from the physical integration of processes

Analysis of the benefits of vertical integration has traditionally emphasised the technical economies of vertical integration: cost savings that arise from the physical integration of processes. Thus, most sheet steel is produced by integrated producers in plants that first produce steel, then roll hot steel into sheets. Linking the two stages of production at a single location reduces transportation and energy costs. Similar technical economies arise in pulp and paper production and from linking oil refining with petrochemical production.

Consider the value chain for steel cans, which extends from mining iron ore to delivering cans to food processing companies (see figure 6.6). Between the production of steel and strip steel, most production is vertically integrated. Between the production of strip steel and steel cans, there is very little vertical integration: can producers such as Visy in Australia are specialist packaging companies that purchase strip steel from steel companies on contracts.[42]

| FIGURE 6.6 | The value chain for steel cans |

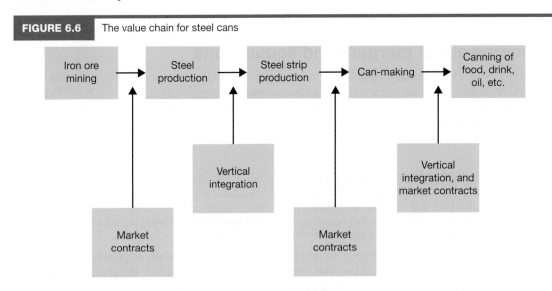

The predominance of market contracts between strip steel production and can production is the result of low transaction costs in the market for strip steel: there are many buyers and sellers, information is readily available, and the switching costs for buyers and suppliers are low. The same is true for many other commodity products: there are only a few large retailers, such as Woolworths and Wesfarmers, that own food manufacturing companies. Likewise, only a couple of flour-milling companies, such as AWB in Australia, own wheat farms.

In the semiconductor industry, some companies specialise either in semiconductor design or in fabrication, while other companies are vertically integrated across both stages (e.g. Intel and ST Microelectronics).

Which is more efficient? Again, it depends on the characteristics of the transaction between the designer and the fabricator. The more technically complex the integrated circuit and, hence, the greater the need for the designer and fabricator to engage in technical collaboration, the better the relative performance of integrated producers.[43]

Developing distinctive capabilities

A key advantage of a company that is specialised in a few activities is its ability to develop distinctive capabilities in those activities. Even large, technology-based companies such as BHP Billiton, AMP Limited and Coles Group, cannot maintain IT capabilities that match those of IT services specialists such as Microsoft, Apple Inc. and Unisys Australia. The ability of these IT specialists to work with many different customers stimulates learning and innovation. If Holden's IT department only serves the in-house needs of Holden, this does not encourage the rapid development of its IT capabilities.

However, this assumes that capabilities in different vertical activities are independent of one another. Where one capability builds on capabilities in adjacent activities, vertical integration may help develop distinctive capabilities. Thus, IBM's half-century of success in mainframe computers owes much to its technological leadership in semiconductors and software. The efficiency of Wal-Mart's retailing operations depends critically on specialised IT and logistics from its in-house departments.

Managing strategically different businesses

Most of the world's leading retailers — Wal-Mart, ALDI and Carrefour — do not integrate backward, that is, they do not manufacture. Not only do manufacturing and retailing require very different organisational capabilities, they also require different strategic planning systems, different approaches to control and human resource management, and different top management styles and skills.

Strategic dissimilarities between businesses have encouraged a number of companies to vertically de-integrate. Marriott's decision to split into two separate companies, Marriott International and Host Marriott, was influenced by the belief that owning hotels is a strategically different business from operating hotels. Similarly, Britain's major brewing companies have all de-integrated: Whitbread Plc divested its breweries and specialised in pubs, restaurants, and hotels; Scottish & Newcastle sold off most of its pubs and hotels to become a specialist brewer.

The incentive problem

Vertical integration changes the incentives between vertically-related businesses. Where a market interface exists between a buyer and a seller, profit incentives, as well as the emphasis on quality and reliability of supply, can ensure that the buyer is motivated to secure the best possible deal and the seller is motivated to pursue efficiency and service in order to attract and retain the buyer. Under vertical integration there is an internal supplier–customer relationship that is governed by corporate management systems rather than market incentives.

One approach to creating stronger performance incentives within vertically integrated companies is to open internal divisions to external competition. Many large corporations have created shared service organisations where internal suppliers of corporate services such as IT, training and engineering compete with external suppliers of the same services to serve internal operating divisions.

Competitive effects of vertical integration

Monopolistic companies have used vertical integration as a means of extending their monopoly positions from one stage of the industry to another. The classic cases are Standard Oil, which used its power in transportation and refining to foreclose markets to independent oil producers; and Alcoa, which used its monopoly position in aluminium production to squeeze independent fabricators of aluminium products to advantage its own fabrication subsidiaries. Such cases are rare. As economists have shown, once a company monopolises one vertical chain of an industry, there is no further monopoly profit to be extracted by extending that monopoly position to adjacent vertical stages of the industry. A greater concern is that vertical integration may make independent suppliers and customers less willing to do business with the vertically-integrated company, because it is now perceived as a competitor rather than as a supplier or customer.

Flexibility

Both vertical integration and market transactions can claim advantage with regard to different types of flexibility. Where the required flexibility is rapid responsiveness to uncertain demand, there may be advantages in market transactions. The lack of vertical integration in most companies in the construction industry reflects, in part, the need for flexibility in adjusting both to cyclical patterns of demand and to the different requirements of each project. Vertical integration may also be disadvantageous in responding quickly to new product development opportunities that require new combinations of technical capabilities. Some of the most successful new electronic products of recent years — Apple's iPad, Nintendo's 3DS portable game console, Dell's range of notebook computers — have been produced by contract manufacturers. Extensive outsourcing has been a key feature of fast-cycle product development throughout the electronics sector.

Yet, where system-wide flexibility is required, vertical integration may allow for speed and coordination in achieving simultaneous adjustment throughout the vertical chain. American Apparel is a fast-growing clothing manufacturer in the United States with an internationally known brand — especially for T-shirts. Its tightly coordinated vertical integration from its Los Angeles design and manufacturing base to its 160 retail stores allows a super-fast design-to-distribution cycle. In Australia, similar situations can also be found.

Designing vertical relationships

The discussion so far has compared vertical integration with arm's-length relationships between buyers and sellers. In practice, there are a variety of relationships through which buyers and sellers can interact and coordinate their interests. Figure 6.7 shows a number of different types of relationship between buyers and sellers. These relationships may be classified in relation to two characteristics. First, the extent to which the buyer and seller commit resources to the relationship: the arm's-length nature of spot contracts means that there is no significant commitment; vertical integration involves substantial investment. Second, the formalisation of the relationship: long-term contracts and franchises typically involve complex written agreements; spot contracts may involve little or no documentation, but are bound by common law; collaborative agreements between buyers and sellers are by definition informal, while the formality of vertical integration is at the discretion of the company's management.

| **FIGURE 6.7** | Different types of vertical relationship |

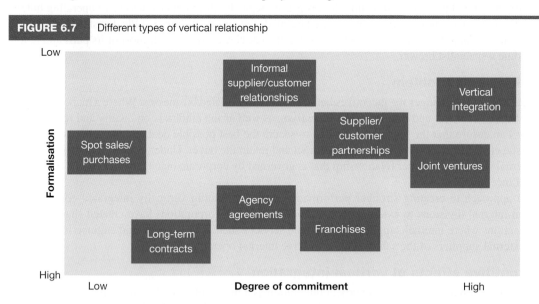

Different types of vertical relationship

Different types of vertical relationship offer different combinations of advantages and disadvantages. Consider, for example, the following.

- *Long-term contracts.* Market transactions can be either spot contracts — buying a cargo of crude oil on the Rotterdam petroleum market — or long-term contracts that involve a series of transactions over a period of time and specify the terms of sales and the responsibilities of each party. Spot transactions work well under competitive conditions (many buyers and sellers and a standard product) where there is no need for transaction-specific investments by either party. Where closer supplier–customer ties are needed — particularly when one or both parties need to make transaction-specific investments — then a longer term contract can help avoid opportunism and provide the security needed to make the necessary investment. However, long-term contracts introduce their own problems. In particular, they cannot anticipate all the possible circumstances that may arise during the life of the contract and run the risk either of being too restrictive or so loose that they give rise to opportunism and conflicting interpretation. The inflexibility problems of long-term contracts are particularly evident in IT outsourcing when the agreement may be for a period of 10 years or more.[44]

- *Vendor partnerships.* The greater the difficulties of specifying complete contracts for long-term supplier–customer deals, the more likely it is that vertical relationships will be based on trust and mutual understanding. Such relationships can provide the security needed for transaction-specific investments, the flexibility to meet changing circumstances and the incentives to avoid opportunism. Such arrangements may be entirely relational contracts with no written contract at all. The model for vendor partnerships has been the close collaborative relationships that many Japanese companies have with their suppliers. During the late 1980s, Toyota and Nissan directly produced about 20 to 23 per cent of the value of their cars, whereas Ford accounted for 50 per cent of its production value and GM for about 70 per cent. Yet, as Jeff Dyer has shown, the Japanese automakers have been remarkably successful in achieving close collaboration in technology, quality control, design, and scheduling of production and deliveries.[45]

- *Franchising.* A franchise is a contractual agreement between the owner of a trade mark and a business system (the franchiser) that permits the franchisee to produce and market the franchiser's product or service in a specified area. Franchising brings together the brand, marketing capabilities, and business systems of the large corporation with the entrepreneurship and local knowledge of small companies. The franchising systems of companies such as McDonald's, Century 21 Real Estate, Hilton Hotels, and Seven-Eleven convenience stores facilitate the close coordination and investment in transaction-specific assets that vertical integration permits with the high-powered incentives, flexibility and cooperation between strategically dissimilar businesses that market contracts make possible.

Choosing between alternative vertical relationships

Designing vertical relationships is not just a 'make or buy' choice. Between full vertical integration and spot market contracts, there is a broad spectrum of alternative organisational forms. Choosing the most suitable vertical relationship depends on the economic characteristics of the activities involved, legal and fiscal circumstances, and the strategies and resources of the companies involved. Even within the same industry, what is best for one company will not make sense for another company whose strategy and capabilities are different. While most food and beverage chains have expanded through franchising, Starbucks, anxious to replicate precisely its unique 'Starbucks experience', directly owns and manages its retail outlets. While most banks have been outsourcing IT to companies such as IBM and Fujitsu Australia, US credit card group Capital One sees IT as a key source of competitive advantage: 'IT is our central nervous system . . . if we outsourced tomorrow we might save a dollar or two on each account, but we would lose flexibility and value and service levels.'[46]

In addition to the factors already considered, the design of vertical relationships needs to take careful account of the following.

- *Allocation of risk.* Any arrangement beyond a spot contract must cope with uncertainties over the course of the contract. A key feature of any contract is that its terms involve, often implicitly, an allocation of risks between the parties. How risk is shared is dependent partly on bargaining power and partly on efficiency considerations. In franchise agreements, the franchisee (as the weaker partner) bears most of the risk — it is the franchisee's capital that is at risk and the franchisee pays the franchiser a flat royalty based on sales revenues. In oil exploration, outsourcing agreements between the oil majors (such as Shell, BP and Exxon Mobil) and drilling companies (such as Schlumberger and Halliburton) have moved from fixed-price contracts to risk-sharing agreements where the driller often takes an equity stake in the project.

- *Incentive structures.* For a contract to minimise transaction costs it must provide an appropriate set of incentives to the parties. Thus, unless a contract for the supply of ready-mixed concrete to construction projects specifies the proportions of cement, sand and gravel, there is an incentive to supply substandard concrete. A company's reliance on its reputation for future contracts, however, may mitigate such risk. However, achieving completeness in the specification of contracts also bears a cost. The $400 toilet seats supplied to the US Navy may reflect the costs of meeting specifications that filled many sheets of paper. Very often, the most effective incentive is the promise of future business. Hence, in privatising public services — such as passenger rail services or local refuse collection — the key incentive for service quality is a fixed-term operating contract with regular performance reviews and the prospect of competition at contract renewal time. Toyota and Marks & Spencer's vendor partnerships depend on the incentive that satisfactory performance will lead to a long-term business relationship.

Recent trends of integration

The main feature of recent years has been a growing diversity of hybrid vertical relationships that have attempted to reconcile the flexibility and incentives of market transactions with the close collaboration provided by vertical integration. Although collaborative vertical relationships are viewed as a recent phenomenon — associated with Silicon Valley and Japanese supplier networks — closely linked value chains in which small, specialist enterprises collaborate are a long-time feature of craft industries in Europe, India and elsewhere. The success of Japanese manufacturing companies with their close collaborative relationships with suppliers — including extensive knowledge sharing[47] — has exerted a powerful influence on American, European and Asia–Pacific (including Australian) companies over the past two decades. There has been a massive shift from arm's-length supplier relationships to long-term collaboration with fewer suppliers. In many instances, competitive tendering and multiple sourcing have been replaced by single-supplier arrangements. Vendor relationships frequently involve supplier certification and quality management programs and technical collaboration.

The pace of outsourcing has been intensified by companies' enthusiasm for exploiting international cost differences. Large companies in North America, Europe and Australia are increasingly outsourcing manufacturing to China and services (including call centres and IT) to India. The mutual dependence that results from close, long-term supplier–buyer relationships creates vulnerability for both parties. While trust may alleviate some of the risks of opportunism, companies can also reinforce their vertical relationships and discourage opportunism through equity stakes and profit-sharing arrangements. For example, the Commonwealth Bank of Australia took an equity stake in its IT supplier, EDS Australia; pharmaceutical companies often acquire equity stakes in the biotechnology companies that undertake much of their R&D; and, as already noted, oilfield services companies are increasingly equity partners in upstream projects.

While the form of vertical relationships has changed, the trend towards increasing outsourcing has continued. The result is that most companies have specialised in fewer activities within their value chains. Outsourcing has extended from components to a wide range of business services including payroll, IT, training, and customer service and support. Increasingly, outsourcing involves not just individual components and services, but whole chunks of the value chain. In electronics, the design and manufacture of entire products are often outsourced to contract manufacturers such as Hon Hai Precision Industry Co., which makes Apple's iPads and iPhones, Nokia's mobile phones, and Sony's PlayStation 4 consoles.

The costs and benefits of vertical integration

Is vertical integration a beneficial strategy for a company to pursue? As with most questions of strategy, it depends. This chapter has observed that there are costs and benefits associated with both vertical integration and with market contracts between companies. Table 6.2 summarises some of the key criteria for determining the factors that affect the relative advantages of the two approaches to managing vertical relationships. Yet, even within the same industry, different companies can be successful with very different degrees of vertical integration. The key issue here is that, even when external circumstances are the same, the fact that different companies have different resources and capabilities and pursue different strategies means that they will make different decisions with regard to vertical integration.

TABLE 6.2   **Vertical integration (VI) versus outsourcing: some key considerations**

Characteristics of the vertical relationship	Implication
How many companies are there in the vertically adjacent activity?	The fewer the number of companies, the greater are the transaction costs and bigger the advantages of VI.
Do transaction-specific investments need to be made by either party?	Transaction-specific investments increase the advantages of VI.
How evenly distributed is information between the vertical stages?	The greater are information asymmetries, the more likely is opportunistic behaviour and the greater the advantages of VI.
Are market transactions in intermediate products subject to taxes or regulations?	Taxes and regulations are a cost of market contracts that can be avoided by VI.

How uncertain are the circumstances of the transactions over the period of the relationship?	The greater are uncertainties concerning costs, technologies and demand, the greater the difficulty of writing contracts, and the greater the advantages of VI.
Are two stages similar in terms of the optimal scale of operation?	The greater the dissimilarity, the greater the advantages of market contracts as compared with VI.
Are the two stages strategically similar (e.g. similar key success factors, common resources/capabilities)?	The greater the strategic similarity, the greater the advantages of VI over outsourcing.
How great is the need for continual investment in upgrading and extending capabilities within individual activities?	The greater the need to invest in capability development, the greater the advantages of outsourcing over VI.
How great is the need for entrepreneurial flexibility and drive in the separate vertical activities?	The greater the need for entrepreneurship and flexibility, the greater the advantages of high-powered incentives provided by market contracts, and the greater the administrative disadvantages of VI.
How uncertain is market demand?	The greater the unpredictability of demand, the greater the flexibility advantages of outsourcing.
Does vertical integration compound risk, exposing the entire value chain to risks affecting individual stages?	The heavier the investment requirements and the greater the independent risks at each stage, the more risky is VI.

Strategies towards vertical integration have been subject to shifting fashions. For most of the twentieth century, the prevailing wisdom was that vertical integration was generally beneficial because it allowed superior coordination and security. During the past 20 years there has been a profound change of opinion and the emphasis has shifted to the benefits of outsourcing in terms of flexibility and the ability to develop specialised capabilities in particular activities. Moreover, it has been noted that most of the coordination benefits associated with vertical integration can be achieved through intercompany collaboration.

However, as in other areas of management, fashion is fickle. In the media sector, vertical integration between content and distribution has become viewed as a critical advantage in the face of rapid technological change. The resulting wave of mergers between content producers and distributors (TV broadcasters, cable companies and internet portals) has transformed the industry. Telstra is a good example of this form of integration, being both vertically and horizontally integrated into telecommunications, pay TV networks and related content markets. Since it owns one of the two largest Australian cable networks and holds an interest in pay TV content, this may hinder intermodal competition.[48]

Horizontal integration strategy

Horizontal integration is a form of expansion by which a company expands its business activities by taking over or merging with another business in the same industry and at the same level in the supply chain.

A company can achieve horizontal growth through mergers and acquisitions of companies that offer similar products or services. Examples of horizontal integration include a large manufacturer that acquires other similar smaller manufacturers, or a media company that owns various types of media including television, radio, newspapers and magazines.

Advantages of horizontal integration

Through acquisition of competitors and the accompanying amplification of operations, horizontal integration offers companies a number of advantages. The most obvious of these is increased market share; others include economies of scope, economies of scale and increased market power. Economies of scope are achieved by sharing resources across similar products. Economies of scale are achieved by selling more of the same product; for example, by selling across more geographical regions. Horizontal integration gives a company more power over its suppliers and distributors. Additional benefits can be derived through the promotion of several products under the one brand name, capitalising on the perceived linkages that the consumer makes.

Drawbacks of horizontal integration

In some countries, over-expansion horizontally may cause some problems related to competition or antitrust laws. These laws attempt to protect free competition by investigating and punishing companies that have become overly dominant in a particular market. A company, therefore, has to be very careful by restricting its dominance in a market to avoid governmental intervention.

Aside from legal issues, another concern is that very often the anticipated economic benefits never materialise. There may be problems in the integration process. Although business units are producing similar products, the operations may be totally different. For example, computer hardware manufacturers who attempt to enter the software business may find out that there is not much synergy between hardware and software if they are not compatible.

In addition, two different business units in the same company may have different histories of operational problems. For example, there may be a labour union agreement in one business unit that may preclude a wage reduction. By integrating this business unit into the company, not much benefit, in terms of cost saving, can be achieved.

Finally, even when the potential benefits of horizontal integration exist, they may not be able to materialise immediately. There must be an explicit horizontal strategy in place. Such strategies generally do not arise from the bottom-up, but rather must be formulated by corporate management.

6.6 Turnaround and retrenchment strategies

LEARNING OBJECTIVE 6.6 Understand the purpose of turnaround and retrenchment strategies.

Turnaround strategy

When a company is not performing well enough, its management will have to consider either a **turnaround** or a retrenchment strategy.

The overall goal of a turnaround strategy is to return an underperforming company to acceptable levels of profitability and long-term growth. A turnaround strategy enables senior managers of underperforming companies to understand the causes of poor performance, with a view to reducing loss. A well-designed turnaround strategy involves redefining strategic objectives, reducing cost and restructuring organisational processes.

Retrenchment strategy

Retrenchment is a corporate-level strategy that seeks to reduce the size or diversity of an organisation's operations. It includes all activities involving contraction of a company's operations or changes in its assets or financial structure. Retrenchment often involves a reduction of expenditures in order to become financially stable. Retrenchment is a pullback or a withdrawal from offering some current products or serving some markets. Retrenchment usually revolves around cutting costs. It is often a strategy employed prior to or as part of a turnaround strategy.

A retrenchment strategy enables senior managers of underperforming companies to understand the critical causes of poor results in order to stem losses and restore growth. A well-crafted retrenchment strategy leads companies to quickly achieve their full potential. Typically, this involves removing costs, restructuring finances and redefining strategic objectives. Retrenchment often calls for building a stronger management team, making acquisitions or devising an exit strategy.

Turnaround and retrenchment activities

There are four activities that characterise turnaround and retrenchment.
- *Restructuring.* If a company is steadily losing profit or market share, a turnaround strategy is needed. There are two forms of turnarounds. First, a company may choose contractions (e.g. cutting labour costs, marketing and promotion expenses). Second, it may decide to consolidate its businesses by closing unprofitable ones.
- *Divestment.* This is a form of retrenchment strategy used by businesses when they downsize the scope of their business activities. Divestment usually involves eliminating a portion of a business. Companies may elect to sell, close or spin-off a strategic business unit, major operating division, or product line. This move often is the final decision to eliminate unrelated, unprofitable or unmanageable business operations.

- *Liquidation or bankruptcy.* This is very simple. Take the book value of assets, subtract depreciation and sell the business. This may be hard for some companies to do because there may be untapped potential in the assets.
- *Tie to a large company.* For some companies, the only way to stay viable is to act as an exclusive supplier to a giant company. A company may also be taken captive if its competitive position is irreparably weak. Strategy capsule 6.1 shows what can be learned from Kmart's turnaround and retrenchment strategy.

Kmart's turnaround and retrenchment strategy

Kmart had occupied a beleaguered position in the Australian retail arena until its owner, Wesfarmers, decided to appoint Guy Russo as the chain's CEO. The former McDonald's Australia boss brought with him a multiphase plan to boldly turn around an unprofitable company that had not experienced growth in a decade.[49]

When Russo took over, he found that Kmart's competitors Big W and Target were vastly outperforming it. In addition to a lack of strong company identity, he observed that Kmart's greatest problems were due to major flaws in its business model.[50]

Kmart had too much inventory, which meant that its cash was tied up in stock and not accessible as working capital. Russo's solution was to reduce the average store's stock of 100 000 items down to around 75 000 by cutting out those lines that were making a loss.[51] By targeting lines that were not selling, the actual range of products was reduced to 12 000 (from about 50 000) and 40 off-site warehouses holding unwanted big-ticket items were able to be closed down. This allowed the company to more effectively manage its stock control, merchandising and logistics.

As many of Kmart's customers are often time-poor and unwilling to traipse through large stores to find what they want, the company has opted to downsize its larger outlets, preferring footprints of 5000–6000 square metres rather than the traditional 8000 square metres.[52]

Russo observed that Kmart's pricing strategy was a major issue — for too long it had been stocking both very cheap and expensive items, and selling the latter only when they were heavily discounted. Rather than relying on drawing customers in on particular days for sales, the company's pricing model was reconfigured so that consistently low prices were offered, thus reducing its reliance on discounts. During Russo's first three years in charge, prices dropped 30–50 per cent across Kmart's product range and the company's profits doubled.[53] Most recently, Kmart has consolidated its pricing strategy through a new positioning campaign, 'Low prices for life', which reinforces to customers that Kmart will continue to offer great products and exceptionally low prices.[54]

In 2019, Kmart's parent company Wesfarmers acquired the online retailer Catch Group. With this they acquired not only the online platform and warehouses, but also the systems and expertise associated with them. Kmart will benefit from this through accelerated digital and e-commerce capabilities, and improving their supply chain, fulfilment and online execution.[55]

6.7 Corporate parenting

LEARNING OBJECTIVE 6.7 Critically evaluate corporate parenting and synergy connection in diversified portfolios.

So far, we have dealt extensively with different kinds of corporate strategy and the drivers and means by which companies produce profits. Figure 6.1 introduced the framework for corporate strategy, which includes types of corporate strategy, corporate parenting and types of business portfolios. This section looks specifically at corporate parenting. While diversification implies parenting — that is, how corporate parents manage their business portfolios — we need to examine how this occurs. As noted earlier, corporate parents need to add value to their business portfolios or range of SBUs. The notion of expansion and scope are therefore paramount in assisting the corporate parent. The product/market matrix (growth vector) provides strong directional settings for growth. If the decision is to diversify — which is basically what corporate strategy is about — different parenting skills will be needed for each SBU in the portfolio. Synergy such as the sharing of complex know-how that cannot occur in stand-alone SBUs will be critical.

Disney's strategies enabled them to acquire more than brands and franchises that could be leveraged across all their businesses, they also acquired the capabilities associated with these businesses that were needed in order to future-proof their entire organisation. For example, the acquisition of Pixar in 2006 brought with it digital animation capabilities Disney needed to remain competitive. Their latest acquisition of Fox in 2019 widened the scope of Disney's direct-to-consumer network, a high priority for Disney as the demand for cable services was in decline. In any competitive environment — for example, competition for investment resources within the mining industry in Australia in which other corporate parents compete, competition in the footwear industry between Nike and Adidas, or competition among Asia–Pacific retailers for retailing space and location — a corporate parent must achieve a closer fit with its businesses than that achieved by its rivals.[56] They achieve this through increased value creation insights, distinctive parenting characteristics, and by creating high levels of new value through 'heartland' businesses. The **parental advantage** that can be created by corporate parenting is illustrated in figure 6.8.

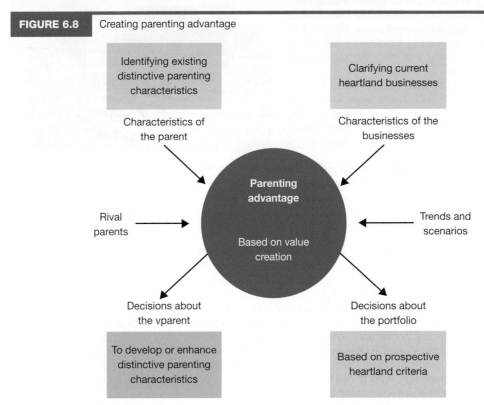

FIGURE 6.8 Creating parenting advantage

Source: Adapted from Goold, et al., 1994.

In figure 6.8, distinctive parenting characteristics refer to the way parents add value to the SBU (e.g. Disney offers a global distribution network and expertise across a number of industries). Global structures (e.g. global matrix structures) may add value because they allow resources to be shared where they are needed the most. Similarly, the strategic planning process or management information system provided by the parent may be a key to being successful in different markets. For example, a parent's ability to access comparable data over long periods, its challenging organisational culture, as well as the CEO's personal characteristics and devotion by the senior management group may give it an edge over rival parents. The linking of core technologies (including technological advantage across production processes) is an example of heartland business characteristics that the parent can use to add value to SBUs. For example, B. Braun in Malaysia implements their German parent's specific production knowledge and processes in their factories located in Penang. So, this knowledge is transferred from heartland businesses and used as a competitive advantage in the offshore SBUs.

Value-creating synergies

Value-creating synergies between parents and SBUs can be tackled on a number of different fronts.
- *SBU inefficiency.* Corporate parents can move to rectify SBU inefficiencies such as management problems related to performance. Parents can move more precisely and quickly to change circumstances in ways that assist the SBU and protect the portfolio.

- *Intermediary role*. Parents play a constructive intermediary role since they can add value through the sharing of unique resources and capabilities. Also, intermediary processes are an effective means for creating value. Processes including functions and services tend to support and contribute to value creation. Focusing on value creation insights, distinctive parenting advantages and heartland business criteria (see figure 6.8) can expose the difference between related parents while underscoring the underlying pattern of similarity.[57]
- *Sizing up distinctive capability*. Corporate parents size up their distinctive capabilities with those of other parents. It is important to note that value creation will be different for just about every corporate parent. Some parents will be able to make well-judged and timely general-management appointments. Some will be better at sizing up opportunities and sharing cost savings and economies of scale (e.g. shared manufacturing economies or R&D). In minerals investments in Australia, companies such as Rio Tinto are masters at identifying funding and helping to carry major risky (but profitable) investments that other companies may not support. Accordingly, such companies will be comfortable with joint ventures and be able to share collective experiences. Thus, corporate parents can play an important role that SBU managers might miss.

Value-destroying synergies

While parent–SBU synergies can contribute to value creation, there are also value-destroying synergies that can easily disrupt business, such as the following.

- *Excessive managerialism*. Here, the nature of standalone parenting perverts business decisions. That is, it can be easily argued that a corporate parent who spends, say, approximately 10 per cent of its time managing ten different businesses will not be as effective as business managers who devote 100 per cent of their time to their respective SBUs.
- *Competition for resources*. When parents are so busy managing the whole portfolio while at the same time seeking to add value, unnecessary competition for corporate attention is often created. Information and presentations of SBU performance and resource allocations might be biased in order to gain the necessary attention from the parent. For example, business managers might place unnecessary emphasis on 'selling' the business units' ideas to parents in an effort to prevent corporate managers asking difficult questions. Consequently, they avoid being asked the right questions by parents.
- *Urgency to perform*. SBUs, as part of a broader conglomerate parent organisation, may not feel the same sense of urgency to perform as independent companies.[58] In some cases, an SBU's performance targets and goals would not be considered acceptable if they were a standalone company. However, corporate parents often tolerate poor SBU performance.
- *Short termism*. Corporate parents can place SBUs under heavy financial pressure to increase quarterly targets because of corporate goals for growth and shareholder expectations. An emphasis on short-term goals and profits may lead to SBU managers losing sight of developing capabilities and new products for sustained competitive advantage in favour of pushing short-term sales targets and products that may become toxic to the company over time.

Collectively, corporate parents face a balancing act between value-creating synergies and value-destroying ones. In value-creating synergies, the parent focuses on sharing resources (such as superior corporate research, investment financing, joint manufacturing facilities or global marketing activities) in ways that help SBUs. Where value-destroying synergies are apparent, corporate parents actually get in the way of SBU managers by adding unnecessary lines of reporting and failing to understand the real needs of SBUs.

Linfox acquisition of Aurizon Intermodal Business

Linfox Logistics operates across 12 countries, with 5000 vehicles and over 24 000 employees, making it Asia–Pacific's largest privately owned logistics company. Linfox famously began as 'a man and a truck' and has since grown into a vertically integrated business providing the full range of supply chain services including warehousing, distribution centre management, transportation and logistics.[59]

Aurizon is Australia's largest rail freight operator. They are a privately owned, public listed company providing logistics services across an extensive network. They offer transport, logistics and supply chain services to the mineral, industrial and agricultural industries as well as intermodal transport for general, industrial and specialised freight.[60] In 2017, Aurizon made the strategic decision to dispose of their intermodal and bulk freight business based on a history of significant losses. Management believed that they lacked the 'fundamental characteristics for success' in the sector (i.e. trucking and logistics systems) and that their focus should remain on their core business of bulk haulage and below rail operations where they held a comparative advantage.[61]

In January 2019 Linfox purchased Aurizon's Queensland intermodal business, including existing customer contracts, rail wagons, shipping containers, trucks, trailers and machinery as well as access to 12 freight terminals across Queensland. The business added considerable value to Linfox, extending the scale and scope of their already extensive road

and rail network in Australia and providing them with greater pick-up, delivery and warehousing capabilities throughout Queensland.[62] The clear synergy between Aurizon's intermodal business and Linfox's operations and capabilities supported this horizontal integration strategy and positioned Linfox for the future growth of inland rail haulage in Australia.

6.8 Portfolio analysis

LEARNING OBJECTIVE 6.8 Demonstrate applied knowledge of portfolio strategy by performing high-level analysis of diversified businesses at various growth phases.

Portfolio analysis is one of the principal means for analysing a diversified company's scope of activities. This generally occurs because of a need to analyse an SBU's relative market share versus market growth. One well-known method is the BCG or Boston Consulting Group matrix which enables managers to analyse various costs per unit in SBUs versus their growth potential, or customers' relative market share versus growth of the businesses.

The BCG matrix

In the BCG matrix shown in figure 6.9, the vertical axis represents the growth of a product market in the next planning period — this is evaluated on the horizontal axis by the market share of a company in a defined product market divided into that of the largest competitor or relative market share.[63]

FIGURE 6.9	The BCG matrix

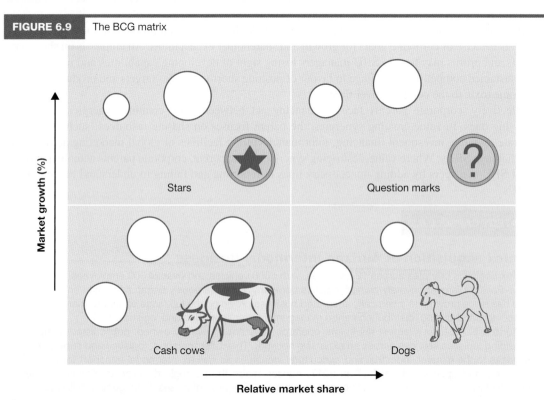

Source: Adapted from Clarke & Brennan, 1998

The circle sizes in figure 6.9 represent the revenue generated in each SBU product for the company. While this may be useful to size up and evaluate business products by moving from one to another more profitable business, high growth vectors can often be chosen bearing no relationship to the existing business.[64] The other issue with the BCG matrix is that by focusing on the most profitable businesses, corporate parents — perhaps unintentionally — drive out synergies for sharing resources between SBUs. The logic of synergy is the creation of a beneficial relationship between businesses. However, as scholars have noted:

> The biggest problem of the product portfolio strikes at the heart of the SBU concept. What happens if a dog and a star, or a cash cow, share key productive resources or technologies? Killing the dog can butcher the economics of the cash cow.[65]

Conversely, the BCG matrix may be useful in circumstances where businesses are seeking clarity about which products are more profitable and where to place investments or how to make savings in overheads. In terms of diversification strategy, the BCG matrix concepts potentially drive out synergies in related businesses. The BCG matrix might accordingly be best used in conglomerate unrelated businesses with very few synergies. However, even conglomerates need to share resources, so viewing diversification from a single-business perspective suggests that managers might view the BCG matrix in context-specific situations.

The GE–McKinsey matrix

While the BCG matrix has been useful in terms of product and market growth in diversified businesses, the *GE–McKinsey nine-box matrix* by comparison provides a more useful way of determining where corporate companies should invest their cash. Produced in the early 1970s by McKinsey & Company, the nine-box matrix (see figure 6.10) enables a diversified company to examine a business unit's projection of its future prospects in an industry.

FIGURE 6.10   The GE–McKinsey nine-box matrix

Competitive strength of business unit

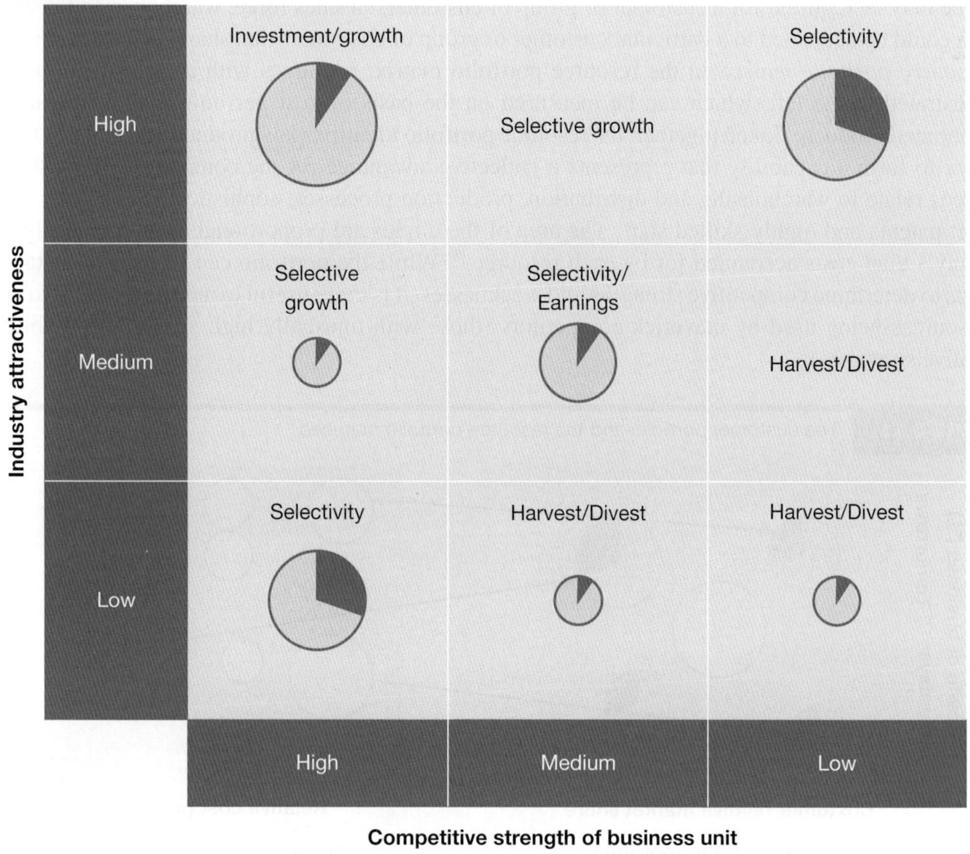

Source: Partnership for Public Service and McKinsey & Company, 2012.

With respect to the matrix, the *x*-axis denotes the competitive strength of a business unit against the *y*-axis, which represents industry attractiveness. Each business can be placed inside the matrix. Those business units placed above the diagonal are generally those recognised for increased investment and growth potential. In figure 6.10, the size of the circle represents the size of the market and the darker shaded area of the pie represents the company's market share. In the middle of the diagonal, the company is careful about its investments. Managers might be willing to believe in these 'selective investment' businesses; however, they are a second priority to those in the top of the diagonal. At the bottom of the diagonal are businesses to be sold, liquidated or 'milked' for cash. The GE–McKinsey matrix is not normally used as an 'end-game' to determine where best to invest cash. It was developed before Porter's five forces model and well before more useful research was based on industry attractiveness. So, analysis should be conducted of industry attractiveness factors coupled with competitive strength of a business unit using other means as well. McKinsey notes that judgement is required to weight the trade-offs involved in deciding where to invest cash in competing businesses and that a strong unit in a weak industry is in a very different situation to a weak unit in a highly-attractive industry.[66] The other point to note about figure 6.10 is that the matrix can easily be converted into a *parenting opportunity matrix*. If one changes the *x*-axis to represent 'Value-creation potential' (as a percentage of current value) and the *y*-axis to reflect 'relative ability to extract value', then each circle represents a business in the portfolio. The circle size of a business in a parenting opportunity matrix is proportionate to its current value.[67] Corporate parents would accordingly want to add value-creating synergies to those businesses that offer the most value going forward.

The customer and resource portfolio matrices

The *customer portfolio matrix* (see figure 6.11a) is a useful tool to evaluate a customer's market share of the overall business they are in relative to competitors and the value of purchases the customer buys.[68] The *x*-axis indicates the customer's market share and the *y*-axis is the projected growth of the customer's businesses based on yesterday's and tomorrow's customers. A company will need to evaluate tomorrow's customers since these customers will make major purchases of the company's products. A customer portfolio could also be compared to a resource portfolio (see figure 6.11b) because this type of analysis can reveal further opportunities for creating synergies across businesses. For instance, a particular kind of resource may be required for a customer or group of customers: a sales force, warehouse and distribution system could be dedicated to a particular customer or group of customers that share resources identified in the *resource portfolio matrix*. In the resource portfolio matrix, resources with a competitive advantage are illustrated to the left, which can be measured on the basis of cost per unit or their impact across differentiated products. Taken together, the resource portfolio identifies key productive resources that work together to form a capability that represents a collective advantage for the company. The most obvious resources relate to warehousing and distribution, production processes, sophisticated computer systems, product patents and highly skilled staff. The area of the circles are proportional to the percentage of the company's total costs accounted for by each resource.[69] While the portfolio can be used as a standalone analysis to determine competitive strengths and weaknesses, it is more useful to use the matrices to identify the resources being used by maverick competitors (those with unusually high growth, profitability and innovative strategies).

| FIGURE 6.11 | The customer portfolio and the resource portfolio matrices |

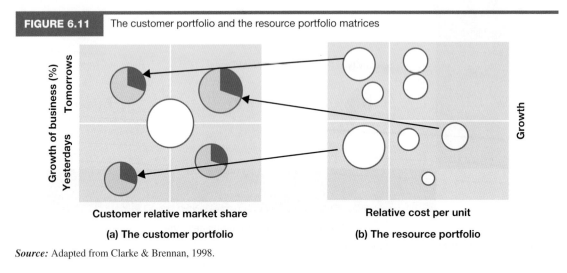

Source: Adapted from Clarke & Brennan, 1998.

SUMMARY

Corporate-level strategy is the master plan of a company and includes diversification, integration, merger and acquisition, turnaround and retrenchment strategies. The most critical long-run consideration is the development of organisational capability in deciding which parts of the value chain to engage in. In relation to the latter, diversifying through merger and acquisition is popular for decisions relating to integration or outright growth. These combinations present companies with some of their most difficult strategic decisions.

Diversification decisions have traditionally been based on vague concepts of synergy that involved the identification of linkages between different industries. More specific analysis of the nature and extent of economies of scope in resources and capabilities have given greater precision to analysis of synergies that add value. At the same time, it is recognised that economies of scope are insufficient to ensure that diversification creates value. A critical issue is the optimal organisational form for exploiting these economies.

Vertical integration decisions revolve around two key questions. First, which activities will be undertaken internally and which will be outsourced? Second, how should vertical arrangements with both external and internal suppliers and buyers be designed? Both types of decision are critically dependent on the company's competitive strategy and the capabilities it possesses. The conventional analysis of vertical integration has looked simply at the efficiency of markets as compared with the efficiency of companies: if the cost of transacting through the market is greater than the cost of administering within the company, then the company should vertically integrate across the stage. Horizontal integration involves buying a company in the same industry and at the same level in the supply chain. It can provide economies of scale and scope and increased market power.

A merger or acquisition to expand a company's business requires careful consideration. While there are definite merits in mergers and acquisitions, a company may face various problems of synergies and economies of scale.

When a business is not doing well, it will need to consider adopting a turnaround and/or retrenchment strategy to survive and revitalise its operations.

KEY TERMS

acquisition The purchase of one company by another (also known as a takeover or a buyout).

diversification strategy A company's decision to expand its operations by adding new products and services, markets or stages of production to the existing business.

horizontal integration The expansion or addition of business activities in the same industry and at the same level of the supply chain.

merger The combination of two companies into a bigger company.

parental advantage A parental advantage exists where diversified companies generate more value and a closer fit overall with their SBUs than any of their competitors as rival parents owning the same businesses.

retrenchment strategy A corporate-level strategy that seeks to reduce the size or diversity of an organisation's operations.

turnaround strategy The plan and effort to return an underperforming company to acceptable levels of profitability and long-term growth.

vertical integration Integration up or down a supply chain through which a company will control the production and distribution of products.

SELF-STUDY QUESTIONS

1 What is corporate-level strategy? Why is corporate-level strategy important for a company seeking rapid growth?

2 Why is a diversification strategy in the Asia–Pacific region not as easy in 2020 as it might have been in the early 2000s?

3 What are the merits of vertical integration? What are the differences between horizontal and vertical integration?

4 What are the differences between a merger and an acquisition? When and why are they useful?

5 Compare and contrast related and unrelated diversification. When will unrelated diversification be more useful?

6 When is a retrenchment strategy necessary?

DISCUSSION QUESTIONS

1 An ice cream manufacturer is proposing to acquire a soup manufacturer on the basis that, first, its sales and profits will be more seasonally balanced and, second, from year to year, sales and profits will be less affected by variations in weather. Will this spreading of risk create value for shareholders? Under what circumstances could this acquisition create benefits for shareholders?

2 Tata Group is one of India's largest companies, employing 203 000 people in many different industries, including steel, motor vehicles, watches and jewellery, telecommunications, financial services, management consulting, food products, tea, chemicals and fertilisers, satellite TV, hotels, motor vehicles, energy, IT and construction. Such diversity far exceeds that of any North American, western European or Australian company. What are the conditions in India that might make such broad-based diversification both feasible and profitable?

3 Giorgio Armani is an Italian private company owned mainly by the Armani family. Most of its clothing and accessories are produced and marketed by the company (some are manufactured by outside contractors). For other products, notably fragrances, cosmetics and eyewear, Armani licenses its brand names to other companies. Armani is considering expanding into athletic clothing, hotels and bridal shops. Advise Armani on whether these new businesses should be developed in-house, by joint ventures or by licensing the Armani brands to specialist companies already within these fields.

4 General Electric, Berkshire Hathaway and Richard Branson's Virgin Group each comprise a wide range of different businesses that appear to have few close technical or customer linkages. Are these examples of unrelated diversification and do the corporate and ownership links within each of the groups result in the creation of any value? If so, what are the sources of this value creation?

5 Zara manufactures close to half of the clothes sold in its retail stores and undertakes all of its own distribution from manufacturing plants to retail outlets. Gap outsources production and distribution. Should Zara outsource its manufacturing and distribution? Should Gap backward integrate into production and distribution? Why?

6 If you were VP of strategic planning for a large multi-business company, would you use portfolio planning techniques in your work? If so, for what purposes? If not, why not? Would your preference be to use the GE–McKinsey nine-box matrix or the BCG matrix? Explain the rationale behind your choice.

EXERCISES

1 Form a group of three to four members with your peers. Identify a company that has recently undertaken some major changes in its operations (e.g. major takeover or restructuring). Assess the characteristics of such changes and analyse whether they were successful or not.

2 Collect information on at least five large companies in Australia (BHP Billiton, Rio Tinto, Telstra etc.). Identify recent examples of strategies of these companies that are related to merger, acquisition, diversification, and vertical and horizontal integration.

3 Write a short essay (750–1000 words) on the importance of formulating an appropriate corporate-level strategy. What are the possible options for such formulation?

4 Identify some major merger or acquisition cases from the past few years. Evaluate the success of such cases and analyse whether they have achieved their objectives.

5 Explore the Australian Competition and Consumer Commission (ACCC) website, www.accc.gov.au. Discuss why the Australian government pays so much attention to mergers and acquisitions in Australia.

6 'Don't put all of your eggs in one basket!' You've probably heard that over and over again throughout your life. Are companies following this premise? Investigate the diversification strategy of some major companies and assess to what extent they are successful.

7 Investigate companies that have diversified into the Asia–Pacific region recently. How do the drivers for diversification explained in this chapter match the corporate strategies adopted by these companies?

FURTHER READING

Bettis, RA & Prahalad, CK 1995, 'The dominant logic: Retrospective and extension', *Strategic Management Journal*, vol. 16, 5–14.

Balogun, J, Hope-Hailey, V & Gustafsson S 2015, *Exploring strategic change*, 4th edn, VLeBooks.

Fernhaber, SA & Patel, PC 2012, 'How do young firms manage product portfolio complexity? The role of absorptive capacity and ambidexterity', *Strategic Management Journal*, doi: 10/1002/smj

Goold, M & Campbell, A 1998, 'Desperately seeking synergy', *Harvard Business Review,* Sept–October. 131–143.

Goold, M Campbell, A, & Alexander, M 1994, *Corporate-level strategy — Creating value in the multi-business company,* New York: John Wiley & Sons, Inc.

Hamel, G & Prahalad, CK 1994, *Competing for the future,* Boston: Harvard Business School Press.

Kaplan, R & Norton, D 2001, *The strategy-focused organization,* Boston: Harvard Business School Press.

Parmigiani, A & Holloway, SS 2011, 'Actions speak louder than modes: Antecedents and implications of parent implementation capabilities on business unit performance', *Strategic Management Journal,* 32, 457–485.

Porter, ME, *Competitive strategy: Techniques for analyzing industries and competitors,* New York: Free Press.

Porter, ME 1991, 'Toward a Dynamic Theory of Strategy', *Strategic Management Journal*, vol. 12, Winter Special Issue, 95–118.

ENDNOTES

1. Walt Disney Company, '2019 annual meeting of shareholders', 2019, https://thewaltdisneycompany.com/app/uploads/2019/03/2019-asm-transcript.pdf.
2. ibid.
3. Walt Disney Company, 'Fiscal year 2018 annual financial report', 2019, www.annualreports.com/HostedData/AnnualReports/PDF/NYSE_DIS_2018.pdf.
4. M Goold, A Campbell, and M Alexander, *Corporate-level strategy: Creating value in the multibusiness company*, New York: John Wiley & Sons, 1994.
5. I Ansoff, *The new corporate strategy*, New York: John Wiley & Sons,1965.
6. A Campbell and K Sommers Luchs, *Strategic synergy*, 2nd edn, Thomson Business Press, 1998.
7. ibid.
8. Goold, Campbell and Alexander, op. cit.
9. ibid.
10. RP Rumelt, *Strategy, structure and economic performance*, Cambridge, MA: Harvard University Press, 1974.
11. C Park, 'The effects of prior performance on the choice between related and unrelated acquisitions', *Journal of Management Studies*, vol. 39, 2002, 1003–1019.
12. For a discussion of relatedness in diversification, see J Robins and MF Wiersema, 'A resource-based approach to the multibusiness firm: empirical analysis of portfolio interrelationships and corporate financial performance', *Strategic Management Journal*, vol. 16, 1995, 277–300; J Robins and MF Wiersema, 'The measurement of corporate portfolio strategy: analysis of the content validity of related diversification indexes', *Strategic Management Journal*, vol. 24, 2002, 39–59.
13. RM Grant, 'On dominant logic, relatedness, and the link between diversity and performance', *Strategic Management Journal*, vol. 9, 1988, 639–642.
14. RM Grant, 'On dominant logic, relatedness, and the link between diversity and performance', *Strategic Management Journal*, vol. 9, 1988, 641.
15. DA Ravenscraft and FM Scherer, 'Divisional selloff: a hazard analysis', in *Mergers, selloffs and economic efficiency*, Washington, DC: Brookings Institute, 1987; ME Porter, 'From competitive advantage to corporate strategy', *Harvard Business Review*, May–June 1987, 43–59.
16. SM Bartram, 'Corporate risk management as a lever for shareholder value creation', *Financial Markets, Institutions and Instruments*, vol. 9, 2000, 279–324.
17. M Hayward and DC Hambrick, 'Explaining the premiums paid for large acquisitions', *Administrative Science Quarterly*, vol. 42, 1997, 103–127.
18. A study of 68 diversifying ventures by established companies found that, on average, breakeven was not attained until the seventh and eighth years of operation: R Biggadike, 'The risky business of diversification', *Harvard Business Review*, May–June 1979.
19. ME Porter, 'From competitive advantage to corporate strategy', *Harvard Business Review*, May–June 1987, 46.
20. The formal definition of economies of scope is in terms of 'sub-additivity'. Economies of scope exist in the production of goods $X_1, X_2, ..., X_n$, if $C(X\Sigma_i C_i(X_i)$
    where:

    $$X = \Sigma_i \left(x_i \right)$$

    $C(X)$ is the cost of producing all n goods within a single company
    $\sum_i C_i(x_i)$. is the cost of producing the goods in n specialised companies.
    See WJ Baumol, JC Panzar, and RD Willig, *Contestable markets and the theory of industry structure*, New York: Harcourt Brace Jovanovich, 1982, 71–72.
21. Economies of scope can arise in consumption as well as in production: customers may prefer to buy different products from the same supplier. See T Cottrell and BR Nault, 'Product variety and firm survival in microcomputer software', *Strategic Management Journal*, vol. 25, 2004, 1005–1026.

22. More generally, research intensity is strongly associated with diversification. For the United States, see CH Berry, *Corporate growth and diversification*, Princeton: Princeton University Press, 1975; for the United Kingdom, see RM Grant, 'Determinants of the interindustry pattern of diversification by UK manufacturing companies', *Bulletin of Economic Research*, vol. 29, 1977, 84–95.

23. There is some evidence to the contrary; see H Park, TA Kruse, K Suzuki, and K Park, 'Long-term performance following mergers of Japanese companies: the effect of diversification and affiliation', *Pacific Basin Finance Journal*, vol. 14, 2006; PR Nayyar, 'Performance effects of information asymmetry and economies of scope in diversified service firms', *Academy of Management Journal*, vol. 36, 1993, 28–57.

24. The role of capabilities in diversification is discussed in CC Markides and PJ Williamson, 'Related diversification, core competencies and corporate performance', *Strategic Management Journal*, vol. 15, Special Issue, 1994, 149–165.

25. This issue is examined more fully in DJ Teece, 'Towards an economic theory of the multiproduct firm', *Journal of Economic Behavior and Organisation*, vol. 3, 1982, 39–63.

26. JP Liebeskind, 'Internal capital markets: benefits, costs and organisational arrangements', *Organisation Science*, vol. 11, 2000, 58–76.

27. D Scharfstein and J Stein, 'The dark side of internal capital markets: divisional rent seeking and inefficient investment', *Journal of Finance*, vol. 55, 2000, 2537–64; V Maksimovic and G Phillips, 'Do conglomerate firms allocate resources inefficiently across industries?' *Journal of Finance*, vol. 57, 2002, 721–767; R Rajan, H Servaes, and L Zingales, 'The cost of diversity: the diversification discount and inefficient investment', *Journal of Finance*, vol. 55, 2000, 35–84.

28. C Kaye and J Yuwono, 'Conglomerate discount or premium? How some diversified companies create exceptional value', Marakon Associates, 2003.

29. 'Microsoft on trial', *The Economist*, 28 April, 2006, www.economist.com.

30. ED Cavanagh, 'Reciprocal dealing: a rebirth?' *St. Johns Law Review*, vol. 75, 2001, 633–647.

31. US Senate, Subcommittee on Antitrust and Monopoly Hearings, Economic Concentration, Part 1, Congress, 1st session, 1965, 45.

32. In the US airline industry, extensive multimarket contact resulted in a reluctance to compete on routes dominated by one or other of the airlines. See JAC Baum and HJ Korn, 'Competitive dynamics of interfirm rivalry', *Academy of Management Review*, vol. 39, 1996, 255–291.

33. S Jayachandran, J Gimeno, and PR Varadarajan, 'The theory of multimarket competition: a synthesis and implications for marketing strategy', *Journal of Marketing*, vol. 63, July 1999, 49–66.

34. RM Grant, AP Jammine, and H Thomas, 'Diversity, diversification and performance in British manufacturing industry', *Academy of Management Journal*, vol. 31, 1988, 771–801.

35. LE Palich, LB Cardinal, and CC Miller, 'Curvi-linearity in the diversification-performance linkage: an examination of over three decades of research', *Strategic Management Journal*, vol. 22, 2000, 155–174.

36. N Harper and SP Viguerie, 'Are you too focused?' *McKinsey Quarterly*, 2002 Special Edition, 29–37.

37. G Andrade, M Mitchell, and E Stafford, 'New evidence and perspectives on mergers', *Journal of Economic Perspectives*, vol. 5, no. 3, 2001, 103–120.

38. JD Martin and A Sayrak, 'Corporate diversification and shareholder value: a survey of recent literature', *Journal of Corporate Finance*, vol. 9, 2003, 37–57.

39. CC Markides, 'Consequences of corporate refocusing: ex ante evidence', *Academy of Management Journal*, vol. 35, 1992, 398–412; CC Markides, 'Diversification, restructuring and economic performance', *Strategic Management Journal*, vol. 16, 1995, 101–118.

40. GA Jarrell, JA Brickly, and JM Netter, 'The market for corporate control: empirical evidence since 1980', *Journal of Economic Perspectives*, vol. 2, no. 1, Winter 1988, 49–68.

41. T Straub, 'Reasons for frequent failure in mergers and acquisitions — a comprehensive analysis', DUV Gabler Edition, 2007.

42. The situation is different in aluminium cans, where aluminium producers such as Alcoa and Pechiney and users such as Coca-Cola and Anheuser-Busch are major producers of beverage cans.

43. JT Macher, 'Technological development and the boundaries of the firm: a knowledge-based examination in semiconductor manufacturing', *Management Science*, vol. 52, 2006, 826–843; KMonteverde, 'Technical dialogue as an incentive for vertical integration in the semiconductor industry', *Management Science*, vol. 41, 1995, 1624–1638.

44. R Johnston and PR Lawrence, 'Beyond vertical integration: the rise of value adding partnerships', *Harvard Business Review*, July–August 1988, 94–101.

45. JH Dyer, 'Effective interfirm collaboration: how firms minimize transaction costs and maximize transaction value', *Strategic Management Journal*, vol. 18, 1997, 535–556; JH Dyer, 'Specialized supplier networks as a source of competitive advantage: evidence from the auto industry', *Strategic Management Journal*, vol. 17, 1996, 271–292.

46. L Willcocks and C Sauer, 'High risks and hidden costs in IT outsourcing', *Financial Times*, Mastering Risk, 23 May 2000, 3.

47. JH Dyer and K Nobeoka, 'Creating and managing a high-performance knowledge-sharing network: the Toyota case', *Strategic Management Journal*, vol. 21, 2000, 345–368.

48. CRN Australia, Australian Consumer Competition Commission (ACCC) believed the National Broadband Network (NBN) project reinforced the need for a review of Telstra's operation, www.crn.com.au.

49. K Southam, 'Guy Russo puts Kmart on the road to recovery', 23 December 2010, www.news.com.au.

50. M Hawthorne, 'Man from Maccas has new-look Kmart sizzling', *The Age*, 4 March 2010, www.theage.com.au.

51. ibid.

52. J Thomson, 'What your business can learn from Kmart's turnaround strategy', *SmartCompany*, 21 April 2009, www.smart company.com; M Pallisco, 'Kmart leading trend towards less is more', *Sydney Morning Herald*, 5 May 2012, www.smh. com.au.

53. K Southam, 'Guy Russo puts Kmart on the road to recovery', 23 December 2010, www.news.com.au; J Thomson, 'Kmart boss slams retailers' outdated model: Here are three leadership strategies', *Leading Company*, 8 May 2012, www.leadingcompany.com.au.

54. V Mitchell, 'Kmart launches new brand positioning, campaign', CMO, 31 July 2019, www.cmo.com.au/article/664750/kmart-launches-new-brand-positioning-campaign.

55. Wesfarmers, 'Completion of acquisition of catch group holdings limited', 12 August 2019, www.wesfarmers.com.au/util/news-media/article/2019/08/12/completion-of-acquisition-of-catch-group-holdings-limited.

56. McKinsey & Company, 'Innovating in China's automotive market: an interview with GM China's president', *McKinsey Quarterly*, February 2012.

57. ibid.

58. loc. cit., p. 95

59. IBISWorld, 'Linfox Proprietary Limited — Australian Company Profile', www.ibisworld.com.au/australian-company-research-reports/transport-postal-warehousing/linfox-proprietary-limited-company.html.

60. IBISWorld, 'Aurizon Holdings Limited — Australian Company Profile', www.ibisworld.com.au/australian-company-research-reports/transport-postal-warehousing/aurizon-holdings-limited-company.html.

61. Aurizon, 'FYR2017 Presentation Transcript', www.aurizon.com.au/investors/documents-and-webcasts/2017.

62. Linfox, 'Linfox secures strategic purchase of Aurizon Queensland intermodal business', www.linfox.com/article/linfox-secures-strategic-purchase-of-aurizon-queensland-intermodal-business.

63. See J Clarke and K Brennan, 'Four portfolio analysis'. In A Campbell and K Sommers Luchs, *Strategic synergy*, 2nd edn, Thomson Business Press, 1998.

64. ibid.

65. McKinsey & Company, February 2012, op. cit.

66. McKinsey & Company, 'Enduring ideas: The GE–McKinsey nine-box matrix', *McKinsey Quarterly*, 2008.

67. McKinsey & Company, February 2012, op. cit.

68. ibid.

69. ibid.

ACKNOWLEDGEMENTS

Photo: © nikkimeel / Shutterstock.com

Photo: © Nils Versemann / Shutterstock.com

Photo: © Judah Grubb / Shutterstock.com

Figure 6.2: © I Ansoff, *The new corporate strategy,* John Wiley & Sons, 1965.

Figure 6.8: © M Goold, A Campbell & M Alexander, *Corporate-level strategy: creating value in the multibusiness company,* John Wiley & Sons, New York, 1994.

Figures 6.9 and 6.11: Adapted from J Clarke & K Brennan, 'Four portfolio analysis', In A Campbell and K Sommers Luchs eds, *Strategic synergy,* 2nd Edition, Thomson Business Press, 1998. For all subscription inquiries please phone, from Australia: 1300 304 195, from Overseas: +61 2 8587 7980 or online at legal.thomsonreuters.com.au/search. The official PDF version of this article can also be purchased separately from Thomson Reuters.

Figure 6.10: 'Mission-Driven Mobility: Strengthening Our Government Through a Mobile Leadership Corps.' Copyright © 2012 by Partnership for Public Service and McKinsey & Company. All rights reserved.

CHAPTER 7

Cooperative strategies and alliances

LEARNING OBJECTIVES

After studying this chapter, you should be able to:

7.1 explain the need for intercompany cooperation, partnerships, alliances and networks in the new competitive landscape, and understand how strategic alliances can serve as tools for market entry and achievement of operational goals

7.2 describe the advantages that companies can achieve through strategic alliances

7.3 describe different types of collaborative arrangements and explain how they can enable companies to create and co-create value

7.4 appreciate the role of ecosystems in value creation

7.5 discuss some of the reasons for the success or failure of strategic alliances

7.6 explain the role of governance mechanisms and relational governance in managing strategic alliances and collaborative platforms.

Alibaba Group's Taobao — emerging ecosystems enabler

Alibaba Group, the largest e-commerce company in China, started out as a business-to-business service provider, created to help Chinese companies find export channels online. It established its operations as an intermediary helping to connect entrepreneurs with global markets. The arrival of eBay in the Chinese market represented a potential threat to Alibaba. In response to this threat, Alibaba launched its Taobao business, a business-to-business Taobao Marketplace, and its business-to-consumer sister Tmall.com. Together, these two businesses dominate online shopping in China. The initial entry into

the consumer world was a defensive move to survive international competition. Gradually, Alibaba Group has emerged as the dominating e-commerce platform in China with 666 million active users each month. An initial model linking buyers and sellers was supported by related operations, such as a safe payment platform, Alipay, which has become the largest and the most active online payment service provider, counting for over 50 per cent of all electronic transactions in China.[1]

Alibaba developed its websites to suit the Chinese culture. Indeed, these websites include a lot of unstructured, visually cluttered information, pictures and graphics. Such presentation is very different to the clear and easy-to-follow websites of Amazon or Google. To be able to see the whole page, users have to scroll down several times. This overwhelming presentation of Alibaba's websites is further reinforced by the availability of the most exotic products, products which would be typically discovered in street markets. Alibaba is used by thousands of sellers from the most remote locations in China and beyond who were all attracted to the chance to find their consumers online.[2] Alibaba has built its electronic platform to look like a huge hardware stockpile.[3]

Alibaba's websites were deliberately made differently to those of its Western competitors. They are made to suit Chinese users. Alibaba has cultivated the creation of a business ecosystem by welcoming investment and innovation from its network partners, including sellers of merchandise, delivery and payments enabling companies and influencers. Alibaba encouraged the ecosystem by supporting efficient interfaces between partners and reducing barriers to joining its electronic platforms, such as Taobao and Tmall.com. Alibaba has created the potential for new sources of generating profits and ensuring growth for itself as well as for its ecosystem participants.[4]

Alibaba has deliberately facilitated the development of its business ecosystem and secured investments by its business partners. This ecosystem has allowed partners to learn from each other through knowledge spillovers and speedy exchange of innovative solutions. Alibaba has emerged as a facilitator and supporter of the ecosystem. This was a distinctive difference from its initial role of acting as an intermediary. Alibaba became very efficient in developing and utilising its governance mechanisms to ensure that its partners use efficient interfaces which, in turn, lower entry barriers and make it easier to join the Taobao and Tmall.com ecosystems. New participants have learnt that the platforms of Taobao and Tmall.com are not only easy to operate but also secure and trustworthy and this perception allowed active engagement of new participants, retaining existing participants and active growth. By investing resources into developing the ecosystem's scale, survival and commitment to innovation, both Alibaba and its partners became technologically advanced, popular among users and profitable. Taobao, a successful business platform, has learnt to move away from the role of being a manager of the emerging ecosystem of business partners and become a catalyst for development.[5]

In 2001, Taobao experienced severe cash drain (US$2 million a month, with US$10 million on the bank). In order to generate much-needed cash, Taobao introduced fees-based membership packages to those business partners who signed up for priority placement in online directories and search rankings. These partners of Taobao were also offered extra promotion on Taobao's site for an additional fee and opportunities of a credit-rating and review mechanism. These innovations introduced by Taobao resulted in its shift from a pure electronic platform to a service provider. Taobao was acting as an intermediary or 'middleman' between buyers and sellers and took a commission for this connection. Taobao took the network advantages associated with large numbers of buyers and sellers. To grow the number of players, Taobao would have to reduce its control while instead encouraging the shop owners to take more initiative in working with other participants in the ecosystem. If there are problems or opportunities, third parties need to be encouraged to profit by providing an improved service.[6]

Alibaba has grown and developed its competitive advantage by utilising its distinctive business model. The most critical element of Alibaba's business model is its ability to grow together with other members of its ecosystem, including customers, service providers and logistics companies. Alibaba was highly responsive to feedback of customers and other network players. At the early stages of Alibaba's operations, the vast majority of Chinese customers were skeptical about e-commerce and were not used to online shopping. Similarly, Chinese suppliers were reluctant to make their products available online because they were concerned that once their products were sent to customers, payments would not be made. The introduction of the Alipay platform with its money freezing capability became a critical measure to address these concerns and build trust between buyers and sellers. Alipay manages online transactions with the overall amount of money, which is three times higher than that of PayPal.[7]

Introduction

Increased market uncertainty demands that companies identify new opportunities in the market and respond to them quickly if they wish to sustain their competitive advantage. Many successful companies prefer to pursue innovations in a collaborative way — because collaboration allows them to be more flexible, pool the required resources and spread competitive risks. Alliances allow companies to develop new capabilities and competencies. A *strategic alliance* is a cooperative relationship between companies involving the sharing of resources in pursuit of common goals. Strategic alliances are viewed as an alternative to diversification and the choice of strategy mode depends on a comparison of the added value and the bureaucratic costs associated with each strategy.

Alliances may involve formal agreements or they may be entirely informal — they may or may not involve ownership links. *Networks* are similar to alliances in that they involve a degree of cooperation, but, unlike alliances, cooperation is not necessarily formalised in a contractual agreement. This chapter will examine the opportunities and challenges of various forms of cooperation.

7.1 Call for partnerships in the new competitive landscape

LEARNING OBJECTIVE 7.1 Explain the need for intercompany cooperation, partnerships, alliances and networks in the new competitive landscape, and understand how strategic alliances can serve as tools for market entry and achievement of operational goals.

The scene setter describes how Alibaba, the largest e-commerce company in the world, has established their competitive advantage based on a distinctive business model. The most critical element of Alibaba's business model is its ability to grow together with other members of its ecosystem, including customers, service providers and logistics companies. There has been a trend over recent years whereby competitive advantage stems from collaborative arrangements rather than product portfolios or independent product offerings.[8]

The current dynamic market environment requires companies to focus on their core competencies while forming cooperative relationships with other companies to access and build resources. Contemporary developments in the field of strategy acknowledge that the resources residing outside the company's boundary are also potentially available to the company.[9] To benefit from resources external to the organisation, it is crucial to establish, develop and maintain lasting business relationships with customers, suppliers and other important parties.[10] Companies can no longer be isolated and independent; rather they must be flexible and cooperative. This has resulted in a new interconnected and interdependent environment with intercompany partnerships that help companies to access required resources and develop new capabilities to respond to the rapidly changing business environment. This increasing interest in cooperative models reflects an important shift in strategy formulation and implementation. This understanding of the importance of collaboration of companies with various groups of stakeholders not only challenges former views on the company owning and controlling all aspects of its own activities, but it also means that the responsibilities of companies are extended outside of its boundaries. As Araujo, Dubois and Gadde put it, 'firms' resources are partially controlled by the demands and requirements of counterparts, while "external resources", owned by counterparts, are partially controlled by the firm'.[11]

The growing understanding of the importance of cooperative models has also resulted in another development: within local and regional economies, clusterings of companies (and the social environment within which they are embedded) have become engaged in a wider set of interactions to advance the local context. This clustering of companies reflects that intercompany collaborations are able to produce, improvise and innovate more effectively than companies would otherwise do independently. These local production systems are viewed as important to local economies as they create a basis for regional growth and development. The collaboration at the local and regional levels illustrates the changing landscape of company management based upon partnerships, cooperation and inter-dependence and highlights a significant difference from the previous competitive landscape.[12] While the competitive approach was concerned with how a company could gain advantage over its competitors through favourable industry conditions[13] or by protecting its core resources and capabilities,[14] the cooperative approach expects that competitors explore how they can work together to learn new capabilities and create new products and processes that expand their capabilities beyond their independent capabilities. The previous understanding of a competitive advantage viewed companies as autonomous entities, as explained by Gulati, Nohria and Zaheer:[15] 'Strategy research has generally not looked to place the source of differences in intercompany profitability as arising from the varying participation of firms in strategic networks.' This view is in contrast to the approach taken nowadays in which there is a growing understanding that a company's performance may be strongly influenced by its intercompany ties or its 'strategic networks'.[16] Strategic networks and interfirm collaboration have been under focus in both the academic and business worlds for a considerable time. It is widely acknowledged that networks are forming a major area in the field of strategic management. Strategically guided networks provide companies with excellent support to grow their business and develop innovation. For example, software company Sun Microsystems grew to A\$3.2 billion in sales and A\$284 million in profits in ten years via the company's strategic web of alliances. Indeed, strategic networks provide a company with valuable information and knowledge which would not be possible for the company to create in isolation. Intercompany cooperation is particularly important for small companies and niche players that cannot compete on scale; they need to participate in more efficient and effective mechanisms of production and marketing in order to achieve and sustain a competitive advantage in the global economy. This is especially evident in collaborative platforms of high-tech companies such as Apple, Google, Intel and Microsoft. These platforms unite various network members, which function around the lead companies and other network members. Collaboratively, these network members develop and regularly update technology, innovate and extend product offering, manage their marketing, operations and information system.[17] While traditionally the platform concept has been technology and product-based, focused on industries of complex systems,[18] at present, platforms are evolving from joint creation of the features and attributes of product to joint actions of network members that create value collaboratively. These network-centric collaborative platforms are referred to as *value platforms* where network members create value through a variety of specific activities orchestrated by the lead firm.[19]

Strategic alliances and networks as vehicles of strategy

Strategic alliances refer to interorganisational cooperative activities to achieve one or more goals linked to the organisations' strategic objectives. The literature commonly uses the terms alliances and partnerships interchangeably. However, generally the term *partnership* is broader and refers to collaborations based on formal agreements/contracts as well as to other types of informal collaborations. Informal collaborations are those in which partners do not use a formal agreement or contract. The term *alliances* is generally used to describe cooperation based on agreements and contracts. An alliance can mean any kind of cooperative activity between two or more independent organisations. The activity may revolve around manufacturing or marketing or both. Alliances may involve sharing resources related to only one key activity in the partners' value chain, such as outbound logistics. Recall the value chain mentioned in the chapter on internal analysis of capabilities and core competencies (see figure 3.1). The various definitions of alliances in the literature highlight the fact that there are different types of alliances, with different purposes and methods of execution. For example, alliances can be 'strategic' in the sense of entry into a new market, or 'strategic' in the operational sense — involving access to resources otherwise unavailable. Regardless of these differences, the main characteristics of an alliance are exclusivity (it is exclusive to the parties who are involved in it) and inimitability (it cannot be copied by the parties that are not members of the alliance).[20]

A company entering a strategic alliance must also have the managerial capabilities to create economic value through cooperative models. Alliances require certain skills to create value for partners and these are not just limited to the activities that are external to the company. This chapter will discuss the characteristics of successful alliances and the capabilities required of companies to manage them.

It is very important to understand that alliances are not strategies in and of themselves. Instead, an alliance is a tool to realise the company's strategy. Strategic alliances are a means of vertical integration and/or diversification and hence are part of corporate-level strategy. In this sense, they are a mode of entry once a company has made the decision to enter a new business.

The term **strategic networks** is used to describe a wide range of relationships. Many authors representing the resource-based view (RBV) argue that large organisations proactively create, adapt and control a specific network structure.[21] This is consistent with the arguments of Amit and Zott,[22] following Gulati, Nohria and Zaheer,[23] that strategic networks represent stable interorganisational networks that are strategically crucial to participating organisations. Interestingly, such an understanding of strategic networks as intentionally created collaborative forms distinguishes them from evolutionary networks. For example, Lorenzoni and Lipparini[24] pointed out that the previous researchers considered networks as a given context, rather than a structure that can be deliberately designed by companies. Möller and Svahn[25] add to this definition by asserting that networks are designed by companies 'deliberately for specific purposes', explaining that those networks come in many forms — such as supplier networks, technology development networks, distribution networks and competitive coalitions. Furthermore, Möller et al.[26] argue that many strategic networks are also interrelated through actors and their capabilities, and liaisons have multiple roles in several networks. This kind of engagement in multiple strategic networks assists innovative companies to form temporal strategic networks for specific development purposes. The strategic networks are continuously evolving in the process of supporting well-established value operations as well as emergent value operations.

7.2 Why alliances? Advantages achieved through strategic alliances

LEARNING OBJECTIVE 7.2 Describe the advantages that companies can achieve through strategic alliances.

Companies enter into an alliance to get access to complementary resources that enable each partner to increase economies of scale and gain greater market power. Alliances can also help a company reduce competition, enhance their competitive advantage, gain access to resources, take advantage of opportunities and build strategic flexibility. As noted by Dacin, Oliver and Roy,[27] 'strategic alliances continue to grow in popularity, recent years have witnessed a burgeoning interest in the functions and advantages of strategic alliance formation'. In summary, the main advantages attributed to alliance creation are:[28]

- entry into new markets
- increased market power and economies of scale and scope
- the acquisition and exchange of skills
- strategic renewal
- risk and investment sharing
- reductions in liabilities of foreignness
- the ability to overcome government or trade barriers
- the acquisition of institutional legitimacy.

Entry into new markets

Alliances allow companies to enter new markets more quickly.[29] Most (if not all) companies lack the full set of resources and capabilities needed to reach their objectives. Lack of all the required resources makes entry to a new market slower if companies undertake this entry on their own (as opposed to making alliances with partners who can contribute required resources to enter a new market). Alternatively, to make a more speedy entry to a new market, companies might reallocate their resources from other areas, for example, from new product development, modernisation and so on, but this potentially has a negative impact on the areas where resources were decreased. In the dynamic competitive environment, the speed of market entry is an important source of competitive advantage. Strategic partnerships are commonly used in various industries, for example, in the global airline industry, Australian airline Qantas is partnering with China Eastern Airlines to gain access to China's domestic airline routes. Many international manufacturing companies outsource production in new international markets to local producers in these markets for the purpose of further market penetration and sharing risks and investments. For example, PepsiCo Inc., the world's second largest food and beverages business, is using a strategic beverage alliance with Tingyi (Cayman Islands) Holding Corporation, one of the leading food and beverage companies in China, for stronger presence at this market.

Increased market power and economies of scale and scope

Alliances can increase market power by jointly offering products and services to customers or by jointly purchasing from suppliers. For example, Independent Grocers of Australia (IGA) was formed by independently owned supermarkets and has more than 1400 stores. The IGA group was able to increase the market power of its members through joint purchasing from suppliers combined with establishment of common standards for the freshness of the produce they buy.[30] This is an example of *explicit* cooperation; however, sometimes companies engage in *implicit* cooperation. Tacit collusion is an example of an implicit form of cooperation. **Tacit collusion** exists when several companies in an industry cooperate tacitly to reduce industry output below the potential competitive level, thereby increasing prices above the competitive level.[31] Most strategic alliances pursue other objectives, such as facilitating learning, speeding growth and improving returns and market position.

Economies of scale are attributed to the ability of the company to increase the volume of its production and sales which leads to the reduction of the cost of production per unit. A single company, for various reasons, may not have the scale to benefit from these economies. By combining the production or sales (or both) with another company, the efficient scale can be reached.

The acquisition and exchange of skills

It is common that in alliances partners learn new knowledge and skills from each other. As Hamel, Doz and Prahalad argue:[32]

> Learning from partners is paramount. Successful companies view each alliance as a window on their partners' broad capabilities. They use the alliance to build skills in areas outside the formal agreement and systematically diffuse new knowledge throughout their organisations.

Sun Microsystems also uses technologies 'borrowed' from its partners and developed further within the company, for example to build a new workstation delivering 'more power with less cost'. Sun Microsystems also internally advances technologies brought from outside and then licenses them to third parties for development and sale under the Sun Microsystems brand.[33]

Strategic renewal

Many companies bring in new ideas from the outside. Academics and practitioners alike have argued that no individual, nor the organisation, has a monopoly on useful knowledge. To access external knowledge, companies have to interact with their stakeholders throughout the innovation process.[34] *Open innovation* is defined as 'a distributed innovation process based on purposively managed knowledge flows across organisational boundaries, using pecuniary and non-pecuniary mechanisms in line with the organisation's business model'.[35] Open innovation allows R&D spillovers and knowledge inflows and outflows. Companies can develop processes to explore and transfer external knowledge into developing new capabilities and competencies[36] and, in some cases, it forces the company to re-invent itself. The core benefit of such an approach to innovation is that useful knowledge can be distributed to and accessed beyond the company's boundaries. Nintendo uses carefully selected contributions made by its partners to create high-quality, rapid innovation. The companies that are the most skilful and speedy with implemented innovations use fewer and different resources in newer combinations. By stretching and leveraging modest resources to achieve better performance, these companies often demonstrate technical achievements such as lean production, technical innovation, or flexible manufacturing and service delivery.[37]

Risk and investment sharing

Alliances can motivate companies to make investments by sharing risks. For example, a supplier may not be prepared to make an investment outside an alliance agreement if it would link its company closely to one buyer due to the risks involved in such a decision: the buyer might not be committed to buy a supplier's products or might force a supplier to reduce its price due to its dependence on the single buyer.[38] To make an investment, some element of trust is required for any transaction in which simultaneous exchange is unavailable to the parties.[39] This condition applies to most modern business transactions, and many strategy scholars and practitioners acknowledge the utility of trust.[40] This chapter will later discuss the role of trust as a strategic asset and how trust can be developed in strategic alliances.

Reductions in liabilities of foreignness

Research into foreign direct investment shows that foreign subsidiaries face disadvantages or experience liabilities of foreignness relative to domestic companies due to various factors.[41] For example, Zaheer[42] was first to tie liability of foreignness to the failure to adopt host country practices. To overcome the liability of foreignness and gain a better knowledge of a foreign market, the company planning to begin its operations in a new foreign market will be more successful by partnering with a local company or other companies with experience in this market. Dell and Hewlett Packard, for example, formed alliances with foreign computer manufacturers to reduce the liability of foreignness and improve their competitiveness in foreign markets.

The choice between alliances, international development and acquisitions

Both internal development ('going it alone') and acquisitions can substitute for alliances under certain circumstances. If the risks of new investments are known with certainty and the company has the resources to implement the desired activity, it may 'go it alone' or, in other words, vertically integrate into the activity. Alliances are preferred over 'going it alone' when the potential partner has valuable resources that are costly to acquire. Further, alliances offer a great deal more flexibility compared to 'going it alone'.

Under certain conditions, forging a strategic alliance is a better option than an acquisition. One such circumstance is when there are legal (antitrust/competition law) constraints on an acquisition. A second circumstance is when an acquisition would allow for less flexibility under conditions of uncertainty. A third circumstance is when an acquisition may bring 'undesired' parts of the acquired company to the acquiring company. This 'extra load' may make the acquisition less preferred. Ultimately, in some cases, the value of a company is maximised when it is an independent entity. This value may be reduced when it is owned by another company. Since strategic alliances allow the company to retain its independent status, they may be preferred over acquisitions. One study on intercompany resource combination[43] emphasises the importance of three factors that make an alliance a more attractive option than an acquisition: (1) the resource similarity and complementarity between the two companies, (2) the combined relational capabilities of the two companies, and (3) the partner-specific knowledge between the two companies.

7.3 The types and structure of alliances

LEARNING OBJECTIVE 7.3 Describe different types of collaborative arrangements and explain how they can enable companies to create and co-create value.

Table 7.1[44] presents a wide range of intercompany relationships that can be categorised as strategic alliances. Generally, there are three main types of strategic alliances: joint venture, equity strategic alliance and non-equity strategic alliance.

TABLE 7.1   Strategic alliances

Strategic alliances		
Contractual arrangements	**Equity arrangements**	
Contractual partnerships	**No creation of new company**	**Creation of separate entity**
Joint R&D, joint manufacturing, joint marketing	Minority equity investment	Joint ventures
Arrangements to access mutually complementary assets or skills	Equity swaps	50–50 joint venture
Standard setting or R&D consortia		Unequal joint venture

A **joint venture** is a strategic alliance in which two or more cooperating companies (the 'parents') create a legally independent company in which they invest and from which they share any profits created. Joint ventures allow companies to establish long-term relationships and achieve their strategic goals, such as market penetration. For example, in 2019, Alibaba, China's largest electronic commerce company, launched AliExpress Russia, its joint venture with three Russian partners: RDIF (Russia's sovereign wealth fund), mobile network operator Megafon, and internet services company Mail.ru Group. Alibaba and RDIF each contributed $100 million and, in addition, Alibaba contributed its existing AliExpress business in Russia to this joint venture. Alibaba maintains the controlling 47.8 per cent stake in this partnership, whereas RDIF has the option of investing $194 million in future to purchase an additional stake to its current 12.9 per cent stake in the joint venture.

This joint venture will allow Alibaba to accomplish its growth targets in Russia, which was not possible for Alibaba to achieve on its own. The Russian joint venture is part of Alibaba's strategy to broaden its international presence as the company looks to international markets to support its growth, as it's dominated the Chinese market, and e-commerce growth in China's major cities has slowed. Alibaba's domestic rival JD.com (JD) is also expanding overseas. JD has also favoured partnerships in its battles with Alibaba in and outside China.[45]

In 2005, two leading international technology giants, Google and NASA's Ames Research Center, formed a joint venture to conduct research: the outcome of this collaboration resulted in Google Earth.

Many joint ventures have 50–50 ownership and control; however, there is no need for an equal partnership. It is more important that the partners specify certain aspects of the alliance they are most interested in. By investing in a separate entity, both parent companies have a financial interest in the joint venture. If one cheats the other, the joint venture suffers. Losses incurred by the joint venture affect the financial results of both companies. Joint ventures are the preferred mode of alliances when the possibility of cheating is high.

The most common form of strategic alliance is associated neither with a separate entity nor equity interests. Arrangements such as licensing, franchising and supply contracts are examples of non-equity alliances. **Non-equity alliances** are agreements under which companies collaborate in order to supply, produce, market or distribute products over an extended period of time but without substantial ownership investment in the alliance. For example, two car manufacturers, Chrysler and Nissan, have production deals involving two small cars and a pick-up truck. Dell has a partnership agreement with Federal Express to ensure the just-in-time delivery of its made-to-order computers to customers.

Another example is Amazon, who used this type of alliance with UPS. Both UPS and Amazon benefit from this alliance: Amazon counts for 5–10 per cent of UPS's total revenue and UPS is the primary carrier delivering most of Amazon's shipments. Amazon benefits by receiving steep shipping discounts from UPS and UPS benefits by generating reliable revenue from the millions of Amazon orders shipped continuously, but these two strategic partners do not take equity positions within each other's business.[46]

The next type of strategic alliance, the **equity alliance**, is a cooperation in which one or more partners assume a greater ownership interest in either the alliance or another partner. Many of Amazon's alliances originated as equity alliances, which later resulted in full acquisitions. Amazon uses equity alliances to understand the business of its partners before fully aligning itself to all operations. For example, Amazon and Ring, the home security camera company, entered into an equity alliance in 2016. Amazon provided finances to Ring and in return it demanded a portion of their revenue. This resulted in a full acquisition in 2018. Amazon is skilful at identifying underfunded opportunities and ultimately acquiring them after testing them in equity alliances.

Equity investments increase the stake for companies involved in the alliance. Because one partner has invested in the equity of another as part of the alliance, this company is not likely to cheat on the joint-venture partner. If it does, then its equity in the joint-venture partner loses value. Equity arrangements are very common among Japanese companies. These cross-holdings (the network is called a *keiretsu*) reduce the chances of one company cheating the other for short-term gains.

It is also common that alliances involve multiple partners. In **consortia**, several companies and possibly governments, collaborate towards a shared strategic purpose. Inputs to these cooperative agreements include information and sharing of other resources. The development of technology, for instance, often requires the collaboration of multiple players. For example, the global Wi-Fi Alliance was created to promote wireless local area network (WLAN) technology and certify products for conformance to certain standards of interoperability. This technology is now widely installed in personal computers, video game consoles, smart phones, tablets, and many other devices. Such common use of the technology requires cooperation of various players involved in the production and service of electronic devices.

Alliances of multiple players are particularly common in environments in which there is a competition to establish the technical/industry standard, where companies are increasingly focused and where speed of exploiting capability across industries is possible. The global media is an example of such an environment. For example, in setting standards for digital TV, wireless internet or mobile phones, only one or two standards can be accepted due to the need for having usable and connectable products everywhere in the world. Thus, industry leaders — individual companies or networks, such as the Wi-Fi Alliance — set the standards and others have to adapt or they will be forced out of the industry. The understanding of how technology standards are set leads to the recognition that it is the networks that are competing, not just single companies.[47] In some cases, the development of global strategic alliances is moving the nature of competition as well as strategy development from the business to the alliance level.[48] Moreover, conducting business as part of an alliance or strategic network implies that instead of competing with each other, companies — as part of a network — compete against other networks.[49] Many industries are witnessing the formation of multiple-partner alliances, or constellations, competing against each other for the attraction of new members and for the penetration of their products or services in customer markets. Global airlines, in particular, have aggressively formed alternative groups competing in international markets for both passengers and member airlines through the combination of international routes, joint coordination of operations, and consolidation of marketing tools such as frequent flyer programs. Membership in airline constellations has a positive impact on carriers' operational performance; particularly it improves carriers' load factors or their ratio of passenger traffic to seat capacity. When a carrier belongs to a multiple partner alliance, most of its internalised traffic comes from partners. In airline constellations, as agreements become more comprehensive and general, the extent of passenger traffic that carriers can capture from other members through bilateral (airline to airline alliance) deals should not differ much across companies. In other words, the multilateral nature of constellations apparently substitutes for the need of extensive bilateral partnering. 'Non-members of an airline alliance, in contrast, will have to establish bilateral connections to carriers handling large traffic flow (including, in some cases, members of explicit groups) in order to increase their operational performance.'[50]

Competition at an alliance or network level also has significant implications from the perspective of the end customer. Although the total value perceived by the end customer is an outcome of a complex set of integrated value activities and companies, the end customer evaluates them as one entity or offering. As a consequence, poor performance, or failure, by a participating company weakens the image of the final offering and, in the long run, the competitiveness and business performance of the entire alliance or network. This creates demands for formation of a strategic alliance, the selection of its members, agreement on member roles and responsibilities, and development of its operating principles. The more the quality and competitiveness of the alliance offering depends on seamless collaboration between members, the more critical the alliance formation process and its management.[51]

7.4 The role of ecosystems in value creation

LEARNING OBJECTIVE 7.4 Appreciate the role of ecosystems in value creation.

The ever-increasing connectivity of the modern world, combined with the interdependence of diverse organisations, technologies and institutions, challenges managers to understand and apply new business models. The idea of understanding 'markets as networks'[52] was introduced earlier to view the changes in organisations' customer and supplier relationships as existing within a broader context involving deeper supplier networks, cooperative arrangements and competitive coalitions. According to Möller and Halinen, 'The competitive environment of firms is undergoing a fundamental change. Traditional markets are being rapidly replaced by networks'.[53] Along these lines, both scholars and practitioners consider the ecosystem approach, which has recently attracted a lot of attention in strategic management, innovation and technology management, and industrial marketing. The term 'ecosystem' was originally introduced to the business context by Moore[54], who adapted this term from biology and used 'business ecosystem' to explain the interdependence and coevolution of contemporary business activities. The most important managerial implications of understanding ecosystems are in recognising the ability of organisations to develop flexibility and resilience while working together to coevolve.

A **business ecosystem** is defined as a part of the business environment where a variety of organisations co-exist with one another and coevolve on the basis of their ongoing interaction.

In his thought-provoking book *The Death of Competition: Leadership and Strategy in the Age of Business Ecosystems*, Moore maintained that the performance of companies requires understanding how they have been embedded into the business ecosystem and how well the entire system is performing.[55] The concept of a business ecosystem allows managers to redefine the notion of competitive advantage, specifically in the understanding that competitive advantage can be achieved from 'cooperative, co-evolving relationships with a network of contributors to the overall economic scene'.[56] The ecosystem approach was adopted in theoretical and empirical context for various purposes but it commonly refers to the value-adding characteristics of business-to-business interactions. In recent years, interest in ecosystems has extended to the concepts of *innovation ecosystem, platform ecosystem* and *service ecosystem*,[57] and to the role of ecosystems in systemic value creation.[58] For example, Apple is using the ecosystem approach to increase demand for their products. All of their products are interrelated and easy to use, due to the compatibility of hardware and software. After purchasing a new iPhone, for example, customers can easily transition to additional Apple products, such as an Apple Watch or iPad.

Business-to-business (B2B) and business network scholars use a notion of ecosystem to address the increasing interdependence and coevolution of contemporary business and innovation activities. The following four categories can be identified in the ecosystem approach: (a) competition and evolution; (b) emergence and disruption; (c) stable business exchange; and (d) value co-creation. Using an ecosystem as a perspective in the management of business and innovation networks allows managers to identify new models for value creation. Value co-creation is a central question within the ecosystems approach; therefore, managers have to recognise how value can be captured and co-created.

Value co-creation in ecosystems

Chesbrough and his co-authors emphasised the significant role of the customer in determining the value of a market offering, which they defined as 'a customer's willingness to pay or the benefit the consumer experiences'.[59] The idea of the value of a market offering was extended by strategy scholars who introduced the demand-side perspective of strategy.[60] The strategy literature has stressed the specific characteristics and aspects of benefits beyond the purely monetary, which companies perceive through their interactions with other members of ecosystems.[61] Moreover, value can be created by companies through contributing to open-innovation projects. Examples of perceived benefits to companies of such contributions include emotional rewards such as fun and intellectual challenge, a sense of identity with the project or community, the sense of being a good citizen, improved reputation, and the ability to learn and develop new ideas.

7.5 Success and failure of alliances

LEARNING OBJECTIVE 7.5 Discuss some of the reasons for the success or failure of strategic alliances.

Alliances present a remarkable paradox for companies. On the one hand, studies show that the number of alliances increases by 25 per cent per year and that those alliances account for one-third of many large companies' revenue and value; on the other hand, alliances demonstrate surprisingly low success rates.[62] By the early 2000s, the world's largest companies had over 20 per cent of their assets and over 30 per cent of their annual research expenditures realised through their alliances.[63] Many senior executives believe that alliances are a main vehicle for company growth. In some industries, such as the global airline industry, there is increasing competition — not among single companies — as networks and alliances compete against each other.[64] However, despite the large number of studies on how to make alliances work published in the last two decades, the failure rate for alliances hovers between 30 and 70 per cent.[65] Studies have shown that often alliances neither achieve the objectives of their parent companies nor deliver on the operational or strategic benefits they were expected to provide.[66] Alliance termination rates are reportedly over 50 per cent,[67] and in many cases forming such relationships has resulted in shareholder value destruction for the companies that engage in them.[68] Some of the reasons that alliances fail, and how to make them successful, are now discussed.

Why do alliances fail?

Some alliances fail due to the cultural clashes between partners, particularly when Western companies try to partner with Asian companies. These companies often have different objectives. For example, some Western managers are satisfied with collaboration based on the opportunity to complement their own manufacturing capabilities with the distribution capabilities of their Asian partners and have no ambitions to invest upstream. However, for their Asian partners, collaboration is viewed as a 'second best' option. Asian companies wish to have these manufacturing skills themselves and strive to 'digest' their partners' skills. 'When the commitment to learning is so one-sided, collaboration invariably leads to competitive compromise.'[69] National characteristics of partners influence alliance formation and moderate the relationship between perceived technological uncertainty and alliance formation. When General Motors formed its *New United Motor Manufacturing, Inc. (NUMMI)* joint venture with Toyota, its motive was to learn Toyota's 'lean' approach to manufacturing.[70] Though in this case the alliance was successful, in circumstances in which both alliance partners are trying to acquire one another's capabilities, the result may well be a 'competition for competence' that ultimately destabilises the relationship.[71]

Partnering for the wrong reason (e.g. adopting an 'everyone else is doing it' herd mentality) also might lead to alliance failure.[72] Partnering is often a result of offensive motivation, for example, to achieve greater market power and ward off competitors. However, the fact that the company is entering into an alliance might be interpreted by others to mean there may be problems in the company, and the deal causes media scrutiny which leads to more competition.

Companies may demonstrate opportunistic behaviour in their alliance formation, ignoring responsibilities and free-riding (expecting that their partners will do the job), distorting information or having hidden agendas (partners in an alliance also compete with each other and have very different characteristics). Staff may display their loyalty to their respective companies rather than to the alliance. Partners may be entering into an alliance with an objective to test the market before the launch of a wholly owned subsidiary. Companies believe that their successful experience in alliances with other partners can be transplanted to their new alliances without working on the implications of such transplantation.[73]

What makes alliances successful?

The success of any single alliance is determined by some key factors that are relevant at each stage of alliance evolution.[74] These key factors include:

1. the phase of formation — companies select a partner or partners
2. the phase of design — the alliance governance mechanism is being established
3. the post formation phase — the company manages the alliance on an ongoing basis and creates value.[75]

Table 7.2[76] presents an overview of the main phases of the alliance evolution and some success factors at each phase.

TABLE 7.2   The main phases of the alliance evolution and their success factors

The alliance outcome	Achievement of alliance objectives Greater alliance performance		
Phase of the alliance life cycle	Alliance formation and partner selection	Alliance governance and design	Post formation alliance management
Key success factors of alliance	Partner complementarity Partner compatibility Partner commitment	Equity sharing or ownership Contractual provisions Relational governance	Use of coordination mechanisms Development of trust and social capital Conflict resolution and escalation

The rest of this section will briefly review the critical success factors of alliances. Many studies show the importance of selecting the right partners.[77] Partner complementarity is the extent to which a partner contributes resources and capabilities to the alliance which the other partner lacks and vice versa. Recall the resource-based view of strategy and the role of resources and capabilities in the ability of the company to create a competitive advantage (discussed in the chapter on internal analysis of capabilities and core competencies). These resources and capabilities can be accessed by the company via alliances and networks. According to the resource-based view of strategy, the greater the complementarity between the partners, the more likely the alliance will be a success. In addition, a joint-venture partner has to be compatible with the focal company and committed to the relationship.[78] Partner compatibility requires a similarity in styles of doing business and cultures. Commitment requires that partners not only be willing to contribute their resources to the alliance, but also be able to make short-term sacrifices to achieve the desired long-term outcomes.[79]

The choice of alliance governance and design also plays an important role in determining alliance success. Equity sharing or ownership refers to the arrangement in which partners own an equity stake in the other (equity alliances) or create a separate venture (joint venture). Such arrangements prevent opportunistic behaviour of partners because they are not only committed to the alliance, but they also are concerned about each other's performance.[80] Contractual provisions establish partners with mutual rights and obligations by specifying each partner's expected inputs into the alliance, the processes by which exchanges will occur and disputes will be resolved, and the expected outputs of the relationships. Contracts also limit information disclosure by partners during the period of the alliance by specifying the interaction of each partner with any third parties, and regulating the way in which the alliance will end.[81] Relational governance refers to self-enforcing governance based on goodwill, trust and reputation.

Further, partners create *social capital* that affords them flexibility:[82] they can rely on their partners and call for help when they need it. Social capital also means that reciprocity exists: partners can ask for assistance and they are expected to provide it when asked.[83] Trust based on interpersonal trust is referred to as *relational capital*. Relational capital is developed through the constructs of trust and trustworthiness, norms and sanctions, obligations and expectations, and identity and identification. It has a significant effect on the resource exchange process in alliances. Overall, the relational dimension of social capital allows actors to determine the amount of capital and level of risk when exchanging resources.[84] Although alliance success is reliant on collaboration between companies, trust is developed by interpersonal communication, such as between managers or professionals of the joint-venture partners, and also contributes to the successful collaboration at the joint-venture level. This is particularly relevant for joint-venture collaboration in Asia where partners prefer to do business with familiar counterparts and often business deals are based on interpersonal relationships.[85] Williamson emphasised the greater value of partnering relationships when they are based on personal trust. He observed that 'other things being equal, idiosyncratic exchange relations that feature personal trust will survive greater stress and will display greater adaptability'.[86] The next section will discuss the importance of trust for alliance success.

Trust in alliances

The partner relationships in an alliance are always evolving and, thus, not everything can be predicted and presented in a formal contractual agreement. This leads to an understanding that partners have to develop trust in their relationships. Trust depends on reputation effects or on multilayered relations between the parties to a transaction that can create low-cost enforcement opportunities.[87]

The development of trust between partners:

- limits transaction costs, particularly in organisational situations where there is a high level of uncertainty[88]
- facilitates long-term relationships, reducing conflicts that are non-functional to the partnership goals[89]
- stimulates collaboration among companies, increasing the likelihood of the success of alliances[90]
- simplifies knowledge transfer and joint learning
- enables the company to obtain a sustainable long-term competitive advantage.

Table 7.3 summarises the factors of alliance success and failure based on a study of 30 companies in the computer, telecommunications and media industries in Europe and the United States.[91]

TABLE 7.3   The factors of success and failure of alliances

Success factors	Failure factors
Specific goals, life span, tasks, responsibilities and achievement measures	Conflicting interests
Use of pilot ideas	Lack of clearly defined objectives and responsibilities
Ongoing management, coordination, transparency and communication	Ill evaluation of the achievements
Commitment	Under-resourcing
Value chain alignment	Cultural issues
Active team work and staff training	(Perceived) underperformance

Source: Dodourova, 2009.

7.6 Governance of alliances: how to make alliances successful

LEARNING OBJECTIVE 7.6 Explain the role of governance mechanisms and relational governance in managing strategic alliances and collaborative platforms.

Given the growing use of alliances and the low success that companies usually have with them, a company can create a significant competitive advantage over its rivals if it can achieve greater overall alliance success. This explains why both academics and practitioners are so interested in understanding the factors that explain how companies have alliance capability and greater alliance success.[92] In the past decade, a large number of studies have been written on how to make collaborations with competitors or suppliers successful. Successful alliances must accomplish two goals: coordination of the optimal combination of productive resources across parties and mitigation of the risks of opportunistic behaviour.[93] The literature on managing alliances provides a wide range of studies in which two main approaches seem to be dominating. One is drawn on transaction cost economics, which argues that successful exchange can be achieved by reinforcing formal governance mechanisms.[94] **Governance mechanisms** are concrete managerial and control activities that describe in detail how the required behaviour of the partner will become motivated, influenced and established, or in which ways the desirable or predetermined gains are to be fulfilled. Another stream of research emphasises the role of more relational governance mechanisms that are based on building of trust and social identification such as forming teams, frequent direct managerial contact, shared decision making and joint problem solving.[95] Recent studies have shown that these approaches are not mutually exclusive.[96] There is no conclusion about when one approach is more effective than the other. However, Hoetker and Mellewigt[97] argue that the optimal choice of governance mechanisms depends on the type of assets involved in the alliance being governed. They recognise that the primary types of assets include knowledge-based and property-based assets. **Knowledge-based assets** are a company's intangible know-how and customer service expertise. **Property-based assets** are legal properties owned by companies including physical resources, such as buildings, and financial capital. Both property-based and knowledge-based assets may enable partners to achieve the alliance's objectives. Formal governance mechanisms require less prior interaction of partners compared to relational governance mechanisms. As the relationships of partners develop and grow over time, relational governance mechanisms become more feasible and facilitate more intensive use of knowledge-based assets.

Considering alliances as an inherently dynamic process, many studies focused on exploring the organisational determinants of alliance capability and alliance learning processes for the success of alliances.[98] Research has shown that some companies are much more successful at managing alliances, or creating value through them, than other companies. For example, mining companies Rio Tinto and BHP Billiton, grocery retailers Coles and Woolworths, and retailer David Jones are companies that belong to the former category — they manage their alliances successfully and create value through those alliances. Companies with greater alliance success are presumed to possess superior **alliance capability** — the ability of companies to effectively manage intercompany alliances and create value through them. The next section will discuss the role of a dedicated alliance function for alliance success.

The role of a dedicated alliance function for alliance success

Dyer, Kale and Singh[99] argue that a dedicated alliance function, which is responsible for supervising and managing a company's overall alliance activity, positively contributes to greater alliance success. Other research and case-based studies[100] have also demonstrated that companies with a dedicated alliance function achieve greater alliance success.

> An *alliance function* is essentially a structural mechanism, in the form of a separate organizational unit or team of managers, responsible for managing and coordinating a firm's alliance activity, that provides several benefits to firms. First, it facilitates strategic and operational coordination between the firm's numerous alliances. Second, it becomes a focal point for attracting, screening, and identifying appropriate alliance opportunities. Third, it guides individual business units on a variety of alliance related issues such as searching and selecting appropriate partners, drafting legal agreements, etc . . . Fourth, it can serve as a focal point for initiating organization-wide efforts to learn and accumulate alliance management lessons and best practices within a firm. Collectively, these actions not only enable better integration across all alliances in a firm, but also help to improve its alliance management skills. Hewlett-Packard, Oracle, Siebel, Citibank . . . are some of the companies that have created an alliance function and achieved greater alliance success.[101]

Having a dedicated alliance function is a more effective tool for building alliance management know-how in large companies than in small companies.[102]

Recent studies show that companies can develop alliance capability by learning and accumulating alliance management skills and best practices by articulation, codification, sharing and internationalisation of relevant alliance know-how. Kale and Singh[103] introduced a term 'alliance learning process' to assess the role of knowledge articulation and transfer in the development of alliance capability and in gaining more power over competitors. Although alliances are viewed as guided by calculation, collaboration with partners is a crucial tool to improve the company's competitive profile. For example, Hamel, Doz and Prahalad[104] argue that alliances with competitors can make partners stronger against outsiders, and Lorenzoni and Baden–Fuller articulate that companies should create strategically guided networks and act as coordinators of their partners, or, in their words, 'create a strategic centre to manage a web of partners'.[105] The next two sections are based on the articles 'Collaborate with your competitors — and win' of Hamel, Doz and Prahalad and 'Creating a strategic centre to manage a web of partners' of Lorenzoni and Baden-Fuller respectively.

How to collaborate with competitors and win

Hamel, Doz and Prahalad[106] stress that the companies that benefit most from competitive collaboration are those that adhere to a set of simple but powerful principles.

Collaboration is competition in a different form.
Successful companies never forget that their new partners may be out to disarm them. They enter alliances with clear objectives, and also understand how their partners' objectives will affect their success.

Harmony is not the most important measure of success.
Indeed, occasional conflict may be the best evidence of mutually beneficial collaboration. Few alliances remain a win–win undertaking forever. A partner may be content even as it unknowingly surrenders core skills.

Cooperation has limits.
Companies must defend against competitive compromise. A strategic alliance is a constantly evolving bargain whose real terms go beyond the legal agreement or the aims of top management. What information gets traded is determined day by day, often by engineers and operating managers. Successful companies inform employees at all levels about skills and technologies that are off-limits to the partner and monitor what the partner requests and receives.

Learning from partners is paramount.
Successful companies view each alliance as a window on their partners' broad capabilities. They use the alliance to build skills in areas outside the formal agreement and systematically diffuse new knowledge throughout their organisation.

The role of a strategic centre in managing a web of partners

Lorenzoni and Baden-Fuller[107] emphasise the importance of companies to act as a strategic centre for theirpartners. They explore vertical relationships of companies in which companies cooperate and compete simultaneously. These scholars argue that it is necessary for a network of companies to have a strategic centre that can function as builder and coordinator. This role's main features include the following.

- *Strategic outsourcing.* Outsource and share with more partners than the normal broker and traditional company. Require partners to be more than doers, expect them to be problem solvers and initiators.
- *Capability.* Develop the core skills and competencies of partners to make them more effective and competitive. Force members of the network to share their expertise with others in the network, and with the central company.
- *Technology.* Borrow ideas from others which are developed and explained as a means of creating and mastering new technologies.
- *Competition.* Explain to partners that the principle dimension of competition is between value chains and networks. The network is only as strong as its weakest link. Encourage rivalry between companies inside the network, in a positive manner.

Apple, Benetton, McDonald's, Nike, Nintendo and Toyota are examples of companies that act as a strategic centre in relation to their network members. The idea of having a web of partners is consistent with understanding contemporary alliances as a web of relationships, a 'web' being an interdependent set of alliances'.[108] Further, this web of partners can be considered as constellations of companies or multi-company alliances, which are more complex to manage.

Exit from alliances

There is an increasing research interest in the break-up of alliances,[109] but literature on the dissolution of alliances is currently sparse.[110] Lacking an exit strategy is viewed as a common mistake that partners have when starting an alliance. Exit strategies should be a part of any alliance agreement. Exit strategies should meet the test of fairness while protecting key resources of joint-venture partners. Yet, the study of Gulati et al. on exit planning in strategic alliances found that many companies fall into the trap of having no exit plan and other companies take too simple a planning approach, wondering if the exit will be unconditionally easy or hard.[111] This study offers a framework that represents contingency-specific exit situations for each partner in the alliance, situations in which exit can be:

- symmetric and easy for both partners — where the alliance term expires, or its objectives are met or acknowledged as impossible to attain

- symmetric and hard for both partners — where the alliance has been advancing towards its goals, and its success is contingent upon both partners' unique expertise and capabilities
- asymmetric (hard for the firm and easy for the partner) — where the partner is heavily dependent on the alliance, and the firm either breaches the alliance contract or observes better prospects elsewhere
- asymmetric (easy for the firm and hard for the partner) — where the firm is heavily dependent on the alliance, and the partner either breaches the alliance contract or observes better prospects elsewhere.[112]

Exiting an alliance should be performed the same way the company enters it — in a spirit of cooperation, openness, trust, mutual benefit and assistance, and in accordance with the original guiding principle.[113] The alliance does not dissolve automatically into nonexistence. Partners may help each other to find alternative suppliers, customers or partners. The best approach to exit is when partners agree up front what the 'rules of disengagement' are for an alliance. These rules set out each partner's responsibilities and obligations when the relationship is to be terminated or is to be downsized to a less critical or strategic position. These accepted rules will clarify a wide range of issues with regard to people and other resources allocation, fair access to training equipment and sites, appropriate confidential information, and fair pricing for intellectual property issues, and maintenance and service issues.

SUMMARY

The new competitive landscape with dynamic markets makes companies interdependent and interconnected: companies have to focus on their core competencies while forming cooperative relationships with other companies to access and build internal resources. Partnerships and alliances with customers, suppliers and competitors enable companies to access the required resources outside the company's boundaries in order to learn and develop new capabilities and respond to the rapidly changing business environment. The increasing interest in cooperation reflects an important shift in strategy formulation and implementation, and challenges former views on the company owning and controlling all aspects of its own activities. The company's management is based upon partnerships, cooperation and interdependence, and the company's responsibilities are extended outside of its boundaries.

The term 'strategic alliances' refers to interorganisational cooperative activities to achieve one or more goals linked to their strategic objectives. Strategic alliances are viewed as vehicles of the company's strategies. The term 'strategic networks' refers to stable inter-organisational arrangements that are intentionally created by participating organisations for specific purposes. The main advantages that can be achieved through alliances are entry into new markets, increased market power and economies of scale and scope, the acquisition and exchange of skills, the company's strategic renewal, risk and investment sharing, reductions in liabilities of foreignness, overcoming government or trade barriers and the acquisition of institutional legitimacy.

The main types of alliances are joint ventures, equity alliances and non-equity alliances. There are also multiple members' alliances or constellations. A joint venture is a strategic alliance in which two or more cooperating companies (the 'parents') create a legally independent company in which they invest and from which they share any profits created. An equity alliance is an alliance in which one or more partners assume a greater ownership interest in either the alliance or another partner. Equity investments increase the stake for companies involved in the alliance. Non-equity alliances are agreements under which companies collaborate in order to supply, produce, market or distribute products of the partner over an extended period of time but without substantial ownership investment in the alliance. It is also common that alliances involve multiple partners. In consortia, several companies, and possibly governments, collaborate for a shared strategic purpose. The inputs of these cooperative agreements include information and sharing of other resources.

Although the number of strategic alliances is increasing, many of them fail: they do not achieve the objectives of their parent companies nor deliver on the expected operational or strategic benefits. Alliances fail due to being formed for the wrong reason, incompatible objectives of the parent companies, choosing the wrong partner, opportunistic behaviour and cheating of partners. Alliance success factors include partner complementarity and compatibility, an effective governance mechanism and development of trust between partners.

Alliance success can be achieved by reinforcing formal governance mechanisms as well as by using relational governance mechanisms. Formal governance mechanisms are concrete managerial and control activities which describe in detail how the required behaviour of the partner will be motivated, influenced and established, or in which ways the desirable or predetermined gains are to be fulfilled. Relational governance mechanisms are based on the building of trust and social identification such as forming teams, frequent direct managerial contact, shared decision making and joint problem solving. These approaches are not mutually exclusive.

A dedicated alliance function positively contributes to the success of alliances. An alliance function is a separate organisational unit or team of managers, responsible for managing and coordinating a company's alliance activity, that provides the following benefits to companies: it facilitates strategic and operational coordination between the company's numerous alliances; it becomes a focal point for attracting, screening and identifying appropriate alliance opportunities; it guides individual business units on a variety of alliance related issues such as searching and selecting appropriate partners and drafting legal agreements; and it serves as a focal point for initiating organisation-wide efforts to learn and accumulate alliance management lessons and best practices within a company. Collectively, these actions not only enable better integration across all alliances in a company, but also help to improve its alliance management skills.

To collaborate with competitors and win, companies should adhere to the following principles: collaboration is competition in a different form, harmony is not the most important measure of success, cooperation has limits, and learning of partners from each other is paramount.

Lacking an exit strategy is viewed as a common mistake that partners make when starting an alliance. Exit strategies should be a part of any alliance agreement. Exit strategies should meet the test of fairness while protecting the key resources of joint-venture partners. Exiting an alliance should be performed the same way the company enters it — in a spirit of cooperation, openness, trust, mutual benefit and assistance, and in accordance with the original guiding principle.

KEY TERMS

alliance capability The ability of companies to effectively manage intercompany alliances and create value through them.

business ecosystem A part of the business environment where a variety of organisations co-exist with one another and coevolve on the basis of their ongoing interaction.

consortia Companies, and possibly governments, that collaborate for a shared strategic purpose.

equity alliance An alliance in which one or more partners assume a greater ownership interest in either the alliance or another partner.

governance mechanisms Concrete managerial and control activities which describe in detail how the required behaviour of the partner will become motivated, influenced and established, or in which ways the desirable or predetermined gains are to be fulfilled.

joint venture A strategic alliance in which two or more cooperating companies (the 'parents') create a legally independent company in which they invest and from which they share any profits created.

knowledge-based assets A company's intangible know-how and customer service expertise.

non-equity alliances Agreements under which companies collaborate in order to supply, produce, market or distribute products of the partner over an extended period of time but without substantial ownership investment in the alliance.

property-based assets Legal properties owned by companies including physical resources, such as buildings, and financial capital.

strategic alliances Interorganisational cooperative activities to achieve one or more goals linked to the organisations' strategic objectives.

strategic networks Stable interorganisational arrangements that are intentionally created by participating organisations for specific purposes.

tacit collusion When several companies in an industry cooperate tacitly to reduce industry output below the potential competitive level, thereby increasing prices above the competitive level.

SELF-STUDY QUESTIONS

1 Explain why competition is moving from a company level to an alliance, network and ecosystem level. What implications does this have from the perspective of the end customer?

2 Explain how strategic alliances assist companies in implementation of their strategies. What are the collaborative advantages that can be achieved through alliances?

3 What types of alliances can be formed by companies? How does the choice of a certain type of alliance impact the possible behaviour of partners in an alliance?

4 Why do some alliances fail while others succeed?

5 Why and how should companies plan for their exit from an alliance?

DISCUSSION QUESTIONS

1 Discuss moral hazards that can derail an alliance and prevent one partner from doing its best in the alliance. What can be done to deal with it?

2 'Strategic alliances will not survive in the long term if the participating partners do not share clearly-defined objectives.' Discuss this statement in relation to any alliances that have been featured in this chapter or have recently been highlighted by the media.

3 Alliances can be used to assist companies to analyse the economic potential of entering a new industry or market. Why would a company seeking to analyse these opportunities simply not hire market analysts and industry experts to evaluate the economic potential of entering into a new market? Is there anything that makes an alliance a better way to evaluate entry modes than alternatives (i.e. by doing it alone or through acquisitions)?

4 There is a growing popularity of strategic alliances as a vehicle to access international markets. Review the reasons that make alliances fail. Do you think these reasons are more relevant to international strategic alliances? Why, or why not?

5 How do stable and dynamic environments make alliances and other collaborative platforms different? How is success of alliances and collaborative platforms affected by the characteristics of the environment? Support your statements by using examples of alliances and other collaborative platforms in stable and dynamic environments.

EXERCISES

1 Identify a co-working centre, an innovation hub or a business incubator in your city or local area. Investigate collaborative activities for members of this platform. How is value created there? Is this platform successful? Explain your reasoning.

2 Using one local business in your area as an example, think of new partners that would perform one primary or support activity of the value chain of this company. What type of strategic alliances would you recommend to them and why? How should the company choose the right partner or partners among the alternatives? Can partners run their joint activities online? If so, explain how. Support your answers by using examples.

3 Review partnerships/alliances in which your university is involved. What are the objectives of these partnerships/alliances and how are they being achieved?

4 Go to the Cochlear website at www.cochlear.com.au. Study how Cochlear implements its strategy for continuous innovation using alliances with other companies. Identify the types of Cochlear's alliances based on the information in this chapter. Explain how Cochlear manages to make its alliances successful.

5 Search the websites of business periodicals such as *Business Week, Fortune* and *The Wall Street Journal* and look for strategic alliance announcements. Identify the motivation(s) for the alliance.

FURTHER READING

Aarikka-Stenroos, L & Rittala, P 2017, 'Network management in the era of ecosystems: Systematic review and management framework', *Industrial Marketing Management*, vol. 67, 23–36.

Gulati, R, Sytch, M & Mehrotra, P 2008, 'Breaking up is never easy: planning for exit in a strategic alliance', *California Management Review*, vol. 50, no. 4, 147–163.

Chesbrough, H, Lettl, C & Ritter, T 2018, 'Value creation and value capture in open innovation', *Journal of Product Innovation Management*, vol. 35, no. 6, 930–938.

Scillitoe, JL & Chakrabarti, AK 2010, 'The role of incubator interactions in assisting new ventures', *Technovation*, vol. 30, no. 3, 155–167.

Schreiner, M, Kale, P & Corsten, D 2009, 'What really is alliance management capability and how does it impact alliance outcomes and success?', *Strategic Management Journal*, vol. 30, no. 13, 1395–1419.

Zollo, M, Reuer, JJ & Singh, H 2002, 'Interorganizational routines and performance in strategic alliances', *Organization Science*, vol. 13, no. 6, 701–713.

ENDNOTES

1. J-M Dru, *Thank you for disrupting: the disruptive business philosophies of the world's great entrepreneurs*, Wiley, 2019, 256; C Smith, '40 amazing Alipay statistics and facts (December 2018)', ExpandedRamblings.com, 7 December 2018, https://expandedramblings.com/index.php/alipay-statistics.
2. Dru, op. cit.
3. Interview of Kishore Biyani with IndiaKnowledge@Wharton, 'Retailer Kishore Biyani: "We believe in destroying what we have created"', knowledge.wharton.upenn.edu, 1 November 2007; Dru, op. cit.
4. P Williamson and MW Jingji, 'Alibaba Group's Taobao: from intermediary to ecosystem enabler.' In B De Wit, *Strategy: an international perspective*, 6th Edition, Cengage Learning, 2017.
5. B De Wit, *Strategy: an international perspective*, 6th edn, Cengage Learning, 2017.
6. Williamson Jingji, op. cit; De Wit, op. cit.
7. Dru, op. cit.
8. H Perks, C Kowalkovski, L Witell, and A Gustafsson, 'Network orchestration for value platform development, *Industrial Marketing Management*, 67, 2017 106–121.
9. R Gulati, 'Network location and learning: the influence of network resources and firm capabilities on alliance formation', *Strategic Management Journal*, vol. 28, no. 1, 1999, 17–37; GK Lee, 'The significance of network resources in the race to enter emerging product markets: the convergence of telephony communications and computer networking', 1989–2001, *Strategic Management Journal*, vol. 20, no. 5, 2007, 397–420.

10. D Ford, P Berthon, S Brown, L-E Gadde, H Håkanson, P Naude, et al., *The business marketing course: managing in complex networks*, Chichester: John Wiley & Sons, Ltd, 2002; D Ford, L-E Gadde, H Håkansson, and I Shenota, *Managing business relationships*, Chichester: John Wiley & Sons Ltd, 2003.

11. Araujo, Dubois, and Gadde, 1999, p. 880, cited in E Baraldi, R Brennan, D Harrison, A Tunisini, J Zolkiewski, 'Strategic thinking and the IMP approach: a comparative analysis', *Industrial Marketing Management*, vol. 36, 2007, 879–894.

12. K Pavlovich and M Akoorie (eds), *Strategic alliances and collaborative partnership (a case book)*, New Zealand: Dunmore Press, 2003.

13. ME Porter, *Competitive strategy*, New York: Free Press, 1980.

14. This statement is known as the resource-based view of strategy, discussed in the chapter on business-level strategy and competitive positioning; see, for example, JB Barney, 'Firms resources and sustained competitive advantage', *Journal of Management*, vol. 17, 1991, 99–120; B Wernerfelt, 'A resource-based view of the firm', *Strategic Management Journal*, vol. 5, no. 2, 1984, 171–180.

15. Gulati, Norhia, and Zaheer, op. cit.

16. JH Dyer and H Singh, 'The relational view: cooperative strategy and sources of interorganisational competitive advantage', *Academy of Management Review*, vol. 23, no. 4, 1998, 660–679; JH Dyer and NW Hatch, 'Relation-specific capabilities and barriers to knowledge transfers: creating advantage through network relationships', *Strategic Management Journal*, vol. 27, 2006, 701–719.

17. A Gawer and MA Cusumano, (2014)'Industry platforms and ecosystem innovation', *Journal of Product Innovation Management*, vol. 31, no. 3, 2014, 417–433.

18. ibid.

19. H Perks, C Kowalkovski, L Witell and A Gustafsson, 'Network orchestration for value platform development', *Industrial Marketing Management*, 67, 2017, 106–121.

20. M Forsgren, 'The concept of learning in the Uppsala internalization process model: a critical review', *International Business Review*, vol. 11, no. 3, 2002, 257–277; Pavlovich and Akoorie, op. cit.

21. KR Möller, A Rajala and S Svahn, 'Strategic business nets – their type and management', *Journal of Business Research*. 58, 2005, 1274–1284; JH Dyer and H Singh, 'The relational view: cooperative strategy and sources of interorganisational competitive advantage', *Academy of Management Review*. vol. 23, no. 4, 1998, 660–679.

22. R Amit and C Zott, 'Value creation in e-business', *Strategic Management Journal*, vol. 22, no. 6/7, 2001, 493–520.

23. R Gulati, N Nohria and A Zaheer, 'Strategic networks', *Strategic Management Journal*, vol. 21, no. 3, 2000, 203–15.

24. G Lorenzoni and A Lipparini, 'The leveraging of interfirm relationships as a distinctive organisational capability: a longitudinal study', *Strategic Management Journal*, vol. 20, no. 4, 1999, 317–338.

25. KE Möller and S Svahn, 'Role of knowledge in value creation in business nets', *Journal of Management Studies*, vol. 43, no. 5, 2006, 987.

26. Möller, Rajala and Svahn, 2005, op. cit.; KE Möller and A Halinen, 'Managing business and innovation networks — From strategic nets to business fields and ecosystems', *Industrial Marketing Management*, vol. 67, 2017, 5–22.

27. JH Dyer, P Kale and H Singh, 'How to make strategic alliances work', *MIT Sloan Management Review*, vol. 42, 2001, 37–43.

28. Table adapted from MT Dacin, C Oliver and J-P Roy, 'The legitimacy of strategic alliances: an institutional perspective', *Strategic Management Journal*, vol. 28, 169–187, 2007.

29. L Fuentelsaz, J Gomez and Y Polo, 'Followers entry timing: evidence from the Spanish banking sector after deregulation', *Strategic Management Journal*, vol. 23, 2002, 245–264.

30. IGA home page, www.iga.net.au.

31. JB Barney, *Gaining and sustaining competitive advantage*, Addison-Wesley, 1997, p. 255.

32. G Hamel, Y Doz and CK Prahalad, 'Collaborate with your competitors — and win', *Harvard Business Review*, January–February, vol. 67, 1989, 133–139.

33. G Lorenzoni and C Baden-Fuller, 'Creating a strategic center to manage a web of partners', *California Management Review*, vol. 37, no. 3, 1995, 146–163.

34. H Chesbrough, 'The era of open innovation', *Sloan Management Review*, vol. 44, no. 3, 2003, 35–41.

35. H Chesbrough and M Bogers, 'Clarifying an emerging paradigm for understanding innovation', in H Chesbrough, W Vanhaverbeke, and J West, *New frontiers in open innovation*, 3–28. Oxford: Oxford University Press, 2014.

36. ibid.

37. ibid.

38. OE Williamson, *The economic institutions of capitalism*, New York: New Press, 1985.

39. PS Ring and AII Van de Ven, 'Developmental processes of cooperative interorganizational relationships', *Strategic Management Journal*, vol. 13, no. 7, 1992, 483–498.

40. Williamson, op. cit.

41. JM Mezias, 'Identifying liabilities of foreignness and strategies to minimize their effects: the case of labor lawsuit judgments in the United States', *Strategic Management Journal*, vol. 23, no. 3, 2002, 229–244.

42. S Zaheer, 1995, op. cit.

43. L Wang and E Zajac, 'Alliance or acquisition? A dyadic perspective on interfirm resource combinations', *Strategic Management Journal*, vol. 28, no. 13, 1291–1317.

44. P Kale and H Singh, 'Managing strategic alliances: what do we know and where do we go from here?', *Academy of Management Perspectives*, vol. 23, no. 3, 2009.

45. N Gupta, 'Alibaba's Russia joint venture takes shape', *Market Realist*, online June 27, 2019, https://marketrealist.com/2019/06/alibabas-russia-joint-venture-takes-shape.

46. A Irwin, 'Amazon's strategic alliances', 19 April, 2019, https://abbyirwin.blogspot.com/2019/04/amazons-strategic-alliances.html.

47. For example, see R Garud and A Kumaraswamy, 'Changing competitive dynamics in network industries: an exploration of Sun Microsystems' open strategy', *Strategic Management Journal*, vol. 14, 1993, 351–369.

48. R Gottliebsen, 'The global search for allies', *Business Review Weekly*, 8 March 1999, 10.

49. AP De Man, *The network economy: strategy, structure and management*, Aldershot: Edward Elgar, 2004; W Vanhaverbeke, and NG Noorderhaven, 'Competition between alliance blocks: the case of the RISC microprocessor technology', *Organization Studies*, vol. 22, no. 1, 2001, 1–30; J Partanen and K Möller, 'How to build a strategic network: a practitioner-oriented process model for the ICT sector', *Industrial Marketing Management*, no. 41, 2012, 481–494.

50. Reproduced from SG Lazzarini, 'The impact of membership in competing alliance constellations: evidence on the operational performance of global alliances', *Strategic Management Journal*, vol. 28, no. 4, 2007, 364–365.

51. Partanen and Möller, 2012, op. cit.

52. LG Mattsson, 'Relationship marketing and the "markets-as-networks" approach — A comparative analysis of two evolving streams of research', *Journal of Marketing Management*, vol. 13, no. 5, 1997, 447–461.

53. KE Möller and A Halinen, 'Business relationships and networks: managerial challenges of a network era', *Industrial Marketing Management*, vol. 28, no 5, 1999, 413–427; L Aarikka-Stenroos and P Rittala, 'Network management in the era of ecosystems: Systematic review and management framework', *Industrial Marketing Management*, 2017, vol. 67, 23–36.

54. JF Moore, 'Coevolution in business systems', in *The death of competition: Leadership and strategy in the age of business ecosystems*, New York: Harper Collins, 1996.

55. ibid.

56. L Aarikka-Stenroos and P Rittala, 'Network management in the era of ecosystems: Systematic review and management framework', *Industrial Marketing Management*, vol. 67, 2017, 23–36.

57. ibid.

58. SL Vargo, H Wieland and MA Akaka, 'Innovation through institutionalization: A service ecosystems perspective', *Industrial Marketing Management*, 44, 2015, 63–72.

59. H Chesbrough, C Lettl and T Ritter, 'Value creation and value capture in open innovation', *Journal of Product Innovation Management*, vol. 35, no. 6, 2018, 930–938.

60. ibid.

61. ibid.

62. J Hughes and J Weiss, 'Simple rules for making alliances work', *Harvard Business Review*, vol. 85, no. 11, 2007, 122–131.

63. D Ernst, 'Envisioning collaboration', in J Bamford, B Comes-Casseres and M Robinson (eds), *Mastering Alliances Strategies*, San Francisco: Jossy-Bass, 2004.

64. SG Lazzarini, 'The impact of membership in competing alliance constellations: Evidence on the operational performance of global airlines', *Strategic Management Journal*, vol. 28, no. 4, 2007, 345–367.

65. It is interesting that J Dyer, P Kale and H Singh in their famous work ('How to make strategic alliances work', *Sloan Management Review*, vol. 23, no. 4, 2001, 660–679) have indicated the failure rate of alliances between 30 and 70 per cent; whereas J Hughes and J Weiss ('Simple rules for making alliances work', *Harvard Business Review*, vol. 85, no. 11, 2007, 122–131) reported it as between 60 and 70 per cent.

66. J Bamford, B Comes-Casseres and M Robinson (eds), *Mastering alliances strategies*, San Francisco: Jossey-Bass.

67. R Lunnan and S Haugland, 'Predicting and measuring alliance performance: a multidimensional analysis', *Strategic Management Journal*, vol. 29, no. 5, 2008, 545–556.

68. P Kale, J Dyer and H Singh, 'Alliance capability, stock market response and long-term alliance success: the role of the alliance function', *Strategic Management Journal*, vol. 23, no. 8, 2002, 747–767.

69. Hamel, Doz and Prahalad, op. cit., 134.

70. JA Badaracco, *The knowledge link: how firms compete through strategic alliances*, Boston: Harvard Business School Press, 1991.

71. G Hamel, 'Competition for competence and inter-partner learning within international strategic alliances,' *Strategic Management Journal*, vol. 12, Summer Special Issue 1991, 83–103.

72. D Elmuti and Y Kathawala, 'An overview of strategic alliances', *Management Decision*, vol. 39, no. 3, 2001, 205–217.

73. Pavlovich and Akoorie, op. cit.

74. R Gulati, 'Alliances and networks', *Strategic Management Journal*, Special Issue, vol. 19, no. 4, 1998, 319–321.

75. M Schreiner, P Kale and D Corsten, 'What really is alliance management capability and how does it impact alliance outcomes and success', *Strategic Management Journal*, vol. 30, no. 13, 2009, 1395–1419.

76. Adapted from Kale and Singh, 2009, op. cit., 48.

77. MA Hitt, D Ahlstrom, MT Dacin, E Levotas and L Svobodina, 'The institutional effects of strategic alliance partner selection in transition economies: China versus Russia', *Organization Science*, vol. 15, 2004, 173–185.

78. P Beamish, 'Joint ventures in LDCs: Partner selection and performance', *International Management Review*, vol. 27, no. 1, 23–27.

79. G Gundlach, R Achrol and J Mentzer, 'The structure of commitment in exchange', *Journal of Marketing*, vol. 59, no. 1, 1995, 78–92; Gulati, 1998, op. cit.

80. Williamson, op. cit.

81. J Reuer and A Arino, 'Strategic Alliance Contracts: Dimensions and determinants of contractual complexity', *Strategic Management Journal*, vol. 28, no. 3, 2007, 313–330.

82. PS Adler and SW Kwon, 'Social capital: prospects for a new concept', *Academy of Management Review*, vol. 27, no. 1, 2002, 17–40.

83. SC Yang and CK Farn, 'Social capital, behavioural control, and tacit knowledge sharing — a multi informant design', *International Journal of Information Management*, vol. 29, 2009, 210–218.

84. B Butler and S Purchase, 'Use of social capital among Russian managers of a new generation', *Industrial Marketing Management*, vol. 38, no. 5, 2008.

85. H Li and Y Zhang, 'The role of managers' political networking and functional experience in new venture performance: evidence from China's transition economies', *Strategic Management Journal*, vol. 28, no. 8, 2007, 791–804.

86. Williamson, op. cit.

87. M Storper and AJ Venables, *Clusters, network and innovation*, New York: Oxford University Press.

88. R Dore, 'Goodwill and the spirit of market capitalism', *The British Journal of Sociology*, vol. 34, no. 4, 1983, 459–482; PM Doney, JP Cannon and MR Mullen, 'Understanding the influence of national culture on the development of trust', *Academy of Management Review*, vol. 23, no. 3, 601–620.

89. Ring and Van de Ven, op. cit.; S Ganesan, 'Determinants of long-term orientation in buyer-seller relationships', *Journal of Marketing*, vol. 58, no. 2, 1994, 1–19.

90. JC Anderson and JA Narus, 'A model of distributor firm and manufacturer firm working partnerships', *Journal of Marketing*, vol. 54, no. 1, 1990, 42–58; RM Morgan and SD Hunt, 'The commitment–trust theory of relationship marketing', *Journal of Marketing*, vol. 58, no. 3, 1994, 20–38; Gulati, 1995, op. cit.

91. M Dodourova, 'Alliances as strategic tools. A cross-industry study of partnership planning, formation and success', *Management Decision*, vol. 47, no. 5, 2009, 843.

92. P Kale and H Singh, 'Building firm capabilities through learning: the role of the alliance learning process in alliance capability and firm-level alliance success', *Strategic Management Journal*, vol. 28, no. 10, 2007, 981–1000.

93. See, for example, W Mitchel, O Dussauge and B Garrette, 'Alliances with competitors: how to combine and protect key resources', *Journal of Creativity and Innovation Management*, vol. 11, no. 3, 2002, 203–223; JA Nickerson and TR Zenger, 'A knowledge-based theory of the firm: the problem-solving perspective', *Organization Science*, vol. 15, no. 6, 2004, 617–632.

94. KJ Mayer and NS Argyres, 'Learning in contract: evidence from the personal computer industry', *Organization Science*, vol. 15, no. 4, 2004, 394–410.

95. Gulati,1998, op. cit.; B Uzzi, 'Social structure and competition in interfirm networks: the paradox of embeddedness', *Administrative Science Quarterly*, vol. 42, no. 1, 1997, 35–67.

96. G Hoetker, 'How much you know versus how well I know you: selecting a supplier for a technically innovative component', *Strategic Management Journal*, vol. 26, no. 1, 2005, 75–96; L Poppo and T Zenger, 'Do formal contracts and relational governance function as substitutes or compliments?', *Strategic Management Journal*, vol. 23, no. 8, 2002, 707–725.

97. G Hoetker and T Mellewigt, 'Choice and performance of governance mechanisms: matching alliance governance to asset type', *Strategic Management Journal*, vol. 30, no. 10, 2009, 1025–1044.

98. B Anand and T Khanna, 'Do firms learn to create value? The case of alliances', *Strategic Management Journal*, vol. 21, no. 3, 2000, 295–316; Kale, Dyer and Singh, 2002, op. cit.

99. Dyer, Kale and Singh, 2001, op. cit.

100. Doz and Hamel, 1998, op. cit.; J Draulans, A-P deMan and HW Volberda, 'Building alliance capability: management techniques for superior alliance performance', *Long Range Planning*, vol. 36, no. 2, 2003, 151–166; J Bamford, B Gomes-Casseres and M Robinson, *Mastering alliance strategy: a comprehensive guide to design, management and organisation*, San-Francisco: Jossey-Bass, 2002.

101. Kale and Singh, 2007, op. cit.

102. H Hoang and FT Rothaermel, 'The effects of general and partner-specific experience on joint R&D project performance', *Academy of Management Journal*, vol. 48, no. 2, 2005, 332–345.

103. Kale and Singh, 2007, op. cit.

104. Hamel, Doz and Prahalad, 1989, op. cit.

105. Lorenzoni and Baden-Fuller, op. cit.

106. This section draws on Hamel, Doz and Prahalad, 1989, op. cit.

107. This section draws on Lorenzoni and Baden-Fuller, op. cit.

108. Doz and Hamel, 1998, op. cit.

109. K Aljoutsijärvi, K Möller and J Tähtinen, 'Beautiful exit: How to leave your business partner', *European Journal of Marketing*, vol. 11/12, no. 34, 2000, 1270–1289; R Gulati, M Sytch and P Mehrotra, "Breaking up is never easy: planning for exit in a strategic alliance', *California Management Journal*, vol. 50, no. 4, 2008, 147–163.

110. S Hertz and L-G Mattsson, 'Collective competition and the dynamics of market reconfiguration', *Scandinavian Journal of Management*, vol. 20, 2004, 31–51.

111. Gulati, Sytch and Mehrotra, op. cit., 2008.

112. ibid.

113. T Lendrum, *The strategic partnering handbook*, North Ryde: McGraw-Hill, 2003.

ACKNOWLEDGEMENTS

Photo: © Frederic Legrand - COMEO / Shutterstock.com

Extract: © P Kale and H Singh, 'Building firm capabilities through learning: the role of the alliance learning process in alliance capability and firm-level alliance success', *Strategic Management Journal,* vol. 28, no. 10, 2007, 981–1000.

Extract: © G Hamel, Y Doz and CK Prahalad, 'Collaborate with your competitors — and win', *Harvard Business Review,* January–February, vol. 67, 1989, 133–139.

Table 7.3: © Emerald Group Publishing Ltd; Table 3 'Partnerships: success and failure factors' from M Dodourova, 'Alliances as strategic tools. A cross-industry study of partnership planning, formation and success', *Management Decision,* vol. 47, no. 5, 2009, 843.

CHAPTER 8

Global strategies and the multinational corporation

LEARNING OBJECTIVES

After studying this chapter, you should be able to:

8.1 understand the context for a global strategy, using industry analysis tools to identify the global influences on industry structure and competition

8.2 identify the environmental conditions in specific countries that a multinational organisation may utilise to increase its competitiveness

8.3 formulate strategies for exploiting overseas business opportunities, including overseas market entry strategies, partnerships and overseas production strategies

8.4 understand how strategic alliances can be used to balance global integration and national differentiation in global strategies

8.5 design organisational structures and management systems for global strategies

8.6 describe the capabilities necessary for an effective global business leader.

Tata group — a multinational with ideals

The Tata Group was an international company from the outset. Founded in 1868 as a trading business, it now includes almost thirty companies distributed globally across a range of industries. It made sales in 2019 of US$113 billion. The Tata Group comprises 28 publicly listed companies including: Tata Consultancy Services, Tata Motors, Tata Steel, Tata Chemicals, Tata Consumer Products, Titan, Tata Capital, Tata Power, Tata Advanced Systems, Indian Hotels and Tata Communications. Tata operates in 100 countries, operating in the information technology, automotive, aerospace, infrastructure, financial services, tourism and travel, telecommunications and media, investment, consumer and retail industries.[1]

Tata's original operations were trade between India and England. The UK, along with the US, is still one of the major revenue sources for Tata. Each company in the Tata Group has an individual international strategy which reflects the current state of that industry, and the opportunities available to it. Tata has made a number of significant acquisitions as part of its international expansion, including acquiring Tetley tea in 2000, Corus, Jaguar, Land Rover, Daewoo commercial vehicles (Korea) and national steel (Singapore), General Chemical Industrial Products, Tyco and many other large international organisations. These complement some of its more successful homegrown businesses, such as Tata Steel and Tata Consultancy Services, which are spread across Europe, the US and Asia.[2]

Tata is unique among the world's largest multinationals as it also has a significant philanthropic component to its structure, and operates with the mission 'To improve the quality of life of the communities we serve globally, through long-term stakeholder value creation based on Leadership with Trust'. Sixty-six per cent of the equity of the Tata group is owned by philanthropic trusts that support education, health, skill development, disaster relief, environment, sports, social justice, nutrition, income generation, arts and culture.[3] This is supported by the core values of integrity, responsibility, excellence, pioneering and unity.[4] Tata's values-based approach has generated enormous community support for its initiatives and, more importantly, is also the foundation of its internationalisation strategy.

Tata's successful and sustained international expansion resulted from the development of a strong range of socially and economically beneficial industries in India, combined with a focus on trade and, when the opportunity arose, highly related acquisitions. For example, the trading company originally opened by Tata was soon underpinned by the establishment of a textile mill to supply trading items and provide much-needed employment. This was soon followed by a hotel (which was a symbol of national pride), a steel manufacturer (providing much-needed steel in India) and a hospital. Then came an Institute of Science, the country's first (clean) hydroelectric plant and a range of social initiatives and other industrial developments that created a strong platform for its industrial expansion — which had been continuing since the 1930s, but took off strongly in the 1980s when the opportunity to internationalise from India increased. This foundation-building focused approach to internationalisation helped Tata to achieve continual success in its foreign investment activities.[5] Developing most of its industrial capabilities in India also provided Tata with the knowledge and capability necessary to support the expansion of operations into other countries and acquire businesses in other countries — in the same industries. Although Tata is moderately diverse, it still focuses on its core areas of capability development, centring strongly around technology capability, and restricts its internationalisation activities to areas of strong capability. Tata's international expansion is an excellent example of the use of internal resources to create capabilities that enable it to respond effectively to global industry conditions.

Introduction

Global forces are the key factors affecting competition in almost every single industry. They introduce new competitors and create new business opportunities for organisations of every size. Global forces are strongly influenced by international trade and **direct investment**. For the last decade, the growth of world trade has outstripped the growth of total global output, meaning that the ratio of exports and imports to total sales in most countries has increased. For example, Australian imports moved from 15 per cent of manufactured goods in 1960 to 69 per cent in 2018.[6] Trade in services such as travel, communications, information and financial services has grown even faster. **Foreign direct investment** into Australia has increased dramatically as well, with a total foreign investment in Australia in 2017 of A$850 billion, which was 47 per cent of total gross domestic product (GDP).[7]

Global forces on industries result from companies attempting to exploit larger scale regional market opportunities (such as most segments of the Chinese manufacturing industry) and exploiting operational opportunities by locating activities wherever they can be conducted most efficiently and effectively. **Global businesses** create flows of international transactions comprising goods and services, trade and factor payments (payments, interest, profits and licensing fees) and flows of capital.

Global forces have been present as long as there has been international trade, although many industries were not strongly exposed until the 1960s. At this time, even though international trade was significant, local companies still dominated most domestic markets. Rapid increases in communication technology and falling transportation costs encouraged the development of global forces after this time. Now the market leaders in every industry are generally global businesses and the niches where single-country companies can compete are rapidly shrinking. The ability to globalise operations and markets has become a key criterion for the success of large businesses, such as BHP Billiton, HSBC Bank and Qantas. Global forces generate many challenges for businesses, requiring them to be knowledgeable about many markets and possess substantial capital resources.

International trade has made huge contributions to many economies and enabled the growth of large businesses, such as Tata, described in the scene setter. Even developed countries benefit strongly from international trade. The trade war between China and the US, for example, is an attempt to influence whether the US or China gains the greatest benefit from the international trade between them. Brexit is a result of the concern by the UK government that international trade with increasingly competitive European countries did not benefit the UK as much as it once did, and a desire to disconnect from the EU trade constraints.[8]

Global operations bring different organisations possessing very different **national resource bases** into the same markets, making it possible for organisations to access resources from outside their home country. For this reason, operating globally is more than accessing larger markets or improving operational efficiency through growth — it also introduces entire new resources and means of competing. This chapter examines the resource impact of global conditions and how organisations can utilise these conditions to improve their resource base.

Global strategy is focused on the global market, rather than individual country or regional markets. It may still consider modes of competition and resources used in specific country markets, but is primarily focused on competition through global-scale resources and operations. By comparison, *international strategy* is the decisions that relate to interactions between subsidiaries in specific countries.

8.1 Global strategic management

LEARNING OBJECTIVE 8.1 Understand the context for a global strategy, using industry analysis tools to identify the global influences on industry structure and competition.

Global strategic management assumes that the world is a single segmented market in which a company can compete through its combined resources, responding to the opportunities and risks it offers. The process is similar to that of single-country strategic management, however, conditions and resources cannot be considered to be uniformly distributed across the industry. In other words, an organisation will not have access to the same resources, or resources at the same level, across global markets and conditions will vary across global markets to a greater extent. The elements of global strategic management include:

- assessing the environment in the global market
- assessing the capability of the organisation to compete in that environment, which will include the effect of political, social and foreign exchange risks
- setting objectives and desired outcomes
- establishing policies and procedures that will enable the organisation to meet those objectives
- designing a structure for the organisation and allocating resources
- implementing the actions necessary to create the new structure and allocate resources
- providing leadership and direction during implementation and ongoing operations
- monitoring results and comparing performance to the desired objectives.

Identifying the objectives and structure for a global strategy is one of the more challenging tasks. They need to be suitable for activities that span the globe, yet flexible enough to adapt adequately to regional conditions. For example, the Comprehensive and Progressive Agreement for Trans-Pacific Partnership (CPTPP) which Australia entered in 2018 provides opportunities for global expansion of Australian businesses into the 11 member countries, which include Japan, Canada and Vietnam. These opportunities result from relaxed investment conditions which are similar to those applied to local companies in those countries.[9] Opportunities such as these influence the structure and objectives of global strategies.

Developing an appropriate global strategy takes time and so companies which are global from the onset (**born global**) are rare. Acquiring sufficient knowledge about the global environment is one of the key reasons that global strategies cannot normally be constructed quickly. Global strategies involve establishing global resources, which puts the organisation at a higher level of risk than a single-country company and so a greater degree of knowledge and certainty is necessary.

Transference of business operations to environments offering the best conditions (such as access to skilled staff) is one of the key characteristics of a global strategy. This is known as **offshoring operations** and can offer significant performance and operating cost benefits.[10] This can include shifting low complexity operations such as call centres to low labour-cost environments or transferring complex operations such as RD to countries such as China and India where large numbers of employees with specialised skill sets are available. Strategy capsule 8.1 notes that Fonterra established dairy and dairy product manufacturing operations in China to take advantage of low-cost operations in that country as part of its global strategy.

The uncertainty about conditions in different countries means that offshored operations are often established as part of international partnerships — particularly if technology or skill transfer is important. Unfortunately, international partnerships tend to have a high failure rate; often as high as 50 per cent.[11] The failure rate of international joint ventures can be reduced by:[12]

- identifying the objectives of the joint venture
- establishing appropriate partnership contracts
- thoroughly screening and selecting potential partners on the basis of their compatibility with other partners
- devoting sufficient time and effort to negotiation on the details of the partnership, including purpose, form, scope, duration and administrative structure
- ensuring that problems are dealt with as they occur during the life of the joint venture, rather than ignoring the problems or assuming the other partner will deal with them
- understanding that partnerships will usually have a limited life, only being valuable while they service the objectives of all parties. These objectives will change much more rapidly than is anticipated.

Fonterra — supplying the world with milk

New Zealand–based dairy producer Fonterra employs 20 000 people globally, generating sales of A$10 billion per year in 140 countries — 30 per cent of the world's total dairy trade. In China alone, Fonterra sells A$5 billion worth of dairy products annually, which is 11 per cent of all dairy consumption in China. Fonterra sells to 20 000 stores across China and operates a large number of dairy farms in China as well.[13] Fonterra commenced operations in 2001, as a result of the merger of two New Zealand dairy co-operatives and the New Zealand dairy board.[14]

Soon after its formation, Fonterra established a formalised international strategy to coordinate all its international activities. Fonterra's international strategy is based on establishing a combination of direct and indirect relationships in all aspects of its operations. For example, its entry to China was the result of a deal with a major Chinese dairy distributor, which consolidated a growing indirect presence in China.[15] Fonterra principally uses indirect relationships to develop markets and then establishes direct relationships. Its strategy is geographically segmented to assist with resource allocation. This approach protects the Fonterra group from the challenging dynamics of the global dairy industry, which were the cause of the forced sale of Australian dairy producer Murray Goulburn, in 2018. Despite global sales of A$3 billion per year across 100 countries and farm operations in China, Murray Goulburn was unable to maintain profitable operations in the global dairy industry due to downturns in markets in which it had invested.[16]

Fonterra manages downturns and problems in individual global regions through its segmented global strategy, which enables it to quarantine the effect of regional problems and protect the performance of the remainder of the organisation. With this system in place, Fonterra has managed to survive a number of challenging experiences internationally.[17] Other core competencies are the ability to manage a fully integrated supply chain, large number of suppliers, distribution partnerships, joint ventures and regional manufacturing partnerships. This has enabled them to introduce regional innovations to their product range to increase their competitiveness in individual markets.[18] The combination of economies of scale in the production of the raw milk ingredients internationally, market-led innovation and regional production and manufacturing has enabled Fonterra to remain competitive in a very challenging global industry.

The benefits of a global strategy

Although a global strategy creates challenges, it can also increase the chances of success. Global strategies can take advantage of the global nature of customer preferences, scale effects, resources, customer servicing and knowledge acquisition opportunities not available to single-country companies.

- *Customer preferences are becoming globalised.* Customer preferences are responding to the global forces of technology, communication and travel, and becoming homogeneous. Global strategy can take advantage of this development and focus on products and services that follow these global trends.

- *Superior economies of scale.* Global operations excel in large economies of scale due to their large markets. This does not mean that they also require a large product range, although many do, such as General Electric, which operates in sectors as diverse as power, aviation and healthcare,[19] or the Tata Group which operates in even more industries (see scene setter). Global economies of scale can be achieved for even a single product or service, as Facebook and PayPal have demonstrated. The Australian hearing aid implant manufacturer Cochlear, discussed in the chapter on internal analysis of capabilities and core competencies, was not really successful until it expanded its markets to include the United States and Europe and achieved sufficient economies of scale in its niche market to support the high costs of its RD.

- *Access to more resources.* Different locations offer access to different resources — people, technology and raw materials. They also offer regional markets which support the development of regional operations. Industry knowledge is an increasingly important feature of globalisation in which market and technological information in different regions is aggregated by global organisations to support a portfolio approach to global activities.[20]

- *Serving global customers.* In several industries, such as banking, audit services and advertising, the primary driver of global forces has been servicing global customers. For example, the large accounting firms have established branches in most major economies so that they can provide auditing services to multinational companies in each of their locations. In many instances, global customers demand their suppliers globalise alongside them.[21]

- *Achieving a global-level knowledge of the industry.* Global businesses tend to learn much more quickly about their external environment as a result of operating within different country environments. This is because specific features of the environment (such as carbon trading or consumer demand profiles) will be more prominent in one country than in others. This also applies to larger and different geographical regions. For example, pollution management and recycling have been standard management activities across most of central Europe for much longer than in other regions. Companies wishing to learn more about these practices benefit from establishing operations in several European locations. Operating across several markets will provide maximum exposure to all of these factors. A critical requirement for this learning is that the company possesses global communication and knowledge transfer infrastructure that permits new experiences, ideas and practices gained in individual country markets to be transferred and integrated into the rest of the organisation. Access to this information is one of the competitive advantages of global businesses over single-country businesses.[22]

- *Increasing the range of competitive options available.* One of the reasons that the Roman's were successful in competing against the tribes of Gaul (now France and Germany) was the Roman's ability to draw upon the vast military and economic resources of the Roman Empire to support their pursuit for expansion. Similarly, global businesses possess a key strategic advantage over their nationally focused competitors. Global businesses can fight aggressive competitive battles in individual national markets using their global resources, including finance and skills. For example, McDonald's was able to use its global knowledge regarding establishing fast food retail chains, its huge financial capacity and its global brand to successfully establish a McDonald's retail chain in India where many of its competitors had failed.

- *Following the industry.* As industries such as the fashion industry become broadly globalised, organisations that follow their industry's internationalisation paths and patterns gain benefits such as technology transfer, strategic alliance options, market information and development concentrations, such as technology parks. The organisations that are 'in the game' gain significant competitive advantages over their rivals who do not follow their industries.[23]

Analysing a global industry

Understanding the nature of the global industry is the first step towards globalisation. Global industries can be analysed using the same tools as domestic industries — starting with Porter's five forces of competition framework. This analysis tool is discussed in detail in the chapter on external and industry analysis. Here we will briefly consider how each of Porter's five forces translates to the global context.

Competition from potential entrants

Barriers to entry into most national markets have fallen substantially, particularly through global trade arrangements such as ASEAN and CPTPP (Comprehensive and Progressive Agreement for Trans-Pacific Partnership), as well as the free trade agreements between countries such as Australia and China. These trade simplifications, the continuously falling costs of transportation, globalisation of standards and the convergence of customer preferences have dramatically lowered the barriers to entering the global market in most industries. Creating entry barriers by continually improving company capabilities through acquisition can create an effective barrier against new entrants.

Global rivalry

Global forces increase internal rivalry within industries in the following three ways.
- *Lowering seller concentration.* At the global level, there are more suppliers competing, which reduces the dominance of any one supplier. For example, although there are two principal microprocessor manufacturers (Intel and AMD), there are over 100 companies manufacturing or subcontracting the manufacture of microprocessors globally. As all of these producers supply the global market, there is a wide range of potential suppliers for many computing applications.
- *Increasing diversity of competitors.* The size of the global market creates many opportunities and niches, which increases the diversity of competitors. In the microprocessor industry, for example, Intel and AMD service a broad section of the market, but microprocessor manufacturers such as Google produce specialist microprocessors for specific applications and are more competitive in these niches than Intel or AMD.[24] Unlike many domestic market niches, a global niche still provides enough activity to sustain a large-scale business unit.
- *Increasing global capacity.* Global capacity in most industries has continuously grown. This has been offset by increasing demand from several new markets including the Chinese and Indian middle-class markets.[25] Reductions in demand from global markets due to economic downturns in the EU, China, US or India following COVID-19 can quickly turn this into global excess capacity and reduce industry profitability.

Global buyer power

Global sourcing provides a key tool for cost reduction because of the low concentration of competitors in global markets allowing global organisations to access many suppliers. This encourages global suppliers to increase the diversity of their offerings in response to buyer needs.

Greater power of substitutes

Global markets are very attractive and easily identified. In addition to attracting direct competitors, these markets also attract suppliers of substitutes. This is very evident in the global consulting industry in which some of the work of traditional management consulting firms is being provided by IT companies using artificial intelligence to interpret data.[26]

Reduced power of suppliers

As a direct result from increased buyer power, supplier power in most global industries is reduced by the diversity of suppliers available on the global market. Only where there is a rarity or shortage in what is being supplied, such as the rare-earth metals used in car brake systems and robotics, do global suppliers retain a high level of power.[27] Very large producers, such as BHP, also retain supplier power as a result of their capacity to supply much greater quantities than other competitors in the global market to major customers such as China.

8.2 Effect of regional conditions on global competitiveness

LEARNING OBJECTIVE 8.2 Identify the environmental conditions in specific countries that a multinational organisation may utilise to increase its competitiveness.

Comparative advantage

The global competitiveness of an organisation is strongly affected by the advantages provided to it from the national-level industries in which it operates. The relative benefits gained from the regions in which a global business operates is the **comparative advantage** provided by its individual operations. The concept of comparative advantage has a venerable history, having been first proposed in economist David Ricardo's *Principles of Political Economy and Taxation*, published in 1817. Comparative advantage can result from physical resources, human resources or technological resources. For example, Australia has a comparative advantage against most other countries in highly specialised technology areas, such as mining technologies, aspects of horticulture and vaccine manufacture. The concept of comparative advantage has developed in recent years to focus on national value chains and incorporates effects such as public institutions, labour market efficiency, transport infrastructure and financial markets.

National competitive advantage

Another way of looking at the advantages provided by the countries and regions in which a business operates is Porter's theory of national competitive advantage, which was introduced in the chapter on external and industry analysis as part of the analysis of the external environment. This theory identifies four dimensions of the business environment, or business system, of a particular country or region which provide a competitive advantage to organisations operating there: factor conditions; related and supporting industries; industry strategy, structure and rivalry; and demand conditions.

Governments now refer to these four factors as elements of industry value chains, and invest significantly in improving the strengths of their value chains, in order to attract more global business investment. Internet infrastructure is a *related and supporting industry* which the governments in most countries are developing as quickly as possible in order to attract business activity. Studies have shown that this infrastructure has significant effects on a large range of industries, including public health and creative industries.[28] The four components of national competitive advantage will now be considered in relation to global strategy.

Factor conditions

Factor conditions reflect the innate heritage of resources. The most valuable factor conditions are unique and highly country-specific resources, followed by specialised but not unique resources. For example, Porter points out that the success of Hollywood is due to the local concentration of skilled labour supplied by the universities of California, Los Angeles and Southern California schools of film. Constraints can also lead to the development of unique resources. For example, Italy is a leading[29] adopter of automation because of the cost penalties of restrictive labour regulations.

Related and supporting industries

For many industries, a critical resource is the presence of related and supporting industries. One of the most striking of Porter's empirical findings is that national competitive strengths tend to be associated with 'clusters' of industries. One such industry cluster in the United States is semiconductors, computers and computer software. For each of these industries, critical resources are the other related industries. In Germany, a mutually supporting cluster exists around chemicals, synthetic dyes, textiles and textile machinery.

Demand conditions

Demand conditions in the domestic market are the primary driver of innovation and quality improvement. For example:
- demand for electric vehicles and sports cars in the US led to the development of the Tesla roadster, which Tesla claims is the fastest car in the world
- regional demand for technology in Korea enabled Samsung to develop beyond textile supply to include heavy industry, chemicals and aerospace, before expanding into electronics and ultimately becoming one of the leading mobile phone manufacturers.

Strategy, structure and rivalry

Porter suggested that intense industry competition encourages innovation and efficiency improvement, which Christiansen referred to as disruptive innovation.[30] These conditions can provide valuable development opportunities for a global organisation in specific areas of its product range. In other environments, such as the EU, government support through systems such as subsidies encourages increases in industry scale, but discourages increasing competitiveness through efficiency.

Comparing comparative and national competitive advantage

Comparative advantage identifies the activities in which organisations operating in a particular country or region will perform strongly at that time. It does not consider the factors that led to that condition, how quickly it will change and the ways in which that advantage functions. For example, Puerto Rico previously possessed a comparative advantage in its medical industry, which offered high skill levels and low wages. These conditions, however, have led to an exodus of its medical practitioners in the last few years, significantly reducing the country's medical capabilities and eliminating this comparative advantage. By comparison, *national competitive advantage* considers the systems and features of the country or region that led to the competitive advantage. Applying this as a systematic review can allow global business to interpret trends in factors such as regional demand and related and supporting industries to develop longer term strategies for the activities they will conduct in those regions. For example, the China–Australia free trade agreement which came into force in 2015 changed the strategy, structure and rivalry conditions in China for Australian multinational and global companies.[31] This **free trade agreement** took many years to negotiate and global Australian-based companies watching the progression of these negotiations had the opportunity to plan for the free trade agreement in their global strategy. Figure 8.1 summarises the implications of national competitive advantage as it might be incorporated in a global strategy.

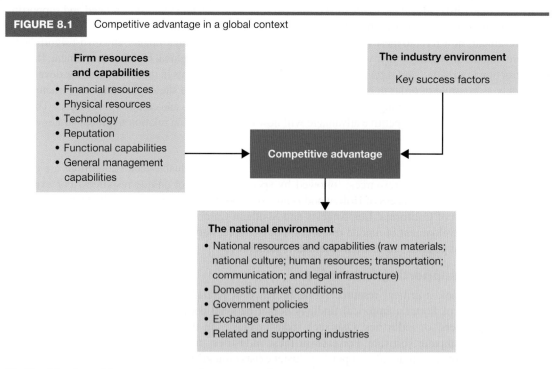

FIGURE 8.1 Competitive advantage in a global context

8.3 Selecting an entry mode

LEARNING OBJECTIVE 8.3 Formulate strategies for exploiting overseas business opportunities, including overseas market entry strategies, partnerships and overseas production strategies.

While global strategy is based on the concept of global markets, Porter's theory of national competitive advantage indicates that the business conditions in different regions can vary significantly, even if the market is essentially global (such as the global market for mobile phones). We have seen that a global strategy should match specific operations to the different regions in which the business operates to gain the greatest overall competitive advantage. This leads to an important decision for each region — how to enter that particular region. The common entry modes for global businesses are:

- *exporting* — manufacturing a product or producing a service in the home country and then transporting/making it available in a foreign market, possibly with the assistance of an export agent
- *contracts* — project-based activities such as the building agreements of global construction companies
- *licensing* — making proprietary technology and systems available to partners on a fee basis
- *franchising* — a more developed version of licensing which can include a global brand, specifically developed technology and systems and use of global supply networks; McDonald's is a good example of global franchising
- *joint ventures* — a partnership that contributes finances and resources such as staff, technology and market knowledge to joint operations in the particular region
- *wholly owned subsidiaries* — a regional division of the organisation that could vary from a regional marketing and sales division through to a fully self-contained division designing, producing and financing its own operations in the foreign market.

Figure 8.2 shows how the resource commitment required is affected by the entry mode selected for that region.

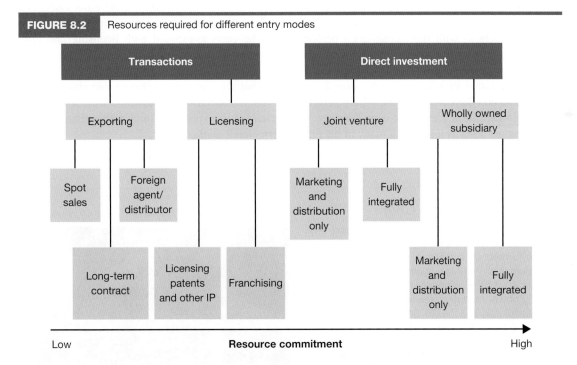

FIGURE 8.2 Resources required for different entry modes

The best entry mode for each region in which the global business operates can be identified by considering the following five questions.

1. *Is the organisation's competitive advantage based on organisation-specific or country-specific resources?* If the organisation is relying on sources of competitive advantage linked to specific countries it should exploit that advantage in other countries by exporting. For example, the Ethiopian coffee industry sells coffee globally and has a competitive advantage resulting from good growing conditions and very low labour costs (in many cases, Ethiopian coffee is grown on family-owned farms). Therefore, Ethiopian coffee producers selling coffee in countries such as Australia (10 per cent of coffee consumed in Australia comes from Ethiopia) need to export their coffee to Australia to maintain their competitive advantage.[32]

2. *Is the product tradable and what are the barriers to trade?* If the product or service is difficult or expensive to transport or there are trade barriers to importing it into a region, it is necessary to have regional operations or a joint venture, or to license a regional operator to produce the same product or service in that market. For example, Fonterra (see strategy capsule 8.1) exports dried milk powder to China as a high-quality imported product and produces fresh milk in China because milk is too perishable and expensive to export.

3. *Does the organisation possess the full range of resources and capabilities for establishing a competitive advantage in the region?* Global scale resources and competencies do not always match the needs of regional conditions sufficiently well to create a strong competitive advantage. This often leads to the need to adopt a combination of global and regional resources — referred to as **glocalisation**.

For example, the Mars group trades its chocolate under a different brand in the US, UK and Australia (Dove, Galaxy and Mars) to allow it to adapt the flavour to regional preferences.

4. *Can the organisation directly appropriate the returns from its resources?* The choice of regional production, licensing or exporting influences the ease with which profits can be returned to the head office of a global company. Money transfer and regional taxation conditions can add costs to transferring money from one region to another and exchange rate variations can introduce the risk of lost revenue. Loss of intellectual property (IP) is another form of risk which can reduce the returns that the company can gain from a particular region. When successful return of profits is risky or there is the potential for loss of IP, exporting becomes more attractive. Starbucks (a global US-based coffee chain) established outlets in Australia without glocalisation, but found that these operations were unsuccessful because Starbuck's global operations did not provide them with a sufficient competitive advantage in Australia. In the end, the licence was sold to a local company.

5. *What are the transaction costs?* All global operations have associated **transaction costs**. Exporting specific transaction costs include holding export licences, transportation costs, local agent costs and import duties. Operating in a foreign region transaction costs include the management costs associated with operating a subsidiary, exchange rate risks and income transfer fees and taxes and the investment risks associated with that subsidiary's performance. The costs associated with licensing and joint ventures includes the costs of managing the partnership and IP risk. Minimising the transaction costs is often a key motivation for choosing a particular entry mode. Starbucks established operations in Australia rather than importing because it concluded that the currency exchange rate risk between Australia and the US and the subsidiary performance risk for operations in Australia were low.

Strategy capsule 8.2 explains why Treasury Wines decided to export to China, rather than locating operations in China as it had with many of his other international markets.

Network view of global strategy

The insights that Porter's theory of national competitive advantage and entry mode selection shows us that an effective global strategy needs to comprise more than an independent collection of subsidiaries in a number of attractive locations. The varying opportunities and conditions around the globe require activities and operations layouts that resemble a network, rather than a collection of independent businesses. The network approach to global strategy allows activities to occur at the nodes in the network (regions) where the conditions are most attractive, and still be integrated. As a result, some nodes could span several regions and other nodes could be focused on a single location. Some nodes may be responsible for a significant range of operations and other nodes might be highly specialised.

The network approach to global strategy results in a number of important benefits, as follows.

1. It supports glocalisation in every area of the global market. Global businesses will often establish large-scale operations that service a segment of the global market, operating in the location that offers the greatest advantages. Subsidiaries of the large-scale regional operation service smaller sections of that region. This approach enables the organisation to customise to regional conditions in key areas such as product/service design, but retain the benefits of global economies of scale. Regionalised subsidiaries allow for even further globalisation. For example, major fertiliser manufacturers produce fertiliser for the South-East Asian region in Thailand where the conditions for manufacturing fertiliser are very attractive and the key customers in the South-East Asian region are relatively close.[35] This reduces transportation costs and delivery delays, while still allowing for regional level economies of scale.

2. It allows for intermediate nodes in the global business operations that can provide an important interpretation and coordination function. The global variation in accounting practices, regulations and negotiating approaches, as well as culture and language, create significant challenges for the head office of global business in understanding regional conditions and coordinating operations globally. Intermediate nodes in the network can interpret and coordinate head office's systems and rules with the regional regulations, requirements and customer expectations of the region. For example, global organisations with head offices in Europe may choose to establish an intermediate node in Hong Kong. This intermediate node is then used to manage subsidiaries on the mainland of China. The value of the Hong Kong node is that it can be reasonably easily staffed with employees familiar with both Chinese and European business practices, regulation, culture and language. This enables the Hong Kong node to understand the head office rules, systems and expectations as well as the regulations, conditions and opportunities in China and harmonise them to improve coordination. Direct control of business nodes in mainland China has proven to be very difficult for organisations headquartered in Europe.[36]

Analysing conditions in different regions

Analysing the conditions prevalent in different regions of the globe is a key to developing an effective global strategy. Business conditions in any region are rarely as attractive as initial assessments suggest because negative aspects of the conditions can be overlooked. In addition, competition in individual regions can change from when the analysis was conducted due to the subsequent entry of other global competitors. A sensitivity analysis will determine whether the regional business conditions are only attractive in their optimal conditions or remain attractive when they are better understood. This can consider the likely variation in key factors such as economic conditions, labour availability and market conditions to see how attractive the region is across the normal scope of variation.

The analysis should be constructed using knowledge of the region to ensure that the analysis approach is culturally matched to the region and that well-informed information sources are involved. As the organisation is usually unfamiliar with the region, a third party will normally be engaged to supply the information for the analysis. It is also important to consider how many other foreign competitors are operating in the region. Increased numbers of competitors will lead to supporting industry and possibly also supportive government policy, as well as greater competition for regional demand.

Emerging region analysis

The analysis of an **emerging region** is particularly challenging due to the rapidly changing and often unique conditions. These regions can be attractive both in terms of operational costs as well as growing markets, however, other business conditions normally taken for granted, such as roads and power reliability, may not be suitable for the organisation's plans. Analysis of these regions needs to carefully consider the political and social systems, cultural openness, labour skill levels and business infrastructure.

Assessing regions using Dunning's eclectic theory

Dunning's eclectic theory (also known as the ownership, location, internationalisation — OLI — model) provides a simple but helpful framework for analysing regional conditions. This framework draws attention to the importance of:

1. the opportunities to use the organisation's key strength in that region
2. the overall benefit from operating in that region
3. the regional conditions that are compatible with the key strengths of the organisation.

8.4 Global strategic alliances

LEARNING OBJECTIVE 8.4 Understand how strategic alliances can be used to balance global integration and national differentiation in global strategies.

Global strategies can incorporate partnership agreements, which offer some challenges but many advantages. These partnerships are usually referred to as **strategic alliances**.

Strategic alliances are frequently mandatory for establishing operations in emerging economies. For example, until recently, all foreign businesses in India needed to be in a partnership or license their technologies, designs, etc. to a local company. The lifting of this restraint has had a profound effect on foreign investment in the country as well as elevating India's role in global strategies.[37]

Global strategic alliances provide companies with access to technologies, processes, products or services and better access to regional markets. For example, it is very difficult to make sales in Japan unless an agreement can be struck with a Japanese distribution company. These agreements are difficult to achieve and require time, patience and excellent contacts, making a local partner very important.

Strategic alliances have inherent associated risks, including the loss of intellectual property. In addition, strategic alliances rarely prohibit either partner from forming new strategic alliances with the first partner's competitors or from exiting the partnership at any time, irrespective of the investment made by the other partner. The objectives of both partners may diverge as the partnership progresses. They will be subject to many other influences and opportunities which will be unlikely to be the same for both partners.

Strategic alliances can best be maintained by a combination of approaches. These include regular partnership agreement reviews, commencing the alliance with a good mutual understanding and allocating the authority and responsibility for the alliance to specific managers. The partnership reviews can both consider whether the objectives of the partnership are being met and establish future objectives. Where partnership contracts are used for a strategic alliance, the duration, scope of responsibilities, inputs (including investment), expected outputs and purpose of the alliance must be clearly defined. Contracts specify constraints (boundary conditions) for partnerships but do not provide clear explanations of how they operate on a daily basis or what constitutes success. Care must be taken to ensure that the contract is an addition to a shared understanding, rather than substituting for that understanding. Contracts are helpful when the strategic alliance is dissolved.

The personal contacts between staff members of alliance partners can introduce social capital into the partnership, which can significantly improve communication and trust between the partner organisations. This social capital can be built on professional connections and strengthened through shared experiences and exchanges which lead to increased trust.[38] Professional associations, industry conferences and trade shows are excellent ways of establishing initial connections with staff from partner organisations. These connections are called 'weak ties' because they represent a professional relationship but do not carry enough strength to influence decisions or generate trust.

International joint-venture partnerships

Joint-venture partnerships are a very important subset of strategic alliances — particularly in countries such as China where much of the investment by foreign companies has been through joint-venture partnerships. Major Chinese initiatives, such as China's Belt and Road initiative, have formed the foundation for thousands of joint-venture partnerships, ranging from China through Turkey to central Europe.[39] Even though Australia is not a physical part of the Belt and Road region, there have also been related joint agreements between the countries. For example, the Victorian government has struck an agreement with China's National Development and Reform Commission which increases the number of joint-venture activities between the two countries in both Australia and China.[40]

The longevity and overall success of international joint ventures is affected by political uncertainty in the region and in the partnership arrangement, the share of equity of the partners and the future investment or divestment opportunities.[41] This last factor is particularly important as joint ventures are usually a stage in the globalisation process. If joint ventures in specific regions prove successful, the organisation is likely to continue its globalisation through further joint ventures. If not, the organisation will move quickly to other approaches for globalising.

Organising global operations

Managing a global business is complex and the success of global strategies depends on how well the organisation can implement them. One of the key features of this is the orientation of the global strategy. This can include a product and service, regional or customer orientation. Each of these will now be considered.

Product and service orientation

If the global strategy is product and service-oriented, divisions will be based around products and services, and will focus on developing the capabilities to excel in its products or services. It will also be able to achieve high levels of customisation in each of the regions in which the organisation operates. Google is generally considered to be one of the best companies at developing excellence in its product range. Its product-oriented global strategy achieves this through a high degree of interconnectivity across all the regions in which it operates and by employing only the most capable and motivated staff.[42]

Regional orientation

A regionally oriented global strategy will lead to divisions in the organisation which focus on specific regions and are coordinated at the top levels of the organisation. For example, Citibank has Asian, South-East Asian, European and North American divisions, each of which develops products and services that appeal to the economic, business and regulatory conditions in their respective region.[43] These regional divisions may even be listed on local stock exchanges as independent corporate entities and only treated as parts of a global business in the annual report. For example, the Australian Coca-Cola division, Coca-Cola Amatil, is a partnership and is listed on the Australian Securities Exchange (ASX).

Increasingly, organisations are moving towards regional strategies within economic trade agreement-based regions such as ASEAN and the EU. Research has determined cultural differences within regions which are connected by trade agreements do not seem to interfere with coordination across the region.[44] This presumably reflects the understanding between the member countries that they are expected to cooperate because of the trade agreement. The UK's exit from the EU has had an interesting effect on the global strategies of its companies, which were previously heavily oriented towards the EU and are now directing their regional orientation more strongly to new key regions.

Customer orientation

A customer-oriented global strategy will frequently lead to the formation of customer service divisions that coordinate the relationship between the organisation and key customer groups. This has the effect of making the organisation more open to customer influence than with other orientations. Cathay Pacific, a global airline, established a customer service division that is primarily concerned with creating sales. Lufthansa airlines rearranged its structure to establish a dedicated commercial transportation division and a catering division to enable it to focus on providing these highly customer-focused activities. Both of Lufthansa's divisions have regional subsidiaries in all the important locations it services, such as the United States and, of course, Europe.

8.5 Global business structures

LEARNING OBJECTIVE 8.5 Design organisational structures and management systems for global strategies.

Another factor contributing to the success of global strategy is the business structure. For example, an organisation that chooses to operate internationally through franchises would find a flat structure much more suitable than a hierarchical structure. A hierarchical structure will not provide sufficient communication and information transfer with its franchisees. In the context of international partnerships, a flat structure is also desirable as it is more flexible and more likely to match the structure of the business partner. Hierarchical structures tend to result in narrowly defined systems and management roles and limited flexibility.

Global businesses from different regions frequently adopt similar global business structures. European-origin global businesses tend to have a high regional concentration in their structures, which allows them to strongly adapt to the conditions in the region. This, however, leads to integration challenges. For example, Phillips has had to continuously reorganise its structure to maintain coordination across its ever-growing range of regionally focused business units.[45] US multinationals take a different approach and adopt business structures that facilitate the transfer of technology and proven products. In more recent times US global businesses such as Procter Gamble have begun to transfer technology, design and products from subsidiaries back to their head office. Japanese global businesses continue to compete through the efficiency of their global production and new product development and global businesses based in China and India are beginning to adopt similar structural approaches.

The structures adopted as part of global strategy typically fit into one of four forms:
- multidomestic
- matrix
- global
- transnational.

Multidomestic business structure

The multidomestic approach is a simple approach comprising separate, autonomous business units in different countries (see figure 8.3). The structure reflects a focus on creating adequate channels through which resources (finances, capability and knowledge) can flow. In this structure, the head office becomes a centralised coordination authority that deals with the issues of communication, report comparison and resource allocation among the regional divisions. Income is collected from each business area and combined into overall profit. This approach has several drawbacks, which include:
- poor communication between regions
- possibility of accidental replication of key activities (e.g. RD) in different divisions
- internal competition (global customers may encourage the individual country divisions of the organisation to compete to reduce prices)
- inequitable allocation of resources to each subsidiary.

FIGURE 8.3   A multidomestic business structure for an electronics company

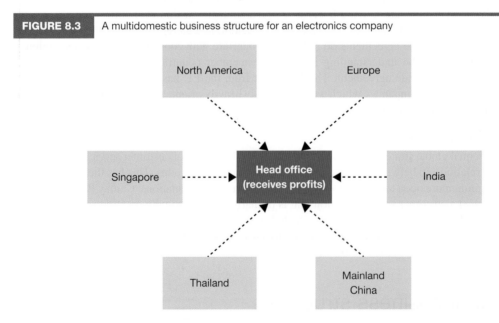

An advantage is that this approach frees up the head office to relocate to more attractive locations, for example, to capital markets (to access finance) or where tax levels are lower. For example, HSBC moved from Hong Kong to London and Tetra Pak moved from Lund, Sweden to Lausanne, Switzerland.[46]

Matrix structure

Global strategies that focus on both products and regions require a matrix structure. The matrix structure increases the level of coordination between different business lines and regions. For most organisations, however, this is only a temporary solution as reporting for every activity goes to two different divisional heads — the product line and the regional division heads. The different objectives of the divisions make this structure difficult to manage in practice. Figure 8.4 shows a matrix structure for a hypothetical electronics manufacturer — with interests in Asia, Australia, the United Kingdom and India. In this instance, each manager must respond to two divisional heads — a regional divisional head and a market divisional head.

FIGURE 8.4 Matrix structure for a global electronics manufacturer

Due to the challenges associated with matrix structures, alternative forms that achieve the same level of coordination are appearing. A good example of this is the helix structure. Instead of tensions between different organisational objectives, the dual management roles are split between capability development and value creation. The capability development management role has long-term objectives and the value creation management role has short-term objectives.[47]

Globally integrated structure

A global strategy that balances integration and national differentiation requires differential management of products, functions and location. By comparison, globally integrated operations enable organisations to take advantage of resources and capabilities from different parts of the organisation and combine them with activities in other environments. This results in the ability to compete through capabilities as well as economies of scale. The constraints of integration mean that the products and services produced by these organisations are generally standardised and, while meeting the fundamental requirements of each region (such as regulatory requirements), they usually cannot accommodate a high level of regional preferences. Figure 8.5 demonstrates the central role of head office in providing a range of centralised services for the different regions in which an organisation operates. Figure 8.5 also shows that a globally integrated structure does not support the network characteristics of a fully developed global strategy, as discussed earlier in this chapter.

Nestlé uses a globally integrated structure and achieves a reasonable level of regional customisation combined with global-level economies of scale. This makes it very competitive in all its global markets and allows it to apply global-scale resources to the development and capture of new markets.

Procter Gamble uses a similar approach, which has resulted in some global standardised products (e.g. Pringles potato chips and high-end perfumes) and some highly regionally customised products, such as hair colouring products and laundry detergent. Its RD is globally integrated while sales operate at the regional level to provide it with the information necessary to achieve regional customisation.

Transnational business structure

The transnational structure produces the greatest possible benefits from a global strategy. It is characterised by a fully integrated network of distributed and interdependent resources and capabilities (see figure 8.6)

and allows a global strategy to operate without the constraints of the previously discussed structures. Important characteristics of this structure are that:

- each national unit is a source of ideas, skills and capabilities that can be harnessed for the benefit of the total organisation
- national units access global scale economies by being designated as the company's world source for a particular product, component or activity
- head office coordinates relationships among units in a highly flexible manner. Its primary role is to create an organisational culture and communication channels that are conducive to the coordination and resolution of differences. It focuses on establishing 'clear corporate objectives, developing managers with broadly based perspectives and relationships and fostering supportive organisational norms and values'.[48]

FIGURE 8.5   A globally integrated structure for an electronics company

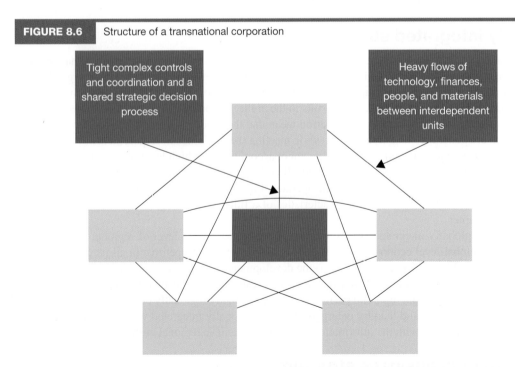

FIGURE 8.6   Structure of a transnational corporation

The transnational structure requires all areas of the business to operate in harmony. This requires resources to be allocated to activities rather than regions. This requires broad spans of control (covering regions, products or resources) and a sophisticated approach to prioritisation.

Vertical and horizontal differentiation

The adoption of a particular business structure to support a global strategy will require consideration of the organisation's **vertical differentiation**, **horizontal differentiation**, **spatial boundaries** and governance mechanisms.[49] Decisions about the level of integration up and down the value chain (vertical differentiation), the breadth of market coverage (horizontal differentiation) and the regions in which the organisation operates (spatial boundaries) determine the opportunities to apply the organisation's technological and skill-based resources, form partnerships, alliances and networks, and align resource allocation with the global strategy.

8.6 Global leadership

LEARNING OBJECTIVE 8.6 Describe the capabilities necessary for an effective global business leader.

Global leadership skills are central to creating a successful global organisation. Global business leaders need multifaceted skills and a focus on coordinating the different cultures, country-level conditions, technologies and disciplines represented by the organisation.[50] But is this capability innate, or is it the result of experience? Leadership attribute theory suggests that effective leadership skills can result from the personal characteristics of the leader and do not change significantly with experience.[51] In the global context, however, inherit traits are unlikely to be sufficient to enable the leader to coordinate effectively across different cultures and different business systems. Experience is necessary to enable them to fully understand all the different approaches across the organisation that they are coordinating. As a result, we can conclude that global leadership requires a combination of experience and personal characteristics.

As the world changes, and especially post COVID-19, gaining these experiences results in shifting focuses for global leaders. The 2019 YPO global leadership survey found that global leaders were focused on external factors, such as creating a global impact. They were also concerned by external constraints, such as global levels of corruption and political barriers.[52] Interestingly, integration of global operations was not one of their ten greatest concerns. This is explained by the findings from Ernst & Young's 2018 global leadership survey, which determined that the top concern for global leaders was developing new leaders, due to the complexity of leading the global environment. The importance of developing leadership capability in the global context was underscored by the finding that only 32 per cent of the companies in the survey with nationally effective leadership could navigate complexity and respond to the competitive environment adequately.[53]

Global leadership requires that leaders possess cultural intelligence, which enables them to understand how to act ethically in the different cultures in which the organisation operates. Several studies have shown that this requires humbleness, commitment, responsibility, respect and a clear sense of ethically desirable outcomes.[54] Cultural backgrounds provide a strong contribution to the development of cultural intelligence. The rapid internationalisation of Chinese industry has required Chinese business leaders to develop their global leadership capability extremely rapidly. These leader's home country cultural backgrounds are composed of Confucianist, socialist, free-market, legalist and Buddhist dimensions.[55] This creates a relatively complex context from which to develop cultural intelligence. The multiple viewpoints this provides lead to a strong capability for understanding conditions, although the value systems on which they are based also create barriers to changing leadership approaches to accommodate different value systems. These experiences are common to global companies with extensive international experience as well. For example, global subsidiaries operating in Thailand — such as DaimlerChrysler, Siemens, Bayer and GM — found that providing leadership and direction that was consistent with the expectations of head office and compatible with the regional corporate culture was the greatest challenge that they faced.

In addition to experience, global leaders require specific traits, particularly tolerance of ambiguity, flexibility and low ethnocentrism.[56] These competencies can be increased though language skills, which add to cross-cultural sensitivity and improve the accuracy of the information gained by a leader.[57] Global leaders need to be aware of the assumptions and limitations of the information on which their decisions are made. Information sourced from different contexts and prepared according to different conventions can be correctly interpreted only with a good understanding of the contexts.[58]

Both the YPO and Ernst Young surveys also found that ethical and social considerations were important foci of global business leaders. The ethical and responsible characteristics of an effective global leader are reflected in the leader's knowledge and ability to build relationships; their values, ethical positions, courage and discipline; their ability to inspire trust; and the community to which they appeal. Ethical and socially considerate leadership involves setting an ethical compass for the organisation.

In a global organisation with different cultural perspectives, setting this compass can be particularly challenging. Global leaders need to create an active dialogue among stakeholders and, at the same time, assess and balance the different claims so that outcomes are mutually positive.[59]

Global leaders are most effective in communities where their relationship is strong enough to influence and exchange information. Positivity is another important characteristic for global leaders, reflecting a desire for change and strongly held viewpoints. This can take the form of a systematic approach to decision making which accommodates the different contexts and cultures that exist across a global organisation.[60] This means that global leaders must first motivate and facilitate involvement, and then judge the contributions that result from that involvement. To achieve this, global leaders must have both entrepreneurial and moderator skills.

Creating global strategy success

This chapter has explained that a number of factors are required for a successful global strategy, including:
- planning based on accurate global and regional market information
- locating operations where the political, economic, market, technology and workforce skill conditions are attractive for the business
- a flexible organisational structure that will allow the regional parts of the business to adapt to regional conditions
- supportive global business capabilities including global and major capital finance skills and global human resourcing capabilities
- access to sufficient global leadership capabilities to implement the strategy
- ability to provide leadership at the global level, with appropriate globally relevant values and ethical standards
- global supply chains.

Following on from the global effect of COVID-19, we will see a continuing relaxation of many of the previous barriers to global business, as the increased opportunities for global business which developed in years following the 2008 GFC demonstrated. This means that all the above factors will become increasingly important over the next five years and that organisations should start strengthening these capabilities in anticipation of greater future opportunities. The continuing growth of the Australian consulting industry globally (the Australian consulting industry is the fourth largest consulting industry globally — it grew 9 per cent over the 12 months 2019–20) demonstrates how attractive global scale business has become for service organisations.[61]

The upsurgence of AI and forms of automation demonstrate that advanced technology can provide a competitive advantage, even if it is quickly claimed by competitors. For example, (as noted in the chapter on external and industry analysis) the major astronomical observatories compete globally for major international astronomical projects offering the largest supercomputers available.[62] These observatories typically gain a two-year competitive advantage from this technology before another observatory acquires a faster machine. The rapid shifts in economic development across regions, post COVID-19, confirms that a global organisation must have a flexible structure in order to take advantage of new rapidly growing markets and retreat from markets which have poor economic growth.

Employing a global workforce is an excellent approach for developing the type of flexible skills necessary for success in the global market. According to the 2019 PwC annual global CEO survey, the availability of key skills (in staff) was the third top threat identified by global CEOs.[63] A global workforce facilitates communication with every market, as well as introducing regional business knowledge to the organisation. More important than all of these, however, is the organisation's leadership and the culture it creates. At a global level, creating an effective culture is a major leadership challenge. Engaging generation Z, for example, requires the ability to provide a constant source of opportunity as they are highly motivated but have high expectations.[64] Providing the opportunity for staff to use initiative across a global organisation and generating a level of trust are particular challenges leaders have to face.

SUMMARY

The global business environment is complex. It is highly dynamic and comprises pockets of resources of which the organisation needs to take advantage in order to be competitive, as well as voids where there is an absence of supporting infrastructure or supporting industries. In addition, competitors will have different strengths in different regions of the global market, and so an organisation may be a leader in one market and a follower in another. The ability to coordinate and take advantage of these opportunities and respond to these challenges is a key for competitiveness in the global business environment.

Understanding how to position the organisation's resources as part of a global strategy requires the ability to analyse global environmental conditions, as well as individual conditions in each region of the business. Global operations can generate large economies of scale and allow key operations to be located in regions offering resources that create the greatest competitive advantage.

The business structures adopted by a global business have a strong influence on the value a global strategy can generate. At its most effective, a global strategy requires a network of resources and operations, functioning both globally and regionally. A multidomestic strategy isolates resources into specific regions and significantly reduces the economies of scale in both operations and resources. Matrix and globally integrated structures provide combinations of resources and regional customisation that increase economies of scale in capabilities and operations. The transnational structure is a network structure. It allows fluidity in resource allocation to either capabilities or regions and provides the greatest integration of both scale of operations and resources, globally.

The implementation of global strategies by many companies is very much hit and miss, reflecting inadequate understanding of the conditions that they are facing, inadequate preparation and insufficient resources. Although partnerships are challenging to coordinate and can lead to inequities, they also significantly reduce risk and accelerate global expansion. Global partnerships can provide complementary regional knowledge and resources if the relationship can be maintained.

Events such as COVID-19 demonstrate the importance of global networks and connections that support the business when markets change and channels close. Access to alternative resources, markets and the ability to arrange operations at the global level provides an invaluable survival mechanism at times of crisis. Leadership is an important dimension of a successful global strategy as well — providing direction in ambiguous contexts, incorporating diverse views and offering a systematic openness to unexpected opportunities are the key leadership characteristics that drive a global strategy.

KEY TERMS

born global Companies that plan and achieve global operations in just a few years.

comparative advantage Relative competitive advantages provided to business operations in one country/region relative to other countries/regions.

direct investment Investing in business operations in a market, for example, by establishing a regional subsidiary to service that market.

emerging region A new or developing region.

entry mode The approach taken to enter an international market.

foreign direct investment Direct investment in a market located in a different country.

free trade agreement Unrestricted international trade between countries.

global businesses (usually) Large businesses operating in many countries or regions with a global market objective. By comparison, international businesses focus on individual foreign country markets.

global forces Forces resulting from the integration of markets and economies globally which affect conditions in every single market and industry.

glocalisation Using a combination of global and regional company resources to efficiently provide a focused regional competitive advantage.

horizontal differentiation Differences in resources and operational activities between sections of the business at the same level.

joint-venture partnerships Partnerships in strategic projects where the partners share equity.

national resource bases The competitive assets a country can offer global businesses.

offshoring operations Transferring specific operations to another country.

spatial boundaries The physical boundaries of the regions that subsidiaries service.

strategic alliances Partnerships whichallow (global) organisations to share resources, risks and opportunities.

transaction costs Cost of global business operations outside the home country.

vertical differentiation Differences in the levels of hierarchy that comprise the organisation. The fewer the levels of hierarchy, the greater the vertical differentiation.

SELF-STUDY QUESTIONS

1 What are the special challenges associated with global strategic planning?

2 What is the impact of global forces on international market entry strategies?

3 What is the importance of management competency in international market entry?

4 Describe the various international market entry modes. Briefly list the pros and cons of each mode.

5 Contrast the classic structured approach to market entry with alternative approaches.

6 Identify and discuss the success factors for establishing global business.

7 What are some of the organisational structures that are appropriate for global business? Why are these structures more appropriate for global operations than other kinds of structures?

8 What are the advantages for global businesses of operating in different regions?

9 Describe the factors that are shaping international joint ventures.

DISCUSSION QUESTIONS

1 Identify an industry that has limited imports or foreign direct investment. Explain why the industry has escaped the influence of global forces. Explore whether there are opportunities for successful global forces within the industry and, if so, identify the strategy that would offer the best chance of success.

2 Select two countries to compare (e.g. Japan and Germany) and identify a natural resource that you can argue creates a specific comparative advantage for each country.

3 According to Porter's *Competitive advantage of nations*, the United Kingdom possesses a comparative advantage in several industries including: advertising, auction trading of antiques and artwork, distilled alcoholic beverages, hand tools and chemical preparations for gardening and horticulture. Use Porter's theory of national competitive advantage to explain this pattern of international competitive advantage.

4 When Porsche decided to enter the SUV market with its luxury Cayenne model, it surprised the industry by locating its new assembly plant in Leipzig in eastern Germany. Many observers believed that Porsche should have located the plant either in central or eastern Europe where labour costs were very low, or (like Mercedes and BMW) in the United States where it would be close to a major market. Use Porter's theory of national competitive advantage to explain Porsche's decision.

5 As Swiss International Air Lines discovered, using matrix structures for global operations can be challenging. However, it can be made to work — as the Siemens Group has demonstrated. Identify the major advantages and disadvantages of a matrix structure for Wesfarmers (a large diversified organisation). Visit the Wesfarmers website (www.wesfarmers.com.au) and identify the various industries and locations in which this organisation operates.

6 British expatriates living in the United States frequently ask friends and relatives visiting from the United Kingdom to bring with them bars of Cadbury's chocolate on the basis that the Cadbury's chocolate available in the United States is manufactured under licence by Hershey's and is inferior to 'the real thing'. Should Cadbury-Schweppes maintain its licensing agreement with Hershey or should it seek to supply the US market itself, either by export from the United Kingdom or by establishing operations facilities in the United States? Explain your reasoning.

7 Consider the characteristics required of a global leader in an Indonesia-originating global steel producer that is both interested in and affected by the growing economic and market significance of China and India.

EXERCISES

1 Consider a global business that you may wish to operate yourself one day or with which you have had some experience. Discuss the comparative pros and cons of licensing your product or service in China. You should particularly consider the advantages of lower setup costs and avoiding barriers to other forms of market entry, as well as the disadvantages of lower control over operations and protection of intellectual property.

2 Suppose an organisation has decided to enter a new international market. Choose a product line or service that you could conceivably find a market for in another country and choose a likely country. What sort of business structure is suitable?

(a) Begin your determination by making some brief notes on how you would analyse the market for your chosen product line or service in that country. What factors would you test in a sensitivity analysis?

(b) Using Dunning's eclectic theory, determine whether direct foreign investment is the best strategy.

(c) In trying to decide whether exporting or direct investment in the country would be the better strategy, what factors relating to this product or service would sway you against exporting?

(d) Would an export intermediary assist with some of the issues you identified in (c)? If so, what sort of agent would best suit your purposes? What characteristics would you look for in an agent?

(e) What factors might attract you to a licensee to make and/or market your product/service in the other country? And what factors would make you reject this option? Why?

(f) Are there any other entry strategies that might work? Consider each of the strategies in the following table and list factors for and against each (especially in terms of risk, control, cost and benefits).

Strategy	Factors for	Factors against
Joint venture		
Acquisition		
Agent/distributor		
Contract		
Franchise		

3 Consider and identify the locational advantages resulting from international investment in the United States, China and Europe. Use the other two components of Dunning's theory (ownership and internationalisation advantage) to explain why China is such an attractive location for foreign direct investment (FDI) and why the United States is the least attractive of the three.

4 BHP Billiton currently exports 200 million tonnes of iron ore and metallurgical coking coal to China each year. These raw materials are converted into steel for the Chinese construction and automotive market. The price of steel is much higher than the cost of the raw materials required to produce it. This means that BHP Billiton's profits from its sales to China would be much greater if the product was sold as steel. Unfortunately, the cost of manufacturing steel in Australia is higher than the cost of manufacturing steel in China. If BHP Billiton wished to successfully sell steel in China, it would have to produce it locally, using raw materials imported from Australia. BHP Billiton has considerable research and development capability and many patents relating to steel production which it could transfer to China. Investigate the other major steel producers operating in China and determine the best structure for BHP Billiton to use to establish a steel production subsidiary in Shanghai.[65]

5 Go to the GE website at www.ge.com and find the company's annual report. Identify its approach to global business. Consider what GE is trying to achieve through its international business (growth, profit etc.) and in the global business factors that GE believes will enable it to achieve this.

6 Most agreements by nations to reduce trade barriers are reciprocal. To explore the impact of one such agreement, go to the Australian Department of Foreign Affairs and Trade website at www.dfat.gov.au. Review the recent free trade agreements between the United States and Australia. Locate and read the following articles and summarise the key benefits to Australia from this free-trade agreement.
– 'Advancing Australia's economic future'
– 'Economic analysis of AUSFTA: Impact of the bilateral free trade agreement with the United States'
– A series of 'fact sheets on each of the key chapters of the agreement'
– 'AUSFTA — Frequently Asked Questions'

7 Go to the World Trade Organization (WTO) website at www.wto.org. Select the Doha development agenda and identify:
(a) the key objectives and issues of this round of trade talks
(b) the countries that were most active in the discussions
(c) the ease of resolution of these discussions.

There is no need to look into much detail to identify the last point, so just try to gain a sense of the level of mutual agreement between the countries principally concerned with each of the issues. Try to explain why this round took so long to reach resolution.

FURTHER READING

Blanton, R & Dursun, P 2017, 'Dying for globalization? The impact of economic globalization on industrial accidents', *Social Science Quarterly,* vol. 98, no. 5, 1487–1502.

Zhu, H, Qi, Z & Ding, Z 2020, 'The roles of Chinese CEOs in managing individualistic cultures in cross-border mergers and acquisitions', *Journal of Management Studies,* vol. 57, no. 3, 664–697.

Lama, M 2020, 'On markets and pandemics: a view from India', *Global-e: A Global Studies Journal,* vol. 13, no. 21.

Pascal, W 2020, 'The importance of global business hubs on internationalizing SMEs: an empirical analysis of psychic and geographic distance', *Technology Innovation Management Review,* vol. 10, no. 4, 35–47.

Dzwigol, H, Barosz, MD & Kwilinski, A 2020, 'Formation of global competitive enterprise environment based on industry 4.0 concept', *International Journal of Entrepreneurship,* vol. 24, no. 1.

Ekman, P, et al. 2020, 'Digital transformation of global business processes: the role of dual embeddedness', *Business Process Management Journal,* vol. 26, no. 2, 570–592.

ENDNOTES

1. Tata, 'Business profile', 2020, www.tata.com/content/dam/tata/pdf/The_Tata_group_Business_Profile_2020v2.pdf.
2. Tata, 'Business overview', 2020, www.tata.com/business/overview.
3. Tata, 'Values and purpose', 2020, www.tata.com/about-us/tata-values-purpose.
4. ibid.
5. Tata, 'Our timeline', 2020, www.tata.com/about-us/tata-group-our-heritage/Our-Timeline.
6. The Australian Industry Group, 'Australian manufacturing in 2019 local and global opportunities', 2019, https://cdn.aigroup.com.au/Economic_Indicators/Economic_Outlook/Australian_Manufacturing_in_2019.pdf.
7. Austrade, 'Australia's inward FDI stock surged to almost A$850b', 2018, Australian Trade and Investment Commission, www.austrade.gov.au/international/invest/investor-updates/2018/australias-inward-fdi-stock-surged-to-almost-850-billion-in-2017.
8. A Crawford, 'Brexit exposes painful disconnect between England and Britain', Bloomberg.com, 2019, www.bloomberg.com/news/articles/2019-04-12/brexit-exposes-painful-disconnect-between-england-and-britain.
9. Australian Investment Council, 'How the CPTPP will benefit Australian businesses', 2020.
10. J Pla-Barber, E Linares and PN Ghauri, 'The choice of offshoring operation mode: A behavioural perspective', *Journal of Business Research*, 2019, 103, 570–580.
11. S Perkins, R Morck and B Yeung, 'Innocents abroad: the hazards of international joint ventures', *Global Strategy Journal*, 4, 2012, 310–330.
12. A Soulsby and E Clark, 'Instability and failure in international joint ventures in post-socialist societies: Power, politics and strategic orientations', *Competition Change*, vol. 15, no 4, 2011, 296–314.
13. Fonterra, 'Doing business in China', 2013, www.fonterra.com/nz/en/what-we-stand-for/global-reach/doing-business-in-china.html.
14. Fonterra, 'NZ dairy timeline', 2020, www.fonterra.com/nz/en/campaign/nzdairytimeline.html.
15. UABS Knowledge, 'Fonterras audacious global master plan', *University of Auckland Business School*, 16 September, 2014, www.uabsknowledge.ac.nz/en/research-and-comment/research-and-analysis/fonterra-s-audacious-global-master-plan.html; A Scott, S Bowden and J Rowarth, 'Critical success factors when going global: New Zealand dairy companies', Proceedings of the New Zealand Grassland Association Conference 75, 2013, 61–66, www.grassland.org.nz/publications/nzgrassland_publication_2529.pdf.
16. Australian Food News, 'Murray Goulburn, what went wrong?', *Australian Food News*, 18 May 2016, www.ausfoodnews.com.au/2016/05/18/murray-goulburn-what-went-wrong.html.
17. S Smith, 'Fonterra rings up $562m loss, announces focus will shift across the ditch', 26 September 2019, *ABC News*, www.abc.net.au/news/rural/2019-09-26/fonterra-dairy-company-reports-$562-million-loss/11550886.
18. A Scott, S Bowden and J Rowarth, 'Critical success factors when going global: New Zealand dairy companies', Proceedings of the New Zealand Grassland Association Conference 75, 2013, 61–66, www.grassland.org.nz/publications/nzgrassland_publication_2529.pdf.
19. GE, '2019 Annual Report', General Electric, 2019.
20. S Tallman, Y Luo and PJ Buckley, 'Business models in global competition', *Global Strategy Journal* vol. 8, no. 4, 2018, 517–35.
21. A Verbeke, R Coeurderoy and T Matt, 'The future of international business research on corporate globalization that never was . . .', *Journal of International Business Studies* vol. 49, no. 9, 2018, 1101–1112.
22. M Sewak and A Sharma, 'Performance implications of MNE subsidiary federation: evidence from India', *Journal of International Management*, vol. 26, no. 1, 2020.
23. A Taira, 'Beyond the cluster: a case study of pipelines and buzz in the glocal relational space of the glove-related industry of Shikoku, Japan', *Geographical Journal*, vol. 186, no. 1, 2020, 45–58.
24. J Porter, 'Google may have just ushered in an era of quantum supremacy', *The Verge*, 23 September, 2019.

25. Export Finance Australia, 'India—Middle class unlikely to rival China; but export opportunities present', 2018, www.export finance.gov.au/resources-news/news-events/world-risk-developments/2018/world-risk-developments-february-2018/india-middle-class-unlikely-to-rival-china-but-export-opportunities-present/.

26. The Economist, 'AI providers will increasingly compete with management consultancies', *The Economist*, 28 March, 2018.

27. Freedonia, 'World rare Earths', *The Freedonia Group*, 2015 Report, www.freedoniagroup.com/industry-study/world-rare-earths-3349.htm.

28. J Reiter, '4 ways governments can develop digital infrastructure', *World Economic Forum*, 15 September 2017, www.weforum.org/agenda/2017/09/governments-develop-digital-infrastructure-vodafone.

29. F Tiraboschi and M Tiraboschi, 'Italy's industry 4.0 plan: an analysis from a labour law perspective', *E-Journal of International and Comparative Labour Studies'*, vol. 7, no. 1, 2018.

30. CM Christensen, ME Raynor and R McDonald, 'What is disruptive innovation?', *Harvard Business Review*, December 2015.

31. DFAT, 'China–Australia Free Trade Agreement', 2018, Dfat.gov.au, www.dfat.gov.au/trade/agreements/in-force/chafta/Pages/australia-china-fta.

32. AgriFutures Australia, 'Coffee', 2017, www.agrifutures.com.au/farm-diversity/coffee.

33. A Madigan, 'Treasury Wine Estate's BEN FU trademark registered in China', *WBM Online*, 10 April 2020, https://wbmonline.com.au/treasury-wine-estates-ben-fu-trademark-registered-in-china.

34. Nine Finance, 'Treasury Wine boosts China ops', *Nine Finance*, 2017, https://finance.nine.com.au/business-news/treasury-wine-strengthens-china-ops/2bb20cb7-4f66-4b33-bf20-5430ab0a2523.

35. Chemical Online, 'Demand for fertilizer on the rise in Southeast Asian countries', Chemical Online.com, 19 April 2001.

36. F Froese, D Sutherland, JY Lee, Y Liu and Y Pan, 'Challenges for foreign companies in China: implications for research and practice', *Asian Business Management*, vol. 18, 2019, 249–262.

37. BBC, 'India overhauls foreign ownership rules', *BBC News*, 20 June 2016, www.bbc.com/news/business-36575755.

38. S Orr, J Menzies and J Paul, 'International networking and success-versus failure-based learning of SMEs', *Management International Review*, 2020.

39. OEDC, 'China's Belt and Road Initiative in the global trade, investment and finance landscape', *OEDC Business and Finance Outlook*, 2018 OECD Publishing, Paris.

40. Premier, 'Victoria and China take partnership to the next level', *Premier of Victoria*, 23 October 2019, www.premier.vic.gov.au/victoria-and-china-take-partnership-to-the-next-level.

41. E Lukas, 'Dynamic market entry and the value of flexibility in transitional international joint ventures', *Review of Financial Economics*, vol. 16, no. 1, 2007, 91–110.

42. Fortune Editors, 'The 25 best global companies to work for', *Fortune*, 26 October 2016, https://fortune.com/2016/10/26/best-global-companies.

43. Citibank, 'Countries and jurisdictions', 2020, www.citigroup.com/citi/about/countries-and-jurisdictions.

44. A Schuh, 'Regionalization in Central and Eastern Europe: searching for regiocentric orientations in MNC strategies', *Journal of East–West Business*, vol. 13, no. 2/3, 2007, 143–166.

45. Philips, 'Philips realigns the composition of its reporting segments', *Philips News Center*, 10 January 2019, www.philips.com/a-w/about/news/archive/standard/news/press/2019/20190110-philips-realigns-the-composition-of-its-reporting-segments.html.

46. J Birkinshaw, P Braunerhjelm, U Holm and S Terjesen, 'Why do some multinational corporations relocate their headquarters overseas?', *Strategic Management Journal*, vol. 27, 2006, 681–700.

47. A De Smet, S Kleinman and K Weerda, 'The helix organization', *McKinsey Company*, 3 October 2019, www.mckinsey.com/business-functions/organization/our-insights/the-helix-organization.

48. CA Bartlett and S Ghoshal, *Managing across borders: the transnational solution*, 2nd edn, Boston: Harvard Business School Press, 1998.

49. M Jones, 'Globalization and organizational restructuring: a strategic perspective', *Thunderbird International Business Review*, vol. 44, no. 3, May/June 2002, 325.

50. RW Service and K Kennedy, 'A comprehensive global leadership model', *Business Renaissance Quarterly*, vol. 7, no. 1, 2012, 75–106.

51. P Behrendt, S Matz and AS Göritz, 'An integrative model of leadership behavior', *Leadership Quarterly*, vol. 28, no. 1, 2017, 229–44.

52. YPO, '2019 YPO Global Leadership Survey', *YPO*, 22 January 2019, www.ypo.org/global-leadership-survey.

53. Ernst Young, 'Global Leadership Forecast 2018', *Ernest Young*, The Conference Board and Development Dimensions International, 2018.

54. T Tyre, 'Ethical leadership in the global marketplace', *Global Education Journal*, 2018, no. 4, 83–96; J Haar, M Roche and D Brougham, 'Indigenous insights into ethical leadership: a study of Māori leaders', *Journal of Business Ethics*, 2019, vol. 160, no. 3, 621–640.

55. P Liu, 'A framework for understanding Chinese leadership: a cultural approach', *International Journal of Leadership in Education*, 2017, vol. 20, no. 6, 749–761

56. P Caligiuri and I Tarique, 'Dynamic cross-cultural competencies and global leadership effectiveness', *Journal of World Business*, vol. 47, no. 4, 2012, 612–622.

57. D Burkus, 'Essay: developing global leadership: a review of barriers and adjustments for international expansion', *International Management Review*, vol. 8, no. 2, 2012, 83–84.

58. TS Kee, V Islam, TF Said and SW Azimah, 'Leadership skills and competencies of global business', *Independent Business Review*, 2017, vol. 10, no 1, 1–20.

59. C Voegtlin, M Patzer and A Scherer, 'Responsible leadership in global business: a new approach to leadership and its multi-level outcomes', *Journal of Business Ethics*, vol. 105, no. 1, 2012, 1–16.

60. CM Youssef and F Luthans, 'Positive global leadership', *Journal of World Business*, vol. 47, no. 4, 2012, 539–547.

61. Consultancy, 'Australia's consulting market punching above its weight', *Consultancy*, 23 March 2020, www.consultancy.com.au/news/1802/australias-consulting-market-punching-above-its-weight.

62. 'World's fastest supercomputer processes huge data rates in preparation for mega-telescope project — ICRAR', *ICRAR,* 22 October 2019, www.icrar.org/summit.

63. PWC, '22nd Annual Global CEO Survey', *Price Waterhouse Coopers*, 2019, www.pwc.com/gx/en/ceo-survey/2019/report/pwc-22nd-annual-global-ceo-survey.pdf.

64. S Percy, 'An international perspective: top leadership challenges for 2020', *Forbes*, 7 January 2020, www.forbes.com/sites/sallypercy/2020/01/02/an-international-perspective-top-leadership-challenges-for-2020/#5719b526d0c9.

65. BHP Billiton, www.bhpbilliton.com.

ACKNOWLEDGEMENTS

Photo: © MyStockVideo / Shutterstock.com
Photo: © Imaginechina Limited / Alamy Stock Photo
Photo: © TnkImages / Shutterstock.com

PART IV

STRATEGIC EVALUATION AND IMPLEMENTATION

CHAPTER 9

Strategic evaluation, implementation, structure and control

LEARNING OBJECTIVES

After studying this chapter, you should be able to:

9.1 discuss the role and importance of structural building blocks for structural arrangements and how these are embedded in organisation design

9.2 distinguish how specialisation, coordination and cooperation support structural arrangements, both local and global

9.3 illustrate and discuss how different organisational structures support business and corporate-level strategies, both local and global

9.4 describe the strategy evaluation process

9.5 explain how scenario planning can be used for strategy evaluation

9.6 recognise how different evaluation frameworks such as the McKinsey 7-S support the strategy evaluation process

9.7 discuss the importance of strategy evaluation in uncertain times.

BP — organisational structure and management systems

When John Browne stepped down as CEO at BP in January 2007, he was credited with having transformed an inefficient, bureaucratic, state-owned oil company into the world's most dynamic, entrepreneurial, performance-focused, and environmentally aware oil and gas major. Since Browne took up the job in 1995, BP's market capitalisation had increased fivefold and its earnings per share by 600 per cent.

A brief history of BP

BP began as the Anglo-Persian Oil Company, which had been founded in 1909 to exploit a huge oilfield that had been discovered in Iran. At the outbreak of the First World War, the British government acquired a controlling interest in the company, which it held until the company (by then renamed British Petroleum) was privatised by Margaret Thatcher's government in 1979.

Under a series of chief executives — Peter Walters, Bob Horton and David Simon — BP went from being a highly centralised, bureaucratic organisation to becoming less hierarchical and more financially oriented. Under John Browne's management BP was transformed into a truly innovative environmentally conscious company. This strategic transformation was accompanied by radical changes to BP's structure, systems and culture.

The atomic structure

At the heart of Browne's transformation of BP were high aspirations to become a leader in the petroleum industry.

Through a series of mergers and acquisitions, by 2000 BP emerged as the world's seventh biggest company in terms of revenues. Browne's approach was built upon the following three principles.

- BP operates in a decentralised manner, with individual business unit leaders (such as refinery plant managers) given broad latitude for running the business and direct responsibility for delivering performance.
- The corporate organisation provides support and assistance to the business units (such as individual refineries) through a variety of functions, networks and peer groups.
- BP relies upon individual performance contracts to motivate people.[1]

At the time, most of the oil majors had a corporate head office that coordinated and controlled a few major divisions. This divisional structure typically comprised: upstream (exploration and production), downstream (refining and marketing) and petrochemicals. BP had been similar; its divisional structure had been described as a 'collection of fiefdoms'.

Browne was keen to break away from the management conventions of the oil industry. His inspirations were the management styles of Silicon Valley and the corporate transformation that had been unleashed by Jack Welch at General Electric. The structure created by Browne was radically different: the divisions were dismantled and the company was organised around 150 business units, each headed by a business unit leader who reported directly to the corporate centre. According to the deputy CEO, this was 'an extraordinarily flat, dispersed, decentralised process of delivery' that reflected a division of responsibility between the business unit heads who were responsible for operational performance and senior management who were responsible for strategic direction and managing external relations — especially with governments. The 150 business units were organised into 15 'peer groups' — networks of similar businesses that could share knowledge, cooperate on matters of common interest and challenge one another.

Adapting the management model, 2001–08

In 2001 and again in 2003, BP's organisational structure underwent significant revisions designed to address excessive decentralisation and to improve coordination and control.

Instead of the individual business units reporting directly to top management, the peer groups were replaced by 'strategic performance units', which were more formalised organisational units with their own budgets and with responsibility for the business units beneath them.

The strategic performance units were organised within three business segments: exploration and production; refining and marketing; and gas, power, and renewables. Thus, while BP's individual refineries remained as separate business units, they reported to refining, which itself was one of the three strategic performance units that comprised the refining and marketing segment.

In addition to the business structure, there was a regional structure. BP had four broad geographic areas: (1) Europe; (2) the Americas; (3) Africa, the Middle East, Russia, and the Caspian; and (4) Asia, the Indian subcontinent, and Australasia. The head of each region was responsible for ensuring regional consistency of the businesses within that region, managing BP's relations with governments and other external parties, and conducting certain administrative functions relating to tax and compliance with local laws.

Further changes took place when Tony Hayward took over from John Browne in 2007. A consulting report from Bain and Co. declared that BP was the most complicated organisation that the consultants had ever encountered. Bain identified more than 10 000 organisational interfaces. Haywards 'forward agenda' emphasised cost cutting and simplification. Regional structures were eliminated, functional structures streamlined, and the number of senior executives was reduced from 650 to 500.

Introduction

Why, in the same market environment, do some companies prosper while others struggle to survive? How does a company's internal characteristics, such as resources, capabilities and core competencies, enable it to create a competitive advantage? Some Australian companies, such as One.Tel (telecommunications), Virgin Australia Airlines, Air Australia and Shoes of Prey (a customised shoe wear producer) have failed in recent years, while other Australian companies, such as Wesfarmers and David Jones, have remained successful despite ups and downs in performance. There are many factors that contribute to the success or failure of companies.

In this chapter, we will address the role of many organisational components, including strategy evaluation, for the success of the company. Most organisational structures rely predominantly on the type of strategy an organisation employs. So, organisations with innovative strategies may have to adopt the most appropriate structure that supports their innovative activities. For example, organisations that have single product lines will survive with a functional-type structure whereas organisations with multiple products and product areas will require different structures to help them achieve more efficient implementation. The formulation of strategy cannot be separated from its implementation. Indeed, formulating a strategy without taking into account the conditions under which it will be implemented will result in a poorly-designed strategy because it will not be supported by the best structure. A fundamental flaw in the corporate planning systems of three decades ago was separating strategy formulation — the task of corporate executives and strategic planners — from its implementation by divisional heads and middle managers, and from other key components or building blocks of structure that were necessary to make it work. As the opening scene setter suggests, while the right kind of innovative organising model is critical, it is equally critical to consider that many other elements support the implementation of successful innovation.

The design of organisational structure and management control systems is the key component of strategy implementation. Hence, the view of strategy formulation and strategy implementation as a sequential process is summed up in the adage 'structure follows strategy'. Management guru Thomas J. Peters argues the reverse: if capabilities are the primary basis of strategy, and if capabilities are a product of organisational structure, then strategy follows structure.[2] Yet, as Hamel and Prahalad explain, capabilities and competencies help to provide a competitive advantage that supports the long-term vision largely dictating what structure will be required.[3] The key point, however, is not whether strategy or structure takes precedence, but the recognition that the two are closely interdependent.[4] For companies such as fashion retailer Inditex, with its closely-coordinated network of local suppliers and worldwide network of franchised retailers, or BHP, with its diverse portfolio of high quality assets and commodities located in low-risk locations around the world, organisational structures are determined by strategy and high standardsof governance.

Having established that the understanding of how companies organise themselves is fundamental to their strategy and their performance, this chapter will introduce the key concepts and ideas necessary to develop companies' structures and systems, as well as possible changes to them. The fundamental principles of organisational design support a range of strategy implementation techniques.

Understanding a company's performance involves evaluating its strategies. Managers evaluate a company's strategies three times: first, managers evaluate the mission statement (is it still current?) and objectives; second, they evaluate strategic alternatives while making strategic choices in selecting the strategy alternative; and third, managers evaluate strategy performance. This chapter discusses the role of strategy evaluation for successful performance of the company. This is supported by consideration of the role of scenario planning for strategy evaluation. Next, approaches used by companies to value evaluation are given, followed by a discussion of the two widely used frameworks of strategy formulation and implementation — the McKinsey 7-S model and the balanced scorecard model. Lastly, the need for ongoing strategy evaluation in uncertain times is considered.

9.1 Building blocks of organisational structure

LEARNING OBJECTIVE 9.1 Discuss the role and importance of structural building blocks for structural arrangements and how these are embedded in organisation design.

While flexibility and responsiveness are critically important characteristics of modern organisations, both are dependent on coordinated activities of the company. These, in turn, depend on the types of strategic plans performed in a company and the intensity of collaboration needed. Coordination across the organisation, roles of personnel and the degree of flexibility and responsiveness required is a collective decision. Together with other coordinated tasks, the building blocks of structure need to be formulated in response to an organisation's strategy (see figure 9.1). Building block components will be similar (but not necessarily the same) across structures. Some building block components will be more pervasive, depending on the type of organisational arrangements required. For example, a functional structure places much more emphasis on the coordination between each department whereas a matrix structure will require more cooperation across departments. It is important to note as well that with any structure, the connecting horizontal lines suggest that cooperation between functions is paramount. For instance, the output of one department becomes the input of another. Within each department, a marketing and sales section exists alongside a manufacturing section. So, sales and marketing will promote and sell the output and goods produced from manufacturing and, for its part, manufacturing will rely on sales and marketing as a guide to how many products to produce.

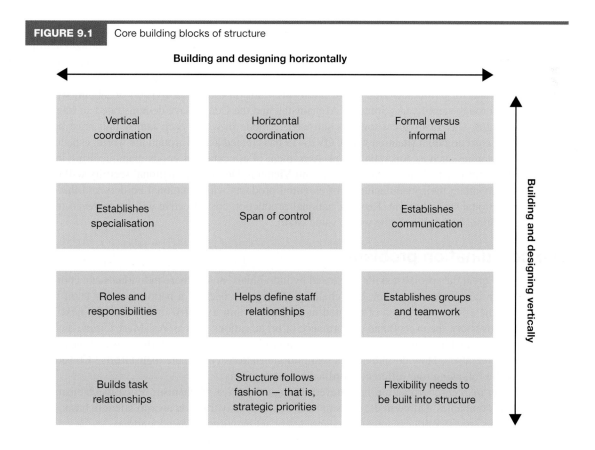

FIGURE 9.1 Core building blocks of structure

9.2 Specialisation, coordination and cooperation

LEARNING OBJECTIVE 9.2 Distinguish how specialisation, coordination and cooperation support structural arrangements, both local and global.

There are two fundamental problems in designing organisational structures. According to Mintzberg:

> Every organized human activity — from making pots to placing a man on the moon — gives rise to two fundamental and opposing requirements: the division of labor into various tasks, and the coordination of these tasks to accomplish the activity. The structure of the organization can be defined simply as the ways in which labor is divided into distinct tasks and coordination is achieved among these tasks.[5]

Specialisation and division of labour

The fundamental source of efficiency in production is specialisation, especially the division of labour into separate tasks. The classic statement on the gains due to specialisation is Smith's description of pin manufacture:

> One man draws out the wire, another straightens it, a third cuts it, a fourth points it, a fifth grinds it at the top for receiving the head; to make the head requires two or three distinct operations; to put it on is a peculiar business, to whiten the pins is another; it is even a trade by itself to put them into the papers.[6]

Smith's pin makers produced about 4800 pins per person each day — 'but if they had all wrought separately and independently, and without any of them having been educated to this peculiar business, they certainly could not each have made 20, perhaps not one pin, in a day'. Similarly, Henry Ford experienced huge productivity gains by installing moving assembly lines and assigning individuals to highly specific production tasks. Between the end of 1912 and early 1914, the time taken to assemble a Model T fell from 106 hours to just over 6 hours. More generally, the difference in human productivity between modern industrial society and primitive subsistence society is the result of the efficiency gains from individuals specialising.

However, specialisation comes at a cost. The more a production process is divided between different specialists, the greater are the costs of coordination. The more volatile and unstable the external environment, the greater the number of decisions that need to be made and the higher are these coordination costs. Hence, the more stable is the environment, the greater is the optimal division of labour. This is true both for companies and for entire societies. Civilisations are built on increased division of labour, which is only possible through stability. As Somalia, Afghanistan and the Congo have demonstrated so tragically, once chaos reigns, societies regress towards subsistence mode in which each family unit must be self-sufficient. The current global situation with COVID-19 has created a need around the world, especially in developed economies such as Australia, for re-assessment of allocation of goods manufacturing in more cost-efficient countries, such as China, Malaysia and Vietnam. Demand for national security will require companies to maintain their manufacturing of essential products within national borders and this might change international specialisation. Keeping national production cost effective will be achieved through innovative solutions and agility in the whole value chain.

The coordination problem

No matter how great the specialist skills possessed by individuals, unless these individuals can coordinate their efforts, production cannot occur. The challenge for every coach of a national soccer team is how to coordinate the efforts of a group of talented individuals within a limited time before the next World Cup finals. Conversely, the exceptional performance of organisations such as Wal-Mart, Cirque du Soleil, BHP and the Berlin Philharmonic Orchestra are primarily the result of superb coordination between organisational members. How do individuals within organisations coordinate their efforts? Consider the operation of the following four different coordination mechanisms.

- *Price.* In the market, coordination is achieved through the price mechanism. Price mechanisms also exist within companies. Different departments and divisions may trade on an arm's-length basis, where internal prices (transfer prices) are either negotiated or set by corporate headquarters.
- *Rules and directives.* A key feature of companies is the existence of employment contracts. Unlike self-employed workers, who negotiate market contracts for individual tasks, employees enter general employment contracts where they agree to perform a range of duties as required by their employer.

Authority is exercised by means of general rules (e.g. 'Employees will report for work not later than 9 am') and specific directives (e.g. 'Mr A, please show Miss B the way to her new office').

- *Mutual adjustment.* The simplest form of coordination involves the mutual adjustment of individuals engaged in related tasks. In soccer or doubles tennis, each player coordinates with fellow team members without any authority relationship among them. Such mutual adjustment occurs in all teams and work groups where there is no formal leader.
- *Routines.* Where activities are performed recurrently, coordination based on mutual adjustment and rules becomes institutionalised within organisational routines. These regular and predictable sequences of coordinated actions by individual workers are the foundation of organisational capability. If organisations are to perform complex activities at extreme levels of efficiency and reliability, coordination by rules, directives or mutual adjustment is not enough — coordination must become embedded in routines.

Price mechanisms also work well in situations of 'arm's length' coordination. For example, in coordinating production and sales, it may be sufficient to offer sales personnel simple price incentives such as higher commission rates on those products where inventories are high. Rules tend to work well for activities where standardised outcomes are required and the decision-making abilities of the operatives involved may be limited — most quality control procedures involve the application of simple rules. Routines form the basis for coordination in most activities where close interdependence exists between individuals, whether a basic production task (supplying customers at Dreamy Donuts) or a more complex activity (performing a heart bypass operation or implementing a systems integration project for a multinational corporation).

The cooperation problem: incentives and control

The discussion of coordination has dealt only with the technical problem of integrating the actions of different individuals. However, coordination problems are not entirely solved by implementing coordination mechanisms. There is also the problem of different organisational members having conflicting goals. This is referred to as the **cooperation problem**. Overcoming goal conflict requires creating incentives and controls.

Goal misalignment can be analysed in terms of agency problems.[7] An agency relationship exists when one party (the principal) contracts with another party (the agent) to act on behalf of the principal. The problem is ensuring that the agent acts in the principal's interest. Within the company, the major agency problem is between owners (shareholders) and managers. The problem of ensuring that managers operate companies to maximise shareholder wealth is at the centre of the corporate governance debate. During the 1990s, changes in top management remuneration — in particular the increasing emphasis given to share options — were intended to align the interests of managers with those of shareholders.[8] However, at Enron, WorldCom and HIH Insurance, these incentives encouraged managers to manipulate reported earnings rather than to work for long-term profitability.

Agency problems exist throughout the hierarchy. For individual employees, systems of incentives, monitoring and appraisal are designed to encourage pursuit of organisational objectives and overcome employees' tendency to do their own thing or simply shirk. The organisation structure may create its own problems. Organisational departments create their own sub-goals that do not align with one another. The classic conflicts are between different functions: sales wishes to please customers, production wishes to maximise output, RD wants to introduce mind-blowing new products, while finance worries about profit and loss. Thus, a combination of coordination and cooperation factors requires careful alignment (see figure 9.2).

Several mechanisms are available to management for achieving goal alignment within organisations, as follows.

- *Control mechanisms* typically operate on the basis of managers supervising groups of subordinates. Managerial supervision involves monitoring behaviour and performance, while subordinates are obliged to seek approval for actions that lie outside their area of authority. Such hierarchical supervision and control rests on both positive and negative incentives. Positive incentives are typically the reward of promotion up the hierarchy in return for compliance; negative incentives are dismissal and demotion for failing to acquiesce to rules and directives.
- *Financial incentives* are designed to reward performance. Such incentives extend from piece-rates for production workers to share options and profit bonuses for executives. Such performance-related incentives have two main benefits: first, they are high powered — they relate rewards directly to output — and second, they economise on the need for costly monitoring and supervision of employees.

The problems of pay-for-performance arise where employees work in teams or on activities where output is difficult to measure. Linking pay to individual performance may discourage collaboration; linking it to group performance may encourage free riding.

- *Shared values* are the commonality of goals between organisational members. Some organisations (churches, charities, clubs and most voluntary organisations fall into this category) are able to achieve high levels of cooperation and low levels of goal conflict without extensive control mechanisms or performance-related incentives. The role of corporate culture as a control mechanism that is an alternative to bureaucratic control or the price mechanism is very important in encouraging conformity to organisational goals.[9] Examples are Wal-Mart, Coles Group, Amway and the Shell Group, which all show the presence of shared values and principles that encourages the alignment of individual and corporate goals without necessarily undermining the individuality of organisational members. Such control saves on monitoring costs: self-control and informal monitoring by co-workers substitute for managerial supervision and financial incentives. Similar observations can be made about companies driven by a common technological vision. At Apple Computer Inc. (now Apple Inc.) in the 1980s, the belief that Apple was leading a computer revolution that would transform and democratise society permitted intense cooperation with very little formal control. By 2013, Apple's shared values are not so much a well-articulated mission statement. Rather, shared values are embedded within the products and accomplishments that define the future of mobile media and computing devices such as the iPods, iPhones and iPads. Steve Jobs was once quoted as saying 'Man is the creator of change in this world. As such, he should be above systems and structures, and not subordinate to them.'[10]

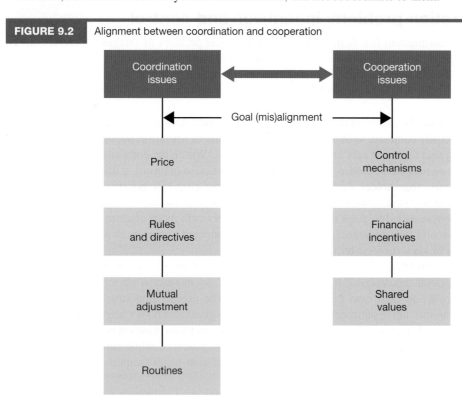

FIGURE 9.2 Alignment between coordination and cooperation

9.3 Types of structure in focus

LEARNING OBJECTIVE 9.3 Illustrate and discuss how different organisational structures support business and corporate-level strategies, both local and global.

In this section, we will introduce the more commonly-used structures and discuss them in greater detail. As indicated earlier, the key point to remember is that any structural configuration depends on the type of strategy employed, the nature of products and services sold, the number of reporting relationships required, and the degree of geographic expansion. These facts mostly influence the 'how and why' of structure. Here, we describe four common organisational forms: the simple structure, the functional structure, the multidivisional structure, and the matrix structure.

The simple structure

A simple structure is the simplest way of organising people to perform a certain task. This can happen in a small retail store or a small factory run by a family. It is a structure with a minimum level of division of labour. Decision making is largely centralised in the hands of a single person (usually the founder) with very little formalisation (see figure 9.3).

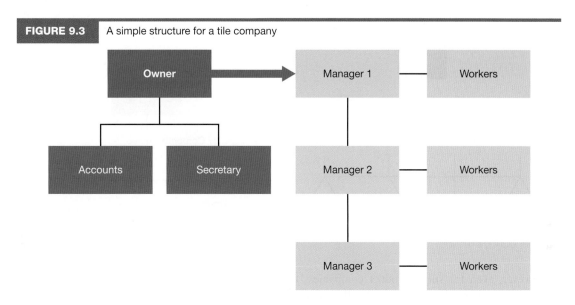

FIGURE 9.3 A simple structure for a tile company

Figure 9.3 provides an example of an owner of a small tile business with several managers. Each manager is responsible for a number of other workers. This simple structure is functional from a coordination and cooperation perspective since the business specialises in only one type of product (tiles), and can easily be managed. The major advantage of a simple structure is its flexibility and adaptability (see table 9.1). As long as the founder approves, the organisation can alter itself very quickly and effectively to cater to changes in the market, without the burden of any formality that will obstruct its speed in making decisions. Since the flow of information within the organisation is very fast, so too is the decision-making process.

TABLE 9.1 Advantages and disadvantages of simple structures

Advantages	Disadvantages
Flexible and adaptable	Too reliant on owner
Responsive to change	Lack of consistency
Quick decision making	Erratic decision making

The simple structure's major weakness is a possible lack of consistency and sustainability. The organisation's entire operations may be over-dependent on a single person (usually the founder). Depending on the founder's disposition, the decision-making can be erratic and irrational. In terms of sustainability, any problems experienced by the owner may influence business survival.

When the business expands, more orders accumulate and more work is required. To meet the demands of customers, more people will need to be employed, necessitating more complicated production processes. As the organisation grows, division of labour and coordination become important, and so a more complicated structure becomes a necessity.

The functional structure

Single-business companies tend to be organised along functional lines. Grouping together functionally similar tasks is conducive to exploiting scale economies, promoting learning and capability building, and deploying standardised control systems. Since cross-functional integration occurs at the top of the organisation, functional structures are conducive to a high degree of centralised control by the CEO and top management team. In figure 9.4, many of the building blocks discussed earlier are apparent. Typically, functions are coordinated at the top of the organisational apex, with each function existing with unbroken lines from top to bottom.

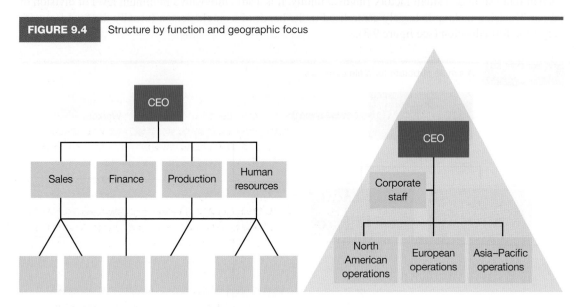

FIGURE 9.4 Structure by function and geographic focus

However, even for single-product companies, functional structures are subject to the problems of cooperation and coordination (see table 9.2). Different functional departments develop their own goals, values, vocabularies and behavioural norms, which make cross-functional integration difficult. As the size of the company increases, the pressure on top management to achieve effective integration increases. Because the different functions of the company tend to be tightly coupled rather than loosely coupled, there is limited scope for decentralisation. In particular, it is very difficult to operate individual functions as semi-autonomous profit centres.

TABLE 9.2 Advantages and disadvantages of functional structures

Advantages	Disadvantages
Best in stable environments	Problems of cooperation and coordination
Supports in-depth skill development	Slow response time
Ideal for single-product lines	Bottlenecks caused by sequential tasks
Specialists freed from administrative and coordinating work	Decisions pile at the top
	Poor cross-functional integration
	Stability results in less innovation
	Problems when company grows products

The real problems arise when the company grows its range of products and businesses: once a functionally organised company expands its product range, coordination within each product area becomes difficult. For example, a company that wishes to expand by geographic growth may use a functional-type structure in different countries. However, this may become difficult over time if different countries require adaptation to products and quicker response times. Table 9.2 shows the advantages and disadvantages of functional structures.

Although the long-term trend among very large companies has been for product-based, divisionalised companies to replace functionally organised companies, the trend is not entirely one way. As companies mature, the need for strong centralised control and well-developed functional capabilities has caused some companies to seek greater integration between a strictly functional structure and geographic scope.

The multidivisional structure

The product-based multidivisional structure emerged during the twentieth century in response to the coordination problems caused by diversification. The key advantage of divisionalised structures (whether product based or geographically based) is the potential for decentralised decision making. The multidivisional structure is the classic example of a loose-coupled, modular organisation where business-level strategies and operating decisions can be made at the divisional level, while the corporate headquarters concentrates on corporate planning, budgeting and providing common services.

Central to the efficiency advantages of the multidivisional corporation is the ability to apply a common set of corporate management tools to a range of different businesses. At ITT Corporation, Harold Geneen's system of 'managing by the numbers' allowed him to cope with over 50 divisional heads reporting directly to him. At British Petroleum, John Browne's system of 'performance contracts' allowed direct reporting by over 20 'strategic performance units'. Divisional autonomy also fosters the development of top management leadership capability among divisional heads — an important factor in CEO succession.

The large divisionalised corporation is typically organised into three levels: the corporate centre, the divisions and individual business units, each representing a distinct business for which financial accounts can be drawn up and strategies formulated. This form of organisation replaced both the centralised, functional structures that characterised most industrial corporations and the loose-knit holding companies created in the merger wave of the early twentieth century. So, the problems with integration that organisations with a purely functional structure encountered were solved by creating greater autonomy as companies became larger. DuPont and Boral Limited provide examples of this.

- At DuPont, increasing size and a widening product range strained the functional structure and overloaded top management:

  > the operations of the enterprise became too complex and the problems of coordination, appraisal and policy formulation too intricate for a small number of top officers to handle both long-run, entrepreneurial and short-run, operational administrative activities.[11]

  The solution devised by Pierre du Pont was to decentralise: ten product divisions were created, each with their own sales, RD, and support activities. The corporate head office headed by an executive committee took responsibility for coordination, strategy and resource allocation.[12]

- At Boral Limited, the primary feature of its divisional structure was the separation of operating responsibilities (which were vested in divisional managing directors at the divisional level) from corporate strategic responsibilities (which were located at the head office) (see figure 9.5). The divisional structure reconciles central coordination with the efficiencies and responsiveness of operational decentralisation. For Boral, the key is to decentralise into areas where there is the most growth. Both the US and Asian markets are important to support particular strategies related to Boral. Boral has made major acquisitions in Asia's plasterboard business and also acquired other businesses as part of an intensive distribution strategy in its home country. At the same time, the company's structure provides enough flexibility and scope in order to divest or get rid of non-performing areas in different parts of the world, to the extent that the company looked forward to 'consolidating the benefits of recent acquisitions and restructuring by continuing a Group wide performance improvement plan to maximise cash flow from existing assets'.[13]

It is relatively easy to see the advantages of a multidivisional structure in companies such as Boral Limited (see table 9.3). Decentralised multidivisional structures help to ensure rapid response to fast-changing environments that require multiple tasking across projects and programs. At the same time, however, innovation is more confined to a division and it is difficult for the corporate parent to allocate pooled resources and share synergies across divisions.

Matrix structures

Whatever the primary basis for grouping, all companies that embrace multiple products, multiple functions and multiple locations must coordinate across all three dimensions. Organisational structures that formalise coordination and control across multiple dimensions are called **matrix structures**.

Many diversified, multinational companies, including Telstra, Philips, Nestlé and Unilever, adopted matrix structures during the 1960s and 1970s, although in all cases one dimension of the matrix tended to be dominant in terms of authority. During the past two decades, most large corporations have either dismantled or reorganised their matrix structures. For example, Shell abandoned its matrix during 1995 and 1996 in favour of a structure based on four business sectors: upstream, downstream, chemicals, and gas and power.

FIGURE 9.5   Multidivisional structure for Boral

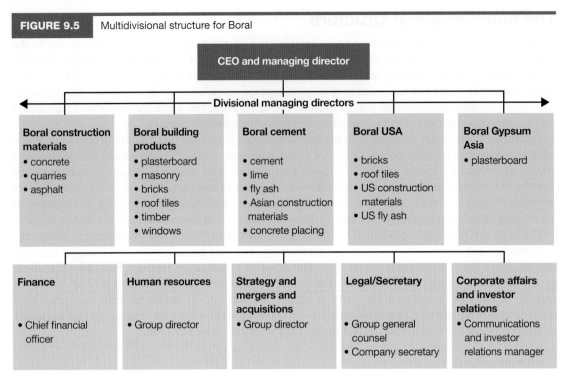

Source: Boral Australia, 2012.

TABLE 9.3   Advantages and disadvantages of multidivisional structures

Advantages	Disadvantages
Suited to fast change	Innovation growth restricted to existing divisions
High product, project or program visibility	Difficult to allocate pooled resources
Task responsibility and contact points are clear	Shared functions hard to coordinate
Multiple tasks are processed in parallel	Possible internal task conflicts
Focus is on performance in SBUs	Difficult for parent to add value

In fast-moving business environments companies have found that the benefits from formally coordinating across multiple dimensions have been outweighed by excessive complexity, larger head office staffs, slower decision making and diffused authority. Some management researchers observed that matrix structures 'led to conflict and confusion; the proliferation of channels created informational logjams as a proliferation of committees and reports bogged down the organisation; and overlapping responsibilities produced turf battles and a loss of accountability'.[14] Yet, a successful example is the Commonwealth Scientific and Industrial Research Organisation (CSIRO), which is an Australian research organisation that effectively adopts a matrix structure by providing good organisational support for innovative research and the teams undertaking it.[15] The innovation required to build, say, a helicopter may warrant the adoption of a matrix structure in order to reap the greatest benefits. Taking this example (see figure 9.6), the establishment of different project teams suggests that project managers will be responsible for specific projects; however, project staff might work across multiple projects as well, since sharing expert opinions is vital. Notice that a helicopter is a complex innovative 'whole' in terms of its frame, engine, rotors and electrical components. Therefore, it makes sense in such a complex project that managers and project teams will be required to work in a multidimensional way.

The current trend is that the matrix structure is used carefully and discretionally. In fact, complex organisations that comprise multiple products, multiple functions and multiple geographical markets need to coordinate within each of these dimensions. The problem of the matrix organisation is not that it attempts to coordinate across multiple dimensions — in complex organisations such coordination is essential — but that this multiple coordination is over-formalised, resulting in excessive corporate staffs and over-complex systems that slow decision making and dull entrepreneurial initiative. Currently, companies tend to focus formal systems of coordination and control on one dimension, and then allow the other dimensions of coordination to be mainly informal.[16] Generally, matrix organisations can be complex to manage because both project and traditional functional area managers are involved in the organisation, and good interpersonal skills are required (see table 9.4). Task team personnel are often required to work across projects because of the knowledge-sharing opportunities this provides; however, as a result, people may have two bosses and there is a potential for conflict. Nevertheless, when the information and technological requirements are such that a full-time focus on the market or product is needed, a matrix organisation can be helpful[17], mostly because it unleashes the innovation, learning and knowledge required to make complex projects work.

| FIGURE 9.6 | Matrix structure for a helicopter manufacturer |

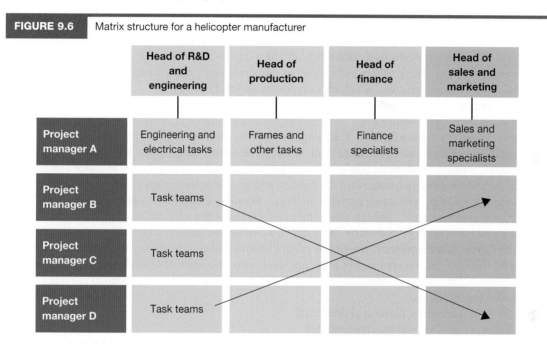

| TABLE 9.4 | Advantages and disadvantages of matrix structures |

Advantages	Disadvantages
Full-time focus of personnel on actual project	Costly to maintain personnel pool to staff matrix
Managers/workers can work across projects	Participants experience dual authority
Knowledge sharing	Little interchange with functional groups outside the matrix, causing duplication of effort
Reduces information requirements as focus is on single product/market	Participants in matrix require good interpersonal skills to maximise work efforts
Brings together specialised technical skills to the product/market	

9.4 What is the strategy evaluation process?

LEARNING OBJECTIVE 9.4 Describe the strategy evaluation process.

Many strategy scholars present the strategic management process as a consequence of several distinctive steps. At the start, companies make decisions about their mission and the objectives of their strategy. The next step is an analysis of the external environment of the companies, which allows managers to identify opportunities and threats. This is followed by an analysis of the internal environment to determine the strengths and weaknesses that companies possess in responding to the opportunities and threats of the external environment. By matching the external opportunities and threats with internal strengths and weaknesses, managers make strategic choices by selecting from the range of strategy alternatives. Top managers compare and evaluate the strategy alternatives to determine their appropriateness for achieving the mission and objectives of the company. As a result of their strategic choices, managers select the strategy alternative that is the most appropriate to the company's mission and goals. This choice is the strategy that will be implemented by the company.

This task requires managers to identify what organisational capabilities have to be developed to achieve the company's goals. **Strategy implementation** is a continuous, hands-on, action-oriented, 'make-it-happen' process that incorporates the following main activities:

- allocating company resources to organisational structures so that the latter have the required funds and staff members to perform the assigned value-creating activities
- initiating strategy-supporting policies and operating procedures
- developing organisational capabilities to reach the company's targeted objectives on schedule
- setting up information, communication and operating systems that enable company staff members to perform allocated tasks effectively and efficiently on a day-to-day basis
- facilitating a positive work culture and climate to support strategy implementation
- establishing a reward structure, which encourages the targeted outcomes.

Strategy implementation requires a strong 'fit' between strategy and organisational capabilities; strategy and the reward structure; strategy and information, communication and operating systems; and strategy and culture. Strategy only matters if it is properly implemented. Strategy implementation is the most time consuming task of strategy management. It has to be supported by many levels and points within the company. Strategy implementation is followed by evaluating the strategy's performance to determine whether the chosen strategy has satisfied the mission and goals that the company set out to achieve.

As Moroney[18] noted, 'evaluation pervades strategy'. **Strategy evaluation** is an important part of strategy. According to Rumelt,[19] 'strategy can neither be formulated nor adjusted to changing circumstances without a process of strategy evaluation'. Strategy as a deliberated pattern, which shows the direction and the performance of the company, would not exist without strategy evaluation. Strategy evaluation was defined by Rumelt[20] as 'the appraisal of plans and the results of plans that centrally concern or affect the basic mission of the enterprise'. Rumelt[21] also stated that the evaluation of strategy should provide answers to the following questions.

- Are the objectives of the business appropriate?
- Are the major policies and plan appropriate?
- Do the results obtained to date confirm or refute critical assumptions on which the strategy rests?

Further, Rumelt[22] identified the following four criteria that managers need to use when selecting from strategic alternatives.

1. *Consistency.* The strategy must not present mutually inconsistent goals and policies.
2. *Consonance.* The strategy must represent an adaptive response to the external environment and to the critical changes occurring within it.
3. *Advantage.* The strategy must provide for the creation and/or maintenance of a competitive advantage in the selected area of activity.
4. *Feasibility.* The strategy must neither overtax available resources nor create unsolvable sub-problems.

In the current dynamic external environment, which exhibits a fast rate of change, companies should be particularly focused on emphasising the second criteria of strategy evaluation: consonance. Indeed, managers have to determine how the chosen strategy is performing: Does it allow a company to achieve its strategic goals? Is it within the set budget? Does it dictate any change of direction? Managers should prioritise a timely evaluation of strategy performance after it has been implemented. In addition, two approaches to strategy evaluation have to be distinguished: (1) an ongoing adjustment of the companys strategy to the changes in the dynamic environment, and (2) an emergent approach to strategy formulation, evaluation and implementation. On the other hand, a strategy evaluation that took place when a certain strategy was implemented can be described as an intended or planned approach to strategy evaluation.

Moroney[23] argues that strategy evaluation should take three forms at different stages of the strategic management process.

1. *Performance evaluation and strategic appraisal* — the first step in developing a new strategy or in the fundamental reappraisal of existing strategy. This involves 'gap' analysis.[24]
2. *Strategy evaluation and selection* — the prospective appraisal of strategy options and the selection of a preferred strategy.

3. *Evaluation and control of strategy outcomes* — this follows strategy implementation to ensure strategic goals are met.

Evaluation also involves the determination of the value of the company's strategy. Managers can compare the value of a strategy before it was chosen with the value of the strategy after it has been implemented. By doing so, managers identify whether the strategy has achieved what it was expected to achieve.[25] Evaluation of strategy performance should be made after the strategy has been implemented, but it has to be an ongoing activity in the company. This ongoing evaluation is commonly known as monitoring. **Monitoring** is an ongoing activity performed within the company to check if a strategy which is being implemented is on the right track. This is particularly critical in the dynamic environment where companies' need for greater flexibility is indisputable. As the chief executive officer (CEO) of Estée Lauder, Peter Jueptner, explained:[26]

> We have a sort of ongoing strategy discussion and a quarterly budget discussion . . . discussing what to do and potentially reallocating some of the resources. It is so much shorter term in terms of how you do your resource allocation . . . Now we are basically changing quarterly and adjusting quarterly.

This approach to flexibility is also relevant to Visa. As its CEO, Niki Manby, explained:[27]

> This word *flexibility* and how we all drive it into our businesses — the word that I think we have to pair that with is *alignment*. You want to be nimble, but at the same time you want to make sure you're turning whole ships and not parts.

Incorporating flexibility and alignment into strategy implementation and ongoing monitoring will help to ensure that any problem does not go undetected and is corrected in a prompt manner. Such ongoing corrections are particularly relevant for an *emergent* approach to strategy formulation, evaluation and implementation which was discussed earlier.

In many instances, managers do not evaluate strategies if the company performs successfully — the company is making a profit, customers are satisfied and employees are content. However, it can be argued that managers still need to evaluate successful strategies in order to determine the key success factors. Strategies can be successful due to external factors. For example, many resource sector companies in Australia have enjoyed high growth rates in the 2000s due to China's growing demand for natural resources. Such success might be temporary and the companies have limited control over it. In order to sustain successful performance and competitive advantage, companies have to understand the factors determining successful performance. The tools used to evaluate strategy are also used in other management processes, such as strategy formulation and performance measurement. Moroney[28] categorises the three groups of evaluative tools as:

1. *strategic* — using techniques such as 'SWOT analysis', 'achievement of objectives' and 'closing the planning gap' to develop the strategic alternatives being evaluated at the stage of strategic choice
2. *financial* — returns on investments, level of risk, based on standard measures of organisational performance
3. *organisational* — acceptability, involvement, internal fit and consistency, motivational.

These three groups of evaluating tools can be applied to a company mentioned in the introduction of this chapter. At Inditex, one of the largest fashion retailers in the world, the *strategic* goal is 'to create beautiful, ethical, quality products that are not only right for our customers, but right for the people who work for us, right for communities and right for the environment'.[29] *Financial* categories of evaluation include standard measures of performance: targeted profit margin, payments on schedule and controllable economic growth. *Organisational* categories include maintaining a friendly, informal culture, building and maintaining strong partnerships with business associates (supplier and delivery companies), and involving customers and fashion influencers in the company sales.

9.5 Scenario planning in strategy evaluation

LEARNING OBJECTIVE 9.5 Explain how scenario planning can be used for strategy evaluation.

In a complex market and dynamic environment, Makridakis and Gaba argue, 'traditional tools of strategic planning, such as extrapolations of past trends, are unlikely to produce reliable forecasts in the medium or long term'.[30] Furthermore, such techniques do not allow companies to make accurate estimates about the level of uncertainty that is associated with these forecasts. On the contrary, **scenario planning** can be used to avoid the pitfalls of more traditional methods. The US Army developed scenario planning and war gaming in the 1950s. Scenario planning involves the structural use of management judgement to construct multiple 'script-like characterisations of possible futures'.[31] These characteristics focus on the dynamics of how a particular future might unfold by studying causal relationships, dominating trends, the behaviour of key players and internal consistency. 'The resulting multiple scenarios attempt to bound the uncertainties that are seen to be inherent in the future',[32] write Goodwin and Wright. This tool enables companies to evaluate a given strategy under the range of possible futures that might develop.

Most commonly, scenario planning is used in the evaluation of proposed strategies and the strategic choice of the most appropriate strategic alternative. The process of evaluation may identify and include new ideas and, therefore, lead to the formulation of new strategies.[33] The ticks in the matrix shown in Figure 9.7[34] reflect positive performance of a strategy under a given scenario — the more ticks, the better the performance. Crosses show negative performance. Of the three strategies being evaluated Goodwin and Wright suggest 'strategy 1 [with the least number of crosses] offers the least worst negative performance, or in other words, maximum option'. Note that the table is constructed for the purpose of comparison of the three numbered strategies — after this comparison 'the strategy' will be selected. The selected strategy may be judged as the most robust option; however, a decision to adopt strategy 1 would mean high aversion to risk on the part of the decision makers. The new ideas generated in the process of strategy evaluation have led, in figure 9.7, to the design of a new strategy that clearly prevails over the alternatives in that it will perform at least as well under the entire range of scenarios.[35]

FIGURE 9.7 Testing the performance of strategies against scenarios

	Scenario 1	Scenario 2	Scenario 3
Strategy 1	✔✔✔	✔	✘
Strategy 2	✘✘	✔	✔
Strategy 3	✔✔	✘✘	✔✔✔
New strategy	✔✔✔	✔✔✔	✔✔✔

Source: Goodwin & Wright, 2001.

The evaluation of strategy within the scenario planning process has to meet the following criteria.[36]

- *Transparency* — the presentation of results that can be understood and trusted. The process of scenario planning should be clear to all managers from various divisions of the company. The decision makers can share common knowledge and enhance communication among them.
- *Ease of judgement* — less chance of errors in the process of questioning and reasoning. This can be achieved by judgement performed in a number of simple steps familiar to the decision makers. Simplicity of the judgement process and the limits placed on its duration will also avoid boredom and fatigue among the decision makers.
- *Versatility* — the evaluation should be able to incorporate both financial and nonfinancial objectives. It is important to avoid focusing only on the more easily measured financial outcomes and include a broader range of attributes, such as risk, interest rates, currency exchange and government warranties to certain businesses.
- *Flexibility* — changes in perspective can be accommodated as insights and understanding increase, and alternative perspectives of different participants in the decision-making process can be modelled and compared.

Scenario planning should be primarily used as a preliminary phase in the decision-making process.[37] This will enable decision makers to clarify their ideas before moving on to a formal decision analysis method that has been designed to support decision making under conditions of uncertainty.

9.6 The McKinsey 7-S model for strategy evaluation and execution

LEARNING OBJECTIVE 9.6 Recognise how different evaluation frameworks such as the McKinsey 7-S support the strategy evaluation process.

The discussion so far has focused on choosing the most appropriate strategy among alternatives; however, in order to achieve the desired performance targets, companies should support their chosen strategies with the appropriate mechanisms of strategy implementation. Strategy implementation should incorporate a broad range of interrelated changes. Often changes occurring only in some selected areas are hardly able to make any significant organisational change. To change organisational course, managers have to deal with interrelated and often overlapping attributes.

If the various areas and processes of a company are all in complete alignment, the company is successful. A good way of presenting these various elements is through the '7-S model'. This model was introduced by McKinsey Company partners' Peters and Waterman in their book *In Search of Excellence*. The model describes the following seven factors critical for effective strategy execution.[38]

1. *Strategy*. The positioning and actions taken by an enterprise in response to or anticipation of changes in the external environment, intended to achieve competitive advantage.
2. *Structure*. The way in which tasks and people are specialized and divided, and authority is distributed; how activities and reporting relationships are grouped; the mechanisms by which activities in the organization are coordinated.
3. *Systems*. The formal and informal procedures used to manage the organization, including management control systems, performance measurement and reward systems, planning, budgeting and resource allocation systems, and management information systems.
4. *Staff*. The people, their backgrounds and competencies; how the organization recruits, selects, trains, socializes, manages the careers, and promotes employees.
5. *Skills*. The distinctive competencies of the organization; what it does best along dimensions such as people, management practices, processes, systems, technology, and customer relationships.
6. *Style/culture*. The leadership style of managers — how they spend their time, what they focus attention on, what questions they ask of employees, how they make decisions; also the organizational culture (the dominant values and beliefs, the norms, the conscious and unconscious symbolic acts taken by leaders (job titles, dress codes, executive dining rooms, corporate jets, informal meetings with employees).
7. *Shared values*. The core or fundamental set of values that are widely shared in the organization and serve as guiding principles of what is important; vision, mission, and values statements that provide a broad sense of purpose for all employees.

Prior to the introduction of the 7-S model, the authors tried to search for a perfect organisational structure that would enable the company to achieve excellent performance. They concluded, however, that structure alone could not solve the problem of how to coordinate resource allocation, incentives and actions across large companies. The 7-S model sends the message that companies are successful when they achieve an integrated harmony among the three 'hard Ss' of strategy, structure and systems, and the four 'softer Ss of skills, staff, style and superordinate goals (now referred to as shared values). The main contribution of this model is that (1) it posits that there are many factors that determine a company's performance, (2) these factors have to align with each other and (3) all these factors are equally important and there is neither a start nor a finish in this model.

The 7-S model continues to be used in practice as a diagnostic and prescriptive framework for organisational alignment. Within the academic literature, economists and strategy scholars tend to emphasise the tangible and measurable 'hard Ss' of strategy, structure and systems through studies of the impact of mergers, alternative organisational forms, and incentive and reward systems. Scholars in other social sciences (organisation behaviour, psychology and sociology) pay more attention to the intangible and difficult-to-measure 'softer Ss' of skills, staff, style and shared values.[39]

The 7-S model can be used to evaluate strategy implementation by identifying the strategy and assessing whether changes need to be made to any of the factors for a better alignment. If the company's strategy is not working, it could demand a re-evaluation of the strategy. If a companys strategy is cost leadership, then the 'staff' should ensure that people are rewarded for cost savings, using fewer resources and making fewer mistakes. The 'systems' should ensure that the monitoring measures track cost savings and efficiency. The 'structure is flat and allows the combination of functions. The 'style' should encourage looking for innovations and efficiency.

The 7-S model is well aligned with another model, the balanced scorecard (BSC), which was introduced by Norton and Kaplan[40] in 1992, ten years after the introduction of the 7-S model. The balanced scorecard methodology provides an integrated framework for balancing financial and strategic goals, and extending these balanced performance measures down the organisation to individual business units and departments. Both the 7-S and the balanced scorecard models articulate that effective strategy implementation requires a multidimensional approach. Both models stress interconnectedness and assist managers to align their organisation for effective strategy execution. As Kaplan argues:

> The BSC is not only fully consistent with the 7-S framework, but can also enhance it in use. The BSC's most obvious benefit arises when managers use it to design a customized reporting and performance management system. (…) The BSC also influences other organisational systems when managers use it to align their planning, budgeting, and resource allocation systems, and their incentive and reward systems to strategy.[41]

9.7 Strategy evaluation in uncertain times

LEARNING OBJECTIVE 9.7 Discuss the importance of strategy evaluation in uncertain times.

Companies require flexibility in decision making in uncertain times. This is also relevant to strategy evaluation. In a time of a rapid, fundamental, and universally perceptible change, expanding roles of governments, re-evaluation of imbalances in global trade and capital markets, and pervasive uncertainty, companies have to continuously reassess their business models to unlock unexpected opportunities. It is imperative that companies engage in uncertainty and use scenario planning in order to become resilient and flexible to contend with any factors of the environment.[42] The dynamic environment makes it critically important for the company to make decisions when the time is right. Companies have to develop and sharpen their skills of truly 'dynamic management'.[43] If companies delay their decisions, the costs of opportunities may rise, the costs of investments may escalate, and losses can accumulate. At the same time, decisions made too early can lead to bad choices or excessive exposure to risks. Furthermore, companies have to be able to evaluate their performance in a much shorter time frame and respond appropriately. The role of an emergent strategy is to assist managers to adjust their companies to the fast changing, unpredictable and uncertain environment. The environment also changes organisational goals. As a result, managers have to evaluate their strategies against the changed goals rather than their original goals. Managers should adopt 'decision making under uncertainty' techniques such as scenario planning and decision science (using decision trees is beyond the scope of this book; this special knowledge can be gained from textbooks and courses on decision science). This will allow managers to gain a greater appreciation of the power of collective insight in volatile times, when information is fragmentary and fast moving.[44]

Strategy evaluation requires managerial responsibility and accountability for those decisions and actions. This means assessment of the ability of managers to identify factors critical to the success of their companies, execute chosen strategies, communicate the company's goals and objectives to the people at all levels of their organisation, motivate their personnel, and facilitate knowledge transfer within the company as well as throughout the entire value creation network. Uncertainty of the external environment demands an ongoing strategy evaluation and appropriate adjustment to a chosen strategy and its implementation.

SUMMARY

Companies perform evaluation of their strategy three times: first, company managers assess the mission statement and objectives to understand if it is still relevant; next, strategic alternatives are assessed and the best one chosen; and last, when a certain strategy is implemented, managers evaluate performance of that strategy. Strategy formulation and further adjustments to the changing environment require strategy evaluation.

Strategy evaluation is defined as 'the appraisal of plans and the results of plans that centrally concern or affect the basic mission of the enterprise'. Managers have to evaluate strategies, not only in the case of unsuccessful performance, but also if the company performs successfully. Managers need to evaluate successful strategies in order to determine the key success factors.

The fast-moving market environment and market complexity challenge companies to look for alternatives to the traditional tools of strategic planning and for new methods of forecasting, as well as estimating the uncertainty that is associated with these forecasts. For example, scenario planning can be used to get a comprehensive picture of possible developments of the company associated with the choice of various strategic alternatives. Scenario planning involves the structural use of managerial judgement to construct multiple 'script-like characterisations of possible futures'. Scenario planning is used in the evaluation of proposed strategic alternatives and the choice of the best strategic alternative.

The McKinsey 7-S model represents a framework for effective management and evaluation of the company's performance. It describes the seven factors critical for effective strategy execution: strategy, structure, systems, staff, skills, style/culture and shared values. Organisational structure alone could not solve the problem of how to coordinate resource allocation, incentives and actions across large companies. The 7-S model sends the message that companies are successful when they achieve an integration of the three 'hard Ss' of strategy, structure and systems, and the four 'soft Ss' of skills, staff, style and superordinate goals (now referred to as shared values). The main contribution of this model is that (1) it argues that there are multiple factors that determine a company's performance; (2) these factors are interrelated with each other and have to align with each other; and (3) all these factors are equally important and there is neither a start nor a finish in this model.

Strategy implementation is inseparable from strategy formulation. Organisational structure and systems are central to the fundamental issues of competitive advantage and strategy choice. In particular, the existence of organisational capability is critical to strategy implementation. While business enterprises continue to experiment with new organisational forms, some fundamental principles need to be observed carefully. These include the need to reconcile specialisation with coordination and cooperation, understand the hierarchy in and principles of organisation design, and select the appropriate structural forms. Effective management systems for coordination and control are important. This refers especially to information, strategic planning, financial planning and control, and human resource management systems. There is an obvious need to integrate different control mechanisms and implement effective change management.

KEY TERMS

cooperation problem The problem of different organisational members having conflicting goals.

matrix structures Organisational structures that formalise coordination and control across multiple dimensions.

monitoring An ongoing activity performed in the company to check if a strategy that is being implemented is on the right track.

scenario planning The structural use of management judgement to construct multiple script-like characterisations of possible futures.

strategy evaluation The appraisal of plans and results of plans that centrally concern or affect the basic mission of the enterprise.

strategy implementation Putting a chosen alternative into place, carrying it out proficiently and producing desired outcomes.

SELF-STUDY QUESTIONS

1 What are the advantages and disadvantages of functional, multidivisional and matrix-based organisational structures in strategic management? Support your answer with relevant examples.

2 Identify and describe the various possible forms of strategic control that are relevant to organisational restructuring.

3 Explain why companies have to use strategy evaluation to formulate and adjust their strategies. What are the stages of the strategic management process at which companies evaluate strategies?

4 What is scenario planning and how does it assist companies in making informed strategic choice while assessing alternatives?

5 What are the factors of successful performance of companies according to the McKinsey 7-S model?

DISCUSSION QUESTIONS

1 'Formulating strategy used to be a one-off task, but nowadays it is an ongoing and continuous process.' Do you agree with this statement? Explain your reasoning.

2 'The company value is more important than the shareholders' value.' Do you agree with this statement? Why or why not?

3 Do you think speed of organisational response to market changes is the most critical factor for company performance? Explain your position.

4 'In uncertain macroeconomic conditions, scrutiny of the relationship between business and society is higher and companies focus their corporate social responsibility efforts to boost their impact in a resource-constrained environment.' Discuss this statement.

5 Consider a scenario where a company shifts to become more innovative, but retains its current divisional-product based structure. What things might have to change inside the company? Why?

6 Explain (with reference to a diversified, divisionalised company such as Wesfarmers, Australia's biggest diversified company) the extent to which the multidivisional company may be regarded as a modular organisation. To what degree is each division an independent entity?

EXERCISES

1 Visit the Shell website at www.shell.com and identify how the company uses scenario planning techniques in strategy evaluation.

2 Collect information regarding Ford Australia. Explain how the company's business model has evolved over the years. What strategies has the company adopted in recent years? What underlying economic logic explains the company's choice of business strategy?

3 Identify a company that has recently undertaken organisational restructuring. What are the major changes and are they successful?

4 Obtain the organisational charts of two corporations. Compare and contrast their similarities and differences. Explain the underlying rationale as to why they are different.

5 Review the latest annual report for a Malaysian bank. Analyse how the bank is structured and how it links structure and strategy.

6 Form a small group of three to four members. With reference to your university, each try to analyse the management systems for coordination and control (such as information, strategic planning, financial planning and control, and human resource management systems). Report your findings back to the group. As a group try to identify the basic hierarchy and structure of the university.

7 Collect information on the management control system of a specific company. Based on your online searches, how does this management control system relate to the organisational structure of the company?

8 Describe the stated culture of the multinational company Rio Tinto. Examine recent analyst reports or articles about this company and explain the gaps between the company's stated culture and how it is reported in the media.

FURTHER READING

Barnet, ML & Salomon, RM 2012, 'Does it pay to be really good? Addressing the shape of the relationship between social and financial performance', *Strategic Management Journal,* vol. 33, no. 11, 1304–1320.

Daniels, JD & Krug, JA 2008, *Multinational enterprise theory: Volume III, Organizational structure and control,* JD Daniels (ed.), SAGE library in marketing.

Diefenbach, T & Sillence, JAA 2011, 'Formal and informal hierarchy in different types of organization', *Organization Studies,* vol. 32, no. 1, 1515–1537.

Jacobides, MG, Winter, SG & Kassberger, SM 2012, 'The dynamics of wealth, profit, and sustainable advantage', *Strategic Management Journal,* vol. 33, no. 12, 1384–1410.

Manzoni, JF 2012, 'Building and nurturing a high performance – High integrity corporate culture', in MJ Epstein, JF Manzoni and A Davila (eds.), *Performance and management control: advancing global practice,* Emerald.

Ming, G & Tse, E 2010, 'Building innovative organizations in China: The "execution+" organization', *Asia Pacific Journal of Management,* vol. 27, no. 1, 25–53.

Nandakumar, MK, Ghobadian, A & ORegan, N 2010, 'Business-level strategy and performance: the moderating effects of environment and structure', *Management Decision,* vol. 48, no. 6, 907–939.

Parnell, JA, Lester, DL, Zhang, L & Mehmet, AK 2012, 'How environmental uncertainty affects the link between business strategy and performance in SMEs', *Management Decision,* vol. 50, no. 4, 546–568.

Yip, G 2004, 'Using strategy to change your business model, *Business Strategy Review,* vol. 15, no. 2, 17–24.

Zand, DE 2009, 'Strategic renewal: how an organization realigned structure with strategy', *Strategy Leadership,* vol. 37, no. 3, 23–35.

ENDNOTES

1. See *The Report of the BP U.S. Refineries Independent Safety Review Panel* (January 2007).
2. T Peters, 'Strategy follows structure', *California Management Review,* vol. 26 (Spring 1984): 114–128.
3. G Hamel, CK Prahalad, 'Strategic intent', *Harvard Business Review,* May–June, 1989.
4. R Whittington, A Pettigrew, S Peck, E Fenton, and M Conyon, 'Change and complementarities in the new competitive landscape', *Organisation Science,* vol. 10, 1999, 583–596.
5. H Mintzberg, *Structure in fives: designing effective organisations,* Englewood Cliffs: Prentice Hall, 1993, p. 2.
6. A Smith, *The wealth of nations,* London: Dent, 1910, p. 5.
7. S Ross, 'The economic theory of agency, *American Economic Review,* vol. 63, 1973, 134–139; K Eisenhardt, 'Agency theory: an assessment and reviews', *Academy of Management Review,* vol. 14, 1989, 57–74.
8. M Conyon, S Peck, G Sadler, and L Read, 'The structure of executive compensation contracts: UK evidence', *Long Range Planning,* vol. 33, 2000, 478–503.
9. WG Ouchi, *Theory Z,* Reading, MA: Addison-Wesley, 1981.
10. 'Apple Inc mission statement is not very innovative and barely a mission at all', http://retailindustry.about.com.
11. AD Chandler, Strategy and structure, Cambridge: MIT Press, 1962, 382–383.
12. http://heritage.dupont.com/floater/fl_management/floater.shtml.
13. *Boral Limited Annual Report, 2012,* Boral Limited, 2012, p. 5.
14. CA Bartlett and S Ghoshal, 'Matrix management: not a structure, a frame of mind', *Harvard Business Review,* July–August 1990, 138–145.
15. G Syme, 'Integration initiatives at CSIRO: reflections of an insider', *Journal of Research Practice,* vol. 1, no. 2, 2005.
16. 'A survey of the company: the new organisation', *The Economist,* 19 January 2006.
17. R Duncan, 'What is the right organization structure? Decision tree analysis provides the answer', *Organizational Dynamics,* Winter, 1979, 59–80.
18. M Moroney, 'Strategy evaluation: towards an updated paradigm', *Irish Business and Administrative Research,* vol. 21, no. 1, 2000, 103–129.
19. RP Rumelt, 'Evaluating business strategy', in H Mintzberg et al., *The strategy process,* London: Prentice Hall Europe, 1998, 91–100.
20. ibid., 100.
21. ibid., 91.
22. ibid., 92.
23. Moroney, op. cit., 108–110.
24. J Billsberry, 'Gap analysis', in V Ambrosini with G Johnson and K Scholes (eds), *Exploring techniques of analysis and evaluation in strategic management,* London: Prentice Hall Europe, 1998, 219–228.
25. J Rose and M Hayne, 'A soft system approach to the evaluation of complex interventions in the public sector', *Journal of Applied Management,* vol. 8, 1999, 199–216.
26. 'Navigating the new normal: a conversation with four chief strategy officers', *McKinsey Quarterly,* December 2009.
27. ibid.
28. Moroney, op. cit.
29. Inditex, 'How we do business. Right to wear', www.inditex.com/en/how-we-do-business/right-to-wear.
30. S Makridakis and A Gaba, 'Judgement: its role and value for strategy', in G Wright and P Goodwin, P. (eds.), *Forecasting with judgement,* Chichester: John Wiley Sons, Inc., 1998.
31. PJH Schoemaker, 'When and how to use scenario planning', *Journal of Forecasting,* vol. 10, iss. 6, 549–564.
32. P Goodwin and G Wright, 'Enhancing strategy evaluation in scenario planning: a role for decision analysis', *Journal of Management Studies,* vol. 38, no. 1, 2001, 1–16.

33. ibid.

34. ibid., 4.

35. ibid.

36. ibid., 1–16.

37. Schoemaker, op. cit.

38. R Waterman, T Peters, and J Phillips, 'Structure is not organization', *Business Horizons, Business Horizons*, vol. 23, no. 3, 14–26; R Kaplan, 'How the balanced scorecard complements the McKinsey 7-S Model, *Strategy Leadership*, vol. 33, no. 3, 2005, 41–46.

39. Kaplan, 2005, op. cit.

40. RS Kaplan and DP Norton, *The strategy focused organization*, Boston: Harvard Business Review, September-October, 1993.

41. RS Kaplan, 'How the balanced scorecard complements the McKinsey 7-S Model', *Strategy Leadership*, vol. 33, no. 3, 2005, 41–46.

42. AP Webb, 'Setting strategy in the new era: a conversation with Lowell Bryan and Richard Rumelt', *McKinsey Quarterly*, June 2009, 1–4.

43. L Bryan, 'Dynamic management: better decisions in uncertain times', *McKinsey Quarterly*, 2009, 4.

44. ibid.

ACKNOWLEDGEMENTS

Photo: © Tommy Lee Walker / Shutterstock.com

Extract: 'Mission-Driven Mobility: Strengthening Our Government Through a Mobile Leadership Corps.' Copyright © 2012 by Partnership for Public Service and McKinsey Company. All rights reserved.

Figure 9.5: © Boral Australia

Figure 9.7: © P Goodwin and G Wright, 'Enhancing strategy evaluation in scenario planning: a role for decision analysis', *Journal of Management Studies,* vol. 38, no. 1, 2001, 1–16.

CHAPTER 10

Leading strategically and developing corporate culture

LEARNING OBJECTIVES

After studying this chapter, you should be able to:

10.1 identify what it means to lead strategically in the global corporation

10.2 review how leaders build adaptive capacity, and how they acquire and assimilate knowledge in ways that transform current stocks of knowledge

10.3 distinguish between the principles of operational and strategic agility that enable organisations to effectively cope with change and uncertainty

10.4 review how CEOs achieve transformational behaviours, build top management teams, encourage adaptation and innovation, and acquire and share knowledge

10.5 think about leading strategically as a human capital resource for building global talent and building shared knowledge

10.6 ascertain how to develop a company's corporate culture and to integrate its benefits, and classify the relationship between leading strategically and corporate culture

10.7 apply ethical leadership principles to leadership in action.

Leading strategically at Shire Pharma

The following quote from the CEO of Shire, a leading global pharmaceutical company, encapsulates the strategic leadership priority of any global leader.

If we don't adapt as an industry, someone else will do it for us. Take logistics; if you have a medicine you keep in your refrigerator at home, it will have a chip that says it's a week from expiring so you should think about reordering it, or it will automatically reorder for you. That's not so far out. But how will it affect the way we operate? What does a CEO need to do?[1]

This quote, particularly in relation to adaptation and keeping ahead of fast-moving technological breakthroughs in both logistics and technological application, is the thought topic of leading CEOs.[2] For instance, 75 CEOs and board chairs recently indicated that two major challenges involved (1) how to prepare for constant disruption, and (2) how to manage the transition into the top job by assessing whether to make moves early versus taking the time to assess and reflect. Take Shire, for instance. As a leading global biotechnology organisation, Shire focuses on serving people with rare diseases and highly specialised conditions with a charter to develop and deliver breakthrough therapies for people with life-altering conditions.[3] With so many stakeholders to please, from patients, to their families, to physicians, to employees plus a range of diverse suppliers and biotech partners around the world, the former CEO of Shire (Flemming Ørnskov) reflected on how to lead strategically and how the pharma company had lifted its margins to 44 per cent from 36 per cent. Leading strategically was reflected across a number of complementary themes from developing a cohesive culture, targeting strategic acquisitions, creating 'scale' by developing a diversified portfolio through manufacturing capabilities and commercial infrastructure in different countries, and by creating a clear vision to be the leading biotech in rare diseases and highly specialised conditions. Ørnskov achieved these goals by creating a more unified 'One Shire' out of many separate businesses, including by relocating different companies to other countries to achieve the scale objective. By establishing fact-based relationships and rules of interaction, the CEO was able to build trust with the board, resulting in a $4 billion acquisition in similar and supporting industries. In addition to other acquisitions, this evolved from $160 million to almost $50 billion in acquisition spending.[4]

Leaning on the notion that CEOs need to be leaders not managers, the CEO was able to build a story that the company was on a journey to deliver a leading-edge global pharma company which he continuously repeated to his staff and the board. The idea of storytelling led to investors 'going the distance' and understanding Ørnskov's long-term goal direction and why certain decisions needed to be taken. This led to increasing trust as results improved and investors and staff came to appreciate how the CEO and his team delivered on their transition-to-growth goals. Strategic focus was how science collided with unmet needs, with Ørnskov adopting a 'physician' approach to taking notes, analysing the symptoms, looking at the findings, and building pictures about what this might look like. According to Ørnskov, he needed to be three steps ahead of his organisation by leading the integration of ideas, having small groups of thought partners, and by moving away from disparate devices for solving health problems to clusters of products that combined up-to-date expertise and interactivity through cutting-edge manufacturing, devices and diagnostics. Here, leading strategically was less about sales and marketing and more focused on technology, R&D, new commercial models and support. The CEO saw himself as the face of the company with a need to build an organisation that was open to change, that was adaptable, which in turn could contribute to change in the industry. The successes of Shire are an example of what it takes to lead strategically within an environment of constant disruption, which is the daily reality for many global leaders.

Introduction

The opening scene setter tells us much about leading strategically, touching on the key themes of adaptation and change, knowledge acquisition and staying close to the customer, storytelling and building corporate culture, communicating and establishing vision, and embracing technological change, among others. First, leading strategically invokes leader actions that assist any organisation to achieve both short- and long-term goals and to adapt to complex situations through strategic agility. **Leading strategically** — which is often called 'strategic leadership' — is about how to communicate a vision for the future, and how to apply strategic decisions in ways that develop an organisation's capabilities and competencies as a bedrock for strategic action. It also concerns how to build an effective culture[5] while simultaneously acquiring and sharing knowledge as a basis for strategic action. *Strategic agility,* on the other hand, concerns how organisations as a whole flexibly respond to complex, global and dynamic environments.[6] Leaders are tasked with establishing the long-term direction for their companies while developing the capabilities for their organisations to adapt and the means to respond to global events and constant disruption.

In this chapter, we introduce several leadership themes related to strategic, transformational, adaptive and agile leadership. Based on contemporary research, we espouse the ideas and principles of adaptive leadership and strategic agility and then discuss how these principles are part of transformational leadership. Because of the constant disruption being increasingly realised in international environments, we explain how leadership actions can be applied in transformational situations and we provide many examples of leading strategically. We also discuss how adaptive leadership principles relate to global change and disruption.

In this chapter, we discuss the key themes and priorities that must be established by top leaders to invoke a number of performance measures. We also examine how leaders build internal dynamic capability, the importance of acquiring and sharing knowledge that increases a company's adaptive ability, and how leaders develop and identify global talent. We discuss how different forms of human capital become critical for building an organisation's human capital resource, which is the responsibility of top leaders, especially if they are going to be competitive within global environments.

Within the strategy and change literature, experts highlight the key relationship between leadership and culture.[7] Accordingly, we discuss this unique relationship within the context of developing corporate culture, creating core values, how norms are embedded and how basic assumptions provide meaning and purpose to global organisations. Leading strategically is after all how top leaders communicate meaning and purpose internally and externally. The chapter outlines several key principles related to ethical leadership since leading strategically cannot occur within a vacuum of behaviour that is devoid of corporate responsibility and developing the moral actions of the leader.

Taken together, this chapter explores these key themes in ways that help global leaders to develop a set of actions that can be applied in practice. Here, we are less interested in talking *about* leading strategically and developing corporate culture than highlighting through practical explanation *how* the principles outlined can be applied. All of the ideas and themes embodied in this chapter are based on contemporary research, which informs the discussions. We integrate the ideas of this chapter with the strategic development, formulation and implementation of earlier chapters. For instance, leading strategically is critical for the success of corporate-level strategy and building the diversified company, and relevant to the discussions of global strategies and the multinational corporation. This chapter is also functionally related to how the company engages in the internal analysis of its capabilities and core competencies and is the basis of how companies determine and build their competitive advantage through the actions of top leaders. We now turn to the first broad topic and the dynamics of leading strategically.

10.1 Leading strategically

LEARNING OBJECTIVE 10.1 Identify what it means to lead strategically in the global corporation.

To lead strategically means to understand how a number of different leadership approaches can be applied in contemporary contexts. First, the context that underpins all of the discussions in this chapter is one of *constant change and disruption*, be it continuous change within the global company, or the need to manage crisis in the face of wider global events. An example of such an event was the COVID-19 global pandemic of 2020 that left many organisations and their managers with urgent change agendas, leading to company closures, significant workforce losses, and an over-reliance on government-led bailouts on the back of falling sales and market share. Here, companies that had been better prepared strategically were able to adapt relatively quickly while those that were merely repeating their business models from one year to the next, often with very large corporate debt, found it difficult to survive. So, a useful question to consider is what kinds of leadership actions enable global organisations to survive within a constant state of unrest? Additionally, what kinds of capital are important to enable survival in times of crisis and constant disruption? To answer these questions, we need to ask ourselves what it means to lead strategically.

What does it mean to lead strategically?

To lead strategically means to move away from a number of supervisory leadership approaches that focus on tasks and person-oriented behaviours designed to provide feedback, guidance and support to subordinates.[8] Some of these include path–goal theories, leader–member exchange and servant leadership with a specific focus on motivating followers to achieve higher order behaviours[9] and to be highly engaged. While motivating followers within the day-to-day activities of the company is very important, leading strategically, by comparison, concerns the creation of meaning and purpose for the organisation.[10]

Leading strategically has five foundational pillars (see figure 10.1).

1. *Adaptive capacity* — the ability of the global company to change by focusing on innovation and continuous learning.[11] Here, adaptive leaders understand how to change the internal dimensions of the company in response to external events.
2. *Absorptive capacity* — the ability to continuously learn and build dynamic capability through the capacity to recognise new information, assimilate it, and apply it to new ends and means, while offensively and defensively improving the fit between a company and its environment.[12]
3. *Operational* and *strategic agility*[13] — constantly improving existing products and inventing market-creating innovations.
4. CEO *behavioural dimensions, responsibilities and performance* — the ability of the CEO to empower the team for innovation, manage human talent and plan for succession.[14]
5. *Building the corporate culture*[15] — integrative leadership priorities with guiding values and behaviours throughout the organisation.

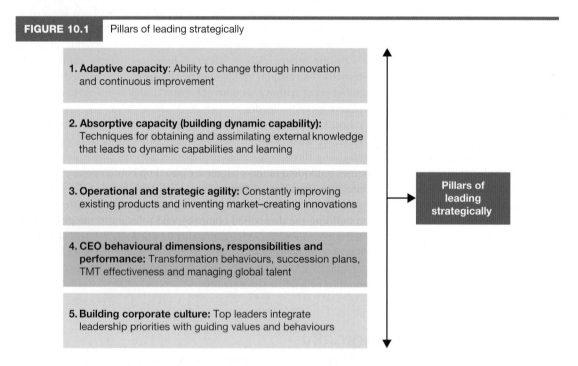

FIGURE 10.1   Pillars of leading strategically

1. Adaptive capacity: Ability to change through innovation and continuous improvement

2. Absorptive capacity (building dynamic capability): Techniques for obtaining and assimilating external knowledge that leads to dynamic capabilities and learning

3. Operational and strategic agility: Constantly improving existing products and inventing market–creating innovations

4. CEO behavioural dimensions, responsibilities and performance: Transformation behaviours, succession plans, TMT effectiveness and managing global talent

5. Building corporate culture: Top leaders integrate leadership priorities with guiding values and behaviours

Pillars of leading strategically

Without these collective pillars, the capacity to lead strategically will be severely limited.

Let's now turn to discussing adaptive capacity as the first of these pillars for leading strategically.

10.2 Adaptive capacity and transformational learning

LEARNING OBJECTIVE 10.2   Review how leaders build adaptive capacity, and how they acquire and assimilate knowledge in ways that transform current stocks of knowledge.

Adaptive capacity

Adaptive leaders help people deal with change and their response to changing environments[16] in ways that better enable the organisation to effectively cope with uncertainty. *Adaptive capacity*, by comparison, refers to the ability of any organisation as a whole to unleash the potential of its systems and people in ways that allow it to adjust and adapt to shifting environments.[17] Strategy capsule 10.2 illustrates how a company might achieve this. Adaptive capacity involves a complex process comprising multiple dimensions, including situational challenges, leader behaviours and adaptive work.

As shown in figure 10.1, adaptive capacity is the first pillar of leading strategically. It comprises a systems perspective, a sociological perspective, a service orientation and a psychological perspective. From a *systems perspective*, problems are often embedded within a range of internal systems. For instance, when a company is slow to react to change and tends to converge around well-known decision paths, its management information system may be too slow to receive signals from the environment in ways that demand change, possibly filtering out important information.[18] Similarly, think of any internal system such as an inventory system (often called a material condition). If a leader changes and updates the inventory system to increase efficiency in response to external demand, she or he needs to also update the social system (often called a social condition), which might concern, for instance, the job specifications and daily routines of employees. So, in addition to a systems perspective, adaptive leaders need to be cognisant of the *sociological perspective*. In such situations, we can see how the adaptive capacity of the company and its leaders results in timely internal change. Adaptive leaders must also consider a *service orientation* where they use their expertise to 'serve the people by diagnosing their problems and by helping them to find solutions to real-world problems'.[19] Adaptive leaders may also rely on a *psychological approach* to enable change, which means helping people to accomplish adaptive behaviour.[20]

Adaptive leaders are confronted by different kinds of situation challenges. *Technical challenges*, for instance, are constant and are defined by what we don't know as explained in the opening scene setter, and *adaptive challenges* require shifts in thinking and changes in perceptions, attitudes and beliefs, which we will discuss further in relation to the second pillar, absorptive capacity. For now, however, we can see how the work of adaptive leaders is to confront the different kinds of adaptive challenges particularly related to the internal dimensions of the global organisation.

CFOs as strategic leaders

Many chief financial officers now have to build skills in areas of their business that are not regarded as traditional finance priorities. What this illustrates is that, increasingly, strategic leaders such as CFOs are required to be resourceful and adaptive to changing needs and new business requirements. This means leaders have to adapt continuously in order to overcome external pressures by finding new investment opportunities for their companies, and by being resourceful internally. In a recent survey of 193 CFOs, more than half suggested that many new priority areas such as risk, regulatory compliance, mergers and acquisitions are part of their responsibility, while 38 per cent included IT in this list.[21] That is, CFOs are now increasingly shifting work priorities to strategic leadership (46 per cent), organisational transformation (45 per cent) and performance management (35 per cent) while responsibilities for capital allocation (24 per cent) are also increasing. These strategic shifts in the work of CFOs suggests that while some traditional job-type roles in companies have been relatively confined to one functional area, new work demands require strategic leaders to work across cross-functional units, suggesting that the work of these strategic leaders is changing. More than ever, they are increasingly required to assert proactive and strategic leadership actions, adopt an investor's mindset for more innovative practices and returns, and embrace technological advances over and above their traditional finance responsibilities.

Absorptive capacity — building dynamic capability

The second pillar of leading strategically shown in figure 10.1 is **absorptive capacity (AC)**. Generally, AC is the ability to learn, recognise new knowledge, assimilate it and apply it to new ends.[22] Many writers expand this definition in the context of leading strategically. For instance, from a learning perspective, AC is the capacity to assimilate knowledge in ways that allow the knowledge learned to be imitated.[23] Since building a stock of knowledge and leveraging it in new and better ways often leads to competitive advantage, finding ways to increase AC is a capability that a company wants to acquire. The AC of a company can become a 'dynamic' capability when it is geared towards creating organisational change, that is, those changes that are strategic in nature[24] which other companies may not possess. AC is thus about developing a set of organisational routines and processes by which companies acquire, assimilate, transform and exploit knowledge in superior ways that lead to dynamic organisational capability[25] and competitive advantage (see the chapter on the nature and sources of competitive advantage).

So, what are the priorities for strategic leaders as a result of creating AC? A 'capacity' is something that is built, developed and learned, so it is useful to understand how strategic leaders achieve this. First, effective leaders enable acquisition skills and routines to be developed so that the top leadership team, middle-level teams and individuals can identify and acquire new knowledge from the environment and embed it within a company's routines, systems and processes. Thus, *acquisition skills* relate to speed, intensity and direction which help determine the quality of a company's acquisition capabilities.[26] A company's routines, systems and processes have to be sophisticated enough to embrace the knowledge that is acquired.[27] While the speed and the quality of what is learned is important in the acquisition stage, the capacity of the company and its leaders to interpret and comprehend the information becomes critical in the *assimilation stage.* If, for instance, human, organisational and social resources are not mature enough to embed the knowledge learned, then the lack of these complementary assets will thwart the potential of the knowledge to be captured and applied.[28]

It is important to note from a learning perspective that acquisition skills, notably intuition and interpretive ability, are mostly attributed to individuals and teams, whereas assimilation and the capacity to explore the insight gained from external sources is mostly a group or team-level ability.[29] AC is also about *transformation* skills, that is, recombining new and existing knowledge in ways that recognise two inconsistent forms of knowledge that foster new innovation(s) and change.[30] While transformation will lead to the internalisation of capabilities while recombining the old with the new, *exploitation* skills emphasise the ability to refine, leverage and extend existing capabilities or competencies. Here, such routines will relate to the structural, systemic and procedural mechanisms that enable companies to exploit their existing knowledge base over extended periods of time. Importantly, however, researchers note that while acquisition and assimilation skills relate to the potential of companies to gather, collect and assimilate new knowledge (sometimes called potential AC), realised AC[31] will relate to whether they possess enough resources to capitalise on knowledge potential. For strategic leaders, this means that they have to establish a culture of learning that enables their employees to think innovatively (intuition skills), and constantly scan the external environment for new information (interpreting ability). Similarly, developing and recombining internal routines with new routines that enable the company to transform their existing knowledge (integration skills) will be critical, along with exploiting the knowledge they already have through leadership action and resource commitment of a number of existing processes, structures and systems (institutionalisation skills). Figure 10.2 outlines the relationships.

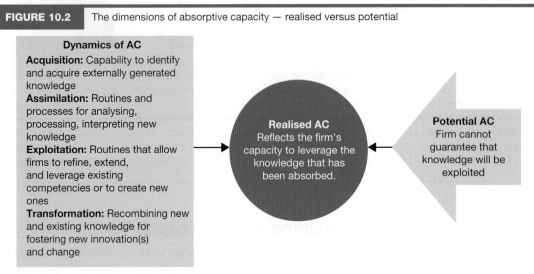

FIGURE 10.2   The dimensions of absorptive capacity — realised versus potential

Dynamics of AC

Acquisition: Capability to identify and acquire externally generated knowledge
Assimilation: Routines and processes for analysing, processing, interpreting new knowledge
Exploitation: Routines that allow firms to refine, extend, and leverage existing competencies or to create new ones
Transformation: Recombining new and existing knowledge for fostering new innovation(s) and change

Realised AC
Reflects the firm's capacity to leverage the knowledge that has been absorbed.

Potential AC
Firm cannot guarantee that knowledge will be exploited

Source: Adapted from Zahra & George, 2002.

Thus far we can see that dynamic capabilities depend on the four AC factors shown in figure 10.2: acquisition, assimilation, exploitation and transformation. We also note that certain skills underpin these capabilities. That is, the capabilities themselves do not just happen. They have to be developed. As competition becomes more knowledge-based, strategic leaders must develop a thorough understanding of their organisation's knowledge base, the processes by which it converts knowledge to capabilities, and the capacity of those capabilities to meet the demands of its environment.[32] For instance, in situations where companies form alliances, a top leader and her team needs to be cognisant of at least three ways to acquire new external knowledge:

1. *passive knowledge* — acquiring externalised knowledge from journals, seminars and consultants
2. *active learning* — acquiring knowledge from benchmarking and competitor intelligence by developing a sophisticated management information system
3. *interactive learning* — where a company can get close enough to its competitor or allied company that the more tacit components of knowledge (the how and why) are more observable.[33]

We also noted earlier that routines underpin skills. Here, it is useful to reflect on what we know from past learning techniques that have assisted strategic leaders for decades. In table 10.1, notice the link between building shared vision and strategic leader actions described earlier. Also, in testing and surfacing how we think and act (mental models), notice how this is similar to transformation AC and the ability to assimilate new knowledge. Leaders help their managers to align what they espouse or say with what they truly believe, suggesting that honesty, trust, and integrity are critical in building AC ability. Finally, in systems thinking, you will notice how this is similar to pillar 3 on building operational and strategic agility described below.

TABLE 10.1 Learning techniques for leading strategically

Building shared vision	Surfacing and testing mental models	Systems thinking
Encouraging personal vision	Seeing leaps of abstraction	Seeing interrelationships, not things, and processes, not snapshots
Communicating and asking for support	Balancing enquiry and advocacy	Moving beyond blame
Visioning as an ongoing process	Distinguishing espoused theory from theory in use	Distinguishing detail complexity from dynamic complexity
Blending extrinsic and intrinsic visions	Recognising and defusing defensive routines	Focusing on areas of high leverage
Distinguishing positive from negative visions		Avoiding symptomatic solutions

Source: Senge, 1990.

An additional way for leaders to develop routines to build dynamic AC is by being aware of the actual behaviours that inhibit their capacity to acquire knowledge, assimilate the knowledge in existing systems, exploit existing knowledge, and transform their thinking in ways that lead to new innovations. Table 10.1 represents some of the defensive routines that restrict how top leaders think and act. Some scholars note that renewal and transformation require the removal of obstacles and that paralysed behaviour in companies often suggests that there are too many managers and not enough leaders.[34] Some obstacles will be reflected by the organisational structure's capacity to assimilate knowledge, suggesting that processes, routines and procedures are outdated. Other obstacles are embedded within the performance management and remuneration system to the extent that employees will prioritise self-interest over change goals. A useful way for strategic leaders to develop routines for developing dynamic AC is by reverting to a checklist that outlines which behaviours and routines need to be prioritised. Researchers have noted that if different scales of behaviours and skills can be developed that accurately reflect the four AC dimensions, then leaders will be able to systematically develop these within the company.[35] Table 10.2 provides a valid empirical scale that can be used by leaders as a checklist for establishing AC. It refers to everyday-business routines, cross-departmental requirements, employee skills that have to be developed and the degree of management support required. As such, the table illustrates that leading strategically is not only about an individual's personal behavioural style; rather, it is about developing the routines and skills that enable adaptive and AC in ways that help any global organisation develop its unique sets of dynamic capabilities such that rapid disruption and change can be addressed. Table 10.2 can be incorporated into a company's management systems as a guide for auditing their current behaviours. The 'Availability' column in the table shows which routines and skills are currently available in a hypothetical company (denoted by a tick) and which ones need to be developed (denoted by a cross).

TABLE 10.2   A checklist for establishing absorptive capacity

Routines and skills to develop absorptive capacity	Availability
Acquisition	
1. The search for relevant information concerning our industry is every-day business in our company.	✗
2. Our management motivates the employees to use information sources within our industry.	✓
3. Our management expects that the employees deal with information beyond our industry.	✗
Assimilation	
4. In our company ideas and concepts are communicated cross-departmental.	✗
5. Our management emphasises cross-departmental support to solve problems.	✓
6. In our company there is a quick information flow, e.g. if a business unit obtains important information it communicates this information promptly to all other business units or departments.	✗
7. Our management demands periodical cross-departmental meetings to interchange new developments, problems, and achievements.	✓
Transformation	
8. Our employees have the ability to structure and to use collected knowledge.	✓
9. Our employees are used to absorb new knowledge as well as to prepare it for further purposes and to make it available.	✗
10. Our employees successfully link existing knowledge with new insights. Our employees are able to apply new knowledge in their practical work.	✓
Exploitation	✓
11. Our management supports the development of prototypes.	✓
12. Our company regularly reconsiders technologies and adapts them accordant to new knowledge.	✓
13. Our company has the ability to work more effectively by adopting new technologies.	

Source: Adapted from Flatten et al., 2011.

Transformation growth in a materials delivery company

Leading strategically means being strategically agile, developing market-led innovations through external transformation while internally increasing the adaptive practices that support business and corporate strategies. In analysing a materials delivery company, what were some of their key strategies for achieving this external and internal balance, and what were the results?

The problems to be addressed related to achieving more efficient and effective use of their delivery systems, where fleets of trucks carried raw materials to other manufacturing centres. The trucking side of operations was connected to different parts  of their operations, suggesting that the company had to redesign its internal road systems and loaded materials more creatively where every function connected to other functions. The delivery system connected to the company's entire end-to-end process, from understanding its customer needs through to the delivery of the finished product.[36] The transformation strategies of the company related to:

1. introducing systems to share raw-materials information more broadly, which highlights additional possibilities
2. transitioning company culture towards a continuous improvement organisation
3. transformation efforts to be led by frontline employees
4. addressing the entire value chain to grow the business by delighting customers
5. cross-functionalising operations across all connecting areas such as product development, procurement, manufacturing, supply chain, capital productivity, and services.

Collectively, these steps towards implementing an enterprise-wide transformation were not just about cost cutting but about growth initiatives that could generate up to 41 per cent of transformation value as compared to general administrative initiatives involving cost-cutting targets which generated just 9 per cent of gross targets. Other results showed that the cross-functional transformation outperformed its single-function counterparts by between 30 and 40 per cent.

10.3 Strategic agility

LEARNING OBJECTIVE 10.3 Distinguish between the principles of operational and strategic agility that enable organisations to effectively cope with change and uncertainty.

Not all adaptive challenges are internal. When the adaptive capacity of the company and its leaders does not keep pace with the environment in such a way that enables them to readily absorb new knowledge, assimilate and use it, the problem more likely relates to operational agility — in this case, poor operational agility. Scholarly reports[37] notice the distinction between operational agility and strategic agility. *Operational agility* can include a capacity to continuously assess opportunities, make hard choices, opt not to compete in some areas, set and act on iterative targets, and learn from the results. Often consistent with operational agility are agile teams who work towards adding new features and dealing with customer and operational demands. Operational agility is underpinned by the AC dimensions of assimilation and exploitation. Conversely, **strategic agility** means the need to pursue market-creating innovations.[38] Whereas operational agility succeeds in delivering a steady flow of additional value for customers equivalent to filling a series of small cups with water, strategic agility is similar to filling the whole bucket — the shift from cups to buckets is a difference in the scale of the financial impact.[39] Strategic agility is underpinned by the AC dimensions of acquisition and transformation.

In aligning operational and strategic agility, there is a requirement to 'balance the need to innovate versus the need to produce'.[40] Another way of describing this alignment is the need to exploit all the good things that the organisation *has* learned (operational agility) versus exploring all the new things (new knowledge, skills, processes and innovations) that *need* to be learned (strategic agility). For instance, market-creating innovations will stem from developing an exploratory culture and being extremely agile into the future, while different adaptive strategies will focus on a company's internal operational agility, the ability to change internal systems, and the ability to develop employees who are sufficiently motivated and informed to act spontaneously (see the section on building corporate culture below). By applying both operational and strategic agility, this will translate into actions to (1) develop ideation capabilities — generating ideas to develop new innovations, (2) engage employees in experimentation and adaptation, (3) help to capture the learning into the company's knowledge base (4) develop collaboration capabilities by encouraging high collaboration and networking. Leadership priorities are thus more related to (5) accepting and promoting uncertainty, surprise, unknowability and open-endedness, and (6) creating conflicting tension as a basis to develop creativity.[41]

Both operational and strategic agility thus serve as a synthesising capability that creates competitive advantage out of 'conflicting' forces. That is, the leader's job is to connect workers across networks both internal and external where possible because conflicting forces (creating substantive conflict with constructive ideas through a learning culture) enable increased effectiveness in problem-solving groups. Similarly, researchers suggest that based on their observations of top global companies, leaders practise the art of valuing paradoxes (complex situations that are difficult to solve) as vital ingredients of high performance by proactively identifying and raising tensions or conflict.[42] They see paradoxes as a means to raise tension through contradictory, yet interrelated elements that exist simultaneously and persist over time, and as a means to foster novelty, creativity and long-term sustainability.[43] We discuss next that the job of the top leadership team is no easy feat! Yet, the increasing need to be adaptive internally has to be balanced with the need to be innovative externally. On the one hand leaders are adaptive, but they are also agile because they need to explore and innovate. This concept is illustrated in figure 10.3 as a series of strategic inflection points (SIPs) that relate to fundamental, interdependent industry dynamics, technologies and strategies.

FIGURE 10.3 Strategic inflection points for agile companies

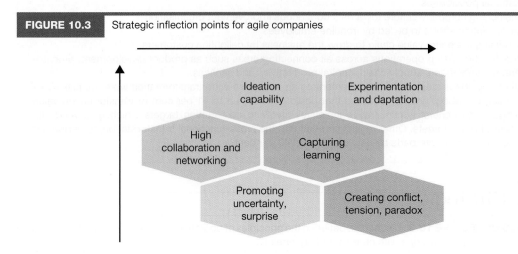

As noted earlier, the context for this chapter is to learn how to lead strategically within an environment of constant change and disruption. This means that the interrelationships between the pillars is important since they should not be viewed as unrelated events. For instance, regarding the first pillar discussed (adaptive capacity), and in lessons from the field of consultancy where leaders apply a range of leadership attributes, characteristics and approaches to dealing with crisis and change, it is useful to ask how leaders respond to global events. In recent research,[44] there is little difference between crisis management and leading through constant disruption. A global virus that the world experienced in 2020 is a crisis in a business sense because it leads to disruption in markets, customers and jobs as well as the flow of imports and exports. Similarly, a global collapse in the finance market as the world experienced in 2008 led to constant disruption and change as companies had to dramatically reinvent their business portfolios.[45] We note in the chapter on the nature and sources of competitive advantage how fast-cycle markets relate to products and innovations that cannot be protected because of intense and rapid competitive moves that erode and destroy competitive advantage. In table 10.3, notice the conventional paths of strategy in the left-hand column and the results of non-conventional strategic agility in the right-hand column.[46] Accordingly, notice the link between our earlier points about leading strategically and leading *with* strategic agility. What does this tell you? It suggests that top leaders have to be agile in order to deal with constant change and disruption.

TABLE 10.3   **Leading with strategic agility**

Conventional strategy	Non-conventional strategic agility
The candle was the only means of light	Thomas Edison made the electric light bulb
Operational agility was about making faster horses	Henry Ford made the model T Ford
Developing better mobile phone (Nokia, Blackberry)	Apple made the multi-functional iPhone
Improving DVDs through operational agility	Netflix pioneered web-based streaming of movies
Improving keyboard-based search (Google)	Amazon pioneered voice-activated search

Source: Adapted from Denning, 2018.

Actions of strategic leaders

While we might better understand the principles that underpin the notion of leading strategically, let's now examine what leader actions support these. There are two parts to leading strategically. The first part is based on specific leader attributes,[47] the second on specific business transformation moves.[48] Let's look at the first part. Based on lessons from the field, leaders have to think first, collaborate on multiple options, act decisively, remain positive, and be humble and courageous. In *thinking first*, leaders take the time to assess what impacts the crisis or fast-cycle market forces are having on their business. Being misinformed is to incorrectly assess these forces and to shift direction too early. When leaders *collaborate on multiple actions*, they are encouraging brainstorming and interpretive skills through ideas creation by gaining a better appreciation of the situation and different options. Within a crisis, leaders *act decisively* by developing a plan of action that is shared with the team and by facing the crisis head on. Similarly, *remaining positive* means expressing trust in the team, and thanking them for their contributions while being positive about the future. Here, time needs to be invested as both leaders and employees work together to confront the current problems faced. Lastly, being *humble and courageous* means making mistakes but owning up to them as crisis and strategies evolve together. It also means staying true to oneself, allowing compromise but not on the core principles so that loyalty and confidence is engendered. While specific leader attributes are thus important, so are the specific transformation moves that address the crisis.[49]

In moving to the second part of what strategic leaders do in crisis and constant change, another shift is in the transformation of portfolio-related moves (see the chapter on corporate-level strategy). Here, given that constant change is underscored by digitisation, advanced technologies and tech-enabled disruption, incumbent companies are not only having to stretch out their financial returns but also remake their businesses.[50] Generally, this is achieved through transformation in five different ways.

1. *Productivity improvements.* Consulting firms suggest that for productivity improvement to qualify as a big move, the relative improvement must outpace 70 per cent of companies in the sector over a decade.
2. *Differentiation such as innovation in products, services and business models.* Here, gross margin improvements must place the company in the top 30 per cent of its industry improvement.
3. *Active resource reallocation.* To qualify as a reallocation that makes a difference, a company must shift at least 60 per cent of its capital spending across its businesses over ten years.
4. *Mergers and acquisitions (M&A).* More reliable increases to company performance are found in M&As relating to at least one deal per year or more than 30 per cent market capitalisation over a ten-year period.
5. *Ratio of capital expenditure to sales.* Here, sales must exceed 1.7 times the industry median over a ten-year period.[51]

Figure 10.4 illustrates how both leadership attributes and transformation define what strategic leaders do. At a minimum, leading strategically is not only about leading effectively by practising those leadership attributes that matter, but also about ongoing transformation. In the next section, we take a closer look at transformational leadership and how this is closely related to strategic agility. Can you also distinguish the difference between the transformation dimension required for AC and the transformation required for strategic agility? What is the difference?

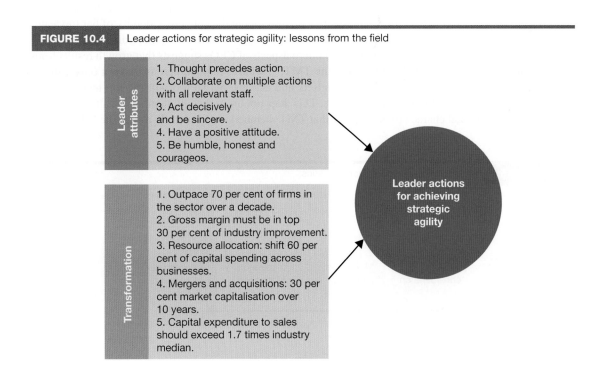

FIGURE 10.4 Leader actions for strategic agility: lessons from the field

Leader attributes
1. Thought precedes action.
2. Collaborate on multiple actions with all relevant staff.
3. Act decisively and be sincere.
4. Have a positive attitude.
5. Be humble, honest and courageos.

Transformation
1. Outpace 70 per cent of firms in the sector over a decade.
2. Gross margin must be in top 30 per cent of industry improvement.
3. Resource allocation: shift 60 per cent of capital spending across businesses.
4. Mergers and acquisitions: 30 per cent market capitalisation over 10 years.
5. Capital expenditure to sales should exceed 1.7 times industry median.

Leader actions for achieving strategic agility

10.4 CEO behavioural dimensions, responsibilities and performance

LEARNING OBJECTIVE 10.4 Review how CEOs achieve transformational behaviours, build top management teams, encourage adaptation and innovation, and acquire and share knowledge.

Transformational behaviours and the top management team

Leading strategically is often associated with transformational and charismatic leaders who focus on building the top leadership team. While the 'strategic' aspect of leaders as noted earlier is about strategic actions and aligning the different functional activities of the company, the transformational leader is able to communicate and connect with people, create meaning, mobilise support, and inspire others in the pursuit of organisational effectiveness.[52] The results of more successful transformations suggest that leaders release and mobilise employee energy and communicate commitment,[53] while at the same time, helping to build the top management team (TMT) based on shared leadership.[54] Old roles related to resource controlling and power broking are redundant; leaders as coaches, information providers, facilitators, supporters and teachers are now the norm.[55] The latter suggests that the top leader or CEO will oscillate between a transformational approach and a day-to-day transactional approach. On the one hand, he or she is trying to lever the company towards strategic agility and transformation, but on the other, is ensuring that their company is highly adaptive within its own internal systems of operation.

In looking at specific CEO characteristics associated with both transformational and charismatic leaders, researchers suggest that intelligence, maturity and breadth (emotional maturity with a broad range of interests), inner motivation and achievement, and honesty are key traits of the leader.[56] Contemporary CEOs and their TMT now have to focus on strategic vision and how to articulate it, have an increased sensitivity to the environment, associate actions with personal risk, and be sensitive to member needs.[57] Generally, transformational leaders are noted for their individualised consideration, charisma or idealised influence, inspiration and intellectual stimulation[58] (see figure 10.5). Interestingly, research indicates that time is an important moderator in considering the effects of CEO charisma on CEO tenure. For instance, charismatic CEOs have a tendency to alter their strategies on a year-to-year basis consistent with the idea that charismatic leaders value opposition to the status quo.[59] Charismatic leaders of peer firms — companies within the same industry — can also affect the leadership and strategic actions of focal firms – a specified company with a charismatic leader. That is, companies often seek to copy the successful leadership attributes of the charismatic CEO of a peer firm.[60] Notably also, researchers in the field contend that leaders influence the self-concept of their followers by associating followers' goals and collective experiences to the leaders mission so that 'they become valued aspects of the followers' self-concept'.[61] The CEO in particular achieves this by developing the collective identity of her top team, changing their perceptions of the nature of work, while working to increase both individual and collective self-efficacy. For instance, recent research on the micro aspects of CEOs suggests that growth results from the creation of stable shared leadership within the TMT;[62] what is implied here is that not only will the CEO embody transformational behaviours, mindsets and actions, but so too will the top team because they are aligned with the CEO's strategic visions. This does not mean that all members of a top team will possess transformational characteristics, rather, that TMT members will generally model the behaviour of the leader.

| **FIGURE 10.5** | Transformational leader characteristics |

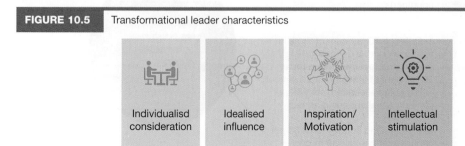

| Individualisd consideration | Idealised influence | Inspiration/ Motivation | Intellectual stimulation |

Source: Adapted from Kouzes & Posner, 2002.

Thus far in the chapter we have been focusing on leading strategically, strategic adaptation and agility, AC and the transformational leader characteristics of CEOs. Innovation and exploration have formed a central part of these discussions, particularly related to acquiring new information and transforming the decisions of the company, if not the company itself. These strategic aspects of the work of CEOs and their teams is confirmed as well by different scholarly findings. Strategic leadership behaviours, for instance, are positively associated with innovation processes beyond organisation size and individual personalities to the extent that strategic leadership behaviours influence both product-market as well as administrative executive innovation.[63] In essence, the effectiveness of CEOs and their heterogenous TMTs (comprising individuals with different backgrounds, experience and education) depends on their capacity to channel disparate viewpoints and perspectives into an engine room of innovation.[64] The value of heterogenous teams is positively associated with innovation and strategic change[65] in many prior studies. Thus we see the value and the formation of the TMT as very important within the domain of what a transformational or charismatic leader does.

Overcoming barriers to strategic leadership actions

Common barriers for achieving effective strategic actions include a lack of unified culture, misalignment of strategic actions and supporting organisation structure, poor AC in receiving and responding to signals from the environment, slow response to external events, problems in the TMT, and cultural norms that are often espoused within an organisation but not practised, creating confusion around work practices and job specifications.

In supplementary actions that strategic leaders need to develop to overcome barriers to change, six additional areas are apparent: the need to *anticipate* external events, *challenge* decisions, better *interpret* uncertain environments, reframe *decision* approaches, *align* dispersed systems, and *learn and experiment*.[66]

For example, it is common practice in top companies such as Du Pont and Royal Dutch Shell to avoid the trap of not responding early enough to disruption. These companies avoid these traps by developing multiple scenarios of future actions, carefully framing a decision approach from the outset by reviewing multiple options that balance rigour with speed, and rallying stakeholders around strategic directions that are potentially polarising. Similarly, many large companies such as Microsoft, Xerox and Google systematically practise the idea that the ability to learn faster than competitors is common and developing a culture of innovation is standard by, for instance, encouraging experiments and 'failing fast' through corrective courses of action as well as fostering collective action. CEOs who are able to deal with these supplementary actions are better able to overcome the barriers to leading strategically.

CEO succession

The selection of the CEO by the board of any company will not be easy in *succession planning*, nor will the CEO effortlessly assemble the right team. For instance, some studies have shown that a CEO is constrained by, first, the need to orient a company to their own strategic agenda, and second, the need to personally connect their visions with that of the company. In relation to the former, new CEOs are often forced to include non-TMT members or a task force of collaborators who are similar to them in terms of attitudes, values and demographic features. This suggests that TMT members are often sidelined in favour of the CEO's preference for critical information and commitment,[67] suggesting that it takes time to assemble the right TMT. Some transformational leaders have not been successful in aligning their vision to coincide with the beliefs of the company, meaning that such leaders have had short tenures.[68] Other considerations for selecting a CEO for succession are based on the company's task demands. That is, CEO selection is often based on prior experiences, age and possibly international background, which will need to match the company's zest for knowledge, mindset and skill requirements, especially depending on a company's degree of internationalisation in its task demands.[69]

Overall, the performance of an effective CEO should not be underestimated, presuming that a company is able to choose a CEO with the right mix of international experience, education, background and leadership characteristics matched to its own internal and external demands. For instance, studies have shown that the effect of a CEO on performance is estimated at 29.2 per cent of the variance in corporate profitability,[70] indicating that the choice of CEO by any company is a critical factor for success, particularly in volatile and disruptive markets.

10.5 Developing human capital — managing talent

LEARNING OBJECTIVE 10.5 Think about leading strategically as a human capital resource for building global talent and building shared knowledge.

One of the key tasks of top leaders is to develop their people and manage talent in such a way that they build the human capital stocks of the business. First, top leaders and their lower-level managers have to identify that there is a difference between individual-level human capital — that is, knowledge, skills and abilities plus other characteristics (**KSAOs**) possessed by individuals — and unit-level or company-level human capital that can be leveraged as an organisational capability.[71] This is because these individual KSAOs cannot be easily transferred into homogenous capabilities that can be turned to a company's competitive advantage. Researchers note that there is an assumed relationship between individual KSAOs and company- or unit-level performance, but there is little research to support this association.[72] While companies spend time developing certain specific skills and attributes in their staff — such as experience, judgement, intelligence, relationships and insight — this often suggests that such skills are not easily attained by competitor companies. Leaders often miss the fact that much of their workforce has many valuable innate general skills, such as high-level problem-solving skills, emotional intelligence and leadership ability, which top leaders need to release by encouraging internal HR policies that help to fully develop the workforce. Recent research suggests, for instance, that firms cannot easily generalise how KSAOs can be applied or accurately represent the total skill set within their organisation. If we examined an organisation's total composite of skills, many represent both KSAOs plus a range of general skills that companies are not always capable of developing.[73]

Company-specific **human capital resources (HCRs)** plus general skills influence the mobility of workers between companies, highlighting the importance of how organisations manage and treat their people as well as manage future talent.[74] Some studies have found that high performance HR practices that enable both specific and general skills increase the perception of employees that the company is committed to them; thus, organisational citizenship behaviour is increased along with a stronger intent to stay in the organisation.[75]

The point is that top leaders need to think less about individual KSAOs and more about how to develop the unit or company-level human resources because company-level resources are created from the emergence of different types of HCRs across the organisation.[76] For instance, given the rise of digital innovation and disruption, technology-driven companies are having to raise workforce productivity by creating a seamless online experience to attract and develop the best talent, which has led to upgrading talent across multiple disciplines, ranging from data scientists to agile coaches, digital marketers, human-centred designers and technology architects.[77] In managing talent, companies have to carefully consider how to attract the best people. This begs the question, what are the requirements for the workforce of the future and in managing talent? In a recent study, 97 per cent of executives surveyed expected an increase in competition for talent and that the standard phrase of 'attract and retain' was being replaced by 'attract and continually attract'.[78] Here, 99 per cent of companies were taking action for change, believing that the highest return on investment on talent will come from redesigning jobs to better deliver value. Similarly, in developing a mindset related to a 'platform for talent', companies were focused on many factors:

1. matching skill supply with work demand across industries
2. thinking more creatively about how to manage older workers given increased automation replacing jobs
3. redesigning awards and compensation models to attract and retain workers
4. transitioning work design to increasing flexible work and away from full-time jobs
5. linking lack of trust and workforce attrition to employee burnout necessitating a higher focus on employee engagement programs.[79]

Notice how many of these factors for developing global talent are significantly linked to strategic agility and adaptability. Figure 10.6 highlights most of the key discussions surrounding developing human capital and managing talent and in building HCRs.

The human capital resource

HCR is a unit-level resource that is created from the emergence of individuals' knowledge, skills, abilities, and other characteristics across the company

Future workforce priorities

- Identifying general and specific skills of future work
- Managing older workers
- Redesigning compensation
- Flexible work trends
- Employee burnout
- Worker skills development
- Competitive advantage of HR metrics

Create an HCR checklist

- Can our capabilities withstand disruption?
- How will they attract the best workers?
- Will our HR systems keep pace with automation?
- How will they develop a highly engaged workforce?

STRATEGY CAPSULE 10.4

Organisational growth mindset for culture change

In the context of building corporate culture as well as AC, cultural change is not easy as it requires shared values, shared assumptions, and alignment between the top leaders and the work patterns of employees. Enabling a *growth mindset* helps because it changes employees' emphasis from 'proving their ability' to 'improving' it, and from focusing on where they are to where they should be.

The Neuro-Leadership Institute suggests that a growth mindset fosters a culture where all employees are seen as possessing potential, encouraged to develop their capabilities and acknowledged once those capabilities have been realised.[80] The following three actions become important to achieve a growth mindset.

1. Define clear priorities that help people buy into the culture change. For example, long lists of skill requirements for employees might be replaced by just three of four skills that form the foundation for growth.
2. Form new habits not by trying to tackle multiple resolutions all at once but rather by acting on new behaviour every day so that it becomes routine.
3. Embed the growth mindset in new systems which are structural implementations that reinforce a desired behaviour.

Driving to work a different way will only become a habit once you practise it, since the moment you forget, your mind will revert to the old route! Taken together, a growth mindset is reinforced by priorities, habits and systems.

10.6 Developing corporate culture

LEARNING OBJECTIVE 10.6 Ascertain how to develop a company's corporate culture and to integrate its benefits, and classify the relationship between leading strategically and corporate culture.

Strategic leaders need to pay attention to what is noticed and commented on within the organisation; what is measured, controlled and rewarded. What messages do leaders want to convey? Developing **corporate culture** is about how leaders create shared social knowledge, which guides the behaviour and actions of employees, including the decisions necessary for internal integration and external adaptation.[81] Role-modelling and coaching place leaders' personal and visible behaviours on display. While language, metaphor, action, behaviours and values are important for leaders to pay attention to, strategic leaders are interested both in what is said or espoused, and what is truly believed within their organisation. Both what is rewarded and punished, and the nature of the rewards and punishments themselves, convey meaning.[82] The capacity for developing culture in any organisation is based on a set of guiding principles or basic assumptions that influence decision making. If basic assumptions about how people are meant to react and behave within a group are strongly held, then a different reaction and behaviour by someone using a different premise within the group may not fit with the basic assumptions. Implicit assumptions that guide behaviour inform group members as to how to perceive, think about and feel about things, while often basic assumptions are not debatable nor confronted because they are taken for granted as a basis for what organisation members believe and how they will act.[83] Top leaders in particular have to determine the extent to which a company's basic assumptions support its stated values. A mismatch between values and assumptions suggests that leaders are promoting confused signals. One of the first acts of successful leaders, whether at the level of the department, team or whole organisation, is to know well how the values and deep-level assumptions that drive routines are practised before trying to change basic behaviours.

Interestingly, studies have found that different types of leaders play different roles in shaping an organisation's corporate culture. In a study of Chinese CEOs facing the existence of state control, as well as the emergence of new companies, and complex and dynamic institutional forces, some CEOs were focused on business and performance with less attention to developing systems and processes, while others created systems to institutionalise the cultural values that were the basis of performance and competition.[84] Typically, the CEOs who focused on business and performance were dynamic, visionary and charismatic. These CEOs contrasted with non-charismatic and information-builder CEOs who were institution builders more focused on establishing institutionalised cultural values. These findings are consistent with research related to American CEOs; that is, a high-profile, charismatic style is not always required to successfully shape a visionary company.[85] Studies have also shown that there is a mismatch between the rhetoric of declared appropriate norms and behaviours, similar to the stated assumptions described above, and behaviours that reflect these.[86] This means that in building corporate culture, often there is a lack of compatibility between vision and reality which can be fixed by a second-order level of change and a shift in governing norms. But it also means that in any company, the CEO and top team need to be aware that cultural assimilation of new values and ideas emerges slowly and gradually with some resistance expected based on different employee and group orientations and motivations. Employees' faith and trust in their organisation's integrity has been shown to depend on observed conformity between what the organisation says it stands for and what it is perceived to do.[87] For example, when this gap is small, the result is committed employees, high retention of staff by reduced absenteeism and turnover, and increased productive behaviour related to attendance, performance and citizenship.[88]

Any top leadership team will seek to build corporate culture alignment by matching the values that are espoused with internal aspects of high-performance routines.[89] These routines include high instances of support for creativity, open communications, respect and integrity, and a change-driven culture, among others. For instance, consistent with the earlier section on adaptive capacity, research shows that adaptive systems (often called organic systems) frequently benefit from work system redesign, new learning and development opportunities, and change-driven cultures, as distinct from rigid systems that discourage employee initiative,[90] all of which create high-performance cultures (see figure 10.7).

FIGURE 10.7   How cultural values build high performance cultures

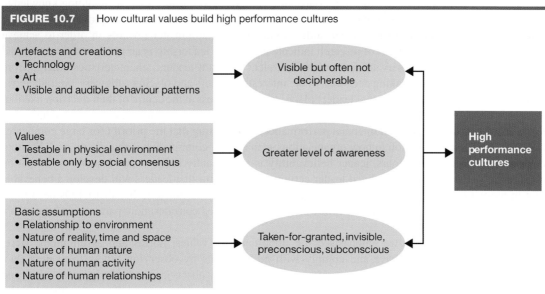

Source: Adapted from Schein, 1985.

Corning Research and Development Corporation

Obsessing with budgets and deadlines kills ideas, according to Dr Waguih Ishak of Corning Research and Development Corporation.[91] With so much research and development as part of innovation, Corning has learned some lessons for creating an innovation culture. First, Ishak suggests that an organisation has to practise 'innovation parenting'; that is, once creative people are grounded with key objectives, focus areas and core capabilities, the next step is to give them broad discretion (what we call *shared leadership* in this chapter) to conduct their work.[92] At Corning, scientists are trusted and accountable for delivering practical products and processes that can be manufactured, which in turn

helps forge an innovation culture. Second, sometimes rules have to be broken to allow innovators to experiment by busting hierarchy in ways that allow people to be creative. Third, unconventional thinking is encouraged such that traditional leading-edge products can be challenged. At Corning, workers are encouraged to work on at least two projects to allow them to shift gears if they hit roadblocks in their innovative efforts. Fourth, developing external capital links through diverse companies from start-ups to venture capitalist to national labs and universities enables more expansive inputs to be part of innovative outcomes; and fifth, Corning hires people who are willing to work on multiple projects and who constantly push for improvements such as inventing the processes that are needed to mass-produce new materials. What this suggests is that innovation culture development requires a number of innovation action-points that are a trigger to change.

10.7 Ethical practices

LEARNING OBJECTIVE 10.7 Apply ethical leadership principles to leadership in action.

Research notes the extent to which leaders share knowledge with their workers as a reflection of their own leadership ethical state, in particular, the extent to which they portray the moral manager and the moral person. **Ethical leaders** tend to be fair, open and trustworthy, by nurturing trusting relationships so that workers feel a fair reciprocation for their contributions.[93] Moreover, rather than withholding knowledge for personal gain, leaders instead engage in controlled motivations towards their employees through the leader's own reward power or his or her ability to control and administer rewards in order to achieve some desired behaviour. Patterns of research indicate that ethical leadership is an important precursor and component of becoming a servant and authentic leader.[94] Servant leaders' characteristics emerge from ethical principles, such as making decisions in the interests of others and placing followers' welfare above their own, while justice demands that leaders place issues of fairness at the centre of their decision making. Research suggests that building positive stakeholder perceptions of an organisation's ethical identity has led to increased satisfaction and financial performance,[95] suggesting that the priority for large companies has shifted from ethical action to how organisations manage and communicate ethical actions.[96] Without demonstrated ethical behaviours, leader believability is significantly reduced and leaders would not be regarded as authentic. Without ethical leader actions, it is doubtful that leaders will develop a believable plot in terms of being authentic to their followers. For instance, we noted earlier that CEOs need to be authentic in order to connect with their followers through idealised consideration, particularly related to a transformational leader.

In the previous section, we emphasised the importance of values, norms and assumptions. Here, employees learn how to behave and comply with moral norms by observing others from their own experience, plus, in the context of their employment, explicitly by observing the leader's moral values and behaviours; they then practise and engage in these moral behaviours themselves.[97] Thus, the ethical leader role-models behaviour that is more likely to lead to moral behaviours such as honesty, trustworthiness, social responsiveness, fairness, caring and so on. Leaders display higher moral identity by sharing knowledge because they are motivated by a sense of moral obligation and prosocial behaviour because they see themselves as a good citizen. They are also increasingly willing to share knowledge, as we noted earlier within the AC pillar. Despite the fact that knowledge sharing from the leader is about risk taking because it implies a loss of the leader's proprietorship of know-how, there is a direct relationship between the extent to which an ethical leader shares knowledge and the extent of their moral relevance as a manager and leader. Leaders pursue prosocial and moral behaviour through knowledge sharing not only because of reward or fear of punishment but because they link their moral identity to their actions. According to scholars, it is possible to classify the different stages of moral reasoning such that it will be important for strategic leaders to assess the stage that accurately reflects their ethical values (see figure 10.8). Conflicts in the leader themselves are visible when one stage conflicts with another. Ethical egoism (a person acts to create the greatest good for her or himself) conflicts with a utilitarian approach of acting for the greatest good for the greatest number. By contrast, altruism suggests that a leader's actions are morally correct in that they promote the best interests of others. A CEO's moral reasoning will be based on internalised universal principles of justice (stage 6), where decisions are made based on the viewpoints of all parties involved. Overall, ethical theories are about the conduct of leaders that addresses the consequences of their actions versus the duty or rules governing their actions. Taken together, leading strategically concerns a highly ethical state given the depth of company commitment to overall responsible citizenship, which always starts with the CEO and the TMT.

FIGURE 10.8   Moral development of the leader

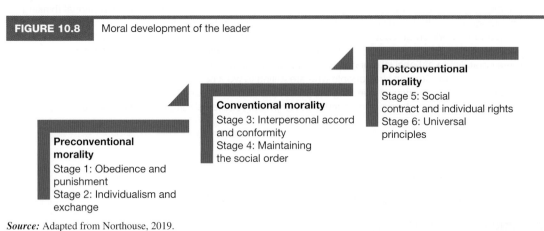

Source: Adapted from Northouse, 2019.

SUMMARY

In this chapter, we have not just talked *about* leadership behaviour. Rather, we have gone the extra step of illustrating *how* and in what circumstances leading strategically matters. First, we saw that companies practise strategic leadership within their daily operations by incorporating five strategic pillars. These were: adaptive capacity, AC and building dynamic capabilities, operational and strategic agility, CEO behavioural dimensions, responsibilities and performance and building corporate culture. We noted in earlier sections of the chapter how leadership behaviours needed to be balanced with specific leadership actions for getting things done, as illustrated by our opening scene setter about Shire Pharma and in the strategy capsules. We illustrated how strategic leaders balance the need for adaptive practice with exploring new market-led innovations by adopting specific agile strategies and we gave examples of these. We illustrated the importance of AC and the ability of any organisation to acquire and capture knowledge and we related much of the discussion to how an organisation learns and builds its capabilities. The emphasis here was on which specific knowledge routines are evident in the organisation and which need to be developed for the future. We noted how knowledge and learning routines do not just happen but have to be created in order for a company to create its own competitive advantage.

We then discussed many of the dimensions of CEO leadership behaviour particularly relevant to the TMT, including which transformational behaviours are more likely to bring about significant strategic change, especially when combined with strategic agility.. We also noted other dimensions within the CEO domain and within the scope of the business, such as succession planning and why the actions of CEOs are critical for the overall performance of the company. Later, we linked the discussions on building corporate culture with leading strategically so that the student of strategy could determine how these were linked. Finally, we highlighted the importance of ethical leadership and why the actions of moral and ethical leadership contribute to the universal principles of postconventional morality.

KEY TERMS

absorptive capacity (AC) Relates to developing a set of organisational routines and processes by which companies acquire, assimilate, transform and exploit knowledge in superior ways that lead to dynamic organisational capability.

adaptive leaders Leaders who help people deal with change and their response to changing environments in ways that better enable the organisation to effectively cope with uncertainly.

corporate culture Shared social knowledge that guides the behaviour and actions of employees, including the decisions necessary for internal integration and external adaptation.

ethical leaders Leaders who tend to be fair, open and trustworthy, by nurturing trusting relationships so that workers feel a fair reciprocation for their contributions.

human capital resources (HCRs) Unit-level resources that are created from the emergence of individuals' knowledge, skills, abilities and other characteristics across the company that strategic leaders must nurture and develop.

KSAOs Knowledge, skills and abilities plus other characteristics.

leading strategically Communicating a vision for the future and applying strategic decisions in ways that develop an organisation's capabilities and competencies as a bedrock for strategic action.

strategic agility How organisations as a whole flexibly respond to complex, global and dynamic environments and the ability to pursue market-creating innovations.

SELF-STUDY QUESTIONS

1 Why is leading strategically different from one-to-one leadership behaviour?
2 What things do strategic leaders do and why?
3 How would you distinguish between adaptive leadership and transformative or innovative leadership?
4 Strategic agility is similar to innovative leader actions but there are differences. What are they?
5 How is absorptive capacity related to learning?
6 What does exploitation mean within the context of absorptive capacity?
7 The human capital resource appears to be different to individual-level attributes. In what ways are they different and why does it matter?

8 Transformational leaders often match CEO characteristics. In what ways?

9 What are the priorities of CEOs with respect to the TMT? What can go wrong and why?

10 Why are values and assumptions important in building corporate culture?

DISCUSSION QUESTIONS

1 A company is falling behind its competitors in respect of capturing external knowledge. When it is able to capture important knowledge, different sections and departments of the business don't really know why this is important. What has gone wrong in the company and what needs to change?

2 A firm practises strategic agility but is still falling behind its nearest competitors. What can the CEO and the TMT do to check if their agile actions are making a difference in competitive markets? What contexts within the firm may need to change and why?

3 The CEO of a company knows that human resource capability is a critical component and that the best talent is highly sought after. What can he or she do to ensure they are keeping the best talent from being poached by rival companies?

4 The CEO is desperately trying to change a company's culture and instil and embed her ideas into those of the TMT as well as assimilate them into the company. The problem is that she is running up against quite active opposition to her plans. What can she do about this situation and why is there opposition to her transformational ideas?

5 The leader and his TMT are determined to increase shareholder value, increase the share price of the company's stock, and settle on a growth phase for the company. Their ideas for expansion into other countries, especially third-world countries so that they can take advantage of the resources in those countries, is being significantly questioned by shareholders on the basis of environmental and ethical concerns. In what ways are different ethical principles of growth-at-all-costs clashing with other company values? What is the solution?

6 The leader wants to embrace a non-conventional strategy of rapid market growth and is generally supported by the TMT. The problem is that the company Board of Directors is not sold on the strategic ideas. What can the leader do to change the mind of the board and to convince them of the overall growth strategy? Why is the board reluctant to agree?

EXERCISES

1 Track and research the strategic agility of Shire Pharma. Given that the company did not suddenly become agile and innovative, what events and major changes occurred over a three-year period that reflected their changed culture? In addition to the information provided in the opening case, what were the specifics of these changes? Compare some figures. What was the return to shareholders and return on assets 5 years ago? What is it now?

2 Before you can assess the effectiveness of your corporate culture, you need to first evaluate it. Think of a company you know or your own company and answer five basic questions listed by Jacob Morgan at Inc.com to evaluate the state of corporate culture. The link is www.inc.com/jacob-morgan/evaluate-your-corporate-culture-with-5-questions.html.

3 Digital transformation is presenting as a major disruptive force in business models. Explain what digital disruption means by exploring the following article: 'Digital Australia: Seizing the opportunity from the fourth industrial revolution', by *McKinsey & Company*, 2017, www.mckinsey.com/featured-insights/asia-pacific/digital-australia-seizing-opportunity-from-the-fourth-industrial-revolution.

Choose at least two industries out of this article in which digital disruption is occurring. Compare and contrast common features that are related to strategic agility.

4 Look at the following two links and read the articles. What are some of the more common features arising from these articles?

– John Pierce, 'Change your company culture for good: how to design a lasting initiative', www.forbes.com/sites/forbeshumanresourcescouncil/2020/01/03/change-your-company-culture-for-good-how-to-design-a-lasting-initiative/#4468273773d3

– David Rock, 'The fastest way to change a culture', www.forbes.com/sites/davidrock/2019/05/24/fastest-way-to-change-culture/#67af12773d50

5 Either in groups of four or at home, draw two columns. The first column should be headed 'Unethical Leadership Practices' and the second 'Ethical and Moral Leadership Practices'. Using some of the research noted in this chapter, note the differences and discuss these.

FURTHER READING

Agote, L, Aramburu, N & Lines, R 2016, 'Authentic leadership perception, trust in the leader, and followers' emotions in organizational change processes', *The Journal of Applied Behavioural Science,* vol. 52, iss. 1, 35–63.

Deinert, A, Homan, AC, Boer, D, Voelpel, SC & Gitermann, D 2015, 'Transformational leadership sub-dimensions and their link to leaders' personality and performance', *The Leadership Quarterly,* 26, 1095–1120.

Hougaard, R & Carter, J 2018, *The mind of the leader*, Boston MA: Harvard Business Review Press.

Jin, S, Seo, M-G & Shapiro, DL 2016, 'Do happy leaders lead better? Affective and attitudinal antecedents of transformational leadership', *The Leadership Quarterly,* 27, 64–84.

Kirubi, M, K'Aol, G & Rana, R 2019, 'Influence of supportive and participative path-goal leadership styles and the moderating role of task structure on employee performance', *International Journal of Research in Business and Social Science (2147–4478)*, vol. 8, no. 5, 76–87.

Steffens, NK, Mols, F, Haslan, SA & Okimoto, TG 2016, 'True to what we stand for: Championing collective interests as a path to authentic leadership', *The Leadership Quarterly*, 27, 726–744.

ENDNOTES

1. 'Leadership and strategic innovation in Pharma', *McKinsey & Company*, July 2017.
2. 'How technology is changing the job of the CEO', *McKinsey & Company*, August 2017.
3. See www.shirepharmaceuticals.co.uk/who-we-are, viewed 15 April, 2020.
4. *McKinsey & Company*, July 2017, op cit.
5. K Boal and R Hooijberg, 'Strategic leadership research: Moving on', *The Leadership Quarterly,* vol. 11, no. 4, 2001, 515–549.
6. MW Lewis, C Andriopoulos, and WK Smith, 'Paradoxical leadership to enable strategic agility', *California Management Review*, vol. 56, no. 3, 2014. Spring.
7. AS Tsui, Z-W Zhang, H Wang, KR Xin, and JB Wu, 'Unpacking the relationship between CEO leadership behaviour and organizational culture', *The Leadership Quarterly,* 17, 2006, 113–137.
8. Boal and Hooijberg, op cit.
9. PG Northouse, *Leadership: theory and practice*, London: Sage Edge, 2019.
10. RJ House and R Aditya, 'The social scientific study of leadership: Quo vadis?', *Journal of Management*, 23, 1997, 409–474.
11. M Uhl-Bien and M Arena, 'Leadership for organizational adaptability: A theoretical synthesis and integrative framework', *The Leadership Quarterly*, 29, 2018, 89–104.
12. WM Cohen and DA Levinthal, 'Absorptive capacity: A new perspective on learning and innovation', *Administrative Science Quarterly*, vol. 35, no. 1, 1990, 128–152.
13. S Denning, 'The four keys you need to achieve strategic agility', *Forbes*, May 22, 2017.
14. A Gupta and V Misangyi, 'Follow the leader (or not): The influence of peer CEOs characteristics on interorganizational imitation', *Strategic Management Journal*, 39, 2018, 1437–1472; DS Elenkov, W Judge, and P Wright, 'Strategic leadership and executive innovation influence: An international multi-cluster comparative study', *Strategic Management Journal*, 26, 2005, 665–682.
15. Tsui et al. op cit.
16. Boal and Hooijberg, op cit.
17. Uhl-Bien and Arena, op cit.
18. ibid.
19. Northouse, op cit.
20. ibid.
21. 'Are today's CFOs ready for tomorrow's demand on finance?', *McKinsey & Company*, December 2016.
22. Cohen and Levinthal, op cit.
23. L Kim, 'Crisis construction and organizational learning: Capability building in catching-up at Hyundai Motor', *Organization Science,* 9, 1998, 506–521.
24. Zahra and George, op cit.
25. SA Zahra and G George, 'Absorptive capacity: A review, reconceptualization, and extension', *The Academy of Management Review*, vol. 27, no. 2, 2002, 185–203.
26. ibid.
27. TC Flatten, A Engelen, SA Zahra, and M Brettel, 'A measure of absorptive capacity: Scale development and application', *European Journal of Management*, 29, 2011, 98–116.
28. PA Murray, 'The domains of intellectual capital: An integrative discourse across perspectives'. In J Syed, P Murray, D Hislop and Y Mouzughi (Eds), *Palgrave Handbook of Knowledge Management*. Palgrave Macmillan, 2018.
29. PY Sun and MH Anderson, 'An examination of the relationship between absorptive capacity and organizational learning, and a proposed integration', *International Journal of Management Reviews,* 2010, doi: 10.1111/j.1468-2370.2008.00256.x

30. Zahra and George, op cit.

31. Sun and Anserson, op cit.

32. PJ Lane and M Lubatkin, 'Relative absorptive capacity and interorganizational learning', *Strategic Management Journal*, vol. 19, no. 5, 1998, 461–477.

33. ibid.

34. J Kotter, 'Why transformation efforts fail', *Harvard Business Review*, January 2007.

35. Flatten et al. op cit.

36. 'The numbers behind successful transformations', *McKinsey Quarterly*, October 2019.

37. RA Heifetz, *Leadership without easy answers*, Cambridge, MA: Belknap Press, 1994.

38. S Denning, 'What is strategic agility?' *Forbes*, January 28, 2018.

39. ibid.

40. Uhl-Bien, op cit.

41. ibid.

42. 'How to lead in times of crisis', Forbes Business Council, April 2020, viewed 12 April, 2020.

43. ibid.

44. op cit. 32

45. 'Global financial crisis, what caused it, and how the world responded', *Canstar*, June 23, 2018.

46. op cit. 28.

47. op cit. 32.

48. 'Why your next transformation should be "all in"', *McKinsey Quarterly*, October 2019.

49. ibid.

50. ibid.

51. ibid.

52. BM Bass, *Leadership and Performance Beyond Expectations*, New York: The Free Press, 1985.

53. L Greiner, T Cummings, and A Bhambri, 'When new CEOs succeed and fail: 4-D theory of strategic transformation', *Organizational Dynamics*, vol. 32, no. 1, 2002, 1–16.

54. R Agarwal, S Brajuinsky, and A Ohyama, 'Centers of gravity: The effect of stable shared leadership in top management teams on firm growth and industry evolution', *Strategic Management Journal,* 41, 2020, 467–498.

55. GG Dess and JC Picken, 'Leadership in the 21st Century', *Organizational Dynamics, Winter*, 2000, 18–33; RJ Allio, 'Learning to be a leader', *Strategy and Leadership*, vol. 44. no. 4, 2016, 3–9.

56. JM Kouzes and BZ Posner, *The Leadership Challenge: How to keep getting extraordinary things done in organizations*, San Francisco: Jossey-Bass, 1995.

57. JA Conger, 'Charismatic and Transformational Leadership in Organizations: An insider's perspective on these developing streams of research', *Leadership Quarterly,* vol. 10, no. 2, 1999, 145–179.

58. ibid.

59. AJ Wowak, MJ Mannor, M Arrfelt, and G McNamara, 'Earthquake or glacier? How CEO charisma manifests in firm strategy over time', *Strategic Management Journal*, 37, 2016, 586–603.

60. A Gupta and VF Misangyi, 'Follow the leader (or not): The influence of peer CEOs characteristics on interorganizational imitation', *Strategic Management Journal*, 39, 2018, 1437–1472.

61. ibid.

62. Agarwal et al. op cit.

63. DS Elenkov, W Judge, and P Wright, 'Strategic leadership and executive innovation influence: An international multi-cluster comparative study', *Strategic Management Journal*, 26, 2005, 665–682.

64. H Li and J Li, 'Top management team conflict and entrepreneurial strategy making in China', *Asia Pacific Journal of Management*, 26, 2009, 263–283.

65. S Nadkami and P Hermann, 'CEO personality, strategic flexibility and firm performance: The case of the Indian business process outsourcing industry', *Academy of Management Journal*, 53, 2010, 1050–1073.

66. PJ Schoemaker and S Krupp, 'Overcoming barriers to integrating strategy and leadership', *Strategy and Leadership*, vol. 43, no. 2, 2015, 23–32.

67. S Ma and D Seidl, 'New CEOs and their collaborators: Divergence and convergence between the strategic leadership constellation and the top management team', *Strategic Management Journal*, 39, 2017, 606–638.

68. J-L Denis, A Langley, and M Pineault, 'Becoming a Leader in a Complex Organization', *Journal of Management Studies*, vol. 37, no. 8, 2000, 1063–1099.

69. S Kunisch, M Menz, and AA Cannella, 'The CEO as a key microfoundation of global strategy: Task demands, CEO origin, and the CEOs international background', *Global Strategy Journal*, 9, 2019, 19–41.

70. A Mackey, 'The effect of CEOs on firm performance', *Strategic Management Journal*, 29, 2008, 1357–1367.

71. RE Ployhart and TP Moliterno, 'Emergence of the human capital resource: A multilevel model', *Academy of Management Review*, 36, 2011, 127–150.

72. AJ Nyberg, TP Moliterno, D Hale, and D Lepak, 'Resource-based perspectives on unit-level human capital: A review and integration', *Journal of Management*, vol. 40, no. 1, 2014, 316–346.

73. Murray, op cit.

74. RE Ployhart and TP Moliterno, 'Emergence of the human capital resource: A multilevel model', *Academy of Management Review*, 36, 2011, 127–150.

75. RR Kehoe and PM Wright, 'The impact of high-performance human resource practices on employees' attitudes and behaviours', *Journal of Management*, vol. 39, no. 2, 2013, 366–391.

76. Ployhart and Moliterno, op cit.

77. 'Digital Australia: Seizing the opportunity from the Fourth Industrial Revolution', *McKinsey & Company*, March 2017.

78. 'Global Talent Trends 2019: Connectivity in the human age', *Mercer*, January.

79. ibid.
80. 'How culture change really happens', *The Neuro-Leadership Institute*, 2018.
81. AA Tsui, Z-X Zhang, H Wang, KR Sin, and JB Wu, 'Unpacking the relationship between CEO leadership behaviour and organisational culture', *The Leadership Quarterly*, 17, 2006, 113–137.
82. E Schein, *Organizational culture and leadership*, Jossey-Bass, 1985.
83. ibid.
84. ibid.
85. JC Collins and JI Porras, 'Building a visionary company', *California Management Review*, 37, 1995, 80–100.
86. H Hofstetter and I Harpaz, 'Declared versus actual organisational culture as indicated by an organisation's performance appraisal', *International Journal of Human Resource Management*, vol. 26, no. 4, 2015, 445–466.
87. A Howell, A Kirk-Brown and BK Cooper, 'Does congruence between espoused and enacted organizational values predict commitment in Australian organizations?' *International Journal of Human Resource Management*, vol. 23, no. 4, 2012, 731–747.
88. ibid.
89. C Kontoghiorghes, (2016) 'Linking high performance organizational culture and talent management: Satisfaction/motivation and organizational commitment as mediators', *International Journal of Human Resource Management*, vol. 27, no. 16, 2016, 1833–1853.
90. ibid.
91. 'Creating an innovation culture', *McKinsey Quarterly*, September 2017.
92. ibid.
93. YL Bavik, PM Tang, R Shao, and WL Long, 'Ethical leadership and employee knowledge sharing: Exploring dual-mediation paths', *The Leadership Quarterly*, 29, 2018, 322–332.
94. Northouse, op cit.
95. N Kleyn, R Abratt, K Chipp, and M Goldman, 'Building a strong corporate ethical identity: Key Findings from Suppliers', *California Management Review*, vol. 54, no. 3, 2012.
96. ibid.
97. Bavik et al., op cit.

ACKNOWLEDGEMENTS

Photo: © motorolka / Shutterstock.com
Photo: © OJO Images RF / Getty Images
Photo: © Narin Eungsuwat / Shutterstock.com
Photo: © Blue Planet Studio / Shutterstock.com
Photo: © Sam Edwards / Caiaimage / Getty Images
Photo: © Eoneren / Getty Images
Extract: Excerpted from 'Leadership and strategic innovation in pharma', July 2017, McKinsey & Company, www.mckinsey.com. © 2020 McKinsey & Company. All rights reserved. Reprinted by permission.
Figure 10.7: © Schein, *Organizational culture and Leadership,* Jossey-Bass, 1985.
Table 10.1: © 1990 from MIT Sloan Management Review/Massachusetts Institute of Technology. All rights reserved. Distributed by Tribune Content Agency.
Table 10.2: © TC Flatten, A Engelen, SA Zahra, and M Brettel, 'A measure of absorptive capacity: Scale development and application', *European Journal of Management,* 29, 2011, 98–116.

CHAPTER 11

Corporate governance and ethics

LEARNING OBJECTIVES

After studying this chapter, you should be able to:

11.1 understand the meaning and boundaries of corporate governance

11.2 appreciate the significance of stakeholder management in the context of corporate governance

11.3 acknowledge the implications of the separation of ownership and management in the modern organisation

11.4 analyse the internal and external governance structure of organisations

11.5 comprehend the structure and major roles of governing boards

11.6 recognise the relationship between managers and governing boards, and assess how this relationship is related to strategic risk and corporate performance

11.7 appreciate the value and importance of corporate governance trends in the public sector and the international arena.

Insights from the Banking Royal Commission

In February 2019 the Royal Commission into Misconduct in the Banking, Superannuation and Financial Services Industry made its final report publicly available. With this report came an end to years of rumours, discussion and debate about potential misconduct by financial institutions in Australia. Central to the investigation were allegations of financial institutions charging unfair fees and aggressively targeting customers in the pursuit of profit, with one of the larger banks allegedly even billing deceased clients knowingly.[1] In the introduction of the Royal Commission's report the following conclusion was provided.[2]

> The conduct identified and described in the Commission's *Interim Report* and the further conduct identified and described in this Report includes conduct by many entities that has taken place over many years causing substantial loss to many customers but yielding substantial profit to the entities concerned. Very often, the conduct has broken the law. And if it has not broken the law, the conduct has fallen short of the kind of behaviour the community not only expects of financial services entities but is also entitled to expect of them.

Unsurprisingly, the report generated public outcry. Not only did the misconduct tarnish some of Australia's most well-known financial brands, the findings also raised critical questions around the role, influence and power of Australia's main financial regulators. Both the Australian Securities and Investments Commission (ASIC) and the Australian Prudential Regulation Authority (APRA) filed multiple criminal and civil cases in the aftermath,[3] but some did consider these steps to be too little, too late.[4]

The banking crisis and its fallout highlight key corporate governance and strategic management issues. First, the crisis raises important questions around the purpose of the corporation; does the corporation solely exists to generate short-term returns for its shareholders or should it balance the returns of multiple stakeholders in the long-run? With a culture of greed[5] being blamed for the misbehaviours, a more balanced approach towards the pursuit of profit and shareholder value appears needed. This probably also requires an overhaul of the reward systems that are currently being used by financial institutions. The Royal Commission in this regard noted that:[6]

> Rewarding misconduct is wrong. Yet incentive, bonus and commission schemes throughout the financial services industry have measured sales and profit, but not compliance with the law and proper standards. Incentives have been offered, and rewards have been paid, regardless of whether the sale was made, or profit derived, in accordance with law. Rewards have been paid regardless of whether the person rewarded should have done what they did.

Second, as the governing board and senior management are ultimately responsible for the control and strategic direction of the corporation, questions have been raised regarding their role in creating and/or preventing the banking crisis. During the hearings and aftermath several CEOs and chairs stepped down, with the most notable ones being the CEO and chair of National Australian Bank (NAB), who resigned days after the release of the final report. During an interview the chair commented that 'we are deeply sorry. We are saying we are deeply sorry. In our departures we are hoping that we will contribute to the development of a better industry that's capable of delivering better outcomes for customers'.[7]

Overall, this case demonstrates the importance of putting appropriate checks and balances in place in corporations and the broader regulatory context. As illustrated by this example, the consequences of illegal and unethical behaviours can jeopardise the reputation of corporations as well as ruin the careers of the managers and directors working for them. As such, corporate governance is essential to the creation of long-term strategic value.

Introduction

The most important strategic management issues concern how companies are led and controlled by corporate leaders. This chapter's scene setter clearly raises a number of issues for corporate governance such as executive and non-executive directors' ethical decision making, the broader regulatory framework, societal pressures and expectations, and matters of corporate governance linked to the overall strategic direction of an organisation. These matters are not only relevant to Australian companies but all companies in the Asia–Pacific region wishing to expand their operations beyond national borders.

This chapter highlights a number of country-specific corporate governance issues and explores and evaluates the importance and contributions of corporate governance with reference to the sustainability of organisations. It introduces the basic concepts and boundaries of corporate governance and highlights the importance of stakeholder management in corporate governance. It then discusses the control mechanisms, both internal and external, of corporate governance to the extent that these are different from one country to the next. The issues of globalisation cannot be ignored in good corporate governance. This chapter attests to many examples of poor corporate governance for companies expanding globally. Consequently, poor corporate governance can threaten the feasibility of corporate strategy and a failure of the relationships between boards and managers can be potentially fatal. However, many Asia–Pacific companies are now changing their legislation to reflect better corporate governance principles — including key changes to the roles and responsibilities of directors. The interaction between managers and governing boards is analysed in the context of the separation of management and ownership, which will form a basis for the analysis of the relationship between effective governance and corporate performance. Lastly, the chapter presents the practices of corporate governance from an international and global perspective and the future trends of corporate governance.

Managers and governing boards are organisations' corporate leaders. By playing an important role in the strategic management of organisations, these leaders are accountable not only to the shareholders, but also to all of the stakeholders and society as a whole. Only by understanding the importance of good corporate governance is it possible to appreciate that the business environment needs to be fair and transparent and that all companies should be held accountable for their actions and their impact on society.

This chapter goes beyond a simple description of the general aspects of corporate governance. It looks more deeply at the contributions of corporate governance to corporate performance and social responsibilities. Poor corporate governance very likely leads to waste, mismanagement and corruption within companies.

11.1 Corporate governance: basic concepts

LEARNING OBJECTIVE 11.1 Understand the meaning and boundaries of corporate governance.

The process of making and controlling strategic decisions is called **corporate governance**.[8] As the foundation on which the modern corporation is built, corporate governance is an umbrella term that includes specific issues arising from the interactions among the governing board, senior managers, shareholders and other corporate stakeholders, which are used to determine and control the strategic direction and performance of organisations.[9] Corporate governance is concerned with identifying ways to ensure that strategic decisions are made more effectively, and is used in corporations to establish order between the company's owners and its top-level managers, whose interests may sometimes be in conflict.

Since corporate governance is about the way corporate entities are governed, as distinct from the way business within these organisations is managed, effective corporate governance is needed to protect shareholders' rights, enhance disclosure and transparency, facilitate effective functioning of the board and provide an efficient legal and regulatory enforcement framework. Corporate governance is about more than just protecting the interests of shareholders; a proper system of corporate governance should go beyond mere profit maximisation and consider the effects of the company's operations on stakeholder groups such as customers, employees, suppliers, regulatory authorities and society at large.

This chapter's study of corporate governance will focus on the ways in which corporate leaders, including both the managers and governing boards, perform their roles in relation to the distribution of power among themselves and shareholders. It is the possible imbalanced distribution of such power that can cause problems with corporate governance.

Governance and sustainability

Corporate governance is closely related to the sustainability of an organisation. It is a key element in enhancing investors' confidence, promoting competitiveness and ultimately improving economic growth. Proper corporate governance requires the effective coordinating effort of all corporate leaders in generating support within the company, motivating active participation of employees, conveying the significance of the strategy and its goals, and maintaining a high level of company-wide awareness of the importance of constant improvement and innovation.[10]

Corporate governance is more than just overseeing the internal operations of a company. From a broader perspective, an appropriate system of corporate governance can promote the interests of organisations so that corporate leaders can use their influence in the market to face the challenge of domestic and foreign competitors and exercise their rights to a voice in government affairs and public policy. In other words, the coordinated efforts of corporate leaders can potentially increase overall market size, gain an advantage related to industry competition, thereby reducing the threats of competitors, and increase their bargaining power relative to suppliers and customers.[11]

What happens when corporate governance is not functioning well enough? Strategy capsule 11.1 shows how a large Japanese multinational company was forced to file for bankruptcy after falsifying product safety information. To ensure the sustainability of companies, a proper system of corporate governance is essential.

Boundaries and relationships of corporate governance

The process of corporate governance starts with an organisation's managers, which includes the chief executive officer (CEO) and senior managers. They are involved, not only in the day-to-day operations of the company, but also the strategic long-range planning process.[19] Their effective performance at the strategic level is essential to the growth and long-term prosperity of the organisation.

As another important component of corporate leadership, the governing board monitors the work of the top managers in strategic planning, under the influence of owners, potential investors, regulators, auditors and other stakeholders. Figure 11.1 shows the boundaries and relationships of corporate governance.

FIGURE 11.1   Boundaries and relationships of corporate governance

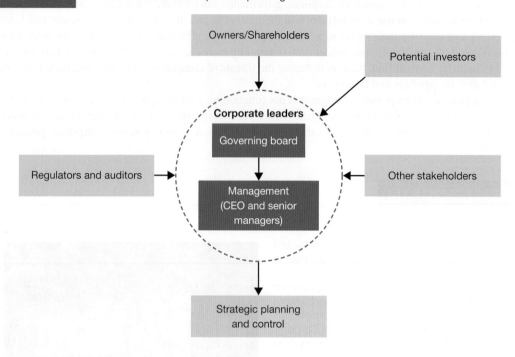

Being a company's source of power and values, corporate leaders (including the managers and the governing board) must take the initiative in planning a broad-gauged, long-range, large-scale and company-wide strategy, based on a vision and direction of where the organisation is heading.[20] The owners or shareholders, who have the option to retain or sell their shares in the market, oversee the work of these corporate leaders. Other potential investors are also closely watching the performance of the company and will take appropriate acquisition actions wherever necessary. For instance, during Telstra's annual general meeting of shareholders in 2018, over 60 per cent of the shareholders voted down the executive remuneration report, as the proposed executive remuneration was not perceived to be in line with the performance of the organisation. The shareholders therewith challenged the corporation to reconsider its remuneration approach.[21] In addition, regulators and stakeholders, who will be affected by the company's activities, are likely to voice concerns and exert their influence to ensure that the company is operating in line with their expectations.

11.2 Corporate governance: social responsibilities and stakeholders

LEARNING OBJECTIVE 11.2 Appreciate the significance of stakeholder management in the context of corporate governance.

Companies are now operating in an environment of intense competition both in the product and capital markets. Investors, governments and regulators are paying more attention to avoid the financial scandals of recent years that have created a significantly more constrained regulatory environment. Management research shows that investors are willing to pay more for a company with good corporate governance practices.[22] Many investors look beyond the balance sheet for ethical and responsible business behaviour — for example, environmental protection; energy efficiency; adoption of health and safety standards; workplace issues such as compensation, benefits and training; as well as charitable giving and community activism.

In addition to the concerns in the business world, increasing public and stakeholder worries about the social and environmental impacts of business practices are forcing companies to come to terms with a much broader set of interests and expectations in society.

Corporate governance and social responsibility

Corporate social responsibility (CSR) is considered to be the continuing commitment by business to behave ethically and contribute to economic development while improving the quality of life of the workforce and their families as well as of the local community and society at large.[23] As such, CSR is related to the need to make a profit, obey the law, be ethical and be a good corporate citizen. To some extent, these actions can be viewed as tools that business organisations can use to meet society's expectations. They are particularly useful when such actions can result in organisational outcomes that affect the social perception in favour of the organisation. This type of social responsibility action is useful in aligning the demands of the external social environment with the organisation's resources and capabilities. Offering the personal services of organisation members to the public sector is an example of such an action — as representatives of the organisation they can serve in some social, trade or professional organisations, or participate in charity activities.

Corporate governance is considered to be more than the mere agenda to lead and control a company. It is related to CSR in which employees and other stakeholders of business companies are important concerns. There are five basic goals for corporate governance to enhance corporate social responsibilities:[24]

1. recognition of ethics and basic human and social rights as part of honourable and honest business practice
2. a proactive stance towards environmental protection
3. protection of the community and social group from over-development and exploitation, often connected to environmental concerns
4. enhancement of social responsibility in employment, including fair labour relations — a mix of minimum labour standards and best practice, job security, equal treatment in labour markets and level playing fields for economic competition
5. sharing wealth creation fairly at local, society and global levels, and economic proof of the socially responsible corporation being both good business and good for society.

Corporate directors' social responsibility roles require they take up CSR actions to produce or induce organisational, social and public policy outcomes that meet society's expectations and are therefore favourable to the company's continued survival and economic success. These roles can be regarded as a stream of top-level decisions that can induce an integrated set of activities intended to produce favourable social outcomes. For example, product stewardship, pollution prevention and sustainable development are new priorities of a board's response to corporate social responsibility and management of a company's image in the environment. Figure 11.2 shows the relationship between corporate governance and social responsibility. In the same way companies attempt to respond to their external environments with social activities, directors of governing boards can help their companies through appropriate social responsibility actions.

Management of stakeholders

Stakeholder management is the process of managing the expectations of people, groups and organisations that have an interest in a company and will be affected by its activities.[25] Stakeholder management is an important issue in corporate governance. In a report presented to the US Council on Competitiveness, Porter, a well-known researcher in strategic management, recommended closer board involvement with stakeholders in order to make the United States more competitive than Japan and Germany.[26]

Stakeholders are groups of people who have an interest in the activity of a certain entity, such as an organisation, a local community, a society or a certain social movement. An organisation's survival and continued success depends upon the ability of its management to create and maintain sufficient wealth, value and satisfaction for all stakeholder groups.[27] There are basically two types of stakeholders: (1) primary stakeholders (which include the company itself, employees, shareholders, customers and suppliers); and (2) secondary stakeholders (which include the media and various special interest groups as well as the general public).

The nature of an organisation's stakeholders, their values, their relative influence on decisions and the nature of the situation are all relevant information for predicting organisational behaviour and outcomes.[28] In line with this view, the objectives of a corporation can only be achieved by protecting and balancing the interests of these different groups of stakeholders.

FIGURE 11.2 Corporate governance and social responsibility

Concern for stakeholders and corporate governance

The concern for stakeholders by corporate directors has some important implications for corporate governance. Corporations can be more responsive to the interests of society as a whole by incorporating the participation of stakeholders in their governing boards. The stakeholder approach to the roles of a governing board expects the organisation leaders, such as corporate directors and senior managers, to negotiate and compromise with stakeholders in the interests of the corporation. Corporate directors can help their companies through appropriate actions, such as disclosure of relevant information, adoption of a code of ethics, respect for environmental concerns, and corporate social activities, which will have positive effects on stakeholders. Global initiatives such as the sustainable development goals of the United Nations are increasingly being adopted by organisations as part of thinking through these responsibilities towards stakeholders.[29]

The concern for stakeholders by organisation leaders is expected to have a significant influence on, and to realistically reflect, the formulation and implementation of a company's mission and strategies. Such concerns will also have significant impact on how the strategies adopted by an organisation that deal with multiple stakeholders will change as the organisation evolves through the stages of formation, growth, maturity, and decline or revival. This will provide a relevant framework for assessing the roles, rights, responsibilities and legitimacies of different actors in the interactions between organisations and their environment.

However, not all corporate leaders are interested in the proper management of stakeholders. Corporate leaders' apathy to stakeholders can be explained with reference to a lack of the perception congruency between different parties. For governance effectiveness, some empirical studies showed that there were significant perception disparities between corporate directors and managers regarding stakeholder management.[30] It is possible that many organisations expect their corporate leaders to play specific roles in relation to taking care of stakeholders but, unfortunately, many corporate leaders may not necessarily perceive such roles as important. This disparity in role perception — understanding why some corporate leaders are not interested in stakeholder management — is important.

Stakeholder analysis

Stakeholder analysis is a process of systematically gathering and analysing qualitative information to determine whose interests should be taken into account when developing and implementing a policy or program. It is a technique that can be used to identify and assess the importance of key people, groups of people, or institutions that may significantly influence the success of a company's activities. It is useful in anticipating the kind of influence, positive or negative, these stakeholder groups will have on the company and will be helpful in developing strategies to get the most effective support possible and reduce any obstacles to successful implementation of corporate strategies.

11.3 The root problem of corporate governance: separation of ownership and management

LEARNING OBJECTIVE 11.3 Acknowledge the implications of the separation of ownership and management in the modern organisation.

While understanding the needs of stakeholders is important for organisational leaders to formulate and design appropriate strategies, the root problem of corporate governance is related to the separation of ownership and management — an unavoidable phenomenon of modern organisations.

In the past, businesses were managed by the owners and their families and there was no problem of conflict between ownership and management. The introduction of the modern public corporation ignited a managerial revolution that led to a separation of ownership and control. It also brought an important challenge of the modern organisation — the agency problem.

In the modern corporation, there is a division of power, duties and rights between shareholders and managers. Shareholders purchase and own shares of a corporation, which entitle them to income from the operations of the companies after all costs and expenses have been paid. Such earnings are called **residual income**.

Shareholders (principals) who invest their capital in a company are inclined towards, and sometimes even design, an effective governance system that protects their interests and thus maximises their rate of return. Professional managers (agents) are contracted to manage corporations, which they do not own.

The relationship between a principal and an agent can be explained by agency theory. **Agency theory** concerns potential conflicts arising between shareholders (principals), and managers (agents) who have effective control over companies. The managers' control may allow self-interest to influence their decision making. Shareholders lack direct control of large, publicly traded corporations. The key issue is that it may not be worth the shareholders' efforts to mind the company's business because the shareholdings may be too small. It is, therefore, difficult or expensive for shareholders to verify whether managers are behaving appropriately. Under these circumstances, managers may not necessarily take decisions that maximise shareholders' wealth. They may choose to pursue their own personal goals, such as avoiding risk, maximising their pay and fringe benefits, and spending money on prestige projects.

Two agency problems arise: managerial opportunism and moral hazard.

Managerial opportunism

The use of corporate resources, whether they are tangible or intangible, for a manager's benefit at the expense of the company's investors is called managerial opportunism. Based on the assumption that a human being is rational, self-interested and opportunistic, managers as agents are inclined to practise managerial opportunism if there is no control mechanism in place. Self-interested behaviours by managers — managerial opportunism — prevent the maximisation of shareholders' wealth, which is the primary goal of shareholders. Shareholders cannot be sure if managers have exerted their maximum effort because people are motivated by opportunities for their own personal gain. That is why governance and control mechanisms are established to prevent managerial opportunism.

Moral hazard

Moral hazard is the situation in which managers do not need to take up the full consequences and responsibilities of their decisions and, therefore, may have a tendency to act less fully in shareholders' interests than they should. This leaves shareholders to face the consequences of undesirable managerial actions. In securing their jobs, managers are inclined to business diversification in order to reduce operational risks. Shareholders, however, expect a good return on their investment — good dividends — and prefer the organisation to take higher risks. They invest in different companies to reduce their personal risk level by holding diversified portfolios. Moral hazard will result in a divergence of interests and risk preferences between the managers and shareholders.

Agency costs

Agency costs are costs incurred to safeguard a principal's interest against the inappropriate actions of an agent.[31] These costs stem from two main sources: reward and control. The reward cost of agency refers to the costs associated with the financial incentives of an agent. Examples are managers' salaries and bonuses, which are reward costs that need to be borne by shareholders. Controlling costs of agents are the costs related to the process of aligning the divergent interests of the managers and shareholders. In other words, the monitoring and sanction of managerial opportunism and moral hazard is related to the controlling cost. Agency costs are inevitable within an organisation because they provide proper material incentives (e.g. performance bonuses and stock options) and moral incentives for agents to properly execute their duties, thereby aligning the interests of principals and agents.

11.4 Corporate governance mechanisms

LEARNING OBJECTIVE 11.4 Analyse the internal and external governance structure of organisations.

Given the significance of the negative implications of the separation of ownership and management, it is important that measures are taken to solve this agency problem. Corporate governance mechanisms are the processes by which strategic decisions of companies are made and controlled. Corporate governance is designed to reduce the conflicts of interest between investors and managers, thereby eliminating barriers that may hinder the growth of the value of the organisation. The governance structure in different countries may differ in accordance with their political, social and economic environment. There are two major types of governance mechanisms: internal and external. Figure 11.3 shows a diagrammatic representation of the internal and external governance mechanisms.

| FIGURE 11.3 | External and internal corporate governance mechanisms |

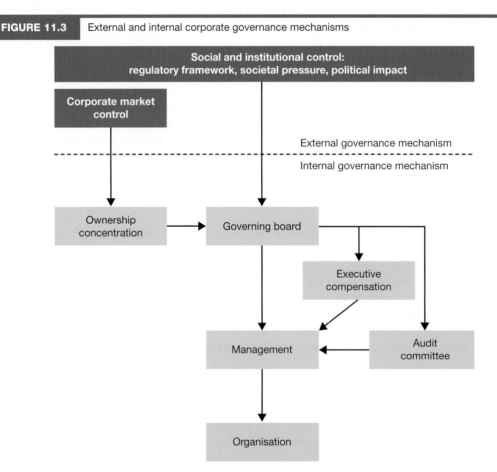

External governance mechanisms

External governance mechanisms primarily refer to the control of managerial activities by the external environment of an organisation. It includes two types of control: institutional control and corporate market control.

Institutional control

Institutional control includes regulatory frameworks, social pressure and political impact. In general, most of the well-developed economies have established some detailed statutory regulatory frameworks of corporate governance, based primarily on a government's legislation (e.g. the Corporations Act in Australia or Companies Act in New Zealand). To ensure an effective corporate governance framework, it is necessary that government, professional bodies and associations have clearly defined rules and regulations, including voluntary codes of practice and guidelines for best practice.

The stock exchange, the regulating agencies and the investing public are constantly urging companies to release more accurate, timely and detailed information about their operations. The improved quality of corporate accounts and annual reports, and the availability of other forms of information to investors and analysts (e.g. company briefings and press announcements), help monitor companies and identify, as well as prevent, inappropriate or unethical actions by managers.

Some examples of internal governance guidelines that are designed to protect shareholders' interests are as follows.

- A governing board is not to be dominated by a single individual acting as both the chairperson and chief executive.
- Independent non-executive directors should have more power to represent shareholder interests.
- A governing board should be careful in making decisions connected with executive compensation and auditing of company accounts.

In addition to other regulatory agencies' and internal governance guidelines, there is, for example, legislation (e.g. the Corporations Act or Companies Act) to protect shareholders' interests. What makes the whole notion of corporate governance messy, however, is relating good governance and better board composition to performance. While there have been increasing calls by shareholders and governments to transform corporate governance rules — such as ensuring the right mix of independent directors — there is a consistency of research to suggest that there is 'no predicate, either in logic or in experience to suggest that a majority of independent directors on a board will guarantee good corporate governance or better financial returns for shareholders'.[32] This relates to the CEO roles and those of the board, and the belief that many of the problems between agents (CEOs, general managers) and principals (the board of directors acting on behalf of shareholders) have little to do with increased company performance.[33]

Institutional control also includes social pressure and political impact. *Social pressure* is the combination of external influences that surround an organisation in the course of its daily operations. *Political impact* comes primarily from the government, including the regulation and deregulation of business activities. Social pressure penetrates into the ambits of an organisation as well as its board through various socialisation and institutionalisation processes. Power struggles in the polity, together with the enforcement of law and order of the regulatory framework, may also exert pressure on corporate governance practices. Institutional forces, in addition to market changes, are likely to influence the rationality and drives for profit-maximisation which mould the economic behaviour of the corporate leaders. In many cases, however, these social, political and institutional forces may not be effective in controlling some of these leaders. Failure of companies, in the form of bankruptcy and fraud, is not uncommon. The best known example is failure of the Enron Corporation in the United States.

Corporate market control

The modern economic system allows the voting shares of companies to be publicly bought and sold through the mechanism of a stock exchange. Economic control of governance is present in the form of **corporate market control**, which refers to the process by which ownership and control of companies is transferred from one group of investors and managers to another.[34] More simply put, it is about the influence of the possible changes in ownership of companies that will affect the practices of corporate governance.

The share prices of publicly listed companies on a stock exchange are often viewed as an indicator of the extent to which managers are efficiently operating the corporation and maximising shareholders' wealth. Managers are hired to make the company's day-to-day pricing, production, investment, marketing and other business decisions. If they are performing in line with investors' expectations, the financial statements of their companies will show their adequacy.

How will the capital market respond if the managers of a listed company are not doing a good job? If this happens, depending on the available information, the share price of the company will be valued low and this will create incentives for a takeover by a more efficient group of managers and shareholders. By taking control and subsequently changing senior managers or management practices and reallocating resources, the assets of the acquired company may be put to uses that create a higher value. The market for corporate control is important in bringing together two important markets — the markets for products and services and the capital market — and can play an important role in promoting market efficiency.

Shareholders of underperforming companies may not be able to expend additional resources to monitor and control all the companies in which they have a shareholding. If they observe that managers of a particular company are not acting in what they regard as their best interests, they will very likely sell the shares they own rather than intervene in the company's operations. This will also result in a lower share price. If this process continues, the company may become vulnerable to a merger bid by another group of managers, resulting in a loss of top management jobs. Fear of being taken over can establish some sort of backstop position to prevent shareholder wealth considerations being totally ignored.

Thus, in the market for corporate control, individuals and companies buy or take over undervalued corporations. Ineffective managers are usually replaced in such takeovers. The threat of takeover may lead the company's manager to operate more efficiently. The purchase of a company that is underperforming relative to industry rivals is desirable because it can improve its strategic competitiveness. In such a case, the market for corporate control is acting in place of the company's internal governance mechanisms. There are various signs that may alert a company to an imminent hostile takeover. The company may suddenly become the target of various inspections carried out by regulatory bodies. Also, the number of transactions in shares of the company may considerably increase in addition to the number of unsolicited offers to purchase shares in the company. In such circumstances, corporate leaders may undertake certain defensive strategies to protect their interests. In most cases, preventive measures against hostile takeovers are much more effective than reactive measures.[35]

Although the market for corporate control is important in the Anglo-American capital market, which is driven by a philosophy that focuses on shareholder wealth maximisation, the non-Anglo-American markets, such as Germany, France, Holland, and Asian markets such as Japan, Thailand and Singapore, are functioning in a way that reflects a higher priority being given to longer term corporate wealth maximisation.[36] In the former philosophy of shareholder wealth maximisation, the short-term share price of a company is critical for assessing the strength of the management of a company, while the latter philosophy of corporate wealth maximisation is more a concern for maximising company wealth in the long term. As such, hostile takeovers are less likely to play an important role in the restructuring process of large companies in the non-Anglo-American markets. While this may be true, many Asian countries have formed national committees on corporate governance in a direct attempt to control fraud and corruption (including improper disclosure). Further, countries such as China, Singapore, South Korea and Malaysia have focused on strengthening their Corporations Act, which varies from one country to the next. For example, developing training programs for directors and management has become mandatory with many Institutes of Directors in those countries.[37] Similarly, corporate governance legislation has been overhauled in Singapore and Japan on the back of increasing evidence of corporate fraud and director oversights (see strategy capsule 11.1).

Internal governance mechanisms

Internal governance mechanisms are the devices of the processes within an organisation that oversee managerial activities and performance. They include ownership concentration, executive compensation, the audit committee and governing boards.

Ownership concentration

Ownership concentration refers to the situation in which a relatively large number of shares are owned by a small number of individual or institutional investors. These owners are called blockholders. Governance mechanisms can be enhanced by blockholders, who have a strong incentive to closely monitor management. Their large stakes make it worthwhile for them to spend time, effort and expense to closely monitor their investments. Occasionally, they also obtain seats on the governing boards, which can further enhance their ability to effectively monitor management. Blockholders are sometimes institutional owners, such as stock mutual funds and superannuation funds. They can have the proxy voting power and incentive to discipline ineffective top-level managers, as well as the power to reward and influence compensation outcomes. They can even affect the company's choice of strategies. For example, it is generally believed that powerful blockholders reward strategic persistence by CEOs over time with higher compensation and incentives. Generally, blockholders/stakeholders have little psychological attachment to a particular strategy because their main interest is financial return or higher share prices.

However, blockholders can create an entrenched position in which the majority shareholders abuse their position of dominant control to the detriment of minority shareholders. This may be facilitated by specific legal arrangements, like differential voting rights, in which some shares 'carry' more votes.[38] Sometimes blockholders unaffiliated with management take a more passive stance by taking the management view, or they can be influenced by already established business relationships with management. Thus, blockholders may have strong incentives to divert resources to their own benefit at the expense of minority shareholders.

Higher ownership concentration can also lessen the likelihood of aggressive company takeovers and more competitive company strategies since the incentive effect interferes with management entrenchment. Consequently, minority shareholders may perceive that higher ownership concentration by large block-holders is a sign of a more successful and better quality company. In established publicly traded companies, these arguments are consistent with the assumption that ownership concentration is a substitute for legal protections, which provide the functions of corporate governance. In other words, a company's ownership structure that is dominated by large blockholders may be a positive response to an individual company's operating characteristics in its competitive and legal environments.

Executive compensation

How should the executive compensation of managers be controlled? Executive compensation is the use of managerial incentives such as salary, performance-based cash and share bonuses, and share options to reward CEOs and senior managers, in order to align their interests with those of shareholders.

- *Salary.* Salary is the basic income of managers — the amount stipulated in their employment contracts. This form of compensation is paid to managers while they are employed even when their performance is not up to the expectations of shareholders.
- *Share options.* Organisations can grant directors and other senior managers share options. Share options permit managers to purchase, by a certain date, shares at a fixed price. If the share price rises significantly between the date when the option was granted and the date when the shares are bought, the manager can make a fortune by buying at the pre-arranged price and then selling in the market place. Managers under such a scheme have a clear interest in achieving a rise in share price with a resulting increase in the value of their shareholdings. An alternative method is to allot shares to managers if they achieve certain performance targets; for example, growth in earnings per share or return on shares.
- *Performance-based cash bonuses.* Any formula-based cash reward that is paid above and beyond salary is called a performance-based cash bonus. Performance incentives such as cash bonuses can inspire an executive to work hard and remain committed to a company. They are discretionary and usually based on pre-established, substantially market-based criteria.
- *Performance-based share bonuses.* Stock options and other similar incentive plans are effective tools for retaining employees because they reward employees based on the company's long-term performance. Very often, managers can only sell these shares after a specified period of time, normally at least one year later. This type of deferred share bonus is an investment vehicle that encourages managers to take a long-term perspective to building and sustaining the share prices of their organisations.
- *Fringe benefits.* In addition to compensation in the forms of cash and shares, there are various types of additional executive compensation plans. These fringe benefits include medical, housing and car allowances, life insurance, relocation payments, use of company-owned holiday accommodation, health-club membership, tuition reimbursements, and other compensation that will make the total remuneration package more competitive and attractive. It will help make managers more satisfied and thus willing to stay with the company.

Executive compensation is a kind of positive reinforcement that provides incentives to managers to work more effectively. Negative reinforcement, in the form of punishment, is also very common. For example, the threat of being sacked with the accompanying humiliation and financial loss may encourage managers not to diverge too far from shareholders' preferences. However, this method is seldom used — it is often difficult to implement due to the difficulties of making a coordinated shareholder effort.

However, what is clearer in recent times is a backlash from governments and society generally about the pay inequality between CEOs and other senior managers versus the average income.[39] Many financial experts suggest that shareholder value and value creation has not increased since 2005 and that, in coming years, various stock exchanges globally will see negative wealth creation. Put simply, there is very little wealth creation for the broader population compared to the rewards and accumulated wealth received by top executives. For instance, the average salary of a CEO of one of the 100 largest public companies in Australia was about A\$4.75 million in 2017; this was about 78 times more than the average worker in Australia.[40] Moreover, despite the Banking Royal Commission publishing its critical findings and shareholders targeting the executive remuneration of companies such as Telstra, the bonuses of ASX100 executives were near long-term record heights in 2019.[41] Both developments signify that there appears to be an increasing divide between societal expectations of executive pay and pay levels for the average worker. Similarly, in Asian countries, widespread anger is noticeable among shareholders who lose significant and sometimes life savings through massive write-downs resulting from poor corporate governance accountability while, simultaneously, executive rewards are not correctly disclosed.[42] A contrasting view to the above is that soaring remuneration has little to do with weak governance but much to do with globalisation.[43]

In the current managerial job market, qualified managers are enjoying more negotiating power than ever. This means a company needs to be flexible and responsive to market demand and keep its executive compensation package as attractive as what the rest of the market is offering. In addition, the performance and reputation of a company is important to help managers do a better job. A company with a clear vision, innovative ideas or quality products has a much better chance of attracting the best managers at all levels. Many managers are committed to organisations by the unique and challenging opportunity offered in these organisations, not just attractive executive compensation packages.

Audit committees

Corporate governance includes the rules and procedures for making decisions on corporate affairs to ensure success while maintaining the right balance with the stakeholders' interest. As one of the important mechanisms to ensure that decisions are made properly, the **audit committee** is a body directly answerable to the governing board and responsible for verifying that the operations of the company have been conducted appropriately and its accounting records are kept in a proper manner.

The governing board needs to ensure that effective arrangements are in place to provide assurance on risk management, governance and internal control of the company. In this respect, the board should be advised by an audit committee with members appointed by the governing board. The audit committee is very often required to issue its statements and reports on the results of its work during the preceding year, which are then sent to the governing board together with the annual report. The audit committee is usually composed of members appointed by the governing board.

Directors of the governing board need to be realistic about their personal legal liability. They need to pay attention to important corporate issues such as accuracy of accounting records, risk management of company assets, and oversight of external and internal auditors. This chapter's scene setter reminds us of these liabilities. Through the proper functioning of the audit committee, directors can thus ensure:

- compliance of directors' activities with laws and regulations
- proper financial reporting of significant issues of the company
- properly conducted internal audits (which includes assessment of compliance and ethics risks in the audit plan)
- ongoing management monitoring of board effectiveness and corporate performance
- recognition of trends, which are then acted upon appropriately.

There are substantial changes in the development of audit committees in many countries. Countries in the Asia–Pacific region, in particular, are eager to follow what the developed countries require to enhance the effectiveness of corporate governance. In 1989, Singapore mandated the adoption of audit committees following the collapse of a major conglomerate and a market crisis; in 1994, Malaysia followed. In 1998, Thailand announced that all listed companies must form audit committees by December 1999. In 1999, South Korea (The Republic of Korea) made audit committees mandatory for the listed subsidiaries of the large conglomerates. Many Asian companies are now required to have audit committees in place.

Governing board

A **governing board** is a group of elected individuals that acts in the owners' interests to formally monitor and control the company's top-level executives. In general, the board has the power to direct the affairs of the organisation, and punish and reward managers, in order to protect shareholders from managerial opportunism. In the absence of legal definition, the directors can protect whomever they choose, be they members of the organisation or an external constituency, depending on their own needs and the pressures to which they are subjected.[44]

In the case of a business corporation, a governing board will stand in place of the shareholders. In the case of a government-owned corporation, the board is appointed to represent the interests of the government. As a representative of the legal owners, the board has the authority to exercise the power of the corporation, subject only to restraints imposed by the law. This power is conferred upon them by the legal owners through the articles of incorporation or statutory provisions. Boards, therefore, have the legal responsibility to use their authority and power in the best interest of the owners.

11.5 The governing board as the core of corporate governance

LEARNING OBJECTIVE 11.5 Comprehend the structure and major roles of governing boards.

A governing board is at the core of the corporate governance of modern organisations. There are quite a few alternative names for a governing board, including board of directors, board of trustees and supervisory board. The shareholders' role in governance is to appoint the directors and the auditors and to satisfy themselves that an appropriate governance structure is in place. A governing board is the point of coordination and interaction where different external influences of the organisation meet regularly, sometimes on a face-to-face basis, with each other and with the managers, to discuss and ostensibly control the decisions and actions of the organisation.

The responsibilities of the board are manifold. They include setting the company's strategic goals, providing the leadership to put them into effect, supervising the management of the business and reporting to the stockholders on their stewardship. Governing boards are often described, or portrayed visually, as the top of an organisation, and endowed with the authority to set objectives and monitor the performance of the management.[45] The board's actions are subject to laws, regulations and the decisions of the shareholders in the company's general meetings.

Structure of a governing board

The structure of a governing board has three basic components: the size of the board, director composition and board demography. This reflects the mainstream of research in board structure and, to some extent, an anatomy of what really constitutes a board. Figure 11.4 illustrates a common framework for the study of the internal structure of a governing board.

FIGURE 11.4 Internal structure of a governing board

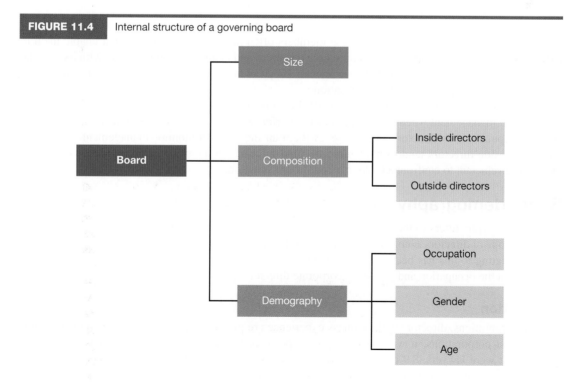

Board size

Board size refers to the number of members of the governing board. The ideal size of a board has been the topic of much debate. The potential advantages of larger boards are that more views are represented and thus discussed, and the board will be able to draw upon the expertise and skills of more directors while making strategic decisions.[46] The potential downside of larger boards is that it might be harder to take decisions and reach consensus among many directors. The ASX principles in Australia recognise this tension and prescribe the following.[47]

> The board should be of sufficient size so that the requirements of the business can be met and changes to the composition of the board and its committees can be managed without undue disruption. However, it should not be so large as to be unwieldy.

In reality, the size of governing bodies varies widely across different countries.[48] The specific nature of the company's competitive environment and managerial team help explain cross-sectional variation in corporate board size and composition. There is a trend that board size increases as companies grow in size and diversify over time, although studies show that the association between the size of governing boards and their performance is very weak.[49]

Board composition

The composition of a governing board is a critical determinant of its ability to carry out its governance responsibilities effectively. Board structure influences the quality of directors' deliberation and decisions, the ability of directors to control CEOs and their capacity to provide strategic directions and performance. There are basically two types of directors:

1. inside (or executive) directors — usually a company's CEO and other top-level managers
2. outside (or non-executive) directors — individuals who are independent of the company's day-to-day operations and have no other direct relationship with the company.

The strengths and weaknesses of inside and outside directors constitute an interesting topic in management literature. Inside directors can bring specialised knowledge and experience gained from their direct involvement in organisational activities to the board.[50] The amount and quality of information possessed by inside directors should be superior to that typically possessed by outside directors, who are supposed to help implement corporate strategies by serving as a direct communication link between the board and other organisational members.

Outside members of the governing board are unable to understand the business of the organisation well enough to be truly effective. However, these members often have external contacts that enable them to enhance the organisation's ability to obtain scarce resources and to align the organisation with its external environment. They can also become change agents. They can help overcome cognitive barriers to change by bringing new perspectives to the organisation.

Outside directors are more vigilant than inside directors and they are more likely than inside directors to challenge management when the company is not performing well. They are also eager to protect their personal reputations as directors and this gives them an incentive to monitor management's activities. Although inside directors tend to have more detailed information about company operations, they are likely to be reluctant to confront a CEO in a boardroom situation.

Board demography

Board demography refers to the occupation, gender and, sometimes, age of the members of a governing board. The age of directors is not a major academic interest in the study of governing boards and very little research relating to this has been done. The demographic features of a governing board therefore focus primarily on the occupation and gender of corporate directors.

Occupation

In most corporations, directors with business experience are preferred. In a survey of the United States' 1300 largest corporations, it was found that 64.5 per cent of the directors were business executives, 6.0 per cent were lawyers, 8.9 per cent were academics and 4.5 per cent were consultants. Being filled mainly with business executives, the governing boards of companies in most developed countries are obviously business-biased.[51]

Gender

A growing body of research investigating gender diversity and governance on corporate boards reveals that, despite the progress made on gender diversity in the workplace, women are still a minority in top management and at board level globally.

Women's representation on corporate boards may be shaped by the larger environment, including the social, political and economic structures of individual countries. Countries with higher representation of women on boards are more likely to have women in senior management and more equal ratios of male to female pay.[52] Countries around the globe have also started to experiment with corporate gender quotas to improve gender equality. A recent OECD study suggests that these gender quotas appear to be working,[53] although some management researchers suggest that companies put women on corporate boards merely for the sake of company image, with little concern for their actual contributions.[54]

Intraboard heterogeneity

Intraboard heterogeneity refers to the diversity in the composition of governing boards such that the directors are different from each other with respect to their professions, gender or age.[55] Despite the collective responsibility of most governing boards, certain individuals or groups of individuals on governing boards are considerably more influential than others. Some are more educated and others can have more relevant business experience and exposure.

Members of governing boards are usually individuals of relatively high social status. However, there is a lack of frequent interaction within a board, which implies a corresponding deficiency of a distinct and persistent culture within these boards. Since strategic decisions to be made by directors of governing boards are usually complex and non-routine, and affect the company over an extended period, not all directors are required to contribute equally.

The directors' expertise and ability to fully comprehend a company's business situation are important factors in determining the board's ability to provide advice to management and to monitor managerial behaviour.[56] The composition of a governing board determines its 'human capital' and leads to different board activities and outcomes. Studies show that differences in prior board experiences are correlated positively with differences in director involvement in strategic decision making.[57] Since directors are different, there is a distinct heterogeneity in the skills set of companies' governing boards. Boards, through their unique combination of skills, are a potential source of knowledge and expertise for the companies they govern.

Heterogeneity is a challenging issue in the study of the structure of governing boards. Some studies show that the more heterogeneous and complementary the individual cognitive traits of board members, in terms of knowledge, skills, beliefs and values, the more efficient and effective are the problem-solving processes in the board.[58] Other research suggests that there is no direct linkage between heterogeneity and board performance.[59] While intraboard heterogeneity as a determinant of company performance has been the subject of extensive research, there is no general consensus that links variations in board size and the type of membership with company performance.[60]

Roles and responsibilities of governing boards

A governing board is considered to be a boundary-spanning control unit. It has important roles in regulating exchanges of information and resources internally and across organisational boundaries.[61] Considerable effort has been spent studying governing boards and many different types of theories and models have been proposed to explain the various roles played by governing boards. In general, the roles and responsibilities of governing boards can be examined from two different perspectives — academic and practical.

From an academic perspective, governing bodies play three sets of interrelated roles. They are strategy, control and service roles.[62] The *strategy* role is involved with the formulation and dissemination of corporate goals and policies as well as the allocation of the resources necessary to implement the board's strategies. The *control* role is concerned with corporate control, which includes monitoring and rewarding executive action and performance. The *service* role is related to the institutional function of governing boards, which includes representing the organisation's interests in society, linking the company with its external environment and securing critical resources.

From a practical perspective, the Australian Independent Working Party into Corporate Governance recommends that the key role of a governing board is to ensure that the corporate management is continuously and effectively striving for above-average performance, taking into account risk.[63] The

Working Party proposes that the functions of a governing board should at least cover the following — appointment of the CEO, formulation of strategies and policies, budgeting and planning, reporting to shareholders on regulatory compliance, and ensuring the board's own effectiveness.[64]

By combining these two different perspectives and addressing the issues faced by governing boards with regard to both the internal and external environments of a company, four major types of roles of governing boards can be identified: controlling, strategy making, networking and coordinating.

As corporate leaders, governing boards need to pay attention to both the internal and external environment of their companies. Internally, numerous studies on corporate governance suggest that governing boards need to control managerial behaviour and activities and, at the same time, provide management with advice and counsel on strategic matters that require the expertise of individual directors. These represent the controlling and strategy-making roles. Externally, governing boards can solicit and maintain business and social contacts for their companies,[65] and are required to consider and coordinate the various interests of stakeholders. These represent the networking and coordinating roles.

Figure 11.5 shows a diagrammatic representation of these four major roles. It should be noted that not every governing board will need to perform all these four roles simultaneously. At different times, governing boards can play a variety of mixed roles to face the challenges of the external environment.

| FIGURE 11.5 | Four major roles of governing boards |

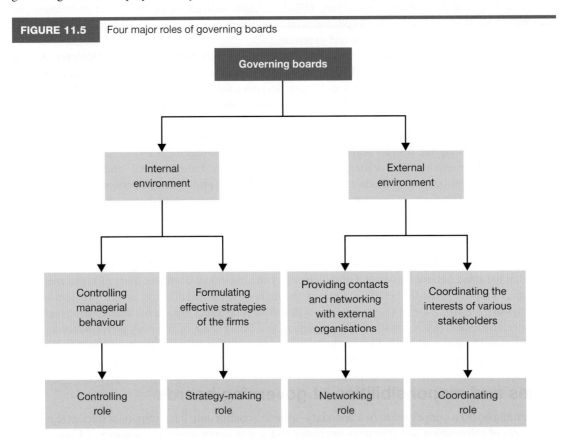

11.6 Interaction between management and the governing board

LEARNING OBJECTIVE 11.6 Recognise the relationship between managers and governing boards, and assess how this relationship is related to strategic risk and corporate performance.

As discussed earlier in this chapter, a governing board acts as a control mechanism to prevent (or detect) managerial opportunism, which is against the interests of shareholders, and assists in the formulation of corporate strategies. The governing board guides and directs management to achieve the corporate mission and objectives.

It is important and beneficial to have active and participative interaction between management and the governing board of an organisation. The effectiveness of corporate directors in monitoring management is critical for the survival of all corporations characterised by the separation of ownership and decision making.[66] In addition, a governing board is considered to be an important information system that allows the organisation to face the challenges of the external environment.

In practice the interaction between management and the governing board of an organisation is an important issue and unfortunately has not been given enough attention in the business or academic arenas. The concerns about this issue are twofold.

1. What is the role of managers in an organisation — an agent or a steward?
2. Should the position of chairperson of a governing board be occupied by the CEO of the organisation?

Agent or steward

There has been a recent trend to reconcile the economic and moral dimensions of management by challenging the prevailing assumptions of human motivation that are derived from agency theory.[67] From an economic perspective, managers are opportunistic and their role as an agent needs to be closely monitored. From the moral dimension, however, many senior managers are diligent and thus motivated to do a good job. If this is the case, it follows that there is no motivation problem or non-alignment of interests between management and ownership, and so the management acts like a steward of an organisation. Given such a case, the control role of the governing board will be less important.

So, what role of management is more effective — agent or steward? There are two factors that influence management to become an agent or a steward.

1. Some managers have transcendent motives of having a strong identification with their companies so that their commitments to these companies are characterised by honesty and decency.[68]
2. There can be a developmental process in which trust and reciprocity are cultivated between the governing board and the managers through a history of cooperative interactions.[69]

Managers can change over time from a position of agent towards a position of steward. An effective governing board is able to manage its relationship with management in a mutually beneficial manner. While in the early stage of the relationship, a governing board needs to control managers more closely, eventually, as interactions become more developed, this control role will become less important. When managers are more committed to their companies, their role as agent will gradually be overshadowed by their strong sense of stewardship.

Managing risk

As responsible stewards of the company's activities, CEOs and managers will want to display an increasing capacity to manage risk. In fact, good corporate governance in every company necessitates the need to identify risks. Corporate collapse is the product of poor strategic oversight by the board in terms of mitigating the risk of major strategic decisions and/or minimising the risk to shareholders through good corporate governance oversight. Research suggests that companies mismanage strategic risk by making premature decisions and limiting their search functions.[70] Figure 11.6 outlines five elements of strategic risk and displays key strategies for aligning strategic risk with sound corporate governance principles.[71] Significantly, figure 11.6 shows how such factors as culture and leadership are critical in preventing strategic risk failures and managerial greed.

Unfortunately, not all managers will eventually become stewards. In many cases, the self-interested behaviours of managers are so dominant that a governing board must be very careful to curb any potential instances of managerial opportunism. A governing board will need to be careful not to allow any management malpractice, and at the same time should try to cultivate the positive aspect of stewardship into the mindset of managers. This, of course, is not an easy task, but can provide great benefits if appropriate strategic risk assessment is in place.

CEO and chairperson of a governing board

In some companies, the chief executive officer or CEO is also the chairperson of the governing board, a situation which is described as 'CEO/chairperson duality'. The chairperson of a governing board sets the tone of the board and their strength as a leader may well determine the effectiveness of the board. The separation of the position of chairperson of a governing board from the CEO position can significantly help directors prevent crises, act swiftly and effectively in the event of a crisis, and evaluate objectively the impact of crises.

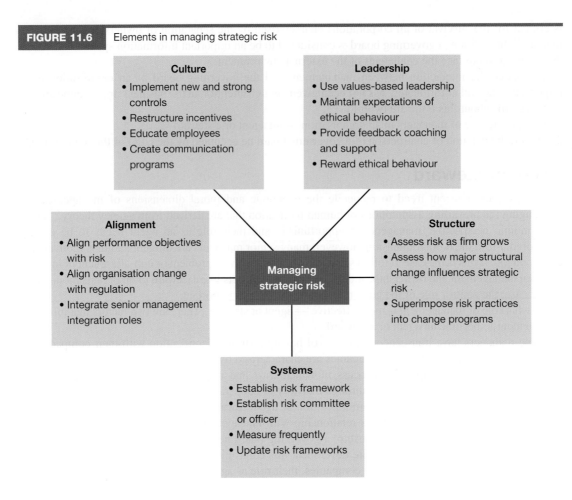

FIGURE 11.6 Elements in managing strategic risk

Culture
- Implement new and strong controls
- Restructure incentives
- Educate employees
- Create communication programs

Leadership
- Use values-based leadership
- Maintain expectations of ethical behaviour
- Provide feedback coaching and support
- Reward ethical behaviour

Alignment
- Align performance objectives with risk
- Align organisation change with regulation
- Integrate senior management integration roles

Managing strategic risk

Structure
- Assess risk as firm grows
- Assess how major structural change influences strategic risk
- Superimpose risk practices into change programs

Systems
- Establish risk framework
- Establish risk committee or officer
- Measure frequently
- Update risk frameworks

Studies show that governing boards tend to be more effective when one person does not simultaneously occupy the positions of CEO and chairperson.[72] CEO/chairperson duality has some adverse effects on organisational performance, and scholars strongly recommend that the positions of the CEO and the chairperson of the governing board of an organisation be occupied by two different persons.

CEO/chairperson duality is a double-edged sword. The negative aspects become apparent where a company's CEO is so powerful that they control everything in the company. Governing boards are charged with ensuring that CEOs carry out their duties in a way that serves the best interests of the shareholders. Therefore, a governing board must maintain equilibrium between management and shareholder interests. Separating the roles of chairperson and chief executive gives a board sufficient power to challenge an overly dominant CEO.

In some cases, there are considerable benefits attributable to CEO/chairperson duality. While some shareholders are put off by the absence of board control and checks and balances, others are reassured by the presence of unity of command and the absence of potentially acrimonious conflict between strong-minded individuals. When the positions of chairperson and CEO are occupied by a single person, it can provide a single focal point for company leadership. A powerful and effective CEO creates an image of stability and instils a sense of wellbeing in the employees as well as the shareholders of the company, projecting a clear sense of direction.

Corporate governance and performance

The contribution of corporate governance to corporate performance is an important issue.[73] Organisational outcomes, such as strategies and performance, are expected to reflect the characteristics of the organisation's leaders. Pressure from institutional investors and other stakeholders, however, will cause governing boards to become increasingly critical of management performance.[74]

As an important component of corporate governance, a governing board very often intervenes in an organisation's strategic planning and decision-making process. A board can play a particularly important and direct role in influencing strategic change, especially when an organisation is at its early stage of development or is encountering a crisis. The overall performance of the organisation is an outcome of the governance process.[75]

It is of crucial importance that companies have strong and effective corporate governance practices, which can help set corporate objectives to generate sustainable economic returns to owners, run day-to-day operations of the business, protect the interests of shareholders and stakeholders, and align corporate activities with applicable laws and regulations. Good corporate governance, complemented by a sound business environment, can strengthen business investment, corporate performance and economic growth.[76] In particular, effective corporate governance practices will enable companies to:
- more easily access capital markets, lowering the cost of capital
- strengthen corporate reputation and raise the trust and confidence of investors and customers
- increase the efficiency of operational activities and minimise risks
- enhance long-term sustainability and growth.

With better transparency and public awareness of minority investors' and stakeholders' rights, the behaviour of corporate leaders will gradually change. The change in behaviour and performance of boards and management will ultimately affect the corporate decisions made by top management. This will have regard not only to corporate fairness but also corporate social responsibilities. Shareholders and stakeholders rely on the exercise of good corporate governance in order to ensure that their companies are performing well enough.

Strategy capsule 11.2 illustrates how incorrect disclosure almost brought down Australian business Centro Properties Group, one of the largest retailing groups in the world. This threatened the long-term sustainability of the company at a time when corporate ethics was under increasing scrutiny. This vignette shows how shareholders are powerful groups that can work together to ensure major companies admit to serious errors. In many cases, shareholders are able to bring lawsuits against companies in the interest of protecting investments and to ensure a company takes the right course of action for long-term sustainability and growth.

Stakeholder power and organisational sustainability

Law firms acting on behalf of hundreds of investors and shareholders levelled claims worth A$200 million against the Centro Properties Group in 2010–11. Centro, known globally as the second largest shopping centre owner behind Westfield, did not disclose A$200 billion of short-term debt. Errors in the annual accounts incorrectly labelled Centro's short-term bank debt as long-term debt. The basis of the claims was that Centro Properties, a division of Centro Group, had breached its obligations for continuous disclosure through alleged deceptive conduct under the Corporations Act.[77] The accounting errors were not discovered until 2008, which immediately saw the value of stocks decline by more than 90 per cent. The group's debt structure was subsequently reviewed and the sacking of its senior executives closely followed.

- What this case exposes, is that the survival and sustainability of a large corporation — in fact, any organisation — can be threatened by inaccurate public statements that shareholders, investors and valuers rely on. By not correctly disclosing the amount of short-term debt, the company's directors had overstated the overall performance of the company by indicating its accounts were in order. However, incorrect accounts overstated Centro's ability to survive in the short term. If short-term creditors had called on the company to pay its debts immediately, this would have threatened shareholder wealth by exposing the company to undisclosed short-term debt commitments. Similarly, existing shareholders would have made investment decisions based on the accounts.
- While Centro Group eventually restructured its activities, changing its name to Centro Retail Australia, this did not prevent the Federal Court in 2012 from finding that eight Centro directors had breached the Corporations Act. This led to the Court awarding a settlement figure of A$200 million to investors and shareholders.[78] In relation to corporate governance and performance, particularly sustainability, the case highlights how directors need to increase the efficiency of operational activities and minimise risks, while enhancing long-term sustainability and growth.

11.7 Current trends in corporate governance

LEARNING OBJECTIVE 11.7 Appreciate the value and importance of corporate governance trends in the public sector and the international arena.

Corporate governance has been a major concern for corporate sustainability for many years. However, it is only recently that corporate governance has begun to have a major effect on businesses — after most governments around the world implemented legislation for the proper control of companies. A number of trends in corporate governance have been observed. First, the extension of the governance practices of private enterprises to the public sector is obvious, and second, there is an international convergence of corporate governance practices. These important issues will be discussed next.

Public sector governance

Public sector governance is concerned with a desire for greater economy, efficiency and effectiveness in the use of public resources. As the public sector plays a vital role in society, it is imperative to develop public sector governance that is conducive to delivering high performance. Good public sector governance requires that the government be held accountable to stakeholders for the proper use and stewardship of public resources, and that there are effective checks and balances for monitoring the government's performance.

There are three key elements of good public sector governance.[79] The first key element is 'leadership oversight'. This refers to the role and performance of the governing board in setting strategic direction, providing leadership, defining control mechanisms, reporting performance and taking overall accountability. The governing board should lead by example by committing to and observing the highest standards of conduct. Phenomena such as low attendance rates at board/committee meetings, which could affect the effectiveness of the operations of the board, and poor documentation on the management of conflicts of interest affecting board members are signs of governance inadequacies.

The second key element is 'control and compliance'. A strong system of control is essential to the efficiency and effectiveness of operations. It requires the management and staff to cultivate and sustain a culture of compliance with the applicable statutory requirements and administrative and internal guidelines and procedures in the day-to-day operations. Some public projects contain inadequate and inaccurate information, project reports are submitted late, and projects that have poor control suffer from inadequate or missing information and late submissions. Control and compliance can prevent (and detect) these problems.

The third key element is 'disclosure and transparency'. The governing board of a public organisation needs to commit to openness and transparency in the operations and performance of the organisation. It should establish clear and effective communication channels with stakeholders to report its mission, objectives and performance and, at times, disclose important information that is of public interest. Disclosure and transparency is particularly important in the public sector and this is illustrated in several of this chapter's strategy capsules. The tightening of legislation relating to Asia–Pacific companies, as discussed earlier, will help to ensure correct disclosure so that risks are mitigated.

Good corporate governance is essential to the credibility, success and sustainability of an organisation, whether it is in the private or public sectors. This requires a strong commitment from the governing board, management and staff at all levels. Good corporate governance may not guarantee success, but without it failure is almost certain.

International corporate governance

From an international perspective, the process of convergence in corporate governance is gathering momentum due to growing concerns regarding the importance of putting appropriate checks and balances in place. Many countries have been adopting international best practices over the past two decades, with international investors and creditors also becoming more comfortable in dealing with economic entities that adopt transparent and globally acceptable accounting and governance standards. Companies that comply with high governance standards invariably develop a better reputation in the global capital market and are thus able to raise capital at lower costs.

Yet, actual practices of corporate governance still differ widely and significantly among countries. The governance mechanism of each country is shaped by its political, economic and social environment, as well as by its legal framework. Strategy capsule 11.3 showcases some of the diversity surrounding ownership rights, remuneration disclosure and director requirements across countries in the Asia–Pacific region.

Corporate governance across the Asia–Pacific region

Despite the growing convergence of corporate governance regulation and practices around the globe, national differences are still significant. The *OECD Corporate Governance Factbook 2019* provides a comprehensive overview of this striking plurality, including the following examples from the Asia–Pacific region.[80]

1. Whereas in Australia and Indonesia the minimum notice period for a general shareholder meeting is respectively 28 days and 22 days, in Japan and Korea the minimum notice period is 14 days. Whereas in all these countries all shareholders need to be informed about the general shareholder meeting, in Hong Kong this is not a requirement.
2. The minimum shareholder requirement for placing items on the agenda of the general shareholder meeting is 3 per cent in China, 5 per cent in Indonesia and 10 per cent in India. The minimum shareholder requirement to request a general shareholder meeting is generally higher; in the mentioned countries, at least 10 per cent ownership is required.
3. Whereas disclosure of the policy and amount of remuneration is merely recommended in Malaysia and Singapore, this is required in countries such as Australia and China.
4. Whereas Australia, Korea and New Zealand do not have any recommendations or requirements around when a long-sitting board member is no longer to be considered independent, in China this is the case after 6 years, and in Hong Kong, Singapore and Malaysia a company needs to explain its position after 9 years.

Understanding these national differences is essential, particularly with the growing significance of Asian capital markets. The described corporate governance recommendations and requirements are not only important in terms of understanding the likely checks and balances companies will put in place, but also in terms of being appreciative about the specific rights you have when doing business and investing throughout the Asia–Pacific region.

Commonwealth Association of Corporate Governance

Corporate governance has received much attention in the past two decades. The Commonwealth Association of Corporate Governance (CACG) was established in 1998 with the objective of promoting the best international standards on corporate governance through education, consultation and information throughout the countries of the Commonwealth as a means to achieve global standards of business efficiency, commercial probity and effective economic and social development. The CACG has established a global appreciation of four generic corporate governance principles:

1. the *responsibility* of directors who approve the strategic direction of the organisation within a framework of prudent controls and who employ, monitor and reward management
2. the *accountability* of the board to shareholders who have the right to receive information on the financial stewardship of their investment and exercise power to reward or remove the directors entrusted to run the company
3. the *transparency* of clear financial and operational information with which meaningful analysis of a company and its actions can be made
4. the *fairness* that all shareholders are treated equally and have the opportunity for redress for violation of their rights.

Based on these generic principles, countries in the Commonwealth set up their own principles and recommendations for proper corporate governance.

OECD Principles of Corporate Governance

The OECD is an intergovernmental international organisation that brings together the most industrialised countries of the global economy. Its objective is to coordinate the economic and development policies of its member nations.

The *OECD Principles of Corporate Governance* were developed to provide guidance for stock exchanges, investors, corporations and other parties that have a role in the process of developing good corporate governance. The *OECD Principles of Corporate Governance* represent a common basis that OECD member countries consider essential for the development of good governance practices. They are intended to be concise, understandable and accessible to the international community. They are not intended to substitute for government, semi-government or private sector initiatives to develop more detailed 'best practice' in corporate governance. There are six basic principles.[81]

1. *Ensuring the basis for an effective corporate governance framework*
   The corporate governance framework should promote transparent and fair markets, and the efficient allocation of resources. It should be consistent with the rule of law and support effective supervision and enforcement.
2. *The rights and equitable treatment of shareholders and key ownership functions*
   The corporate governance framework should protect and facilitate the exercise of shareholders' rights and ensure the equitable treatment of all shareholders, including minority and foreign shareholders. All shareholders should have the opportunity to obtain effective redress for violation of their rights.
3. *Institutional investors, stock markets, and other intermediaries*
   The corporate governance framework should provide sound incentives throughout the investment chain and provide for stock markets to function in a way that contributes to good corporate governance.
4. *The role of stakeholders in corporate governance*
   The corporate governance framework should recognise the rights of stakeholders established by law or through mutual agreements and encourage active co-operation between corporations and stakeholders in creating wealth, jobs, and the sustainability of financially sound enterprises.
5. *Disclosure and transparency*
   The corporate governance framework should ensure that timely and accurate disclosure is made on all material matters regarding the corporation, including the financial situation, performance, ownership and governance of the company.
6. *The responsibilities of the board*
   The corporate governance framework should ensure the strategic guidance of the company, the effective monitoring of management by the board, and the board's accountability to the company and the shareholders.

Key conclusions

The significance of proper corporate governance in the modern world can now be easily observed everywhere. A statement on corporate governance is shown in most of the annual financial reports of listed companies in both developed and developing countries. This has important implications for the disclosure of operational and financial information. A company with a relatively weak system of corporate governance will be less trustworthy in terms of the integrity of its financial statements. This chapter provides many examples of organisations falling short of good corporate governance standards.

Investors need to know and understand both quantitative and qualitative risk factors more systematically. They expect the structure of corporate governance of their target investment to be effective, not merely compliant with prevailing laws or any prescribed code of conduct. Effective corporate governance requires the joint efforts of all corporate leaders, owners, potential investors, regulators, auditors and other stakeholders. What is at stake overall is the short-and long-term sustainability of organisations in the Asia–Pacific region. Good governance is a serious business. Asia–Pacific organisations are increasingly focusing on global activities, therefore it is imperative that they carefully follow various corporate governance guidelines established in various countries across the region.

SUMMARY

Corporate governance is the process by which important strategic decisions are made and controlled in organisations. These important decisions will have to be made with reference to the management of stakeholders, including shareholders, auditors, creditors and others. By paying more attention to these stakeholders, a company can thus maintain its long-term sustainability by enhancing its social responsibility.

The primary cause of problems of corporate governance is the separation of ownership and management. It is countered by several internal and external control mechanisms. These include governing boards, audit committees, executive compensation, ownership concentration and corporate market control. Among these mechanisms, the most important one is the governing board. Its structure, in respect of its composition, demography, roles and responsibilities, has significant influence on the way it performs its roles in corporate governance.

In particular, there is an increasing call for more governing boards to include non-executive directors as a countercheck for the other directors, including the CEO. In this chapter, we have discussed several examples of incorrect disclosure, cover-ups and ill-fated decisions concerning company accounts. In these cases, the inclusion of non-executive directors would have ensured better governance.

Whether managers of a company are acting as the agents or stewards of the company depends on the extent to which they are committed to the company. In both cases, corporate governance will need to ensure that managers are not acting against the interests of shareholders.

The current trends in corporate governance are the extension of practices of governance of private enterprises to the public sector and international convergence of corporate governance practices, although national differences still persist.

KEY TERMS

agency theory The notion that shareholders' and managers' interests are not always aligned and that therefore managers may not always act in shareholders' best interests.

audit committee A body directly answerable to the governing board and responsible for verifying that the operations of the company have been conducted appropriately and its accounting records are kept in a proper manner.

corporate governance The process of how important strategic decisions are made and controlled in organisations.

corporate market control The process by which ownership and control of companies is transferred from one group of investors and managers to another.

corporate social responsibility (CSR) The continuing commitment by business to behave ethically and contribute to economic development while improving the quality of life of the workforce and their families as well as of the local community and society at large.

governing board A committee at the highest level of a company charged with making all major decisions; members are appointed by shareholders at the annual general meeting.

institutional control The control of corporate governance through laws, regulations, social pressures and political factors.

residual income Income from the operations of a company after all costs and expenses have been paid.

stakeholder analysis The process of systematically gathering and analysing qualitative information to determine whose interests should be taken into account when developing and implementing a policy or program.

stakeholder management The process of managing the expectations of people, groups or organisations that have an interest in a company and will be affected by its activities.

stakeholders Organisations and individuals to whom the organisation has a commitment and who have expectations of what the organisation does.

SELF-STUDY QUESTIONS

1 What is corporate governance? Why does corporate governance receive so much attention from various stakeholders, including shareholders, investors, business writers and academic scholars?

2 What is an agency relationship? Explain what assumptions shareholders of modern corporations may make about managers as agents.

3 Explain how the external and internal governance mechanisms — including ownership concentration, executive compensation, audit committee, governing board, corporate market control and institutional control — are used to control and monitor managerial decisions.

4 What are the primary roles of a governing board? Why are these roles important?

5 Which issues of strategic risk are applicable to all global companies, large or small?

6 How can corporate governance facilitate ethical strategic decisions for effective management of stakeholders?

7 How does corporate governance and ethical decision making change depending on how one defines the purpose of the public corporation?

DISCUSSION QUESTIONS

1 In circumstances where boards are faced with powerful and influential CEOs, in what ways (if any) will their strategic priorities change?

2 Are directors on a governing board merely 'rubber stamps'? In other words, do they endorse whatever managers present to the board? Explain.

3 In several Asia–Pacific nations, there is a predominance of family members as powerful shareholders. What corporate governance strategies can be used to ensure that ethical governance holds sway over these dominant interests?

4 If the primary objective of a governing board is to control managerial decisions, who controls the governing board?

5 To what extent do you believe a public company should solely focus on optimising its residual income? Explain and justify your position.

EXERCISES

1 Form a group and prepare a 15-minute oral presentation of a recent case related to malpractice of corporate governance. Try to provide valid solutions to stop such malpractice in future. Use any appropriate audiovisual equipment.

2 Develop an in-depth case study of a governance issue in one of the countries in the Asia–Pacific region.

3 Conduct a governance study on how a specific Asia–Pacific company tries to integrate sustainability initiatives into its strategic decision making and business operations (approximately 1000 words).

4 Collect information on corporate governance issues and standards applicable to China, Australia and India. Highlight the similarities and differences you found between these countries.

5 Select an organisation and access its annual report from its website. Carefully read the chairperson's and chief executive officer's reports. Based on this information, identify how the company designs its strategies. Choose examples from companies such as:
 – an international bank
 – a multinational conglomerate.

FURTHER READING

Boivie, S, Bednar, MK, Aguilera, RV & Andrus, JL 2016, 'Are boards designed to fail? The implausibility of effective board monitoring', *Academy of Management Annals*, vol. 10, 319–407.

Dalton, DR & Dalton, CM 2011, 'Integration of micro and macro studies in governance research: CEO duality, board composition, and financial performance', *Journal of Management*, vol. 37, 404–411.

De Villiers, C, Naiker, V & van Staden, CJ 2011, 'The effect of board characteristics on firm environmental performance', *Journal of Management*, vol. 37, 1636–1663.

Huse, M 2018, *Value-creating boards: Challenges for future practice and research*, Cambridge: Cambridge University Press.

International Corporate Governance Institute (www.icgn.org).

Lorsch, JW 2017, 'Understanding boards of directors: A systems perspective', *Annals of Corporate Governance*, vol. 2, 1–49.

Monks, RAG & Minow, N 2008, *Corporate governance*, 4th ed., Chichester: John Wiley & Sons.

Solomon, J & Solomon, A 2013, *Corporate governance and accountability*, Chichester: John Wiley & Sons.

Vallabhaneni, SR 2008, *Corporate management, governance, and ethics best practices*, Hoboken: John Wiley & Sons.

ENDNOTES

1. 'Commonwealth Bank charged fees to dead clients, inquiry hears', *BBC*, 19 April 2018, www.bbc.com.
2. Royal Commission into misconduct in the banking, superannuation and financial services industry, *Final report*, 2019.
3. D Ziffer, 'Kenneth Hayne's banking royal commission reported a year ago, but are customers any better off?', *ABC*, 4 February 2020, www.abc.net.au.
4. Royal Commission into misconduct in the banking, superannuation and financial services industry, *Interim report*, 2018.
5. ibid.
6. Royal Commission into misconduct in the banking, superannuation and financial services industry, *Final report*, 2019, p. 2.
7. 'NAB CEO Andrew Thorburn and chair Ken Henry resign in the wake of banking royal commission', *ABC*, 7 February 2019, www.abc.net.au.
8. Committee on the Financial Aspects of Corporate Governance 1992, *The Financial Aspects of Corporate Governance* (Cadbury Report), London: Gee and Co. Ltd.
9. H Hung, 'A typology of the theories of the roles of governing boards', *Corporate Governance: An International Review*, vol. 6, no. 2, 1998, 101–111.
10. MC Jensen, 'Organisation theory and methodology', *Accounting Review*, vol. 56, no. 2, 1983, 319–338.
11. RI Tricker, *International corporate governance*, Singapore: Prentice Hall, 1994.
12. P Brasor, 'Japan Post Holdings drags its heels on insurance sales scandal', *The Japan Times*, 11 January 2020, www.japantimes.co.jp; 'The corporate scandals that rocked Japan', *BBC*, 20 November 2018, www.bbc.com.
13. J Ma, E Nobuhiro and M Horie, 'How a billionaire family fell from grace after the Takata airbag scandal', *Bloomberg*, 29 June 2017, www.bloomberg.com.
14. K Alaimo, 'The Takata scandal and the value of diversity', *Bloomberg*, 28 January 2017, www.bloomberg.com; K Alaimo, 'Could board diversity have prevented the Takata scandal?', *Automotive News*, 4 February 2017, www.autonews.com.
15. W Pesek, 'Takata is the real safety hazard, not its air bags', *The Japan Times*, 25 May 2015, www.japantimes.co.jp.
16. H Tabuchi and NE Boudette, '3 Takata executives face criminal charges over exploding airbags', *New York Times*, 13 January 2017, www.nytimes.com.
17. 'Takata Corporation pleads guilty in faulty air bag cover-up scandal, agrees to pay $1.3 billion', *ABC*, 28 February 2017, www.abc.net.au.
18. D Shepardson, 'Takata whistleblowers to share $1.7 million award, lawyers say', *Reuters*, 27 March 2018, www.reuters.com.
19. CWL Hill and SA Snell, 'Effects of ownership structure and control on corporate productivity', *Academy of Management Journal*, vol. 32, no. 1, 1989, 25–46.
20. H Aldrich and D Herker, 'Boundary spanning roles and organisation structure', in PC Nystrom and WH Starbuck (eds.), *Handbook of organisational design*, New York: Oxford University Press, 1981, pp. 217–230.
21. 'Telstra considers executive pay overhaul after investors' first strike against board', *The Guardian*, 16 October 2018, www.theguardian.com
22. JD Westphal and P Khanna, 'Keeping directors in line: social distancing as a control mechanism in the corporate elite', *Administrative Science Quarterly*, vol. 48, 2003, 361–399.
23. World Business Council for Sustainable Development (WBCSD) 2007, Annual Review.
24. R Scott, *Corporate governance and social responsibility: building the links*, London: Union Network International (UNI), 2004.
25. SL Berman, AC Wicks, S Kotha and TM Jones, 'Special research forum on stakeholders, social responsibility, and performance', *The Academy of Management Journal*, vol. 42, no. 5, October, 1999, 488–506.
26. ME Porter, *Capital choices: changing the way America invests in industry*, Washington, DC: US Council on Competitiveness, 1992.
27. AJ Hillman and AH Michael, 'Corporate political strategy formulation: a model of approach, participation, and strategy decisions', *Academy of Management Review*, vol. 24, no. 4, 1999, 825–842.
28. J Alexander, 'Environmental Sustainability versus profit maximization: overcoming systemic constraints on implementing normatively preferable alternatives', *Journal of Business Ethics*, vol. 76, no. 2, 2007, 155–162.
29. United Nations, '28 companies with combined market cap of $1.3 trillion step up to new level of climate ambition', press release, 23 July 2019, www.un.org.
30. Hillman and Michael, op. cit.
31. RV Aguilera, CA Williams, JM Conley, and DE Rupp, 'Corporate governance and social responsibility: a comparative analysis of the UK and the US', *Corporate Governance: An International Review*, vol. 14, no. 3, 2006, 147–158.
32. EM Fogel and AM Geier, 'Strangers in the house: rethinking Sarbanes-Oxley and the independent board of directors', *Delaware Journal of Corporate Law*, vol. 32, no. 1, 2007, 33–72.
33. DR Dalton and CM Dalton, 'Integration of micro and macro studies in governance research: CEO duality, board composition, and financial performance', *Journal of Management*, vol. 37, 2011, 404.
34. Glossary of Industrial Organisation Economics and Competition Law, 1993, compiled by RS Khemani and DM Shapiro, commissioned by the Directorate for Financial, Fiscal and Enterprise Affairs, OECD, 1993.
35. For more information about the defence tactics against hostile takeover see KS Kokot, 'The art of takeover defence', *The Ukrainian Journal of Business Law*, 2006, 18–20; JA Pearce II and RB Robinson, 'Hostile takeover defences that maximise shareholder wealth', *Business Horizon*, vol. 47, no. 5, 2004, 15–24.
36. A Stonehill and KB Dullum, 'Corporate wealth maximization, takeovers, and the market for corporate control', *Nationaløkonomisk Tidsskrift*, Bind 128, 1990.
37. T Shanmugaratnam, 'Corporate Governance developments in Singapore and the region', OECD Asian Corporate Governance Roundtable, Singapore, 27 June 2007.
38. 'Differential voting rights', 9 May 2008, Lawmatters.in, http://lawmatters.in.
39. J Abernathy, 'Barren returns on executive pay', *Business Spectator*, 18 November 2011, www.businessspectator.com.au.

40. M Liddy, B Spraggon and N Hoad, 'CEOs now earn 78 times more than Aussie workers', *ABC*, 6 December 2017, www.abc.net.au.

41. L Henriques-Gomes, 'Australian CEO bonuses at near record highs despite royal commission', *The Guardian*, 17 September 2019, www.theguardian.com.

42. Shanmugaratnam, op. cit., p. 40.

43. 'Money for nothing? Executive pay levels rise because of globalisation, not poor oversight', *The Economist*, 14 January 2012, p. 51.

44. H Mintzberg, *Power in and around organisations*, Englewood Cliffs, NJ: Prentice Hall, 1983.

45. M Mizruchi, 'Who controls whom? An examination of the relation between management and boards of directors in large American corporations', *Academy of Management Review*, vol. 8, 1983, 426–435.

46. CM Dalton and DR Dalton, 'Boards of directors: Utilizing empirical evidence in developing practical prescriptions', *British Journal of Management*, 2005, vol. 16, S91–S97.

47. Australian Securities Exchange Corporate Governance Council 2014, *Corporate governance principles and recommendations*, 3rd edn, ASX, www.asx.com.au.

48. Spencer Stuart, 'Boards around the world', Spencer Stuart, 21 February 2020, www.spencerstuart.com.

49. Hung, op. cit.

50. J Goodstein, K Gautam, and W Boeker, 'The effects of board size and diversity on strategic change', *Strategic Management Journal*, vol. 15, 1994, 241–250.

51. IF Kesner, 'Directors' characteristics and committee membership: an investigation of type, occupation, tenure, and gender', *Academy of Management Journal*, March, 1988, vol. 31 iss. 1, 1988, 66–84.

52. S Terjesen and V Singh, 2008, 'Female presence on corporate boards: a multi-country study of environmental context', *Journal of Business Ethics*, vol. 83, no. 1, 2008, 55–63.

53. Organisation for Economic Co-operation and Development (OECD), *OECD principles of corporate governance*, 2015, www.oecd-ilibrary.org.

54. RJ Burk, 'Women on corporate boards of directors: views of Canadian chief executive officers', *Women in Management Review*, vol. 9, no. 5, 1994, 3–10.

55. T Saito and H Odagiri, Intraboard heterogeneity and the role of bank-dispatched directors in Japanese firms: An empirical study, *Pacific-Basin Finance Journal*, vol. 16, iss. 5, 572–590.

56. MA Carpenter and JD Westphal, 'The strategic context of external network ties: examining the impact of director appointments on board involvement in strategic decision making', *Academy of Management Journal*, vol. 44, no. 4, 2001, 639–660.

57. JD Westphal, and LP Milton, 'How experience and network ties affect the influence of demographic minorities on corporate boards', *Administrative Science Quarterly*, vol. 45, no. 2, 2000, 366–398.

58. CM Treichler, 'Diversity of board members and organisational performance: an integrative perspective', *Corporate Governance: An International Review*, vol. 3, no. 4, 1995, 189–200.

59. H Hung, *Is social responsibility a concern for corporate directors? An empirical study in Hong Kong*, a paper presented at the World Business Ethics Forum, Hong Kong, 2008.

60. W Ocasio and H Kim, 'The circulation of corporate control: selection of functional backgrounds of new CEOs in large U.S. manufacturing firms, 1981–1992', *Administrative Science Quarterly*, vol. 44, no. 3, 1999, 532–562.

61. Carpenter and Westphal, op. cit.

62. SA Zahra and JA Pearce, 'Boards of directors and corporate financial performance: a review and integrative model', *Journal of Management*, vol. 15, no. 2, 1989, 291–344.

63. FG Hilmer, *Strictly boardroom: improving governance to enhance company performance, Report of the Independent Working Party into Corporate Governance*, 2nd edn, Melbourne: Information Australia, 1998.

64. FG Hilmer, *Strictly boardroom: improving governance to enhance company performance, Report of the independent working party into corporate governance*, Melbourne: The Business Library, 1993.

65. G Chitayat, 'The role of the board of directors in practical terms', *Management International Review*, vol. 23, 1983, 71–77.

66. E Fama and M Jensen, 'Separation of ownership and control', *Journal of Law and Economics*, vol. 26, 1983, 301–325.

67. T Donaldson and LE Preston, 'The stakeholder theory of the corporation: concepts, evidence, and implications, *Academy of Management Review*, vol. 20, no. 1, 1995, 65–91.

68. D Pastoriza and MA Ariño, 'When agents become stewards: introducing learning in the stewardship theory', 1st IESE Conference, 'Humanizing the Firm & Management Profession', Barcelona, IESE Business School, 30 June – 2 July, 2008.

69. MD Lynall, BR Golden, and AJ Hillman, 'Board composition from adolescence to maturity: a multitheoretic view', *Academy of Management Review*, vol. 28, no. 3, 2003, 416–443.

70. SA Drew, PC Kelley and T Kendrick, 'CLASS: five elements of corporate governance to manage strategic risk', *Business Horizons*, vol. 49, no. 2, 2006, 127–138.

71. Figure adapted from Drew et al., op. cit.

72. D Vera and M Crossan, 'Strategic leadership and organisational learning', *Academy of Management Review*, vol. 29, no. 2, 2004, 222–240.

73. S Finkelstein and DC Hambrick, 'Top management-team tenure and organisational outcomes: the moderating role of managerial discretion', *Administrative Science Quarterly*, vol. 35, 1990, 484–503.

74. DP Forbes and FJ Milliken, 'Cognition and corporate governance: understanding boards of directors as strategic decision-making groups', *Academy of Management Review*, vol. 24, no. 3, 1999, 489–505.

75. MJ Peel and E O'Donnell, 'Board structure, corporate performance and auditor independence', *Corporate Governance: An International Review*, vol. 3, no. 4, October, 1995, 207–217.

76. Carpenter and Westphal, op. cit.

77. 'Centro class action boosted by court decision', *Sydney Morning Herald*, 28 June 2011, www.smh.com.au.

78. B Butler and L Wood, 'Centro settlement worth $200 m', *The Age*, 8 May 2012, www.smh.com.au.

79. Based on the speech by the Director of Audit, 'Public sector governance: the role of the director of audit' to the Hong Kong Branch', Certified Management Accountants Society of British Columbia, Canada on 12 June 2007.
80. Organisation for Economic Co-operation and Development (OECD), *Corporate governance factbook 2019*, 2019, www.oecd.org.
81. Organisation for Economic Co-operation and Development (OECD), op. cit. p. 83.

ACKNOWLEDGEMENTS

Photo: © Michael Leslie / Shutterstock.com
Photo: © 360b / Shutterstock.com
Photo: © PHOTOCREO Michal Bednarek / Shutterstock.com
Photo: © Sergii Gnatiuk / Shutterstock.com
Extract: © The Treasury
Extract: © OECD 2015, *G20/OECD Principles of Corporate Governance*, OECD Publishing, Paris, http://dx.doi.org/10.1787/9789264236882-en.

FUTURE SKILLS GUIDE

Preface

You are probably wondering what you need to do to gain and retain your dream job once your degree is completed. Industries and individuals have changed dramatically in recent years, in part due to COVID-19; so how do you differentiate yourself, and what can you do to get ahead?

In addition to the specialist knowledge and competencies that you are developing at university, there are certain general skills that are critical for any career you choose to pursue. We created the *Future Skills Guide* to capture and convey these skills, so that you can enter the workplace with confidence.

Here is an overview each of the authors that contributed to the *Future Skills Guide*.

- Steve Sammartino is Australia's leading futurist, an international keynote speaker and an author of three bestselling books on entrepreneurship and technology.
- Nicola Hazell is a technology expert. Hazell is among Australia's leading voices on women in leadership, gender equality and social innovation.
- Co-Director of the Bond Resolution Centre, Professor Rachael Field is internationally renowned for her research and service work in family mediation and student wellbeing.
- Clare Payne is globally recognised for her work in ethics in finance. She was named in the Australian '100 Woman of Influence' in 2016 and a World Economic Forum Young Global Leader in 2014 in recognition of her personal commitment to social issues.
- Swinburne University's Dean of Learning Innovation, Professor Angela Carbone is a passionate advocate and researcher on professional development and student employability skills.
- Michael Eales is the Partner of Business Models Inc and a Strategy Designer who specialises in business design and innovation capacity building.
- Mandy Johnson is an illustrious innovator whose bestselling books, keynote speeches and strategic advisory services provide innovative, evidence-based techniques to improve and transform both private and public organisations.

We hope that this practical handbook will support your wellbeing and help you build resilience and employability skills both now and into the future.

Future of work

QUESTIONS   What changes do you anticipate to the way we work in the next five to ten years? How can we prepare for these changes now?

Professor Angela Carbone

During the recent COVID-19 disruption we have seen those organisations quick to adapt and adopt technology continue to operate and survive while the rest of the world was in shutdown. Advances in technology will continue to change the way we work. Concepts such as artificial intelligence (AI), machine learning, automation, globalisation and collaboration are infiltrating the workplace and will become the norm for the next generation entering the workforce. We are seeing organisations come together to solve extremely complex problems and address global challenges. Problems such as managing health pandemics and climate change are global concerns, not localised in one area. As we increasingly work together across international boundaries, whether to monitor weather patterns, rates of global warming or the spread of viruses, we will need global perspectives and a set of competencies to navigate cultural differences and manage the way we work.

Current and future generations will need to develop digital competencies and literacies so they can seamlessly adapt to the changing nature of work. Technology is capable of capturing, processing, storing and sharing huge volumes of data and information, and we need to prepare to be able to deal with this. The ability to manage and interpret data is becoming an important skill. Making sense of vast amounts of data often requires separating garbage from clean data. As you build these skills, it's a good idea to demonstrate your knowledge and competencies via an e-portfolio. Applying and critiquing models and predictions means working with others, so developing collaboration and communication skills is extremely important.

Participating in industry-based and cross-team projects throughout your university studies is a great way to build your interpersonal skills such as collaboration, negotiation and communication. To deal with the complexities of the global challenges that you will face during your career, you will need to develop more than just deep discipline knowledge; you will require an ability to work across disciplines and collaborate and communicate perceptively and effectively with others across a variety of fields.

Professor Rachael Field

It is clear that working in a post–COVID-19 world will look very different to our work life experiences up to 2020. While a five- to ten-year prediction might have been possible pre-COVID-19, it is now more difficult to anticipate what the future of work will be. However, there are three particular skills that we can develop now that will inevitably be important — whatever our future working environments look like. These are self-management skills, resilience and agility.

Self-management

Self-management skills support our self-regulation — that is, our ability to control our thoughts, feelings and actions. If we have strong self-management skills, we can set goals independently and take the initiative to achieve them, and this can enhance our achievements and career success.

Individual people have their own approaches to self-management that work for them. Generally, people with strong self-management skills will be positive and proactive thinkers who effectively manage their time, their stress levels and their emotional responses to issues and events. It is important to be aware of a range of self-management strategies and then choose ones that work best for you. In the Wellbeing section later in this guide you'll find three key wellbeing strategies that are also positive self-management strategies. Resilience is also a key element of effective self-management.

Resilience

Resilience skills help us to cope well with life and, in particular, with the stressors and challenges at work and in our personal lives. Life in general is naturally stressful — at least to some extent — and stress is something that we all experience, albeit at varying levels and in various contexts. Although stress is often thought of as a negative thing, it can have a positive side, and it is possible to experience healthy levels of stress.

The American Psychological Association has identified work as one of the top two causes of stress. When asked about their personal stressors, around six in ten adults (in the US) identified work and money as significant sources of stress, making them the most commonly mentioned personal stressors.[1] Despite this, developing our resilience skills can help us to use stress positively: as a motivator for achievement, as something that stimulates us to be active and engaged, and as a prompt to develop more effective and efficient ways of working.

Psychologists generally refer to resilience as our capacity to cope with stress, challenges and difficulties. Resilient people can better manage change or loss and deal with negative experiences or events. They can also harness resources (both internal resources within themselves and external resources) in order to steer their way effectively through a difficult time. Resilience is therefore a key predictor of success in life.

Some people are born with greater resilience than others, but everyone can develop and build their resilience and enhance their existing levels of resilience. Developing our resilience basically involves employing some common-sense wellbeing strategies. Some strategies that are easy to enact include:
- adopting a positive outlook
- reframing difficulties as challenges
- staying connected to and engaged with support networks of friends and family
- being prepared to ask for help
- managing goals and priorities
- developing a hobby or interest outside of work
- being organised and balanced
- avoiding procrastination
- sleeping and eating well
- exercising
- practising relaxation techniques (such as stretching, exercise, deep breathing, socialising and mindfulness meditation)
- having a sense of humour and perspective.

Agility

Change is stressful because our natural biological response to change is a stress reaction. The post-COVID-19 world and the future of work will inevitably involve a lot of change. Building our self-management skills can help us cope with these high levels of change. Along with self-management and resilience skills, agility is an important part of coping positively with change.

Dictionary definitions of agility tend to refer to an ability to move, think, understand and respond quickly and easily. Agile people are empowered and agentic. They remain calm when faced with the challenge of change, they process information quickly, they can be proactive and decisive and they take opportunities even if there is a level of potential risk.

So, how can we increase our agility? Generally, agility will follow a positive mindset. If you are proactive, problem-solving-oriented, keen to innovate and focused, this will help you to be agile. All of the approaches to building resilience referred to earlier are also relevant to our levels of agility, as are the wellbeing strategies discussed later.

Michael Eales

We have found ourselves at the epicentre of one of the biggest shifts in human history — that of shaping new systems for the future of human work with machines. To prepare for this future, we need to understand three of the biggest challenges to the way we work: automation and the future of human effort, adaptability and the future of human connection, and AI and the future of human expression.

Automation

Consider how a machine codifies human effort. Effort often manifests itself as jobs that require known and repetitive tasks, processes or calculations. These jobs will decline. The future we are moving towards will require people to work with machines to tackle complex challenges, making sense of nonlinear problems that do not come with a codified approach or guidebook. This is the VUCA world — volatile, uncertain, complex and ambiguous. Developing your skills for critical thinking and critical feeling will prepare you.

Adaptability

There is a future where technology supports our shared wellbeing, sense-making and ability to tackle complex challenges. In this future, trust, responsibility and accountability will be key characteristics to understand. As people continue to navigate work-life balance, the digital-physical divide will continue to widen. Your ability to communicate effectively, both online and offline, will be of increasing importance to navigating the bonds and bridges across individuals and groups, and their interests and intentions. Expect to see more jobs that require you to leverage your innately human attributes of care and compassion, communication and creativity. Developing your skills in managing uncertainty while facilitating individual and group connections will prepare you. Check out www.creative-capital.info and explore the value of the creative industries.

AI

We express ourselves in ways that machines are only just learning to replicate at the simplest level. Our intent to create and shape the world around us sees us make choices every day that shape the future of human expression in a more immersive digital world. These choices, whether they be via online communication or the workflow tools we use to manage our work and life, are pulling us towards a deeper digital-physical fusion. In this future your ability to interpret reality and help the machines you work with understand your interpretation will be key. This is the domain of the storyteller, the translator, the designer. You will choose to follow the programmed reality around you, or inform the programming itself. **Developing a curiosity for 'how you think', your intuitive intelligence, is key to preparing you for this future.** If you're interested in learning more, check out the field of speculative design and transmedia storyworlds.

The future of work is bright, provided we consciously design for humans at the centre.

Mandy Johnson

Predicting the future can be dangerous, as Microsoft's former CEO Steve Ballmer discovered after declaring in 2007: 'There's no chance that the iPhone is going to get any significant market share'. We can, however, confidently say that the world of work is morphing at lightning speed, through the combined power of technological and social forces. In 1950 the life expectancy of a company was around 75 years.

By 2001 it was less than 15 years, and today, the life cycle of any product or service is estimated to be about 5 to 7 years.[2] Given that Instagram, Netflix, Uber Eats, iPads, Google Home and Siri didn't even exist ten years ago, one wonders how we spent our hours before then!

With business evolving at warp speed, time is the victim, becoming an ever-shrinking commodity. Projects, meetings and emails are snowballing each year, and with mobile digital devices connecting us 24/7 there is a corporate expectation and social pressure to 'do it all'. Yet unlike most of history, when humans were hunter-gatherers, there are no natural 'off' times. We can no longer rely on the end of berry season or the annual buffalo migration to take a break.

Self-discipline, then, is a skill required in much greater measure than in past eras. In this new working paradigm, those who can channel their attention and concentrate on real achievement amid this mounting frenzy of activity and distraction — in effect, be thinking 'human beings' rather than mindless 'human doings' — will be the ultimate winners. Those who fail to make the transition — and there are many at present — will find the disruptive technology continually 'disrupts' themselves.

The way we work is also becoming much more fluid and flexible. Unlike employees of the past, who often held a single job for life, with set hours and fixed remuneration, future workers will have much more scope in their professional lives. They may be employees, contract or on-call workers, solo-preneurs, entrepreneurs, multiple job holders or a combination of these. They might work in a corporate office or as part of a collaborative virtual team, or be freelancing in their own business on the side. The hours they work will also be more elastic. Already some companies offer design-your-own shift times, four-day work weeks with three-day weekends, and more micro flexibility where people can have intermittent time off to pursue specific interests or hobbies.

As a result, there will be no predictable climb of the corporate ladder for young employees. This will create more uncertainty, but also more opportunities. Those who are just joining the workforce now will be better able to shape their own career path than previous generations. This self-directed career journey will be more challenging and exciting, and require some forethought in answering questions such as the following.

- What are the things you are good at/are passionate about/enjoy doing?
- What gives you purpose?
- What problems could you solve for companies?
- Where and when and how do you want to work?
- Who do you want to work with/for?

With youth unemployment on the rise, workers that give thought to these kinds of questions and come up with a deliberate, rational way forward will be the ones who flourish in the years ahead.

Another big shift in the future of work will be an increasing war for talent. Leadership surveys continually show that the number one issue keeping CEOs awake at night is finding and keeping great people. An enduring mismatch between skills and jobs means employers continue to struggle to fill positions with the right employees. The projections show this problem escalating. According to demographer Bernard Salt, Baby Boomers are exiting the workforce at a faster rate than the next generations are entering it.[3] Because we have had low birth rates for the last 20 years, we've had people exiting the workforce faster than new generations are entering — so the available labour pool is shrinking.

If forecasts are correct, the COVID-19 pandemic will have caused Australia's unemployment rate to double in the second quarter of 2020.[4] This will expand the talent pool; but for those insomniac CEOs, the battle for the *right* talent will continue to be the new long-term reality. For skilled future workers this creates a lot of incredible opportunities and even bidding wars for their services. For those with limited skills, or who don't constantly evolve, the future is less rosy.

Steve Sammartino

Non-linear work and careers

The infiltration of automation and AI in the workplace will increase the variety of work we do — both within our jobs themselves, and in terms of the variety of roles and positions we will take on over the decade. The number of tasks we need to take on within a job role will escalate. As automation increases, humans will need to become adept at adding skills to what they have learned in previous jobs or via their formal education.

AI will replace some of our previous tasks. Workers will need to take responsibility for ensuring they obtain new skills and knowledge so they can take on tasks that are not replaceable by machines. Many companies are already acknowledging this shift in managing human resources and are attempting to redeploy workers where possible, but smart career management means being proactive and pre-empting these changes to your industry. This is especially the case given automation is now headed for traditional white-collar sectors of employment, which have traditionally been immune to AI intervention.

The period of time we work in certain roles, jobs or industries will also truncate as the pace of change accelerates. **To be successful in your career you will need to develop transferable skills and become adept at moving sideways into related industries, especially given such a large number of industries will likely become disrupted and their business models will become less sustainable.** Climbing the corporate hierarchy vertically is now a far more difficult proposition. Companies are looking for skills outside of their industry — especially those facing changes to their revenue streams and operating models.

In the coming decade we will need to manage our own career rather than relying on traditional advancement and promotion within a single company or even a single industry. As AI becomes more prevalent, specialist skills will be outsourced to the machines. Humans will need to be generalists, providing insight, nuance and variety to the approach of how work is done. Efficiency will be left to the machines, while creativity and flexibility will be the skills in most demand. We'll need to be able to solve problems that haven't been solved before.

The shift to freelance and gig labour

Since industrialisation the place of work has been largely centralised: all the tools to do our jobs resided in factories and offices. Under this model it was difficult to find, train, organise and ratify the skills of people who weren't under a company's direct control. This is no longer the case.

The gig economy we're experiencing in the present day is just an indication of what is to come. The trend will extend beyond low-cost labour and into high-value-added corporate and white-collar roles. In the next five to ten years we will see more well-paid corporate freelancers emerge — modern-day digital craftspeople. Now that people can bring their reputations with them online and are connected, labour will become more fluent. Not only is it possible to have a workplace made up of freelancers, but it's a significant cost saving to employers: the on-costs of employing full-time staff are substantial — usually a minimum of 20 per cent of their salaries.

Both staff and companies can benefit from freelance staff working with more than one company simultaneously: it widens people's skill bases, and also reduces risk for both parties. Companies can contract and expand labour as needed, and employees will have a lower revenue risk by having multiple 'employers' from which they gain revenue. People will become 'projecteers', managing a number of complementary projects across more than one company at the same time.

The human element

Before industrialisation much of our labour was physical. In the past century the highest-paid labour was left-brain logic work. But in the next decade this will shift to emotional labour. With emotional labour, *how* we approach tasks and problems is even more important than *what* we are doing. It means that humans displaying the greatest amount of empathy, adaptability and creativity will become the most valued. **Emotions such as sincerity and authenticity will be valued most highly because they are human traits.** Even in situations where automation may be possible, much of the highest-paid work will be valued 'because a human is doing it' — even if this means it is imperfect. A classic example of this today is the fact that live performances of entertainment artists are worth more than the 'recorded version' of the same performance — it's because the human element is what we really value. Labour that is differentiated by its humanity will rise above automation as we find that our true purpose isn't just efficiency, but connection.

The machines will take care of volume and efficiency, and our ability to look someone in the eye and truly connect at a species level will be a core differentiator of us versus machines. The shift to remote work will also exacerbate the need for connection. People who can maintain a high level of humanity through digital channels and back that up in person will become indispensable. An era of quasi digital isolation will require us to find new ways to connect.

Self-education

The shelf life of any education is in flux. In the new economy, our formal education must be constantly upgraded. There is a wide gamut of learning opportunities available, from our most respected universities to independent YouTube channels. The new investment we need to make for our careers is in ourselves, and in our own time. Think of it as the career equivalent of maintaining your health and fitness. **Learning isn't something you do once and then forget about; you will need to practise it constantly to keep pace.** With self-education we can be nimble and quickly move up the learning curve, staying on the cutting edge of what is valued economically.

Personal branding

These days, your CV is not just the document you email to a prospective employer — it's whatever an internet search says about you. We need to become adept at displaying our proficiency in public forms. Smart career management will increasingly involve using social tools to display qualifications, industry experience and thought leadership. This doesn't just mean using traditional career tools such as LinkedIn; it means understanding that everything you publish online is accessible and fair game for any person or company looking to engage you economically. Everything we publish creates a permanent digital footprint that will work either for or against us in the job market. **To be a competitor in this space you need to manage your personal brand wisely; this means ensuring you present your best intellectual self and stay 'on brand' in all your digital communications channels.** The internet never forgets. Your digital social interactions should be kept to private channels.

The best place to announce your brand is on your personal website that you own and control. Your website is your modern CV, and if you are diligent about search engine optimisation you will be rewarded with having your website at the top of search results. This means you are in the best position to control your own narrative as much as possible.

Project management

Project management is a core skill of the future. Anyone who can lift their skillset above 'being a factor of production' into 'organising the factors of production' will be best placed for a future where AI is inexorably linked to work. Those who are good at managing changing situations and allocating resources, people and processes will be better placed than those undertaking production-based tasks.

Clare Payne

There has been much commentary about the future of work and how it will be different to what we know now. Through an ethical lens, the big changes to the way we work will be as follows.

More collaboration

We will see an increase in collaboration and partnerships across sectors that will help us devise solutions that bring us closer to a better world. The United Nations Sustainable Development Goal number 17, 'Partnerships for the goals', directs the global community to form partnerships for change.[5] The United Nations Sustainable Development Goals are a universal call to action to end poverty, protect the planet and ensure that all people enjoy peace and prosperity. The goals acknowledge that a successful sustainable development agenda requires partnerships between governments, the private sector and civil society. To achieve this, the United Nations promotes partnerships built upon sustainable principles and values, a shared vision, and shared goals that place people and the planet at the centre.

Throughout the COVID-19 crisis, we witnessed positive examples of collaboration for good. In Italy, a specialist scuba diving company worked with medical teams to adapt scuba masks to be used as ventilators. In Australia, the for-profit and not-for-profit sectors united to meet community needs. Supermarket chain Woolworths partnered with community-based not-for-profit Meals on Wheels to ensure the elderly had essential supplies. We also saw CEOs working together to determine how to manage workforce reductions by offering temporary employment in another business, such as CVS Pharmacies in the US taking on hotel staff from Hilton and Marriott. In Australia, companies such as Telstra, Woolworths and Rio Tinto publicly pledged to redeploy Qantas staff laid off due to COVID-19.[6]

These examples of collaboration and partnership for a common good are an indication of what is possible in the future.

Alignment of values and purpose

In recent years we've seen the rise of 'purpose' in business, where long-established businesses have redefined their purpose as providing value beyond the traditional, and often limited, measures of profit and shareholder returns. A purpose-led organisation strives to have a positive impact on society. This business trend was reinforced when the Business Roundtable, a group of 181 business leaders, declared in August 2019 their commitment to leading their companies for the benefit of all stakeholders.[7]

For many, this was long overdue, and the challenge will be for businesses to now ensure their actions match their promises. They would be wise to focus on getting this right, as individuals are increasingly seeking alignment between their own values and the organisation for which they work. Employees and customers expect businesses to take positions — to have a voice — on the big issues of the day that matter to them, such as climate change and human rights.

This drive for alignment between the values of individuals and their employer, and between customers and the products and services they choose, will only increase as new generations enter the workforce and progress to positions of power.

Technology for good

While we have already seen profound changes to our personal and professional lives due to innovations in technology, it is predicted that we will move to a more meaningful application of technology, particularly AI, that will change our lives and world for the better. For example, robots will be used in medicine to relieve medical staff from routine tasks.

Over the last decade, we have seen an increased focus on the ethics of AI and privacy issues related to data and social media. In some ways this process — where guidelines, formal councils and new regulations continue to be established over time — is 'ethics in practice'. While there is not a global consensus on how best to manage our interactions with technology to ensure all rights are protected, it remains on the agenda due to the promise of technology to change our lives for better.

Here are some ideas for how you can prepare for these changes now.

1. *'No-regret' actions.* There are some 'no-regret' actions that you can take to prepare yourself for the work of the future, and others that businesses can implement. For example, employers can accommodate flexible work arrangements to engage a broader workforce. As a new graduate, you can equip yourself to work away from traditional workplaces and become familiar with the technologies that facilitate your performance if you work from a home office or other work hub.

2. *Monitor and pilot.* Employers and individuals don't need to adopt every new technology or program that comes to market. Instead, they need to assess their own needs and determine what is right for them. For example, businesses can pilot the use of new technologies with one team or they can monitor the use of new technologies by competitors and involve stakeholders and staff in deciding what is appropriate for their business. In the spirit of collaboration for good, we've seen an increase in cross-functional teams in the workplace; this can also extend to cross-industry, with businesses working with their competitors in knowledge-sharing for the common good. Individuals should think about the connections and technology that might enhance their performance — for example, actively participating in webinars or joining groups and associations (online or in person).

3. *Investment.* There will be many new technologies and systems that businesses are not ready to implement for a variety of reasons, such as incompatibility with existing systems, lack of expertise or funding limitations. In order to prepare for changes that may become inevitable, businesses and individuals should invest in understanding developments, engaging experts and commissioning or keeping up-to-date with research and developments. Those that have the capacity can invest in innovation labs and collaborator programs that will help them adapt and select the right solutions. For example, in order for businesses to fully leverage customer data and insights they will need to have the right systems in place to extract value. **Those who are new to the world of work should look for opportunities such as emerging leader programs and 'hackathons'; these will allow you to grow your knowledge, impact and network.**

Nicola Hazell

In what has been dubbed the Fourth Industrial Revolution, change is happening at a more rapid pace than we've ever seen before. Amid this change, there are three key areas that will be transformed for the next generation: jobs, careers and skills.

Current estimates indicate around 40 per cent of jobs that exist today will be affected by automation by 2030.[8] This means some jobs will be transformed by technology and others will become obsolete.

The reality is, many of the jobs of the future don't even exist yet. Around 65 per cent of children entering primary school today will ultimately end up working in completely new job types that don't yet exist.[9] This phenomenon is already underway, as many of the most in-demand growth occupations today did not exist ten or even five years ago. The pace of change is predicted to accelerate.

So how do you figure out what your dream job is when that job might not yet exist? The answer is: you don't need to. Shifts in job mobility mean young people are predicted to have an average of 17 jobs across 5 different industries in their lifetime.[10] **It's no longer about 'a career for life', so building a plan to secure that dream job isn't really going to set you up for a long-term sustainable future.**

Not only will the jobs and careers young people experience be diverse, so too will the conditions of work, which are likely to become more fluid.[11] You are likely to hold portfolios of activities, including paid employment, unpaid employment (internships or volunteering), self-employment (including entrepreneurship), and caring for children or the elderly. These different conditions, as well as the different roles, will require a variety of skills — changing from one scenario to the next.

This is where a shift in approach to skills is required. To thrive in this new world of work, you will need more than a single specialist skillset or trade. You'll need to develop transferable 'enterprising skills' such as digital literacy, collaboration, creativity and resilience — which have already become vital assets in the quest to secure *any* job.[12] More than anything, you will need to be ready to hit the ground running.

To prepare for these shifts, you need to invest in skills, mindset and activation. The skills required can't be developed just by reading lots of textbooks. These are skills that have to be learned by *doing*.

So if you're learning about finance and business, be sure to put that learning to the test. **Team up with others and try turning your learnings into a business to see what happens when you apply your skills in the real world. If you're learning to code, don't just follow the study guide — try building something of your own.** Identify a problem that your friends or family members are struggling with and consider what role technology could play in solving that problem — then have a crack at creating the solution.

As you go through these scenarios, there will be other key skills that you develop along the way. How you communicate will be critical — can you listen to others to really understand the challenge they're facing before you set about solving it for them? Once you've built your first idea, can you tell a clear story to others so they understand why this idea is the right one to help them with their problem?

Throughout this process, you'll have moments when what you're working on falls in a heap. What you thought was the solution might not turn out how you planned. This feedback is where the magic sits; the chance to understand what doesn't work, so you can figure out what does. Building resilience is about knowing things will fail, embracing that failure, and using it to fuel you to try again and do better.

The final thing to remember is that no one person will have all the skills required to solve every problem. **You need to be able to collaborate and value the insights and knowledge of people who think differently to you and have diverse experiences or perspectives to share, and work with them to create something truly useful.** Success in the future of work will not be about the individual, it will be about the collective.

Technology

QUESTIONS What effect will future technology have on people entering the workforce over the next five to ten years? How can we prepare for these changes now?

Professor Angela Carbone

It is predicted that 50 per cent of today's jobs will disappear by 2030.[13] Technology will cause most, if not all, repetitive jobs to be automated. Many jobs that exist today will become obsolete, and the nature of work will change as innovation will cause new jobs to be created. As technology replaces jobs of a repetitive nature, people entering the workforce will focus less on job security but more on job opportunity. As technology continues to evolve, flexibility and mobility will matter more than stability and job loyalty. This means that you must prepare to be adaptable and able to transfer your skillset to new environments, as it is extremely unlikely you will have a single job title for your lifetime. Research to date already tells us that the current generation entering the workforce is likely to have 17 jobs and 5 careers over their lifetime.[14]

In the past, disciplines such as English and maths were the core units of study that most students needed to get a job. However, the next generation of students will need more than just deep disciplinary knowledge; they will need a complete set of employability skills — of which digital skills will be a high priority — to effectively operate in the future world of work.

Michael Eales

Technology is a key tool in facilitating personalised, unique and memorable experiences. A solution designed today without technology in mind neglects an integral component of life as we know it. Looking to the future, we will see changes and opportunities for exploration in the physical forms that technology takes, the evolving expectations of the user, and enabling accessibility for all members of society. We are all responsible for the design of responsible technology that realigns technology with humanity.

Check out the Centre for Humane Technology (https://humanetech.com) **to explore the emerging tensions between where technology and humans are going.**

Form — How will hardware be transformed?

As we become more creative in designing technologically enabled experiences, so too does the form in which technology takes in physical environments. From the family computer to the iPhone, we have transitioned from communal to individual technology consumption. We are currently in the process of transitioning from visible technology with set interfaces to technology that is embedded within environments with natural interfaces, presenting exciting challenges in manufacturing and customer experience design.

Expectations — How does technology transform customer expectations?

The uptake and acceptance of e-commerce has had flow-on effects to the expectations of the holistic user in daily life. Website checkouts are seamless — why aren't our local stores the same? No longer are digital channels operating in a complete vacuum; now, seamless experiences facilitated by digital technology are expected even in the real and organic world.

Accessibility — How can we create a world for all?

While participation in the physical world can be limited, the digital world provides exciting opportunities for accessibility. Until relatively recently, participating in sport was difficult for those not physically able; however, the digital sub world of esports now provides the opportunity for people of all abilities to collaborate, communicate and exchange value. The question is how we can further facilitate and embrace this new sub world.

Mandy Johnson

Even though humans have been making shoes for more than 40 000 years, a robot arm can now stitch a shoe together from scratch in just six minutes. This is not good news for all those wannabe cobblers out there, but with automation and AI the new reality, the first major impact is going to involve the kinds of jobs we do. This doesn't mean that there won't be *any* work: technology does threaten jobs that currently exist, but also leads to a whole host of roles that have never been envisaged. Social media managers, data scientists, Uber drivers and podcast producers didn't exist ten years ago.

Technology will, however, transform the types of skills required to get work. Machines remove repetitive tasks so there will be less need for manual labour and lower-level skills like data entry, but more requirement for human, intuitive input such as social and emotional skills. Innovative exploration will require abilities that haven't even been named yet. Elon Musk's Neuralink brain-computer interface, the Amazon Assistant that understands emotions and Li-Fi internet that can download at the speed of light are just a few cutting-edge ideas in development.

So what impact will all of this have on future workers? On average, most humans have a work life of 30-plus years, yet 42 per cent of all current job skills are predicted to be obsolete by 2022.[15] People will no longer be doing one or two jobs for life. In some fast-changing fields it's anticipated that skills taught in university courses will be obsolete before a person even graduates.[16] Lifelong learning, then, is the new way forward. Developing soft skills such as problem solving, communication and critical thinking and focusing on core high-demand technical skills such as data analytics will be key to future employment.

The way employees update and learn new skills will also change. Many organisations still offer training in cringe-worthy PowerPoint formats or tedious videos which, to the digital generation raised on touchscreens and powerful game technology, is like stepping back to the '80s and catching a ride in a DeLorean. More immersive education in things like virtual reality (VR) will see explosive growth, and it's already beginning. US retailer Walmart will VR-train over a million employees in 2020, and companies like Porsche, Boeing and UPS are all following suit.

How people work will also radically change. 'Going online' will be a thing of the past as smart, invisible technology effortlessly connects us everywhere and anywhere. Without the need to go into an office to access corporate IT systems, working from home will become one of the most efficient ways to work — and won't just be seen as a means to stay in one's pyjamas all day. Already over 50 per cent of Australians and New Zealanders do some work remotely and in shared co-working spaces, and future employees will have much more scope to work anywhere, any time.[17] **Consider getting a new desk and setting up an office in your spare room: the workplace of the future is coming to your home.**

Steve Sammartino

Artificial intelligence and automation

AI and automation are about to invade every pocket of our working lives. The cost of accessing software, hardware and data flows (cloud storage and uploads and downloads) is in rapid decline. Technology use in the workplace will be pushed beyond social media and basic software, entering the realm of machine learning and natural language processing (NLP). Computers will start to understand the work environment they are placed in. AI will adapt and change the things it is capable using data, feedback loops and interactions it has within the work context.

Machine learning is software that can learn to perform a task without specific instructions. It does this by using mathematical models that rely on patterns and inference instead of exacting instruction. The machine (AI) learns from the data it is exposed to, which is actually known as training data. So, in many ways, AI has a similar behaviour pattern to humans: it learns from what it sees and makes 'decisions' based on that data. As the data changes, the output changes, resulting in an increasing learning loop and accuracy.

NLP is related to computer languages that can synthesise and process natural human language and configure responses back in human-like form. NLP will become a bridge between people and machine-learning software and create a system where humans start to interact with computers in a collegiate way to solve business problems. We are already seeing this technology replace many of the keypad interactions we would traditionally have using software on the web and inside our homes (it is constantly evolving and improving its functionality). Current examples include voice commands on smartphones, in vehicles and via smart speakers. As NLP improves through these consumer interactions, it will progressively move up the hierarchy and into the workplace. In the coming five to ten years, many of our interactions in the workplace will be with machine-learning algorithms, and we will command these via our voice — much like we do with humans today. In the future, our 'colleagues' will be these new forms of androids.

Automation is the replacement of human activity via machine — in all its forms. Even the most intellectually complex tasks will be automated, and no career is immune. Lawyers, doctors and accountants will all be assisted by intelligent software systems. Technology that was once the reserve of only the largest organisations will become available to everyone as the costs of these services drop due to cloud computing, and ubiquitous low-cost hardware. Humans will need to learn to work with AIs, guiding machines and extracting answers and insight from their non-human partners.

Manufacturing returns to high-cost labour markets

Developed markets have seen a decline in local manufacturing since low-cost labour markets were opened to trading. In Australia, manufacturing as a percentage of the economy peaked in the mid 1960s at around 25 per cent of gross domestic product (GDP). It is now 6 per cent of our local economy.[18] We are about to see a reversal of this trend.

In the next decade, many firms currently relying on overseas manufacturing will re-localise manufacturing as labour becomes a reduced portion of manufacturing costs overall. Developed economies that have increasingly evolved into financial and service-based economies in the past 30 years will see manufacturing grow as a percentage of GDP. While it won't surpass the long-term trend towards services it will become a more important part of the economic mix.

Manufacturing's automation will be assisted by intelligent machinery, flexible manufacturing and advancements in 3D printing capability. Politically this process will be expedited by local firms' desire to reduce risk within global supply chains. Recent times have shown that trade wars and pandemics have exposed firms that are reliant on global suppliers to bring products to market. The next decade will see a shift towards deglobalisation as technology advances erode low labour cost advantage.

Dematerialisation and virtualisation

Software is increasingly replacing the functionality of things that used to be physical. This process is called dematerialisation. The beginnings of this phenomenon were seen in the office when email replaced physical mail, spreadsheets replaced physical ledgers and AutoCAD replaced physical blueprints.

Dematerialisation is the process that has caused the largest amount of disruption in the past two decades. It has reduced the cost of goods dramatically, and upended business models. For example, many hundreds of physical things now live inside smartphones. Many goods that used to require a separate physical item, purchase process and supply chain have become software. Think about it: when did you last use a physical torch, map, newspaper, music player, camera, video camera, GPS device, dictionary or photo album? Dematerialisation and virtualisation will continue as more goods are converted into software.

Digital twins will become a major part of the virtual economy. A digital twin is a virtual replica of any physical thing or process. Their implementation will become economical through the emergence of the Internet of Things (IoT) and advancements in augmented and virtual reality in the next decade. This pairing of the virtual and physical worlds allows analysis of data and monitoring of systems to head off problems before they even occur. Imagine a digital twin for a large industrial machine. Via the twin, anything that goes wrong with the physical version will immediately translate back to the virtual version. If any repairs, maintenance or changes are made to the physical version, the digital twin is automatically updated. Likewise, eventually we'll be able to change the physical version without actually touching it — it will all be done via the digital twin.

When a process starts to be affected by AI or dematerialisation we need to become alert to it immediately. We have to adopt the new virtual version of things, as the efficiency doctrine means that the former physical versions will eventually no longer be able to compete economically and they will be replaced. **It is best to lean into everything virtual as this is the long-term trajectory that can't be fought against.** We need to learn to operate the relevant software so we are not left behind using yesterday's methods; or, worse, seen as a luddite who is unable to adapt to the business world as it evolves.

We must also be prepared for large parts of our jobs — or even our entire jobs — to be replaced by software. Even high-paid roles such as radiography will be replaced by AI. In cases like this, humans need to learn to be able to move up the value chain within a work context — to a more human role where we organise things, rather than do things.

The other major preparation we can undertake is to become a student of business history and changing business models. Technology's trajectory is highly predictable, but the way most businesses react to technological upheavals is by resisting it. **If you closely study the mistakes disrupted industries and companies have made, you will see how certain patterns repeat and how business models can adapt to low-cost innovation, and this will help you prepare.**

By observing the shifts in business models our minds are trained to change and can adapt to disruption more fluidly. By observing history and being prepared for change, we don't suffer from shock when it arrives.

Clare Payne

While it's often tempting to focus on the exact skillset required for a certain job, it is the other skills, sometimes referred to as 'soft skills', that will become even more important as technology increasingly changes our workplaces and professional lives.

The skills most in demand could include the following.

1. *Relationship skills to complement technical skills.* While technology can assist us with our jobs, data still requires interpretation, systems require oversight and decisions need to be made and communicated. Having good communication and relationship skills will be very important in order to work effectively in teams and get the most out of the technology.

2. *Critical thinking and good decision making.* **We know we must remain vigilant in identifying fake news and being aware of the potential for manipulation through misinformation. It will be even more important in the future workplace to apply critical thinking to interpret and understand information and actions.** Individuals will increasingly be held accountable for their decisions and actions, so it is critical to develop good decision-making skills that bring you to conclusions that you can justify and defend.

3. *Openness to technology, rather than fear of it.* Many people fear advances in technology and have concerns for how it will affect our job security. Sometimes these concerns have overshadowed the complementary ways that technology can assist in making performance and work life better. In the future, it will be important to view technology as an enabler rather than being fearful of the changes it might bring. The full adoption of technology will require trust, and the large technology and social media providers will need to consistently demonstrate to us that they are worthy of our trust.

How can we prepare for these changes now?

The reality is that most of us now need a base level of competency in terms of understanding the digital world. We can no longer rely on an IT department to save us. We're fortunate that many programs and devices are designed for the novice and are accompanied by tutorials with the opportunity to ask questions and troubleshoot. Whether someone is 15 or 90 years old, they can learn how to use new technology that has the potential to make their life better.

Nicola Hazell

Technology is no longer a single industry; it has become the underpinning infrastructure and driver of almost *every* industry. This means that digital literacy — an understanding of how technology works, how it can be used and what its limitations are — will be critical for anyone entering the workforce over the next five to ten years.

This has never been so apparent as during the global crisis brought on by the spread of COVID-19 around the world in 2020. The most resilient businesses and organisations during the crisis have been those able to quickly shift their products or services to an online model. The digital maturity of a business has determined its capacity to continue operating and engaging with its customers. This is not just the case for big institutions such as banks; it has proven to be equally important for industries traditionally considered to be service industries defined by their in-person physical experience. For example, restaurants and gyms have had to quickly adapt their delivery and engagement models to an online experience in order to remain afloat. Some gyms have delivered equipment such as exercise bikes and weights to clients' homes to use during online workout sessions, while many restaurants have adopted online ordering and altered their menus to provide customers with produce that they can partially prepare at home, or can be enjoyed fully cooked and delivered to their door. Those without the capability or infrastructure to shift online have been forced to shut down. This is a critical example of the importance of technical knowledge coupled with the ability to *apply* it to solving problems as and when — let alone before — they arise.

Global crises aside, the rapid advancement of technology is making it possible for people with big ideas to conquer problems that have existed for centuries, but have previously been impossible to solve. Every day, the impossible is becoming possible — and this means the future can be seen as a world of possibility ready to be unlocked. But while technology can be a powerful vehicle for solving critical problems, that power is only unlocked by the ingenuity, creativity and empathy of a diverse range of people dedicated to solving those problems. This is why, even in a tech-driven future, it is our humanity that is the most critical factor.

In order to thrive in a tech-driven future of work, we need to understand and embrace the strength of diversity: diversity of thought, diversity of lived experience, diversity of perspective — all generated from ensuring you engage with the talents, insights and skills of people from a diverse range of backgrounds, genders and identities. Those who are curious, have a thirst for learning and a respect for the value that can be found in different perspectives will be best placed to thrive — collectively — in a tech-driven future of work.

Of course, all this is based on the premise of access to technology and the opportunity to use and understand it. Right now, just in Australia, more than one million households do not have access to the internet. While the global shutdown brought about by the rapid spread of COVID-19 has forced families and households around the world to work and study from home, the implications of this shift have not been felt equally. Those without access to internet connectivity, let alone without access to devices such as mobiles and laptops, have been left in the dark in this rapidly digitised world of work, learning and human connectivity.

This has cast a spotlight on one of the greatest challenges faced by many in the tech-driven future — that inequality of access means the impact of technical advancement will be felt asymmetrically across communities and countries around the world, presenting a risk of deepening inequality if the playing field is not levelled through structural intervention.

Wellbeing

QUESTIONS Why is mental wellbeing important? How can work negatively impact your mental wellbeing? What are some strategies for managing stress and maintaining wellbeing at work?

Professor Rachael Field

Mental wellbeing is critical to our success in the world of work. Taking a realistic perspective on the rigours and stressors of working life means that we can intentionally attend to our mental wellbeing. If we purposefully take action to prevent, or address, any decline in our wellbeing, this will improve our chances of being successful in our work-related endeavours, and also in our personal lives.

Professional working life can be rigorous and stressful. As we discussed earlier, the world of work post COVID-19 will incorporate a lot of change and change very often invokes a stress response in humans. Depending on the work context, people experience different stressors; however, some stressors are commonly experienced.

Most of us will feel stressed by the following scenarios:
- uncertainty about employment opportunities or job security
- high workloads
- long hours
- having to manage risk
- ethical dilemmas
- the pressure to stay up to date
- feeling out of our depth in terms of skills and expertise
- the competitive and adversarial nature of some work environments.

As noted earlier, being aware of the importance of mental wellbeing for our work success requires us to intentionally enact self-management skills. This is the key strategy for managing stress and maintaining mental wellbeing at work. Research tells us that up to 40 per cent of our happiness is within our personal control;[19] we need to harness our own agency to manage this 40 per cent through purposeful and informed approaches and activities. If we don't, we may become vulnerable to experiencing anxiety or depressive disorders, which in turn can put us at greater risk of physical and mental ill-health and at risk of adopting unhealthy coping strategies — such as abuse of alcohol.

The resilience and agility-building strategies identified earlier are relevant to maintaining wellbeing at work. Three additional ideas are mindfulness, harnessing hope theory and reflective practice.

Mindfulness

There are many approaches to relaxation and wellness, such as yoga and meditation, that support the development of self-management skills. Mindfulness meditation is a form of meditation that is particularly accepted as an effective approach to managing and coping with stress in professional work contexts. Research shows that mindfulness improves how we feel and enhances performance, as well as helping to unclutter our busy working minds so that there is increased capacity for idea generation, problem solving and engaging with broader and deeper perspectives. For these reasons, mindfulness can also support higher levels of personal satisfaction from work.

Meditation generally involves training the mind to be disciplined and contemplative. Mindfulness meditation involves being immersed in the moment and engaging with the idea of 'simply being'. **It involves taking time to sit quietly and be present, focusing on things such as breathing and cultivating a state of mind that is still — avoiding processes of evaluation, analysis and assessment.** It requires acceptance of thoughts, emotions and feelings, and engagement with our senses.

Mindfulness meditation can be practised anywhere and at any time — as long as there is a space to be quiet and still. While mindfulness meditation is only one of many wellbeing strategies and is not for everyone, it is definitely worth trying given the strong existing evidence base for its effectiveness in helping us cope with stress and pressure.

Harnessing hope theory

Charles Snyder was an expert in hope theory and wrote the book *Handbook of Hope*.[20] According to Snyder, hope is made up of agentic thinking, pathways thinking and goal setting. A person will have hope when they are motivated and have strong willpower (agentic thinking) to generate a range of strategies (pathways thinking) for achieving a goal (an endpoint). Hope theory suggests that hopeful people experience high levels of motivation and draw on their own capacity to control, or at least influence, their own circumstances. They actively work out potential viable strategies to achieve what they want, and are also open to using additional or alternative strategies on the pathway to achieving their goals if necessary.

Hope theory involves intentional approaches that anyone can enact to improve performance and wellbeing. Scholarly rigorous research has established that hope is an important predictor of success, happiness, resilience and motivation. Basically, hopeful people perform better, are more agile and better able to adjust to change and challenges, and they cope better with stressful circumstances. Hope also influences life satisfaction more generally. The research into hope indicates that hope can improve self-esteem and problem solving while supporting better mental health, and social competence and awareness. Hope has also been shown to result in higher pain tolerance thresholds and faster recovery from illness and injury.

So, how can we enact hope theory in our lives? We can do this by formulating goals, by being autonomous and adopting pathways thinking, and by practising agentic thinking.

The first element of hope theory involves goal setting. Setting goals is important for a range of self-management processes. According to the theory of hope, setting *appropriate* goals is the key. Appropriate goals help us to thrive. Inappropriate goals, on the other hand, tend to be unrealistic and unachievable and set us up for disappointment. Appropriate goals are connected to our intrinsic motivation. They are related to something we genuinely want to achieve, and care about. Appropriate goals are concrete, not abstract. A concrete goal is achievable — we can recognise when it has been accomplished, and it creates feelings of success and a sense of affirmation. Abstract goals are too vague to be achievable.

Pathways thinking is the next element of enacting hope theory and is related to our autonomy. Once goals have been set it is important to establish a realistic pathway that gives you a sense of control over achieving them. Pathways thinking involves generating a range of possible strategies for goal realisation — not just one strategy — so there is a back-up Plan B if Plan A doesn't work out. **Even in the most stressful circumstances, taking control of the situation by planning a range of ways to achieve a goal will support you to feel a sense of hope and wellbeing.**

The final element of engaging with hope theory is to adopt agentic thinking. Agentic thinking is the application of mental willpower, determination, motivation and energy. It involves a 'can-do' attitude to achieving success. Positive self-talk — that is, saying to ourselves that we believe in ourselves and backing ourselves to be successful — is a component of agentic thinking.

Reflective practice

Reflective practice is an important way of developing self-management skills such as resilience and agility and can help you to be psychologically well. Reflection involves thinking deeply and carefully in a structured and purposeful way — so that we can learn from experience (both successes and mistakes). Reflective practice is an important part of being successful in many professional work contexts.

Reflective practice is an important self-management skill because:
- it helps us to assess our strengths and weaknesses
- it aids in monitoring performance and interactions with others
- it supports a sense of self-direction
- it helps with processing feedback and assessing successes and failures
- it supports the generation of strategies for success
- it helps us take responsibility for our actions
- it allows us to live out our personal values, beliefs and principles.

Reflective practice is a critical skill for wellbeing in future work contexts because it is a means by which we can control feelings of helplessness, uncertainty, anxiety and stress. It supports the management of our mental processing of complicated or challenging issues. It can be used to help set goals and targets, and to engage in pathways and agentic thinking. Reflective practice can also help with:
- working through unstructured ideas
- solving dilemmas for which there are no obvious answers
- processing knowledge, concepts and emotions in order to make sense of them.

There is no one right or wrong way to do reflective practice. As individuals we can refine our own approach and create our own 'art' of reflective practice. There are, however, some established methods of effective reflective practice that can help with getting started.

Graham Gibbs' model of reflective practice[21] has the following six basic steps.
1. Identify an experience or situation that requires reflection.
2. Describe the experience or situation to yourself.
3. Explore your reactions and feelings in relation to the situation or experience.
4. Analyse and evaluate the situation or experience by asking questions like: 'What was good or bad about that experience?', 'What sense can be made of the situation?', 'What was really going on?', 'Was the experience similar or different to a previous experience?'. This process of evaluation and analysis involves making some value judgements about the experience and drawing on personal catalogues of experiences.
5. Make some conclusions about the situation or experience, starting with general conclusions and moving to conclusions that are more specific.
6. Use the reflections in the first five steps to create a personal action plan, using questions like: 'How will I manage a similar experience next time?', 'What will I do differently?', 'What will I do in the same way?', 'What have I learned from the situation?', 'What steps can I take to make the most of this learning experience?'.

Professor Angela Carbone

Mental wellbeing is extremely important to not just function, but to think clearly and have a positive impact on the world. **It is important to develop a 'professional purpose' mindset** — not only to navigate the complex world of work you'll face, but to have a more meaningful professional life. Professional purpose, as defined by Bates, Rixon, Carbone and Pilgrim, reflects a person's level of commitment to developing a professional future aligned with their personal values, professional aspirations and societal outlook.[22] People who have cultivated this mindset will become more self and socially aware, informed of the changing nature of work, connected through relevant global networks and prepared to pursue jobs that are meaningful to them. Having a professional purpose means that your personal interests and passion will align with your professional goals to shape the impact you have on the world.

Purpose in life has been defined as a central, self-organising life aim that organises and stimulates goals, manages behaviours and provides a sense of meaning.[23] We can think of purpose as operating as an overarching goal manager. The sense of purpose is not linked to the achievement of a designated goal, but operates as a mindset — motivating you to be oriented towards your goals.[24] Having a purpose in life allows you to pursue multiple goals and to generate new goals once a goal is attained, thereby experiencing personal growth. In contrast, having a specific goal that is not based on a sense of purpose makes new goals hard to identify after the goal is reached, and this makes it difficult to sustain the energy needed to pursue a goal.[25]

Here are some tips to manage stress and improve mental wellbeing in the workplace.

- When the pressures of work are demanding and stressful, it is important to have other interests in your life. Interests outside of work give you the chance to broaden your experiences and perhaps discover a new passion. Your interests or hobbies can also be a low-risk way to participate with new groups and cultures. A great way to do this is to join clubs and societies at university, if you haven't already. These provide a safe and fun space to learn about a new culture or skill.
- Make sure you incorporate regular physical activity, heathy food and eight hours of sleep per night into your daily routine. This will give you the energy and focus you need to deal with stress at work.

Michael Eales

Wellbeing is a fundamental aspect of an individual's overall health. Your mental wellbeing is just as important as your physical wellbeing. Mental wellbeing is more than the absence of mental health concerns; it is a dynamic state that encapsulates your social and emotional needs. When you take care of your mental wellbeing, you will have the mental, social and emotional capacity to get closer to your goals, creating a playground for thought, creativity and critical thinking.

Work can be a large part of our lives, playing a significant role in our mental wellbeing and subsequent capacity. It's normal to be busy at work sometimes, or to find yourself working on a project or in a role that wasn't your first choice. However, if your work is negatively impacting you to the point where you aren't able to foster social and emotional relationships or care for your mental wellbeing, it's important to take a step back and re-evaluate your options.

Check out www.healthdirect.gov.au/mental-health-and-wellbeing **to explore the relevance of mental wellbeing, mindfulness and mental health issues further.**

In managing stress and maintaining mental wellbeing at work, it's important to pinpoint what areas of work you find most beneficial, start a dialogue around mental wellbeing and create time to actively pursue activities that will support your mental wellbeing.

Areas of benefit

What gives you the most excitement in your current role or university studies? Think back to what tasks you do that excite you, or where the time seems to fly by; where you're able to get into a 'flow state'. Comparing these to activities where time seems to drag by can help you recognise which activities give you the most enjoyment or fulfilment. While it won't always be possible to only do the tasks you enjoy, recognising this can help you know when to make more time outside — or inside — work to focus on your mental wellbeing.

Start a dialogue

Are you having a bad day? Then tell your team. We aren't all going to be at the top of our game all the time. However, it's not up to your team to know when you have external concerns in your life — it's up to you to tell them. There's no need to go into detail about your concerns if you don't want to, but giving people a head's up will help reduce any additional pressure that you don't need to have.

Time for you

How are you getting fulfilment? From exercise to meditation to chatting with your friends, think about what makes you feel happy and fulfilled. Making sure you're creating time for these activities alongside your work life is important to support your mental wellbeing; meaning you won't burn out at work or at home, and can maintain a work-life balance that best fits your needs.

Mandy Johnson

'Choose a job you love, and you will never have to work a day in your life.' This may be an oft-repeated cliché, but it still holds true today. Managing mental wellbeing begins before you even have a job, because you'll be far happier working for a company with like-minded peers, and in a role that is the best 'fit' for you. If you are an apple working for a company that only values pears you will become stressed and unhappy, so finding an employer that needs, nurtures and appreciates apples will be essential for your personal wellbeing. **Don't be seduced by the job title. The choice of company is far more important than the initial job role, so find one that is a good fit for your talents, aligns with your personal values and has a track record of inspiring and rewarding its people.**

Once you have a started in a role or even set up your own business, the next strategy to maintain mental wellbeing is to manage your workload effectively. Over 2000 years ago the Greek philosopher, Socrates, warned us: 'Beware the barrenness of a busy life'. His message remains relevant today. New employees often believe that success means working themselves to the bone, wearing busyness as a badge of honour. Yet all the evidence contradicts this way of thinking. A Stanford University/IZA study showed that output falls sharply after a 50-hour work week, and declines even further after 55 hours — to the extent that someone who puts in 70 hours produces nothing more than the person who worked 55 hours.[26]

Setting healthy work boundaries allows you to avoid this pitfall and focus on achievement, not just activity. This is often easier said than done, especially for young or new employees. Working long hours is often necessary to meet an encroaching deadline or to help out on a vital team project. If you are forever feeling stretched thin, however, it's usually because you've over-committed, and this is especially true of 'people-pleasers'. Avoiding responding on the spot — for example, by telling your co-workers that you need to check your diary before agreeing to take on more work — is a good way to stop them using you as their 'go to' person for all their needs. **When it's your boss who is continually adding more work to your plate, a good diplomatic response is an enthusiastic, 'That looks like a great project. I'm currently working on A, B and C projects which are all due in the next few weeks — which one of these would you like me to put on hold, to enable me to do this new one for you?'.** As billionaire entrepreneur Warren Buffett famously said, 'The difference between successful people and really successful people is that really successful people say no to almost everything'.

Another strategy for managing stress and maintaining mental wellbeing is to actively develop social connections and satisfying hobbies outside of work. In other words, work to live, don't live to work. Every job is taxing at times but de-stressing in your personal life will enable you to cope better because once tension builds, even the smallest of incidents can lead to uncontrollable outbursts. Playing sport once a week, going out for dinner or just enjoying a laugh with friends — grasp whatever activities help to get you out of your work headspace and stop your work stress bucket overflowing. Those who prioritise themselves high up on their daily 'to-do' list will be the ones who survive and thrive in the future.

Steve Sammartino

For most of human history, our jobs included physical activity. Today, much of what we do is intellectual, and maintaining mental wellbeing is core to success. As our economy has become more complex, flexibility of mind and our ability maintain mental stability is inextricably linked to our ability to perform.

It is also worth remembering that this fact is even more important as work hours have become more fluid in our lives. Every year we do more work outside of traditional hours and our usual place of work. Mental wellbeing is now the bellwether for general wellbeing. In this sense many of us are never *not* working — we are almost always subconsciously working, even when we are not 'at work'. This is why we so often come up with solutions to a work problem at home, or randomly have a new idea we need to write down for work while we are engaged in non-work activities.

Mental wellbeing must be protected because in the modern economy as it is our most vital economic asset. We have to guard it like the bank vault to our future. There are a few main areas in which work can affect our mental wellbeing. The first is the interactions we have with people. Adversarial communication with colleagues, staff, managers or customers can have an impact on how we feel, long after the moment itself has passed. In many cases these interactions become a pattern of behaviour; the negative interactions become typical, so even the thought or expectation of such behaviours can impact our mental state. It becomes a negative cycle.

Stress around the specific tasks we have to do can have a similar impact on us mentally. When we are given a task load and deadline that is unrealistic, or asked to solve a problem without the required resources or that nobody else has been able to solve, the pressure mounts. Recurring patterns of this nature are dangerous for wellbeing if not well managed.

Another element that can impact wellbeing at work is the feeling of insecurity — that we may be dismissed, lose our job or the company might go under. Job insecurity can be an enormous source of stress.

Here are three tips to help you manage stress and improve mental wellbeing in the workplace.

1. *Ensure cultural fit.* Be sure you have a good cultural match with your company, work environment or clients. No amount of managing your career and personalities will ever fix a cultural misfit. It's not about what culture is right — it is about what culture is right for *you*. There is no such thing as the perfect culture, and this is evidenced by the fact there are many successful firms with many juxtaposed cultures. Some cultures are democratic, meritocratic, autocratic, scrappy, startup-like; there are no rules for success. The only rule that matters is finding a culture that matches how you like to operate, and your value system. **Keep switching companies until you find one that matches. If you can't find one, build your own company or work for yourself instead.**

2. *Maintain physical fitness.* Exercise and a healthy diet are key elements to maintaining mental wellbeing. Numerous studies show that exercise releases endorphins and serotonin which can have a positive impact on mood. In addition to this, regular exercise can help conditions including anxiety and depression and improve sleep. Being well rested is vital for work occurring in a high-stress environment.

3. *Invest more in yourself than you do in your job.* If we are constantly upgrading our skills and investing more in ourselves than our jobs, the companies we work for become the ultimate beneficiaries. In addition, this will ensure you have the skills needed to be valued by your next employer or client. This can radically reduce the tension associated with job insecurity.

Clare Payne

The Australian Psychological Society (APS) has found that problems at work can have an enormous impact on an individual's mental health and wellbeing.[27] We spend up to a third of our lives working, so it is crucial to our health and wellbeing that work is a positive and healthy experience.

We have seen a shift in our understanding of workplace health and safety to encompass a broader idea of wellbeing. Many businesses now offer workplace wellbeing programs that focus on work-life balance, support for parental and carer responsibilities and, importantly, mental health initiatives.

In a knowledge economy, people are considered the most valuable resource. For these people to contribute at their best and flourish we need to ensure their physiological wellbeing and safety, which are vital to living a good life.

There are many factors we encounter at work that can negatively impact our mental health and wellbeing, such as unfair pay or conditions, or harassment and bullying. We are also learning about the negative impact of workplace cultures that are psychologically unsafe. For example, cultures that promote a fear of failure and expect people to work with unclear direction, lack of job security or no recognition for a job well done can negatively impact individuals, and ultimately business outcomes as well.

Business in the Community, a UK-based organisation that is part of the Prince's Responsible Business Network, has called for employers to recognise the scale of poor mental health in the workplace.[28] Along with others, it has highlighted the duty of care of employers have to their employees, and the obligation employers have to respond to mental ill health just as they would to a physical illness.

Many organisations are now focusing on how to create positive, inclusive workplace cultures that help rather than harm the mental health of the people who work in them.

Here are some ways you can manage stress and improve mental wellbeing in the workplace.

1. *Understanding your rights.* It is essential for you to understand your rights at work, and also as a citizen. There are many online resources that will help you understand your rights, and the rights of others, so you can confidently protect and assert yourself.

2. *Taking time for what matters.* Many of us find that work can become overwhelming, particularly given that technology has increased expectations of availability and blurred the distinction between work and personal time. While employers should respect people's time, the reality is that we all need to be conscious of balancing our own lives — ensuring we prioritise things that are good for our mental health and wellbeing such as walking, a creative pursuit or just connecting with friends.

3. *Seeking clarification.* Seeking clarity on vision, goals and purpose can remove stress and provide a clear path for you to contribute to your organisation and reach your potential. When you are new to a workplace you will see things with 'fresh eyes'. This is a great advantage, as more experienced workers can slip into unthinking behaviours, which can lead to unethical practices. Asking questions is a powerful tool. For managers, removing ambiguity can drive employee satisfaction and performance.

Nicola Hazell

Stress has been described as the smoking of our generation. It costs the Australian economy more than $15 billion per year in work absenteeism and lost productivity.[29] In the US, that figure is more than $500 billion. Stress is a hidden epidemic, affecting the mental wellbeing — and, therefore, capacity and productivity — of not just our workforce, but our whole community. When there is widespread stress in a work environment, it creates toxic cultures, drives poor decision making and can lead to business failures.

On the flipside, those with strong mental wellbeing are in a far better position to do their best work in stressful situations. Not only do they have the energy and focus to generate great ideas and work well with others, they also develop an inbuilt resilience for the kinds of challenges a rapidly changing world of work can throw at us. Those who pay attention to their own mental health and put in place tools and habits to keep themselves mentally well are more likely to come up with great ideas, bounce back from rejection or failure and build sustainable, game-changing businesses and teams.

Here are some tips to manage stress and improve mental wellbeing in the workplace:[30]

1. *Monitor and manage your workload.* Be aware of what you are working on and how much you may have on your plate. Speak up at an early stage if you are feeling overwhelmed so you can seek guidance and support to share the load.

2. *Don't be afraid to address the hard topics.* You don't have to be the boss to encourage a culture of open communication about mental health and wellbeing so others know that it's okay to talk about stress at work. When people are able to be their authentic selves at work, it fosters positive mental wellbeing. As a member of a team, you can cultivate this within your own organisation by creating safe spaces for others to share, and being willing to do so yourself.

3. *Seek out and use emotional and mental health support tools.* Get to know the activities and tools that help you stay mentally well. Whether it's meditation, exercise, connection with loved ones, or one of the many online tools now available for improving mental wellbeing, it's essential to recognise the things that help you manage stress and keep you in a positive frame of mind and ensure you prioritise them as a consistent part of your routine.

4. *Be accountable.* You can't expect your workplace to help you manage stress and improve your wellbeing if you don't do the same for others. Be accountable for the way you behave and interact with your colleagues and managers, to ensure you're supporting them just as much as you'd like them to support you. Workplace wellbeing is a two-way street — everyone plays a role in creating a healthy environment where we all thrive.

Social intelligence

QUESTIONS What do you consider the biggest social challenge when entering the workforce? What are the traits of people who successfully navigate these challenges?

Nicola Hazell

Throughout childhood, and even during university, we spend most of our time outside the home with people our own age. Our peers may come from different neighbourhoods and backgrounds, but in many ways we have more in common than not. At university, you're exposed to the same learning and curriculum as your classmates, equipped with the same information and insights and tasked with many of the same challenges.

When you enter the workforce, this changes completely. Suddenly, your colleagues and managers come from different walks of life. They are different ages and have vastly different life experiences to you. Their stories are diverse and so, too, is the value they bring to an organisation.

Some of the greatest challenges in adapting to the workforce come in learning to work with such a diverse group of people; figuring out the value you add and when to add it in a much more complex environment; and understanding how to build relationships that are productive, healthy and respectful.

What's more, while you might think it is your technical skills and knowledge that will be the critical factor to your success, in reality, it is the transferable, interpersonal and social skills that will determine whether you thrive in the workforce. Research shows that the majority of modern employers looking to fill graduate positions are more interested in the non-technical skills a person has.[31] Your ability to communicate well, work with others, come up with ideas, solve problems, show resilience under pressure and to learn from your mistakes are the skills in demand. These skills don't just make great workers — they also make great leaders. If you can learn how to translate these skills into opportunities, you can significantly increase your employability.

The best companies to work for are those that create a healthy environment for ideas to be raised — and challenged. The best possible solutions can be found through debate and interrogation. To succeed in this kind of an environment requires a unique mix of skills:

- confidence, so you're not afraid to share your ideas, opinions and insights
- humility, so you recognise that your ideas, opinions and insights may and should be challenged
- collectivism, so you're willing to work together and support others to arrive at the best possible solution — whether it's your original idea or not.

To help develop these skills during your studies and early work experience, seek out opportunities to take part in extracurricular activities or projects that challenge you to develop and demonstrate new skills, allow you to connect and work with others, and provide the opportunity to learn from those who may have more experience or different perspectives. **When given the opportunity, seek feedback from managers, mentors and peers who can help you continue to grow these skills and attributes and offer additional opportunities to learn.**

These will be critical traits for navigating the challenges and opportunities that arise in any workplace of the future.

Professor Rachael Field

Social intelligence involves knowing ourselves and understanding others. High standards of professional performance and civil interaction are expected in the workforce, and this will continue into the future. Managing ourselves and engaging with others appropriately at work can be a big social challenge.

Effective communication is a fundamental skill-set for managing the social side of being in a workplace. Communication skills are important when it comes to professional conduct and building constructive working relationships with colleagues, and they are also critical to preventing, managing and resolving disputes. Conflict and disputes in the workplace can be damaging for productivity and your mental health. Workplace conflict can derive from relatively small matters (such as using all the milk in the fridge and not replacing it) to large, even legal, matters such as bullying.

Proactive leadership is an important element of creating healthy workplaces with low levels of disputation and conflict. Individuals, too, can manage the social challenges of working by building and enacting effective communication skills.

In dispute resolution and mediation training, the acronym LARSQ (listening, acknowledging, reframing, summarising and questioning) is used to describe the basic skills necessary for effective communication. Dispute resolution practitioners and mediators use these skills all the time in their professional practice. They are skills that you can employ as part of exercising social intelligence.

Effective listening involves listening actively and responsively, and letting the speaker know that they have not only been heard but also understood. This requires focus and attention. Acknowledging refers to the recognition of emotions, needs, interests, fears and priorities. When these things are acknowledged a person feels listened to and valued and they are then more likely to collaborate constructively and engage in positive problem solving. Reframing is a complex skill, but basically it involves taking negative words and sentiments and re-expressing them in a way that supports effective communication. For example, instead of saying 'I think you're lying', you might say 'I'm not sure about the accuracy of what you just said'. Summarising is a part of active listening involving repeating back to someone your understanding of what they have said to ensure the accuracy of that understanding and to demonstrate engagement in the communication. Finally, appropriate questioning is critical to effective communication. Effective questions are open and clarifying rather than closed or leading. The book *Mediation Skills and Techniques* by Laurence Boulle and Nadja Alexander is an excellent resource if you would like to learn more about effective communication and conflict resolution.[32]

Successfully navigating the challenges associated with being a socially intelligent work colleague and effective communicator in the workplace calls for a range of positive traits. Three important ones are emotional intelligence, awareness and responsiveness to others, and the ability to receive and give feedback appropriately.

Emotional intelligence

This involves an ability to engage with and use emotions logically and wisely. In order to do this, we need to be able to perceive emotions accurately, assimilate emotion-related feelings, understand emotions and manage them. Emotional intelligence is a form of intrapersonal intelligence involving emotional self-awareness and an ability to regulate your own emotions. It is also related to interpersonal intelligence, which is a person's ability to accurately detect the emotions of another person and to manage responses to those emotions.

Awareness of and responsiveness to others

This builds on emotional intelligence and is an important aspect of communicating effectively. Awareness and responsiveness can be realised through the skill of empathy. Empathy is the ability to understand another person's perspective — in other words, 'put yourself in their shoes'. It goes beyond simply recognising and understanding another person's feelings and experience to entering their world and acknowledging and valuing them as a person with their own individual needs, interests and concerns. Importantly, being empathic is not the same as agreeing with someone or feeling sorry for them. Empathy as a form of awareness and responsiveness can be shown through enacting all the elements of LARSQ — especially if you can incorporate empathic questions and acknowledgement. This approach will contribute to effective communication at work and can be a positive strategy in the prevention, management and resolution of workplace disputes and conflict.

The ability to give and receive feedback

This requires emotional intelligence and reflective practice. It is easy to feel criticised and upset by feedback you receive in the workplace. However, managing feedback (and also giving feedback) appropriately contributes to a socially healthy workplace and can positively support collegiality and your own wellbeing.

Responding to feedback appropriately requires an openness to the opinions of others and a willingness to improve. It is almost always nice to receive feedback on what you have done well; but not so easy to receive feedback that criticises what you have done, or that says something has been done incorrectly or should have been done differently. Building the skills of receiving and giving feedback well is an important aspect of professional self-management and self-regulation.

Some strategies for using the feedback process appropriately include:
- being open to receiving feedback
- valuing the time and effort of the person providing the feedback
- preparing for receiving feedback — having the right mindset to receive it with emotional intelligence
- avoiding taking feedback personally
- using feedback constructively to improve performance
- avoiding arguing with negative or critical feedback
- considering the big picture and keeping things in perspective
- building on the feedback by asking clarifying questions and asking for additional feedback on specific points.

Michael Eales

Having high social intelligence means you have the ability and capacity of knowing your true self, and understanding the core of others in your environment. Considering the dynamic and opportunistic course of a career, establishing and having a concrete and solid level of social intelligence will allow you to market yourself effectively to different audiences in your professional and personal life. This means having deep empathy for those you work with, understanding what makes you and others tick and translating the two as you work across company cultures. Mastering the relationship between social intelligence and empathy is key to better navigating the world around you.

Yourself

While it is important to be able to tailor your approach to different circumstances, your true self should never change. **Invest time in knowing what makes you tick, what your boundaries are and what motivates you, and use this knowledge as a parameter or criteria when presented with new opportunities.** Remember that what makes you, you is invaluable, and you are your best asset. If you're interested in exploring this further, check out https://businessmodelyou.com.

Culture

Having a solid understanding of yourself enables you to figure out how to work effectively in different environments. It's crucial to remember that each company culture is unique — pick and choose the parts you wish to emulate while remaining true to yourself. **Read the book *The Invincible Company* to learn more.**[33]

Relationships

Friction is a natural process of life that enables you to grow and develop as an individual. When confronted with the potential for conflict, embrace the opportunity to proactively manage the relationship through empathy in communication. It is a small world, after all, and if you maintain your relationships well there is decreased risk of 'burning bridges'.

Mandy Johnson

In 1913, the famous car manufacturer Henry Ford established a sociological department to control every aspect of his employees' lives. Investigators would turn up unannounced at employees' homes and if they failed the 'cleanliness evaluation' or were deemed to be consuming too much alcohol, they were sacked. We've come a long way from this kind of tyranny, however the first social challenge new employees face is understanding and dealing effectively with the many unspoken rules and operating norms within their organisation — what is known as workplace culture.

Every business has its own distinct culture, in the same way that people have their own distinct personalities, and this is expressed in daily practices that act as signals to workers. Can I joke around and have fun at work? Is it okay for people to make a mistake or do they try to cover it up? Are tattoos encouraged or frowned upon? Just to make things more confusing, in some cases the culture companies publicly proclaim can be the exact opposite of what happens in practice. Observing, asking questions of approachable co-workers and avoiding making assumptions are some tactics that can help new workers traverse this minefield.

Another area of social challenge for new employees is dealing with co-workers with vastly different personalities, experiences and cultural beliefs to their own. **Don't fall into the cloning trap, believing that everyone should think and communicate just like you.** Social assumptions and biases are also still rife in today's workplaces. Dog lovers like dog lovers, rugby players prefer other rugby players, and they'll often make unhelpful sweeping generalisations about those who don't like dogs or rugby.

Scenarios like these require effective social skills, such as asking questions rather than making assumptions. Compare: 'I know you people all hate loud music' to 'What is your opinion of heavy metal music?' which is far more diplomatic. Good conflict-handling skills are essential, too. These can include managing your emotions (taking deep breaths and keeping your tone of voice at normal levels) and listening and showing empathy ('That does sound frustrating'). Learning good techniques like these allows new workers to overcome natural defensiveness and reduces workplace arguments.

Yet perhaps the biggest factor that affects an employee's social success when entering a new workforce is their own mindset. Those who adopt a victim mentality — blaming others and denying that anything they do is a factor in the equation — bring about their own failure. Those who take responsibility, refuse to externalise and ask, 'How am I contributing to this?' and 'What can I do to change?' can overcome almost any hurdles. By paying attention, doing what you say you will do and being consistent and authentic, you will earn the respect from others that is necessary to achieve success. After all, who would you rather do something for — someone you like or someone you don't like?

Professor Angela Carbone

One of the biggest social challenges you will face when entering the workforce is building strong and trusting relationships with people that hold different cultural, spiritual and ethical values to you. People work well with those that they can trust; however, trust does not come instantaneously: it requires time, multiple interactions, and opportunities to engage in meaningful conversations and negotiate your position around challenging issues. Your values will be tested and questioned. You will encounter differences of opinions and approaches, which might lead to conflict. Being able to understand the sensitivities around an issue and appreciating and respecting the values of others — particularly those who have had different cultural and social experiences to you — will be instrumental in managing. Stellar negotiation, influencing and persuasion skills will be important, and you can hone all of these skills while at university.

Traits of people that can navigate such challenges include the following.
1. *Reliability and honesty.* Performing consistently well and being trustworthy enables you to develop strong relationships with your colleagues and stakeholders.
2. *Emotional intelligence.* Being self-aware and maintaining a positive attitude so that you can empathise with others and respond rather than react to conflict will enable you to successfully navigate relationships with others at work.
3. *Grit and tenacity.* You will need courage and strength to express your point of view when others might disagree and react in an unacceptable manner. It may take time and perseverance to achieve the outcome you want, as you will likely experience delays or difficulties in achieving success.
4. *Resilience.* You need to be able to recover quickly when faced with difficulties or when the outcome is different to what you expected.

Steve Sammartino

One of the biggest challenges you will face when entering the workforce is that workplaces are far less democratic than educational or social institutions. Over the past 20 years we have seen the emergence of a generation that has grown up without meritocracy. We've been taught that equality matters more than performance. But in the workforce, you don't get a ribbon just for participating. While social equality has certainly increased in the workplace, corporate hierarchies are still Darwinist in terms of who rises to the top. Not everyone gets to the 'next grade'.

Rapidly changing norms of acceptability mean that this is a new skill-base people must have to navigate a successful career. To avoid a clash of cultures (between people, media, industries and corporations) we need to understand belief systems outside of what we value personally, or grew up with socially or geographically.

Traits of people that can navigate such challenges include the following.
1. *Keen cultural observers.* People who are keen observers and students of the rapidly changing cultural landscape have a massive social advantage. As global cultures converge and people are more mobile physically and digitally, understanding different cultures and shifts in what is acceptable is now as valuable as being an observer of consumer trends.
2. *Listeners.* People who first want to understand someone else's point of view before they wish to have their viewpoint understood are particularly good at navigating and resolving conflict. As our tasks become more about managing projects and situations, this type of empathy is highly valued.
3. *Data enthusiasts.* In a digital society where algorithms determine what we all see, understanding bias in data is vital. People are increasingly exposed to more of what they already believe as they are served up news and opinions that match their existing viewpoints. It is becoming an important trait to be aware of this, and extend views outside of algorithmic wormholes so that we have a broad understanding of society.

Clare Payne

It can be a challenge to accept others who have different views, backgrounds and skills to your own. The focus on inclusion and diversity at work has been an important development, although there is still much progress to be made.

Recognising that others have a powerful contribution to make, even if their style or approach differs to your own, is an important concept to understand and practise. Looking for and being able to see the strengths in others is a good way to overcome this social challenge. You should take the time to get to know your colleagues and customers and seek to understand them. **Try to avoid using labels or stereotyping, which can be discriminatory and hinder effective connection and performance.**

You might find it helpful to think about the qualities of ethical leaders, as they are more likely to successfully navigate challenges. It's important to note that leaders can exist at all levels of an organisation — you don't necessarily need a title to be considered a leader.

In her book *Setting the Tone: Ethical Business Leadership*, Philippa Foster Back identified five key attributes of an ethical leader:[34]

1. openness
2. fair-mindedness
3. honesty
4. courage
5. the ability to listen.

These attributes set an ethical leader apart from others. We all possess these attributes in varying degrees, however they will be nurtured, developed and supported by an ethical leader.

Developing mental agility, such as the capacity to challenge your perspectives and evolve your opinions when presented with a variety of different perspectives or ideas, is important in developing as an ethical and inclusive worker and leader who is fit for the future.

Ethics

QUESTIONS How will ethics in the workplace evolve over the next five to ten years? What issues will emerge as top priority during this time? How can we prepare for these changes now?

Clare Payne

The issue of ethics will be front and centre as the next generation of leaders emerge — particularly as they question the outcomes that have arisen from past and current practices.

While laws and regulations will remain important, I believe we will see a continued move beyond mere compliance to an expectation of higher ethical standards. In January 2020, the annual credibility survey Edelman Trust Barometer declared that the battle for trust will be fought on the field of ethical behaviour.[35]

As global issues such an inequality and climate change become more pressing, ethics will only become more important. Individuals will look to their employer, in particular their CEO, to have a position and 'take a stand' on the issues of the day. Already, 92 per cent of employees expect their company's CEO to speak up on issues such as income inequality, diversity, ethical use of technology, climate change and immigration.[36] This expectation is predicted to continue to grow, propelling businesses and leaders to action and contribute to a better world.

Three issues that will emerge as a top priority during this time are as follows.

1. *The idea of moral money.* Until recently, morality and money were rarely paired. In June 2019 the *Financial Times* London launched a 'Moral Money' section. Now, one quarter of all investable assets globally, worth $31 trillion, are managed with an environmental, social and governance (ESG) mandate.[37] Our own Responsible Investment Association of Australasia has declared that responsible investment is 'mainstream', with 44 per cent of money managed (totalling $2.24 trillion) under a responsible investment mandate in 2019.[38] The increased focus on whether money is accumulated and spent morally will change investment, influence business practices and improve outcomes for society.

2. *Shifting from a short to long-term focus.* Much of our finance sector and business operations have been focused on short-term outcomes, such as quarterly profit cycles, rather than on the long-term viability and contribution of products and services to society. The COVID-19 pandemic has exposed many of the downfalls of focusing on short-term solutions rather than planning and preparing over a longer timeframe. For example, the drastic shortage of essential items exposed the vulnerability of just-in-time inventory systems, which are common to many businesses and often implemented by private equity in the quest to drive down costs and make a profit in the short term rather than ensuring a business can deliver to society over the longer term.

3. *Addressing inequity.* Inequity across society can't be ignored, in Australia or globally. It has become clear that traditional measures such as gross domestic product (GDP) do not tell us about the extent to which financial growth is shared across the population. Edelman has identified that a growing sense of inequity is undermining trust. It has found that the majority of those living in developed markets do not

believe they will be better off in five years' time, and more than half of globally believe that capitalism in its current form is doing more harm than good in the world. Our experiences during the COVID-19 crisis will likely reaffirm this position and propel us towards positive change.

In order to prepare for these changes, businesses and individuals will need to determine their role in society. Many businesses still remain focused on shareholder and financial returns without considering their impact. Those that work in the field of change and transformation have indicated that it can take a decade for businesses to truly transform their operations to be purpose-led.

As a society, we will need to determine measures and indicators, particularly non-financial, that signify a new idea of success and track progress towards a better world.

There are many ways that individuals can influence for good. Managers can ensure pay equity and fairness, and individuals can ensure they act with honesty and respect the contribution and individuality of those with whom they work and interact.

Professor Rachael Field

Ethics are foundational, fundamental principles on which professional work is based. Ethics in the workplace is about analysis and decision making in terms of what the right, moral or appropriate thing to do is. In the workplace you will be expected to act ethically at all times, and this will continue to be the case in the world post COVID-19 — although we may find that new ethical dilemmas arise in the future work environment that have not yet been anticipated.

Many professions have ethical codes of conduct, and membership of professions is often regulated by these codes. A breach of the ethical code can mean exclusion from the profession — which is generally regarded as a very shameful thing. Ethical decision making in workplaces requires more than simply abiding by a professional code of conduct, however. Ethical dilemmas are complex and don't always fit neatly into prescribed rules. This means that to be ethical at work, you will need an ability to apply ethical rules to real-life situations, a very clear personal commitment to taking the right path, as well as the skills to analyse, process and respond to ethical problems. Your capacity to manage the complexity of ethical challenges may take some time to develop. Even the most experienced professionals will say that they are challenged by ethical dilemmas in their daily work.

The evolution of workplace ethics in the future could force the emergence of three important issues. First, the need for individuals to have a well-developed moral compass; second, increased emphasis on the importance of an ability to exercise appropriate ethical judgement; and third, the critical nature of mentoring in workplaces.

A moral compass

Having a moral compass refers to a person's internal and innate ability to judge what is right and wrong and to act appropriately in accordance with that judgement. In the workplace a moral compass denotes honesty, propriety and competence.

Honesty refers to telling the truth and is related to integrity and candour. It also indicates an absence of deceit. To be ethical, communications and actions in the workplace must be honest and never intended to deceive or convey something known to be false. Propriety relates to the quality of a person's professional character; that is, a suitable and proper professional character. Reflective practice, emotional intelligence, communication skills and empathy are all important to maintaining our propriety in the workplace and behaving ethically. Competency concerns the ability (the knowledge, skills and expertise) to work accurately and effectively using appropriate levels of skill and expertise. An ethical person in the workplace will ensure that they have sufficient knowledge and experience to do the work that is asked of them. If they have concerns that they might not have sufficient competence for the task, they will ask for help and guidance.

An ability to make ethical judgements

Developing an ability to make ethical judgements is something that happens over time and through experience and lessons learned in practice, through reflective practice and through mentoring relationships. Ethical dilemmas in workplaces are hardly ever straightforward; they are messy and complex. 'Deliberative ethical decision making' is an approach that can help with ethical judgement. This approach is useful because it offers some logical steps for processing an ethical problem. It also provides evidence of a thoughtful and careful approach that — even if it isn't agreed with — is justifiable and based on logical reasoning.

The possible steps of a deliberative ethical decision-making process are:
1. identify the ethical issue
2. consider potential initial options for addressing the issue
3. identify the various interests of the relevant people involved in the problem
4. identify the relevant professional sources of authority such as the relevant rules of professional conduct that might apply to the situation
5. consider whether there are any broader ethical considerations
6. consult, seek help and guidance from someone not involved with the problem — possibly a mentor, professional counsellor or more experienced colleague
7. generate some possible courses of action and consider the consequences of each of them
8. on balance, in all the circumstances and informed by all the considerations in steps one to seven, make a decision about the most appropriate action to take
9. summarise a diary note of the decision and the reasons for it on the basis of the ethical deliberations.

Mentoring

Mentoring is an important part of developing a moral compass and the ability to make ethical judgments in professional contexts. A mentor is an experienced person in your workplace, industry or profession who helps and gives advice to you — a younger or less experienced person. Taking the initiative to find a mentor demonstrates an awareness of the importance of learning from peers and more experienced people; it shows a recognition of the complex nature of ethical judgement and the time it takes to develop. All young professionals need help with the development of their ethical and professional judgement, and it's important to know when to ask for help. Some workplaces establish formal mentoring relationships between staff. The most successful approaches to mentoring, however, are often the ones that develop organically.

Managing ethical challenges in future work environments requires intentional approaches to developing the skills discussed in this section. It also requires a positive attitude to developing self-regulation and self-management skills. This is because in the workplace a person who is well, emotionally balanced and coping is more likely to be able to make good ethical decisions.

Michael Eales

Ethics are reflected in the choices we make — both conscious and unconscious — for the greater good or individual rights. The ethical procedures of a company are now regarded as having the same importance as the products and services they deliver. As an employee, you will bear some responsibility for how ethics are upheld at the company you work for, while also needing to align your own personal ethics and values to your daily processes. Therefore, it is important to be aware of your own ethical principles, understand that transparency is the best policy, and regularly reflect on the world we live in today.

Principles

How you project yourself and what you actually do are two different things, and social responsibility is no exception. When reflecting on your own ethical principles, view yourself as if you were judging a company's corporate social responsibility program. Work out what you *say* you do versus what you *actually* do and go from there.

Transparency

As we become more aware and enlightened of human practices we must continually improve. This is only achieved based on true and evidenced information extracted from insights and observations we make of the world around us, and how this world works. To improve we must be aware of our preconceptions and assumptions we often carry around with us. **When in doubt, transparency and honesty is the best policy in both professional and personal circumstances.**

Reflect

With ongoing crises such as climate change, and humans increasing their roles in mitigating its effects, we all have some responsibility in enacting change in the world. **Remain up to date on global information to inform your ethical practices at home and work.** Many hands make light work.

Check out the work of the Ethics Centre — https://ethics.org.au.

Mandy Johnson

Ethics is one area that is changing exponentially and will offer some of the greatest challenges for employees entering the workforce in the next five to ten years. On the one hand, there is a lot of positive change. More companies are taking a public stance on ethical issues: Qantas publicly supported the Australian same-sex marriage bill, the big four banks refused to fund the Adani coalmine and Atlassian vocally supports climate change initiatives.

At the same time, the ethical line is blurring between personal and professional life. Employees can be sacked for posting articles and arguments on their private social media pages that contradict their employer's stance. In Australia, a sawmill worker was sacked after his company introduced a new fingerprint scanning system and he refused to hand over his biometric data, for fear of it being misused. A Chinese organisation even forces its employees to wear helmets with sensors that detect anger, depression and fatigue. A big ethical question in the future then will be where we draw the line between ourselves and our work, especially with employers that adopt Big Brother tactics.

The rise in the use of AI will also create new ethical issues. AI has many benefits such as reducing human error in fields such as weather forecasting, and decreasing risk for humans (think AI robots that defuse bombs in war zones). Yet unchecked, AI can be destructive. Amazon discovered this after it created an AI hiring tool that scored job applicants from one to five stars to automate the search process. It was eventually abandoned when Amazon realised the system was skewed towards male applicants and had been hiring far more men than women.

Decision making will also be more ambiguous in this rapidly changing world. Like pioneers in a new frontier, science is developing faster than ethics, meaning that front-line employees will be dealing with more complex ethical questions. For instance, if a corporation you work for uses neuromarketing to make children dependent on sugary products, is that okay with you? Or if your genetics company creates a cloning system that secretly selects embryos solely on intelligence, is it your duty to tell someone? If your software company uses AI algorithms to manipulate public and political debate in ways that make you uncomfortable, what do you do about that?

We are all dependent on employers for our jobs and salary so speaking up is easier said than done. Yet research shows that people regret *not* acting more than they regret actions not going well. This is certainly true of some General Motors workers who helped develop and install a cheap ignition switch that they knew to be faulty, even in the pre-production phase.[39] The defective part eventually led to over 153 deaths, multiple crashes and 10 million car recalls — all because no-one spoke up. This all goes to show that, even though we aren't taught much about ethics in schools or university, it can have a major impact on our future.

Steve Sammartino

In the coming years, ethics will extend well beyond selling products with ingredients and production histories that are ethically sound. Fair treatment of staff and animals and compliance with workplace health and safety are all now seen as the bare minimum. The next forms of evolution in ethics will pertain to the digital marketplace.

The first of these will be ethics around data. Globally, the regulations around using data for profit are very lax. Even where regulations exist, it is difficult to prove data is being accumulated or misused, and which jurisdiction the data actually resides in. It is also true that the large majority of data breaches remain unknown to the victims at a corporate and personal level.

Much of the data that is accumulated is gathered without the explicit approval of end users. While privacy and service agreements are usually presented prior to using digital services, this quasi-approval is done via legal obfuscation. That is, the agreements include a level of complexity that very few people understand, and most agreements are many thousands of words long — so the reality is, most of us click 'accept' without properly absorbing the information.

This is resulting in massive privacy impingements in consumer society we are yet to see or understand the long-term consequences of. This will be a new battleground for ethics in business in the coming decade. The accumulation of data, how secure it is and the privacy impacts will become a major issue for management.

Three issues that will emerge as a priority during this time are as follows.

1. *Data will become a liability.* Companies that currently gather data on end users do so by providing free services in exchange. Increasingly data is being seen as an asset that end users should own and control. There have even been calls for data to be treated as a form of labour, as those who supply data are essentially creating products for tech companies to use for advertising. Mitigation corporations will increasingly need to reward customers whose data they gather with something beyond free products. Data will need to be treated like a bank deposit, for which some form of interest is paid and that can be fully withdrawn at the request of the data depositor.

2. *Algorithms will be regulated.* Currently algorithms that decide how digital products are served up via advertising are completely unregulated. Algorithms can have a dramatic impact on how internet users behave and react, and what they believe to be true. They have an inordinate influence on civic society. In the future it will become vital to ensure any algorithms used are 'ethical in advance'. Corporations utilising algorithms for any business purpose should be prepared for them to be regulated in a similar way to packaged food. Consumers will eventually have access to information showing how digital decisions are made on their behalf. Dark patterns that are used in hidden algorithms (for example, racial or sexual preference profiling) are likely to be outlawed in any business context.

3. *Criminality of data breaches.* Data security is not taken very seriously by most corporations at this point because the consequences of a breach are so small. In most cases, the profit from misuse of data is greater than the fines most large corporations face when hacks occur. Legislators globally are becoming acutely aware of this flaw and will shift the focus from financial repercussions to hold directors and staff criminally liable for breaches. The focus for corporations will need to shift to securing data like money.

The number one strategy for corporations is to get ahead of the legislation; to act on what is likely to be legislated later, now. It can actually become a point of difference for brands and companies to be ethically proactive.

From a career management perspective, people need to align themselves with corporations that have data ethics — not just because it is the right thing to do, but because large digital brands are less likely to be dominant in a future where they have to have a greater corporate responsibility when the consumer marketplace becomes more aware of data ethics.

Nicola Hazell

Casualisation and the gig economy

Over the past decade, it has become increasingly difficult for young people to get a secure job in their chosen fields — to get that break as they are starting out their working lives.[40] In Australia, people are more in debt at a younger age than ever before; almost one in two are still relying on their parents financially at the age of 24, and one in four graduates are struggling to find full-time employment after completing secondary or tertiary studies.[41]

The under-employment factor is a critical issue that is likely to rise.[42] Already, despite 60 per cent of young Australians holding some form of post-school qualification, 50 per cent of them are unable to secure traditional employment scenarios of more than 35 hours of work per week. Even among those who can secure full-time hours, many are doing so in casual, insecure jobs. Compared to 30 years ago, twice the number of young people are now working full-time hours in casual jobs, and the majority are doing so by holding down multiple jobs at once.

For all the flexibility and opportunity the gig economy can offer, this emerging segment of our global workforce brings with it a great deal of vulnerability for young workers. They may have a job (or jobs) — as a casual barista, an Uber driver or a cleaner on AirTasker – but this work is not fulfilling their social or economic needs, nor creating pathways to quality, full-time employment. Already, there are concerns about the implications of this trend — that it could potentially create a working poor among younger generations.

The traditional social constructs that have been built to provide workplace safety nets — such as workplace rights, minimum wages, government benefits and collective bargaining — have not been built into the frameworks of this new way of working.

The ethical risks of this are significant, presenting serious challenges for government, companies, regulators and the public to confront. **As someone about to take the plunge into this environment, it's essential to be aware of your rights, to be cognisant of the risks, and to consider the flow-on effects of what you are individually willing to compromise on.** Human beings by nature crave and require security. In the middle ages, security was tribal. In the modern day, that sense of security comes from being part of a community, a town, a home or an organisation. In the gig economy, security doesn't really exist. And when a crisis hits, there is no safety net built into systems that sit around it.

In the future of work, the ethics of this model for commerce and work will be increasingly questioned. Just because it offers greater efficiency, independence and flexibility, does that outweigh the loss of security, community and accountability? Or does it instead serve to further deepen the inequalities that have long existed in the modern world of work?

The ethics of this new reality will come further into question in the years ahead. In a post-COVID-19 environment — where the implications of this lack of security will have been brought to light at greater scale — the debate as to how to create a future of work that is ethical, and that increases (not decreases) equality, human connection and security, will be brought to the fore.

The emergence of AI

The growth of AI presents one of the great ethical debates of our time. Ever since the idea of 'robots taking over' was introduced into the public discourse via film and television decades ago, questions of trust, privacy and control have been raised.

Now, as we see technology move rapidly into the realm of AI in ways that are already integrating deeply into our daily lives — think Google Home, Amazon's Alexa, Tesla's self-driven cars and even the way Facebook knows what ads to show you — the question of what constitutes ethical AI is an urgent and pressing issue.

In many ways, the horse has already bolted. Data rights and data privacy are issues that only the most dedicated technology advocates and regulators are deeply engaging with, while most of us simply enjoy the convenience these technologies bring into our lives without questioning what it is we are giving up. Without consumer-driven demand for, and comprehension of, the ethical treatment of data, it becomes increasingly difficult for regulators to challenge.

The implications of this go much further than what it means for our data today. If the algorithms that make up AI are being fed a baseline of knowledge that does not have ethics built in, the AI will continue to perpetuate that baseline. The same can be said of bias. If AI is built to see the world through the eyes of just one 'type' of person, then what AI recognises as true or false, right or wrong, will be intrinsically biased towards that point of view. We're already seeing the way this plays out, with indicators of racism and sexism in the behaviours and insights of some forms of AI.[43]

The ethics of this is critical. If action isn't taken to counter these biases and build a baseline that recognises and respects diversity, then the AI that will increasingly inform our work, our homes, our lives and the information we are fed will continue to perpetuate inequality, growing in a way that is inherently unethical.

Creating a better world

Now more than ever, companies are being forced to demonstrate and earn their social licence to operate. Community expectations of corporate social responsibility are stretching well beyond the charity arms of organisations, requiring businesses and individuals to increasingly look at their operations through a lens of impact. This consideration of impact is then informing and influencing the values of organisations, their business activities and the behaviour of their people.

This shift is not just being driven simply by a desire to 'do the right thing'; nor is it being driven by social causes succeeding in their advocacy. It's being driven in many ways by consumer behaviour and expectations. Therefore, companies that not only consider how to mitigate any negative impact they have, but in fact are built out of an intent to have a net positive impact, will be the ones that come out on top. If this utopian view does not come to fruition, the implications for humanity are perilous. Unless businesses recognise and value the qualities of community and connection, equality and environmental sustainability — and unless employees live out these qualities in the way they work and live their lives — the fabric of society in the future of work will be eroded.

For humanity to evolve, the future of work needs to be played out with a new human-centred model. The social contract of the industrial era will need to be challenged to focus on outcomes over hours, to value contribution in a less transactional way. And on an immediate, personal level, the next generation will need to take this opportunity to question what it means to be human, and what the role of 'work' should be within that greater human experience.

In the meantime, you don't need to worry about climbing ladders that have been put in place by previous generations. **Instead, focus on the impact you can make in the world, then create the path in front of you to get there.** And, importantly, take others along with you when you do.

Skills and development

QUESTIONS Why is staying sharp important? What can happen if you don't stay up to date and continually refine your skills? How will professional development evolve over the next five to ten years? Knowing this, what are some strategies you can use to stay at the top of your game?

Nicola Hazell

Perhaps the most critical attribute for any individual in the future of work is curiosity. Those who are curious and have a constant thirst for learning and growth will be best placed to have a meaningful career and an impactful life. It's no longer a case of studying one university degree or trade to set you up for life. Ongoing professional and personal development will be key over the next five to fifty years.

For those on the frontline of technology — even those who are driving the change — the need to learn and adapt as the tech evolves is constant. But being adaptable and curious will be critical whether you're working in a hands-on technology role or not. As technology shifts, so too do markets. And as our world becomes more and more politically unstable, the conditions we operate in are more volatile and uncertain. Job mobility — the fact we will all have diverse careers in changing roles across changing industries — means we'll constantly be placed in different environments and circumstances and required to upskill or re-skill for the changing scenario.

As we've seen off the back of the COVID-19 global crisis, many workers have already been forced to consider their skills and how they could apply them in a totally different context within a different industry and role. The confronting nature of this situation is an indication of further instability likely to come. The key here is that preparing for instability is not about simply acquiring *more* skills and knowledge — because in a world that is changing so fast, we can never accumulate all the knowledge we might need to confront every task and challenge we will be presented with. No amount of professional development or outside learning will ensure you have the answer to every problem. In this scenario, it's not about what you know; it's about how you respond. Being prepared to make a decision to do something risky, to put yourself out there and take on something you haven't done before when there is no guarantee it will work: this is the mindset you will need in the future of work.

You can't afford to wait for 'perfect'; to wait until you're sure you're making the right call. It's not about being flippant. You can still be considered and deliberate and thoughtful. But you've also got to take a leap of faith and trust your intuition when there is 'nothing but gut' to go on.

Mandy Johnson

Imagine you are sitting in on an executive meeting and the managing director (MD) asks each of her leaders what their plan is for the next 12 months. One worker who has just experienced his most successful year ever says he is going to do exactly what he did last year. The MD replies, 'Well, you're in trouble then!' The point she was making is that knowledge was king for past generations, but when the world of work is changing at a cyclonic pace, it is knowledge *by learning* that will determine someone's effectiveness. If you're just focused on doing the same thing each year, and others are constantly improving, within 12 months you will have gone backwards in comparison without even realising it.

The good news is that once you embrace the concept of lifelong learning you can make it a practical strategy. Start by focusing on aspects of your work you would like to investigate or develop, then ask yourself: 'How am I going to learn more this year?' This might be via bite-sized learning such as TED Talks or YouTube clips, or from observing an expert in the field or finding a mentor who can act as a sounding board.

Yet focusing just on improving technical job skills is a poor strategy if you want to achieve long-term success. Google discovered this when the corporation analysed the characteristics of its best employees.[44] The management team thought technical skills would be the primary driver, but they were wrong. Good communication, effective listening and building good relationships with co-workers were the top three. Despite all the hype about skills in STEM (science, technology, engineering and maths), occupations requiring people skills are growing the fastest, so improving these is a good way to prepare for the changes coming.

Improving your own self-awareness is another vital future skill. Top employees are always the ones with the most accurate understanding of their own abilities. **Assessing strengths and weaknesses, asking trusted colleagues and collaborators for feedback and then addressing these through targeted actions are all activities that can help you more effectively navigate future workplaces.**

Or as French novelist Marcus Proust put it: 'The real voyage of discovery consists not in seeking new landscapes, but in having new eyes'.

Professor Angela Carbone

Staying sharp means that you are quick to notice things; that you're keeping a careful watch for opportunities and possible danger or difficulties. Staying sharp is absolutely necessary to ensure we can realise opportunities for the betterment of society and avoid major disasters that could have a significant impact on our lives. During the COVID-19 crisis we saw actions from sharp-eyed ministers and politicians avoid an overburden of Australia's hospital system.

To succeed in the new world of work you must be sharp, show leadership, act effectively, address challenges and make decisions that contribute in a positive and impactful way. If we don't stay sharp and up to date, our ability to recognise economic and social opportunities will be diminished; in the worst scenarios, we could be faced with potential life-threatening situations. It is important to develop our professional skills and keep them relevant, so we can contribute to the world in a meaningful and positive way.

Over the next five to ten years professional development will evolve in three main ways.

1. Formal education will still be the leading way in which people will develop their knowledge and skills in preparation for work and life, but we may see a shift from multiple-year-long degrees to shorter, more specific training packages.
2. On-the-job training and development with a focus on work-integrated learning will become more prominent as a form of professional development. This will provide people with an additional insight into the nature of the business and why staying sharp is instrumental in decision making.
3. We will become more connected with experts, industry leaders, researchers and other key culturally diverse people that are exploring the same issues. This will help us engage more deeply with current issues and see them from different perspectives, enabling us to become more effective contributors.

To stay ahead of your game you will need to develop a lifelong learning attitude that fosters curiosity and collaboration, taking action and reflecting on processes and outcomes for improvement. **While you are at university, say 'yes' to any opportunities to begin building your professional network such as mentoring, leadership and work integrated learning programs.** These will help you learn about workplace realities and your intended profession.[45] Networking and mentoring activities can help you connect with people who have different personal backgrounds, mindsets or ideas, and this can challenge and inspire you. Networking and mentoring can also provide you will support to help you deal with stressful situations.[46]

Professor Rachael Field

Although it is hard to predict how future workplaces will be changed as a result of COVID-19, it seems inevitable that one development will involve an increased emphasis on individuals taking responsibility for staying current with the knowledge, skills and values that are relevant to their work environment. This means an increased expectation that people will be self-directed lifelong learners.

Lifelong learning involves the voluntary and self-directed pursuit of knowledge and expertise for personal and professional reasons over the course of a lifetime. Lifelong learners are autonomous and self-motivated.

Three possible strategies for staying on top of professional development are as follows.
1. Join a professional society that offers structured, credible and relevant continuing professional development programs.
2. Consider further advanced levels of university study such as a postgraduate degree.
3. Ensure that lifelong learning and continuing professional development are included in regular discussions with your mentor and in professional performance reviews with your supervisor.

Michael Eales

In this rapidly evolving world, the jobs of today do not represent the jobs of tomorrow. This increases the desirability and need for specific skills of unknown value. To prepare for the unknown, a shift in investment from learning processes to acquiring abilities or skills is required. This includes learning to navigate ambiguity, communicate complex information and understand people and contexts at the molecular level.

Ambiguity

The only thing in this world that is constant is the state of change itself. No longer can we rest on our laurels and be comfortable in processes and environments that rely on a state of homeostasis. Learning certain skills — such as the ability to be present in the moment, rapidly reframe problems in relation to new information and find patterns in information to forecast the future — will enable you to not only remain ahead of change, but learn to embrace it in everyday practices. To better understand the way our world is changing, check out the soon-to-be-released book by Business Models Inc and Wiley called *Business Model Shift*.

Communication

The power of information systems, databases and computing analysis has grown significantly in the last 20 years, with organisations now able to leverage unprecedented knowledge to inform day-to-day activities and strategy. Historically, most skills have focused on analysis and application to facilitate understanding of data within siloed teams. As we work in increasingly diverse and multidisciplinary teams, learning the ability to translate, communicate and visualise complex information in a timely manner continues to prove invaluable and transferable across time.

People

In the face of automation, once highly prized skills in analysis can now be achieved at the press of a button. However, the ability to observe, empathise and translate human behaviour remains essential and continues to grow in a world coming to understand the importance of human-centred design principles. Investing in learning the skills that unpack human behaviour and reasoning provides grounding to the only constant in this world: that we are all human. Check out the work of Vince Frost to find out more: https://designyourlife.com.au.

Steve Sammartino

A fundamental shift in work is occurring. In the past, our job was to know how to do something, or to know what the answer actually was. Today, in a world exploding with data, our role is to know where to look to find the answer. As the world increases in complexity there is simply too much for anyone to know in any role, career or industry. As we work with forms of AI, the grunt work will be outsourced to smart machines; the role of humans is to know which path to chose. We need to be able to navigate a territory, rather than choose a specific direction. This requires us to be sharp, to learn on the job and to look beyond what worked yesterday to find answers and efficiencies. The fundamental shift is away from memory towards exploration. This requires increased situational awareness and agility.

People who do not continually update their skills have an increased risk of redundancy, and could face career and income decline. It's also increasingly important to upgrade your skills given that lifelong positions are increasingly rare. We are now expected to hold a number of positions in several different companies to be seen as 'skilled'. Given this reality, it's incumbent upon people to have a CV that is in a constant state of readiness to undertake a new position elsewhere.

Professional development will increasingly become the responsibility of the individual over the next five to ten years. We will all need to upskill ourselves, outside of formal corporate training. This marries up with the emerging trend towards independent and freelance labour and reduced tenure at corporate workplaces. Because we will most likely be working for a number organisations — even simultaneously — corporations will be less likely to invest in employees who are employed on a project or casual basis.

Qualifications outside of formal learning institutions and universities will gain more respect than they have done traditionally. This is due to increased digital access, and the fact that topic-specific thought leaders are becoming educators. Evidence of self-directed learning will also become a sign of the personal qualities of individuals, such as having initiative and being a self-starter. Such qualities are highly desired by employers.

Three strategies that you can use to stay at the top of your game include the following.

1. *Take on a side project.* Don't wait for your company or current customers to provide opportunities. Be prepared to have a side project you launch, lead and complete independently to garner the skills you'll need in the future. Thoughtful design of side projects can build a skill base that can be brought into your work life, improve financial acumen or assist in your next career move. Side projects will also have a positive personal branding impact and show initiative.

2. *Invest in your skills.* In the new world order we will be paid for our skills — not our time on the job. We need to remove the 'punch clock' mentality of value being a time-based factor. This is where the lowest-paid workers are, and will remain. Being able to separate the time taken to do a task and the revenue or payment you receive for it is a fundamental aspect of earning a large income. This is a head's up for workaholics: the correlation people make between time spent at work and income is a false narrative. As labour becomes project-oriented, what we are paid will increasingly be based on outcomes, rather than hours.

3. *ABL.* ABL stands for 'always be learning'. **At least 30 minutes of each day should be allocated towards learning a new skill or concept related to your industry, current role or a career pivot you'd like to make.** This can be done through simple online methods. It could be reading up on emerging trends, listening to podcasts or watching instructional videos. This learning doesn't have to be formal, especially given that emerging trends and technologies take a while to enter formal learning institutions.

Clare Payne

Different people will take to change better than others. It's important to recognise your individual strengths and understand what drives you — your personal purpose — rather than just trying to fit in. The ideal situation is to find a workplace where your individualism is appreciated and benefits others.

We have already seen a shift in the idea of professional development from employer-led to individual-led. This will continue as more opportunities become available through online platforms with access to experts from all over the world and a lower cost barrier.

Three strategies you can use to stay at the top of your game include the following.

1. *Constant learning.* By reading and listening, we can constantly learn and develop, ensuring we stay sharp and up to speed with the state of the world and the role of business within society.

2. *Self-awareness.* Taking time to reflect on what you are seeing, learning and feeling can ensure that you are conscious of your actions and the path that you are taking, as well as your impact on others.

3. *Staying curious.* Asking questions is sometimes the quickest way to understanding. The classical Greek philosopher, Socrates, asked, 'What ought one to do?' It is a question for any situation where choice is being exercised, and propels us to reflect on what we *should* do rather than what we *can* do.

Entrepreneurship and venture design

QUESTIONS How do you see entrepreneurship and venture design changing in the future? What are some emerging trends that will impact the way people start their own businesses?

Michael Eales

Venture design is emerging as the battleground for true creative capital and a more equitable model for entrepreneurial effort. For entrepreneurs, this world continues to provide myriad opportunities for those willing to see it. More so, the fast-paced nature of this world creates both a launching pad and an obstacle to seeing a venture through to the next stage of maturity. Future entrepreneurs must see opportunity in a world of problems, iterate fast and view social responsibility as a core activity of their business.

Opportunity

Venture design is focused on solving a problem worth solving. The arbitrator of this equation is always the customer. When identifying where value is created, it can be tempting to focus on solving a problem you have. In the rear-view mirror, we can see that this is a well-trodden path to entrepreneurial success. However, true value is achieved when you turn a customer problem into an opportunity to add continued value to the customer's life. So think: yes, this solves a problem, but how can we further enhance this value proposition to continue to add value well into the future?

Speed

In this world, speed is the new intellectual property (IP) and it is important to note that lengthy reports don't generate high-speed impact. Let the inner workings of your business reflect the speed of the world around it and you will achieve the level of desired impact at market.

Social responsibility

The customer's perception and evaluation of a company's social responsibility across business practices is of increasing importance. No longer are customers satisfied with a corporate social responsibility program; they want the products they are purchasing to contribute to positive change within the world. Entrepreneurs of the future should consider how their pipeline can create social change to, in turn, generate a more valuable product in the eyes of the consumer.

Want to learn more? Read the book *Design A Better Business*[47] and check out https://design abetterbusiness.tools to learn more.

Steve Sammartino

The Silicon Valley ethic that emerged after the dot-com crash has hijacked the perception of entrepreneurship. In the past 15 years, startups have focused on the venture-funded model. In this model, venture capital is used as an accelerant to grow quickly, establish and dominate a new or emerging digital market. Frequently this model is built around free or subsidised products to increase digital adoption rates. While other more traditional models of entrepreneurship continued to exist, the narrative of modern startups has focused on the potential of building digitally disruptive businesses that could financially displace a large, slow analogue incumbent.

This was strategically correct for the time, and has given birth to a tech sector for which three of the five largest companies by market capitalisation did not exist in a pre-internet world. But now that the internet is beyond its burgeoning phase, and most simple forms of digitisation have already come to market, we will see a return to a new kind of venture where an initial public offering (IPO) or market sale to a larger firm is no longer the objective.

This is in part due to increasing pressure on law makers to regulate powerful tech companies, and the fact that these same large tech firms have built platforms through which new forms of entrepreneurship can be built. These companies have in some part formed a digital infrastructure for new types of small and medium-sized businesses to emerge — businesses that are less likely to create a platform in themselves, but serve as a profit engine to their founders. A return to yield and profit-based business will shape the next decade of entrepreneurship,

An inordinate number of businesses in the past decade have lacked a sustainable business model and have been saved by a few dominant technology firms acquiring them. The evaporation of cheap capital in the form of venture funding as well as financial conservatism in a post-COVID-19 world will also turn future ventures to be more about profit and slow, sustainable growth.

Three emerging changes that will largely impact the way people start their own business are as follows.

1. *Self-funding.* People starting their own business will be far more likely to self-fund their ventures and be focused on profit from the beginning. As the nature of work becomes more short-term and project-oriented, people will become entrepreneurs in the micro sense — firstly, to generate an income; and secondly, to build out a firm bigger than themselves.
2. *Profit over growth.* The economic climate will result in entrepreneurs being focused on immediate profit and growth, which is built through retained profits rather than equity or debt financing. The low-cost production infrastructure that the web has enabled will facilitate this. We'll also see startups less likely to own their own infrastructure but to access it, making their operations more flexible and profitable.
3. *Beyond digital.* Most entrepreneurial ventures have been focused on digital. In the next decade we'll see a return to functional products and services that were seen as declining industries (such as fast-moving consumer goods) — but this time, they will be localised brands, reinventing the geographic-centricity that was destroyed by global conglomerates taking over local brands to grow via acquisition. The future of business will be a more fragmented marketplace of nimble, geographically isolated firms operating for profit.

Mandy Johnson

As 16-year-old environmental activist Greta Thunberg found when her climate change campaign exploded into a global movement, technology can be a great amplifier, connecting people with others outside of traditional structures. This is fuelling an upsurge in 'collaborator' and 'purpose-driven' entrepreneurs. Rather than being confined to jobs within standard organisations, collaborator entrepreneurs work with others, each contributing a component of the solution, yet operating as separate independent entities. Purpose-driven entrepreneurs balance profitability with mission and tackle challenges in areas such as health, the environment and social justice. Both purpose-driven and collaborator entrepreneurs use technology to connect with armies of like-minded peers, advocates and potential customers.

Technology is also the mechanism transforming venture design. Future entrepreneurs won't just be looking to improve features or benefits of an existing product, to outdo competitors. Complete paradigm shifts in an offering's form, transaction or engagement will become the norm, similar to the way movie live-streaming decimated traditional video stores: the product stayed the same, but the method of delivery underwent a radical transformation. Budding entrepreneurs will have to do all this on a shoestring budget. Finding investors is becoming harder, so those who require less cash at startup or are adept at crowdfunding have a real advantage.

For lasting success, elasticity will become an essential feature of venture design, especially in the wake of more frequent crises that impact business such as the global financial crisis (GFC) and the COVID-19 pandemic. Entrepreneurs who can easily ramp up and down in reaction to external events — such as 'dark kitchens' offering restaurant-quality delivery meals without the fixed costs of a traditional establishment — are the startups of the future. Elasticity can apply to all areas of a business, from staff numbers and warehouse goods through to cashflow. Even product offerings can be flexible, as demonstrated during the COVID-19 pandemic when gin distilleries redeployed their alcohol supplies to manufacture in-demand hand sanitiser, and car companies began mass-producing face masks.

Technology's ability to generate more meaningful, quality data will also affect venture design, especially when applied to specific target markets or community sectors. Retailer Lorna Jane uses data mining to determine what its clients really want and has grown into a global multi-million-dollar business for woman who want to wear active wear everywhere. Future entrepreneurs will be able to effectively track their target market's changing needs, and design, shape and alter their physical products to suit.

Those who don't will fail. Even though a Kodak employee invented digital photography, the company took 18 years to make the switch, well after its competitors, and it eventually went bankrupt in 2012. Nowadays some of the only people who use Kodak film canisters are African Masai men, who stuff them with snuff and wear them in their elongated ear holes.[48] It's a cautionary tale, and one that future entrepreneurs would do well to remember. As we know, the one thing that won't change in the workplace of the future is change itself. So enjoy the ride!

Clare Payne

It is now much easier to start a business, however securing funding remains difficult for some. The allocation of venture capital is predicted to become more diversified and fair in the future. For example, a focus on female entrepreneurship will see more female-led businesses come to market and, when matched with venture capitalists with a gender focus, we will see these leaders and businesses flourish. There is hope that having a greater mix of people that reflects our society will bring new solutions to old problems as they can operate outside the constraints of traditional business models.

Starting businesses will only get easier, however the challenge will be for businesses to become sustainable and achieve their purpose.

Emerging changes that will assist this transition are as follows.

1. *Lower-cost entry.* Cloud computing is already meaning the cost of entry capital is far lower than it was historically.
2. *Game changers.* With fewer barriers to entry and more global collaboration there is the possibility of 'game changers', such as new ideas or procedures that affect a significant shift in the current way of doing or thinking about something, rather than incremental innovation. Each new 'game changer' that emerges will likely inspire others to think differently.
3. *Pressing issues.* The pressing nature of big global issues such as health, poverty and climate change will propel new forms of business and partnerships, particularly by the young who are tech savvy and sceptical of the status quo. I believe young people and those who are new to the workforce will play a big role in leading us to a better future.

Nicola Hazell

While many new enterprises created in the tech and startup boom of the past two decades have been driven by what could grow the fastest, attract the most customers and make the most money, increasingly investors *and* customers are looking for more from new ventures. Today, purpose is becoming a core pillar of success. Not just because people are growing a conscience, but because purpose-driven businesses have the greatest potential for impact at scale.

Consider this: in a world where we face huge challenges affecting the future of humanity, those businesses and organisations set up to solve such challenges will be the ones with the largest addressable market and therefore the greatest opportunity to succeed at scale. This has played out clearly during the COVID-19 crisis. While the digital maturity and agility of businesses has been a critical factor in their ability to respond to physical restrictions in civic movement (enabling them to transition immediately to an online operation), the long-term resilience of those businesses will come down to their level of engagement with their community — whether there is a deep ethos of trust that ensures their customers stay with them through the period of transition and back again.

What's more, beyond survival, the businesses that are *thriving* are those with a mission of solving critical issues for humanity. This includes digital businesses focused on education, technology designed to improve access to health and essential services, platforms that enable people to connect and communicate, digital tools to improve workforce productivity and mental health, and technology that delivers insights on community wellbeing and economic resilience. Within Australia's startup community alone, these are the businesses that are growing through the crisis — because they are increasing their impact as they solve critical human-centred problems.

In the ultimate example of survival of the fittest, the businesses that are thriving and will continue to thrive are those driven by purpose, by creating positive impact, by a mission to solve real and tangible problems that will make the world a better place, and built on a framework of trust and ethics. For any young entrepreneur starting or joining a new venture in the years ahead, these will be the critical factors — for investors, for customers, for employees and for themselves.

ABOUT THE CONTRIBUTORS

Angela Carbone

Angela Carbone is a Professor and Dean (Learning Innovation) in the Faculty of Science, Engineering and Technology, Swinburne University, Australia. She has extensive teaching, leadership and research experience, and has held various educational leadership positions throughout her academic career. She was the inaugural Academic Director of Education Excellence for the Office of Learning and Teaching at Monash University. Prior to that she was the Associate Director of the Office of the Pro Vice-Chancellor (Learning and Teaching) and the Director of Education Quality in the Faculty of Information Technology at Monash University. Her teaching achievements have been recognised nationally, awarded the nation's highest teaching award, and securing two national teaching fellowships. Angela led a multi-institutional employability research project capturing innovative approaches to develop students' employability skills and is currently engaged in an externally funded project to support students' development of learner agency during work placement. She chaired the Embedding Employability into Teaching and Learning Conference 2016 and is a member of the International Education, Practice and Employability Network. She has presented her ideas at an international thinktank on graduate attributes and employability and is widely published in peer reviewed journals in the area of education and employability.

Michael Eales

Michael Eales is Managing Director of Business Models Inc. in Australia and New Zealand, an award-winning international business, design and innovation agency. Michael uses strategy design, system design and future-centred design to drive innovation across organisations and push the traditional boundaries of work.

As a design pioneer, Michael supports organisations of all sizes to think better, communicate more effectively and work faster — so their strategy can move as fast as their business. Michael has helped boards of directors, top leaders and innovation teams across government, for profits and not-for profits innovate their business model and design a future strategy. He also specialises in helping organisations navigate uncertainty through scenario planning, and is Good Design Australia's COVID-19 Design Taskforce lead.

Michael inspires people and organisations with his approach to future visioning, while grounding the design and execution of strategy with an evidence-based approach to look at their business (model) from a completely different perspective. In his projects he uses the new tools of business design, like the Business Model Canvas, Vision Canvas, Context Canvas and Value Proposition Designer, and co-creation techniques from the book produced by his team — *Design A Better Business*.

Rachael Field

Rachael is a Professor of Law in the Faculty of Law at Bond University, and Co-Director of the Bond University's Centre for Professional Legal Education. Her areas of research expertise include dispute resolution, legal education, family law and domestic violence. Rachael has received a number of national teaching awards including a national citation in 2008, a national teaching fellowship in 2010 (through which she developed curriculum practices for the promotion of law student wellbeing) and a national teaching excellence award in 2014. Rachael is an Australian Learning and Teaching Fellow, member of the Fellows Executive and a Senior Fellow of the Higher Education Academy. She co-chairs the annual STARS conference, which has a focus on student success in tertiary education. Rachael founded the Australian Wellness Network for Law in 2010 which is now expanding internationally. In 2010, Rachael contributed significantly to the drafting of the Threshold Learning Outcomes for law, which have had national and international impact. Rachael is also co-founder of the Australian Dispute Resolution Research Network. She has a portfolio of more than 100 scholarly publications many of which are legal education focussed, and is co-author of six books. Rachael has volunteered at Women's Legal Service, Brisbane, since 1993, and has been president of the Service since 2004. In 2013 Rachael was named Queensland Woman Lawyer of the Year.

Ideas and content for this piece were adapted from Nickolas James, Rachael Field and Jackson Walkden-Brown, *The New Lawyer* (Wiley, 2nd ed, 2020) and Rachael Field, James Duffy and Anna Huggins, *Lawyering and Positive Professional Identities* (LexisNexis, 2nd ed, 2020).

Nicola Hazell

Nicola Hazell is one of Australia's leading voices on gender equality, social innovation and the future of work. With a career spanning technology, politics, journalism, and civil society, Nicola has a track record of achieving social impact at scale. She has worked with organisations and sectors around the world — from global tech giants and intergovernmental organisations, to emerging start-ups and social enterprises — to design and accelerate new solutions to drive investment in inclusion, diversity and social innovation.

Nicola is a firm believer in collective impact and the power of giving back, acting as a mentor and judge for various leadership and development programs, and as a strategic advisor for a range of women-led start-ups and purpose-driven organisations. She is determined to continue growing the impact and influence of a new wave of leaders, ready to create a more inclusive future of work.

Mandy Johnson

With the world of work changing at lightning speed, Mandy Johnson speaks, writes and advises on the innovative people and leadership strategies that create remarkable workplaces and transform organisational results. A best-selling author, with 'in-the-trenches' experience as a start-up founder and director of global travel retailer Flight Centre's UK operation, she is renowned for her practical approach. Mandy has featured on Sky Business News, Qantas Radio with Alan Kohler and ABC Radio's Conversation Hour, and she's worked with companies from just about every industry. One of only a handful of Australians to present at the Asia–Pacific Talent Conference in Taipei, she also runs signature masterclasses, guest lectures MBA and incubate students and has delivered executive education courses for Bond University and the University of Queensland Business School. Mandy also facilitates the Australian Owner Manager Program and offers advice to global students from 193 countries as part of UQ Business School's edX MicroMasters program. Her goal is to challenge conventional thinking at every opportunity and spread the word that great people practices are the heart, soul *and* balance sheet of every future workplace.

Clare Payne

Clare Payne is the EY Fellow for Trust and Ethics and an Honorary Fellow of The University of Melbourne. Clare advises businesses and leaders on ethics, good governance and trust. She is a former employment lawyer who managed the integrity office of Macquarie Bank and founded The Banking and Finance Oath. Prior to the global financial crisis, Clare's paper titled, '*Ethics or Bust*' was awarded the inaugural Ethics & Trust in Finance Prize by the Observatoire de la Finance, Geneva. She then went on to co-author *A Matter of Trust — The Practice of Ethics in Finance* (Melbourne University Publishing). Clare is a World Economic Forum Young Global Leader and is recognised as an Australian '100 Women of Influence.' Clare has a Bachelor of Communications and Laws and is a Vincent Fairfax Fellow for Ethics in Leadership.

Steve Sammartino

Steve wrote his first lines of computer code at age 10, and is one of Australia's most respected business minds. After graduating from university majoring in economics, he worked in multiple Fortune 500 companies and held many senior positions culminating in directorships, before answering his true calling for independence from The System. Curious about why some people seemed to get richer, regardless of education and income, he delved deeply into the study of personal finance, informally. His experience means he intimately understands small and big business and how to play the game to get ahead and design your own future.

Steve has had multiple technology start-ups, including launching rentoid.com, one of the first 'sharing economy' startups, before Uber or Airbnb. Steve had a successful exit selling the start-up to a public company. He now invests in emerging technologies and has multiple advisory board positions in a variety of disruptive technologies across the airline, automotive, real estate and co-working industries, and the Internet of Things, quantified self, mobile applications, and 3D printing technologies.

A media commentator on technology and the future, Steve is a regular on the ABC and provides expert assessment on the rapidly evolving technology sector. He has also been featured on the BBC, The Smithsonian Institute, The Discovery Channel, Mashable, Wired, and has even had documentaries made about his projects.

ENDNOTES

1. American Psychological Association 2019, *Stress in America*, www.apa.org.
2. Deloitte Center for the Edge 2013, *Institutional innovation: Creating smarter organizations to scale learning*, Deloitte University Press, www2.deloitte.com.
3. Salt, Bernard 2011, 'Baby boom to baby bust', *The Australian*, 28 May, www.theaustralian.com.au.
4. Sullivan, Kath 2020, 'Unemployment rate predicted to reach 10 per cent amid coronavirus pandemic, pushing Australia into recession', *ABC News*, 13 April, www.abc.net.au.
5. The United Nations, 'Sustainable Development Goals', https://sustainabledevelopment.un.org.
6. Marin-Guzman, David and Baird, Lucas 2020, 'Woolworths offers jobs to laid-off Qantas workers', *The Australian Financial Review*, 19 March, www.afr.com.
7. Business Roundtable 2019, 'Business Roundtable Redefines the Purpose of a Corporation to Promote "An Economy That Serves All Americans"', 19 August, www.businessroundtable.org.
8. Committee for Economic Development of Australia (CEDA) 2015, *Australia's future workforce?*, www.ceda.com.au.
9. World Economic Forum 2016, *The Future of Jobs: Employment, Skills and Workforce Strategy for the Fourth Industrial Revolution*, www3.weforum.org.
10. McCrindle 2020, 'Job mobility in Australia', https://mccrindle.com.au.
11. Foundation for Young Australians 2015, *Backing Young Entrepreneurs*, www.pc.gov.au.
12. Foundation for Young Australians 2016, *The New Basics: Big data reveals the skills young people need for the New Work Order*, www.fya.org.au.
13. CBRE Group 2014, *Fast Forward 2030: The Future of Work and Workplace*, www.cbre.com.
14. Foundation for Young Australians 2018, *The New Work Order* report series, www.fya.org.au.
15. World Economic Forum 2018, *The Future of Jobs Report*, www3.weforum.org.
16. Zao-Sanders, Marc and Palmer, Kelly 2019, 'Why Even New Grads Need to Reskill for the Future', *Harvard Business Review*, 26 September, https://hbr.org.
17. McCrindle, 'Teleworking in Australia: Latest Trends and Perceptions', https://mccrindle.com.au; International Workplace Group 2019, *The IWG Global Workspace Survey*, http://assets.regus.com.
18. Reserve Bank of Australia 2020, 'Composition of the Australian Economy Snapshot', www.rba.gov.au.
19. Lyubomirsky, Sonja, Sheldon, Kennon M & Schkade, David 2005, 'Pursuing Happiness: The Architecture of Sustainable Change', *Review of General Psychology*, vol. 9, no. 2, pp. 111–131.
20. Snyder, Charles 2000, *Handbook of Hope : Theory, Measures, and Applications*, Academic Press.
21. Graham Gibbs 1988, *Learning by Doing: A Guide to Teaching and Learning Methods*, Oxford Centre for Staff and Learning Development.
22. Bates G, Rixon, A, Carbone, A & Pilgrim, C 2019, 'Beyond Employability Skills: Developing Professional Purpose', *Journal of Teaching and Learning for Graduate Employability*, vol. 10, no. 1.
23. McKnight, PE & Kashdan, TB 2009, 'Purpose in life as a system that creates and sustains health and well-being: An integrative, testable theory', *Review of General Psychology*, vol. 13, no. 3, pp. 242–251.
24. Elliott, A 2006, 'The hierarchical model of approach-avoidance motivation', *Motivation and Emotion*, vol. 30, no. 2, pp. 111–116.
25. McKnight, PE & Kashdan, TB 2009, *op. cit.*
26. Pencavel, John 2014, *The Productivity of Working Hours*, IZA Institute of Labor Economics, www.iza.org.
27. Australian Psychological Society, 'Stress & wellbeing - how Australians are coping with life', www.psychology.org.au.
28. Business in the Community 2019, *Mental Health at Work 2019*, www.bitc.org.uk.
29. Baldassarre, Gina 2018, 'Pioneera helps address employee stress and burnout with a chatbot', Startup Daily, 16 July, www.startupdaily.net.
30. Owen Whitford, Danielle, www.pioneera.com.
31. Foundation for Young Australians 2016, ibid.

32. Boulle, Laurence and Alexander, Nadja 2020, *Mediation Skills and Techniques*, 3rd edn, LexisNexis.
33. Osterwalder, Alexander et al. 2020, *The Invincible Company: How to Constantly Reinvent Your Organization with Inspiration From the World's Best Business Models*, Wiley.
34. Foster Back, Philippa 2005, *Setting the Tone: Ethical Business Leadership*, Institute of Business Ethics.
35. Edelman 2020, '2020 Edelman Trust Barometer Reveals Growing Sense of Inequality Is Undermining Trust in Institutions', www.edelman.com.
36. ibid.
37. 'A new revolution in finance: introducing Moral Money, the latest FT newsletter', *Financial Times*, https://subs.enterprise.ft.com.
38. Responsible Investment Association Australasia, *Responsible Investment Benchmark Report 2019 Australia*, https://responsibleinvestment.org.
39. Plumer, Brad 2015, 'The GM recall scandal of 2014', Vox, www.vox.com.
40. Organisation for Economic Co-operation and Development (OECD) 2019, 'OECD work on Youth', www.oecd.org.
41. Foundation for Young Australians, The New Work Order report series, www.fya.org.au.
42. Foundation for Young Australians 2018, *The New Work Reality*, www.fya.org.au.
43. Buranyi, Stephen 2017, 'Rise of the racist robots – how AI is learning all our worst impulses', *The Guardian*, 8 August, www.theguardian.com.
44. Strauss, Valerie 2017, 'The surprising thing Google learned about its employees — and what it means for today's students', *The Washington Post*, 21 December, www.washingtonpost.com.
45. Smith-Ruig, T 2014, 'Exploring the links between mentoring and work-integrated learning', *Higher Education Research & Development*, vol. 33, no. 4, pp. 769-782.
46. Stuart, M, Lido, C, Morgan, J & May, S 2009, *Student diversity, extra-curricular activities and perceptions of graduate outcomes*, York, UK: The Higher Education Academy.
47. Van der Pijl, Patrick et al. 2016, *Design A Better Business*, Wiley.
48. Roberts, David 1986, *Moments of Doubt and Other Mountaineering Writings*, Mountaineers Books.

INDEX